The Measure of Multitude

The Measure of Multitude

POPULATION IN MEDIEVAL THOUGHT

Peter Biller

OXFORD
UNIVERSITY PRESS

Great Clarendon Street, Oxford OX2 6DP
Oxford University Press is a department of the University of Oxford.
It furthers the University's objective of excellence in research, scholarship,
and education by publishing worldwide in

Oxford New York

Athens Auckland Bangkok Bogotá Buenos Aires Calcutta
Cape Town Chennai Dar es Salaam Delhi Florence Hong Kong Istanbul
Karachi Kuala Lumpur Madrid Melbourne Mexico City Mumbai
Nairobi Paris São Paulo Shanghai Singapore Taipei Tokyo Toronto Warsaw

and associated companies in Berlin Ibadan

Oxford is a registered trade mark of Oxford University Press
in the UK and certain other countries

Published in the United States
by Oxford University Press Inc., New York

First published 2000

British Library Cataloguing in Publication Data
Data available

Library of Congress Cataloging in Publication Data
Data available

ISBN 0-19-820632-1

1 3 5 7 9 10 8 6 4 2

Typeset by Jayvee, Trivandrum, India
Printed in Great Britain
on acid-free paper by
T. J. International
Padstow, Cornwall

To Miggy, Susie, and Kate

ACKNOWLEDGEMENTS

Earlier versions of chapters 4 and 14 appeared in, respectively, *The Work of Jacques Le Goff and the Challenges of Medieval History*, ed. M. Rubin (Woodbridge, 1997), and *Dante and the Middle Ages: Literary and Historical Essays*, ed. J. C. Barnes and C. Ó Cuilleanáin (Dublin: Irish Academic Press), and I am grateful to Boydell and Brewer and the Foundation for Italian Studies, University College, Dublin, for permission to reproduce.

I am also grateful to the library staff of Corpus Christi and Gonville and Caius Colleges and the University Library, Cambridge; the British Library and the Warburg Institute in London; the John Rylands Library in Manchester; Balliol, Merton, St John's, and the Bodleian in Oxford; the Minster Library in York; the Bibliothèque Nationale and Bibliothèque Mazarine in Paris; the Stadtbibliothek in Erfurt, Stadt- und Universitätsbibliothek in Frankfurt, and the Universitätsbibliothek in Leipzig; the University Library in Bologna; the Laurenziana and Nazionale in Florence; the Ambrosiana in Milan; the Nazionale in Naples; the Vatican Library. Standing for the many who have helped me are those princes among librarians, David Griffiths of York University Library and Sue Reedie of the London Library.

The book was conceived and written in the Department of History and the Centre for Medieval Studies at the University of York, and its research and writing were helped by a Visiting Fellowship at All Souls College Oxford (1990), a British Academy Marc Fitch Readership (1992–4), and a further British Academy research grant. Jean Dunbabin, Nancy Siraisi and David d'Avray lent me microfilms, while Alexander Patschovsky procured me a copy of Engelbert of Admont's *De regimine principum.* Help on particular points has come from John Barnes, Miggy Biller, Jim Binns, Jessalynn Bird, Christopher Dyer, Richard Fletcher, Nick Furbank, Mary Garrison, Jeremy Goldberg, Monica Green, Michael Haren, Richard Helmholz, Bunny Leff, Amanda Lillie, Michael McVaugh, Mark Ormrod, Peter Rycraft, Leslie Smith, Peggy Smith, Pat Thane, and Christopher Tyerman. John Baldwin read Chapter 3, Susie Biller Chapter 1, Jean Dunbabin Chapters 11–13, Christopher Tyerman Chapters 3 and 9, and John Bossy and a remarkable anonymous copy-editor the whole. I am indebted to the friendly efficiency of Ruth Parr, Michael Watson, and others at Oxford University Press. My most significant debt is to Richard Smith, while friendship and support have also come from John Bossy, Barrie Dobson, Anne Hudson, Bunny Leff, Jim McMillan, Christopher Tyerman, Allen Warren, Rob Wyke, Yossi Ziegler and colleagues in York's History Department—including Ron Clayton, who relieved me of my duties as Exam Secretary (alas only temporarily) to help me finish the book.

By the time I was thinking of the chapters on Aristotle, Lorenzo Minio was too ill for real conversation . . . if only. Once when talking with him I ventured the idea that there was an important theme in the demographic elements in the *Politics* and their influence on thought. Lorenzo said, 'Yes'.

Another 'if only' applies to C. S. Walker, 'Steve' to everyone, who died in early middle age. For our A/L History lessons about six of us would crowd into his study, a converted sitting-room in a Victorian house which was part of the school buildings. There we would sit on a motley array of tatty old chairs as Steve ripped open his mail, often the latest medieval history book from Blackwells, and threw the odd quip or query in our direction. He radiated. There was a quizzical manner, humour, steady warmth, questions, and great good sense. But *where* was the teaching? Where the strenuous transmission to us of historical stuff? Something extraordinary was happening, but it was intangible. David d'Avray suggests osmosis. Whatever it was, it helped to produce such medievalists and politicians as Peter Linehan, Edmund King, Chris Patten, Denis MacShane, David d'Avray, and me.

Finally, this book and its author owe most to the dedicatees, Miggy, Susie, and Kate.

P.B.

CONTENTS

PLATES

(between pages 234 and 235)

1(*a*). Nicole Oresme's translation of and commentary on Aristotle's *Politics* (between 1370 and 1374), was dedicated to Charles V, king of France. The second of the king's copies was written in 1376 and produced, like the first copy, by the scribe Raoulet d'Orléans. Oresme and Raoulet worked together on the layout and decorative schema, while the cycle of illustrations, with one miniature at the beginning of each of the eight books of the *Politics*, was executed by the workshop of the Master of the Coronation Book of Charles V. Reproduced here is the frontispiece to book 4 in this manuscript (Bibliothèque Royale Albert 1, Brussels, MS 11201–2, fol. 138r). The upper strip shows three groups in a 'good polity' or political community (see 'bonne policie' in the inscription above the middle compartment), the lower one three groups in a 'bad polity' ('mauuaise policie' in the inscription above the middle compartment). The left-hand compartment of each strip has the 'poor' ('pouvres' in the inscriptions), the central compartment 'middling people' ('moiens'), and the right-hand compartment the 'wealthy' ('riches'). These parts of the multitude of a political community are characterized by their proportional numbers. In a good community middling people are large in number relative to the poor and the wealthy—and the poor, shown here with their occupational tools, get on with their work. In a bad community the middling people are relatively small in numbers—and the poor, shown here with weapons, threaten revolt. On Aristotle's concern with numbers in the population and political stability, see pp. 324 and 358–60, on the manuscript Nicole Oresme, *Le livre des Politiques d'Aristote*, ed. A. D. Menut, Transactions of the American Philosophical Society, n.s. 60, part 6 (Philadelphia, 1970), pp. 34–5, and on the decorative cycle C. R. Sherman, *Imaging Aristotle: Verbal and Visual Representation in Fourteenth-Century France* (Berkeley, Los Angeles, and London, 1995). By permission, Bibliothèque Royale Albert 1, Brussels.)

1(*b*). The earliest appearance in an index of the headings of—in modern terms—'overpopulation' and 'birth-control' is found in the index which Nicole Oresme appended to *Le livre des Politiques d'Aristote*, here shown in Avranches, MS 223, fol. 319r–v. One of its headings is 'Multiplication de peuple', which provides the reader with the book and chapter where there is treatment of 'Why and how one can avoid the people multiplying excessively'. The heading 'Multiplication de peuple' also sends the reader to another heading, 'Multitude denfans', which in turn refers the reader to two discussions, one 'Why it is not good to have too great multiplication of children', and the other of 'Various remedies against too great multiplication of children or population'. (By permission, Bibliothèque-Discothèque Municipale d'Avranches.)

2(*a*) and (*b*). Maps whose principal theme is biblical history often predominate in modern views of medieval cartography. However, most maps of the world contained in medieval manuscripts were not biblical. Set in a tradition which goes back to the Greeks, they assumed the sphericity of the world and represented a hemisphere which was divided into strips of zones or climates. There were five of these zones in the very popular map which illustrated the *Commentary on the Dream of Scipio* by Macrobius (395–436), and these zones or strips provided an elementary map of the habitability of the world. The north and south polar strips were 'cold' and 'uninhabitable'. The central equatorial strip (itself mainly an ocean, but with land both to north and south) was 'too hot' and 'uninhabitable'. The strip lying between the northern zone and the central zone was 'temperate' and 'inhabitable', and contained the known parts of the inhabited world. The strip lying in the southern part of the hemisphere, between the central and southern zones, was also 'temperate' and 'inhabitable', but it was largely unknown. Example (*a*) from a twelfth-century manuscript (British Library, Additional MSS 11943, fol. 38v), which has south at the top, inscribes each of the southern and northern zones as 'frigida inhabitabilis', and each of the two zones lying between the polar zones and the central zone as 'temperata habitabilis'. Example (*b*), from an eleventh-century manuscript (Bayerische Staatsbibliothek, Clm 6362, fol. 74r), shows the flexibility with which the known inhabited world was envisaged as fitting into this schema. While the northern temperate inhabitable contains northern Africa, the Mediterranean, and southern Europe, Ethiopia goes into the nominally uninhabitable central strip, and northern Europe into the nominally uninhabitable northern strip. Inhabitability and uninhabitability were only overarching categories: there were degrees of both in the minds of cartographers and their audience. See Macrobius, *Commentary on the Dream of Scipio*, II. ix, trans. W. H. Stahl (New York, 1952), pp. 214–16. On medieval world maps see M. Destombes, *Mappemondes A.D. 1200–1500*, Monumenta Cartographica Vetustioris Aevi 1 (Amsterdam, 1964), and J.-G. Arentzen, *Imago Mundi Cartographica: Studien zur Bildlichkeit mittelalterlicher Welt-und-Ökumenenkarten unter besonderer Berücksichtigung des Zusammenwirkens von Text und Bild*, Münsterische Mittelalter Schriften 53 (Munich, 1984). (By permission, Bayerische Staatsbibliothek, Munich, and British Library, London.)

3. Given an even distribution of people, each with a strip measuring six feet by one mile, how many people would a quarter of the world's surface contain? In the course of his commentary on Peter the Lombard's *Sentences* the Dominican Richard Fishacre raised this question, and his calculations and his final figure of 33,099,000,000 can be seen here in a manuscript in Cambridge, Gonville and Caius 329/410, fol. 211v. The question is discussed on pp. 244–6 and the text is transcribed in p. 245 n. 118. (By permission, Gonville and Caius College, Cambridge.)

4. John of Freiburg, the author of the *Confessionale* (1297–8), an immensely popular short manual of instruction for confessors, wrote, 'I have judged it useful to provide some things on the enquiries which should be made about some particular sins which are more frequently committed by people of various dignities, estates and occupations.' In the leaves shown here (Oxford, Bodley, MS Laud, Misc. 298, fols. 361v–362r), the second and third columns show the questions he advised should be put *ad coniugatos*, 'to the married', and the third and fourth columns questions to be put *ad mercatores et burgenses*, 'to traders and townsmen'. The last three lines of the questions to the married run thus: 'Item, did the wife effect some impediment to conceiving? And the same [question] about the man, [did he effect some impediment to conceiving?]. Or did she procure an abortion?' (*Item, si mulier aliquod impedimentum fecit ne conciperet; et idem de viro; vel si aborsum procuravit*). The text is discussed on pp. 195–9. (By permission, Bodleian Libray, Oxford.)

5. Around 1300 Montpellier produced a flurry of short sex treatises which examined reasons for failure to conceive. One such treatise, the *Compilatio de conceptione* (dubiously attributed to Arnau de Vilanova), organizes the defects into general headings, sub-headings, and lists, and with concern for clarity reduces them to the tabular form which is seen here in two leaves

of Bibliothèque Nationale, MS Lat. 6971, fols. 70r–v. For example, one general division is 'Ante commixtionem', 'In commixtione', and 'Post commixtionem' (before, during and after intercourse). A curving line runs down the left-hand side of the last column, with the words 'Post commixtionem', and it links defects after intercourse, beginning with *subita erectio mulieris* and *saltus maxime ad posterius* ('sudden getting up by the woman' and 'jump, especially backwards'). See the discussion on p. 154. I am indebted to Michael McVaugh for photocopies of manuscripts of this treatise. (By permission, Bibliothèque Nationale de France.)

6(*a*) and (*b*). Chapter 14 addresses thought about population in the crowded city of Florence, shown here (*b*) in a detail of The Madonna of Mercy, an anonymous fresco painted in 1342, now in the Museo del Bigallo, formerly in the loggia of the Confraternity of the Misericordia. (Permission of Museo del Bigallo, Florence; photograph by Antonio Quattrone.) Prominent (just right of centre) is the Baptistery. In his chronicle, under the year 1338, the Florentine businessman Giovanni Villani described how the numbers of little boys and little girls who were baptized here were counted each year, and he provided figures for the sex-ratio, seen here (*a*) in his *Nuova cronica* in a Vatican manuscript. Pal. Lat. 939, fol. 219r. See Chapter 4 for an account of the origin in the thirteenth century of the idea of sex-ratio, and the discussion of these figures on pp. 411–12. (Permission, Biblioteca Apostolica Vaticana, Rome.)

ABBREVIATIONS

NOTE

Unless stated otherwise, translations are mine. The Latin original is always provided when it only exists in manuscript, but when a printed edition is available I repeat the Latin only where either the precise original wording is crucial or the Latin is unusually inaccessible. English translation of the Bible is given from the Douay version. With Arabic names I follow medieval conventions—for example, Avicenna, not the modern western transliteration of Arabic, Ibn Sina—and with other names I have followed the commonest modern forms. While leaving many titles of medieval works in their original Latin or vernacular forms, I have adopted an English version for the most common ones. Thus Peter the Lombard's *Sententiae in IV libris distinctae* is referred to as the *Four Books of the Sentences* or simply the *Sentences*, and Gregory IX's *Libri Quinque Decretalium* as the *Five Books of the Decretals* or Gregory IX's *Decretals*. References to Canon and Roman Law follow the conventions described in J. A. Brundage, *Medieval Canon Law* (London and New York, 1995), pp. 190–205. The conventions I follow in references to Aristotle are described in Ch. 10 n. 1 and Ch. 11 n. 1, and those I follow in references to Avicenna's *Canon* in Ch. 6, p. 149 and n. 61. See Ch. 14 n. 3 on the edition used of Giovanni Villani, in which book numbers differ from those in older editions. In references to printed editions the absence of folio or page number indicates that the edition is unfoliated or unpaginated.

AFP	*Archivum Fratrum Praedicatorum* (Rome, 1931–)
AHDLMA	*Archives d'histoire littéraire et doctrinale du moyen âge* (Paris, 1972–)
AL	Aristoteles Latinus, Corpus Philosophorum Medii Aevi (Rome, Cambridge, etc., 1939–)
AL *Codices 1*	G. Lacombe, assisted by A. Birkenmajer, M. Dulong, E. Franceschini, *AL Codices Pars Prior*
AL *Codices 2*	G. Lacombe, assisted by A. Birkenmajer, M. Dulong, E. Franceschini, revised by L. Minio-Paluello, *AL Codices Pars Posterior*
AL *Codices 3*	L. Minio-Paluello, *AL Codices Supplementa altera*
Albert, *De animalibus*	Albert the Great, *De animalibus libri XXVI*, ed. H. Stadler, 2 vols., BGPTM 15–16 (1916–20)
Albert, *In sententias*	Albert the Great, *Scripta in IV. libros sententiarum*, 5 vols. (1893–4), in *Opera*, Borgnet, xxvi–xxx
Albert, *Opera*, Borgnet	Albert the Great, *Opera omnia*, ed. A. Borgnet, 38 vols. (Paris, 1890–99)
Albert, *Opera*, Geyer	Albert the Great, *Opera omnia*, ed. B. Geyer and others, 50 vols. (Aschendorff, 1951–)
Albert, *Politics*	Albert the Great, *Commentarii in octo libros Politicorum Aristotelis*, in *Opera*, Borgnet, viii
Albert, *Quaestiones de animalibus*	Albert the Great, *Quaestiones super De animalibus*, ed. E. Filthaut, in *Opera*, Geyer, xii

Albertus and the Sciences	*Albertus Magnus and the Sciences: Commemorative Essays 1980*, ed. J. A. Weisheipl (Toronto, 1980)
Alexander of Hales, *In sententias*	Alexander of Hales, *Glossa in quatuor libros sententiarum Petri Lombardi*, 4 vols., Bibliotheca Scholastica Medii Aevi 12–15 (Grottaferrata, 1951–7)
Alexander of Hales, *Quaestiones*	Alexander of Hales, *Quaestiones disputatae antequam esset frater*, 3 vols., Bibliotheca Scholastica Medii Aevi 19–21 (Grottaferrata, 1960)
Alexander of Hales, *Summa*	Alexander of Hales, *Summa theologica*, 4 vols. in 6 parts (Quaracchi, 1924–79)
AMN	Analecta Medievalia Namurcensia (Louvain, etc., 1950–)
Andrès, *In sententias*	Antonio Andrès, *In quatuor sententiarum libros opus longe absolutissimum* (Venice, 1578)
Aquinas, *In sententias*	Thomas Aquinas, *Scriptum super libros sententiarum*, 3 vols.; *Opera omnia*, vi–viii
Aquinas, *Opera omnia*	Thomas Aquinas, *Opera omnia*, 25 vols. (Parma, 1852–73)
Aquinas, *Summa theologiae*	Thomas Aquinas, *Summa theologiae*, Blackfriars edition, 60 vols. (London, 1964–76)
Aristotle, *De gen. an.* (Scot)	Aristotle, *De Animalibus. Michael Scot's Arabic-Latin Translation. Part Three. Books XV–XIX: Generation of Animals*, ed. A. M. I. Van Oppenraaji, Aristoteles Semitico-Latinus 5 (Leiden, New York, Cologne, 1992)
Aristotle, *De gen. an.* (Moerbeke)	Aristotle, *De generatione animalium: Translatio Guillelmi de Moerbeka*, ed. H. J. Drossaert Lulofs, AL xvii. 2.v
Aristotle, *De longitudine* (James)	Aristotle, *De longitudine et brevitate vite*, in Peter of Spain, *Obras Filosóficas*, ed. M. Alonso, Consejo Superior de Investigaciones Cientificas, Instituto de Filosofia 'Luis Vives', Series A 4, 3 vols. (Madrid, 1941–52), iii. 405–11 [= James of Venice translation]
Aristotle, *Politics*	see below, Sp and Su
Arnau de Vilanova, *Opera*	Arnau de Villanova, *Opera nuperrime revisa* (Lyons, 1532)
Auctoritates Aristotelis	*Auctoritates Aristotelis: un florilège médiéval: Étude historique et édition critique*, ed. J. Hamesse, Philosophes Médiévaux 17 (Louvain, Paris, 1974)
Avicenna, *Canon*	Avicenna, *Liber canonis medicine* (Venice, 1527, repr. Brussels, 1971)
Avicenna, *De animalibus*	Avicenna, *Abbreviatio de animalibus*, in Avicenna, *Opera* (Venice, 1508, rprt. Frankfurt-am-Main, 1961), fol. 29r–64r
Baldwin, *Peter the Chanter*	J. W. Baldwin, Masters, *Princes and Merchants: The Social Views of Peter the Chanter and his Circle*, 2 vols. (Princeton, 1970)
BGPTM	Beiträge zur Geschichte der Philosophie [from 27 (1928–30): und Theologie] des Mittelalters (Münster, 1891–)
BL	London, British Library
BN	Paris, Bibliothèque Nationale
Bonaventure, *In sententias*	Bonaventure, *Commentaria in quatuor libros sententiarum*, 4 vols. (Quaracchi, 1882–9) = *Opera omnia*, 11 vols. (Quaracchi, 1882–1902), i–iv

Boyle, *Pastoral Care*	L. E. Boyle, *Pastoral Care, Clerical Education and Canon Law, 1200–1400* (London, 1981)—reprinted articles, designated by Roman numeral (indicating order of appearance) and title, and separately paginated
Boyle, '*Summae confessorum*'	L. E. Boyle, '*Summae confessorum*', in *Les genres littéraires dans les sources théologiques et philosophiques médiévales: Définition, critique et exploitation*, Université Catholique de Louvain, Publications de l'Institut d'Études Médiévales ser. 2/5 (Louvain, 1982), pp. 227–37
Brady, *Prolegomena*	I. Brady, *Prolegomena*, vol. i, part 1 of Peter Lombard, *Sententiae*
BRUO	A. B. Emden, *A Biographical Register of the University of Oxford to AD 1500*, 3 vols. (Oxford, 1957)
Catto, 'Theology and Theologians'	J. I. Catto, 'Theology and Theologians', *HUO*, i. 471–517
CCCM	Corpus christianorum, continuatio medievalis (Turnhout, 1966–)
Chanter, *Summa*	Peter the Chanter, *Summa de sacramentis et animae consiliis*, I, II, III(1), III(2a), III(2b), ed. J.-A. Dugauquier, AMN 4, 7, 11, 16, 21 (1954–67); references to III are to text edited in III(2a–b), in which pagination is continuous (III(1) contains editorial matter)
Chobham, *Summa confessorum*	Thomas of Chobham, *Summa confessorum*, ed. F. Broomfield, AMN 25 (Louvain and Paris, 1968)
Councils & Synods I	*Councils & Synods with other Documents Relating to the English Church I, AD 871–1204*, ed. D. Whitelock, M. Brett, and C. N. L. Brooke, 2 vols. (Oxford, 1981)
Councils & Synods II	*Councils & Synods with other Documents Relating to the English Church II, AD 1205–1313*, ed. F. M. Powicke and C. R. Cheney, 2 vols. (Oxford, 1964)
CUP	*Chartularium universitatis parisiensis*, ed. H. Denifle and E. Chatelain, 4 vols. (Paris, 1889–97)
d'Avray, *Preaching*	D. L. d'Avray, *The Preaching of the Friars: Sermons diffused from Paris before 1300* (Oxford, 1985)
De proprietatibus rerum	Bartholomaeus Anglicus, *De proprietatibus rerum* (Nuremberg, 1519)
DBI	*Dizionario biografico degli Italiani* (Rome, 1960–)
DHGE	*Dictionnaire d'Histoire et de Géographie Ecclésiastiques* (Paris, 1912–)
Doucet, *Supplément*	V. Doucet, *Commentaires sur les Sentences: Supplément au répertoire de M. Frédéric Stegmüller* (Quaracchi, 1954); references are to numbered entries, which follow those in Stegmüller, *Repertorium*
DSB	*Dictionary of Scientific Biography*, ed. C. C. Gillispie, 16 vols. (New York, 1970–80)
DSp	*Dictionnaire de spiritualité*, 17 vols. (Paris, 1937–95)
DTC	*Dictionnaire de théologie catholique* (Paris, 1903–50)
Dunbabin, '*Politics*'	J. Dunbabin, 'The reception and interpretation of Aristotle's *Politics*', in *The Cambridge History of Later Medieval Philosophy*, ed. N. Kretzmann, A. Kenny, and J. Pinborg (Cambridge, 1982), pp. 723–37

Duns Scotus, *In sententias*	John Duns Scotus, *Quaestiones in libros sententiarum*, 6 vols.; *Opera omnia*, 12 vols. (Lyons, 1539), v–x
Durand, *In sententias*	Durand of St. Pourçain, *In Petri Lombardi sententias theologicas commentariorum libri IV* (Venice, 1571, repr. in 2 vols. (Ridgewood, NJ, 1964)
Engelbert, *De regimine*	Engelbert of Admont, *De regimine principum libri seu tractatus VII*, ed. J. G. T. Huffnagl (Regensburg, 1725)
Esmein	A. Esmein, *Le mariage en droit canonique*, 2nd edn. rev. R. Génestal and J. Dauvillier, 2 vols. (Paris, 1929–35)
Flüeler, *Politica*	C. Flüeler, *Rezeption und Interpretation der Aristotelischen Politica im späten Mittelalter*, Bochümer Studien zur Philosophie 19, 2 vols. (Amsterdam and Philadelphia, 1992)
Friedberg	*Corpus iuris canonici*, ed. E. Friedberg, 2 vols. (Leipzig, 1879)
Giles, *De regimine*	Giles of Rome (Aegidius Colonna), *De regimine principum libri III* (Rome, 1607, repr. Darmstadt, 1967)
Glorieux	P. Glorieux, *La littérature quodlibétique*, 2 vols., Bibliothèque Thomiste 5 and 21 (Paris, 1925–35)
Glorieux, *Arts*	P. Glorieux, *La faculté des arts et ses maîtres au XIIIe siècle*, Études de Philosophie Médiévale 59 (Paris, 1971)
Glorieux, *Théologie*	P. Glorieux, *Répertoire des matres en théologie de Paris au XIIIe siècle*, 2 vols, Études de Philosophie Médiévale 18–8 (Paris, 1933–4)
Golubovich	G. Golubovich, *Biblioteca bio-bibliografica della Terra Santa e dell'Oriente francescano*, 4 vols. (Quarrachi, 1906–23)
Gratian, *Decretum*	Gratian, *Decretum*, ed. Friedberg, i
Gui of Orchelles, *De sacramentis*	Gui of Orchelles, *Tractatus de sacramentis ex eius summa de De sacramentis et officiis ecclesiae*, ed. D. and O. Van den Eynde, Franciscan Institute Publications, Text Series 4 (New York, Louvain, Paderborn, 1953)
Guillaume de Moerbeke	*Guillaume de Moerbeke: Recueil d'études à l'occasion du 700e anniversaire de sa mort (1286)*, ed. J. Brams and W. Vanhamel, Ancient and Medieval Philosophy, De Wulf-Mansion Centre, Series 1, 7 (Louvain, 1989)
Handling Sin	*Handling Sin; Confession in the Middle Ages*, ed. P. Biller and A. J. Minnis, York Studies in Medieval Theology 2 (York, 1998)
Herlihy and Klapisch, *Tuscans and their Families*	D. Herlihy and C. Klapisch-Zuber, *Tuscans and their Families: A Study of the Florentine Catasto of 1427* (French edn., Paris, 1978, Eng. trans. New Haven and London, 1985)
HLF	*Histoire littéraire de la France*, i– (Paris, 1733–)
HUO	*The History of the University of Oxford*, ed. T. Aston and others, i– (Oxford, 1984–)
Isidore, *Etymologiae*	Isidore of Seville, *Etymologiarum sive originum libri XX*, ed. W. M. Lindsay, 2 vols., unpaginated (Oxford, 1911)
Jacquart and Micheau	D. Jacquart and F. Micheau, *La médecine arabe et l'occident médiéval* (Paris, 1990)
Jacques de Vitry, *Historia orientalis*	Jacques de Vitry, *Libri duo, quorum prior Orientalis, sive Hierosolymitanae, alter Occidentalis Historiae nomine inscribitur*, ed. F. Moschus (Douai, 1597, repr. Farnborough, 1971)
JEH	*Journal of Ecclesiastical History* (London, 1950–)

Lampen	W. Lampen, 'L'Italia nel pensiero di Fra Bartolomeo Anglico OFM', *Studi Francescani* 14 (1928), 111–18
Landgraf, *Scolastique naissante*	A. M. Landgraf, *Introduction à l'histoire de la littérature théologique de la scolastique naissante* (Montréal, Paris, 1973)
Mansi, *Concilia*	*Sacrorum Conciliorum Nova et Amplissima Collectio*, ed. J. Mansi, 31 vols. (Florence and Venice, 1759–98)
Matthew Paris, *CM*	Matthew Paris, *Chronica majora*, ed. H. R. Luard, RS 57, 7 vols. (1872–83)
McVaugh, *Medicine*	M. R. McVaugh, *Medicine before the Plague: Practitioners and their Patients in the Crown of Aragon, 1285–1345* (Cambridge, 1993)
MGH	Monumenta Germaniae Historica
Michaud-Quantin, *Sommes*	P. Michaud-Quantin, *Sommes de casuistique et manuels de confession au moyen âge (XII–XVI siècles)*, AMN 13 (1962)
Minio, *Opuscula*	L. Minio-Paluello, *Opuscula: The Latin Aristotle* (Amsterdam, 1972)
Müller, *Paradiesehe*	M. Müller, *Die Lehre des Hl. Augustinus von der Paradiesehe und ihre Auswirkung in der Sexualethik des 12. und 13. Jahrhunderts bis Thomas von Aquin* (Regensburg, 1954)
MS	*Medieval Studies* (Toronto, 1939–)
Oresme, *Politiques*	Nicole Oresme, *Le livre de Politiques d'Aristote*, ed. A. D. Menut, Transactions of the American Philosophical Society, n.s. 60, part 6 (Philadelphia, 1970)
Peter of Auvergne, *Politics*	Thomas Aquinas, *In libros Politicorum Aristotelis expositio*, ed. R. M. Spiazzi (Rome, Turin, 1951); the commentary is Peter's from III. vi (p. 142)
Peter of la Palud, *In sententias*	Peter of la Palud [Petrus de Palude], *In quartum sententiarum* (Venice, 1493)
Peter the Lombard, *Sententiae*	Peter the Lombard, *Sententiae in IV libris distinctae*, ed. I. Brady, 2 vols., Spicilegium Bonaventurianum 4–5 (Grottaferrata, 1971–81). I part 2 contains books 1–2 of the *Sententiae*, and II contains books 3–4 of the *Sententiae*. I part 1 contains editorial matter; see above, Brady, *Prolegomena*
Peter of Tarentaise, *In sententias*	Peter of Tarentaise [Innocent V], *In IV. Libros sententiarum commentaria*, 4 vols. (Toulouse, 1652, repr. Ridgewood, NJ, 1964)
Pietro d'Abano, *Conciliator*	Pietro d'Abano, *Conciliator controversiarum quae inter philosophos et medicos versantur* (Venice, 1565, repr. Padua, 1985)
PL	*Patrologia Latina*, ed. J. P. Migne, 217 + 4 index vols. (Paris, 1841–61)
Properties of Things	*On the Properties of Things: John Tevisa's translation of Bartholomaeus Anglicus De Proprietatus Rerum*, ed. M. C. Seymour *et al.*, 3 vols. (Oxford, 1975–88); I–II contain the text, III variant readings
Reinhardt, *Anselm von Laon*	H. J. F. Reinhardt, *Die Ehelehre der Schule des Anselm von Laon: Eine Theologie- und kirchenrechtsgeschichtliche Untersuchung zu den Ehetexten der frühen Pariser Schule des 12. Jahrhunderts*, BGPTM, n.s. 14 (Aschenbach, 1974)
Richard, *In sententias*	Richard of Middleton, *Super quatuor libros sententiarum Petri Lombardi*, 4 vols. (Brescia, 1951, repr. Frankfurt-am-Main, 1963)

RS — Rolls Series, 253 vols. (London, 1858–1911)

RTAM — *Recherches de Théologie Ancienne et Médiévale* (Louvain, 1929–)

SCH — Studies in Church History (Cambridge, London, Oxford Woodbridge, 1964–)

Schönbach — A. E. Schönbach, 'Des Bartholomaeus Anglicus Beschreibung Deutschlands gegen 1240', *Mitteilungen des Instituts für österreichische Geschichtsforschung* 27 (1906), 54–90

Siraisi, *Taddeo* — N. G. Siraisi, *Taddeo Alderotti and His Pupils: Two Generations of Italian Medical Learning* (Princeton, 1981)

SOPMA — T. Kaeppeli and E. Panella, *Scriptores Ordinis Praedicatorum medii aevi*, 4 vols. (Rome, 1970–93)

Sp — Aristotle, *Politics* (Moerbeke's Latin translation), in Thomas Aquinas, *In libros politicorum Aristotelis expositio*, ed. R. M. Spiazzi (Turin, Rome, 1951)

Su — *Aristotelis Politicorum Libri Octo, cum vetusta translatione Guilelmi de Moerbeka*, ed. F. Susemihl (Leipzig, 1882); references are to Moerbeke's Latin translation

Stegmüller, *Repertorium* — F. Stegmüller, *Repertorium commentariorum in Sententias Petri Lombardi*, 2 vols. (Würzburg, 1947). References are to numbered entries in i

Stephen of Bourbon, *Tractatus* — *Tractatus de diversis materiis praedicabilibus*, ed. A. Lecoy de la Marche, *Anecdotes historiques, légendes et apologues tirés du recueil inédit d'Étienne de Bourbon, Dominicain du XIIIe siècle* (Paris, 1877)

Thomas of Strasbourg, *In sententias* — Thomas of Strasbourg, *Commentaria in IIII. Libros sententiarum*, 2 vols. (Venice, 1564, repr. Ridgewood, NJ, 1965, 2 vols. in 1)

Tolomeo, *De regimine* — Tolomeo of Lucca, *De regimine principum* (= Tolomeo, *Continuatio* to Thomas Aquinas, *De regno*), in Thomas Aquinas, *Opuscula philosophica*, ed. R. M. Spiazzi (Turin, 1954), pp. 280–358

TRE — *Theologische Realenzyklopädie*

TRHS — *Transactions of the Royal Historical Society* (London, 1871–)

Vf — *Die deutsche Literatur des Mittelalters: Verfasserlexikon*, 2nd edn. ed. K. Ruh *et al.* (Berlin and New York, 1979–)

Villani, *Cronica* — Giovanni Villani, *Nuova cronica*, ed. G. Porta, 3 vols. (Parma, 1990–1)

Vincent, *Speculum doctrinale* — Vincent of Beauvais, *Speculum quadruplex, sive Speculum maius*, 4 vols. (Douai, 1624, repr. Graz, 1965), ii

Speculum historiale — Vincent of Beauvais, ibid. iv

Speculum naturale — Vincent of Beauvais, ibid. i

William of Auvergne, *De matrimonio* — William of Auvergne, *De matrimonio*, *Opera omnia*, i. 512b–28b

William of Auvergne — *Opera Omnia*, ed. F. Hotot and B. Le Feron, 2 vols. (Orléans, Paris, 1674, repr. Frankfurt-am-Main, 1963)

William of Auxerre, *Summa aurea* — William of Auxerre, *Summa aurea*, ed. J. Ribailler, 4 vols. in 7 parts, Spicilegium Bonaventurianum 16–20 (Paris and Grottaferrata, 1980–87). The *Summa*'s book numbers and the series numbers co-ordinate thus: Lib. 1 = 16; Lib. 2

	parts 1–2 = 17 (in two parts not differentiated by number); Lib. 3 part 1 = 18a; Lib. 3 part 2 = 18b; Lib. 4 = 19. The editor's *Introduction* = 20
Wyngaert, *Itinera*	*Itinera et relationes fratrum minorum saeculi XIII et XIV*, ed. A. Van den Wyngaert, Sinica Franciscana 1 (only vol. published) (Quarracchi, 1929)
Yule and Cordier, *Cathay*	H. Yule, *Cathay and the Way Thither, Being a Collection of Medieval Notices of China*, rev. H. Cordier, 4 vols., Hakluyt Society, 2nd ser. 33, 37, 38, and 41 (London, 1915–16)
Zeimentz, *Frühscholastik*	H. Zeimentz, *Ehe nach der Lehre der Frühscholastik,* Moraltheologische Studien, Historische Abteilung 1 (Düsseldorf, 1973)

1

INTRODUCTION TO MEDIEVAL DEMOGRAPHIC THOUGHT[1]

1.1 *Autobiographical: the origins of this book*

The idea for this book was conceived by an accidental union of teaching and reading. Trying to keep up with the great learning of one colleague with whom I was teaching,[2] I found myself one evening boning up on one of the political theorists who was going to be discussed in a seminar the following morning, Tolomeo of Lucca. Reading through Tolomeo's continuation of a work by Thomas Aquinas, I kept on coming across demographic themes. Commenting on Aristotle's presentation of Spartan concern with the birth-rate in his *Politics*, for example, Tolomeo tartly said that it was absurd for the state to reward great fertility, which could be found even in a 'vile man'. What did he mean by 'vile'? Was it a moral category? Or an expression of hauteur: disdain for the large families of the lower orders? Why was Tolomeo, a Dominican, not simply following the Old Testament and praising fertility? Even if state intervention in the birth-rate was not a reality of Tolomeo's contemporary world, it was a reality of his *thought*-world. Very odd, I thought. Material for reflection in these surprising passages.

Some time before this, two other colleagues at York, both modern historians,[3] had pioneered the teaching at undergraduate level of women's history. It was 1976, and their's was a collaboratively taught course called 'The Condition of Women in History'. Invited to teach the medieval slot, I soon became weary of the intelligible but arid task of trying to make the scant material that survives about medieval nuns in some way applicable to women in general, and I was unhappy with the lack of attention in the scholarship that then prevailed to many material and vital facts, in particular childbirth and the demographic trends of marriage and death. When it came, in 1979, I found Richard Smith's revolutionary account of marriage-patterns a revelation.[4] Here was something that really made sense and so clearly was of fundamental importance in the lives of the ordinary women of medieval Europe.

Around this time I had been reading one American medievalist, John Baldwin, whose works gave a sharp twist to the character of the theme 'medieval thought'.

[1] While *Measure of Multitude* is not anachronistic, *Medieval Demographic Thought* clearly is, and it is used by preference here and in the conclusion to facilitate thinking about its implications.

[2] Peter Rycraft. [3] Jim McMillan and Jane Rendall. [4] See Ch. 11 n. 12.

Usually conceived as abstract and speculative, 'medieval thought' in Baldwin's hands became something very different: medieval academics looking at and discussing hard contemporary realities, such as government, war, taxation, trade, and marriage.

Jostling together in my mind, then, were these three: the importance of the 'vital facts' of demography, Baldwin's model of thought about concrete contemporary reality, and the example in Tolomeo of an unsuspected world of demographic comment. Coalescing, they gave birth to the theme and the question. '*Medieval* demographic thought' . . .?

In the enquiry which followed I had an occupation and a preoccupation. There was work to be done: identifying and reading the texts that would be most useful. At the earliest stage these seemed to be textbooks used in the theology and arts faculties of universities, Peter the Lombard's *Four Books of the Sentences* in the former, and Aristotle's tract on life-span and his *Politics* in the latter. The first and fundamental labour was looking at commentaries upon these, in chronological order, and using this as the core of an account of the development of ideas.[5] Much more followed as the book developed, but its history needs no further retailing here, for it is made plain in this book's contents.

The preoccupation was the worry about claiming too much or too little. Was I more in danger of overstating or understating the case which seemed to be emerging?

Let me describe the pressures and risks which I felt pushed in one direction or the other. Think of them as two pairs of twins, the first pair being (1) medieval essentialism and (2) changes in our approach to medieval thought. Let me begin with this first set of twins. There is the abiding problem of the word and idea *medieval*. Any medievalist has to heave and strain to stop an enormous boulder falling onto the subject, namely modern people's notion of a medieval mentality and their conviction about its essence, backwardness of some sort.[6] Now, there was the earlier claim by demographic historians that medieval mentality made birth-control literally 'unthinkable' in the middle ages, when in fact and paradoxically, as we shall see,[7] it is medieval *thought* of birth-control, rather than medieval practice, that is easy to establish. This seemed to show that medieval demographic thought would be peculiarly vulnerable to this sort of prejudgement about the nature of *medieval*—a special case, as it were, of Jakob Burckhardt's medieval man, defined as medieval by his lack of consciousness.

Pushing in another direction is the other twin, namely changes in the last forty years in our view of medieval university thought. An abstract version of medieval

[5] See Ch. 11 below for a more qualified description of this method applied to the *Politics*, and on scholastic commentaries in general, see F. Del Punta, 'The genre of commentaries in the Middle Ages and its Relation to the Nature and Originality of Medieval Thought', in *Was ist Philosophie im Mittelalter?*, Veröffentlichungen des Thomas-Instituts der Universität zu Köln 26 (Berlin and New York, 1998), pp. 138–51.

[6] See J. Heers, *Le moyen âge, une imposture* (Paris, 1992), which ruins its case, however, by its extremism.

[7] Chs. 6–8 below.

thought prevailed in most of its study during this century. The grand themes were the rise of the scholastic method, the introduction of Greek and Arabic philosophy, their application to theological truths, the challenges to the Christian faith of such doctrines as the eternity of the world, battles between nominalism and realism, Thomism and Ockhamism, and so on. These have been the contents of the classic histories, from Étienne Gilson to David Knowles and Gordon Leff, and although there have long been subordinate genres such as political thought, for a long time medieval thought's image remained predominantly speculative and remote.

Then came the pioneering efforts of historians in North America. Brian Tierney's account of medieval poor law showed how the glosses of canon law texts, emanating from debate and lecturing in Bologna, contained surprisingly practical and concrete discussions of money and the poor. When properly interpreted, the Bolognese canonists appeared to be debating something like an old Labour versus Thatcher view of charity, the poor, and the dangers of pauperization.[8] In the late twelfth century they were more left-wing, but by around 1300 they had become more Thatcherite. Then came John Baldwin's first-round knock-out of Max Weber and other early twentieth-century economic historians. Baldwin began with their contention that medieval economic notions ignored market realities and were therefore straitjackets on economic development. He then turned to what medieval canonists and theologians actually said about the just price, and had no difficulty in showing just how market-realistic some of their economic views were.[9] Then came his masterpiece of 1970,[10] which demonstrated very comprehensively the concreteness of thought of Parisian academics in the late twelfth and early thirteenth centuries. We know of later continuity of some discussion of such things in the theology faculty largely through the scholarship of Leonard Boyle, a Dominican passionately concerned with the education of medieval Dominicans in practical pastoral matters.[11] Growing attention to other faculties, in particular the illumination of the medical faculty through the brilliant studies of scholars such Danielle Jacquart, Michael McVaugh, and Nancy Siraisi, has added to this broadening view of both theoretical and practical learning in medieval universities, and *The Measure of Multitude* is part of this modern tendency.

Both of the preceding paragraphs make clear one danger: reaction leading to overstatement. Over-reaction against prejudices about *medieval* can lead a medievalist into draining the subject of any difference worth studying,[12] or even in extreme cases into the blind attribution of modernity.[13] The danger of exaggeration

[8] B. Tierney, *Medieval Poor Law: A Sketch of Canonical Theory and Its Application in England* (Berkeley and Los Angeles, 1959).

[9] J. W. Baldwin, *The Medieval Theories of the Just Price: Romanists, Canonists and Theologians in the Twelfth and Thirteenth Centuries*, Transactions of the American Philosophical Society, n.s. 49, part 4 (Philadelphia, 1959).

[10] *Peter the Chanter*, described more fully below.

[11] See below, Ch. 2 and nn. 90–1.

[12] Heers falls into this trap, in the bitter tract cited in n. 6 above.

[13] Exemplified at its most bizarre in the title of an article by one historian of medicine, J. M. Riddle: 'Ancient and Medieval Chemotherapy for Cancer', *Isis* 76 (1985), 319–30.

is clear in the case of academic thought, where the following basic truths need to be kept in mind. The theology faculty was not always so dominated by practical matters as it was during Peter the Chanter's day. The translations of Greek and Arabic philosophy injected a strong speculative and abstract dose. And it would be a travesty to claim that Gilson, Knowles, and Leff do not represent a very large proportion of medieval university thought.

But they do not represent *all* of it. I put forward here, for comparison, the case of the historiography of Aristotle's *Politics*, anticipating a point which is made more fully in Chapter 11 below. The *Politics* contains both what we call political *and* demographic thought; the latter is less important but still a substantial presence. While medieval commentators on the *Politics* looked at *both* parts, modern historians who have studied them have looked only at what they said about political thought, and this pattern in modern study reflects a modern rather than a medieval fact: which parts of medieval commentaries modern historians have chosen to read.

The second set of twins pulling in opposing directions are older and newer styles of doing the history of thought and culture. Where an older history of a particular area of thought took as its theme progress, it picked out the line of ideas which advanced its area and passed over those that did not. One powerful current mode of doing cultural history rejects this older approach, damning it as 'precursorism', and itself upholds what is, in effect, the opposite. It uses the 'bad' but popular scientific ideas of a particular past period to obtain an entrée into the broader outlook of people of the time. Thus the first twin would tell the historian of medieval geographic thought to look at the developing realism of maps and to describe the mariners who were discovering Atlantic islands around 1300.[14] The second would encourage concentration on the monstrous races to be found on the margins of the world in medieval maps and travellers' tales, and the 'otherness' (or 'alterity') of the 'medieval' imagination displayed in such sources.[15] What is the balance of these opposing forces in my account? Some progressive elements remain in my picture, for it is just as unhistorical to omit as to overemphasize progressive elements. Different historiographical areas have different needs. An uncharted area needs first of all the easily intelligible and visible strong lines which are more easily to be found in an older style of intellectual history. I have therefore deliberately given *The Measure of Multitude* something of the character of such a chart, presented to help the future explorers who will redraw it and make it more complex. At the same time, however, I have tried to take a broader view of demographic outlook. My sources were the products of (*a*) the very learned and (*b*) theologians and churchmen. I have tried to widen (*a*) a little, by tracing the ideas and words that were—or became—common property among

[14] See older histories, such as C. R. Beazley, *The Dawn of Modern Geography*, 3 vols. (London, 1897–1906), and more recently in J. R. S. Phillips, *The Medieval Expansion of Europe* (Oxford, 1988).

[15] The approach in M. C. Campbell, *The Witness and the Other World: Exotic European Travel Writing 400–1600* (Ithaca, NY, 1988), and I. M. Higgins, *Writing East: The "Travels" of Sir John Mandeville* (Philadelphia, 1997).

the larger number who were literate in Latin.[16] Although a few learned laymen can be found (they appear in Chapter 14), there is little that can be done about (*b*), except to remember it all the time, and to speculate along the lines I suggest at the end of section 6 below.

1.2 *Scope and definition of medieval demographic thought*

The Measure of Multitude: Population in Medieval Thought could also be titled *Medieval Demographic Thought*, and in this section I am going to use this briefer alternative title. It has a useful affinity with the titles of books in neighbouring areas. While such titles as *Medieval Political Thought* or *Medieval Economic Thought* indicate accounts of people in the middle ages *thinking* about politics or economics, *Medieval Demographic Thought* signals a study of people in Latin Christendom between 1100 and the 1340s, describing them *thinking* about the things we bundle together under the heading 'demography': the populations of different countries, the sex-ratio, life-span, and such-like. So far so good, but more explanation is needed, for *Medieval Demographic Thought* is not so immediately transparent as *Medieval Political Thought* or *Medieval Economic Thought*. This is in part because there are no earlier accounts,[17] whose similar titles would prepare the reader. It is also in part because the modernity of the word *demography* and the intellectual discipline it denotes suggest that an anachronism is

[16] With aims similar to those articulated by Quentin Skinner for the history of political theory, *The Foundations of Modern Political Thought*, 2 vols. (Cambridge, 1978), i, pp. x–xii.

[17] J. and M. Dupâquier's *Histoire de la démographie: La statistique de la population des origines à 1914* (Paris, 1985) is confined to the entry of statistics. Brief treatment of the middle ages can be found in older economic histories, for example C. E. Stangeland, *Pre-Malthusian Doctrines of Population: A Study in the History of Economic Theory* (New York, 1904), Ch. 2 (ii), and there is a brief general attempt by J. C. Russell in his *Late Ancient and Medieval Population*, Transactions of the American Philosophical Society, n.s. 48, part 3 (Philadelphia, 1958), pp. 133–8. J. Cohen has studied one biblical text in his *'Be Fertile and Increase, Fill the Earth and Master it': The Ancient and Medieval Career of a Biblical Text* (Ithaca, NY, and London, 1989), and there is much in J. T. Noonan's classic history of Catholic thought, *Contraception: A History of its Treatment by the Catholic Theologians and Canonists* (Cambridge, Mass., 1966) (see further Ch. 6 below, nn. 4–5). Noonan's 'Intellectual and Demographic History', *Daedalus* 97 (1968), 463–85, examines the impact of ideas (especially moral-theological) on demographic matters. My 'Marriage Patterns and Women's Lives' examined the relations between regionalism in demographic patterns and pastoral theology. The 'ages of man' theme has attracted much study, including R. Sprandel, *Alterss-chicksal und Altersmoral: Die Geschichte der Einstellungen zum Altern nach der Pariser Bibelexegese des 12.–16. Jahrhunderts*, Monographien zur Geschichte des Mittelalters 22 (Stuttgart, 1981); M. Dove, *The Perfect Age of Man's Life* (Cambridge, 1986); J. A. Burrow, *The Ages of Man: A Study in Medieval Writing and Thought* (Oxford, 1986); E. Sears, *The Ages of Man: Medieval Interpretations of the Life Cycle* (Princeton, 1986); H. Dubois and M. Zink, *Les âges de la vie au moyen âge*, Cultures et Civilisations Médiévales 7 (Paris, 1992). Particular ages in themselves have attracted their own literature. See e.g. the old and the elderly in S. Shahar's recent general survey, *Growing Old in the Middle Ages: 'Winter clothes us in Shadow and Pain'* (London and New York, 1997). Because of the dearth of statistical evidence, medieval views are often cited in what are principally straight works of historical demography, such as Herlihy and Klapisch, *Tuscans and their Families*. This book stops before the Black Death, contemporary comments on which have long been the object of study: see *The Black Death*, ed. R. Horrox, Manchester Medieval Sources series (Manchester, 1994).

lurking somewhere. Because of this, and the length and on occasion technical character of this book, its readers deserve a clear summary account of what it is about and a simple guide to its contents. Both are provided here, beginning with elementary definitions.

(i) *Demography* is a certain way of thinking about and studying people, in the first instance people living *now*. A textbook addressed to actuaries defines it thus. 'The study by statistical methods of human populations, involving primarily the measurement of the size, growth and diminution of people, the proportions living, being born or dying within some area or region and the related functions of fertility, mortality and marriage'.[18]

(ii) *Historical demography* is this way of thinking and studying, but applied to past peoples by modern historians, *historical demographers*.[19] The initial definition of *demography* needs to be adapted when applied to *historical demography*, with the phrase 'by statistical methods' replaced by 'according to quantity'. Historical demographers go back in time, before censuses and towards populations in the sixteenth and seventeenth centuries, which can be known only fragmentarily through patient reconstruction of families on the basis of surviving series of registers in some parishes. There are fewer tables of figures. As the historians go back even further, beyond the parish registers and towards populations about which much less is known, statistics dwindle even further and ingenious conjecture on the basis of indirect evidence increases. Unable to write sentences such as 'the data of the census show a 2.3 per cent increase in such and such', the historical demographer who specializes in the central middle ages will write a sentence like, 'many Italian cities found it necessary to build new walls, often doubling or tripling the area enclosed, and this is a rough index of expanding urban population in the mid-thirteenth century'.

(iii) *Medieval demographic thought* is an extension of these definitions—medieval people's *thought* about such matters. While a *historical demographer* who specializes in the middle ages looks at the demographic *realities* of the time, asking such questions as 'Was population declining before the great famines of 1315–17?' and 'How widely can we find evidence for a skewed sex-ratio (more women than men) in immigration from country into town?', an historian of *medieval demographic thought* looks at the demographic *ideas* of the time, asking what people thought about such demographic *realities*.[20] If there is a demographic fact of the past, such as (perhaps) men outliving women, what did they *think* about it?

The first theme of *Medieval demographic thought* is thought, and its first question is 'Did these people have such-and-such a demographic concept?' They may not have thought about one sex outliving the other. They perhaps lacked the word

[18] P. R. Cox, *Demography*, 4th edn. (Oxford, 1970), p. 1.

[19] See T. H. Hollingsworth, *Historical Demography*, The Sources of History: Studies in the Uses of Historical Evidence (Cambridge, 1969).

[20] By 'reality' I mean crude brute facts, facts of life and death in populations, not the inclusive and philosophically difficult 'what really existed'.

or words and the concept, or they may have been developing or acquiring them just then. The possession and appearance and development of such ideas is the stuff of a history entitled *Medieval Demographic Thought*, and the relations between these ideas and contemporary demographic realities are only secondary. However, there is more to be said. First, at a practical level the two are sometimes not distinguished. Often the only evidence available to an historian of medieval demographic *reality* is an *idea*. Lacking data about ages at which girls got married or the amount of practice of birth-control among married couples, this historian may still want to make demographic conjectures based on *ideas*, moralists denouncing birth-control or low age of marriage, and so in practice the *historical demographer* and the *historian of medieval demographic thought* may often look at the same material. Secondly, the distinction must not be pushed too far, for ultimately past ideas are past realities, as *historical demographers* themselves realize. A population that is demographically self-conscious is demographically different from one which is not. Past people having the *idea* of overpopulation may then think of *doing* something active about it, like postponing getting married in order to limit the number of children they have or going off to live in a sparsely inhabited country. Finally, connectedness with reality is part of the character of an idea. But there is a problem in *Medieval Demographic Thought*—how far is it practicable to try to sketch demographic reality? I discuss this in section 4 below.

1.3 *Thought*

This book's scope and shape has been dictated by its restriction to surviving direct sources, learned Latin texts, and by the novelty of the enterprise. Since medieval demographic thought has not been systematically described, I have addressed it generally, trying to identify the principal sources and themes and to provide a general account, while stopping short of the Black Death of 1348–9 in order to keep the enterprise manageable. Naturally there are omissions, of which I shall say something below, and parts of the book are only descriptive, essentially saying no more than this: 'over there is one of the areas of demographic thought, and such-and-such are its contents'. The lines which stand out in this book came to be drawn by my asking general and simple questions. 'What are the most important things?', and then, of each of these, 'What was the impact of this or that on demographic thought?', and then, 'In such and such an area, what are the principal texts?' Here are these questions.

i. The intellectual and educational developments of the time, the renaissance of the long twelfth century and the rise of the universities: how did these bear on demographic thought?

a. These developments transformed most areas of thought and writing. How did they alter theological and canon-legal texts dealing with marriage, in particular as these bore on demographic matters?

b. The translation into Latin of Aristotle (early twelfth to late thirteenth centuries) and Arabic medicine (from the late eleventh century) introduced into western centres of learning a vast array of data and concepts. If their reception was *the* fundamental fact in most areas of medieval thought, what were the specific effects in demographic thought?

ii. What was the impact of experience?

a. Part of this is a question about Latin Christendom. The twelfth and thirteenth centuries saw the Church's further extension of its control over marriage, and increasingly close grappling with marriage and procreation among its millions of faithful, while the thirteenth century experienced an extraordinary development in pastoral expertise and observation, through the coming into existence of two religious orders which specialized in preaching and confession, the Dominicans and Franciscans. What was produced by these developments?

b. Part of this is also a question about diversity, both within and beyond Latin Christendom. How was the Church's thought on marriage and population affected by its experience of various faiths, Cathar and Jewish within the bounds of Latin Christendom, Saracen and Mongol beyond?

c. What, in addition, was the significance of the Israel problem of the time, the existence for a while of Christian kingdoms in the eastern Mediterranean? Settled by westerners, who were surrounded by large numbers of hostile Arabs and concerned with defence, these states were the focus of much western thought. How was thought affected by concern with colonization and military numbers, and by the juxtaposition of Islamic and Christian populations?

d. How did occupation of the Holy Land, far-eastern travel, missionary work and academic developments in geography affect the mapping in people's minds of the inhabitation of the whole world?

The different types of texts which can be used to explore these questions supply the structure of this book. The Church's theological and canon-legal texts concerning marriage and population occupy Part 1 (Chapters 2–8), while texts concerning geography, the Holy Land, conversion, and population beyond Latin Christendom are examined in Part 2 (Chapter 9). Part 3 looks at texts translated from Greek or Arabic, with Chapter 10 focusing on natural-philosophical and medical texts, and Chapters 11–13 on one work of moral philosophy, the *Politics*.

Differences between the settings of the Church's ideas and Aristotle's dictated different approaches in these two parts of the book. The former are introduced and described more elaborately. In the case of the Church there was an intricate relation of experience in dealing with marriage and reflection, a close relation between pastors dealing with millions of lay people and the writings of theologians and canon lawyers in the schools. The introduction of Aristotle's ideas into the world of academics, on the other hand, was just that: an important event, certainly, but to begin with taking place only in a particular and quite confined world. Part 2, therefore, gets its own introduction (Chapter 2), an account of the Church's control of marriage, the various sorts of texts this produced, and developments in these texts. In the following chapters close-ups and panoramas alternate in order further to explore roots and ramifications. Chapter 3 provides a deep reading of one treatise by one theologian who was also a bishop and statesman, William of Auvergne, while abortion and birth-control afford another opportunity to illustrate the relations of various texts and practice, with Chapter 6 sketching what we know of practice, Chapter 7 addressing academic canon law and theology, and Chapter 8 looking at the advice manuals written by and for those pastors who tried to grapple with the behaviour of ordinary people. In Part 3, by contrast, Aristotle's ideas are introduced more simply, through an account of their introduction and reception in the schools.

The final chapter uses an ultra close-up lens: the coda to the book. This chapter takes one city around 1300, Florence, and asks, 'How was demographic thought represented here, in one place?' This chapter, in turn, has its coda, with which both chapter and book end: demographic thought in the work of one former Florentine, Dante.

1.4 *Thought on the one hand and the facts on the other: ideas about births and deaths, and the contemporary realities*

In his *Masters, Princes and Merchants: the Social Views of Peter the Chanter and His Circle*, which he published in 1970, John Baldwin took a group of masters who were living, working, lecturing, and writing in the nascent University of Paris in the closing decades of the twelfth century and the opening years of the thirteenth. These men of the schools were interested to a very remarkable degree in concrete contemporary realities, such as trade and government, and they commented upon them in general and in specific practical detail. When presenting them Baldwin's method was juxtaposition. On the one hand there might be the example of a French king raising money for war in a particular year in the Vexin, while on the other hand there would be the reforming theologian Peter the Chanter looking at different ways of raising money for war and different sorts of war, and making moral distinctions. The ideas of this circle of men, the 'reformist intellectuals' of their time, constituted the theme of the book, and most of the book's space is devoted to a painstaking and brilliant exposition of these ideas, while a much smaller part is taken up with summary expositions of the realities which interested them.

Although Baldwin is pre-eminent in the intellectual pedigree of *The Measure of Multitude*, in practice it has not often been possible to follow the example of his juxtaposition of scholastic ideas and the contemporary world. Occasionally the present book establishes a demographic context—for example, saying, 'This is what some historical demographers have said about medieval life-expectancy', before going on to outline what thirteenth-century commentators made of Aristotle's tract on life-span. But it does not do this consistently, because so much less is known with certainty about medieval population than about how the king of France raised money and waged war.

Historical demographers look at a Europe in whose inhabited parts most people supported themselves by pastoral or arable farming, with only a small proportion of the population living in towns and cities—with regional variation, the urban element being larger in northern and central Italy and parts of the Low Countries than in England.[21] There is an orthodoxy about a trend in population in the central middle ages, which is the following. Many different sorts of evidence point to growth in population in the twelfth and thirteenth centuries.[22] There are new settlements, villages becoming towns, and town and city perimeter-walls expanding, which means increasing numbers if one assumes that density of inhabitation remains the same.[23] Town and city populations are growing, principally with numbers flowing in from the country, rather than births outweighing deaths in families already settled in towns and cities. It is unclear how far twelfth- and thirteenth-century expansion of urban habitation was faster than the overall increase in population. Visible are various expressions of the attempt to cope with larger numbers. New churches and parishes meet the needs of worship and the administration of sacraments,[24] while the clearing of forest and draining of fen increases the fields which can be sown and the amount of grain which can be supplied. In England the pressure exerted by numbers of people upon resources of food was such that by 1300, it has been claimed, more land was under cultivation than has ever been since. There is also external expansion, people on the move to less inhabited areas, and colonization taking place in the wake of crusade against the pagan or the Muslim, whether in the Baltic countries, southern Spain, or the Eastern Mediterranean.[25] The expansion tails off well before the Black Death, but there is debate about decline, and when it sets in—before the extraordinary mortality brought about by famine in 1315–17, or even earlier, before 1300?[26] There is another question-mark when the historical demographer stands back from this general picture of *c.*1100–*c.*1340 and looks backwards towards *c.*800 and Carolingian Europe. From that period there survive detailed surveys of some estates, called polyptyches, which suggest very dense population for the small areas upon which they bear.[27] Their congruence with the later expansionist picture of the twelfth and thirteenth centuries is 'saved' by assuming that there were isolated islands of dense population in Carolingian Europe, surrounded by vast tracts of forest, fen, and other uninhabited lands.

Very sophisticated attention has been paid by historical demographers in recent years to this picture. In England there have been very careful studies of the isolated records in series from which some statistical extrapolations can be made, and also complex debate about the conceptual approaches of various historians of economy and population in this period. At the same time modern historical demography of this period has been becoming much 'thicker', relating numbers to a much denser complex of economic, social, and cultural matters.

[21] See contemporary comment in Ch. 10 below. [22] See Ch. 15 below.
[23] The examples of Paris and Florence appear in Chs. 3 and 14 below.
[24] See Paris in Ch. 3 below. [25] See Chs. 3 and 9 below.
[26] See Ch. 5 below. [27] See Ch. 8 below.

What *The Measure of Multitude* needs to retain from this is, first of all, the cautionary note so often sounded by workers in this field. The data is sparse, its interpretation fraught with difficulty, and where it does yield patterns these in turn suggest much variation in demographic rhythms according to region and according to other variables. Secondly, while the revision of thought about the marriage-rate and age at marriage in medieval Europe is very well-known, we are in need of some steady gazing at the vast and ragged uncertainty which comes in its wake.

Though the revolution is expounded more fully below, in Chapter 12, it needs recapitulation here. It has been suggested that populations could be characterized fundamentally by their possession of *either* a so-called 'non-European marriage pattern', defined by low age at first marriage especially for girls, and very high marriage-rate; *or* the so-called 'European marriage pattern', defined by relatively high age at first marriage, especially for girls, and quite low marriage-rate (many adults remaining single). Data from a fiscal census of 1427, the Tuscan *catasto*, suggested a modified version of the non-European pattern (girls' marriage was very early, but men's was late), and the original propounder of the distinction between the two patterns suggested that *medieval* England had the non-European pattern. I italicize in order to point to the essentialist notions of 'medieval' and 'modern' which may exercise some quiet influence on people's belief in the presence of one or other system. The allocation of the two patterns was overturned by Richard Smith, who established that geography was more significant than chronology. Already in the thirteenth century one could point to a high proportion of the population in England not marrying and girls not marrying early. Some mid-thirteenth-century English villages were broadly the same in these matters around 1250 and 1800. In Italy the pattern was rather different from England, and again Smith could point to long duration in its marriage pattern.

All of this upsets the apple-cart. It raises alarmingly fundamental questions about other parts of the usual picture of the 'nasty, brutish, and short' facts of medieval life and death. Where the 'European' marriage pattern prevails fertility is kept low by the restricted proportion of the population that marries and by the effects of a high age at first marriage, which curtails the number of child-bearing years between marriage and menopause. It restricts fertility further through making a woman's later years—pre-menopause years which are less fertile—a higher proportion of the total number of years during which she can conceive children legitimately. Now, births and deaths have to be in rough balance. If the European *marriage* pattern was in place in England and in other parts of north-western Europe in the thirteenth century, broadly as it was centuries later, was medieval *mortality* in these regions also not quite as *medieval* as is usually thought? What are the further consequences for our view of mortality in those parts of Latin Christendom, southern Europe, where a modified version of the non-European marriage pattern prevailed? It is to the cautious and disciplined conjectures of the experts, historical demographers such as Richard Smith, E. A. Wrigley, and Jeremy Goldberg, that the reader should turn for proper guidance about these speculations. My purpose in raising them here is different, to underline just how little we know about—literally—the facts of medieval life and death.

Hence my policy in this book, in which sometimes and in some cases the thought described will have been a response to demographic realities. For the most part I leave these realities to be inferred and conjectured: out there, in the world in which the commentator was living.

1.5 *Anachronism*

I have not yet addressed anachronism: anachronism of individual words, and anachronism of the intellectual discipline *demographic thought*.

Individual words: this is an important and practical point. So far in this introductory chapter I have freely used phrases like *death-rate* and *birth-control*, but this will not do in an exposition of thoughts which were thought in the middle ages. Most such phrases were newly minted in the late nineteenth or early twentieth centuries, with many threads connecting them to modern thought. If sprinkled liberally in the exposition of a thirteenth-century thinker, they misrepresent through their insidious imputation of modernity of thought. In the rest of the book, therefore, such key-words are mainly avoided. *Vitatio prolis* was a common medieval Latin phrase, so I use a translation of it, 'avoidance of offspring', instead of birth-control. An early fourteenth-century commentator on the *Politics* heads his section on population-control *Quomodo curandum est de multitudine*, roughly 'how one takes concerned thought about the multitude [= population]', and accordingly in the rest of this book my preferred phrase is 'thought about the multitude' or 'thought about population'.[28] For the same reasons my translations of longer passages are deliberately very literal. Anachronism is not the only problem here. Without rigour in avoiding such phrases, it is difficult to come to an adequate understanding of the significance of the translations into Latin of Aristotle's works, much of which lay precisely in the demographic vocabulary that they disseminated.[29]

For the question of anachronism in attributing the individual discipline of demographic thought to medieval people, I refer the reader to the final parts of the book, Chapter 14 and the Epigraph.

1.6 *Omissions*

Although *medieval* as a term of chronological convenience has usually meant anything within 500–1500, this book is quite narrow, beginning around 1100 and

[28] See further discussion of the anachronism of modern key-words in Chs. 6 and 11 below.

[29] See Chs. 10–11 below.

ending in the 1340s, before the Black Death of 1348–9, with two minor chronological exceptions in Chapters 8 and 13.[30] The field is Latin Christendom, and in principle this should mean the geographical area of the over five hundred dioceses of the Latin Church, bordering on Greco-Slavonic Christianity in Eastern Europe and Islam in Spain, and including, outside Europe, the crusader kingdoms of the eastern Mediterranean. In practice, however, in this book it is modern knowledge of the demographic realities of England, the Low Countries, France, Italy, Spain, and the Holy Land that hovers in the background, and thought in Paris, Oxford, Bologna, and Florence that occupies the front of the stage.

I am aware of various direct omissions, and I begin with texts. While privileging theology, Aristotle, geography, and the crusades, I have largely ignored astrology.[31] Astrological texts, in particular the group of Arabic texts which were translated into Latin around 1140, upheld a model of generalizing thought in several areas, notably world sects (= religions),[32] and also populations; and later accounts of medieval demographic thought would benefit from their further study. I also decided to privilege certain demographic themes at the expense of others. So, while there is thought here about population levels, marriage-ages, 'control', life-span, and so on, there is little systematic attention to many other themes. Thought about 'ages of man' was left out because of the existence of several monographs on the theme,[33] and also omitted is thought *about* groups which have been receiving much scrutiny by historical demographers: servants and widows.

When we turn to *who* was thinking and who is represented in this book, omission becomes an enormous theme. Latin-literate males, in themselves forming a tiny group, contain an even tinier group, the very learned who left still extant texts, whom I have been reading and thinking about. I have not made into an autonomous theme, as I could have done, the thought of organizers and administrators: churchmen thinking about numbers of Christians and the sizes of parishes and dioceses, and colonizers thinking about migration and settlement. But gender is a bigger problem. The thoughts of half of Latin Christendom, the people whose bodies bore the next generation, do not feature. Absence of direct evidence makes it difficult to deal with the absence of women. I have hesitated to go down the path of inference from indirect evidence, fearing that my speculations would do no more than display my preconceptions. I restrict myself to alerting the reader to the gender fence which is thrown around my book.

There is the problem of extraordinary and ordinary people. The thoughts of the vast majority of people, ordinary, lay, and illiterate, do not feature. I have tried

[30] Ch. 8 includes Carolingian and post-1348 comment on avoidance of offspring, and Ch. 13 includes Nicole Oresme on the *Politics*.

[31] There is some in Ch. 14.

[32] See J. D. North, 'Astrology and the Fortunes of Churches', *Centaurus* 24 (1980), 181–211, and my 'A "Scientific" view of Jews from Paris around 1300', forthcoming in *Micrologus*.

[33] See n. 17 above.

to chip away at the second of these problems a little in Chapter 9, in allusions to the thought of merchants and crusading soldiers or settlers, and I tackle the problem directly in the final chapter. That addresses demographic thought in Florence, attempting to bring into one picture the thought of mendicant friars in their Latin texts and their vernacular sermons, Florentines who were literate in the vernacular, and ordinary Florentines who have left no texts. However, the sources are usually skewed to learned men, usually churchmen, often members of the mendicant orders. A very high proportion of them were reading, lecturing, and writing in Paris, although Bologna and Oxford and a few other centres of learning also feature.

The effects of this skewing need reflection. Some are not as extreme as they at first appear. Centralization in Paris and a few other centres is not so important. Before the regionalization which was such a marked feature of the later middle ages and which began with the foundation of such local universities as Prague (1348) and Cracow (1365), the major universities drew students from all over Christendom. Flemings, Swiss, Poles, and Hungarians jostled together in the lecture-halls of Paris or Bologna, alongside the English, the French, the Lombards, and the Tuscans. When Chapter 5 below parades Dominicans in Paris around 1250, it is displaying the thoughts of one from Swabia, one from France, and one from southern Italy. Nor is it so significant that these men are working in cities. Many of the men in question came from various strata of the nobility, and had come into the cities after early lives passed on rural estates. It was once thought, but no longer, that the thirteenth-century friars were urban and preoccupied with urban things. In fact, friars thought that one could get at more people through working in towns and cities, and this included the countryfolk that came in regularly.[34] More important is the noble origin of many of the learned, Peter the Chanter, Albert, and Thomas, and the fact that their direct experience was of marriage, family, and kin within this stratum.

And the thought-world of ordinary folk? Very rarely can it be got at. One exception is formed by the men and women of Languedoc whose thoughts, lives, and lies were scrutinized by an inquisitor in Pamiers around 1320, and made famous in a modern best-seller, Le Roy Ladurie's *Montaillou*. Let us muse on the gap between these people and medieval academics, taking three themes, first of all one *non*-demographic proposition.

'Some have fallen into this error, that anyone is saved in their faith, law or sect (= religion)', Saracen, Jew, or Christian. This is reported as the opinion of some people by the Paris master and later bishop, William of Auvergne,[35] presumably alluding to debate in the university of Paris in his time, in the early thirteenth century. And it also appears among the many opinions of unlearned people far

[34] See d'Avray, *Preaching*, Chs. 1 and 4.

[35] William of Auvergne, *De legibus*, xxi: *Opera omnia*, ii. 57: *nonnulli in eum errorem devenerunt, ut credant unumquemque in sua fide, vel lege, seu secta salvari.* William is discussing Jews, Saracens, and Christians.

down in the south, a century later, which crowd into the pages of Fournier's inquisition register. 'Saracens and Jews are saved just like Christians.'[36] Let us move on, then, to a thought about population. The Languedoc records provide us with a vignette of a group of men gathered in a square in Ornolac, six of whom are named. They are discussing the place which receives dead souls, and the problem of numbers of people and room. 'Where could so many souls be received as die every day?'[37] After discussion about what place could be large enough, one person compared the size of paradise, receiving so many, to the space between Toulouse and Mérens, and how many could be held if one enormous house occupied this space. In Chapter 10 we shall be seeing an academic Dominican in mid-thirteenth-century Oxford discussing how many people could have fitted into an earthly paradise, conceived as a quarter of the world's surface. His primary concern is similar. Finally, one woman giving evidence to the inquisitor in Pamiers refers in passing to her future life, 'if she lived as long as she could live by nature' (*si ipsa loquens viveret quantum poterat vivere per naturam*).[38] Here she makes a common-sense distinction between contingent length of life (= actual, taking into account accidents, illness, etc.) and maximum natural length of life. We shall see the same distinction being made more academically by the commentators on Aristotle's *Little Natural Works*.[39] Although much more could be said about these texts, I want only to draw from them a preliminary and elementary message, which is this. There was not an unimaginable distance between the thought-worlds of the academics and these Languedocian men and women.

That is not the end of the matter, though. These men and women thought and spoke in the vernacular. Their thoughts were not dressed up with authorities and glosses. Above all, among a distinct minority of them, those, that is to say, who were not passionate devotees of heresy, there is a distinctly atheist and materialist strand. Their thoughts were these. This life is all there is. When someone dies, that's it.[40]

So, if we take this game further—the people in the inquisitor's register standing for ordinary folk and used as controls on our learned men of the Church—this is what we would conjecture about how most of the evidence skews the picture.

[1] The demographic thoughts of our learned men and ordinary folk do recognizably occupy the same world, [2] but if we could regularly access the minds of ordinary folk, we would find demographic thoughts which would be less connected with faith and less theological in their sources and expression. In other

[36] *Le registre d'inquisition de Jacques Fournier, évêque de Pamiers (1318–1325)*, ed. J. Duvernoy, 3 vols., Bibliothèque Méridionale, 2nd ser., 41 (Toulouse, 1965), and Duvernoy's additional *Corrections* (Toulouse, 1972), ii. 110: *ita salvabuntur sarraceni et iudei sicut et christiani*; similar sentiments on pp. 112 and 113.

[37] Ibid., i. 202: *ubi poterant recipi tot anime, quot homines quotidie decedunt.*

[38] Ibid. i. 461. [39] See Ch. 10 below.

[40] W. L. Wakefield, 'Some unorthodox popular ideas of the thirteenth century', *Medievalia et Humanistica*, n.s. 4 (1973), 23–35; P. Biller, 'Women and Texts in Languedocian Catharism', in *Women, the Book and the Godly*, ed. L. Smith and J. H. M. Taylor (Cambridge, 1995), pp. 171–82 (pp. 180–1).

words, if we take the medieval demographic thought given in Chapters 2–14 in this book, we may be getting quite a lot of the essential shape of most people's demographic thought, but subsumed into and part-hidden by the Church and its learned men: green grass, whose colouring is distorted by our having to peer at it through the deep colours of the Church's stained glass windows. But my comments are now at the very limits of conjecture, and perhaps beyond them.

Part 1

THE CHURCH AND GENERATION

2

MARRIAGE AND THE CHURCH'S MARRIAGE-TEXTS

'I want to be a mother.' Chance survival of the records of a court have preserved for us the longing for a baby felt by a girl in rural Normandy. Thomassie, daughter of William Blancvilain, from a Norman village, brought a case for 'divorce' against Thomas known as Osmeul, on grounds of his impotence. The result is known through the record of the sentence which annulled the marriage, on 21 November 1317, after the court had heard evidence and consulted with men expert in law. Preserved in the sentence is the brief summary of Thomassie's position: 'whereas she is a virgin and wants to be a mother'.[1] Behind Thomassie were the countless young, middle-aged, and older men and women who were alive in Latin Christendom at any given time, married or single, with or without children. While at this time it was a church court which dealt with single cases like Thomassie's, it was church writers who turned the marriages of the many into treatises written in Latin, couched in theological terms and making large statements about Marriage. Here is one of them, a theologian called 'Master A' writing around 1120 and taking his lead from Genesis:

> 'Increase and multiply.' To 'increase' is to accept the fertility of sex. 'Multiplication' happens through the union of man and woman. Nor was reason for this union lacking after the sin and punishment of man, [and] in accordance with this [union] the earth is now full of men.[2]

Here are our two poles, the millions of ordinary Christians on the one hand, and on the other hand the churchmen who dealt with their marriages and wrote academic treatises in which they generalized about marriage and the peopling of the earth.

2.1 *The Church and dealing with marriage*

Some time between 1249 and 1261 a Dominican friar, Stephen of Bourbon, was writing a how-to-do-it book on preaching, and including in it many colourful

[1] *Le registre de l'officialité de Cerisy*, ed. M. G. Dupont, Mémoires de la Société des Antiquaires de Normandie, 3rd ser. 10 (Caen, 1880), p. 322: 'cum sit integra et vellet esse mater'. On this case see Esmein, i. 293 and 293 n. 1, and A. Finch, '*Repulsa uxore sua*: marital difficulties and separation in the later middle ages', *Continuity and Change* 8 (1993), 11–38 (p. 15). See n. 37 below on 'vellet esse mater'.

[2] Reinhardt, *Anselm von Laon*, pp. 170–1; on the treatise, ibid., pp. 3–6.

tales or reminiscences which could be used to liven up sermons. Many are incomplete, only scraps.[3] For example:

i. Stephen recalls listening to a conversation between a knight and a rich money-lender. Stephen's presence probably related to marriage negotiations, for the knight's daughter was going to marry the money-lender's son.[4]
ii. Stephen describes a lady's maid walking into a city to sell in the market. As she approaches the embankment she begins to think about buying and selling. In a day-dream she sees herself rising in the world, going up from milk and chickens to pigs and sheep and getting to trade in oxen. Eventually she is rich enough to catch a nobleman. And so she dreams on. Finally she is in all her finery and on horseback, being led along to marry her lord.[5]
iii. Pouilly (Saône-et-Loire) in the diocese of Mâcon is the setting of another vignette. A young herdsman had promised to marry a girl, 'giving his faith', plighting his troth, and then had his way with her. Afterwards he would not keep to their understanding, and the ecclesiastical official of the place excommunicated him. Stephen himself publicly admonished the herdsman to keep to the agreement and solemnize the marriage. But the herdsman was contemptuous of the sentence of excommunication, and laughed at the public rebukes he was getting.[6]
iv. Stephen was preaching in Dun (Saône-et-Loire), in the diocese of Mâcon. Here the parish priest and a certain man told Stephen about the man's son, who had been living with a woman who was too closely related to him by blood or affinity. Action was taken by the parish priest and neighbours. There was accusation and excommunication, and a Dominican, perhaps Stephen himself, tried unsuccessfully to split the couple.[7]
v. An unknown friar was preaching in the same diocese of Mâcon about couples living together. Men openly living with women were made to promise, on oath, to marry them or leave them. A problem came up. One man *was* willing to marry the woman with whom he lived. The trouble in his case was that the pressure from the friar was not in the direction of marriage. She was a blood relative, and the friar's exhortation to the man was therefore to leave her—which the man was unwilling to do.[8]
vi. When preaching in Vézelay Stephen was given a story. It began with the man's father, who had worked hard to enrich his son and enable him to marry in great style. When all had been handed over, the daughter-in-law persuaded her husband to throw his father out of the house.[9]
vii. There is a murder, the outcome of which, sadly, Stephen never tells us. He just sets the scene. It took place, around the year 1240, outside the doorway of the quite recently built church of the Blessed Virgin Mary at Dijon. A moneylender was

[3] On Stephen of Bourbon, see *SOPMA* ii. 354–5 and iv. 280. How Stephen constructed marriage and how his text was read are themes which cannot be pursued here.
[4] Stephen of Bourbon, *Tractatus*, IV. vii; no. 416, pp. 362–3. [5] Ibid., IV. xi; no. 271, p. 226.
[6] Ibid., I. vii; no. 55, pp. 61–2; see p. 61 n. 2 on Pouilly. [7] Ibid., I. vii; no. 51, p. 59.
[8] Ibid., IV. vii; no. 309, p. 260. [9] Ibid., II. vii; no. 161, p. 138.

about to celebrate marriage, and with great show. His bride-to-be would process to the parish accompanied by organ music. Under the portico of the church she would consent to him and ratify marriage by words of present consent, according to custom. Then bride and bridegroom would enter the church in festive manner, where the marriage would be solemnized with the celebration of mass.[10]

viii. In the last tale there is a couple, who had been married for over thirty years. All we learn about them is that they were a Darby and Joan pair. There had never been quarrels or harsh words in their marriage.[11]

Through Stephen we see two groups, a few ordinary women and men on the one hand, and on the other a few churchmen and Churches in parts of central and southern France in the 1230s to 1250s. There is human comedy, whether in the young girl's dreams or the lusty herdsman. There are glimpses of some general, enduring and intractable realities among these men and women: custom; desire for ceremony; preference for informal arrangements about living together; ignoring of law and convention. There are points where these people meet the Church and churchmen. A church building provides the door outside which consent is exchanged, before bride and groom enter the church for mass. A parish priest and an itinerant Dominican friar are both intimately concerned in individuals' marriages, and they both preach about marriage. The law of the church bears on the degrees of physical or spiritual relationship within which marriage may not be contracted. There are formal oaths and an ecclesiastical official. Behind these, though not explicitly in Stephen's text, there are the church courts which dealt with marriage: establishing whether marriages existed, annulling marriages, adjudicating separations, and, in some times and places, concerning themselves with marriage or financial settlements for deflowered and abandoned girls.[12]

What we are looking at here is a cross-section of a *system*: the Church covering and trying to control most aspects of marriage in Latin Christendom. This system had a long history, in which the main theme is the Church's progression from a smaller and less public role to what we are seeing here in the thirteenth century. The transition from less to more is usually put in the tenth and eleventh centuries, but it is impossible to trace in detail because evidence from these crucial years is scarce, and it is also difficult to recount generally, because traditions and the dates of development varied from region to region. In the earlier middle ages the Church intruded less. Legislation and jurisdiction over marriage were a matter for secular law-codes and courts,[13] not the Church. The Church's concern was more private, with the behaviour of its members, and in particular the sins they might commit in contracting marriage, and in sexual relations in or outside marriage: such matters filled the 'penitential books' which are the textual survivals of its system of confession and penance.[14] The contracting of marriage itself was a

[10] Ibid., I. vii; 53, p. 60. [11] Ibid., IV. iii; no. 245, p. 207.

[12] J.-P. Lévy, 'L'officialité de Paris et les questions familiales à la fin du XIVe siècle', *Études d'histoire du droit canonique dédiées à Gabriel Le Bras*, 2 vols. (Paris, 1965), ii. 265–94 (pp. 283–4).

[13] Esmein, i. 7–26.

[14] See R. Kottje, 'Ehe und Eheverständnis in den vorgratianischen Bußbüchern', in *Love and Marriage*

lay and secular matter, whose essentials were the handing over of a girl, by her father to the groom, the exchanging of gifts, and perhaps the girl's *deductio in domum*, her 'being brought into the house' of the groom or his family.[15] This ceremony involved a house or houses: not a church building. There could be one minor role for a priest in this house, however, blessing the marriage-bed, for which an order was provided in the Church's service-books.[16]

Then followed a long period during which 'the Church is slowly taking over'.[17] The Church's jurisdiction and legislation developed and established a near-exclusive competence over marriage in most regions of Latin Christendom.[18] During the twelfth century we get clear glimpses of Church marriage-courts in action, and some court records begin to survive from around 1200.[19] Implemented in these was the Church's law on marriage. This was systematically stated in the great compilations of canon law, particularly those of Ivo of Chartres (died 1115), Gratian (*c.*1140), and Gregory IX (1234); it was comprehensive; and it was tinkered with or radically overhauled by popes and Church Councils. Prominent among the latter were Alexander III (1159–81) settling the definition of what constituted marriage, consent of the two contracting parties; and the fourth Lateran Council of 1215 reducing the number of degrees within which marriage was prohibited from seven to four, in order to avoid easy divorce.[20]

Symbolizing the Church-takeover and its most important element was a move on the ground: away from a house, and to the building which was the local church. Where people had got married in houses, they were now marrying outside the door of the parish church, in the presence of a priest.[21] Some patterns of regional variation appear. For example, this was probably happening earlier in England and Normandy than elsewhere. In France celebration was inside the church south of a line from Bordeaux-Périgueux to Grenoble.[22] Marriages in Italian cities, especially among the élite, remained private affairs conducted in the presence of a notary.[23] When the move from house to church started is not clear. The legislation of Church Councils required celebration *in facie ecclesie* ('in the face of the Church *or* a church'), which certainly meant 'publicly' and probably usually

in the Twelfth Century, ed. W. Van Hoecke and A. Welkenhuysen, Mediaevalia Lovanensia, Studia 8 (Louvain, 1981), pp. 8–40; A. J. Frantzen, *The Literature of Penance in Anglo-Saxon England* (New Brunswick, NJ, 1983), pp. 11, 15, 40, 55–6, 66–7, 80, 118, 140 and 201 n. 2; P. J. Payer, *Sex and the Penitentials: The Development of a Sexual Code, 550–1150* (Toronto, Buffalo, London, 1984); and Ch. 8 below, pp. 181–2.

15 J.-B. Molin and P. Mutembe, *Le rituel de mariage en France du XIIe siècle au XVIe siècle*, Théologie Historique 26 (Paris, 1974), pp. 25–30. A clear account of medieval western liturgies is provided in K. Stevenson, *Nuptial Blessing: A Study of Christian Marriage Rites* (Oxford, 1983), pp. 35–94.

16 Molin and Mutembe, *Rituel*, pp. 27–8.

17 Stevenson, *Nuptial Blessing*, p. 67.

18 Esmein, i. 27–34.

19 *Select Cases from the Ecclesiastical Courts of the Province of Canterbury c.1200–1301*, ed. N. Adams and C. Donahue, Selden Society 95 for 1978–9 (London, 1981), cases A. 6–A. 9, pp. 18–31; see comment (introduction, p. 3) on the earliness of English records.

20 Baldwin, *Peter the Chanter*, i. 176, 332–6.

21 Molin and Mutembe, *Rituel*, p. 32; Reinhardt, *Anselm von Laon*, p. 98 n. 116.

22 Molin and Mutembe, *Rituel*, p. 44.

23 Esmein, i. 198 n. 2; C. Klapisch-Zuber, *Women, Family and Ritual in Renaissance Italy* (Chicago and London, 1985), pp. 178–212.

meant 'at a church'),[24] and it poses a problem. It comes late in England, beginning in 1175 and 1200.[25] However, already before 1150 there are several English, Norman, and northern French liturgies for celebrating at church door; a manuscript written at Bury St Edmunds 1125–35 contains the earliest rite, which was later used at Laon.[26] Clearly, therefore, the conciliar legislation is not innovating, and this may also be true of the earliest extant liturgies: they may be later witnesses to a ceremony which has already been practised for some time.[27]

2.2 *The Church and writing about marriage*

Different parts of this system had their different texts. Consider the range in the mid-thirteenth century and in north-western Europe, where texts were generated more profusely than elsewhere because of the greater 'churchiness' of marriage in this part of Latin Christendom.

There were liturgical books containing the order of service for church celebration of marriage, according to the use of the region or diocese. A parish priest was obliged to keep a copy of the statutes of synods of his diocese. The few quires of this copy contained brief instructions on the administration of the sacraments. The section on marriage would detail banns to be read out in church on Sundays before the marriage and the basic formula for the exchange of consent, and it could specify sobriety of celebration. It would summarize canon law on prohibited degrees and impediments. It could also include a few theological points about marriage which the parish priest should preach, such as its institution, its goodness, and its purpose. The section instructing a priest how to hear confession would encourage questions on sex under one of the seven deadly sins, lust, and more specific questions about sexual sin and sex inside marriage were being suggested, especially through the independent tracts on confession which were beginning to be inserted into synodal statutes around 1240. Among more miscellaneous provisions there might also be some instructing a priest to hear a woman's confession before childbirth, and, especially in England, some telling a priest to instruct mothers on the feeding and care of babies.

Outside the synodal statutes there are monographic treatises on confession, such as Thomas of Chobham's *Summa confessorum*, which had been written

[24] Esmein, i. 200; M. Sheehan, 'Marriage Theory and Practice. The Diocesan Legislation of Medieval England', *MS* 40 (1978), 408–60 (p. 441). In his *Marriage in the Western Church: The Christianization of Marriage during the Patristic and Early Medieval Periods* (Leiden, New York, Cologne, 1994), pp. 401–12, P. N. Reynolds argues that Carolingian reformers insisted on marriage *in facie ecclesie*, although they did not use this phrase.

[25] *Councils & Synods I*, ii. 980 and 1067. See J. Gaudemet, *Le mariage en occident: Les mœurs et le droit* (Paris, 1987), p. 229, on legislation in Hungary and Sicily.

[26] Molin and Mutembe, *Rituel*, pp. 34–71; Stevenson, *Nuptial Blessing*, pp. 68–71.

[27] Molin and Mutembe, *Rituel*, pp. 31–3, note possible but not certain liturgies from the eleventh century for celebration at a church, and a Rouen provincial synod of 1012 asking for the blessing of a couple at church.

about 1216. It ranges over similar themes but at much greater length and in more detail. The varying licitness of conjugal sex was scrutinized, and much attention was given to a spectrum of care which ranged from avoiding miscarriage to the advantages of mothers' over nurses' breast-milk. From around 1220 such works, written by and for secular priests, had been supplemented by works of instruction for confessors written by mendicant friars, especially Dominicans.

From the mendicants also came instructional works on preaching, which would far outstrip the short statements or hints of the statutes. They contained model sermons, sometimes about marriage or addressed to married people. One such treatise, the *Tractatus de variis materiis praedicabilibus*, was written by the Dominican Stephen of Bourbon, who stated a commonplace in his preface,[28] that preachers needed colourful stories to help instilling items of faith and morals in people's minds and memories. Hence the verbal snapshots of marriages in the tales collected in Stephen's treatise.

There were books containing canon law: the books and specialist knowledge of the lawyers and judges who pleaded and adjudicated in courts which dealt with marriage, the 'men expert in law' whose consultation is formally recorded in the sentence in Thomassie's case. The most important collections of canon law were Gratian's *Decretum* of *c*.1140, the *Quinque compilationes antiquae* of *c*.1191–1226, and Gregory IX's *Libri quinque decretalium* of 1234, one book of which is entirely devoted to marriage, while important monographs by individual canon-legal authors came to supplement these; notable among them at this period was the *Summa aurea* of Henry of Susa (Hostiensis), whose earlier version was written in 1250–1. The standard collections, and the glosses and commentaries which each attracted, acted as pedagogic texts in the training of lawyers in the law faculties at the university of Bologna and elsewhere, and at the same time incorporated new law and formed the basis for its further discussion. In the theology faculty, finally, there were the treatises composed by academic theologians, writing in a tradition which went back to the Master A who was quoted at the beginning of the chapter.

While examining these academic treatises in our later chapters, we shall need to remember three things about them and the pile of Church marriage-texts upon which they sit. First, there were a complex web of interconnections and areas of overlap between all these texts. For example, the fundamental compilations of canon law comprise papal decretal letters or conciliar decrees which decide matters of marriage, and some of this material is repeated in adapted and summary form in local Church legislation, and is compressed and repackaged in various ways in priests' and confessors' manuals. Where lists of rules need to be remembered, there are neat verses to help the pastor who needs to memorize what he is reading.[29] Canon *law* is also a principal source in *theology*, where its details are often the object of discussion.

[28] Stephen of Bourbon, *Tractatus*, p. 4.

[29] See e.g. the index of verses in *Trois sommes de pénitence de la première moitié du XIIIe siècle*, ed. J. P. Renard, 2 vols., Lex Spiritus Vitae 6 (Louvain, 1989), i. 532–4.

Secondly, these are not just old books. These texts were once produced and used in a functioning system, read by many people and an influence upon people's lives: as it were, three- rather than two-dimensional.

Finally, there are great practical difficulties in seeing these texts functioning in this past marriage-system, among real past people.

Take Thomas of Chobham's instructional work as an example. It is accessible to us in an elaborate modern edition, which enumerates the over one hundred manuscripts which still survive, principally in northern European libraries, especially English and German. These hint at a *roughly* similar map of earlier location and readership, but the direct evidence is slight.[30] One manuscript was owned by John, a vicar of Newchurch, who left it to a priory in Bilsington, Kent.[31] So far so good, but now conjecture enters. John could have read the section in Thomas where he discussed marital sex (as was remarked earlier) in considerable detail, analysing it according to the husband's motivation as 'licit', 'weak', or too 'vehement'. The conversation, which a husband or wife had with John in the parish of Newchurch, when confessing their sins to him at the beginning of Lent, could have been shaped by John's reading of the section on sex in this manuscript. But we have no tape-recording.

Here is a tale about confession from another source. Two men from a parish are travelling together along the road to Soest,[32] where they are going to market, and, when the baggage belonging to one of them falls into the mud, its owner starts to swear about his parish priest, who is responsible for all this hard work. A conversation starts. The man had been told he must pay his parish priest eighteen pence to say masses, after confessing having sex during Lent. The other man had had an experience at the hands of the parish priest, who was called Hegennaird, which was similar apart from one point. When confessing he had admitted the opposite—not having sex with his wife during Lent. The dreadful Hegennaird had upbraided him:

> 'You have done very badly, keeping yourself from your wife for such a long time. She could have conceived a child with you, but with your continence you've shut off that possibility'. As is usual with simple people, the man was terrified. When he asked for advice about this crime, the confessor replied, 'You give me eighteen pence, and I'll placate God on your behalf with the same number of masses'.

After this roadside conversation, the two men went to Soest, and laid a complaint with the Dean and canons of St Patroclus.

[30] Chobham, *Summa confessorum*, pp. lxxiv–lxxvi.

[31] Ibid., p. lxxviii.

[32] On *exempla* dealing with confession, see J. Berlioz, 'Les ordalies dans les *exempla* de la confession (XIIIe–XIVe siècles)', *L'Aveu: Antiquité et moyen-âge*, Collection de l'École Française de Rome 88 (Rome, 1986), pp. 315–40 (p. 319 on Caesar of Heisterbaach), and J. Berlioz and C. Ribaucourt, 'Images de la confession dans la prédication au début du XIVe siècle. L'exemple de *l'Alphabetum narrationum* d'Arnold de Liège', in Groupe de la Bussière [= M. Sot and others], *Pratiques de la confession, des Pères du désert à Vatican II: Quinze études d'histoire* (Paris, 1983), pp. 95–115. For earlier use of Caesar's *exempla*, see my 'The Common Woman in the Western Church in the Thirteenth and Early Fourteenth Centuries', in *Women in the Church*, ed. D. Wood, Studies in Church History 27 (Oxford, 1990, pp. 127–57 (pp. 133–7). On Caesar see K. Langosch, 'Caesarius von Heisterbach', *Vf* i. 1152–68.

The abuse in this story is not our point, but rather what it implies about normal practice: a parish priest's questioning of the married, when they came to confession, about their sexual activities, along the lines suggested in the manuscript of a confessors' manual. Enquiry into Newchurch is propped up by material from the Rhineland, suggesting what could have taken place. The slightness of direct evidence leads to so many 'could haves'.

This is only the start of the problems. Consider the relationship between the legislative texts, the practice of courts, and the thoughts of individuals whose statements are recorded. For example, records of marriage-courts show these courts forcing couples living together to 'abjure on pain of marrying' (*abjurare sub pena nubendi*). They must either separate or take an oath that if they ever make love again this will in itself mean that they are married. This was close to Stephen of Bourbon's fifth tale, in which those who lived together were forced to promise on oath to marry or separate. Now, the abjuration's element of compulsion would have been embarrassing in texts which stated that marriage could only be constituted by free consent,[33] and therefore this matter—clearly a reality—is simply absent from canon law texts.

Another example is the legal text on annulment of marriage on the grounds of the man's impotence. The woman says, 'I want to be a mother.' Those drawing up the sentence delivered on Thomassie in 1317 formulated her position briefly, in Latin, and following canon law. Reading this text, we are hearing words in canon law which Thomassie agreed to have presented as what she wanted. We are not hearing a translation, from her Norman French, of her precise words. Or, if we are, we can never know that we are.[34]

Why not stay with the Church's texts as *texts*, and abandon the rest of the medieval marriage-system and the real people who once lived within it? Current preoccupation with textuality and the philosophically problematic nature of history's claims to get at a past reality make such sidelining both intellectually respectable and fashionable. If we resist the sweet temptation of epistemological despair, we must not do so by turning a blind eye to the problems.

2.3 *Writing about marriage in the schools, 1100–1350*

The story of academic theological writing on marriage begins here with a dozen anonymous texts from the 'school of Laon'.[35] Several are independent treatises on marriage,[36] others are the marriage-sections of larger works of theology, in which marriage occurs in connection with the creation or as a sacrament, beside

[33] See R. H. Helmholz, *Canon Law and the Law of England* (London and Ronceverte, 1987), pp. 145–6; J. A. Brundage, *Law, Sex and Christian Society in Medieval Europe* (Chicago, 1987), pp. 369–70 and nn. 215–16, 447 n. 155, and 515.

[34] C. 33 q. 1 c. 2; Friedberg, I, 1149: 'si mulier causatur et dicit, "Volo mater esse, et filios procreare"'.

[35] See Reinhardt, *Anselm von Laon*, and Zeimentz, *Frühscholastik*.

[36] *De coniugio* and *Decretum Dei fuit*.

baptism. The treatises are very short, typically about 2,000 words, and they are made up of collections of 'sentences'—dicta of the fathers and papal and conciliar decisions—and often nothing more than these.[37] The earliest, the *Sententie Magistri A*, is almost completely devoid of comment, connecting phrases, or the raising of questions. Its opening phrase, 'What is marriage?', is one of the few exceptions. Soon, however, there is development. More connecting comments enter, and the phrase 'It is asked', *Queritur*, makes more appearances.[38] And there are phrases like '*Some* understand the sacrament of marriage [in such and such a way]',[39] or 'Different people say different things [on this]', which suggest the existence of debates about marriage in the early twelfth-century schools of northern France.[40]

The manuscript of a Laon academic treatise on marriage can be put beside the manuscript of the liturgy for contracting marriage which was located and used in Laon around this time:[41] scholastic development and Churchification of marriage were going hand in hand. Occasionally these short early treatises open windows onto this growing system. Some refer to variation in the way marriage is contracted among churches of different regions.[42] They provide glimpses of the operations of the law. One refers to the use of witnesses in proving degrees of relationship, while another reports current criticism of confessions and proofs which are produced when ordeal by iron is used to settle a dispute in a marriage case.[43] The manuscripts themselves survive in numbers which are rather large for what are (mainly) twelfth-century copies of twelfth-century texts, and their current location in Britain, Germany, Poland, France, and Italy may still contain some traces of the map of earlier dispersion. What we do know for certain is that the six copies of *Decretum Dei fuit* were once at Heilsbronn, Klosterneuburg, St Emmeram, Windberg, Weingarten, and Ebersberg, and two of the copies of the *Sententie Magistri A* were at Clairvaux: Black monk, Cistercian, and Augustinian monastic communities.

Then came lift-off. Theologians' discussion of marriage developed and proliferated with a rapidity and on a scale which mean that only the most important figures can be mentioned here. In the decades from the 1130s to 1150s these are Walter of Mortagne, Hugh of St Victor, and Peter the Lombard.

[37] The *Sententie Magistri A* is an exception, at 11,500 words. *Deus de cuius principio* is about 1,400 words; ed. H. Weisweiler, 'Le recueil des sentences "Deus de cuius principio et fine tacetur" et son remaniement', *RTAM* 5 (1933), 245–74 (the marriage section at pp. 270–4). The *Sententie Berolinenses* about 2,000; ed. F. Stegmüller, 'Sententiae Berolinenses. Eine neugefundene Sentenzensammlung aus der Schule des Anselm von Laon', *RTAM* 11 (1939), 33–61 (marriage section at pp. 56–61). *Decretum Dei fuit* about 2,600; ed. H. Weisweiler, *Das Schrifttum der Schule Anselms von Laon und Wilhelms von Champeaux in deutschen Bibliotheken*, BGPTM 33, 2 vols. (1936), i. 361–79. The *De Coniugio* about 2,800; ed. F. Bliemetzrieder, 'Théologie et théologiens de l'école épiscopale de Paris avant Pierre Lombard', *RTAM* 5 (1931), 272–91 (pp. 274–87).

[38] *Deus de cuius principio*, ed. Weisweiler, p. 274.

[39] *Intelligunt quidam coniugii sacramentum, Deus de cuius principio*, ed. Weisweiler, *RTAM* 5, 271.

[40] *Diversi diversa dicunt, Decretum Dei fuit*, ed. Weisweiler, BGPTM 33, i. 369.

[41] Molin and Mutembe, *Rituel*, p. 36.

[42] *Deus de cuius principio*, ed. Weisweiler, p. 272; F. Bliemetzrieder, *Anselms von Laon systematische Sentenzen*, BGPTM 18, parts 2–3 (1919), pp. 140 and 149.

[43] *De coniugio*, ed. Bliemetzrieder, p. 282; *Deus de cuius principio*, ed. Weisweiler, pp. 273–4.

Walter's long life spanned several generations of scholars, linking the early 'school of Laon' with later Paris. Forwards: Walter's writings were to influence Peter the Lombard. Backwards: Walter was himself a man of Laon, where he taught and was also bishop (1150–74), and he had earlier been a pupil of Alberic of Rheims, and Alberic in turn had been a pupil of Anselm of Laon.[44] Two of Walter's extant letters were directed to Alberic, and both were on marriage. Irritated at his old teacher, who significantly failed to reply to him, Walter trenchantly called into question views which Alberic had expressed on the contracting of marriage during discussion on a ceremonious public occasion, at a coronation of bishops at Rheims.[45] If Walter's letters attest the remarkable public and important nature of marriage debate, his treatise also shows the rapidly increasing sophistication of its discussion.[46]

In this treatise, which he wrote before 1139, Walter looks at marriage under certain headings. He begins with its origin and causes, proceeds to its goodness and the questions whether there is sin in the married having sex, what the (Augustinian) goods of marriage are, the 'various customs of marriage', and what suffices for contracting marriage, and he continues through impediments, inter-faith marriage, and annulments. In each section material is introduced by a briefly stated theme or question. Thus, 'Because there are some heretics who detest marriage and regard the conjugal union of man and woman as damnable, let us now see whether it is good or bad'.[47] 'Authorities' are then shunted around—those familiar from the tracts which anthologized these 'sentences'—and 'arguments' (*rationes*). Then Walter 'determines' a conclusion. In the thirteenth century the sequence of question-raising, parade of authorities, and statement of conclusion was to become very formally tight, a straitjacket confining both thought and literary expression. But it is not so in Walter. In his treatise the form varies flexibly from theme to theme. Thus 'various customs of marriage' sidesteps scholastic language or echoes of debate, as it smoothly and briefly makes the variation of marriage from the creation onwards into a brief history—we shall look at it in section 2.4.2 below. Walter's writing and thought are direct, brief, and elegant. The treatise itself, as a partly discursive work, is naturally longer than the little Laon anthologies, but it is still only about 8,000 words.

Marriage was a prime concern in the mind of this man who was a master in the early schools, a literary 'humanist', and a bishop. Dying an old man in 1174—for he had already been a tutor in Rheims *c.*1117–20—Walter lived through the period when intellectual life in general and theological discussion of marriage in particular came to be located principally in Paris; and the historical element in his own

[44] I. Brady, *Prolegomena*, pp. 14, 82, and 85;. Reinhardt, *Anselm von Laon*, pp. 62 and 102.

[45] Ed. E. Martène and U. Durand, *Veterum scriptorum et monumentorum historicorum, dogmaticorum, moralium amplissima collectio*, 9 vols. (Paris, 1724–33), i. 834–7; see Reinhardt, *Anselm von Laon*, p. 62.

[46] Walter's *De sacramento coniugii* is printed as book 7 of the *Summa sententiarum*, *PL* 176, 153–74; see on it Zeimentz, *Frühscholastik*, appendix 3, pp. 251–4. The stupid view referred to by Walter, *PL* 176, 160, is probably a jibe at Alberic.

[47] *De coniugio*, II; *PL* 176, 155.

treatise on marriage came to be incorporated into a Paris textbook. The abbey of St Victor in Paris was the setting between *c.*1130/1 and 1137 of the composition by Hugh of St Victor of his *De sacramentis,*[48] one very large section of which was on marriage. This work was to stay in the canon. It was one of the few twelfth-century works whose status is attested by its 'peciae' being priced in the Paris stationers' list,[49] and a thirteenth- or fourteenth-century theologian citing half a dozen 'modern teachers' (*moderni doctores*) is likely to include Hugh.

Then, around 1157–8, the cathedral school of Notre-Dame was the setting for Peter the Lombard's composition of the last part of his *Libri IV Sententiarum, Four Books of Sentences,* which was usually simply called the *Sentences.* A large part of the fourth book of the *Sentences* dealt with marriage, and it incorporated much from both Walter's and Hugh's treatises.[50]

Peter the Lombard 'almost certainly' frequented Hugh's lectures at St Victor in the 1130s,[51] and Peter was in turn heard lecturing in the school of Notre-Dame in the middle years of the century, as he polished off the last book of the *Sentences* (1157–8). Paris was now seeing rather longer writings—about 17,000 words in Hugh on marriage, about 22,000 in Peter. Peter's writing was to become *the* standard text, second only to the Bible. Second? In the eyes of an acrid critic of mid-thirteenth-century scholarship, Roger Bacon, in the schools of the theologians the *Sentences* eventually came to be put above the Bible.[52]

Peter[53] was a Lombard, born probably between 1095 and 1100, and most that is known of his early career is the mechanism of its advancement, through personal patronage and letters of recommendation.[54] Studying at the school in Rheims, he will have had contact with the marriage-teachings of Walter's teacher Alberic. He was in Paris by 1134/6, and by the time of a poem of 1142/4 he is 'the famous Lombard theologian',[55] and a good number of prominent contemporaries refer to his teaching. In 1147 he was consulted personally by the pope, in 1148 he was prominent at the council of Rheims, and at some stage he was elected bishop of Paris, where he died in 1160.

In the *Sentences* Peter was concerned with producing a *useful* compendium, bringing together the material—the 'sentences'—which theologians needed, and

48 *PL* 176, 174–613; trans. R. J. Deferrari, Hugh of Saint Victor, *On the Sacraments of the Christian Faith (De sacramentis)* (Cambridge, Mass., 1951); on the date, D. Van den Eynde, *Essai sur la succession des écrits de Hugues de Saint-Victor*, Spicilegium Pontificii Athenaei Antoniani 13 (Rome, 1960), p. 215.

49 *CUP* i. 644, no. 530.

50 Brady, *Prolegomena,* pp. 16, 84–5, and 119; Hugh's influence is most easily traced through Hugh's index-entry, Peter Lombard, *Sententiae,* ii. 585, and the references therein to the marriage section, pp. 416–509.

51 Brady, *Prolegomena,* p. 15.

52 *Opus minus,* in Roger Bacon, *Opera quaedam hactenus inedita,* ed. J. S. Brewer, RS 15 (London, 1859), pp. 328–30.

53 On Peter's life see Brady, *Prolegomena,* pp. 8–45, and M. L. Colish, *Peter Lombard,* Brill's Studies in Intellectual History 41, 2 vols. (Leiden, New York, and Cologne, 1994), i, Ch. 1.

54 A letter of Bernard of Clairvaux to the abbey of St Victor tells us about an earlier recommendation by the bishop of Lucca, and about Bernard's own effectiveness as Peter's patron ('I brought it about', *effeci,* he wrote); Brady, *Prolegomena,* p. 8.

55 Brady, *Prolegomena,* 17.

arranging them in a way that made finding them easy. In his prologue Peter introduces the work thus:

In it you will find the teaching and *exempla* of great men . . . I have folded together in a short space the sentences of the fathers, together with their testimonies, so that someone who is looking will not have to search through numerous books. The brevity [of my compilation] offers him what he is looking for without effort [on his part].[56]

There was a very clear overall shape to the work, with the first book devoted to God, the second to creation, the third to the incarnation, and the fourth to the sacraments and the resurrection, and the long reign of the *Sentences* was to ensure the dominance both of this fundamental shape (the flow from, and return to, God) and the disposition within it of particular topics. And there was a clear formal structure at each subordinate level—the topics within each book, the subsections of each topic, the sub-parts of each sub-section, and so on.

Peter wrote that the work was divided into four books, and continued, 'so that what is looked for comes up more quickly, we have put at the beginning the titles by which the chapters of each of the books are identified'.[57] There are books and chapters, then, but not yet a rapid system for larger sections, which had to wait until some time between 1223 and 1227, when Alexander of Hales enumerated and divided Peter's four books, and called the sections in each of them 'distinctions'.[58] Alexander may thus be said to have completed the organization of the *Sentences* as a user-friendly data-base designed for rapid retrieval. From this time on a reader who wanted a general account of marriage which was also at the same time a resource-book, simply turned to book 4, distinctions 26–42.[59] Wanting material on different sorts of vows, he would find it in an instant by turning to book 4, distinction 38, chapter 2; and likewise for hundreds of other specific topics. The work is one of the most important examples for the book revolution taking place in this period, brought about by the introduction of alphabetic ordering, tables of contents, running-titles, and the giving of chapters to the Bible: all features of the text, which evolved in schools and then in the universities, under the pressures of a scholar's need to *locate* what he wanted quickly.[60]

Among the many theological treatises, either general or on the sacraments, which were written in the late twelfth and early thirteenth centuries, many had a roughly similar shape to the Lombard's work. Most important among these was a treatise written by William of Auxerre between 1215 and 1229 (probably after 1218),[61] called the *Summa aurea*, which became a standard text, diffused in Paris by the pecia-copying system,[62] and present in large numbers in later medieval

[56] Peter Lombard, *Sententiae*, Prologue; i. 4. [57] Peter Lombard, *Sententiae*, Prologue; i. 4.

[58] Brady, *Prolegomena*, p. 144. [59] Peter Lombard, *Sententiae*, ii. 416–509.

[60] R. H. and M. A. Rouse, '*Statim invenire*: Schools, Preachers and New Attitudes to the Page', in *Renaissance and Renewal in the Twelfth Century*, ed. R. L. Benson and G. Constable (Oxford, 1982), pp. 201–25; R. H. Rouse, 'Le développement des instruments de travail au XIIIe siècle', in *Culture et travail intellectuel dans l'occident médiéval*, ed. G. Hasenohr and J. Longère (Paris, 1981), pp. 115–44.

[61] See Ch. 4 below, n. 32.

[62] L. J. Bataillon, 'Les textes théologiques et philosophiques diffusés à Paris par exempla et pecia', in

libraries; part of it is used in Chapter 4 below. But the *Summa aurea*'s form was far from a carbon-copy of Peter the Lombard's work, and it was still possible for a treatise to be written on marriage without the Lombard's shadow falling across it. One such was the treatise on marriage contained in the remarkably original *De sacramentis*, written by William of Auvergne, probably around 1228.[63] The most significant divergence from Peter the Lombard's tradition, however, had come earlier in Paris, through the discussions and writings of a figure who dominated Paris theology between about 1170 and his death in 1197, Peter the Chanter, and also through the other men under his influence who continued the tradition into the second decade of the thirteenth century, such as Robert de Courson and several authors of instructional treatises for confessors, including Thomas of Chobham.

These men were unusually direct and practical.[64] Preoccupied with particular cases of conscience rather than grand themes, Peter and his circle discussed marriages rather than Marriage.[65] 'When taking a wife, a knight said to him [the author]: "She has a large dowry and is related to me in the third degree of affinity. If she doesn't please me, I can procure a separation".'[66] Here a case is stated in Peter the Chanter's text in a few sentences. It is one of several where Peter and others looked at members of the French nobility manipulating laws of marriage in order to enjoy what was, in effect, a system of divorce. Marriage was prohibited where the contracting parties were within seven degrees of relationship by consanguinity (blood), affinity (through marriage), and spiritual affinity (through the sacraments). People could easily marry within five, six, or seven degrees and then later, if it suited one or both of a couple who had discovered they were themselves ill-suited, suitable witnesses to the relationship could be sought out and the marriage annulled.

Here are some other examples of the miscellany of marriage-topics dealt with by the Chanter and his circle. Each of them is very short—for example, the first is only twenty-six words in Latin—and often only the question is stated, not the answer. In Peter's texts, therefore, there are traces of what must actually have taken place in the theological schools of Paris: longer ventilation of each case and question, and the statement of the reply and reasons for it.

i. Under simony. 'Following good church custom [lay men and women] are obliged to make many offerings, such as in purification [after childbirth]. Should they not also [make offerings] at the blessing of marriages? It seems that they should, and they sin by omission if they can do so and are well off.'

ii. 'A certain priest, who is going to bless two marriages in one day, bears in mind that the neighbours are equally the friends of [the parties of] both weddings, does not want them to come to one mass but separately to two masses [literally: each wedding to its own mass], in

La production du livre universitaire au Moyen Age: exemplar et pecia, ed. L. J. Bataillon, B. G. Guyot, and R. H. Rouse (Paris, 1991), pp. 155–63 (p. 158).

[63] The subject of Ch. 3 below.

[64] The following recapitulates Baldwin, *Peter the Chanter*.

[65] However, see below, Ch. 8's discussion of the passage about Sodom in Peter the Chanter's *Verbum abbreviatum*.

[66] The translation is Baldwin's, in his *Peter the Chanter*, i. 335.

order to increase the blessing of offerings [viz. to get more money]. Similarly about funerals. It is asked whether this is allowed.'

iii. 'Again, the question is raised about a man and a woman who have sworn to marry: can they release each other [from this]?' Various cases follow, including this: 'Assume that a man and a woman have sworn to marry each other. Afterwards she will neither marry him nor release him from the oath. He is youthful and pulsating with physical desire.' Does he have to wait?

iv. About those whose sex is doubtful. 'There can be doubt about the marriages of such people. If someone thinks himself a man and with the permission of the Church contracts with some woman, and afterwards thinks of -self as a woman and as someone capable of being passive [presumably = being the passive partner in sexual union with a man], would there [still] be marriage between them? Further, if the person's wife died and she (*illa*) who had previously married were afterwards to marry, would the Church suffer such a marriage and would it in fact be marriage?'

v. 'A certain woman, the wife of someone who was hanged for forging money, was thrown out of her marriage-portion and her wedding-dowry, together with her children. The children went to the pope. The pope ordered the restoration of the maternal goods to the children. The question is raised, what are the "maternal goods"? Are they only the marriage-portion she brought to her husband, or are they also what the husband gave to her as dowry?'

vi. About a young man and young woman who are unable to restrain themselves from having sex: 'There is a similar question about that sort of youth and that sort of young girl. Does the Church permit them to marry on prohibited days, such as Lent, since the danger of fornication threatens? My counsel would be that this sort of youth should marry this sort of girl, in words of the present [tense]. [However], in order to avoid church scandal [they should do this] in private without any sort of solemnity, and for the sake of witness the priest should bring two discreet and worthy men to wherever the marriage takes place, so that after the vow has been taken neither [party] goes back on it. Afterwards, however, [and] at a suitable time, there should be the [proper] external solemnities in the face of the church.'

vii. 'There is a stupid man and he stupidly spends his money in the pub, and there is someone who drags him into doing this. His wife and children are brought into hardship. Is the man who drew him into this foolish waste of money under an obligation to restore it? Have the wife and children the right to take some action—by the law of heaven (*ius poli*), I say, not by the law of the courts (*ius fori*)—against the man who made a fool of her husband?'[67]

In their treatment of these problems they brought together earlier theological tradition, canon law in Gratian's *Decretum*, and later canon law collections and commentaries from Bologna and elsewhere, but what startles the reader is something produced by their preoccupation with the circumstances of individual cases: sharp, *pointilliste*, observation of the contemporary world. Their discussion of marriages could produce advice in particular cases; echoes are found in several works of instruction written for confessors in Paris, such as Thomas of Chobham's *Summa confessorum*,[68] and through the diffusion of these works Parisian thought spread; and the problem outlined in the previous paragraph led to important legislative reform. In his brilliant study of Peter the Chanter and his

[67] These cases are all from the Peter the Chanter's *Summa de sacramentis et animae consiliis*. No. i: Chanter, *Summa*; iii. 30; no. ii: iii. 69; no. iii: iii. 230 and 235; no. iv: iii. 259; no. v: iii. 266; no. vi: iii. 286; no. vii: iii. 413.

[68] Baldwin, *Peter the Chanter*, i. 35–6 and 58.

circle, John Baldwin showed the ways in which their criticism of this abuse led to its treatment at the 4th Lateran Council of 1215, where the law was reformed and the prohibited degrees of marriage were brought down to four.[69]

Cases of conscience reigned in Paris theology between about 1170 and 1215, and then there was a general swing towards the discussion of very abstract theology and philosophy, as Aristotle and Arabic philosophers came to dominate. This latter fact—and nearly exclusive modern preoccupation with it—can overshadow the pastoral and penitential-case tradition. This continued, even if now as a smaller part of the surviving texts. For there was a persisting relationship between the topics of the theology lecture-room and the future pastoral activities of the mendicant friars, priests, and prelates-to-be who were in the audience. This is evident in one later Parisian academic exercise, the theological Quodlibet ('what you will'), in which questions were raised by anyone about anything.[70] The genre emerged in Paris around 1230, achieved its classic form by around 1250, and flourished up to the 1320s. In the (still mainly unprinted) manuscripts of quodlibets, the questions raised and answered were principally abstract. However, some dealt with ecclesiastical problems; a substantial minority tackled cases of conscience;[71] and among these marriage problems[72] and moneylending predominated.[73]

However, such pointed questions on marriage-cases were thin icing on a massive cake which was constituted, by now, by the 'reading' of Peter the Lombard's text. This text was already attracting many glosses in the later twelfth century, and its place as a text to be formally 'read' (lectured upon) in the schools at Paris was being established in the 1220s. Alexander of Hales took it as the standard text for his lectures between 1223 and 1227.[74] By mid-century the fame of this, and the degree to which it was standard, were sufficient for an encyclopaedia to provide a notice of the *Sentences*, 'which is now publicly read in the schools'.[75] Much of a modern account of medieval universities describes the teaching and progression up an academic ladder in terms of the *Sentences*. What we need to note is this fact and its scale. In 1947 Frederic Stegmüller listed 1,407 different glosses and commentaries on the *Sentences* produced between Peter the Lombard's time and

[69] Baldwin, *Peter the Chanter*, i. 332–7.

[70] J. F. Wippel, 'Quodlibetal Questions, Chiefly in Theological Faculties', in *Les questions disputées et les questions quodlibétiques dans les facultés de théologie, de droit et de médecine*, ed. B. C. Bazan, G. Fransen, D. Jacquart, and J. W. Wippel, Typologie des sources du moyen âge occidental 44–5 (Turnhout, 1985), pp. 153–222.

[71] L. E. Boyle, 'The Quodlibets of St. Thomas and Pastoral Care', in Boyle, *Pastoral Care*, ii. 242–51.

[72] Boyle, 'Quodlibets of St Thomas', p. 249; see the entries for marriage and related matters ('Matrimonium', 'Copula conjugalis', 'Parentes', 'Uxor', etc.) in the indexes of the standard list of quodlibetic questions, Glorieux.

[73] O. Langholm, *Economics in the Medieval Schools: Wealth, Exchange, Money and Usury according to the Paris Theological Tradition, 1200–1350*, Studien zur Geistesgeschichte des Mittelalters 29 (Leiden, New York and Cologne, 1992), pp. 249–98.

[74] Brady, *Prolegomena*, pp. 117–18. See P. Glorieux, 'Sentences (commentaires sur les)', *DTC* xiv (1941), cols. 1860–84, and on the *Sentences* in Oxford, J. I. Catto, 'Theology and Theologians 1220–11320', *HUO* i. 471–517 (pp. 473 and 476–7).

[75] Vincent, *Speculum historiale* XIX. i; p. 1185; quoted by Brady, *Prolegomena*, p. 53 n. 1. On Vincent's encyclopaedia, see Ch. 11 below, pp. 296–7 and n. 2.

Luther's.[76] *Each* of these has survived in several, and frequently many, manuscripts, and listing these manuscripts (in the briefest form, without elaborate description) took Stegmüller over 500 pages. Listen to William of Rubruck, in a Mongol camp during his three-year journey to outer Mongolia (1253–5). 'One thing was a comfort to me, that when I noticed their [the Mongols'] greed, I removed from among [my] books the Bible, the *Sentences* and other books which I particularly loved.'[77] Such treasuring of the book during this 10,000-mile round journey says much about the *Sentences*' importance within the confines of the Latin Christendom which this intrepid Franciscan had left so far behind.

Theologians who wrote on marriage in the thirteenth and fourteenth centuries knew what had been written on it by 'the Master of the Sentences' inside out, and 'Book 4 distinctions 26–42' was written in their minds.[78] But in the thirteenth and fourteenth centuries we can encounter theological treatises and collections of theological questions which are independent in form and do not present themselves as commentaries on the *Sentences*. Although Stegmüller's listing of these in his catalogue of commentaries on the *Sentences* can be criticized for subordinating everything to Peter the Lombard, his scholarly imperialism does nevertheless reflect a broader truth. For scholars felt the shadow of the *Sentences*, even when writing elsewhere. Thus Henry of Ghent's quodlibetic disputation[79] and Peter of John Olivi's question (asking whether virginity should be preferred to marriage)[80] may be in independent genres. But they cannot be understood fully without reference to the raising of this same question in commentaries on chapter 2 of distinction 33.

The *Sentences* formed the second stage in the academic life of a theology bachelor, who would lecture on the Bible and then turn to the *Sentences*, which he would 'read' for at least one year, usually two, and sometimes longer. These lectures were sometimes reduced to writing. If taken down by a student, the written version is known as a *reportatio*, while a commentator's later revision of his commentary is known as an *ordinatio*. A written version might be prepared at the same time as the public reading, as seems to have been the case with Aquinas, but this written version might be prepared for publication many years, even decades, after the public 'reading', as was the case with Giles of Rome:[81] care is needed with dates.

My description of a commentary is of an ideal type, for the genre continued developing and was never frozen in the exact likeness of what follows.

[76] Stegmüller, *Repertorium*.

[77] *Itinerarium Willelmi de Rubruc* XVI. iii, ed.Wyngaert, *Itinera*, p. 204; cited by Brady, *Prolegomena*, p. 118 n. 1.

[78] See the summary of its contents in the appendix to this chapter.

[79] Glorieux, i. 186; ed. G. A. Wilson, Henry of Ghent, *Quodlibet VI*, *Opera omnia* (Louvain, 1979–), x. 143–55. Glorieux' index entries under *Perfectio statuum* take the reader to further discussions of the theme.

[80] Discussed in Ch. 5 below.

[81] On this see V. Heynck, 'Zur Datierung des Sentenzkommentars des Petrus de Palude', *Franziskanische Studien* 53 (1971), 317–27 (pp. 318–20).

First, the commentary goes through the *Sentences* book by book, in order, and within each book distinction by distinction. With any one distinction, Peter's text is transcribed, or a summary is given of what the Master of the Sentences (Peter) says in that distinction. There may then follow the clarification of doubtful things in the text (*dubia in littera*), and the raising of questions. The questions will be formally organized in a way common to scholastic texts of the period. The question is formulated. The proposition 'it seems that *x* is the case' is put forward, and supported by a numbered series of authorities and arguments, and then the proposition 'that *x* is not the case' is stated and supported by a numbered series of authorities and arguments. There follow the reply, which produces the solution and major arguments in its support, and, after the reply, particular replies to the numbered authorities and arguments which were earlier put forward in support of the proposition which lost the game. There are many variants on this, including the additional putting forward of 'little questions' which are shorter and less elaborate, and the breaking up of commentary on a distinction into several articles, each of which is divided into questions. By the first half of the fourteenth century the questions can have sub-divisions of quite extraordinary elaboration and number: mazes, negotiation of which needs a lot of note-taking.

For quite a long time, from Alexander of Hales to the later thirteenth century, the genre seems relatively stable. There are certain commentaries which entered a canon of important ones—often, though not always, those which were later selected for further survival by printing. They are a roll-call of well-known figures from histories of scholasticism, the Franciscans Alexander of Hales,[82] Bonaventure,[83] Richard of Middleton[84] and Duns Scotus,[85] the Dominicans Albert the Great,[86]

[82] On Alexander (*c*.1170/1185–1245), see W. Detloff, 'Alexander Halesius', *TRE* ii. 245–8; the editors of Alexander's *Glossa* place its composition between 1223 and 1227. See *Quaestiones*, i. 36* on the date of his *Quaestiones*, *c*.1220–36.

[83] On Bonaventure (*c*.1217–1274), see 'Bonaventura', *DBI* xi. 612–30 (author not given), and W. Detloff, 'Bonaventura', *TRE* vii, 48–55 (p. 49 on the date of his commentary, usually ascribed to 1248–55). On editions and manuscripts, see Stegmüller, *Repertorium*, and Doucet, *Supplément*, nos. 111–21.

[84] On the Franciscan Richard (*c*.1249–1307 or 1308), see E. Hocedez, *Richard de Middleton: Sa vie, ses oeuvres, sa doctrine*, Spicilegium Sacrum Lovaniense 7 (Louvain, Paris, 1925). See Langholm, *Economics*, pp. 327–7, 330 and n. 27, on suggested dates for the commentary (1282–*c*.1295 or *c*.1285–95), and bibliography, p. 328 n. 20. For manuscripts and editions of his commentary, see Stegmüller, *Repertorium*, and Doucet, *Supplément*, no. 722.

[85] On John Duns Scotus (1265–1308) and his reading the sentences at Oxford (and then perhaps at Cambridge) and Paris between *c*.1298 and 1303, see Catto, 'Theology and Theologians', 505–9. The early printed edition which I am using in this book is analysed by C. Bali, *Les commentaires de Jean Duns Scot sur les quatre livres des sentences: Étude historique et critique* (Louvain, 1927)—Chs. 2 and 4 on the commentaries on books 2 and 4. See Stegmüller, *Repertorium*, nos. 421–32. For a summary of the conclusions of modern scholarship on Duns's sentences commentary or commentaries, see W. Detloff, 'Duns Scotus', *TRE* ix. 219, and for bibliography p. 231.

[86] On Albert (*c*.1200–80), see J. A. Weisheipl, 'The Life and Works of St Albert the Great', in *Albertus and the Sciences*, 13–48; pp. 21–5 on Albert's reading the sentences from *c*.1243/4, and completing his commentary on book 4 after March 1249. On editions and manuscripts, see Stegmüller, *Repertorium*, and Doucet, *Supplément*, no. 51, and W. Fauser, *Die Werke des Albertus Magnus in ihrer handsriftlichen Überlieferung*, i. *Die echten Werke*, in Albert, *Opera*, Geyer, Tomus Subsidiarius, i. 275–87.

Peter of Tarentaise (Innocent V),[87] Thomas Aquinas,[88] Durand of Saint Pourçain,[89] and Peter of la Palud OP,[90] and the Augustinians Giles of Rome[91] and Thomas of Strasbourg.[92] They are acutely aware of each other and their predecessors. The habit of citing the roll-call becomes commoner by around 1300—'as Thomas says', 'as Richard says'—but for a long time there has been a complex interrelation of questions and material: tradition, dependency, and interchange. Thus Albert may raise a question upon marriage and natural law, and include a text from Cicero on primitive marriage, and a filament of both question and text leads through Thomas and Peter of Tarentaise and later commentators. Under these figures are the commentaries of many less well-known men, surviving only in manuscript. Sometimes these are important and original men. One such is Richard Fishacre, the first commentator in Oxford,[93] who tended to incorporate much scientific material, and another example is Vidal de Four, later cardinal, one of the most eager to incorporate Aristotle's *Politics* into his commentary on marriage in the *Sentences*.[94]

What needs to be said here is this. Most of these lesser figures only survive in manuscript form—although survival only in manuscript does not necessarily

[87] On Peter (d. 1276) see *Beatus Innocentius PP. IV (Petrus de Tarantasia OP): Studia et documenta* (Rome, 1943), and, in this, H. D. Simonin, 'Les écrits de Pierre de Tarentaise', pp. 163–213 (p. 95 on the written commentary's date, between 1256–7 and 1259–60); on its edition and manuscripts, see Stegmüller, *Repertorium*, and Doucet, *Supplément*, nos. 690–4, and *SOPMA* iii. 262–2 and iv. 239. Simonin ('Les écrits', pp. 298–316) surveys the very wide reading, excerpting, and copying of Peter over the next century.

[88] On Aquinas (*c.*1224/5–74), see J. A. Weisheipl, *Friar Thomas d'Aquino, his Life, Thought and Works* (Oxford, 1975); Weisheipl discusses Thomas's reading the sentences in Paris between 1252 and 1256 (pp. 67–78) and his composition of a written version at the same time (pp. 358–9). On manuscripts and editions, see Stegmüller, *Repertorium*, no. 846, and H. F. Dondaine and H. V. Shooner, *Codices manuscripti operum Thomae de Aquino*, 3 vols. (Paris and Rome, 1967–85).

[89] On Durand (*c.*1270/75–1334), see *HLF* 37 (1938), 1–38; on his sentence commentaries and their revisions (1307–27), see J. Dunbabin, *A Hound of God: Pierre de la Palud and the Fourteenth-Century Church* (Oxford, 1991), pp. 36–9; on manuscripts and editions, see Stegmüller, *Repertorium*, and Doucet, *Supplément*, nos. 192–5, and *SOPMA*, i. 340–3. The printed editions are of the third (1325–7) version.

[90] On the Dominican Peter (*c.*1275/80–1342), see Dunbabin, *Hound of God*; see pp. 31–52 on Peter's reading and commenting upon the sentences, pp. 42–52 on book 4 in general, and p. 42 on the date of its completion, not before the beginning of 1315; see also Heynck, 'Zur Datierung'. On the editions and manuscripts, see Stegmüller, *Repertorium*, and Doucet, *Supplément*, no. 677; *SOPMA* iii. 243–5 and iv. 234.

[91] Giles of Rome (1247–1316), also often referred to as Aegidius Romanus or Aegidius Colonna, read the sentences in 1276–7. Writing the commentary on the second book began before 1280 and was completed between 1309 and 1312; G. Bruni, 'Saggio bibliografico sulle opere stampate di Egidio Romano: 2', *La Bibliofilia* 37 (1936), 253–4, discusses the date of Giles's *scriptum* on the *Sentences* in relation to its dedication to Robert of Sicily, who ascended the throne in 1309. See also Stegmüller, *Repertorium*, and Doucet, *Supplément*, no. 43. On Giles in general see F. Lajard, 'Gilles de Rome, Religieux, Augustinen, Théologien', *HLF* 30 (1888), 421–566; M. A. Hewson, *Giles of Rome and the Medieval Theory of Conception: A Study of the 'De formatione corporis humani in utero'* (London, 1975), ch. 1; F. Del Punta, S. Donati, and C. Luna, 'Egidio Romano', *DBI* lxii. 319–41; C. F. Briggs, *Giles of Rome's De regimine principum: Reading and Writing Politics at Court and University, c.1275–c.1525* (Cambridge, 1999), ch. 1.

[92] On Thomas of Strasbourg (d. 1357), see P. B. Lindner, *Die Erkenntnislehre des Thomas von Strassburg*, BGPTM 27 (Münster, 1930), pp. 1–10; A. Zumkeller, 'Thomas de Strasbourg', *DSp* xv. 872–3; K.-H. Witte, 'Thomas von Straβburg', *Vf* ix. 889–92. Thomas finished reading the sentences in 1337 (Lindner, p. 2). On its editions and manuscripts, see Stegmüller, *Repertorium*, and Doucet, *Supplément*, no. 895.

[93] See Ch. 9 below, pp. 244–6.

[94] See below and n. 170.

mean that the figure had been unimportant, nor does printing necessarily mean the opposite. In the vast majority of the commentaries by lesser figures most of the text reproduces, with only slight omission, abbreviation, and addition, the text of one of the major figures. Bernard *Lombardus* mainly follows Thomas (both are Dominicans), Peter *de Trabibus* mainly follows Peter of John Olivi (both are Franciscans), and so on. Acres of text simply copy or copy and slightly adapt. Frustrating to the historian looking for a new because further *development* of an idea, these are fundamental materials for the historian looking at the *impact* of an idea. For, through such copying by authors whose own commentaries were in turn diffused in many manuscript copies, the thoughts of the major figures pervaded the Latin-reading world of the later middle ages to a quite extraordinary degree.

By the early fourteenth century commentaries can be quite cavalier in the location of a commentary. We need our wits to spot a particular commentary on distinction 33, because in fact it may well be attached, quite arbitrarily, to distinction 35. Some academic theologians still give marriage their full attention—Durand of St Pourçain, for example—but among others there is a parting of the ways. There are the extremes. On the one hand this period saw the production of the most acutely pastoral of all *Sentences* commentaries, Peter of la Palud's, whose value was to be demonstrated by the extensive way in which one of the sharpest pastoral specialists of the fifteenth century, Antoninus of Florence, plundered it. On the other hand the speculative and abstract-minded contemporaries of William of Ockham simply bypass Peter the Lombard's marriage material when producing their *Sentences* commentaries, and substitute questions on matters of speculative philosophy and logic. An example of an in-between figure is the Carmelite John Baconthorpe, interested in many of the more abstract questions but also rooted in the concrete and pastoral world. He comments on parts of the marriage section and disdains others.[95]

This sketch began with Laon anthologies, which were usually around 2,000 words in length, surviving in each case in about half a dozen or a dozen copies. It ends with *Sentences* commentaries whose marriage section is of a much larger order of magnitude. In the mid-thirteenth century, Peter of Tarentaise wrote about 77,000 words on marriage, Aquinas 87,000, Bonaventure 100,000, while in the early fourteenth century Thomas of Strasbourg wrote 48,000, and Peter of la Palud 143,000.[96] And these later works achieved mass diffusion.

[95] John Baconthorpe, *Quaestiones in quatuor libros sententiarum et quodlibetales*, 2 vols. (Cremona, 1618, repr. Farnborough, 1969), ii. 533–63. On the Carmelite Baconthorpe (*c.*1300–pre-1352), see B. Xiberta, *De scriptoribus scholasticis saeculi XIV ex ordine Carmelitarum* (Louvain, 1931), pp. 167–240 (p. 171 on his reading the sentences, before 1318). See Stegmüller, *Repertorium*, no. 402, on manuscripts and printed editions.

[96] Each estimate is based on an average of a few sample pages of text which is then multiplied by the number of pages in the printed editions used here: Peter of Tarentaise, *In sententias* IV. xxvi–lxii (iv. 281–403); Aquinas, *In sententias*, IV. xxvi–xlii (iii. 916–1055); Bonaventure, *In sententias*, IV. xxvi–xlii (iv. 659–880); Thomas of Strasbourg, *In sententias*, IV. xxvi–xlii (ii. 144r–168r); Peter of la Palud, *In sententias* IV. xxvi–lxii (138rb–95va). Electronically stored editions will provide greater precision.

2.4.1 *Development in the schools writings (a): direct infiltration of the contemporary world*

It was a long journey from the brief quires of Laon to Peter of la Palud's encyclopaedic effort. There was continuity in content but also change. New material had to enter, as areas of law acquired clarification (such as consent forming marriage) or alteration (such as the reduction of prohibited degrees in 1215). There were also direct infiltrations from the changing milieux in which the treatises were written, in particular the world of courts, lawyers, and experts. Turn first to marriage courts. There is the glimpse, already quoted from a Laon text, of doubts about a system in which ordeals are used in marriage-cases—before a court whose identity is unclear. Hugh of St Victor used a lawsuit to introduce the topic of secret marriage. A man put away a wife, whom he had married without witnesses. Then he married another woman with due pomp in a church wedding and had children by her. Finally the first wife came to the Church asking for judgement. The husband denied her account, and there were no witnesses to prove the first marriage.[97] Sketched in the academic treatise, then, is an ecclesiastical court, witnesses, proof, and the sort of case which post-1200 records have shown to be the standard fare of the Church's marriage courts.

In later texts, while it would be unusual to catch a glimpse of the practising lawyers or judges, there is another legal class which enters: the specialist group of the lawyers who wrote, commented upon, and debated canon law. Earlier on they are a silent presence, implied simply through the heavy use of their texts, while later they are explicitly present, in the many references to 'the legists', 'the jurists', or 'the decretists'. By 1300 they are increasingly imported by name, 'Gratian', 'Geoffrey' (of Trani), and so on. The content of canon law saturates many of the distinctions on marriage, and the smell of its practice and knowledge of it both by lawyers and parish priests comes with the inclusion in these distinctions of mnemonic verses on matters like impediments to marriage.[98]

Apart from law and lawyers, learned medicine and doctors (*medici*) are another discipline and group increasingly present in the sentence commentaries. While the general setting for this is the 'medicalization' of Europe around 1300,[99] the particular context is a concomitant medicalization of 'religious discourse'.[100] The commentators of the 1250s, especially Bonaventure, are grounded in knowledge of the complexional make-up of bodies, and they make some reference to medical authors and the use of medicine. Bonaventure, for example, refers to debate among *medici* about determination of sex,[101] while Peter of

[97] *De sacramentis*, II. xi. 6; *PL* 176, 488; *On the sacraments*, trans. Deferrari, p. 333.

[98] An example is Bonaventure, *In sententias*, IV. xxxiv, art. 1, qu. 2; iv. 769. On such verses in confessors' literature, see n. 30 above.

[99] McVaugh, *Medicine*, pp. 87–95. See further Ch. 6 below.

[100] J. Ziegler, *Medicine and Religion c.1300: The Case of Arnau de Vilanova* (Oxford, 1998).

[101] See Ch. 5 below.

Tarentaise introduces 'medicine's aid' (*beneficium medicinae*) for temporary impotence.[102]

By the early fourteenth century the commentator's own medical knowledge seems more technical, and the *medici* appear more often. Their views on a miscellany of sexual matters are found scattered in the texts. *Physici* are cited on the increased sexual desire experienced by a pregnant woman;[103] a *medicus* recounted the case, which is then reported by Peter of la Palud, of a man who always made love to his wife after eating.[104] The distinctions which parade the *medici* most are no. 32, on the question of the payment of the marriage debt to a leprous spouse, and no. 34, on such impediments as impotence and madness. 'If there is certainty about this frigidity, based on the observation of doctors (*per experientiam medicorum*)', wrote Thomas of Strasbourg, a judge may abbreviate the usual three years of failure after which a court would annul a marriage on the grounds of the man's impotence;[105] Duns Scotus's phrase was 'by the judgement of doctors' (*per iudicium medicorum*).[106] The opinions of *medici* are cited on the comparison of degrees of infectiousness of leprous men and women and on the last stages of the progression of the disease.[107] Doctors should be consulted on whether infection may follow from having sex with a leprous spouse, and they should be believed. 'Each is expert in his own field' (*Unusquisque enim in arte sua sapiens est*), write both Peter of la Palud and Durand of St Pourçain, alluding to Ecclesiasticus 38, 'Honour the doctor'.[108] Witnesses to 'medicalization' elsewhere—whether of evidence in courts or the enhanced prestige of the medical profession—these commentaries had also themselves been 'medicalized'.

We can read the texts further, trying to get glimpses, beyond the courts and experts, of the millions of marrying, married, concubinary, widowed, parents, childless, or single men and women who were the contemporaries of any particular commentary. A marriage-case conjures some up, on occasion, conflated into fictional individuals who are given simple names: 'If John says to Margaret . . .'. Where a famous and earlier tricky canon-legal case comes in, it may bring with it a royal or noble person, but without name or date: 'There was the case of the heir

[102] Peter of Tarentaise, *In sententias*, IV. xxxiv, art. 2; iv. 342; similar point in Hostiensis' *Summa aurea*, quoted by Esmein, i. 270–1 n. 4.

[103] Peter of Tarentaise, *In sententias*, IV. xxxii, art. 3; iv. 329.

[104] *In sententias*, IV. xxxii, art. 3; fo. 162va. More examples of the intrusion of medicine are given in Ch. 7 below.

[105] *In sententias*, IV. xxxii, art. 2; ii. 157va; Thomas refers at this point to the standard gloss on *Laudabilem*, the text on impotence in Gregory IX's *Five Books of the Decretals* (X. 4. 15. 5; Friedberg, ii. 705–6). Cases of such use of doctors appear in McVaugh, *Medicine*, pp. 205–7, and Lévy, 'Officialité de Paris', p. 1267 n. 9.

[106] *In sententias*, IV. xxxii; ix. 730.

[107] Durand, *In sententias*, IV. xxxii, q. 1; ii. 375rb. Bonaventure (*In sententias*, IV. xxxii, art. 2, qu. 1; iv. 734) does not cite *medici* explicitly, but his technical terminology, *morbus contagiosus*, suggests medical knowledge, as does also Aquinas's insistence on frequent cohabitation rather than sex as the speedy source of infection (*In sententias*, IV. xxxii, qu. 1, art. 1, ad 4; iii. 961).

[108] Peter of la Palud, *In sententias*, IV. xxxii, qu. 1, art. 2; 162rb; Durand, *In sententias*, IV. xxxii, q. 1; ii. 375rb.

to the throne of Aragon who became a monk, but an heir was wanted . . .'.[109] Such reminders of the individual are few, and it is rather generalizations about groups that are introducing an air of realism. 'We see', writes Richard of Middleton, 'that while those born of fornication [outside marriage] may have known parents, nevertheless they are generally neglected [by these parents]'.[110] The category of the poor enters with the theme of their having and supporting children, especially in the conditions prevailing after 1300, of poverty and overpopulation. 'Some who [already] have offspring do not gratefully receive [more]', writes Guiraud d'Ot, 'like the poor, who do not have the wherewithal to feed [any more].'[111] Such statements are found more readily from the late thirteenth century, by which time pastoral thought about the moral behaviour of different estates and professions was encouraging the growth of 'sociographic' generalization.[112]

There is also a deeper change in these works on marriage.

2.4.2 *Development in the schools writings (b): historical variation*

Both the sacrament itself and the particulars of the regulation of marriage pressed themselves upon theologians and canon lawyers as originating in and changing through time. The creation of man and woman, their fall, God's repeated injunctions to increase and multiply, and the supersession of the Old by the New Law, all encouraged the theology of marriage as something historical. The contracting and regulation of marriage and attitudes towards marriage and virginity in the Old Testament and under the new dispensation contrasted in fundamental areas. On the one hand the Old Testament contained the permission of divorce, the plurality of wives of some of the patriarchs, the regulations about degrees of relationship within which one could marry, and praise of fertility and curse on sterility. On the other hand there was the new dispensation: the indissolubility and singleness of marriage, many different regulations, and the praise of virginity. Mediating these topics for our authors were acres of patristic texts, mainly Augustine's discussions in his *On Genesis*, *On the Conjugal Good*, and *The City of God*. Resounding through all medieval theological discussions of marriage was, then, the vocabulary of the fundamental history of marriage: 'Marriage was instituted twice . . . first as office, second as remedy.' Side by side with this were a large number of specific areas where theologians and canon lawyers had their noses pressed against change through time. For, alongside the contrasts of the Old Testament,

[109] Durand, *In sententias*, IV. xxxiii. 1; ii. 377ra; Peter of la Palud, *In sententias*, IV. xxxviii, qu. 4; 183vb; see Dunbabin, *Hound of God*, pp. 44–5.

[110] *In sententias*, IV. xxvi, art. 1, qu. 1; iv. 401.

[111] *In sententias*, IV. xxxi, BN MS. Lat. 3068, fol. 62va: 'aliqui qui prolem habent sed non gratanter acceptant, sicud pauperes qui non habent unde nutriant.' On the Franciscan Giraud d'Ot (Geraldus Odonis, late 13th cent.–1349), see *HLF* 36 (1927), 203–25, and *DTC* xi. 1658–63. Guiraud read the sentences in 1326; on the manuscripts, see Stegmüller, *Repertorium*, and Doucet, *Supplément*, no. 253.

[112] See below, Ch. 8.

there was a deposit of papal and conciliar texts containing decisions about marriage, which had sometimes changed its regulation.

These commonplace but fundamental elements constituted an irreducible minimum of history. But it did not remain a minimum. In the central decades of the twelfth century the accounts of marriage by the most influential writers—Walter of Mortagne, Hugh of St Victor, and Gratian—all heavily emphasized its history. 'In this sacrament one should know that many things once were licit which now are not. For in the Old Testament it was licit for one to have many wives, so that the people of God should be increased, not for a woman to have many husbands, because many women can be fecundated by one (man), but not one woman by many (men). Now, however, this is not allowed, because the people of God has increased.' Here in a work written between 1139 and 1141, the *Sententie Parisienses*, the point being argued is a simple and stark then and now contrast.[113] But by this time there is also something more ambitious: the statement that there *is* a general history of marriage, and a stab at doing this history. Here is chapter 5 of Walter of Mortagne's treatise, which is headed *On the various customs of marriage*:

Because we know that men of different times have had different laws and customs in marriages, let us briefly run over the states of marriage varying according to varieties of times. Marriage was started at the beginning of time between two. . . . And it is probable that it would have been contracted between two through all periods (*per omnem successionem temporis*). If the first men had remained in obedience, then men would have come together without the incitement of the flesh, and they would have generated children subject to God. And there would never have been need for one man to be joined at the same time to two wives in order to spread the cult of God, since all would have known and loved the one God. After the union of the first man and first woman their sons and daughters were joined in marriage: but only one to one. It is clear that the fact that at this time brother was united to sister arose for this reason, that no other men or women were to be found to whom the sons and daughters of Adam could be united. Lamech is the first one reads about who was united to two wives at the same time . . . [in his case for lust]. Later, however, when the human race had multiplied, since at that time nearly everyone worshipped false Gods, there was permission—in fact, command—for [each man among] the very few who remained in the cult of the one God to contract marriage with two or three [women]. This was done for this reason, to avoid the knowledge and cult of God being forgotten and destroyed through the declining [numbers of] these few and their children. Nor was this contrary to the Lord's institution. Although the Lord had started marriage between two, he had not however forbidden it to be among several, in the case or urgent necessity. Moses however, from the time of the Law, forbade marriages with one's own mother, with one's step-mother, sister, niece, father's sister, mother's sister, daughter-in-law, wife's own daughter. Separation was permitted . . . with a bill of divorce. And I think that, at that time, all that was needed to contract marriage was a man and a woman's shared provision in necessary things and [shared] consent to pay the debt of the flesh . . . With the time of Grace coming, however, when faithful people had grown into a copious multitude, the law of marriage was returned to its earlier and more decent institution, so that only one was united to one . . . It was also forbidden for anyone to be joined in

[113] *Écrits théologiques de l'école d'Abélard: Textes inédits*, ed. A. Landgraf, Spicilegium Sacrum Lovaniense 14 (Louvain, 1934), p. 44; see p. xl on the date.

marriage within the seventh degree of relationship . . . This was done so that the love (*caritas*) which arises out of conjugal society should bring together strangers [who are not otherwise] joined in affection through kinship.[114]

The lofty historical note struck by the chapter's title and opening sentence is higher than what follows, but the aim remains in the mind. Marriage has a history and it varies through time. Set within this history are monogamy, polygamy, degrees of relationship, separation, and the progression of God's people from few to many. Historical erudition is suggested by the explicit note of speculation: 'I *think* that at that time . . .'

Hugh of St Victor based his historical account of the sacraments on the three ages of natural law, written law, and grace, and thus where Walter's history flows, Hugh's is more schematic, a matter of numbers, ages and stages.[115] One chapter looks at marriage's origin and institution, and another at its double institution. It was instituted before sin to multiply nature, as its institutor and ordainer God showed when he said, 'Increase and multiply and fill the earth', and it was instituted again after sin, when it was granted as a remedy for the weakness of both sexes. Hugh puts the particulars of its regulation under successive stages. In its first institution, there were only two people and no prohibitions. Later there came the second institution, made by law: some persons were excepted. From then on prohibition made illicit what had previously been allowed by nature. Later debate makes him speculate about what may have applied in the past. Thus he refers to a school of thinkers, probably the heretic Henry of Le Mans and his followers, who hold that even consent between 'unlawful' persons—meaning those who are not 'lawful' persons to contract marriage—makes a marriage. This leads him to raise the question whether this might have applied 'in those times' when men were more ashamed to sin.[116]

Although its formal structure—statement of cases, counterposing of authorities and their solution—gives Gratian's *Decretum* a formal appearance which contrasts strongly with Walter of Mortagne's supple prose, both men underline history in very similar ways. In the *Decretum* there is a general statement of historical variation which parallels Walter's. Introducing his reply to the problem about plurality of wives in the Old Testament, Gratian writes, 'a varying dispensation of the Creator is found for various times.' Variation is linked to small or large numbers of the faithful. Thus Gratian's explanation of plurality of wives continues:

it was promised to Abraham that all peoples would be blessed in his seed . . . The multiplication of God's people was sought religiously through the fertility of many women, because the

[114] *De coniugio*, v; *PL* 176, 157–8.

[115] See R. W. Southern, 'Aspects of the European Tradition of Historical Writing: 2. Hugh of St. Victor and the idea of Historical Development', *TRHS* 5th ser. 21 (1971), 159–79 (p. 165 on the history of another sacrament, penance).

[116] *De sacramentis*, I. viii. 13 (*PL* 176, 314); II. xi. 3 (*PL* 176, 481); II. xi. 4 (*PL* 176, 483); II. xi. 12 (*PL* 176, 499 and 502). *On the sacraments*, trans. Deferrari, pp. 151, 325, 327, 345, and 348. On Henry see Ch. 3 below and n. 59.

succession of faith was in the succession of blood. Whence in the law it was said, 'Cursed is the sterile, who will not have left his seed on earth' [see Deuteronomy 7]. Marriages were also decreed for priests . . . However, since the grace of faith is [now] spread everywhere through Christ's incarnation . . . virginity is [now] preferred to fertility, [and] the chastity of continence is commanded for priests.

In support are texts from Ambrose. Abraham sought to propagate offspring for 'there was still, after the flood, a rarity of the human race'; 'just as Abraham was then pleasing [to God] in marriage, so now virgins are pleasing [to God] in chastity'; 'the patriarchs had many wives not out of concupiscence . . . but for the sake of numerous offspring'.[117] And the particulars of the regulation of marriage are described historically. Take two examples, firstly divorce for adultery:

in the Old Testament many things were permitted on account of weakness, which have been eliminated in perfection of the Gospel: such as the permission to anyone to give a bill of divorce, to avoid the spilling of innocent blood through hatred. Later the Lord forbade this in the Gospel, saying that a wife was not to be put away by her husband, except for fornication.[118]

And again, on consanguinity, the problem of the marriage of consanguines in the Old Testament is posed and then treated historically:

Abraham married his brother's daughter . . . In the law the Lord ordered Moses that no one should marry a wife unless she was of his own tribe and family . . . The reply to these [points] goes thus. Marriages with consanguines were permitted by reason of necessity, or commanded for just reason. Since there was one man at the beginning, and one woman was formed from his side, necessarily sisters were joined to brothers. . . . With necessity ceasing . . . the Lord spoke through Moses, 'Do not uncover the nakedness of your sister'.

The point is then underlined by quotation of part of *The City of God* [15.16], where Augustine makes the same historical point, the introduction of prohibited degrees as the human race grew and multiplied.[119]

Of the highest significance for thirteenth- and fourteenth-century discussions was the receptivity of Peter the Lombard to this historical approach. An early brief work of his on marriage contained in his *Gloss on Corinthians* already shows him looking at variation, here for example on the topic of persons who may lawfully contract marriage: 'others were lawful at the beginning and before Moses, others under the law, others in the time of grace.'[120] When he came to compiling the section on marriage in book 4 of the *Sentences* his leading sources were Walter, Hugh, and Gratian. Extensive use of them made two of his distinctions (26 and 33) into generalizing historical accounts. The distinction which opens the section on marriage, 26, after using chapter 1 to introduce the topic, gets down to business in chapter 2. Composed mainly from Hugh and Gratian, this deals firstly with the double institution of marriage, and the double statement of 'Increase and multiply', the second 'after sin when nearly all men had been consumed in the flood'.

[117] C. 32 q. 4 d. p. c. 2; Friedberg, i. 1127.

[118] C. 31 q. 1 d. p. c. 7; Friedberg, i. 1110.

[119] C. 35 q. 1; Friedberg, i. 1261–2.

[120] Copied by Peter into his *Sententiae*, IV. xxxiv. 1; ii. 462 (see the editor's note to this passage).

And then marriage first as precept and later as indulgence: '"Increase and multiply" was said to the first men before sin by way of precept. They were bound by this after sin, until the multiplication had taken place. After this, marriage was contracted by indulgence.' Peter has added the phrase 'until the multiplication has taken place', and continues as follows. 'Thus, after the Flood, in which virtually the whole human race was wiped out, the second precept was said to the sons of Noah, "Increase and multiply". When man had multiplied [again a phrase added by Peter], marriage came to be contracted according to indulgence . . .'[121]

Distinction 33's chapter 1 is given a title, *On the diverse laws of marriage*, which is virtually Walter's *On the diverse customs of marriage*. There follows a short sentence raising the problem of plurality of wives in the Old Testament, and then comes Gratian's answer: 'A varying dispensation of the creator is found for various times.' Peter puts together the parts of Walter and Gratian quoted above: the fewness of the earliest humans, and therefore marriages between brothers and sisters; plurality of wives in order to multiply God's people, at a time when the sterile person was cursed and priests had to marry; and the rarity of the human race after the flood. In chapter 2, the question of preference between the virginity of the (not procreating) John and the chastity of the (procreating) Abraham continues the theme of variation in relation to time. Through Augustine, who is quoted via Hugh, the text says that 'the celibacy of the one and the marriage of the other have fought for Christ [in different ways] according to the condition of the period' (*pro temporum distributione*).[122] Chapter 3 asks 'What was custom under the Law?' Its answer, prohibited degrees in Leviticus and the bill of divorce, can be juxtaposed to the historical material on other points of marriage regulation, which appear miscellaneously in other distinctions.[123]

Thus Peter the Lombard took a path down the middle of the terrain which had been marked out by these other mid-twelfth-century theologians, adopting and incorporating their words. Their notably historical account of marriage became his as well, dominating the two generalizing distinctions of what was to be the most influential of all textbooks in the thirteenth and fourteenth centuries. Combined with the implicit history of other distinctions, which dealt with past and varying papal and conciliar decisions, this encouraged more history in later treatises on marriages and commentaries on the *Sentences*. We encounter increasing historical erudition devoted to minutiae—for example, in a discussion of marriage liturgy, which moves on to comment on the use of rings long ago among the Romans[124]—and increasingly we come across pat little histories of particular aspects of the Church's law or policy. Thus, for example, when Thomas of Strasbourg turns to the theme of disparity of cult and the question of what happens to marriage when one from a Jewish couple or a gentile [pagan] couple converts to Christianity, he discerns three stages in the Church's advice or

[121] *Sententiae*, IV. xxvi. 2–3; ii. 417–18.

[122] See further discussion of this in Ch. 5 below.

[123] *Sententiae*, IV. xxxiii. 1–3; ii. 456–61.

[124] Alexander of Hales, *In sententias*, IV. xxviii; iv. 428–9.

teaching: the Apostle Paul, the time of Constantine, and now. Each of these corresponds with three stages in the history of conversions: rapidity and ease of conversions of Jews and gentiles in the early Church; growing difficulty of converting Jews by the time of Constantine; and extreme difficulty now in converting either Jews or gentiles, in particular Saracens.[125] Another example, the history of consanguinity, will be given in Chapter 5 below, which will also examine the later development of the principal general theme of distinctions 26 and 33, historical variation in relation to the *numbers* of God's people.

2.4.3 *Development in the schools writings (c): natural law*

By the mid-thirteenth century natural law had become a central theme in the general fundamental discussions of marriage. Natural law had not had this role in Peter the Lombard, nor in his contemporaries, nor in the other later twelfth-century authors I have read. The first example I have met is in Simon of Tournai (d. *c*.1201), who raised the question, whether the 'union of male and female [is by] natural law'. Odon Lottin's history of natural law begins with William of Auxerre around 1220 and concludes in the time of Aquinas.[126] The authors who figure in this earlier stage of the history of natural law and marriage are Guy of Orchelles,[127] Philip the Chancellor, Hugh of St Cher, Roland of Cremona, Guerric of St Quentin, Jean de la Rochelle, the author of the *Summa* attributed to Alexander of Hales, Albert the Great, and then, from the 1250s, Bonaventure, Aquinas, and Peter of Tarentaise. The next stage of the history features, in part, simply the later tradition and influence of the most widely read of these, and it also shows elaboration after the translation of Aristotle's *Politics* and (attributed) *Economics*. In the later thirteenth and early fourteenth centuries some of the *quaestiones* raised on the Aristotelian moral texts—by Peter of Auvergne,[128] Bartholomew of Bruges,[129] Jean of Jandun,[130] and various anonymous authors[131]—are formulated exactly as the

[125] *In sententias*, IV. xxxix, art. 2; ii. 165rb.

[126] Simon of Tournai, *Disputationes*, XCVIII. ii, ed. J. Warichez, *Les Disputationes de Simon de Tournai*, Spicilegium Sacrum Lovaniense 12 (Louvain, 1932), p. 284; O. Lottin, *Le droit naturel chez Saint Thomas d'Aquin et ses prédécesseurs*, 2nd edn. (Bruges, 1931), p. 28 n. 8. On Simon see Baldwin, *Chanter*, i. 43–4.

[127] Although Lottin mentions Guy (*Droit naturel*, p. 31 n. 2), he omits his treatment of marriage and natural law, *De sacramentis*, ix, art. 1; p. 195, no. 214.

[128] *Questiones* on the *Politics*, Paris, BN, MS Lat. 16089, fol. 276ra: *utrum conbinacio maris et femine sit a natura*. See Flüeler, *Politica*, ii. 102. On Peter see Ch. 11 below, and on Peter's and associated *Questiones* now see Flüeler, *Politica*, i. Ch. 2.

[129] *Questiones* on the *Economics*, BN, MS Lat. 16089, fol. 123va, and Vatican, MS Vat. Lat. 2167, fol. 155va: *utrum conbinacio viri et mulieris sit naturalis*. On Bartholomew (d. 1356), see *HLF* 37 (1938), 238–50 (pp. 245 ff. on his writings on the *Economics*).

[130] *Questiones* on the *Economics*, Erfurt, Stadbibliothek, MS Quart 188, fol. 71rb: *utrum combinacio viri et mulieris sit naturalis*. On Jean, see L. Schmugge, *Johannes van Jandun 1285/9–1328*, Pariser Historische Studien 5 (Stuttgart, 1966); see p. 130 on the *Questiones*, written in 1319.

[131] The question is in Peter of Auvergne's terms in Frankfurt-am-Main, Stadt- und Universitätsbibliothek, MS Praed. 52, fol. 174ra, and Bologna, Biblioteca Universitaria, MS 1625, fol. 68v; Milan, Biblioteca

Sentences commentary questions are. 'Is marriage from natural law?', and 'Is the marriage of one to one from natural law?' And there is considerable overlap of material.

Here our interest is the impact of this line of thought on the character of discussions of marriage. To this end, let us look at two mid-century figures, Albert and Bonaventure, whose writings point both to the past and to the future. They show the point that had been reached fifty years after Simon of Tournai, and they were themselves fundamental texts for the following period. Bonaventure was much read and copied, and much of Albert acquired diffusion through Aquinas's reworking of his text.[132]

Albert raises the theme under distinction 33,[133] Bonaventure under both distinctions 26 and 33.[134] The questions are these. Is marriage from the law of nature or peoples (Albert)? If marriage was under precept will it have remained under precept, since natural law is immutable (Bonaventure, distinction 26)? Is concubinage against natural law? Is plurality of wives against natural law? (Both in Bonaventure on distinction 33.) Treatment of these questions proceeds in familiar fashion. Authorities and arguments are listed under counterposed theses, a reply comes down on one side, and there are particular responses to particular points which had been advanced in support of the losing thesis.

Here is Albert arguing for and against marriage being from natural law. First, marriage is not from natural law. One point in support of this is that, according to Aristotle in the second book of the *Ethics*, natural things are the same among all. But marriage contracts are not the same among all. Another point is that 'Cicero, in the *Rhetoric*, says that in the beginning men were forest-dwellers, and at that time no one knew who their own children were, and no one [had] fixed marriages.[135] However, it is clear that then men were living by nature, ergo.' Again, 'at the beginning of the *Old Digest* and the *Institutes* it is said that natural law is what nature teaches all animals.[136] But nature does not teach marriage to all animals. The proof of the middle term is that we see many dogs following one bitch, and that some animals do not have particular females with whom they mate.'

Then, in the other direction, there are points supporting the thesis that marriage *is* from natural law. In the ninth book of the *Ethics* Aristotle said that, 'Man is more naturally a conjugal than a political animal . . .' 'And the meaning is this. Man is more naturally conjugal than political—more, in the sense that setting a house in order comes before and is more necessary than setting a city in order. But man is naturally political, as Aristotle and Avicenna prove. Therefore he is more naturally conjugal. Therefore . . .' Again: 'Aristotle puts forward another

Ambrosiana, MS A. 100 Inf., fol. 2va: *utrum matrimonium sit naturale et aliter utrum concubitus* [Flüeler, *Politica*, ii. 112, reads *concubinacio*] *marius* [r. *maris*] *et femelle sit naturale.*

[132] *In sententias*, IV. xxvi, qu. 1, art. 1; iii. 917–18.

[133] *In sententias*, IV. xxxiii, art. 1; v. 289–90.

[134] Ibid., IV. xxvi, art. 1, qu. 3; iv. 664–5; IV. xxxiii, art. 1, qu. 1–2; iv. 747–50.

[135] See Cicero, *De inventione*, I. ii, Loeb edn. (London, Cambridge, Mass., 1949), p. 4.

[136] Dig. 1. 1. 1. 3; Inst. 1. 2 pr. See Lottin, *Droit naturel*, pp. 7–9, on these Roman legal definitions.

argument, saying, "procreation is common to all animals". To those to whom procreation of children is common by nature, the method of guaranteeing children is natural—[the method] for example, by which among birds [one] is united to one female bird in a particular nest. Therefore it is natural for man to be united to one female in a particular house.' There follow further arguments about natural division of labour between the sexes, and the necessity of long union for the rearing and education of perfect offspring. The last point is given in the words of Aspasius's commentary on the *Ethics*.

In the next article of his commentary on distinction 33, Albert asks, 'Is it natural to have several wives?' There are nine points, first of all, in support of the proposition that it is natural. Among these the second is that 'we frequently see in other animals [= animals other than man] that many females are had by one male', while the seventh is that 'among men who follow nature and reason in excellent fashion, we see many who once upon a time had and many who [now] have several wives, such as Cato and some Arabs'; and, among 'Arabs many used to have and have, many wives.' Against the proposition are eight points. Among these the second takes as an example birds and the need of chicks to be fed by both parents, presenting this as an argument that there should be one female to one male. Later, the question of the naturalness of several husbands again brings an example from animals. 'Among many animals we see many males following one female, for example dogs and wolves.'

Here is Bonaventure, first replying to the problem of natural law and precept. Will the *precept* of marriage have remained without change, since natural law is immutable? Natural law dictates some things absolutely, such as loving God, and some things only for a particular period, such as things being owned in common. Thus this particular law was only for a particular period. That is to say, marriage *was* a precept. While there were few faithful people it was compulsory to marry to bring about multiplication of people. Secondly, here is Bonaventure on 'whether it is against natural law to have a concubine'. Definitions of natural law are produced, Isidore's 'what is common to all nations', and what is 'according to the customs of all'. Bonaventure's reply distinguishes three levels of law, what is in the Law and Gospel, what is common to all nations, and what nature has taught all animals. When we look at animals we see some single and permanent unions, as in turtle-doves.

Now, from these particular glimpses, and also the longer and intricate story of thought about natural law, we need to disengage three general points. First, marriage is central to the general history of thought about natural law. In the general and fundamental definitions of natural law in Isidore (or Isidore as read in Gratian's quotation of him in the *Decretum*)[137] the union of the sexes is the first and elementary example which is given of natural law. Similarly, in the wider treatises whose marriage-sections we are reading, it is marriage which is often *the* principal topic in discussion of natural law.

[137] Isidore, *Etymologiae*, V. iv; D. 1 c. 7; Friedberg, i. 2. See Lottin, *Droit naturel*, pp. 9–12.

Secondly, the properties attributed to natural law are these: applicability at all times; to all men; and to all animals. When these are systematically applied to the theme of the union of human males and females, the result is a formalization and extension of historical and comparative thought about marriage. There had been tendencies to think in these ways, but the thought had been in a vaguer guise. Now form dictates comparison. In present time: comparison of concubinage with marriage, comparison of marriages in Latin Christendom and marriages among other faiths and peoples, and comparison of human mating with animal mating. And in past time: changes in human mating through history. Under the heading of 'disparity of cult' there had long been discussion of marriage between infidels—did it exist?—and of marriage between an infidel, or a converted infidel, and a Christian. Such discussion now falls under the heading 'what is common to all is natural'. Albert's 'marriage contracts are not the same among all' is underlined by Aquinas. 'Marriage is not the same among all, since marriage is celebrated in diverse ways according to the diversity of laws', where 'laws' means 'religions' in the modern sense.[138] The move is from discussion of a canon-legal and practical problem to comparison of marriages in different 'religions'. There had long been curiosity about the mating habits of animals and attribution to them of human characteristics, of sins and ideals, for example chastity to elephants. All of this had been found in bestiaries and still had a long history to come, which would include much exploitation in sermons. Now, however, natural law is driving academic theologians, when writing about marriage, systematically to locate human mating within the wider setting of all animal mating, and it is doing this precisely when more scientific data is becoming available, as we shall see later.

Finally, natural law slightly alters and significantly adds to an already historicized view of marriage. As in other areas, it applies more pressure. There is a problem about natural law if marriage has varied. In definitions of natural law the juxtaposition of sexual union and the early commonness of things, later superseded by property, provided mutual encouragement: variation in one encouraged an historical view of the other. Most significantly, natural law discussions of marriage introduced another (and non-Christian) account of the origin and early history of marriage. Introducing a point against the naturalness of marriage, Aquinas writes that 'marriage did not exist in every period of men', and then follows Albert in quoting Cicero on the lack of marriage among primitive forest-dwellers. In his reply to this point Aquinas quickly brings it up against scripture and scripture's attestation that marriage began with the first man and woman. Unsurprisingly none of our extant theologians' texts ever show an attempted integration of the notion of development from primitive men and a Christian theological history of marriage. 'They wouldn't, would they': with acknowledgement to Mandy Rice-Davies, we need to be cynical about their silence. Through their condemnation we know that unorthodox views about sexual union and

[138] P. Biller, 'Words and the Medieval Notion of "Religion"', *JEH* 36 (1985), 351–69 (pp. 360–3).

what was natural in sex were circulating widely in later thirteenth-century Paris, including the proposition that there was not a first man, nor will there be a last man, but that there always was and always will be generation of man by man.[139] We can only conjecture that since at least Albert's time—his commentary dates from 1249—academic theologians had been allowing their minds at least briefly to dwell on a non-biblical history, one which began with indiscriminate sexual unions among primitive men, and then went on to the growth of laws, ordered communities, and defined marriages. Cicero's text was available in many places, transmitted as it was through Albert, Aquinas, and those whose commentaries adapted them: a constant encouragement to think this history.

2.4.4 *Development in the schools writings (d): the impact of translations from Greek and Arabic*

> In general, with regard to their lives, one may observe many imitations of human life in the other animals . . . The [swallow] builds the nest just as men build . . . On the feeding of the young, both birds carry out the work . . . With regard to pigeons there are other things that give scope for this kind of study. For they are neither willing to pair with more than one, nor do they abandon their partnership prematurely except through becoming a widow or widower . . . as a rule they have this kind of family devotion to each other.

Accompanying this general statement in Aristotle's *History of Animals* (612b18–13a8) was a lot of data on the mating of all animals, including human ones. Translated by around 1220, this and Aristotle's other zoological works were increasingly available as the demand for systematic comparison in discussion of natural law became more pressing. The material was sucked in and soon became commonplace. Examples are the plurality of female partners among hens, cows, and pigs in Thomas of Strasbourg's commentary on the question of plurality of wives (in distinction 33),[140] and examples of animal monogamy in most commentaries on this distinction; and Aquinas and Duns Scotus looking at some animals' abhorrence of relations between mothers and sons in their treatment of prohibitions of blood relationship (in distinction 40).[141]

This is but one example of an elementary and fundamental point about this period. The marriage treatises whose development we are surveying were being written during a period much of whose intellectual history can be written in terms of the impact of translations from Greek and Arabic into Latin. They were written while the vast corpus of Arabic medicine and the logical, natural, philosophical, and moral works of Aristotle and his Greek and Arabic commentators were being made available in the west, and then, with translation, entering

[139] Most quickly accessible through the edition and commentary on the condemned articles in R. Hissette, *Enquête sur les 219 articles condamnés à Paris le 7 Mars 1277*, Philosophes médiévaux 22 (Louvain and Paris, 1977), nos. 138 and 205–10, pp. 216 and 294–300.

[140] *In sententias*, IV. xxxiii.3; ii. 156ra.

[141] Aquinas, *In sententias*, IV. xl, art. 3 (III, 1033); Duns Scotus, *In sententias*, IV. xl (ix. 800–1).

discussion and writing in universities. The influence on marriage treatises is a tiny part of the broader history of this, that is, a tiny part of the history of the single most important fact in the development of thought in the medieval west.

At a quite early stage there is infiltration of logical language. In Peter Lombard's *Sentences* marriage has its efficient cause (consent) and final causes (purposes for which it should be contracted).[142] Medicine, whose intrusion has already been noted, joined the biological parts of Aristotle's natural philosophy in providing the commentaries with a scientific colouring. Aquinas refers to Aristotle's *On animals* on varying patterns of fertility in women during their generative spans, some more fertile when older, some more so when younger.[143] Distinction 36's treatment of minimum ages for contracting marriage, or the discussion of this appended to age for engagements in distinction 27, attract discussions by Bonaventure[144] and Aquinas[145] in which Aristotelian biology and the quicker maturing of females justifies the different ages in female and male, twelve and fourteen. And, as we have already noted, increasingly in view are not only past medicine but current doctors, *medici*, and their specialist professional knowledge.

Finally, there was the influence of the moral works, especially the *Ethics* at an earlier stage and later the *Politics*. We have already seen in the example quoted above of Albert's discussion of natural law, how importation of Aristotle's treatment of marriage as natural and prior to political association, and Greek commentary on this, laid the foundation and provided the vocabulary for a particular treatment of marriage as the first fundamental association in human communities. Later we shall be looking more closely at the *Politics*, and here we need only a brief overview. Translated by at least 1270 and rapidly becoming widely available, *Politics* offered more extensive analysis of marriage and house as prior to wider political associations, speculation about alternative systems (in particular the idea of a community of wives), and systematic treatment of marriage-ages and control of population in book 7. As we read texts approaching and going past 1300, we find the use of the *Politics*, by theologians commenting on the marriage section in the *Sentences*, becoming wider and eventually quite commonplace, though not universal. Richard of Middleton uses the first book when discussing the naturalness of marriage.[146] Duns Scotus,[147] Hugh *de Novo Castro*,[148] Peter

[142] *Sententiae*, IV. xxvii. 1 and 3 (ii. 421 and 422); IV. xxx. 3 (ii. 441).

[143] *In sententias*, IV. xxxii, qu. 1, art. 2; iii. 962.

[144] Ibid., IV. xxxvi, art. 2, qu. 1; iv. 796.

[145] Ibid., IV. xxvii, qu. 2, art. 3 (iii. 932); IV. xxxvi, art. 5 (iii. 997–8).

[146] *In sententias*, IV. xxvi, art. 1; iv. 401.

[147] *In sententias*, IV. xxvi; ix. 576.

[148] *In sententias*, IV. xxvi; Vatican, MS Chigi. B. VI. 96, fol. 84vb. On the Franciscan Hugh see V. Heynck, 'Der Skotist Hugo von Novo Castro OFM. Ein Bericht über den Stand der Forschung zu seinem Leben und seinem Schrifttum', *Franziskanischen Studien* 44 (1962), 244–70, where (p. 267) Lotharingian or German origin is suggested, and years following 1310 in Paris are given as the possible origin of the commentary. See also Stegmüller, *Repertorium*, and Doucet, *Supplément*, no. 366.

Aureoli,[149] Guiraud d'Ot,[150] and John Baconthorpe[151] all bring into their discussions Aristotle's reporting of the suggestion of a community of wives, together with the themes of peace among citizens, the 'good of the household', and the 'good of the city'. Aureoli sets traditional theology beside an idea culled straight from the *Politics*, envisaging the marriage tie as arising either out of the will of the two parties, or through being imposed by the legislator. Thomas of Strasbourg uses the first book of the *Politics* for his discussion of men ruling over women.[152] Duns Scotus[153] and Antonio Andrès[154] cite material on servitude in their commentaries on servile condition and marriage in distinction 36. Vidal de Four[155] and an anonymous writer in an Erfurt manuscript[156] import Aristotle's comments on ideal ages of marriage into their discussion of age of contracting. When a *Politics*-reader such as Thomas of Strasbourg cites exposing and not feeding offspring as an example of something against the good of offspring, Aristotle's discussion of this not feeding offspring in book 7 of the *Politics* is immediately called to mind.[157] Aristotle can be present in this way without direct reference or quotation, but the infiltration should not be exaggerated. Peter of la Palud was not an avid Aristotelian,[158] and I have been able to notice in him only one passing allusion to the *Politics*, the tag that man is a 'civil political animal'.[159]

The moral works, in particular the *Politics*, had a threefold significance. The idea of a community of wives and its criticism, or various ages the legislator could suggest for marriage, gave added impetus to what was already suggested by the observed variation of marriage in history or among different peoples and faiths. This was the idea of marriage as a system to be tinkered with. The idea was an invitation: theorize about marriage's ideal forms; think about permutations; imagine a legislator, and see what happens if he does this or that to it. Secondly, the picture of marriage as the first and most necessary community in a pyramid of communities encouraged analysis which used such terms and approached marriage as a building-block in the human community.[160] When Giles of Rome links husband's dominion over wife with a king's in a kingdom we see what is at least latent in this:

149 *In sententias*, IV. xxvi–xxvii. 2, where Aureoli states that *illa obligatio* [= the marriage contract] *vel nascitur ex impositione legislatoris vel ex propriis voluntatibus.* I am using an edition of his commentary, which according to Stegmüller (*Repertorium*, no. 653) was falsely attributed—Peter of Aquila, *Quaestiones in quatuor libros sententiarum* (Speyer, before 1487, unfoliated). On the Franciscan Aureoli, who read the fourth book in Paris in 1317, see Stegmüller, *Repertorium*, and Doucet, *Supplément*, no. 657, and P. Aureoli, *Scriptum super Primum Sententiarum*, Franciscan Institute Publications (New York, Paderborn, and Louvain, 1953), pp. vii–xxi.

150 *In sententias*, IV. xxvi; Paris, BN, MS Lat. 3068, fols. 48r and 48v.

151 Ibid., IV. xxvii, art. 2; ii. 536.

152 Ibid., II. xvi; i. 161ra.

153 Ibid., IV. xxxvi, qu. 1; ix. 755.

154 Ibid., IV. xxxvi, qu. 1; 161vb. On the Aragonese Franciscan Antonio Andrès (ob. *c.*1320), see Stegmüller, *Repertorium*, and Doucet, *Supplément*, no. 71.

155 Vatican, MS Vat. Lat. 1095, fol. 36ra.

156 Erfurt anonymous, *In sententias*, IV. xxvii; Erfurt, Stadtbibliothek, MS Fol 108, fol. 190ra–b; Stegmüller, *Repertorium*, no. 990.

157 *In sententias*, IV. xxxii. 1; ii. 155ra.

158 Dunbabin, *Pierre*, p. 31.

159 *In sententias*, IV. xxx, qu. 1; 156va; *Politics*, 1253^a 2–3; *Auctoritates Aristotelis*, p. 252, no. 3.

160 See Ch. 3 below for a discussion of the comparable influence of Avicenna's *Philosophia prima* on William of Auvergne's discussion of marriage.

the idea of a link between the cement in this community and the cement of a kingdom, just as there is, more explicitly, the idea of a link between monogamy and peace in the city. Thirdly, as we shall see later, ideas about good, private good, common good, and the good of the republic, which were derived from Aristotle as well as Cicero, came to be applied to marriage and procreation.[161]

2.4.5 *Development of the schools writings (e): diversity of marriage regionally and in various faiths or laws*

Let us turn to experience as a source of change in the marriage treatises, and first to the experience of diversity in marriage during the central medieval period: differences within Christendom, and between various non-Christian faiths. At the beginning of our period Latin Christendom had within it Jewish communities and peoples on the geographical margins, pagan or only recently Christianized, and, beyond the borders, the Muslims. During the twelfth and thirteenth centuries there were two major additions. Within Latin Christendom there grew up a counter-Church, that of the Cathars, from just after 1100 in northern France, but establishing deepest and most enduring roots in southern France and northern and central Italy, where it had organized ecclesial structures which survived to around 1300. Beyond the borders there were the Mongols, attacking eastern parts of Christendom from the early thirteenth century.

The validity of one theme upon which modern study focuses, ignorance and bizarre fantasy in western views of these groups, should not be allowed to obscure another which co-existed with it: the theme of progressively greater knowledge and clearer vision of other faiths. During the twelfth century there were some writers—of whom Gerald of Wales is a late and distinguished example—who wrote almost ethnographically about the customs and faiths of peoples regarded as barbarous: in Gerald's case, the Welsh and Irish. At the same time there was a growing supply of polemical treatises in which articles of faith, Jewish or Muslim or heretical, were sharply described and refuted.

With the Muslims, for example, early milestones were a sharp formal description in the fifth book of the *Dialogi* of Petrus Alfonsi (1108 or 1110) and a campaign to grapple with their faith, animated by Peter the Venerable, the abbot of Cluny, who commissioned a translation into Latin of the Koran which was completed in 1143. The first real scholarly engagement with the Cathars comes in the 1160s. By around 1200 we find one four-book treatise in which one book is devoted to each of four faiths: Jewish, Muslim, Cathar, Waldensian. The path to comparative writing on different 'faiths' is clear, and by the mid-thirteenth century we can find, in the Franciscan Roger Bacon, some comparative writing about the world's 'sects' or 'laws'. Writers also show a growing capacity systematically to analyse particular 'sects' or 'laws', breaking them up into 'articles of faith', 'cult', 'way of life', and

[161] See Ch. 5 below.

treatment of sin. Intrepid Franciscans made the long overland journey to the far east to visit the Mongols, and on their return wrote down accounts of this strange people, which are even more startlingly ethnographic than their predecessors of the previous century, and include set-piece descriptions of Mongol 'religion'.[162] At the same time, there was a significant backcloth in the wider dissemination in thirteenth-century encyclopaedias of classical material on far-flung peoples, their customs, and faiths.

When we turn to the place of marriage, we see least innovation with Jewish marriage. Old Testament marriage had long been the object of attention, although aspects of its law are now being given increasingly ordered discussion in academic treatises on marriage, and Jewish emphasis on fertility and hostility to virginity emerge more clearly. There is a question-mark over knowledge of later developments in Jewish law, and any real observation of marriage in the contemporary and nearby Jewish communities of, say, Paris or Oxford. New, however, was knowledge of marriage among the Muslims, which was given its first and quite detailed account in Petrus Alfonsi's *Dialogi*. Later, in our examination of William of Auvergne, we shall look more closely at reaction to the theme which was not only new but dramatic, Muslim polygamy. Then a Franciscan returned from his journey to China, talked about it in convents in Italy, and produced the first and very remarkable description of marriage among the Mongols—of which more in a moment. An increasingly rich tapestry lies behind these, with the exoticisms of the marriage customs of far-flung peoples which were described in the encyclopaedias, such as Indians' practice of suttee.

Comment on local variation *within*[163] Latin Christendom is seen very early. The Laon texts are so short that their inclusion of comment[164] on variation of celebration of marriage in different regions would in any case be significant. Such awareness is raised to the level of principle: '[there are] different customs and laws of different Churches and countries, [and] the solemnities of marriage vary accordingly.'[165] When Walter of Mortagne comments on marriage customs observed in many Gallican churches,[166] regional variation hovers as a commonplace. The sense of a general northern (French) and southern (Italian) divide came to acquire strong expression. During the middle decades of the twelfth century, when one northern academic centre and one southern upheld contrasting views of the formation of marriage, with Paris emphasizing consent and Bologna the fact of consummation, contemporary canonists expressed their acute awareness of the contrasting regional realities which lay behind the academic tussle. 'In this question the Gallican and transalpine Churches disagree.'[167] 'A certain custom is found which is today observed one way in *Francia* [northern France or the

[162] See my 'Words and the medieval notion of "religion"'.

[163] Outside the Latin church: comment on the marriage of priests among the Greeks is commonplace.

[164] See e.g. comment about Roman and Gallican difference on separation, *De coniugio*, ed. Bliemetzrieder, p. 280.

[165] *Coniugium namque*, quoted by Reinhardt, p. 97 n. 113.

[166] *De coniugio*, xiv; *PL* 176, 165.

[167] *Summa Coloniensis*, just before 1170; Esmein, i. 137; otherwise known as the *Summa 'Elegantius'*, Brundage, *Law, Sex*, p. 259 n. 19.

kingdom of France], and another way in the Roman Church.'[168] And, 'now through God's grace and the authority of Alexander [III] and Urban III this bad custom [marrying according to Bolognese doctrine] has been abolished beyond the Alps and practically throughout Italy, but even today it still taints Bologna, Imola, Modena, Reggio, and Parma'.[169] Nothing else quite matches the force of this twelfth- and early thirteenth-century regional controversy. One example in a late commentary on the *Sentences*, whose sheer length encouraged the inclusion of more comment, suggests to me that more might be found in these texts on marriage defined by region. The comments are by Peter of la Palud, who refers to Spanish noblemen marrying high-born Saracen girls, and who includes the vernacular word *cherivari* when discussing old people being mocked when they got married.[170]

Within Latin Christendom there were several further sources of a sense of diversity of practice or opinion. One was the lens of 'barbarism' through which a Christian people living on the edges of Europe would be viewed and constructed as being, in their marriages and sexual customs, the opposite of what was Christian or normal. Thus the Irish (or 'Scots') fornicated like pigs, without a system of marriage, or practised incest.[171] In another case perception and reality were closer: heresy, which put forward various propositions about marriage and stimulated debate and writing. From the founder of the Henrician heresy came proposals for practical reform. More dramatic were the Cathars, strong in northern France from shortly after 1100, and later very prevalent in Languedoc and Italy. Among them marriage was detested, procreation was utterly evil, pregnant women who died in this state were damned, and it was forbidden for a Cathar to touch—literally—the flesh of a woman. Known with increasing clarity, Cathar doctrine in this area was subject to much detailed description and rebuttal, most penetratingly and exhaustively by Moneta of Cremona around 1241, and it achieved wide diffusion through its description in one of the most popular works ever written, Guillaume Peyraut's *Summa virtutum et vitiis*, written between 1236 and 1249.[172] Already noted as another source of diversity of opinion was the university of Paris, where in the late thirteenth century 'free-thinking' academics made radical statements about sex being natural and its practice free of sin.

Present, then, among our theologians when they were writing their marriage treatises was a sense of the diversity of the practice of marriage in various faiths and peoples as well as, sometimes, diversity of opinion. Their knowledge or experience is this area stimulated, and was stimulated by, the intellectual development which was described earlier: natural law's question of 'always and everywhere

[168] *Summa Parisiensis*, *c*.1169; Esmein, i. 138.

[169] Huguccio, pre-1190; Esmein, i. 141 n. 3.

[170] *In sententias*, IV. xxvi. 1 (139ra); IV. xxviii. 3 (153ra).

[171] See the chapter 'The Face of the Barbarian', in R. Bartlett, *Gerald of Wales, 1146–1223* (Oxford, 1982), pp. 158–77, and pp. 170–1 on 'barbarous' marriage.

[172] P. Biller, 'Cathars and Material Women', in *Medieval Theology and the Natural Body*, ed. P. Biller and A. J. Minnis, York Studies in Medieval Theology 1 (York, 1997), pp. 61–107.

the same' or 'not'. The experience of diversity trickles into the treatises.[173] For example, we have seen Walter of Mortagne smoothly using a quick reference to contemporary heretics detesting marriage. These almost certainly were Cathars rather than Henricians, another set of contemporary heretics whose concern, as we shall see, was reform, not detestation, of marriage. However, *direct* examples of infiltration are not impressive. One apparent example—the question whether marriage can exist between infidels—is an ancient commonplace, and contemporary examples are rare. Peter Lombard's casual decision to refer to past heretics, *Tatiani*, and not to specify as 'heretics' the 'some' in the present who held marriage as a sin, nor to name them as Cathars, was very influential.[174] Most later *Sentences* commentaries follow him in referring to past heretical objections, giving these texts an illusory air of detachment from contemporary heresy. This air was illusory because even someone like Aquinas—one of the authors least likely to lard his writings with specific contemporary allusions—was acutely aware of contemporary heresy and its objections to marriage.[175] Some *Sentences* commentators refer to the polygamous Muslims explicitly—as we saw Albert doing, when discussing plurality of wives—but this is not usual. Alongside the Cathars the Muslims are ever-present shadows in the background of discussions of marriage.

However, direct entry of references to marriage in other faiths is not the principal issue here. I am making this point first at the broader level, about faiths, and then about marriage. Let us stand back from these faiths, Christian, Jewish, Muslim, Cathar, Mongol, and views of them in the central middle ages. There was a broad development in the central middle ages in the capacity to envisage these faiths. In the earlier middle ages people were was born and baptised into and lived inside a Christian faith and participated in its cult in a local Church. Their experiences were expressed in several specific words—'belief', 'cult', 'prayer'. A counterpart of their inability to see this as a single system or entity, and as an entity generically similar to or comparable with a Jewish or Muslim entity, was their lack of a single word for such an entity, 'religion', or -ism words for particular 'religions'. The experience of more and more divergent faiths in the twelfth and thirteenth centuries brought about converging and mutually influencing developments: a sense of number and variety, and thus of Christianity as one among many; a sense of the faith, cult, and customs of each as an entity, one among several such entities; the expression of this on the one hand in literary form—systematic descriptions of heretical or Mongol 'faith', 'cult', 'customs'—and on the other hand in words for such an entity. The words 'laws' or 'sects' are taken in the modern meaning of 'religions'. The word 'religion', hitherto meaning 'devotion',

[173] 'Trickles' is not the right word for Old Testament Jewish law, whose abundant presence is a commonplace in the treatises.

[174] *Sententiae*, IV. xxvi. 5 (ii. 419); IV. xxxi. 6 (ii. 447).

[175] He showed knowledge of the contents of a treatise by the contemporary Italian Cathar Desiderius—L. Paolini, 'Italian Catharism and Written Culture', *Heresy and Literacy, 1000–1530*, ed. P. Biller and A. Hudson (Cambridge, 1994), pp. 83–103 (p. 101)—and refers to heretics condemning marriage in his *Summa contra gentiles*, III. cxxvi.

'cult', or 'monasticism', creeps towards its early modern sense as a possible particular religion, e.g. 'The Jewish religion'; and there are words for particular 'religions', 'Christianity', 'Judaism', and even, though rarely, 'Islam' (*Saracenitas*).[176]

Now, awareness of diversity of *marriages* in different 'religions' encouraged a similar qualitative change in the character of thought about marriage, albeit not one which was expressed by an analogous development in words. Consider the formal description of the Mongols by the Franciscan John of Pian di Carpine. The general section in which marriage is described begins thus:

> First we shall describe the form of their persons [this means formal description of shape of parts of their faces], secondly their marriage, thirdly their clothing, fourthly their habitation, fifthly their things... Each has as many wives as he can maintain... in general they are united with any relatives, except with a mother, daughter or a sister by the same mother.... All other women they take as wives without any discrimination, and they buy them at a very high price from their parents. After husbands' deaths [widows] do not easily transfer to second marriages, unless some man wants to take his stepdaughter as wife.... [Now in the next section, on clothes] Women who are married wear a very ample tunic, slit in the front down to the ground... Girls and young women can be distinguished from men [only] with great difficulty, because they are dressed in everything just like men.

A later chapter, 'On their good and bad morals, customs and food', describes the high chastity of their women and the punishments for adulterers.[177]

If we try to read a work on marriage in the early twelfth century, it will be a short theological tract or part of a canon-law collection, and inside it the word *coniugium*, 'marriage', will mean principally the particular marriage contracted between two individuals, which can be to some degree translated into an abstraction when it is seen and discussed as one of God's sacraments. Here in the mid-thirteenth century *coniugium* can now be the 'marriage-system' of a people, an entity with its own distinctive characteristics, the subject of disciplined formal description and analysis. It is distinctly, though very early, on a path which leads to Malinowski on Trobriand islanders and a comparative *Encyclopaedia Britannica* article on marriage.

Clearly, the essentializing of 'marriage' into 'marriage-system', which was brought about by experience of diversity, was intricately interwoven with the alterations wrought by an increasingly historical view, the theme of natural law, and the impact of Greek and Arabic thought. The shift of outlook which I have tried to identify should not be exaggerated. It is usually only discernible in the overall temper and quality of thought in the works which are being described, and not in their *form*. *Sentences* commentaries were very conservative texts. It would be anachronistic to expect an outgrowth from them, for example, of comparative treatises on marriage.

There was, however, a moment when one very original author was writing. He was singularly free from the shackles not only of the form of *Sentences* commentaries but also the scholastic method in general. Amidst his vast literary output is

[176] See the article cited in n. 162 above.

[177] John of Pian di Carpine, *Ystoria Mongalorum*, II and IV, ed. Wyngaert, *Itinera*, pp. 32 and 33–5.

a treatise on marriage, to which we shall now turn. It shows some of the developments we have been describing in general in marriage treatises, and the author's sense of marriage-systems appears in his systematic comparison of Christian, Jewish, and Saracen marriage. Embedded in this are some extraordinarily 'demographic' contrasts between the Christian and Muslim systems. At the same time these are based on the author's wide-reading and experience. He was a churchman of one of the most populous cities in the west, Paris, and soon to be its bishop. He looked out upon and observed a geographically and politically very wide world, as a man who was about to be the confidante of one of its most important rulers, the king of France.

Appendix to Chapter 2
Guide to Peter the Lombard's Four Books of Sentences

Peter treated marriage and generation in two places. In book 2's account of the creation, distinctions 17–20 dealt with the first man and woman. Distinction 17 (their location in paradise), distinction 18 (woman's creation), and distinction 19 (their paradisal condition, in particular their immortality) lead up to the material of distinction 20. Here Peter used Augustinian texts to hold up for inspection various themes which come under the general question 'what would have happened if man had not sinned?': how children would have been procreated (chapter 1) and what sort of children would have been born (chapter 6).[178] Here was an area where imperfections of marriage and generation in the postlapsarian world could be seen and explored through their opposite, the perfection of sexual union and generation in the prelapsarian world.

The sacrament of marriage occupies distinctions 26 to 42 of book 4.[179]

26. This distinction deals with the double institution of marriage: 'Increase and multiply' *before* the Fall, and (harking back to book 2) marriage as it would have been before the Fall; and its institution *after* the Flood, again 'Increase and multiply'. Marriage, twice as a precept with the repetition of 'Increase . . .', and then later as an indulgence, occupies chapters 3–4. The opposition of second-century heretics (the *Tatiani*) and the goodness of marriage occupy chapter 5, and the sacrament chapter 6.

27. In this distinction chapters 2–5 and 10 parade definitions of marriage as something formed by consent, and divisions of opinion about this (similar to that which divided Alberic and Walter). Chapters 6–8 deal with entry of the married to monasteries, and chapter 9 discusses how the word *sponsa* is being used. Is a *sponsa* one who has made a promise concerning the present, or the future?

28. Chapters 1–3 go further into consent. Does a promise about the future make a marriage? In sub-section four of chapter 1 a commentary on a text of Pope Evaristus leads to a dictum on consent as a necessary part of marriage, with Pope Evaristus's 'handing over by parents' and 'blessing by priests' as pertaining only to due form (*decor*) of marriage. Chapter 4 harks back to book 2 distinction 18, basing a comment on relations between man and woman on the question why woman was formed from man's side.

[178] Commentaries on these distinctions were scrutinized in Müller, *Paradiesehe*, and they are used in Ch. 5 below.

[179] Peter Lombard, *Sententiae*, ii. 416–509. The section is discussed by Colish, *Peter Lombard*, ii. 628–98.

29. This distinction is devoted to force eroding consent.
30. In this distinction disparate themes are juxtaposed. First there is error eroding consent. Is one's consent invalid if one contracts with someone who in reality is different from what one thinks she or he is? Different in identity? Fortune (viz. poor rather than rich)? Condition (e.g. a serf rather than free)? Or different in [moral] character? Secondly there is the problem of Mary and Joseph's marriage. Was this a marriage if there was not consent to sex? Thirdly there is a chapter on the 'causes' (= purposes) of marriage: offspring and other worthy 'causes' such as the reconciliation of enemies and restoration of peace.
31. Chapter 1 defines St Augustine's three 'goods' of marriage, faith (fidelity), offspring, and sacrament. Chapter 2 deals with inseparability, and whether there is really a marriage when the pair have come together without the intention of one of these goods (offspring), or when they deliberately avoid offspring. Chapter 3 continues this theme with a question about those who procure poisons of sterility, as does also chapter 4 on the question of abortion as homicide. Chapters 5–8 are on how the goods of marriage 'excuse' sex, and the degrees and types of this excusing.
32. The principal theme of this distinction is payment of the marriage debt, that is to say, the reciprocal duty of sexual relations. But chapter 4 is on the appropriate times for celebrating marriage in the Church's calendar.
33. This distinction reverts to the general level of distinction 26, forming as it were an arch. It is about history, taking its title, *On the various laws of marriage*, from Walter and Hugh of St Victor and much of its contents from Walter, Hugh, and Gratian. Chapter 1 deals with the plurality of wives of the Old Testament, compared to later marriage, while chapter 2 uses a question based on St Augustine's statement that the 'virginity of John [the baptist] should not be put above the chastity of Abraham'—'John who never experienced marriage and Abraham who generated children'—to explore the respective status and variation through history of virginity, which does not generate, and chaste marriage, which does. Chapter 3 raises the history of marriage in the Old Testament, prohibited degrees, and bills of divorce, and chapter 4 returns to plurality of wives.

From distinction 34 onwards the reader is principally immersed in a theologian's appropriation and presentation of what are mainly the particulars of canon law.

34. This distinction, 'on legitimate persons', provides the history of variations in this, and then goes on to deal with the impotent, frigid, and mad.
35. Chapters 1–3 deal with separations on the grounds of adultery and fornication; men's and women's parity in law on this; and reconciliation. Chapter 4 examines the question whether one can marry someone with whom one has committed adultery.
36. Chapters 1–3 go into details of the problems of marriage and servile condition: for example, the marriage of male and female serfs of different lords. Annexed in chapter 4 is treatment of the minimum age for contracting marriage and engagement to marry. This theme should have been treated in one of the consent distinctions (numbers 27–30). It was partly obscured by Peter's location of it in this distinction, which was both late and mainly concerned with serfs, and this probably explains why commentators paid comparatively little attention to it.
37. This distinction has disparate topics, on the one hand marriage and Holy Orders, on the other hand spouse-killers.
38. This deals with vows, defining and distinguishing them. Rather awkwardly it also includes in chapter 2 a text from Augustine on unnatural sex. This would have been more sensibly placed earlier, alongside excusing of sex through the goods of marriage or avoiding one of the goods, offspring, in distinction 31.
39. This distinction deals with disparity of cult: marriage between infidels, and between an infidel and a Christian.

40–42. The last three distinctions deal with the three types of relatedness which impede marriage.

40. This deals with blood relationship, including the counting of degrees; the reasons for counting six or seven degrees; and Gregory the Great's dispensation to the English.

41. This deals with relationship of affinity, that is, between the relatives of two people who have had sexual relations.

42. The distinction which rounds off the sacrament of marriage deals with spiritual relationship, brought about through god-parenthood, natural (illegitimate) and legally adopted children, and remarriages of the widowed.

3

WILLIAM OF AUVERGNE

In this chapter we are looking only at William, and at one work of his, *On the sacrament of marriage*. William and this work in part exemplify the suggestions which conclude the previous chapter. William took a remarkable comparative and historical-geographic view of different *faiths* and *laws* in the world, and this is the background for an equally remarkable treatment of the sacrament of marriage. In effect much of this is a comparison of Christian, Jewish, and Saracen marriages, and a great deal of it is 'demographic'. There is acute and original comment on fertility, numerousness, avoidance of birth, and the numerical proportion of men and women in the population. William, then, constitutes one phase in the history of medieval demographic thought, as one of the most important figures writing in the 1220s and 1230s. But 'exemplify' can be taken too far. William wrote outside the mainstream of theological writing of this period, whose forms and conventional themes he bypassed. The marriage treatise's freedom from these means that there is an unusually thin veil between the modern reader and William's thoughts, and William's 'demographic' thoughts are themselves unusually acute: taken as more widely representative of 'thinking demographically', they would mislead. While it is not difficult when looking at other Paris theologians at this time, figures such as Gui of Orchelles, William of Auxerre, and Hugh of St Cher, to find areas of overlap which suggest mutual awareness, reference and influence, it is more difficult to bring William into the picture. Since this period in the history of thought at Paris is quite dark, this impression which I have gained—of an almost uncanny silence among contemporary academics—*may* be incorrect.

3.1 William, and his treatise On marriage

There has been no modern attempt to write a general account of William,[1] and there is little precise knowledge of his scholastic career. Born probably around

[1] The starting-point is still N. Valois, *Guillaume d'Auvergne évêque de Paris (1228–1249): Sa vie et ses ouvrages* (Paris, 1880). Access to modern work is provided through P. Viard, 'Guillaume d'Auvergne', *DSp* vi (1967), cols. 1182–92, and *DHGE* xxii (1988), col. 848. Useful characterization of William appears in B. Smalley, 'William of Auvergne, John of La Rochelle and St Thomas Aquinas on the Old Law', repr. in her *Studies in Medieval Thought and Learning from Abelard to Wyclif* (London, 1981), pp. 121–81

1180, by 1223 William was a canon of Notre-Dame, and in 1228 he became bishop of Paris. He played major roles in the affairs of the University of Paris and as a familiar of the French royal court, and he died in 1249. The treatise analysed in this chapter[2] is a part of a larger treatise on the sacraments, which is conjecturally dated to around 1228.[3] In establishing contexts for parts of the treatise I shall refer to William's life *after* 1228 as well as before, partly because the possibilities of early versions and later revisions have not been explored by modern scholarship, and partly because strong continuities will have predominated over sudden change in at least some areas of William's experience—for example, his pastoral view of Paris. The treatise on marriage, 14,500 words long, is divided into ten chapters,[4] and we must first explore the quite extraordinary distinctiveness of the work.

There are several treatments of marriage by theologians who were writing in Paris near this time which can be compared to William's treatise. These are the sections on marriage in the *De sacramentis* of Gui of Orchelles (written not long after 1216/17), in the *Summa aurea* of a much more famous Paris teacher, William of Auxerre (written after about 1218),[5] and Alexander of Hales's 1220s gloss on the Lombard's *Sentences*. These works have much in common. Though neither Gui's nor William of Auxerre's works are glosses on the *Sentences*, the *Sentences* hang heavily over both, and it would be absurd to read either without having a copy of the *Sentences* open beside you. For both Gui and William of Auxerre write within the Lombard's world. The topics, the order of treatment, the questions raised, the texts adduced (and therefore the very words used): all these are *principally* the Lombard's.

William of Auvergne's treatise cannot avoid some overlaps with the tradition within which Gui, William of Auxerre, and Alexander of Hales were writing. There are a few utterly standard questions. 'There is a debate (*quaestio*) among some' about the consent given by those who are driven only by lust, whether this consent

(pp. 137–56), and in L. Smith's 'William of Auvergne and the Jews', *Christianity and Judaism*, ed. D. Wood, SCH 29 (1992), pp. 107–17, and 'William of Auvergne and confession', in *Handling Sin*, pp. 95–107. Lesley Smith is preparing a general study of William.

[2] I have used the text in the 1674 edition of William's *Opera omnia*, which I have compared with two manuscripts, BN, MS Lat. 14842, fols. 173rb–201va (once owned by the abbey of St Victor) and Vatican, MS Vat. Lat. 849, fols. 55va–64rb (described in *Codices Vaticani Latini*, vol. 1 (Vatican, 1902–), II, 219–20). Variations between the printed text and the Paris manuscript are noted, but not the readings of the Vatican manuscript, which is late (1434) and interesting mainly for showing how unintelligible William's text could be made. Manuscripts of the treatise *De sacramentis*, of which *De matrimonio* forms a part, are listed in Smith, 'William of Auvergne and Confession', p. 98 n. 8.

[3] Smith, 'William of Auvergne and Confession', p. 98 and n. 6.

[4] Ch. 1 defines marriage. Ch. 2 addresses the necessity of marriage for fertility, whose enemies are sodomy and prostitution (there is much more emphasis on the second). Ch. 3 attacks unions outside marriage, union for *voluptas*, and Muslim polygamy. Ch. 4 is devoted to the necessity of laws about contracting marriage, and Ch. 5 summarizes what has been said so far. Ch. 6 deals with marriage's holiness and perfection as society, while chs. 8–9 attack carnal pleasure, Ch. 8 pointing out that its pursuit impedes generation. Ch. 9 raises four questions about marriage, its sacramental virtue, virginity and continence, access to wives during pregnancy and childbirth, and Old Testament polygamy; and Ch. 10 concludes with divorce and repudiation.

[5] On this date, see below Ch. 4, p. 97 n. 35.

is matrimonial or only 'amatory' (*amatoria*), and 'Some ask whether someone who knows his wife only for *voluptas* sins mortally';[6] and there are the questions on the sacramental virtue of marriage, the virtue of virginity and continence, and the plurality of the wives of the patriarchs.[7] On the last, as we shall see, William was reluctant to accept the conventional line. Occasionally William deigns to use the Lombard, albeit silently, as in his use of the commonplace of Jews' hardheartedness to explain Old Testament permission of divorce. However, virtually all of William's treatise simply bypasses the topics covered by the Lombard (and Alexander's gloss), Gui of Orchelles, or William of Auxerre. The double institution of marriage is discussed in Peter the Lombard's first distinction on marriage, Gui of Orchelle's first article on marriage, William of Auxerre's first chapter on marriage: it is not to be found in William of Auvergne. Consent as the efficient cause of marriage is discussed in the Lombard's second distinction, Gui of Orchelle's second article, William of Auxerre's second chapter: not in William of Auvergne. Further, even on the few topics where overlap is inevitable, William nearly always adopts his own tack and his own vocabulary.

Aloof from these more conventional works, William's treatise is also distinguished by the importance it accords to marriage in other major faiths, Jewish and Saracen. Especially the latter. William had a world-view of the *variety of laws* (*diversitas legum*), *faiths*, and *sects*, the subject of his treatises *De fide* and *De legibus* (*On faith*, *On laws*), and he read widely and deeply on Saracens and the law of Mahomet.[8] William used the Koran, and he uses and cites by title the revelations of the pseudo-Methodius, the *Risālat 'Abdillāh ibn-Ismā'īl al-Hāshimi ila 'Abd-al-Masīh ibn Ishāq al-Kindi wa-Risālat al-Kindi ila al-Hāshimi* (henceforth referred to as the *Risālat* of Al-Kindi), a treatise, purporting to be an exchange of letters between a Christian and a follower of Mahomet,[9] and Avicenna's *Philosophia prima*.[10] His knowledge of many more authors and texts is clearly indicated by passing allusions to Arab philosophers, the 'many of the wise men of his race' (*multi de sapientibus gentis suae*) who have believed in Mahomet, and to the many western accounts of Mahomet, 'the others [in whose writings] much is read about his life and deeds' (*de vita ejus et gestis apud alios multa leguntur*).[11] More light would be thrown on William if it could be established whether these

[6] *De matrimonio*, VI; p. 519b. They are rooted in Peter the Lombard, *Sententiae*, IV. xxx. 3. 2–3 and IV. xxxi. 7; ii. 44 and 448–51.

[7] *De matrimonio*, X; pp. 527b–8b.

[8] I am taking into account evidence of reading displayed by William in his *De fide et legibus* as well as the treatise on marriage. The Arab authors read and cited by William are listed in Valois, *Guillaume d'Auvergne*, pp. 205–6, and R. de Vaux, *Notes et textes sur l'Avicennisme latin aux confins des XIIe et XIIIe siècles*, Bibliothèque Thomiste 20 (Paris, 1934), pp. 19–22 (Ch. 2 is devoted to William, Avicenna and western 'Avicennism'). See further M.-T. d'Alverny's discussion, 'La connaissance de l'Islam au temps de saint Louis', in *Septième centenaire de la mort de saint Louis* (Paris, 1976), pp. 235–46 (pp. 241–3).

[9] *De legibus*, XVIII; *Opera omnia*, i. 49b and 50a–b. On Pseudo-Methodius, see B. Z. Kedar, *Crusade and Mission: European Approaches toward the Muslims* (Princeton, 1984), p. 29 and n. 68. On the *Risālat*, see n. 89 below.

[10] *De legibus*, XIX; *Opera omnia*, i. 54a; Valois, *Guillaume d'Auvergne*, p. 205 and n. 6.

[11] *De legibus*, XVIII; *Opera omnia*, i. 50b.

'others' included Jacques de Vitry's *Historia orientalis*. Unusual in William was not only the extent of such reading but the combination—on the one hand Arab philosophers, whom he respected, and on the other hand the polemical and partly fantasy-ridden Christian accounts of Mahomet and his followers. He handled this wide range of sources like an academic, listing and distinguishing sources.[12]

Several effects are detectable in William, first of all *some* moderation. Certainly, there was opprobrium in his account of the followers of Mahomet,[13] and two sentences in the marriage treatise contain flashes of the lurid, tabloid, material on the Saracens. One is a passing reference to eastern slave-markets, where William alludes to the inhumanity and contempt for children of men who use their wives to breed children like breeding pigs, to sell in the market.[14] The other comes in one of his arguments, based on equity, against a multiplicity of wives, where the vast numbers he envisages—ten men to twenty-thousand women—recall the spirit of western fantasizing about Saracens and sex.[15] However, in the treatise on marriage that is all, and William put considerable weight upon the other scale. Mahomet's law contained unworthiness, certainly, but it *also* contained 'worthiness' (*honestas*), and 'many true and good things', and one point weighing on this scale was that Mahomet forbade sodomy.[16]

Strongly influencing William and providing some of this moral balance was his reading of the calm philosophic discourses of Arabic *sapientes*, philosophers, whom he also knew and saw as followers of Mahomet: wicked Saracens and wise Arabs were not coralled into separate parts of his mind. Chief among the wise Arabs was Avicenna, and chief among Avicenna's works, in its influence on William's view of Saracen marriage, was one part of Avicenna's *Metaphysics* which was known in its western Latin translation as the *Philosophia prima*.

At the end of this work the Arab philosopher dealt briefly with the qualities of the prophet (or legislator), and the prophet's dispositions for human communities. Here Avicenna writes of the 'city', the need for 'laws' and 'conventions', and the necessity of 'communication in human association'. He deals with 'the binding together of the city and the binding together of the house and sex and about general constitutions concerning this', mentions the relation between the right

[12] In his account of Mahomet, in *De legibus*, XVIII (*Opera omnia*, i. 50a), where he precedes the birth of Mahomet with a prophecy of his rise, he carefully attributes this to [the pseudo-] Methodius. He then distinguishes Mahomet from another one, 'Mahomet the Philosopher', pedantically footnoting the latter as the author of a work which was translated by Plato of Tivoli. He notes discrepant views. 'It is believed by some' that he was a disciple of Sergius, William writes, before giving a reference in the work by the Pseudo-Methodius and then continuing, 'however others say that . . .' He cites various sources and, while not quite providing a list for further reading, he was tending in this direction, when referring to the 'others' who had written more about Mahomet.

[13] *De legibus*, I; *Opera omnia*, i. 22a–b. The treatise on marriage attacks Saracens for their dedication to *voluptas*.

[14] *De matrimonio*, VIII; p. 524b. Other western authors on the theme are assembled in N. Daniel, *Islam and the West: The Making of an Image*, 2nd edn. (Oxford, 1993), pp. 164–9.

[15] *De matrimonio*, III; p. 516a.

[16] *De legibus*, XVIII and XX; *Opera omnia*, i. 50b and 54b. In the second of these passages he also noted that prohibition and the multitude of wives had not exterminated sodomy among them.

ordering of marriage and peace in the community, states that 'there should be laws concerning this union', and then proceeds to outline these laws.[17] The principal source of Aristotle's approach to marriage within the city, the *Politics*, had not been translated into Arabic, and it was therefore the only important work of Aristotle's not available to Avicenna. But enough survives in his other 'moral works', especially the *Ethics*, for Avicenna to be able to absorb and reproduce something of the style of Aristotle's approach.[18] Thus to some degree reading the *Philosophia prima* did for William what the *Politics* was to do for later western authors, in holding up a model of a particular style of discourse about marriage's place in the human community, its relation to peace, and the necessity for legislation about it. Clearly indebted to the *Philosophia prima* is the style of discussion of marriage which William's treatise sometimes displays, when describing marriage as a building-block in wider human communities, with whose 'public good' it is linked, and when taking as a theme the necessity of laws and magistracy dealing with marriage.[19] Some parallels are very close. For example, Avicenna's identification of fornication and sodomy, as marriage's two enemies in the city, is echoed by William's identification of 'prostituting fornication' and 'sodomy' as the two enemies of marriage's fertility.[20] While most western authors wrote of 'sin against nature', 'sin of Sodom', 'sodomite' (*sodomita*), or confined their use to the adjective 'sodomitic', the translation of the *Philosophia prima* used a noun which is rare in western Latin, *sodomia*, and William, ever a lover of essentializing nouns, took this over from Avicenna.[21] Again, William's description of Saracens' grounds for repudiation, when wives become odious in various ways to their husbands, is close to the three reasons listed by Avicenna.[22] Even the centrality of the word *voluptas* in his treatise, especially in chapters 7–8—rather than *concupiscentia* or *luxuria* (concupiscence, lust)—probably came about through William's sharp reaction to a brief reference in the *Philosophia prima* to *voluptas* as natural.[23]

William's form is equally independent. Although William does raise 'questions' and 'determines' them in a few chapters, what is remarkable is the very small proportion of his treatise that is momentarily shaped by such exercises, and also what these lack. For there is scarcely a trace of the usual scaffolding—the posing of thesis, counter-thesis and reply, with authorities and reasons paraded under each. It is difficult to convey to anyone who has not read both William of Auvergne and contemporaries, such as William of Auxerre, writing within strict

[17] Avicenna, *Liber de philosophia prima sive scientia divina*, X. iv, ed. S. Van Riet, Avicenna Latinus, 3 vols. (Louvain and Leiden, 1977–83), ii. 542–8. The heading of the section is *Capitulum de ligatione civitatis et de ligatione domus scilicet de coitu et de constitutionibus generalibus in hoc* ('Chapter on the binding together of the city and the binding together of the household, that is to say, on sex and general laws on this matter'). For the translation of the work into Latin, after 1150, and the twenty-five extant mss., see ibid., i. 124*–125*.

[18] F. E. Peters, *Aristotle and the Arabs: The Aristotelian Tradition in Islam* (New York and London, 1968), p. 61.

[19] *De matrimonio*, IV; pp. 516b–18a.

[20] Ibid., II; pp. 513a–14a.

[21] Ibid., II and IX; pp. 513a and 524a.

[22] Ibid., X; p. 528a.

[23] See his reference to the *Philosophia prima* on the Koran's permission of *gaudia corporum* ('bodily pleasures'), *De legibus*, XIX; i. 54a.

and constricting forms, the extraordinary air of freedom which blows through William of Auvergne's prose. Throughout the treatise William writes in a very simple and free form. He expounds and comments; then he expounds and comments further and further,[24] with some of the developments of comments leading into a digression. When this has happened, he simply cuts straight back to the previous point, at its last stage. With similar simplicity he links arguments by signalling that he is going forward, writing 'further' (*amplius*), or that he is returning after a digression, writing, 'now let us return to where we were' (*Nunc autem revertamur ad id in quo eramus*). It has been suggested that his style was influenced by Avicenna.[25]

It is also difficult to convey the distinctiveness of William's vocabulary, and the insidious ways in which his characteristic thesaurus of words shapes the character of the thought which he expresses. Take first the beginning of any theological treatise on marriage—the question, what is marriage?—and the effect of William's disdaining of what was conventional. *Matrimonium* [*est*] *viri mulierisque coniunctio maritalis, inter legitimas personas, individuam vitae consuetudinem retinens* ('Marriage is the marital union of man and woman, [a union] between lawful persons [= persons who may lawfully contract marriage], involving [their] individual association in life').[26] This is the definition a reader would find in Gratian and in the Lombard:[27] and therefore in virtually every canon-legal or theological treatise on marriage written in the central or later middle ages. William's definition? *Matrimonium est sancta, sanctificativa, et perfecta societas maris et foeminae in genere humano, sive vinculum, sive necessitudo quae eos hujusmodi societatis facit invicem sui in alterutrum debitores* ('Marriage is the holy, sanctifying, and perfect society of male and female in the human species; or bond or necessity which makes them debtors to each other in this sort of society').[28] Right at the start, then, William shows his independence by ignoring the stock phrase which his readers will have expected. That will have made them alert to the implications of his unusual formulation. 'Society', William's favourite word for the relation, will have had less impact than the substitution of 'male' and 'female' for 'man' and 'woman' and the addition of 'human species'. These signalled to the reader the approach of a mind which thought in terms of comparisons with mating in the animal world, and in biological and medical terms.

A high proportion of William's words and phrases is vivid or unusual. Many of the nouns are formed by suffixes from shorter words, often based on adjectives

[24] E. Gilson's characterization, in his *History of Christian Philosophy in the Middle Ages* (London, 1955), p. 251: 'the patristic style of continuous exposition'.

[25] This example from *Opera omnia*, p. 3. Many examples are given by E. Gilson, 'Avicenne en Occident au moyen âge', *AHDLMA* 36 (1970), 89–121 (pp. 92–3), who suggests Avicenna's influence. There was earlier comment on William's style in Valois, *Guillaume d'Auvergne*, Ch. 3.

[26] I have adapted the translation in Hugh of Saint Victor, *On the Sacraments of the Christian Faith (De sacramentis)* (Cambridge, Mass., 1951), trans. R. J. Deferrari, p. 327. See the alternative in J. B. Moyle's translation of the *Institutes of Justinian* I. ix, 5th edn. (Oxford, 1913), p. 12.

[27] See J. Gaudemet, 'La définition romano-canonique du mariage', no. XIV in his *Église et société au moyen âge* (London, 1984).

[28] *De matrimonio*, I; pp. 512b–13a.

themselves formed from nouns. If writing now and in modern English, William would look at the words 'ruin-ruinous-ruinousness' and pick out 'ruinousness' for use. Writing in medieval Latin, William stocked his personal thesaurus with words such as these: *ruinositas, studiositas, contrarietas, aerumnositas, pretiositas, quaerulositas, numerositas, commensalitas, irreligiositas, rumusculi.* Sharpest, perhaps, is his pressing into use an adverb and a verb from the noun which denotes a faith. He does this in order to be able to write that men live 'Saracenically' or 'Jewishly' (*Saracenice, Judaice*), or that they 'Saracenicize' or 'Judaize' (*Saracenizant, Judaizant*), and so that he can use 'Judaism' and 'Saracenism' (*Judaismus, Saracenismus*).[29] These last two nouns are more inclusive than the usual words used by William's contemporaries—'faith' (or 'law') 'of the Jews', 'faith' (or 'law') 'of the Saracens'[30]—and they tend to essentialize the ensemble of peoples, faith, and cult which they denote. Should we compare one pair of contrasting styles, the plainer Latin of William's contemporaries and William's Latin, to a modern pair of contrasting styles, where one author writes plain English and another is addicted to adding 'ific' or '-isticize' to words? The drift in the latter modern example, towards abstraction and essentializing things, may convey *something* of William and his mind. But the modern analogy misleads if it obscures the precision of William's use of words, and the motive of his selection—concern to press language into expressing *more* things.

Some of the thesaurus, and even more of the compound phrases and similitudes, arise from an original mind and its desire for pungent expression. This word-smith, who tosses off phrases like 'bent love' (*curvus amor*) and 'parading and trying-out of females' (*praesentatio et* [. . .] *probatio foeminarum*),[31] has both mordancy and a certain jagged or raw quality. To illustrate the proposition that anything can be re-cleaned, he chooses as his example 'a menstruating woman's rag'.[32] The vividness of the similitudes, which William used in his sermons, was itself the theme of some contemporary *exempla.*[33]

Finally, there is perhaps a more ambitious use of language to express a theme. The images for generation and reproduction, images of fields, trees, fruit, cheese and rennet, are sometimes developed lengthily and recur. William may have been encouraged, in his use of the image of the coagulation of cheese for the generation of the human embryo or the image of women as fields for ploughing and sowing by their appearance in, respectively, Aristotle's *On Animals*[34] and the Koran:[35] but tracing sources is not all. William says something about human generation not

[29] *De matrimonio,* VI; p. 519b.

[30] P. Biller, 'Words and the Medieval Notion of "Religion"', *JEH* 36 (1985), 351–69 (pp. 362–3 and 366).

[31] *De matrimonio,* VIII and X; pp. 524a and 528a.

[32] *De legibus,* XXVIII; *Opera omnia,* i. 97b.

[33] Stephen of Bourbon, *Tractatus,* IV. xi; no. 444, p. 383. On William's lively preaching style, see A. Lecoy de la Marche, *La chaire française au moyen âge,* 2nd edn. (Paris, 1886), p. 64.

[34] Aristotle, *De animalibus* (Scot), XVI; p. 83 [739b21–5]. See J. Needham, *A History of Embryology,* 2nd edn. (Cambridge, 1959), pp. 50, 64 (on the image in Job 10: 10), 76, 84–5, and 87.

[35] On other western authors' preoccupation with this metaphor in the Koran, see Daniel, *Islam and the West,* p. 351.

just through the proposition of a sentence, but also through effects of language—the mystery, richness, and potency of the words in which the proposition is clothed.[36]

3.2.1 *William the pastor, in Paris (a): Christians other than prostitutes*

William's main theme was fertility: fertility among married Christians in the west, among prostitutes in the west, and in countries in which Saracens lived. William's comments on fertility in these milieux need the setting of his own experience.

The first setting is Paris, where William lived for an unknown number of years before becoming bishop. Thereafter, for twenty-one years, he resided in an episcopal palace at the heart of one of the largest cities of Latin Christendom, exercising authority over a diocese which covered not only Paris but some of the smaller towns and villages of the fertile Île-de-France.[37] The numbers of inhabitants had increased and were still increasing. Philip Augustus's new walls for Paris were going up, and there was the construction and extension of commoner as well as grander buildings. In Paris itself inhabited areas were becoming fuller, and there were more people living along particular roads. For a clergyman who was involved in administration all this was not just something to look at. It meant thinking, planning, and trying to organize new parish boundaries. In Paris there was a growth in the number of parishes, accelerating in the later twelfth century, when the enormous parish of St Germain-l'Auxerrois—which was eventually cut into eight parishes—had its first three dismemberments.[38] With the Clos du Chardonnet, the history of the expansion of Paris parish boundaries, under the pressure of expanding population, reached and directly involved William. There was a growing number of people living along the road leading to Saint-Victor, parallel to the canal of La Bièvre, and from April 1230 William was active in getting a parish for the inhabitants of Chardonnet.[39] Since the problem was general, William set about getting general papal permission for what he was doing. His action is known from Gregory IX's bull, given at Perugia on 18 December 1234. This granted William licence to make two parishes of one in his diocese, as he saw fit. The bull makes it clear that William had urged the excessive size of parishes when applying for the power to divide them.[40]

Within the diocese of Paris growing numbers, reflected in alteration to structures, whether town walls or parish boundaries, will certainly have produced the commonplace 'populous' in an observer's mind, and they may also have

[36] *De matrimonio*, I; p. 513a.

[37] The fundamental physical description of Paris in this period and account of the evidence usable on this theme is Baldwin's *Peter the Chanter*, i. 63–72 and ii. 46–50.

[38] A. Friedmann, *Paris, ses rues, ses paroisses du moyen âge à la révolution* (Paris, 1959), pp. 71–3, 91–8, and 277–8.

[39] Friedmann, *Paris*, pp. 238–9.

[40] Valois, *Guillaume d'Auvergne*, pp. 41 and 369, no. 55; Friedmann, *Paris*, pp. 415–16.

suggested some estimating of numbers in parishes, if only in schematic and rough mental approximations. And for a cleric lifting his eyes beyond the diocese of Paris, there was something more. This was the simple concept, which was ubiquitous in classical and medieval geographical description, 'populous', 'more populous', 'less populous', and the possible linking of this with observation of the contrasting populousness of areas which were defined ecclesiastically. Take the case of the archdiocese of Embrun. This was a very large diocese, taking in 3750 square kilometres of south-eastern France, and much of it was mountainous. Its low level of populousness had already in the 1140s encouraged an abbot of Cluny, Peter the Venerable, to make a demographic comparison. To Peter its 'deserted [areas] and little villages' (*desertis et villulis*) contrasted with what one encountered to the west, as one entered the province of Narbonne, 'great gatherings [of people] and populous cities' (*magnis conventibus et populosis urbibus*).[41] The point was made again, a century later, by the great canonist Henry of Susa (Hostiensis), writing after he had become archbishop of Embrun. He commented on Embrun's low population by comparing it with that Paris parish which we have already seen being dismembered, whose vast size made it known up to the eighteenth century as 'la Grande Paroisse': St Germain-l'Auxerrois. The comparison is now numerical. Henry wrote, 'the parish church of St Germain l'Auxerrois, whose rector has the care of more than 40,000 souls, possibly has more than the archbishop of Embrun with all his suffragans.'

The sight of town walls encircling larger areas was a commonplace of western experience at this time. So was the increase of numbers of parishes, which was most dramatic on the boundaries of Christendom. For example, Génicot has noted parishes, in the diocese of Cracow, going from 174 in 1200 to 467 in 1327.[42] The Paris parishes were under very tight episcopal government, and tight observation. Parish priests were ordered to appear in twice-yearly synods, to refer much to the bishop, to bring details of parishioners' bequests to Notre-Dame and possibly much else to synods; and to reduce a lot to writing—rents and possessions, names of dying priests, names of parishioners belonging to a particular confraternity. Now, at this date we are beginning to see the ideal being upheld of pastors knowing the numbers of their flocks.[43] With Henry of Susa and the estimation of numbers in St Germain we move right into the circle of people whom William of Auvergne knew and with whom he dealt—for Henry was teaching law in Paris in 1239 and was one of William's three archdeacons. Henry's estimate clearly goes back to his archidiaconal days in Paris, and it is a reasonable conjecture that some sorts of estimates of St Germain-l'Auxerrois go back—and go back as commonplaces—to the beginning of its dismemberment.

The bishop and priests of the diocese of Paris were working within a great reforming code, the synodal statutes issued by Eudes de Sully a few years before

[41] Peter the Venerable, *Contra Petrobrusianos liber*, VI, ed. J. Fearns, CCCM 10 (1968), p. 10.

[42] L. Génicot, *Le XIIIe siècle Européen*, Nouvelle Clio 18 (Paris, 1968), p. 91.

[43] This is discussed in Ch. 4 below.

1215,[44] and later additions, including those of Guillaume de Seignelay (1219 × 1224). Parish priests met in synods twice a year, and they were required to keep booklets containing the synodal statutes. These laid down their duties, and bore upon such themes as the contracting of marriage, problematic marriage cases, and sin and confession, including major sexual sins. This setting is glimpsed in William's marriage treatise. Behind an admonition that marriage should never be celebrated without the priest's prayer and blessing lie the elementary words of the synodal statute on the same theme, as familar as three times three.[45] Behind the theme of ecclesiastical magistracy over marriage and a brief discussion of separation on the grounds of a husband's cruelty lie sessions of the diocese's marriage court.[46] And behind William's sharp, wide, and miscellaneous knowledge of marriage lies not only direct pastoral experience but also the implementation of the statute that 'A priest should always refer to him [the bishop] all doubts and problems of marriage'.

This, then, was the general framework within which a cleric in the diocese of Paris, and then its bishop, learnt about the marriages and sexual behaviour of ordinary lay men and women in the diocese: synodal meetings, marriage-courts, and confession. And it is through sources of this sort thatWilliam claims knowledge. After describing the lower potency or impotence of some men with their wives and other women, he writes, 'We have learnt this same thing from women, not from men's rumours or [general] opinion, from experience in itself and certainty', in statements given in confession.[47]

Paris also contained one extraordinary family, whose marriages were much observed and commented upon. When William became intimate with it is not clear, but the depth of familiarity which he eventually gained was underlined in contemporary stories. When those attending the queen in childbirth were

[44] *Les statuts de Paris et le synodal de l'ouest (XIIIe siècle)*, ed. O. Pontal, in *Les statuts synodaux français du XIIIe siècle* (Paris, 1971–), i. p. lxviii.

[45] 'Priests should frequently forbid lay people from exchanging consent except in front of a priest and in a public place, that is, in front of the doors of the Church and in the presence of many people.... Those who hold this in contempt and decline it, except through fear or other good cause, should not be regarded as married people but fornicators. And their children should not be regarded as legitimate', *De matrimonio*, VI; p. 520a. We do not find adjudications of illegitimacy, for this reason, in the records of marriage-courts. The presence of the threat suggests that William may have shared something of the extremism in reform of his friend and contemporary bishop of Lincoln, Grosseteste. See R. W. Southern, *Robert Grosseteste: The Growth of an English Mind in Medieval Europe*, 2nd edn. (Oxford, 1992), pp. 9–10 and 260–1.

[46] The first substantial survival of court records from the diocese of Paris is much later—the six hundred cases of a register covering 1384–7; J.-P. Lévy, 'L'officialité de Paris et les questions familiales à la fin du XIVe siècle', in *Études d'histoire du droit canonique dédiées à Gabriel Le Bras*, 2 vols. (Paris, 1965), ii. 1265–94. In these later cases the suits for separation 'from bed and board' mainly involved the adultery of either party and the husband's cruelty. It is to these two categories that William refers in his treatise. For example, his treatment of the married as 'companions' leads him briefly to consider the opposite case. Where a husband is oppressive a wife may not go off to other vows (meaning another marriage or entry into a religious order), 'but if she is weak and cannot bear her husband's molestations', she may leave him for a while, with the Church's counsel and authority and wait for and prudently try to bring about his reform; *De matrimonio*, VI; p. 520b.

[47] *De matrimonio*, IX; p. 525a.

unwilling to break the news of a daughter's birth to the king, William was described as taking on the task, and playing the role of adroit courtier ready with a gentle and clever form of words to jolly along the king: 'Today the crown of France has gained a king, for you have a daughter through whose marriage you will gain a realm.'[48] Although analysis of literary commonplaces may undermine the literal truth of such stories, they convey a broader point, William's closeness to the royal family.

Let us now juxtapose these areas of William's experience with William's 'demographic' statements in the treatise.

The treatise's most remarkable comment on fertility compares the population of countries in which Saracens live and other countries. The 'Saracens do not achieve the multiplication of their people, which they aim at through this [plurality of wives].' Morally the setting and explanation for this is Saracen intentness on carnal pleasure. But William appeals to experience of these other countries to support his point. 'In whatever realm of another people', he wrote, 'of the same amplitude and fertility of soil, [and] unless things are otherwise through disease, the sword or another [source of] damage [to the people], just as great a numerousness (*numerositas*) of indigenous peoples is to be found as in any other realm of the people of the Saracens.' 'Whatever' helps to underline the argument, but the ideal of marriage in William's treatise is that of good Christians in Latin Christendom, as opposed to Jews and Saracens, and his direct experience was the realm of France, especially the Île-de-France: those he refers to in the next sentence as 'our people'. 'So it is clear', he continues, 'that the multiplication of wives and the efforts they devote to generation do not bring about the multiplication of their people at which they aim, and conjugal chastity and singleness of marriages [=monogamy] do not bring about decrease or loss to our people—the decrease they dread so much [happening] in their people.'[49] Remarkable in William's claim is his hardheadedness concerning large Saracen population (which we will discuss below). Remarkable also his careful spelling out of what needs control in the kingdom which is to be compared: geographical size, agricultural fertility, and freedom from particular events which bring about population decline. This man was drawing upon the experience of an adult life which was passed in a capital city whose administrative reorganization, under population pressure, was to be (or had been) a matter of direct personal concern. He chose to ally a general demographic statement about 'our people' with a word which is a half-way house between a standard contemporary phrase, 'great multitude' (*multitudo magna*) and the modern demographer's word 'density': *numerositas.*

[48] Stephen of Bourbon, *Tractatus*, p. 388 n. 1.

[49] *De matrimonio*, VIII; p. 524a: *multiplicationem gentis sue, quam per hoc intendunt sarraceni, non assequantur* [MS: *assecuntur*]*: in quocunque enim regno alterius gentis ejusdem amplitudinis et fertilitas terre, invenitur tanta numerositas populorum indigenarum quanta in quocunque regno gentis sarracenorum, nisi forte peste, aut gladio aut alio incommodo secus contingat. Quare manifestum est, quod multiplicatio uxorum et opera quam dant generationi non efficiunt* [MS adds: *eis*] *gentis sue multiplicationem, quam intendunt, neque* [MS adds: *nobis*] *castitas conjugalis et singularitas matrimoniorum diminutionem aut detrimentum parit gentis nostrae, quam diminutionem in sua gente tantopere formidant* [MS: *reformidant*].

William turns from *numerositas* in a realm and addresses fertility in individual families, and in families of different estates or degrees of wealth. Here he faces in two directions. Pressure to look one way comes from his concern to combat *voluptas*, which he does by demonstrating an inherent opposition between the pursuit of sexual pleasure and fertility. Here ordinary layfolk with whom William was acquainted are put alongside two other groups who are being used in the argument (prostitutes and Saracens), and their sexual practices paraded. There are people who deliberately avoid conception because their 'bent love' is directed towards a pleasure which might be diminished by offspring:

> How much more fitting it was for the Creator to strengthen this hope and love, which, while they are aimed and directed only at the due end, are right, than that bent love, viz. the love of sexual pleasure! Especially since this [bent] love impedes that end and the fruit of children. [Bent love] draws the act of generation into itself, forcing it to stay there—[that act of generation] which was to be directed and exercised towards the end of fruit and offspring: so that not only is the fruit of offspring not looked for by those who are mingling [sexually], but care is taken to stop [such fruit] resulting, to avoid [such procreation] diminishing or totally doing away with sexual pleasure.[50]

In their pursuit of sexual pleasure they apply themselves to avoiding conception. The practice will have been known to William through confession, and perhaps was ventilated in talk at synods. Although William does not try to estimate its extent, its importance to him can perhaps be gauged by the fact that the practice is lined up for discussion alongside fertility among prostitutes and Saracens.

Pressure to look another way, however, came from William's concern to combat Saracens' preoccupation with multiplication, and their confusion, as he saw it, between city and household. William is thereby driven towards upholding an ideal which, whatever it is precisely, will be *smaller* than a Saracen ideal. William, therefore, looks at moderation in the size of families. In William's discussion four things can be distinguished, (i) an ideal size of princely families, (ii) their size in reality, (iii) an ideal size of families lower down the scale, (iv) their size in reality. On (i–iii) there is some illumination, on (iv) nothing. William the courtier came to know a lot about one royal family. When he turns to an example of size he chooses a figure, twelve, which is both round and also close to the number of children Louis IX was to father—eleven.[51] William was in a position to know more than most about the size of families, and his comments on poorer families are tantalizing, for they show a realist and observer: he could have discussed (iv), that

[50] *De matrimonio*, VIII; p. 524a: *Quanto autem magis decuit creatorem hanc spem et amorem augere, qui recti sunt, dum in finem debitum solummodo intendunt et respiciunt, quam istum curvum amorem, scilicet voluptatis* [MS adds: *adicere maxime*]? *Maxime cum iste amor istum finem et fructus prolis impediat* [MS: *fructus . . . impediat / fructum plerumque impediat*], *et opus generationis, quod in finem fructus et prolis dirigendum et exercendum erat, ad se rapiat et in se stare cogat: ita ut non solum fructus prolis non curetur a comiscentibus, sed ut etiam non proveniat procuretur, ne voluptatem ipsam aut minuat aut ex toto etiam tollat.*

[51] The reader is reminded about the (conjectural) date of the treatise on marriage, 1228, earlier than the completion of Louis IX's family. See below Ch. 8 n. 55.

is to say numbers in reality, but does not. All we are left with is his views on their ideal size.

William first of all looks at household numbers:

It is manifest to those who carefully look at this [matter], that a man of any condition and also of any power or wealth is sufficiently burdened [*ornatus* = equipped; possibly mistake for *oneratus* = burdened] with the production and support of one house of a medium number of people, which is [a house] containing twelve children and the necessary and appropriate household [viz. servants and others]. Even a powerful and wealthy prince could hardly provide for twelve children decently and competently in a way which was appropriate to his glory and magnificence. Undoubtedly he could provide clothing and food for them as though they were servants, and [do] this without burden or difficulty—but not for them as the king's children, nor as befits royal highness.

William has begun at the highest point in rank and wealth, a king, and the number twelve. He now moves down strata of rank and money, suggesting proportion between these on the one hand and on the other hand size of family and its support. 'And because the burdens of this sort of wealth and power are proportional to the wealthy and the powerful, it is clear that a house of this size burdens the rich of every sort, and the poor insupportably. One can hardly find a man and a woman taking twelve children through to adult age while rearing them and instructing and providing in every way.'

Having skirted this dangerous theme, William continues with words about oneness which recall the reader to what is being opposed, marriage among the Saracens. 'And what a nest or the like of a nest is among birds is what a house is among men. On the one hand just one male and one female hatch their young in one nest. And so, [on the other hand], just one male and one female only generate in one house. And this is in itself the essential characteristic of marriage, building one house; through marriage, male and female "leave father and mother and adhere" to each other [see Genesis 2: 24], in order to build another house for themselves.'[52] William then doubles back to the danger area, spelling out his advocacy of reason and limit. 'It is manifest therefore that single marriages, that is to say, between one man and one woman [monogamous marriages], require the limits

[52] *De matrimonio*, VIII; p. 524a: *Diligenter autem attendentibus* [MS: *intendentibus*] *in hoc manifestum* [MS adds: *est*] *satis ornatum esse virum, cujuscumque conditionis et etiam quantecunque potentiae aut opulentie, sit provisione et exhibitione domus unius etiam mediocris numeri, que est 12 [c]ontinens* [MS: *XII continens*] *sibi liberos cum familia* [MS adds: *sibi*] *necessaria et* [MS: *et / atque*] *decenti; etiamsi Rex sit praepotens atque ditissimus pro congruentia gloriae suae ac magnificentie vix poterit duodecim* [MS: *XII*] *filiis decenter atque competenter providere. Poterit utique eis tamquam servis vestitum et cibaria providere, et hoc absque onere et difficultate: non autem ut regis filiis, nec ut decet celsitudinem regiam. Et quia proportionalia sunt onera hujusmodi divitiarum seu potentiarum ipsis divitiis et potentiis, manifestum est hujus numeri domum* [MS: *hujus . . . domum / illas*] *omnis generis divites* [MS adds: *pro exigencia mirum*] *onerare, pauperes vero importabiliter. Vix autem invenitur vir et uxor, qui educando et erudiendo omnique modo providendo duodecim* [MS: *XII*] *liberos ad virilem perducant etatem. Et quia quod est nidus* [MS adds: *in*] *avibus aut nido simile, hoc est domus* [MS adds: *in*] *hominibus. Unus autem et una tantum in uno nido pullificant; sic unus et una tantum in una domo generant. Et hoc est per se proprium* [MS adds: *ipsius*] *matrimonii, domum scilicet unam aedificare, propter quod mas et foemina patrem et*

and the constrictions of means and [degrees of] affluence; and that [marriages] sufficiently weigh down the amplest of resources; and that their extension or multiplication is either insupportable or utterly unfit for human nature.'[53] William finally moves away from the theme of numbers that befit levels of wealth and rank and towards the more commonplace themes of women's and men's pain and toil. These are 'the great pain of childbirth, unhappiness of pregnant women, hard work and misery of feeding',[54] and 'for husbands . . . the not light work of supporting pregnant, childbearing and breast-feeding women, and similarly looking after, feeding and educating little children'.[55] In the third of the four questions which William raised and determined in the following chapter, he returned to the advocacy of moderation from the point of view of health, writing of the greater robustness and health of offspring who are generated when 'sowing' is less frequent.[56]

Outwardly, William's discussion is about Christian monogamy versus Saracen polygamy, and it is the latter's 'extension or multiplication' whose insupportability is being demonstrated. But within this argument there is another discussion, about the appropriate size of *Christian* monogamous families. At the centre are two things. One is a view of a direct relation between on the one hand means (and probably rank) and on the other hand numbers of children to be generated and provided for. The other is what is allied to this, the notion of a sliding scale. Both the wording of William's description of supporting a household and bringing up children and his notion of a sliding scale find parallels in discussions of almsgiving. The amount which one should give related to one's superfluity, and the assessment of one's superfluity related to one's station in life: men of higher rank had to maintain greater estate.[57] 'Marriages . . . require limits and constrictions'. William's view of ideal family size seems essentially similar. One may envisage twelve for a prince—though even this is difficult—and such size is insupportable lower down. Lower ideal figures are not spelled out, but a downward sliding scale, as with the obligation to charity, is clearly implied. It seems that a polemic against Saracens licensed a Christian theologian to raise a theologically sensitive topic: an ideal of limit and moderation. If William seems to be advocating an ideal, what of demographic reality? All we can say is that William is close to reality when talking

matrem relinquunt, sibique ad [*ad*: MS omits] *invicem adhaerent, ut sibi* [MS: *sibi / per se*] *aliam domum edificent.*

Guillaume Peyraut seems to have used this in the chapter *De inseparabilitate matrimonii*, in his *Summa de virtutibus et vitiis*, I. iii. 18, 2 vols. (Antwerp, 1571), I, fo. 182r.

[53] Ibid., VIII; p. 524b: *Manifestum ergo est matrimonia singularia, scilicet* [MS: *scilicet / id est*] *inter unum et unam, ipsos limites et angustias facultatum ac divitiarum requirere, et quantumcunque ampla* [MS: *amplam*] *ipsarum opulentiam satis onerare, et extensionem seu multiplicationem ipsorum aut non satis esse portabilem aut nullatenus decere humanam naturam.*

[54] Ibid., VIII; p. 524b: *tantus . . . dolor partus, tanta aerumnositas praegnantium, tantus labor et miseria nutrientium.*

[55] Ibid., VIII; p. 524b: *de viris: non enim est leve onus providere praegnantibus, enixis, et nutrientibus; similiter custodire parvulos, nutrire et erudire.*

[56] Ibid., VIII; p. 526a.

[57] See B. Tierney, *Medieval Poor Law: A Sketch of Canonical Theory and Its Application in England* (Berkeley, 1959), pp. 35 and 146 n. 23.

about high-ranking families and is acutely aware of poorer families' problems when rearing large numbers of children. Further than this we are in the dark.

3.2.2 *William the pastor, in Paris (b): prostitutes*

Through the moral-literary lenses of the reforming theologians studied by John Baldwin there appear sharp vignettes of Paris around 1200. There are poor prostitutes in brothels, offering themselves to transients for a low price; half a penny or a penny are two prices discussed. There are young men losing their virginity to prostitutes. Brothels are in buildings, in which on another floor lectures take place. There is brawling in brothels, and prostitutes shout after men who had turned them down, crying out 'Sodomites!' And during the building of Notre-Dame, the prostitutes of Paris are offering to devote some of the money they earn to paying for a stained-glass window. Later, the fiscal and criminal records studied by Bronisław Geremek allow one to plot the precise areas and streets, as well as the different levels and sorts of prostitutes, the professionals, rich and poor, the part-timers, the pimps, the brothels, the 'sin-shops' (*bouticles au pêchié*).[58]

This was one concern shared by both the more and less radical wings of the 'apostolic' religious movements of the twelfth and early thirteenth centuries.[59] In the early twelfth century one of the principal activities of Vitalis, founder of the order of Savigny, was reforming prostitutes and finding them marriages, while Robert of Arbrissel received reformed prostitutes, alongside other women, in his new foundation of Fontevrault. 'The heresiarch Henry' worked among prostitutes in Le Mans around 1115. He urged men to marry reformed prostitutes, who were to burn their clothes; Henry would provide each with four shillings for new clothing. Possibly connected to this project was Henry's reported opposition to the need for dowries in marriages. Then, at the end of the twelfth century, sisters of a mendicant religious Order most of which became heretical, the Waldensian Order, may have included reformed prostitutes.

[58] Baldwin, *Peter the Chanter*, i. 133–7 and ii. 91–6 (see also the index-entry 'prostitutes'); B. Geremek, *The Margins of Society in Late Medieval Paris*, trans, J. Birrell (Cambridge and Paris, 1987), Ch. 7. See also J. Longère, *Oeuvres oratoires des maîtres parisiens au XIIe siècle: Étude historique et doctrinale*, 2 vols. (Paris, 1983), i. 351.

[59] A. Simon, *L'ordre des pénitentes de S. Marie-Madeleine en Allemagne au XIIIe siècle* (Fribourg, 1918), pp. 1–10; H. Grundmann, *Religiöse Bewegungen im Mittelalter*, 2nd edn. (Hildesheim, 1961), p. 523; H. Leyser, *Hermits and the New Monasticism: A Study of Religious Communities in Western Europe, 1100–1150* (London, 1984), p. 49; G. G. Merlo, 'Sulle "misere donnicciuole" che predicavano', *Valdesi e valdismi medievali II, Identità valdesi nella soria e nella storiografia* (Turin, 1991), pp. 93–112; B. M. Kienzle, 'The Prostitute-Preacher: Patterns of Polemic against medieval Waldensian Women Preachers', in *Women Preachers and Prophets through Two Millenia of Christianity*, ed. B. M. Kienzle and P. J. Walker (Berkeley, Los Angeles, and London, 1998), pp. 99–113. On Henry see also Ch. 2 above and n. 116. Modern accounts of medieval prostitution downplay reform: see L. L. Otis, *Prostitution in Medieval Society: The History of an Urban Institution in Languedoc* (Chicago, London, 1985), pp. 72–6; V. L. Bullough, 'The prostitute in the early middle ages', in *Sexual Practices and the Medieval Church*, ed. V. L. Bullough and J. Brundage (Buffalo, NY, 1982), pp. 34–42 (p. 41); R. M. Karras, *Common Women: Prostitution and Sexuality in Medieval England*, Studies in the History of Sexuality (Oxford, 1996).

By this date we also meet what is, for a few decades, the most striking part of the prostitute-reform movement, in a succession of reformers in Paris. The practical moral theologian, Peter the Chanter, debated various themes to do with prostitutes. A later student at Paris, Jacques de Vitry, devoted part of the account of the western church which he wrote in the 1220s, his *Historia Occidentalis*, to Paris, the sins of usury and prostitution, and the popular preacher Fulk. His chapter 6 has this rural illiterate, Fulk, going to study in Paris. The condition of Paris 'in those days' is thus set up for chapter 7: like other cities it is deeply wrapped in sin, especially sexual sin, prostitution in particular. Chapter 9 has the dénouement. Fulk imbibes moral teaching from the one lily among thorns, Peter the Chanter, and begins to preach in the vernacular. Public prostitutes admit their shame and cut their hair off. 'Virtually all public prostitutes . . . he in large part handed over to marriage, while others he enclosed in religious houses so that they could live under [religious] rule. The monastery of St Antoine, of the Cistercian Order and not far outside Paris, . . . started to receive such women'.[60]

The chronicler Rigord put Fulk's preaching under the year 1198. In May of the same year Innocent III produced a bull, which was to enter the standard collections of canon law,[61] specifying the act of drawing women from prostitution and marrying them as something which helped in the remission of one's sins. Baldwin has attributed the sources of Innocent III's reforming ideas in general to his days of study in Paris, and the same may well apply to this bull and Innocent's ideas about reform of prostitutes. The years of Fulk's activities were conflated in Rigord's and Jacques' accounts, with St Antoine only adopting Cistercian constitutions in 1204.

When looking at William of Auvergne's writing on prostitutes it is crucial to remember both the prostitution of the Paris in which he lived and the tradition of reform and comment on prostitutes in Paris which stretched back over at least forty years into the 1180s. Further, there was William's own contribution to reform. According to an entry of late 1225 in Aubri of Trois Fontaines' chronicle, a Master of Theology 'by his preaching withdrew many common women from sin'. This man was William of Auvergne. William 'started the new house of the "Daughters of God"' (Filiae Dei, Filles-Dieu) for these reformed prostitutes. Following the example, wrote Aubri, 'this Order began to spread in other cities'.[62] The principal historian of the movement's manifestation in Germany, André Simon, stated that it was not easy to establish the connections between the Paris house and others in France, although it was probably their model. And he set the Paris house also as the model for what was about to take place in Germany, where the houses for reformed prostitutes not only spread rapidly but acquired quickly the contours of an Order, the 'Order of the Penitent Sisters of Blessed Mary

[60] *Historia occidentalis*, VIII; ed. J. F. Hinnebusch, *The Historia Occidentalis of Jacques de Vitry: A Critical Edition*, Spicilegium Friburgense 17 (Fribourg, 1972), p. 287.

[61] X 4. 1. 20; Friedberg, ii. 668; Baldwin, *Peter the Chanter*, i. 137 and ii. 96 n. 152.

[62] Quoted by Simon, *Pénitentes*, p. 5: *novam domum filiarum Dei inchoavit et plures communes mulierculas predicatione sua a peccato retraxit; et horum exemplo in aliis civitatibus cepit hic ordo dilatari.*

Magdalen'. Surviving documents from the Paris Filles-Dieu provide glimpses of William at work.[63] In the first text William obtains permission, from the prior of Saint-Martin-des-Champs and the parish priest of Saint Laurent, to set up the house outside Paris—to take them near the religious of St Lazare; and far from sin? The prior and the priest had opposed the move, and they had been overcome: presumably by William. The later documents show the Filles-Dieu acquiring property during the first years of William's episcopate (up to the year 1236): bearing his name, these texts attest William's continuing intervention and support.

In his writing William often turned to prostitutes, their way of life and official treatment of them. In his *De moribus* he writes of their customary ornamentation,[64] while in chapter 4 of the treatise on marriage one of his two examples of repressive measures by magistracy is the expulsion of pimps from cities: a reference to Cardinal Robert de Courson's measure in the legatine Council which he held in Paris in 1213.[65] William appealed to observation as the ground of what he said about prostitutes, for example underwriting his assertion in *De fide et legibus* that 'brawls, robberies, and murders' are associated with prostitutes and brothels. '[The statements of] these things are not just based on belief or opinion: they have the certainty [which is gained] through daily experience.'[66]

When William wrote about prostitutes he saw himself, then, as writing from experience, and in his treatise on marriage he identified prostitution and sodomy as the two chief enemies of generation of 'fruit'. He made two points about the way they depressed fruit. The first is a point about early extinction. 'Not hoping for these seeds of human generation, they choke and extinguish in advance what comes forth or the foetus . . . and [thus] they deprive human nature of its most precious fruit [in the form of] innumerable offspring.'[67] This seems to cover actions both before and after conception, avoidance and abortion. The former, implying something to do with the sexual act, is amplified by a brief reference to prostitution and sodomy 'not only turning away from the industry of fruits [application to fruiting] but twisting the act which ought to be [an act] of generation into shame and making it completely useless for fruit'.[68] The suggestion seems to be spilling of seed, whether withdrawal and emission outside in sex with prostitutes, or otherwise in sodomy—it needs to be noted that here and elsewhere in the treatise William is far more concerned with prostitution than with sodomy.

William's second point is lack of survival through the inadequate rearing which one would expect from such women. 'Although fruit *sometimes* arises from the work of generation, [it is likely] in part or in whole to perish, through lack of

[63] See 'Couvent des Filles-Dieu. Notice historique', in E. Raunié and M. Prinet, *Epitaphier du vieux Paris*, 4 vols. (Paris, 1890–1914), iv. 317–52.

[64] *De moribus*, VII; *Opera omnia*, i. 219b.

[65] *De matrimonio*, IV; p. 517a.

[66] *De legibus*, I; *Opera omnia*, i. 25a: *de his est non solum credulitas aut opinio, sed per quotidianam experientiam certitudo.*

[67] *De matrimonio*, II; p. 513b: *ipsa semina humane generationis non expectantes, exortum sive partum praefocant et praeextinguunt . . . humanam naturam fructu suo preciosissimo innumerae prolis orbant.*

[68] Ibid., IX; p. 525b: *non solum de industria fructuum declinantes sed etiam ipsum opus, quod debuit esse generationis, in turpitudinem detorquentes et ad fructum penitus inutile efficientes.*

care. [It perishes], because there is no one to look after the child, to rear, bring up, teach and provide [it] with other necessary and wholesome things.'[69] William's continuation shows that he is principally thinking of prostitutes, and not utterly without sympathy and compassion for them. 'What woman, placed in such misery and want, would provide [properly], since she does not know from whom she will have got the child? Given that she will have been prostituted all over the place and indiscriminately to all lusting men, what man, impregnating her, would have taken on [the job of support], the starting-point of great misery and deprivation?'[70]

The low fertility of prostitutes was a theme in learned writing before William, beginning with two early twelfth-century works by William of Conches.[71] In one, a dialogue begins thus—'Since prostitute women have sex most frequently, how is it that they rarely conceive?'—and the following discussion centres on changes to the womb, through frequent sex, which make it reject seed.[72] In the late 1220s and in Paris William is likely to have known of this. It is probably in this tradition, and certainly with the mantle of the man learned in natural philosophy and medicine, that William turned again to the theme in another section of the marriage treatise, when dealing with the opposition between the pursuit of sexual pleasure and fertility. 'Further', he wrote, 'through its increase and vehemence the pursuit of sexual pleasure impedes the fruit of generation. For those who burn mostly with this sort of concupiscence are of little generation and little or no fruit, and they are quickly rendered sterile and inept for generation. [This happens] either for this reason, that the seed of generation is consumed in the heat of such ardour. Or [it happens] because the frequency of such [sexual] mingling stops seed of this sort coalescing into life. This occurs in prostitute women, who rarely or never conceive: either they are exhausted through excessive ardour, or the excessive

[69] Ibid., II; p. 514a: *etsi fructus interdum ex opere generationis exoritur, aut ex parte aut ex toto perit, cum non sit qui custodiat, nutriat, educet, erudiat et alia necessaria et salubria proli provideat.*

[70] Ibid., II; p. 514b: *quis enim enixe in tanta miseria constitute provideat, et in tanta indigentia positae, cum ignoretur de quo prolem susceperit? Quis autem impraegnando eam, occasiones tantae miseriae et indigentiae dederit, cum passim et indifferenter fuerit omnibus libidinantibus prostituta?*

[71] The observation and the question 'Why do prostitutes infrequently conceive?' seem to go back in western learned literature to William of Conches (died after 1154). See D. Jacquart and C. Thomasset, *Sexuality and Medicine in the Middle Ages*, trans. M. Adamson (Oxford, 1988), pp. 25 (on the theme in William of Conches), 64 (Vincent of Beauvais), and 81 (Albert the Great). Additional to the references given here are Albert, *In sententias*, IV. xxxiii. 3 (xxx. 295a); J. Cadden, *Meanings of Sex Difference in the Middle Ages: Medicine, Science and Culture* (Cambridge, 1993), pp. 93–4 (on the theme in a group of twelfth-century anonymous questions, influenced by William of Conches); J. W. Baldwin, *The Language of Sex: Five Voices from Northern France around 1200* (Chicago, 1994), pp. 216–17 (on the theme in William of Conches, *The Prose Salernitan Questions*, and the fabliau *Richeut*); P. Biller, 'Birth-control in the West in the Thirteenth and Early Fourteenth Centuries', *Past and Present* 94 (1982), 3–26, at p. 18 and n. 64 (on the theme in Vincent of Beauvais and Giles of Rome); R. J. Long, 'Richard Fishacre's *Super s. Augustini Librum de Haeresibus Adnotationes*: An Edition and Commentary', *AHDLMA* 60 (1993), 207–79 (p. 251); J. Rossiaud, *Medieval Prostitution* (Oxford, 1988), p. 124 (Jean Gerson). I am grateful to Faramerz Dabhoiwala for drawing my attention to the speculations in T. Laqueur, *Making Sex: Body and Gender from the Greeks to Freud* (Cambridge, Mass., and London, 1990), pp. 230–3.

[72] William of Conches, *Dialogus de substantiis physicis*, VI (Strasbourg, 1567), p. 240: *Cum prostitutae meretrices frequentissime coeant, unde est quod raro concipiunt?*

frequency of [their] shamefulness prevents the seed in them having life or coalescing.'[73] After William the tradition continued. William of Conches's works survived, and his statements were to be excerpted and copied into Vincent of Beauvais's encyclopaedic *Speculum doctrinale* in the 1240s, under the rubric, 'Why prostitutes rarely conceive'. In his *On animals* Albert the Great commented on 'excessive use of sex, as for example in prostitutes, on account of which they only rarely conceive'.[74] Giles of Rome observed, in his *De regimine principum*, that 'we see that prostitutes are more sterile [*sic*] than other women',[75] the reason being that union with many men impedes fertility. An unprinted arts faculty quodlibet from Paris around 1300 ventilates the question 'Whether a prostitute can conceive',[76] as does also a collection of medical and natural-philosophical problems known as *Omnes homines*, which is probably from the same period.[77] Thus natural-philosophical discussion of prostitutes' low fertility continued to *c.*1300, much of it being aired by men who wrote and lectured close to the streets where these women worked.

When William links the rarity of conception among prostitutes with exhaustion and seed not 'coalescing', he is writing within this natural-philosophical tradition. But when he turns to prostitutes' use of forms of sex opposed to conception and abortion, and their poor rearing of children, he is drawing upon what he knew as a pastor deeply concerned with the reform of the prostitutes of Paris.

3.3.1 *William and Saracen population (a): earlier thought*

If William's comments on Saracen population need a specific context, contemporary reflection on the Saracen problem, this reflection in itself can only be understood within a wider and longer story which goes back to around 1100 and the aftermath of the First Crusade. Fighting, colonization, and defence of the settlements in the eastern Mediterranean had all had a large impact, providing one deeply coloured and detailed sector of a word-view of population and a large topic to worry about: Saracen numbers. In order to describe this we must digress,

[73] *De matrimonio*, VIII; p. 524a: *Ipsa voluptas suo augmento et vehementia impedit fructum generationis. Qui enim maxime ardent hujusmodi concupiscentia, paucae generationis sunt et pauci fructus aut nullius, et cito steriles efficiuntur et ad generationem inepti, sive propter hoc, quia ex hujusmodi ardore semen generationum consumitur, sive quia frequentatio ipsius commixtionis ne in vitam coalescat hujusmodi semen impedit. Quod apparet in mulieribus prostitutis, que raro vel nunquam concipiunt, vel nimio ardore exhauste, vel nimia frequentia turpitudinis semen in se vitam habere et coalescere prohibente.*

[74] *De animalibus*, X. ii. 1; i. 745: *nimius usus coitus, sicut est in meretricibus, propter quod etiam rarissime concipiunt.*

[75] Giles, *De regimine*, I. ii. 10; p. 248 (arguing the bad effect of a woman being united to more than one man): *Impeditur enim ipsa foecunditas filiorum, si una foemina pluribus coniungatur viris, unde et meretrices conspicimus esse magis steriles, quam alias mulieres.*

[76] BN, MS Lat. 16089, fol. 54r: *Alia questio fuit utrum meretrix possit concipere.*

[77] *Problemata Varia Anatomica: MS* 1165 The University of Bologna, ed. L. R. Lind, University of Kansas Studies, Humanistic Publications 38 (Lawrence, Kan. 1968), p. 65: *Quare mulieres publice non concipiunt.*

leaving the early thirteenth century and William's Paris, and going backwards and onto a larger map. The theme anticipates the treatment of the west's view of world population in Chapter 9 below.

Among modern historians of the First Crusade, the capture of Jerusalem, and the setting up of Latin kingdoms, Joshua Prawer in particular has emphasized how the settlement which followed this and defence were conditioned by fundamental facts of numbers. A charter for a colony of western men, many from southern France—Lambert the cobbler, Stephen the carpenter, Pons the cameler—provided for their settlement 'so that the land should be better populated' (*ut terra melius populetur*).[78] But settlement in the countryside was thin, a very high proportion was in fortified towns, and the settlers were always a minority in relation to the indigenous populations. In defence a perennial problem, which was diminished whenever a crusade was assisting, was the lack of numbers.[79] It has been estimated that at other times the Franks could not usually muster more than two thousand mounted soldiers, while the total resources of the Aiyubid empire of Saladin's brother and nephews were about twenty-two thousand men, of whom ten to twelve thousand were cavalry.[80] Ellenblum has recently attacked part of this view, using archaeological as well as documentary evidence to suggest denser rural settlement by the Franks.[81]

Turning from modern historians, we also find fundamental facts about numbers stressed in the twelfth-century texts, the histories of the first great triumph which spread so widely in the west (especially Fulcher of Chartres's), and the letters from a patriarch of Jerusalem or a master of a military order 'on the state of things' which crowd western monastic chronicles. 'We, a *few* people in the lands of our enemies':[82] Fulcher's words become a commonplace, which applies first of all to battles, in which small numbers of Franks fight a much larger number of Turks, often 'a vast multitude' or 'an infinite multitude'. A minor exception to small versus large is pride in the size of the initial Frankish forces. The commonplace was also applied to settlement in defence, of which Fulcher provided a remarkable survey.[83] Some Franks remained, but some went back. Jerusalem was depopulated; there were not enough men to defend it if the Saracens attacked, and this could so easily happen. Could they not gather from Egypt at least a 100 times 100,000 fighters? The Franks were living among so many thousands and thousands of enemies.

While the picture of small numbers of valiant Franks was becoming common currency, there was a general growth of knowledge of Mahomet's faith and law

[78] J. Prawer, *Crusader Institutions* (Oxford, 1980), p. 121.

[79] J. Prawer, *The Latin Kingdom of Jerusalem: European Colonialism in the Middle Ages* (London, 1972), pp. 129–30, 139, 151–2, 154, 161, 163, 166, 188, and 190. An earlier account of settlement and population is in R. C. Smail, *Crusading Warfare (1097–1193)* (Cambridge, 1956), pp. 40–62.

[80] C. Marshall, *Warfare in the Latin East, 1192–1291* (Cambridge, 1992), pp. 32–3.

[81] R. Ellenblum, *Frankish Rural Settlement in the Latin Kingdom of Jerusalem* (Cambridge, 1998).

[82] Fulcher of Chartres, *Historia Hierosolymitana*, Prologue, IV, in *A History of the Expedition to Jerusalem, 1095–1127*, trans. F. R. Ryan, ed. H. S. Fink (Knoxville, 1969), p. 58.

[83] Fulcher, *Historia Hierosolymitana*, II. vi; *History of the Expedition*, pp. 149–50.

and the geography of the Saracens. Although earlier western Christian ignorance of Mahomet and the Saracens has been overstated, it is clear that clerics became better informed during the twelfth century.[84] The milestones in this development were a chapter in the *Dialogi* of Petrus Alfonsi (1108 or 1110), and the massive effort of comprehension by Peter the Venerable in the 1140s, which brought about the translation into Latin of the Koran and several other works, including the important *Risālat* of Al-Kindi. The first significant element in this developing picture had come very early. It was simple and fundamental: the view of the Saracens as occupying a very large proportion of the world. This view was already being put across—and put across emphatically—in the early twelfth century, and as remotely as in the west of England. It may have been based in part on the reports of men returning from pilgrimages and armed expeditions to the Holy Land, whose distant journeys had deeply impressed them with the size of the world which lay beyond Latin Christendom and how much of it lay under Saracen rule. Or such reports may have reinforced an earlier but no longer documented view.

As a result, views of the proportions of the world and its inhabitants tilted, Christians and Christendom shrinking in numbers and size as Saracens and *Saracenitas* expanded. This is very clear in the west-countryman William of Malmesbury. Writing between 1118 and 1123, he put into the mouth of Urban II, when calling for an armed expedition at Clermont in 1095, a geography of the populations of the two faiths. It took the form of the classic geographical division of the world into three parts. 'They inhabit as their hereditary nest a third part of the world, Asia, which was not incorrectly estimated by our ancestors as equalling the remaining two parts—by virtue of the length of its tracts [of land] and the width of its provinces . . . There, once upon a time, branches of our faith flourished . . . They hold another part of the world, Africa . . . There remains the third climate [part] of the world, Europe—how big a part of this do we Christians inhabit?'[85] Writing elsewhere, in 1127, William was willing to concede a possible polemical point, Mahomet's capacity to work miracles, because this could explain how his faith had conquered so many peoples.[86] In the 1140s Peter the Venerable set generalizations, given in fractions, against the tripartite division of the world. Mahomet's 'very large people' (*gens maxima*) are now 'almost a third part of the human race', and, at the end of the same tract, 'are now thought to be almost half the world'.[87] Was Peter being consistent, thinking of a third (in numbers of

[84] M.-T. d'Alverny's articles provide the fundamental account of western theologians' knowledge of Islam; in her 'Alain de Lille et l'Islam. Le "Contra Paganos"', *Cahiers de Fanjeaux* 18 (Toulouse, 1983), pp. 323–50; see the survey, pp. 304–5, and the material cited in nn. 14–18. See also Daniel, *Islam and the West*, with the caveat that cited sources can be difficult to trace; R. W. Southern, *Western Views of Islam in the Middle Ages* (Cambridge, Mass., 1962); J. Kritzeck, *Peter the Venerable and Islam* (Princeton, 1964); Kedar, *Crusade and Mission*.

[85] *Gesta regum Anglorum*, ed. W. Stubbs, 2 vols., RS 90 (1887–9), ii. 395; R. M. Thomson, 'William of Malmesbury and Some Other Western Writers on Islam', *Medievalia et Humanistica*, n.s. 6 (1975), pp. 179–87 (p. 184).

[86] Ibid., p. 181; Kedar, *Crusade and Mission*, p. 88 n. 125.

[87] Peter the Venerable, *Summa totius haeresis Saracenorum*, ed. J. Kritzeck, *Peter the Venerable*, pp. 205 and 210: *iam pene terciam humani generis partem . . . iam pene dimidia pars mundi reputari potest.*

people) inhabiting a half of the (geographical) world? Or being general, vague—and inconsistent?

This broad population-geography of the two faiths came to unite with the commonplace about disparity of numbers in particular battles. Crusading propaganda in 1185 envisaged Saracen thought in this way: 'Let us silence the name of Christ on earth, and take away [his] place and people. Come, and let us in [all] our great multitude disperse the smallness of the Christian people.'[88] Several English chronicles contain the texts of a purported exchange of letters between the emperor Frederick Barbarossa and Saladin in which boasts of size and number are exchanged. To the Christian emperor's 'do you not know how many have been subject to us?' Saladin hurls back sarcasm and more. Counting is the issue—'if you compute . . . and name . . . if we wanted to enumerate' (*si computatis . . . et nominatis . . . si nos vellemus dinumerare*). Our numbers 'could not be reduced here to writing'. 'If you count the names of the Christians, those of the Saracens are more and more abundant than those of the Christians.' The point is brutally and simply numbers and geography, underlining the elementary military fact. 'And if there is the sea between you and those whom you name as Christians, there is no sea or any barrier between the Saracens—who cannot be estimated [=counted]—and coming to us. And with us there are the Bedouins, who would be enough, if we set them on our enemies; and we have the Turcomans . . .' And so the text goes on, rubbing in the advantage of Saladin's resources over Christian forces.[89]

The theologians were not cut off. Some visited the Holy Land, and they lived alongside and were often close relations of men whose long experience lay in raising and recruiting armies, fighting in Spain or out in the Holy Land, and there facing opposing armies whose comparative strength was a fundamental and commonplace matter of interest. At a certain stage concern with number began to impinge on theologians' treatment of Mahomet's law.

In western views of marriage in Mahomet's law, a role had been played by serious knowledge: the plurality of women who were allowed in lawful marriage and the further unspecified number of slave-women, and tahlîl (divorce). Roles had also been played by the notion of Mahomet's own possession of fifteen wives and two slave-girls, and the promise of beautiful and untouched women to enjoy in paradise, which provided the raw materials for fantasy and the attribution to Mahomet and to the Saracens of sensuality and sexual licentiousness. This had became the root of one early explanation of Mahomet's appeal to so many men, and the rapid spread of his followers. Crude promises of 'infinite sex' (*infiniti*

[88] *Quiescere faciamus nomen Christi a terra: tollamus locum et gentem. Venite et disperdamus in multitudine gravi Christiani populi paucitatem*; letter of Baldwin, archbishop of Canterbury, *PL* 207, 307. See N. Daniel, 'Crusade Propaganda', in *A History of the Crusades*, ed. K. M. Setton, 6 vols. (Madison, 1969–89), VI, 39–97 (p. 49).

[89] On the authenticity of these letters, see H. E. Mayer, 'Der Brief Kaiser Friedrichs I. an Saladin vom Jahre 1188', *Deutsches Archiv* 14 (1958), 488–94 (p. 488 and n. 7 on Saladin's letter). Whether authentic or not, they attest western thought.

concubitus), in the words of the *Risālat* of Al-Kindi,[90] drew in droves of 'men [at the level of the] herd' (*pecorini homines*), and thus the early battles were won. We need to put aside the fantasy, and keep in mind the important progression of thoughts which had thus been set in place, in a sequence which was especially clear in the *Risālat*.[91] This sequence was, first, from a particular point in Mahomet's law to appeal to very large numbers; and, secondly, from very large numbers to military success and dominion.

The theme of polygamy had had a longer and more serious history. The law had already been spelled out clearly and quite precisely by Petrus Alfonsi,[92] and Peter the Venerable's enterprise had then made available to western readers its basis in the Koran, and its more polemical expression in the *Risālat*.[93] Quite apart from the possibilities of observation in Spain and Latin kingdoms in the east, there came to be opportunities to see and hear in north-western Europe, as is clear from Peter the Chanter's reminiscence about one Saracen who had been taken prisoner in the Holy Land and then brought back to Beauvais. There in the Beauvaisis (which was Peter's home) the Saracen was baptised, and married—but later he confessed that he had left behind in Parthia five living wives! Elsewhere Peter the Chanter was probably envisaging the case of a Saracen, while covering possibilities in other faiths, when asking questions about a 'pagan', who has several wives and wishes to convert. Which is his wife? Answer: the one he married first. And if he married them at the same time, which is his wife? Answer: the one he 'knew' first. Thus the practical problem of what happened after conversion was bringing about discussion of plurality of wives in the theological schools of late twelfth-century Paris.

Among the theologians, two very familiar but separate areas began to be linked in the late twelfth century. This is evident in Alain de Lille's treatment of Saracens' marriage in his *De fide catholica*, composed in the fifteen years, or so, before his death in 1202. Alain wrote that 'they assert that it is licit to have several wives at the same time'. Alain does not spell out precise numbers,[94] probably because he can assume his readers' familiarity, by now, with the plurality allowed in the Koran. The words of his own formulation, however, recalled a different but theologically very familiar tradition. They are the words with which Peter the Lombard and many others, in a tradition which goes back to Augustine, had stated the

[90] Ed. J. Muñoz Sendino, 'Al-Kindi, Apología del Cristianism', *Miscelánea Comillas* 11–12 (Comillas, Santander, 1949), pp. 337–460; see M.-T. d'Alverny, 'Deux traductions latines du Coran au moyen âge', *AHDLMA* 16 (1948), 68–131 (pp. 87–90), and 'Alain de Lille et l'Islam. Le "Contra Paganos"', p. 322 n. 15; Kritzeck, *Peter the Venerable*, pp. 31–2, 34 and n. 110, 56 and n. 26, and 101–7; Kedar, *Crusade and Mission*, p. 19 n. 37.

[91] Sendino, 'Al-Kindi', p. 419.

[92] *Dialogi*, V; *PL* 157, 598. On Alfonsi's use of the Koran and the *Risālat*, see G. Monnot, 'Les citations coraniques dans le "Dialogus" de Pierre Alfonse', *Cahiers de Fanjeaux* 18 (Toulouse, 1983), pp. 261–77. On Alfonsi's influence, see J. Tolan, *Petrus Alfonsi and His Medieval Readers* (Gainesville, etc., Fla. 1993).

[93] Sendino, 'Al-Kindi', p. 389.

[94] *De fide, Liber quartus contra paganos*, ed. M.-T. D'Alverny, *Cahiers de Fanjeaux* 18 (Toulouse, 1983), pp. 323–50 (pp. 339–40); see d'Alverny's comments in her 'Alain de Lille', p. 310.

problem of the plurality of wives among the patriarchs of the Old Testament: how could this have been licit? The Lombard's answer to this was the standard one. *Then* it was licit to have several wives in order to bring about the [more rapid] multiplication of God's people. Now, this had been standard only in discussion of Old Testament, patriarchal, plurality of wives, not so far in speculation about the followers of Mahomet. The convergence of the two strands, evidenced by Alain's use of the language of plurality among the patriarchs when writing about the followers of Mahomet, shows how a new thought was becoming possible (or probable) among the theologians.

3.3.2 *William and Saracen population (b): the early thirteenth century*

We now turn to look at the direction such thought was taking around the time of William's composition of his marriage treatise,[95] beginning with Jacques de Vitry. Jacques united Paris theology with eastern experience: a student in Paris, where he was a master by 1193, Jacques was elected to the bishopric of Acre in 1216. In the Holy Land he was active, preaching, participating in the deliberations of the council of war at Acre in 1217, urging the utility of attacking Egypt in a letter of 1218, and witnessing the siege of Damietta.

In his *Historia orientalis*, probably written during 1220,[96] Jacques gives a conventional view of the small numbers of the first generation of Franks, compared to the surrounding 'multitude of Saracens', as well as the small number, the 'few' who faced Saladin's numbers.[97] The key elements of western accounts of early success (small numbers plus God's will) and later failure in 1187 (small numbers without God's will) have a third element spelled out by Jacques: the Saracens, through many engagements with the Franks, had lost their earlier technical inferiority in fighting. Thus, in the directly military part of Jacques' account, the removal of the two elements of God's help and technical military superiority leaves the theme of numbers on its own, bare.

Jacques follows the general emphasis on size in his account of Mahomet, who spread 'in such a great multitude of peoples'. Why did God allow him to take away 'so *many* thousands of souls'?[98] Followings the *Risālat* (directly or indirectly?) on the appeal to many of the permission to indulge lust, he emphasizes the proneness to lust of those who live in warm regions,[99] and underlining the effect of this on number. Those 'ensnared by carnal lures were multiplied beyond number'. But then, after providing a brief and conventional account of the permission of three

[95] Some of the texts examined here may slightly postdate William's treatise.

[96] C. Cannuyer, 'La date de rédaction de l' "Historia Orientalis" de Jacques de Vitry (1160/70–1240), évêque d'Acre', *Revue d'Histoire Ecclésiastique* 78 (1983), 65–72 (p. 71); the outer limits are March 1219 and April 1221.

[97] Jacques de Vitry, *Historia orientalis*, I. xcv; pp. 228–9.

[98] Ibid., I. iv; pp. 8–9.

[99] Ibid., I. vi; pp. 25–6. Similar comment in Gerald of Wales, *De principis instructione*, I. xviii, ed. G. F. Warner, in *Opera omnia*, 8 vols., RS 21 (1861–91), viii. 70.

or four free women as wives and a further number of concubines and slaves, he proceeds to two points which are new. One is a particular Saracen emphasis on high fertility, regarded as a matter of duty or devotion. 'Among them [the Saracens], the more [women] a man can impregnate the more *religious* he is regarded' (*Magis autem religiosus iudicatur inter eos qui plures potest impraegnare*); *religious* could be paraphrased as *devoutly dutiful*. The other is his spelling out of the connection between Saracen emphasis on fertility and the military need for many people. 'Regarding the use of sex and lust as meritorious, they mingle with their wives and concubines [even] more frequently during a fast, either to satiate their lust, or *so that they can generate more children for the defence of their law* [my emphasis]' (*quoniam usum veneris et luxuriam meritorium reputant, frequentius in tempore ieiunii concubinis et uxoribus commiscentur, vel causa libidinis explendae, vel ut plures filios ad legis suae defensionem valeant generare*).[100]

Next to be examined is one of two texts which Matthew Paris inserted into the chronicle he wrote at St Albans between 1235 and 1259, under the year 1236. It was a 'certain writing' (*quoddam scriptum*), which had been sent to Pope Gregory IX (1227–41) by *praedicatores* who had been travelling in the Holy Land. It is not clear whether *praedicatores* meant Dominicans (who were called *Preachers*) or non-Dominican preachers. The *scriptum*, which has overlaps with both the *Risālat* and Jacques, is notable for its formal division and layout—it has a section headed 'On marriage among the Saracens'—which recall the development in the description of marriage-systems which was discussed in Chapter 2 above. The *scriptum* is then followed immediately by another text which derives from an anonymous man, one whose life and actions, as they are given by Matthew Paris, resemble those of Jacques de Vitry. He was a 'famous preacher' (*celebris praedicator*), who was sent to those parts to preach against Mahomet's law. This text opens with fertility, which is presented as *the* principal point of Mahomet's teaching. Mahomet, in the Koran, taught that God's first and principal command was to increase and multiply. Therefore, to bring about the multiplication of the Saracen people, Mahomet ordered the Saracens to have as many wives and concubines as they could support. 'In this way, then, in multiplying wives Mahomet instituted polygamy.' And he did this 'only so that by propagating he could increase his race and people, and thus strengthen his law by number'.

In this way, then, the old and commonplace emphasis on the very large numbers of the Saracens had been set in relation to polygamy, given as the explanation of Saracen multiplication. During the 1220s and 1230s procreating large numbers was coming to be depicted as the first duty enjoined in the Koran, directed towards the increase of Saracen 'law' and its military defence.

If this was the general climate of thought, what was the situation in the eastern Mediterranean when William was writing, and how would he have known about it? There is no evidence that William himself ever travelled to the eastern Mediterranean, or to southern Spain, but there were other people who both did so and

[100] *Historia orientalis*, I. vi; pp. 27 and 30.

probably talked to William. During the years leading up to the conjectured date of the marriage treatise, 1228, a long shadow was cast by the events of 1217–21. The key to retaking Jerusalem had been identified as Egypt, with its rich resources, and the key to conquering Egypt as Damietta, which was taken after a long siege, on 19 November 1219. Throughout the affair manpower had been a crucial issue, and in 1221 huge Muslim reinforcements and the trapping of the army in the summer at Mansurah led to capitulation and the handing back of Damietta. A large number of French ecclesiastics had been out there. Arrivals at Damietta in August 1218 had included the bishop of Laon and the bishop-elect of Beauvais, Milo. Taken prisoner on 19 August 1219 and not released until 1222, Milo apparently became an expert on the military situation. He (and also the bishop of Laon) participated in a council in Paris in 1223, when he could have talked to William, and in November 1224 the two men, Milo and William, were directed to be together in a commission of enquiry. A decade later, in 1233–4, several texts bring together William of Auvergne and Peter des Roches as negotiators between the French and English kings.[101] Now, Peter des Roches spent three years in the Holy Land, on his return spreading texts and knowledge—for example, a copy of William of Tyre's account of events in the Holy Land came through him to the abbey of St Albans.[102] While we cannot establish that Milo and William talked about the Holy Land in 1224, or that William and Peter in fact met, both are examples of William's likely sources of information and ideas.

William was in any case living in one of the best centres of news and information in Latin Christendom, Paris, and it is important also to remember what he clearly was *eventually*, a regular at the royal court and participator in discussions of high matters of policy. Matthew Paris described William haranguing the French king, exhorting him not to go on crusade, and put into William's mouth a summary of the general political situation which ranges over two western monarchs, two areas in France, Germany and Italy as a whole, and the problem of access to the Holy Land.[103] Even if Matthew Paris invented this, his historiographer's concern with verisimilitude (literally) will have made it near the truth. Elsewhere we see the pope advising queen Blanche to consult William of Auvergne about the Latin Kingdom of Constantinople, and a letter about the Mongols in Bohemia and Hungary, which was sent to the count of Lorraine, being sent on to William, with whom it becomes the source of a general conversation between Blanche and Louis about the Mongol threat to the world.[104] All show William, at least *later* in his life, as an expert and adviser to the French king, who took a world-view of affairs, especially to the east.

[101] Valois, *Guillaume d'Auvergne*, pp. 113 and 352–4; T. Rymer, *Foedera, Conventiones, Literae . . .*, 3rd edn. 10 vols. (Hague, 1745, repr., Farnborough, 1967), i, part 1, 114b–5a.

[102] C. J. Tyerman, *England and the Crusades 1095–1588* (Chicago and London, 1988), p. 94.

[103] *Chronica Majora* [1248], V, 3–5.

[104] Valois, *Guillaume d'Auvergne*, p. 116; Matthew Paris, *Chronica Majora* [1241], iv. 109–11; see also vi. 75–6, a letter from a Hungarian bishop to William, reporting to him about the land and military numbers of the Mongols.

With the Saracens, William's first interests was their numbers. William in any case liked numbers: large numbers, 'a thousand thousands', a sequence, 'many, a thousand thousands, infinity',[105] and numbers expressing proportions. He likes to use these morally, as in 'ninety-nine out of one hundred' persons are on their way (morally) to death.[106] Characteristic, therefore, is his explanation why the belief, which he wishes to combat, 'that each person is saved in their own *faith* or *sect*', is so widespread. It is because people are bothered by numbers. Believing that people outside your faith or sect are damned consigns such an extraordinary proportion of all people to hell, compared to the tiny number of people who will be saved. And William goes on, characteristically, to spell it out: how could hell contain the total remaining multitude of men, evil Christians, Jews, Saracens, pagans, and others?[107] William, further, showed a propensity for one set of magnitudes, even though he did not apply figures to them: generation, death balancing generation, and population. Writing about paradise according to the law of Mahomet, he poured sarcasm on the suggestion that it would contain so much 'use of women'. With such generation and no death to balance it, population would grow to infinity: which would be impossible within the bounds of paradise.[108]

William addressed Saracens' concern with large numbers in this world, partly at the level of the individual household. They try to shoe-horn a city [large numbers] into a house [a small number]. 'The Saracens, however, aim at building not houses but individual cities, [they aim thus] at enclosing cities within the narrow confines of individual houses. In their wretched blindness they conflate city and house, since they do not try to build a house before a city but rather, as we have said, a city within a house. For every city is in fact a multitude of houses.'[109] Avicenna's juxtaposition of 'city' and 'marriage', without intervening words for 'house' or 'household' may have inspired this passage.

William's central comparative 'demographic' statements were quoted earlier as part of an enquiry into his observation of western Christian conditions. Here they are repeated in order to see their relation with earlier and contemporary western observation of Muslim population. In his *De fide et legibus*, William quoted Avicenna, citing the *Philosophia prima*, on the role of 'bodily pleasures in our law', and in the marriage treatise he addressed the followers of Mahomet, who are dedicated to sexual pleasure.[110] They aim at achieving higher levels of population, and fail in this aim. William writes thus, in a passage much of which we have already quoted:

[105] *De legibus*, I; *Opera omnia*, i. 27a–b. [106] *De legibus*, XXI; *Opera omnia*, i. 59b.

[107] Ibid.; *Opera omnia*, i. 57a–b. See J. Le Goff, *La naissance de purgatoire* (Paris, 1981), p. 327, on the populousness of the purgatory envisaged by William.

[108] *De legibus*, XIX; *Opera omnia*, i. 52b. [109] *De matrimonio*, VIII; p. 524b.

[110] We should note the presence in the treatise of a contemporary Parisian theologian of a question 'whether fornication is a mortal sin'; William of Auxerre, *Summa aurea*, IV. xvii. 3 Q. 2; iv. 397–9. The question ventilates arguments about natural law and the naturalness of sexual union outside marriage, and, together with William of Auvergne's writings, suggests some presence in the Paris of the 1220s of the naturalist arguments which are better known from later thirteenth-century Paris, where they were condemned in 1277.

There is a manifest indication of this [pursuit of sexual pleasure impeding generation]. [This is] the multiplication of concubines, whom they [the Saracens] call by a false name 'wives' ... the Saracens do not achieve the multiplication of their people, which they aim at through this [plurality of wives]. In whatever realm of another people of the same amplitude and fertility of soil, [and] unless things are otherwise through disease, the sword or another [source of] damage [to the people], just as great a numerousness of indigenous peoples is to be found as in any other realm of the people of the Saracens. So it is clear that the multiplication of wives and the efforts they devote to generation do not bring about the multiplication of their people at which they aim, and conjugal chastity and singleness of marriages [= monogamy] do not bring about decrease or loss to our people—the decrease they dread so much [happening] in their people.

The substratum of William's thought is not spelled out. Let us recapitulate. William was fully aware of Christian concern with the vast 'multitude of Saracens'. He had a long and in part apocalyptic view of this, which he presented in his *De fide et legibus* in terms of the Pseudo-Methodius's prophecy, first of the strength of their multiplication in the time of Charlemagne, and lastly of their resurgence at the end of the world 'in a vast multitude'. And in recent history and commentary on current events he will have known as a commonplace what is so emphasized by Jacques de Vitry, the counterposing in military engagements in the Holy Land of small numbers of Christians and large multitudes of Saracens. The particular insistence upon multiplication, and this for military reasons, which is variously expressed by Jacques de Vitry and in the *scriptum* cited by Matthew Paris, represents a line of thought William was clearly aware of, though not necessarily in these particular texts. And it is this line of thought against which he is, deliberately, setting himself. Now, however independent-minded William was, he is unlikely to have rejected expert military assessment of the populations from which Saracens drew their military manpower.

What, then, was William thinking? The explanation is simple, provided we do three things. We should remember that William's knowledge and interest in the world-wide history and distribution of faiths gave him a better world-view of population than most people had; impute to him a simple distinction (reminiscent of Peter the Venerable's fractions) between *numbers* and *area*; and take his words literally. First, William was not denying that the world contained a vast multitude of Saracens. He would have referred an enquirer about that fact to the *geography* of the world, and those parts of it over which the Saracens held dominion. What he was pointing out, secondly, was that this was a matter of space, conquest, and vast tracts of land, not a matter of higher fertility. Despite the greater overall multitude of Saracens in the world, in any given area of land, and given certain conditions, there is not a higher *numerositas* of the polygamous Saracens than in a similar area which is inhabited by monogamous Christians. Where others were not pausing to think, William was, and his characteristic contrariety and originality were displayed in the penetrating and fundamental distinction which his observation and reflection produced.

William went further, thinking out the fundamental implications of a law which permitted plurality of wives and the notion of more rapid increase, through this, of a people. In what conditions of population could this work? In part of the marriage treatise[111] William followed the conventional theme of the plurality of wives of the patriarchs in the Old Testament: to amplify God's people. However, William fretted. He introduced an unusual alternative explanation, which was partly rooted in the polemicist's opprobrium (Jewish lust), and partly in 'demographic scepticism'. He conceded the possibility, but only reluctantly: 'there *could have been at some time* a greater multitude of women among the people of God than men'. However, elsewhere in the marriage treatise,[112] when he dealt with plurality of wives according to the law of Mahomet, there were no reins upon him, and he mounted three powerful arguments against it. Two were arguments of equity, parity for women, and equity among different men. But the most powerful argument was that 'there was not such a disparity in nature' between the numbers of men and women. In this he prevaricated, between 'no disparity' and 'not such a great disparity'. Here he was writing at the very beginning of western grasp of the concept of a ratio between the sexes, and his views will be more fully explored in the next chapter, which is devoted to the birth and development of the concept of sex-ratio.

[111] *De matrimonio*, IX; p. 526b. [112] *De matrimonio*, III; p. 515b.

4

EQUAL OR UNEQUAL NUMBERS OF MEN AND WOMEN

When looking at the demographic outlook of Florentines in the last chapter of this book we shall come across the startling and famous statistics which the chronicler Giovanni Villani gave for Florence under 1338, including this statement:

> We find from the parish priest who baptised the babies—inasmuch as he put down a black bean for each male he baptised in San Giovanni and for each female a white [bean], in order to have the number—he found that in these times there were each year from five thousand five hundred to six thousand, [with] the male sex most times surpassing [the female] by three hundred to five hundred each year.

Historians have examined Villani's figures in order to reconstruct past demographic reality,[1] but not to ask what the practice, figures, and phrases used by Villani represented in his and other people's minds: a notion of 'sex-ratio'. If we go backwards in time from Villani—say, into the twelfth century—do we find anything in this area? Did people 'think' the thought 'sex-ratio'? The concept has its semantic history in the modern world, where, for example, the *Oxford English Dictionary* first registers an occurrence of the conveniently brief and numerical phrase 'sex-ratio' in 1906.[2] Villani had his phrase—*avanzando* [. . .] *il sesso masculino*: did those before him have words for this concept? If we cannot find the notion of sex-ratio in the twelfth but can in the thirteenth century, when and how did the notion emerge?

4.1 *Commentaries on Book 2 of the* Sentences

The first part of our answer is a parade of the texts which most clearly show a phrase for the concept 'sex-ratio' and continuity in discussion of it: commentaries on distinction 20 of book 2 of the *Sentences.*

Several distinctions dealt with the creation of the first man and woman and with paradise. Among the questions ventilated were several which went back to Augustine.[3] Distinction 17: how old was the Adam who was created by God, and

[1] See Ch. 14 below, n. 124.

[2] *A Supplement to the Oxford English Dictionary*, ed. R. W. Burchfield, 4 vols. (Oxford, 1972–86), iv. 83.

[3] Müller, *Paradiesehe*, pp. 19–32.

what sort of place was paradise? Distinction 19: was Adam's immortality from nature or grace? Distinction 20: how would the first man and woman have procreated, if they had not sinned, and to what sort of children would they have given birth?[4]

Such literal-mindedness may attract derision from the reader whose view of 'the medieval mind' is a compound of discussions of the numbers of angels on the head of a pin and Jakob Burckhardt's sleeping medieval man. In fact, the commentators' attitudes to these questions included guardedness. Introducing the 'many things' which 'are usually asked about the first state of man before sin', Peter the Lombard used words borrowed from Hugh of St Victor but made slightly more tart. 'Although enquiring into these things is sometimes [just idle] curiosity, knowing these things is not pointless' (*quae non inutiliter sciuntur, licet aliquando curiositate quaerantur*).[5] It is tempting to expand to 'utterly pointless', because the Lombard just leaves it there. He does not say what the point might be. What of one of these things, the size of children who would have been born in this state? 'I say that this is not something about which there should be much concern', wrote one of the Lombard's disciples, Peter of Poitiers.[6] Commentators could also see these themes as the opportunity for dry humour, witness a Franciscan, Humbert of Garda. Humbert (or his source) is dealing with Adam's immortality. Would it have continued if he had not sinned? By this time there was a long tradition of discussing physical conditions in paradise as contributing, in part, to longer life. Joining this was Humbert's reading—probably in Bartholomew the Englishman's *On the properties of things*—about the marvels of Ireland, including immortality in an island in Ireland. Solemnly Humbert advances his thesis, 'That, yes' (Quod sic) and 'I prove because' (*Probo quia*). 'Man would have been able to live for ever in paradise, [at least longer] than men who now live in Ireland. I prove [this thus], because earthly paradise is a place more suitable for habitation than that island, but men cannot die in that island, ergo etc.'[7] Humbert manages both to joke about Ireland and to use this joke to poke fun at 'what would have been if' questions.

What the commentators brought to the framework of these distinctions—a joke or the hint of a smile—contrasted with the seriousness which they displayed

[4] Lombard, *Sententiae*, II. xx. 1. 1 and II. xx. 4. 1; ii. 427 and 429: 'De modo procreationis filiorum si non peccassent et quales nascerentur filii'; 'Quales procrearent filios'. Distinction 19 is discussed in J. Ziegler, 'Medicine and Immortality in the Terrestrial Paradise', in *Religion and Medicine in the Middle Ages*, ed. P. Biller and J. Ziegler, York Studies in Medieval Theology 3 (forthcoming).

[5] Lombard, *Sententiae*, II. xix. 1; ii. 421.

[6] Peter of Poitiers, *Sententiae*, II. viii, ed. P. S. Moore, J. N. Garrin, and M. Dulong, 2 vols., Publications in Medieval Studies, The University of Notre Dame 7 and 11 (Notre Dame, 1943–50), ii. 47: *Hoc, inquam, non est multum curandum.* He was writing before 1170.

[7] Vatican, MS Vat. Lat. 1098, fol. 114v: *Quod sic, quia vero* [blotted word, probably *primus*] *homo potuisset in paradiso terrestri perpetuo* [r: *diucius*] *vivere quam modo homines in insula vivencium in hibernia. Probo, quia paradisus terrestris est locus magis aptus pro habitacione humana quam illa insula, sed illa* [r: *illi*] *in insula non possunt mori, ergo, etc.* On Humbert see Stegmüller, *Repertorium*, no. 362. Bartholomaeus, *De proprietatibus rerum*, XV. liv, copies a passage from Gerald of Wales on immortality in an island in Ireland.

when importing natural philosophy and science into their answers to these questions. Here a sea-change had occurred by the 1250s, by the time of Bonaventure's commentary and the *Summa* ascribed to Alexander of Hales. The texts are flecked with the names of Greek and Arabic natural-philosophical and medical authors and their works. On the topics of length of life and death medicine and natural philosophy supply the themes and the vocabulary. There are the 'equality of elements' in the 'complexion' of a man's body and the reading of Avicenna's *Canon of Medicine.* A distinction between natural and accidental death is taken from Aristotle's little *On death.* This precedes discussion of the essence of decline and dying, the decline of 'radical humidity', and Aristotle's *On the length and shortness of life* is pressed into use. Another area is described in Chapter 9 below, where one Oxford theologian, Richard Fishacre, is described applying data derived from an Arabic astronomer-geographer to the question of earthly paradise. In the 1250s, these Greco-Arabic sources are up-to-the-minute, and they are naturalizing commentaries upon these distinctions.

These distinctions dealt with the state of humans before sin, and as they would have been before sin. That is to say, they dealt with the opposite of the world after sin: the opposite of what actually happened and happens. Then there was no sterility; then there were no hermaphrodites;[8] and so on. Comments on what there was or was not *then* therefore self-evidently provide glimpses of what the commentator assumes or thinks to be the case in the imperfect and real world, a world extending from after the fall to now. In the early fourteenth century a Thomas of Strasbourg writes of the contrast between prelapsarian perfection of birth and growth and 'the modern condition' (*status modernus*).[9] The theme of prelapsarian perfection and 'what would have happened if' gave commentators extraordinary freedom to think and speculate about *this*-worldly things: generation, birth, ageing, and inhabitation in their own real world. On one theme this meeting-point of counterfactual speculation, new Greek and Arabic science, and thought about population fizzed and crackled, producing something important and new.

4.2 *Bonaventure on Book 2 of the* Sentences

My starting-point is Bonaventure, who lectured on the *Sentences* between 1250 and 1252. In his commentary on distinction 20 Bonaventure raises a question about the distribution of the sexes, which he answers with a mixture of theological and natural philosophical propositions.[10] At the beginning—and of fundamental

[8] Peter of la Palud, commenting on book 2, distinction 19, and the question whether children would have been born in both sexes, Vatican, MS Lat. 1073, fol. 86ra: *nullus fuisset hermafroditus, quia est monstrum in natura . . . nec aliquis frigidus, nec aliquis sterilis.* The counterfactual was found in other genres; for example, in Henry of Ghent's commentary on Genesis 2: 16 he wrote that 'then everyone would have generated . . . then no woman would have suffered a miscarriage' (*omnes tunc generassent . . . nulla mulier tunc aborsum passa fuisset,* BN, MS Lat. 15355, fol. 248vb.

[9] Thomas of Strasbourg, *In sententias,* II. xx. 3; i. 170rb.

[10] Bonaventure, *In sententias,* II. xx. 6; ii. 485–7. See also Müller, *Paradiesehe,* pp. 229–38, on

significance—there is Bonaventure's provision of a phrase: 'whether there would have been an equal multiplication of men and women' (*Utrum aequalis fieret multiplicatio virorum et mulierum*). There follow four arguments for an equal multiplication, which rest upon symmetries implicit in divine institution, nature's intention in generation, preservation of similars from first man and woman, and marriage as originally a universally binding precept. The four arguments which run *contra*, suggesting a greater number of men, rely on juxtaposing Aristotle's notion of woman as a defective male and what natural philosophers and medical authors (*medici*) say about the generative force of seed, and the perfection of instituted nature. Here is an illustrative example, taken from the fourth argument:

Since man's seed prevails over the woman's seed, it therefore draws and converts it to its own nature; but according to the order of nature, the male is stronger than the female. Therefore, while [instituted] nature lasted, male seed would always have prevailed, or more often. Therefore nature would have generated more males than women.

Cum semen viri praedominatur semini mulieris, tunc ad propriam naturam trahit et convertit; sed secundum ordinem naturae masculus potentior est femina: ergo, natura stante, semper vel pluries vinceret semen virile: ergo plures generaret natura masculos quam mulieres.

Bonaventure's general reply is that if instituted nature had remained, there would have been as many women as men. Following Augustine, he says that conception would have been dependent upon reason before the fall, when it would have dictated parity of numbers. No woman would have lacked a man, nor would a man have lacked a woman, nor would there have been one woman for more men, nor more women for one man. The postlapsarian, real, world is different:

Now, however, generation is not completely subject to the conscious, that is to say, imaginative *virtus* (force), nor to the rational *virtus*, though it does in some way conform. Rather, it varies according to the disposition of the member and external conditions. For this reason, then, there is no set limit to the number of men or females who are to be generated.

Nunc autem, quia generativa non omnino subest virtuti animali, id est imaginarie, nec etiam rationali, licet ei aliquo modo conformetur, sed magis variatur penes dispositionem membri et exterioris adiutorii; hinc est, quod non est certa determinatio numeri nec in viris nec in feminis generandis.

Notable is what Bonaventure tells us of the context of his thought on this point, in the Paris of his day. He says that one can investigate the question if one turns to the principles of other sciences, natural [philosophy] and medicine, each of which has to serve theology. For there is a great debate (*quaestio*), he writes, among the natural [philosophers] and the *medici*, about the diversity of generation of the male and female. When one asks why now a male, now a female, is generated, a threefold answer is given by various men. Bonaventure then proceeds to incorporate a large amount of medical and natural-philosophical material on sex-determination, and also the scriptural example of the colouring of Jacob's sheep, dependent upon what was seen at the moment of conception.

Bonaventure's commentary on distinction 20, and in particular pp. 230–1, on Bonaventure's discussion of the ratio.

To recapitulate what we have by around 1250–2: a cumbersome but usable phrase, 'an equal or unequal multiplication of men and women'; an elaborate formal discussion; the importation of medical and biological data on sex-determination; a contrast of perfect and imperfect worlds in which the clear implication is lack of perfect symmetry in the postlapsarian world. And, finally, we have the possibility raised of more of one sex than another—in this example, more men than women.

4.3 *Commentaries on the* Sentences *up to the early fourteenth century*

One chapter in the history of early thought about the sex-ratio would have to trace the path of *Sentences* commentaries after Bonaventure. What would be its contents? One theme would be the massive manuscript diffusion of Bonaventure's text in itself, or abbreviations of it, from the second half of the thirteenth century onwards. Bonaventure's commentary was present and read above all in theology faculties and mendicant convents.[11] I am suggesting that this will have meant the massive diffusion of Bonaventure's phrase for 'sex ratio', and his biology and reasoning about it, and that these will have become commonplaces of

[11] On Bonaventure's *Sentences* commentary, see Ch. 2 above, n. 103. Fifty-seven MSS of abbreviations (of which fifty-four are from the 13th and 14th centuries) are listed by Z. Alszeghy, 'Abbreviationes Bonaventurae. Handschriftliche Auszüge aus dem Sentenzkommentar des hl. Bonaventura im Mittelalter', *Gregorianum* 28 (1947), 474–510. On some of Bonaventure's works, including his *Sentences* commentaries, in the price-list of the Paris stationers of 1272/6 but not the list of 1304, see L. J. Bataillon, 'Les textes théologiques et philosophiques diffusés à Paris par *exemplar* et *pecia*', in *La production du livre universitaire au moyen âge: exemplar et pecia*, ed. L. J. Bataillon, B. G. Guyot, and R. H. Rouse (Paris, 1991), p. 156. Bonaventure's influence in theology faculties is a commonplace of histories of medieval universities. See d'Avray's comment on the diffusion of Bonaventure's *Sentences* commentary through his sermons, *Preaching*, p. 183. Franciscans who addressed the question include the following. William de la Mare, *Utrum tantum mares generarentur*, Florence, Biblioteca Nazionale, MS Conv. Sopp. A. 2. 727, fols. 120vb–21ra. (Stegmüller, *Repertorium*, and Doucet, *Supplément*, no. 289). Nicholas of Ockham, *An esset equalis multitudo virorum et mulierum*, Oxford, Merton College, MS 134, fol. 84ra (Stegmüller, *Repertorium*, and Doucet, *Supplément*, no. 552). Petrus de Trabibus, Florence, Biblioteca Nazionale, MS D.6.359, fol. 25vb: *Quinto queritur utrum esset equalis multiplicatio virorum et mulierum* (Stegmüller, *Repertorium*, and Doucet, *Supplément*, no. 696). William of Nottingham, *Utrum in statu innocentiae fuisset aequalis multiplicatio mulierum et virorum* (Stegmüller, *Repertorium*, no. 293), M. Schmaus, 'Neue Mitteilungen zum Sentenzkommentar Wilhelms von Nottingham', *Franziskanische Studien* 19 (1932), 195–223 (p. 201). John of Erfurt, Leipzig, Universitätsbibliothek, MS 556, fol. 158va, and MS 558, fol. 46rb–vb: *Utrum equalis fuisset multiplicacio virorum et mulierum* (Stegmüller, *Repertorium, Supplément*, no. 444). John de Bassoles, *Opera in quatuor libros sententiarum*, 2 vols. (Paris, 1516–17), ii. 118va–b: *Utrum pueri nati in statu innocentie statim fuissent perfecti quantum ad corpus et quantum ad animam. . . . Tertio, an in illo statu fuisset generatio mulierum* (Stegmüller, *Repertorium*, and Doucet, *Supplément*, no. 406). Guillem Rubió [Guillielmus de Rubione], *Disputatorum in quatuor libros Magistri Sententiarum libri quatuor* (Paris, 1518), 346va, vb: *An fuisset tunc aequalis multiplicatio virorum et mulierum* (Stegmüller, *Repertorium*, and Doucet, *Supplément*, no. 302). The following anonymous commentators formulate the question in a Bonaventuran spirit. BN, MS Lat. 14307, fol. 192ra–vb: *Utrum fieret virorum et mulierum equalis multiplicacio . . . utrum primi parentes si stetissent filios et filias sub equali numero genuissent* (Doucet, no. 132). Leipzig, Universitätsbibliothek, MS 418, fol. 359rb: *Utrum homines si permansissent in paradiso generassent masculos et femellas in equali numero, sic quod tot fuissent masculi quam femine et e converso* (Stegmüller, *Repertorium*, no. 1073). Leipzig, Universitätsbibliothek, MS 558, fol. 46rb–vb: *Utrum equalis fuisset multiplicatio virorum et mulierum* (Stegmüller, *Repertorium*, no. 1083).

vocabulary and thought, shared in the decades after 1250 by more and more among those who were literate in Latin. Another part of the chapter would take note of the culs-de-sac: authors in whose writings the potential of Peter the Lombard's theme was not realized in the direction of the 'sex-ratio', or was realized only rather faintly. Many Dominicans would feature here, following in the path which had been taken by Thomas Aquinas, both when he was writing on the *Sentences* (1252–6) and again when he was dealing with the theme in the first part of his *Summa theologie* (1266–8): and also an occasional Franciscan, such as Hugo de Novo Castro.[12] Aquinas's formulation and treatment of the question showed the Aristotelian theme of the imperfection of woman predominating over the theme of proportional numbers. The question was 'Whether those who would have been born would have had all bodily perfection . . . [including perfection] of sex' (*Utrum in statu innocentiae homines habuissent omnem perfectionem corporis quoad . . . sexum*). The numerical answer was the simple one of equality among those who would have been born. 'It was fitting for some women to be born, and in equal number with the men' (*mulieres aliquas nasci opportebat, et in aequali numero cum viris*).[13] Number does not return in the discussion in the *Summa theologiae* about whether women would have been born.[14]

Aquinas and later commentators who were more interested in the Aristotelian theme of woman as an imperfect male were less likely to produce thought about ratio in a hypothetical or real population. Those more likely to produce such thought were, as we shall see, those who were less interested in this Aristotelian theme, such as some Franciscan theologians, and the earlier William of Auvergne, who had been openly contemptuous of it. A third part of the chapter would look at those commentators who *did* add to thought about sex-ratio in the population. There were some developments, both of vocabulary and substance, and they are summarized here.

Aquinas's discussion, like Bonaventure's, did contain and therefore help to transmit medical and natural-philosophical material on sex-determination. One

[12] On Aquinas's lecturing on the *Sentences* and his *scriptum* on them, see Ch. 2 above, n. 107. On the precise date and circumstances of composition of the *Summa theologiae*, see L. E. Boyle, *The Setting of the 'Summa theologiae' of Saint Thomas*, The Étienne Gilson Series 5 (Toronto, 1982), p. 14. Hugo's question was *utrum in statu innocencie fuisset generacio mulierum*; BN, MS Lat. 15865, fo. 78va.

[13] *In sententias*, II. xx. 2. 1; i. 564.

[14] *Summa theologiae*, 1a Q. 99 art. 2; xiii. 164–6: 'Whether women would have been born in the first state [of mankind]' (*Utrum in primo statu feminae natae fuissent*). The treatment in the *Summa theologiae* is discussed by K.-E. Børresen, *Subordination et equivalence: Nature et rôle de la femme d'après Augustin et Thomas d'Aquin* (Oslo and Paris, 1968), pp. 154–5. Dominicans who addressed the question include the following. John Quidort of Paris, *Commentarium in libros sententiarum*, II. xx. 3, *Utrum natae fuissent tunc mulieres sic, et forte tot quot et viri*, ed. J.-P. Muller, 2 vols., Studia Anselmiana 47 and 52 (Rome, 1961–4), i. 154. John of Sterngassen, MS Vat. Lat. 1092, fol. 38vb, *Utrum in tali statu nate fuissent mulieres* (Stegmüller, *Repertorium*, and Doucet, *Supplément*, no. 499). Guillaume de Peyre Godin, *Utrum in statu innocencie pueri per generacionem nati habuissent perfectionem corporis . . . quantum ad sexum*, Naples, Biblioteca Nazionale, MS VII. C. 30, fol. 56r–v (Stegmüller, *Repertorium*, and Doucet, *Supplément*, no. 299). Durand of Saint Pourçain, *Utrum in statu innocencie fuissent geniti pueri in utroque sexu, In sententias*, ii. 164va–5ra (Stegmüller, *Repertorium*, and Doucet, *Supplément*, no. 192). One anonymous formulating the question in Aquinas's spirit is in BN, MS Lat. 3681, fol. 60vb: *utrum tunc alique mulieres generarentur* (Stegmüller, *Repertorium*, and Doucet, *Supplément*, no. 1232).

positive addition came through Aquinas's incorporation of some additional material from Aristotle, the notion of early or late ages of the generating male affecting sex: men generating before the age of 21 producing more females.[15] Then, some time in the late 1250s, a treatise inserted into a text by the Franciscan Alexander of Hales formulated the question more elaborately, doing this in order to spell out the three elementary possibilities of the ratio: more, equal, and less. 'Would they [those in paradise] have generated as many boys as girls or more boys than girls or the reverse' (*utrum tot generassent filios quot filias vel plures filios quam filias aut e converso*). The discussion indicated the existence by this time of strongly divided debaters on this issue: 'On this question various [men] hold various opinions' (*de hac questione diversi diversa sentiunt*).[16]

Some time between 1285 and 1295 the Franciscan Richard of Middleton develops the theme slightly while following in Bonaventure's footsteps. 'That they would have been multiplied in equal number is clear from this', Richard writes, 'that one man would have only had one wife, one wife only one husband', in a situation where all dedicated themselves to multiplying the species (*Quod etiam in pari numero multiplicati fuissent, patet ex hoc, quod unus vir non habuisset nisi* [*unam uxorem*], *una uxor nisi unum virum*). Slightly later, in his reply to the first objection to equal multiplication, he states that both sexes were intended, 'for more numerous multiplication of individuals' (*propter numerosiorem multiplicationem individuorum*).[17] Elsewhere, in his commentary on the theme of plurality of wives in the Old Testament in distinction 33 of the fourth book of the *Sentences*, Richard showed that he subscribed to the commonplace that this had been allowed to bring about more rapid population increase.[18] If he was bearing this in mind when discussing prelapsarian ratio, he was saying only that fertility increases as one proceeds from a surplus of men towards parity.

The Franciscan Duns Scotus followed Richard, adding in an original and sharp fashion when attempting to envisage an imbalance in paradise. There could 'have been [males and females] not in an equal number in this manner. A husband could have lived longer, and when his wife was dead he would have married another; and thus in that state there would have been more women, or, if the converse, more men' (*quod non fuissent in numero aequali in statu innocentiae, per hunc modum, quod maritus diu vixisset, et accepisset aliam uxorem, sua mortua: et*

[15] *In sententias*, II. xx. 2. 1; i. 565: *ut in XVIII* De animalibus *sive IV* De gener. anim. . . . *unde ante tertium septennium, ut Philosophus dicit, viri ut in pluribus feminas generant.* The cited text seems to be Aristotle, *De animalibus*, Michael Scot's translation, p. 171: *iuvenes generant feminas plusquam provectioris aetatis.* There is discussion of Aristotle on sex-determination in J. Cadden, *Meanings of Sex Difference in the Middle Ages: Medicine, Science and Culture* (Cambridge, 1993), pp. 23–5.

[16] Alexander of Hales, *Summa Theologica*, 2. 1a. 4. Tractatus. Q. 2, ed. V. Doucet, 4 vols. (Quaracchi, 1921–48), i. 723–7. On the character and date of this treatise, *De coniuncto*, which was inserted after Alexander's death, see V. Doucet, *Prolegomena* (= vol. 4 part 1 of the Quaracchi edn), pp. cxx–cxxi and cclxxvi–cclxxx.

[17] Richard, *In sententias*, II. xx. 1; ii. 254–5. On Richard see Ch. 2 n. 104 above, and E. Hocedez, *Richard de Middleton: Sa vie, ses oeuvres, sa doctrine*, Spicilegium Sacrum Lovaniense 7 (Louvain and Paris, 1925), where pp. 133–4 discuss his becoming a standard authority by the early fourteenth century.

[18] Richard, *In sententias*, IV. xxxiii. 11; iv. 466.

sic fuissent in statu illo plures foeminae: vel si econverso, plures viri).[19] This attempt to link different life-spans, remarriage, and the numerical proportion of the sexes was new. Elsewhere, when setting a discussion of bigamy in the context of a population containing fewer men, Duns briefly indicates conditions he sees bringing about such an imbalance between the sexes: 'if the case should come about—through war, disaster, or disease—that the multitude of men were to decline and the multitude of women remain ...' (*Si tamen contingeret casus per bellum, vel cladem, vel pestem, quod multitudo virorum caderet, et multitudo mulierum remaneret* ...).[20]

With Giles of Rome the story reaches a specialist. In 1276 Giles had written a treatise on the formation of the foetus which included an elaborate reworking of Aristotle's treatment of sex-determination. In his writing on the *Sentences* (1309–12)[21] Giles discussed the question of ratio at length,[22] ranging quite freely, and when dealing with sex-determination he referred with appropriate author's pride to 'many other ways, as we have said in our treatise *On the formation of the human body*'.[23] His most important contributions to the theme were his emphatic engagement with various models of excess in the fourth group of arguments, and his new phrases for this. Apart from William of Auvergne, previous commentators or writers indicated excess by saying the opposite of 'equal multiplication', 'equal number' and 'as many as', or stated, as a positive, 'more than'. Giles sometimes uses the phrase 'more than' but he also heavily relies on the verb 'exceed': 'if one sex exceeded the other' (*si unus sexus superasset alium*), 'if males exceeded females' (*si masculi superassent foeminas*), 'if females exceeded males' (*si foeminae superassent masculos*), 'females ... multiplied beyond men' (*feminas ... multiplicatas supra viros*). Hand in hand went new phrasing, verbal convenience, and 'excess' on its way to becoming a more readily present and available concept. Giles, we should recall, had been one of the earliest thinkers to absorb William of Moerbeke's translation of Aristotle's *Politics*, a work which he used so heavily in his *De regimine principum*. Now, rich in demographic concepts and phrases (though devoid of the ratio),[24] the *Politics* so frequently deals with 'excess of multitude' (*excessum multitudinis*) that it is worth suggesting the possibility that the numerous occasions of 'excess' of particular 'multitudes' encountered by Giles in his reading of the *Politics* may have influenced this semantic-conceptual development in Giles's handling of the ratio. Giles concludes the story of progress. I have not yet found further significant development of thought on the ratio in later *Sentences* commentaries in the period up to 1350.

[19] Duns Scotus, *In sententias*, II. xx. 2; vi. 821–2. See above, Ch. 2 n. 105.

[20] Duns Scotus, *In sententias*, IV. xxxiii. 1; ix. 706.

[21] See above, Ch. 2 n. 111.

[22] Giles of Rome, *In secundum librum sententiarum*, XX. ii. 1 (Venice, 1581), pp. 156b–8b.

[23] Ibid., p. 158a. Giles's embryological treatise was analysed in M. A. Hewson, *Giles of Rome and the Medieval Theory of Conception: A Study of the 'De formatione corporis humani in utero'* (London, 1975).

[24] The statement in Aristotle's *Politics*, p. 117, 1269^{b}15, that one should think of a city as being near to a division into two, the multitude of women and multitude of men, is in Moerbeke's Latin *civitatem prope ei quod est in duo dividi oportet putare ut ad virorum multitudinem et mulierum*. Although the passage

4.4 *Before Bonaventure*

Whatever the gaps in this sketch of *Sentences* commentaries, it is a matter of clarity and sunlight when set beside the murkiness of the two other parts of the enquiry. What precedes Bonaventure? And what is accompanying and helping to produce thought about a ratio?

What went before in theology? I have not found the ratio in Augustine, though many passages in the obvious works seem to cry out for ratio as their next development. But I cannot be sure of this void. As Isidore of Seville said, if anyone tells you he has read all the works of Augustine he is a liar.[25] Since reformulations of the question 'what sort of children would have been' were readily present in various standard twelfth-century texts, especially Hugh of St Victor[26] and Peter the Lombard, it would also be foolhardy to assert that there is a certainty that no one raised the sex-ratio at this period. A lesser claim is being made. Whereas thought about sex-ratio was widely pervasive from 1250, it is difficult to find earlier. The question about children does not lead to ratio with Hugh of St Victor or Peter the Lombard, nor later with Roland Bandinelli,[27] Gandulph of Bologna,[28] Peter of Poitiers,[29] Simon of Tournai,[30] Master Martin,[31] Prepositinus of Cremona,[32] nor—with the last of these, writing around 1215—Geoffrey of Poitiers.[33] None of these had referred to the sex of the children, but by 1250 the developed state of Bonaventure's discussion and his reference at one point to 'some' who raise other possibilities indicate that the theme is not brand-new. We are driven to look at the three decades leading up to the 1240s, and to Paris.

There are four theologians in Paris in this period whose writings contain the ratio, and they are to my knowledge the earliest figures in the history of thought about the ratio. But earlier authors may turn up, for the history of scholasticism in these decades is still very uncharted.[34] The earliest figure is William of Auxerre, whose *Summa aurea* (written between 1215 and 1229, and probably after 1218)[35]

does not make an issue of ratio, one might expect an interested commentator to develop it in the direction of the ratio. I have not found any *Politics* commentator doing this.

[25] Quoted by P. Brown, 'St Augustine', in *Trends in Medieval Political Thought*, ed. B. Smalley (Oxford, 1965), p. 1.

[26] Hugh of St Victor, *De sacramentis*, I. vi. 26; *PL* 171, 1122b.

[27] *Die Sentenzen Rolands nachmals Papstes Alexander III*, ed. A. M. Gietl (Freiburg-im-Breisgau, 1891), p. 122.

[28] Gandulph of Bologna, *Sententiarum libri quatuor*, II. clxxv, ed. J. von Walter (Vienna and Wrocław, 1924), p. 248.

[29] Peter of Poitiers, *Sententiarum libri quinque*, II. viii; ed. Moore, Garvin, and Dulong, ii. 46–7.

[30] R. Heinzmann, *Die 'Institutiones in sacram paginam' des Simon von Tournai: Einleitung und Quästionsverzeichnis*, Münchener Universitätsschriften, Theologische Fakultät, Veröffentlichungen des Grabmann-Instituts, n.s. 1 (Munich, Paderborn, and Vienna, 1967), pp. 56–7.

[31] BN, MS Lat. 14526 contains his *Summa*, where fol. 82ra contains a counterfactual conditional questions, on the procreation of children in paradise.

[32] BN, MS Lat. 14526, fol. 20rb; BL, MS Harley 3596, fol. 21ra–va.

[33] BN, MS Lat. 15757, fol. 29ra. See on him and his *Summa* Baldwin, *Chanter*, i. 31–2, and ii. 22 n. 157.

[34] A. M. Landgraf, *Introduction à L'histoire de la littérature théologique de La Scholastique naissante* (Montreal and Paris, 1973), p. 184.

[35] On the date of the *Summa aurea*, see J. Ribailler's *Introduction Générale* to his edition, Spicilegium

touched upon the ratio when discussing the question whether the marriage of one to one was grounded in natural law.[36] Listed last among the arguments *contra* is this. 'Suppose that there are only two men and infinite women, it is clear that natural reason will dictate to the men that they should multiply the human race as much as they can, as with Lot's sons; therefore it will dictate that each should have many wives.' William comes down against this as unreal:

> This position does not hold [*or* happen], because God ordained it thus, that there should be more males than females, because from the males he wishes some to be rulers and teachers, who are signified by Noah, some to be virgins, who are signified by Daniel, and some to be married, who are signified by Job.[37]

While the order in the text proceeds from God's providence to this proposition about the ratio in the population of the Church, analysis of the text suggests that the order in William's mind was the reverse, starting with a schematization about the population of the Church and working back towards providence. William's text shows him thinking in three ways: (i) one to one; (ii) more of one sex than another; (iii) extraordinarily more of one sex than another. If we apply these to his thoughts about the Church, we are (probably) finding him thinking the following. The population of the Church is made up of (i) rulers and teachers, all male, but a small proportion of all in the Church, (ii) virgins [= religious celibates], more male than female, and (iii) the married, whose ratio is one to one and who constitute the largest proportion of the Church's population. And the sum of all three groups adds up to 'more males than females' but not extraordinarily more. William might be including the increasingly celibate secular clergy in the second group; their large numbers compared to the religious could prevail over any thoughts he might have about areas of intense concentration of numbers of female religious (these are discussed later).

Where William of Auxerre gets attention through probably being the first, William of Auvergne gets it for penetration and 'demographic' realism. Here, held over from Chapter 3 above, are his statements about sex-ratio. The

Bonaventurianum 20, p. 16; Landgraf, *Introduction, pp.* 173–4. See the editors' comments in Gui de Orchelles, *Tractatus de sacramentis*, ed. D. and O. Van den Eynde (New York, Louvain, and Paderborn, 1953), p. xli: ignoring of important canon-legal material on marriage of 1216–17 suggests a date for Gui's *Tractatus* hardly after 1216–17—and thus not after 1220—and William of Auxerre's use of Gui's work in the fourth book of the *Summa aurea* (but not earlier) suggests a date for the *Summa aurea*'s completion a little after 1220, that is to say, between 1222 and 1225. There seems no good ground for the *double* chronological slide. On the reasoning of the Van den Eyndes, the fourth book of the *Summa aurea*, in this picture, could have been undergoing influence from a Gui work composed in 1216–17. Why could it not be as early as 1218?

[36] William of Auxerre, *Summa aurea*, IV. xvii. 3 Q. 2; iv. 394–7.

[37] *Ponatur quod non sint nisi duo viri et infinite mulieres, constat quod viris dictab[i]t ratio naturalis quod debeant humanum multiplicare genus, quantum possunt, sicut patet in filiis Loth; ergo dictabit quod quilibet habeat plures uxores . . . Nec illa positio contingit, quia sic ordinavit Deus, ut plures sint mares quam femine, quia de maribus vult quosdam rectores vel doctores, que significantur per Noe, quosdam virgines, qui significantur per Danielem, quosdam coniugatos, qui significa[n]tur per Iob.* See the annotation of a passage similarly interpreting Noah, Daniel, and Jacob in Alexander of Hales, *In sententias Petri Lombardi*, IV. xxxiii. 3; iv. 532 and n. 3, which indicates the origin in a gloss of Gregory the Great on Ezechiel 14: 20.

theme came up in three of the chapters in his *De matrimonio*. He was nearest to conventional theological thought in the tradition of Peter the Lombard's *Sentences* when raising a question on the licitness of plurality of wives in the Old Testament, upon which the commonplace was God dispensing with monogamy to bring about a more rapid increase in the numbers of his people. While it is difficult to find commentators being sparked into thought by this, William was. In the preceding chapter in his treatise William had just stated that when one compared polygamous as opposed to monogamous kingdoms of similar size and fertility one did not find greater numerousness in the polygamous kingdom, unless the monogamous kingdom had been cut down by war or plague. Reluctance to see population expansion following polygamy in a population with parity or near parity in the ratio led him to state a possible imbalance in the ratio at some point in history, where women exceeded men in the population, as the demographic condition. 'For there could have been at some time a greater multitude of women than men in God's people, and therefore it was necessary for one man to marry many' (*Potuit autem esse in aliquo tempore major multitudo mulierum in populo Dei, quam virorum, et ideo necesse fuit unum virum multas ducere*).[38] William is clearly thinking of a large imbalance. In contrast with his eager discursiveness when exploring the sex-ratio against the Saracens, William is brief here. William does not reject a long tradition about Old Testament plurality of wives. But his brevity and his tentative opening words suggest hesitancy and unease.

An earlier chapter had contained William's principal treatment of the ratio.[39] There it was the main thrust of his onslaught on the plurality of wives or concubines in Islam. Note, before reading him, that there is sometimes a perceptible gap between the thesis he happens to be upholding at a particular moment and what he says in fact happens. He is arguing, self-evidently, to establish a parity of one to one, but his statements are hedged with qualifications. Let us follow him. After a first argument based on the similarity of the condition of the sexes he moves to nature, which contradicts such bizarre numerical disproportions as are implied by Islam: 'Nature herself contradicts this, since there is not naturally such a greater multitude of women than men that each man can have a multitude of wives' (*ipsa natura contradicit, cum naturaliter non sit tanto major multitudo foeminarum, quam virorum, ut unusquisque virorum posset habere multitudinem mulierum*). As William continues he uses either the doubt implied by 'probably' or the qualification of 'almost' to erode one-to-one parity. 'Therefore nature herself manifestly contradicts this error, [nature] which puts males and females in the human species almost at the same level in number, without perceptible or observable excess' (*Natura ergo ipsa manifeste contradicit huic errori, que mares, et foeminas in specie humana numero pene parificet absque excessu sensibili seu perceptibili*), writes William. Having produced a qualification in 'almost' and withdrawn it in 'without perceptible excess', he immediately goes back to 'almost':

[38] *De sacramento matrimonii*, IX; *Opera omnia*, i. 526b–7a.

[39] *De sacramento matrimonii*, III; *Opera omnia*, i. 515b–6a.

Where doubtless an excess of number on the part of males is probable in the human species, which is ruled and ministered by Divine providence; and just as she [nature] helps the male and female in the work of generation, so also she procreates one [male] and one [female], not one [male] and many [females] nor one [female] and many [males].
Ubi nec proculdubio excessum a parte masculorum numeri esse verisimile est speciei humanae, que providentia divina regitur et administratur; et sicut adjuvat masculum et foeminam ad opus generationis, ita etiam procreat unum, et unam, non unum, et multas, neque unam et multos.

William soon backtracks again, writing of the probability (*verisimile est*) for the perfection of nature and convenience of providence 'that males and females naturally are born equal in number in the whole of the human species' (*ut naturaliter numero pares nascantur mares et foeminae in universitate generis humani*). He contemptuously kicks out of court Aristotle—'Nor should one listen to Aristotle, who says in his book on the natures of animals that a female is an imperfect male' (*nec est audiendus Aristot*[*eles*], *qui dicit in libro suo de naturis animalium, quod foemina est mas imperfectus*)[40]—and continues to argue for a ratio of 1:1. While his final argument relates to justice (if the powerful men of a region have twenty thousand wives, many men will have to do without wives), his penultimate argument again shows William glimpsing the broader lines of demographic reality: 'sometimes males, sometimes females die by disease or the sword beyond the intention of nature', that is to say, producing a ratio other than 1:1 (*pereunt vel peste, vel gladio interdum mares interdum foeminae preter intentionem naturae*).

William of Auvergne may have known and been influenced by William of Auxerre's argument about providence. However, his originality, his acute observation of other aspects of population, and his twisting on the hook of 1 : 1 parity suggest the possibility that his notion of an excess in number of males was also rooted in a broad awareness of the ratio at birth. And he is clearly aware of the possibility of imbalances in a given adult population.

Writing on the *Sentences* around 1231–2,[41] the Dominican Hugh of St Cher raised the question whether the marriage of one to one was grounded in natural law in the same words as William of Auxerrre, and the ensuing discussion repeats William of Auxerre's, altering one detail. 'Suppose that there are only two men and infinite women' becomes the less fantastic 'Suppose that there are only two men and many women' (*ponatur quod non sint nisi duo viri et multe mulieres*).[42] Writing a *Summa* around 1232[43] the Dominican Roland of Cremona again raised the same question, though not in identical wording. Roland echoes Hugh (he prefers 'some women') and William of Auxerre, but his text marks a new stage. Roland's question of the marriage of one to one leads on to the further question: 'Here one can ask why more males than females are generated. It is supposed by

[40] Aristotle, *De animalibus*, XVI, Michael Scot's translation, p. 76 [= *De generatione animalium*, II. iii, 737a27–8], where the text runs thus: *femina est quasi mas occasionatus.*

[41] Landgraf, *Introduction*, p. 175, gives pre-1234, and *SOPMA* ii. 271 gives *c.*1231–2; see n. 47 below.

[42] BN, MS Lat. 3073 fol. 108rb, and MS Vat. Lat. 1098, fol. 181rb.

[43] Landgraf, *Introduction*, p. 177. In his 'Roland de Crémone et Hugues de Saint-Cher', *RTAM* 12 (1940), 136–43, O. Lottin argues that Hugh's commentary was earlier than Roland's.

the Masters that that there are more males than females since God wishes to make some [of them] teachers . . .' (*Hic potest queri quare plures mares generantur quam femine. Supponitur enim a magistris quod plures sint mares quam femine, quoniam quosdam vult Deus facere doctores . . .*).[44] The argument Roland is summarizing here is, as we saw earlier, William of Auxerre's, and 'the Masters' are William and those, perhaps including Hugh, who echo him. There is, then, a prevailing view among the Masters, that there is a ratio, and now this view is to be expounded, amplified, and criticized, a process that leads to the formulation of a new question: why is there this ratio?

The second ground stated by William for divine ordination of more males, that God wanted some males to be virgins (celibates), was criticized by Roland, who pointed out that this also applied to women. Roland briefly evokes the real world, whose varying ratios do not help—'For in some countries there are more males than females, and in others the reverse' (*In aliquibus enim terris sunt plures mares quam femine, in aliquibus enim econverso*)—before looking for other possible explanations. It could be that men are better able to be chaste than women, 'and therefore more men than females can be celibate' (*et ideo plures viri possunt esse celibes quam femine*). He also looks at determination of sex, supposing, for example, that 'because the female seed . . . may more often help the male [seed], a male is more often born than a female' (*semen femineum . . . quia sepius iuvet masculinum sepius nascitur masculus quam femina*).

So far, then, as I have been able to discover, it was in the years around the dates of the texts of these four theologians, between 1218/1229 and around 1232, that the thought of the ratio emerged and became a topic of discussion: and in Paris.

But what lay behind this? William of Auvergne and Roland of Cremona (perhaps under the former's influence) take into account a wider world, and William of Auxerre, Hugh, and Roland all think about celibates inside Latin Christendom. Beyond these the texts point to one academic development, and it is with this that we will start. We saw Bonaventure, between 1250 and 1252, referring to a large debate about sex-determination among natural philosophers and medical authors. Let us look at chronology, first among our authors. There is no trace in the first, William of Auxerrre. While the second, William of Auvergne, only briefly quotes Aristotle's *On the generation of animals*, on the generation of females, and does not import further medical or natural-philosophical material on sex-determination, he will have been aware of such material, both from his further reading of this work by Aristotle and also, probably, from Avicenna's *De animalibus*, sometimes known as his *Abbreviatio de animalibus* in recognition of its role as a compendium of Aristotle's treatises on animals. Although a

[44] Paris, Bibliothèque Mazarine MS Lat. 795, fol. 133vb. On Roland, see preceding note; F. Ehrle, 'S. Domenico, le origini del primo studio generale del suo ordine a Parigi e la somma teologica del primo maestro, Rolando da Cremona', in *Miscellanea dominicana, in memoriam VII anni saecularis ab obitu patris Dominici (1221–1921)* (Rome, 1923), pp. 85–134 (pp. 99–133); E. Filthaut, *Roland von Cremona O.P. und die Anfänge der Scholastik im Predigerorden* (Vechta, 1936), pp. 201–19.

compendium, there is also marked independence in this work. The style with which Avicenna can kick Aristotle out of court (*Non putes*, 'do not think' what Aristotle thinks) is echoed in William of Auvergne's 'Aristotle is not to be heard [on this point]', and William of Auvergne's rejection of the notion of the female as imperfect male is paralleled by this theme's non-appearance (I think) in Avicenna's work. The heaviness of William's reading of Avicenna elsewhere lends plausibility to this conjecture. Hugh does not use material on sex-determination in his discussion.

Finally, there is lift-off with Roland, who made heavy use of arguments from medicine and natural philosophy. One earlier part of William of Auxerre's general question had concerned divine dispensation of a plurality of wives in the Old Testament in order to bring about more rapid increase of God's worshippers, to which the logically obvious subsequent question was, why not a plurality of husbands? Here Roland argued that 'if one woman had several husbands, conception would not thereby be multiplied, rather it would be diminished. Prostitutes, in fact, cannot conceive on account of the large amount of intercourse and the diversity of seeds of diverse men' (*si una haberet plures viros, per hoc non magis muliplicaretur fetus, imo pocius diminueretur. Vero meretrices non possunt concipere propter multitudinem coitus et propter diversitates seminum diversorum hominum*).[45] Galen on qualities of hot and cold in male and female was imported by Roland into his discussion of varying male and female chastity (and hence numbers of celibates), and Hippocrates and Galen were cited in Roland's discussion of determination of sex (and the greater generation of males).

Let us stand back from these details. The most general point is the great expansion in the stock of learned medicine and natural philosophy which was acquired by Latin Christendom through translations from Greek and Arabic between the second half of the eleventh century and the first half of the fourteenth. Although Chapter 10 below surveys this phenomenon and addresses in general the way it supplied and stimulated demographic thought, two points need to be anticipated here on the specific topic of sex-determination.[46] The first is about chronology and quantity. Whereas in the early middle ages very little was available on sex-determination, an extraordinary amount came to be available—and this availability itself was accelerating around and just after 1200. Set side by side the knowledge readily available in the earlier middle ages and the knowledge readily available by around in the mid-thirteenth century. In the early middle ages, what can be *most* easily found is material on a related but distinct theme, the effect of what was seen at the moment of conception on what was conceived. Isidore's *Etymologies* exemplified this with Jacob's sheep, conceiving lambs which were

[45] Paris, Bibliothèque Mazarine MS Lat. 795, fol. 133va.

[46] Accounts of ideas about sex-determination are provided in Hewson, *Giles of Rome*, pp. 174–5, 182–7, and 228–30; L. Demaitre and A. A. Travill, 'Human Embryology and Development in the Works of Albertus Magnus', in *Albertus and the Sciences*, pp. 427 and n. 91; D. Jacquart and C. Thomasset, *Sexuality and Medicine in the Middle Ages*, trans. M. Adamson (Oxford, 1988), pp. 50, 59, and 145; Cadden, *Sex Difference* (n. 15 above), pp. 130–4.

coloured with the colours seen when they were being conceived (Genesis 30: 35–42).[47] Among the Hippocratic treatises translated into Latin in the fifth and sixth centuries, 'only the *Aphorisms* seem to have had considerable diffusion',[48] and this diffusion will have helped circulate the brief statement in *Aphorism* 5.48 that the male foetus is usually found on the right and the female on the left of the womb.

The mid-thirteenth century? In Vincent of Beauvais's *Speculum Maius* a reader could find gathered on the theme of sex-determination a wealth of lengthy extracts from texts dealing elaborately with the theme:[49] an unidentified Hippocratic *Epistola de Anatomia*,[50] Avicenna's *Canon of Medicine*, Haly Abbas's *Liber Regalis*, Thomas of Chantimpré's *Liber de natura rerum*, and so on. The massive expansion in available material which has taken place by the time of Vincent de Beauvais had had its milestones, some of them very recent ones. One milestone was the study in Paris by at least the early 1180s of the basic collection of medical texts later known as the *Articella* (including the *Aphorisms*).[51] Another was the diffusion of what William of Auvergne was quoting around 1228, Aristotle's *On the generation of animals*, with its whole book on sex-determination, which had been translated by Michael Scot before or by 1220. This had been followed by Scot's translation, between about 1220 and 1232, of Avicenna's compendium of Aristotle's biological works; books 15–19 resumed Aristotle's *On the generation of animals*.[52] Another milestone was constituted by Avicenna's *Canon*, with its section on sex-determination. Translated before 1190, the work had begun to be cited in the second quarter of the thirteenth century.[53] Each of these works brought together various influences on determination of sex. Avicenna's *Canon*, for example, briskly listed position in womb, the quality of male and female seed, the temperature of a region, or season, and the influence of wind, and periods of life (youth and old age tending more to the generation of women).

This is the second point, its devotion of massive 'scientific' (in contemporary terms) attention to sex-determination in conceptions. Care is needed on the second point, care in delineating both the limitation of scope and also the suggestiveness of these texts in guiding readers towards the specific notion of ratio. Let us

[47] Isidore, *Etymologiae*, XII. i. 58–60.

[48] D. Jacquart, 'Principales étapes dans la transmission des textes de médecine (XIe–XIVe siècle)', in *Rencontres de cultures dans la philosophie médiévale: Traductions et traducteurs le l'antiquité tardive au XIVe siècle*, ed. J. Hamesse and M. Fattori (Louvain and Cassino, 1990), pp. 251–71 (p. 253).

[49] Vincent, *Speculum naturale*, XXXI. xxxvi–lx; 2319–21; *Speculum doctrinale* XIII. xxxvi; 1192. Vincent composed between 1244/6 and 1256/9.

[50] P. Kibre, *Hippocrates Latinus: Repertorium of Hippocratic Writings in the Latin Middle Ages*, rev. edn. (New York, 1985), p. 153.

[51] C. O'Boyle, *The Art of Medicine: Medical Teaching at the University of Paris, 1250–1400*, Education and Society in the Middle Ages and Renaissance 9 (Leiden, Boston, and Cologne, 1998), pp. 12–13 and 116–20.

[52] Avicenna, *De Animalibus*, XVIII; 52v–3v.

[53] Avicenna, *Canon*, Lib. 3, Fen 21, Tract. 2, cap. 12, *De causis masculinitatis*; 289va. D. Jacquart, 'La réception du *Canon* d'Avicenne: comparaison entre Montpellier et Paris au XIIIe et XIVe siècles', in *Histoire de l'école médicale de Montpellier: colloque* (Paris, 1985), pp. 69–77.

follow both in the fundamental text, Aristotle's *On the generation of animals*, in Michael Scot's translation. Attention is given principally to individuals: the 'causes' of the generation of (a) female, singular, or (a) male, singular. As the text turns from the 'causes' which determine sex in principle to the 'accidents' (*accidentia*) which affect it in contingent reality, plurality enters: 'more women' are generated by very young or very old women; or by the moister-bodied; or when or where south winds prevail. Plurality is also implied in the statement that there is regional diversity in sex determination. There is one point, but one point only, where Aristotle's text explicitly approaches ratio, where it compares defective births among humans and other animals. 'In men [i.e. humans] more males than females are born defective, in other animals not' (*In hominibus vero occasionantur mares plus quam feminae, in aliis autem animalibus non*).[54] Reading of this may have contributed to William of Auvergne's statement of nature providing more males. This is as far as the Greek and Arabic texts go. The theme of ratio in the population as a whole is not present.

These texts, then, provided the stimulus of a scientific approach to the bordering theme of individual sex-determination, and Aristotle's treatise in particular put forward contingent variation and one point about a ratio of defective births. More broadly, there was a sharp change in the quality and a massive increase in the quantity of this biological material in the early to mid-thirteenth century, at the time when examples of thought about the ratio are first to be found. My suggestion is that this material was available and ready to fuse with the theme of human population as a whole in theologians' speculations about Old Testament history. And this fusion helped to produce the notion of sex-ratio in the population. Only 'helped'—because other factors may also have been present.

4.5 *The context*

Observation of the world outside is present in the writings of the two Williams. Western observation of contemporary Islamic countries and the permission of polygamy is at the heart of William of Auvergne's acute discussion of proportional numbers. Our obvious starting-point is the skewed sex-ratio which has long been attributed by historical demographers to some medieval towns: an excess of women brought about by the movement of larger numbers of women than men from country into town. Roger Mols stated this ratio as one of the 'general laws' of urban immigration in pre-industrial Europe.[55] We must begin, however, with what our writers noticed. In William of Auxerre what is implied is awareness of a relation between a surplus of one sex or another and observation of celibacy in the

[54] 775a 4–5; Aristotle, *De gen. an.* (Scot), p. 201.

[55] R. Mols, *Introduction à la démographie historique des villes d'Europe du XIVe au XVIIIe siècle*, 3 vols. (Louvain, 1954–6), ii. 183–9, 218–22, 374, and 532. See the cautious discussion in P. J. P. Goldberg, *Women, Work and Life Cycle in a Medieval Economy: Women in York and Yorkshire c.1300–1520* (Oxford, 1992), Chs. 6–7.

church, whether secular clerical (broadly, William's 'rulers and teachers') or religious (William's 'virgins').

One rare modern consideration of the secular clergy from the demographic point of view was Christopher Brooke's study of the slow implementation of the campaign for a celibate secular clergy—in other words, the shift of one small portion of the adult male population from being (probably) predominantly married or concubinary to being predominantly not married or concubinary.[56] In the case of England he suggested a broad chronology for the lower clergy: 'by the second half of the thirteenth century married clergy seem to be an exceptional problem . . . if married clergy were common in eleventh-century England, the Gregorian reform, had, over two centuries, a considerable effect.' And he suggested for the higher clergy a falling off of those with families by the mid-twelfth century.[57] Contemporary awareness of this shift may be one of the things to be found immediately underneath the thought about ratio which is exemplified in William of Auxerre, while another suggested by his text is awareness of ratio among the religious.

There was a long tradition of writing and thinking about the state of 'religion' (viz. monasticism) in terms of rise and fall and rise, and to some degree quantitative ups and downs.[58] Are the numbers of female religious and the rise in the curve on the graph—for example, the great expansion in Cistercian nunneries in north-western Europe in the period from about 1220 to 1240[59]—the phenomena which were most likely to have focused the minds of the clerics who were beginning to write about ratio in the early thirteenth century?

Herbert Grundmann's chapter on the statistics of female religious in the thirteenth century gathered various testimonies to bear on the numbers in reality, but these texts can also be taken as evidence of large numbers of usually highly-placed thirteenth-century clerics *thinking* about abundance or numbers of women.[60] Look at two of these men, first of all Jacques de Vitry. Writing in the *Historia Occidentalis* (possibly around 1220) about the rise in numbers of Cistercian nuns after women's exclusion from the Premonstratensians, he notes the foundation of seven abbeys in the diocese of Liège, adding that these could have been three times as many. When generalizing about their numbers, he writes, 'The religion of the order of Cistercian nuns was multiplied like the stars of heaven and grew immensely, with the Lord blessing them and saying, "Increase and multiply and fill heaven"' (*multiplicata est sicut stelle celi et excrevit in immensum cysterciensis ordinis religio sanctimonialium, benedicente eis domino et dicente, 'Crescite et*

[56] C. N. L. Brooke, 'Gregorian Reform in Action: Clerical Marriage in England, 1050–1200', repr. in his *Medieval Church and Society: Collected Essays* (London, 1971), pp. 69–99.

[57] Ibid., pp. 78, 90.

[58] See Guibert de Nogent, *Autobiographie*, I. vii, ed. E.-R. Labande, Les Classiques de l'Histoire de France au Moyen Âge (Paris, 1981), pp. 50 and 52.

[59] S. Roisin, 'L'efflorescence cistercienne et le courant féminin de piété au XIIIe siècle', *Revue d'Histoire Ecclésiastique* 39 (1943), 342–78.

[60] H. Grundmann, *Religiöse Bewegungen in Mittelalter* (2nd edn., Hildesheim), pp. 312–18.

multiplicamini et implete celum'). In part, clearly, pointing to providence is what Jacques is doing. But the concern which drives him to this precise form—weaving into his text God's original command to multiply and his promise 'I will multiply thy seed like the stars of heaven' (Genesis 22: 17)—is the immenseness of these female numbers.[61]

The second is Matthew Paris, whose observation of beguines in Germany has often been quoted. Matthew Paris not only made this observation in the *Chronica Majora* under the year 1243 but also in his general summary of 1250, and preserved it in his abbreviated version.[62] Now, Matthew Paris deployed three elements in these accounts—sex of the religious, the area in which they lived, and their number. In all he writes either of 'religious, particularly women' or straightforwardly just of religious women. The emphasis throughout is on high number, but the number and area vary, as follows:

i. 'Cologne alone': 'thousand or more'[63]
ii. 'Cologne and adjoining parts': 'two thousand'[64]
iii. In general, but 'especially in Germany': 'up to a thousand thousands'.[65]

The entries in the *Historia Angliae* do not help my point.[66] However, in these two works quoted we see inside the mind of a monk at St Albans, and there we see two things. One is an elementary linking of area and number at three different levels of magnitude, while the other is a willingness to envisage an enormous number, not yet available in one word (a million)[67] for the female religious in general although mainly in one country. Is this articulation at various levels and envisaging of large numbers representative of the kind of thought which could have been the springboard for thought about the ratio?

The fact that female religious constituted only a tiny proportion, in reality, of the population does not controvert my suggestion that their numbers may have stimulated clerics to think of the ratio overall. Contemporary awareness of great numbers of female religious is manifest. However, William of Auxerre was writing of an excess of males, not females, and therefore the suggested model of the

[61] Jacques de Vitry, *Historia Occidentalis*, XV, ed. J. F. Hinnebusch, *The Historia Occidentalis of Jacques de Vitry: A Critical Edition*, Spicilegium Friburgense 17 (Fribourg, 1972), p. 117; see pp. 16–20 for discussion of the date.

[62] R. W. Southern, *Western Society and the Church in the Middle Ages* (Harmondsworth, 1970), pp. 319–20 and nn. 22–24.

[63] *Chronica Majora* under the year 1250: *adeo ut solam Coloniam mille vel plures inhabitarent*; *CM* v. 278.

[64] *Chronica Majora* under the year 1243: *in civitate Coloniae et partibus adjacentibus duo milia invenirentur*; *CM* iv. 278.

[65] *Abbreviatio Chronicorum*, under the year 1243, in M. Paris, *Historia Anglorum*, ed. F. C. Madden, 3 vols. (= RS, London, 1866), iii. 288: *Numerus quarundam mulierum, quas Beguinas vulgus nominat, in Alemannia praecipue, usque ad milia milium incredibiliter multiplicabatur.*

[66] The entries in the *Historia Anglorum*, ii. 476, and iii. 93–4, provide under 1243 *in civitate Coloniae plura milia* and under 1250 the *ecclesia militans* (geographical area not specified) producing *quasdam mulieres.*

[67] A. Murray, *Reason and Society in the Middle Ages* (Oxford, 1978), p. 196. An appearance in French in the form *millon* as early as *c.*1266 is given in *Grand Larousse de la Langue Française*, 7 vols. (Paris, 1975), iv. 3378.

earliest thought about ratio being stimulated by this awareness has to be complex rather than simple. It would have to be something like this: thought about numbers of religious of one sex, *therefore* thought about religious of both sexes overall, and *therefore*, with the inclusion of the more predominantly male and still very numerous older monastic foundations, thought about an excess of males overall. One of the discussions of ratio in paradise examined earlier raised the issue of providential generation of females only, rather than males, because they were the more devout sex.[68] The author is unlikely to have been unaware of the commonplace of his time, the extraordinary numbers of contemporary female religious, but the relationship between observation of a contemporary fact and hypothesizing an extreme for the purposes of debate was complex—and in this case perhaps tenuous.

A well-known memorandum from Ghent, from 1328, recalling the general situation of Flanders and Hainault in the early thirteenth century and the foundation of beguine houses, said that this area 'abounded greatly with women' (*multum habundabat mulieribus*) who could not marry.[69] Though it should be noted that the memorandum ascribes the consideration of this problem to the countesses of the two counties, not to men, this late text does hold up a model of what *could* have been happening earlier. That is, (*a*) reflection on female religious, which moves back towards (*b*) their source, an abundance of women, and this rumination taking place (*c*) in the minds of men living in the largest cities of the most highly urbanized parts of northern Europe, where the ratio was skewed, perhaps, by the ratio of immigration. If our thinkers were clerical, usually members of religious orders, we would expect an inverse relationship between what was largest in their thought (an abundance of female religious) and what was largest in reality (in some towns an excess of lay women), and we can conjecture that both of these phenomena together, in a now no longer precisely discoverable way, provided the creative fizz when these men began to look at the numbers of the sexes in paradise.

The Florentine figures of 1338 were based on evidence compiled by the rector of the baptistry of San Giovanni, and obviously more straightforward than speculations about the religious would be earlier examples of observing, listing, or counting in a parish, at baptism or later. There is no direct evidence and, as is well known, parish registers do not survive till the precocious example of Givry—in 1334, so close to the date of Villani's entry![70] How likely is it that there was thought and observation in the parish? One important point is that although the Givry

[68] Alexander of Hales, *Summa Theologica* 2. 1a. 4. Tractatus. Q. 2; ed. Doucet, i. 727: *videtur quod tantum genitae fuissent, sic: Ut habetur a B. Augustino, sexus muliebris devotior est.*

[69] P. Fredericq, *Corpus Documentorum Inquisitionis Haereticae Pravitatis Neerlandicae*, 5 vols. (Ghent and 'S Gravenhage, 1889–1906), i. 176; E. W. McDonnel, *The Beghards and Beguines in Medieval Culture, with special emphasis on the Belgian Scene* (New Brunswick, NJ, 1954), p. 83.

[70] L. Lex, 'L'enregistrement des décès et des mariages au XIVe siècle', and P. Gras, 'Le registre paroissial de Givry (1334–1357) et la Peste Noire en Bourgogne', *Bibliothèque de l'Ecole des Chartes* 51 (1890), 376–8, and 100 (1939), 295–308; Mols, *Introduction à la démographie*, i. 76–95, on the origin of registers (p. 78 on Givry).

register is the first to survive, there is much earlier evidence that parish priests were required to keep registers listing their parishioners for pastoral reasons—reasons other than birth, marriage, and death.[71] Keeping registers was forced on in Languedoc by a combination of heresy and the Lateran IV decree on annual confession and communion. In the Council of Narbonne (1227) parish priests were required to keep a register of the names of those who confessed (in this case, three times a year).[72] Two years later the Council of Toulouse stated that 'the names of all men and all women in each parish are to be written down' (*nomina autem omnium virorum ac mulierum in qualibet parochia conscribantur*), where this means males of 14 and over and females of 12 and over. It is assumed in the next canon, about confession and communion, that a parish priest will know 'from looking at the names . . . as indicated above' (*ex nominum inspectione . . . ut superius expressum est*) who is avoiding these duties.[73] In other words, the parish priest is to check those confessing and taking communion against his register. The Council of Béziers in 1232 assumes that this system is in operation, and by the later thirteenth century there are statutes specifying the form of registers: *rotuli* and *chartularia*.[74] None of these registers survives, but it is worth remembering a copy which does survive of parts of an inquisitorial enquiry into the Toulousain in 1245/6. This, which contains the names and depositions of 5741 witnesses, in principle organized by parish, can be seen as a later inquisitorial parallel of the registers which the Councils had asked parish priests to compile.[75]

A broader point about the possibility of observation in the parish was one element in the ideal of the *cura animarum*, that a pastor, bishop or priest, should know the number of his flock.[76] Several *exempla* illustrate this. Into a story about

[71] I have not investigated the keeping of written records of names in relation to their duty to pay tithes, which goes back—at least as an ideal—to the Carolingian period. See the diocesan statute of Gerbald, bishop of Liège, issued between 801 and 802: *ut ipsi sacerdotes populi suscipiant decimas et nomina eorum, quecumque dederint, scripta habent*; *Capitula Episcoporum*, ed. P. Brommer, MGH, I- (Hanover, 1984–), I, 17.

[72] Canon 7, in Mansi, *Concilia*, xxiii. 23: *nomina illorum omnium, qui peccata sua confessi fuerint, scribantur a capellanis, qui confessiones audiverunt eorundem, ut laudabile testimonium de confessionibus eorum valeant perhibere.*

[73] Council of Toulouse, canons 12–13, in Mansi, *Concilia*, xxiii. 196–7; annotated edition in *Texte zur Inquisition*, ed. K.-V. Selge, Texte zur Kirchen- und Theologiegeschichte 4 (Gütersloh, 1967), pp. 32–3. Though registration of parishioners' names in Languedocian parishes is usually overlooked in accounts of conciliar measures against heresy, it attracts brief comment in L. Kolmer, *Ad Capendas Vulpes: Die Ketzerbekämpfung in Südfrankreich in der ersten Hälfte des 13. Jahrhunderts und die Ausbildung des Inquisitionsverfahren*, Pariser Historische Studien 19 (Bonn, 1982), pp. 75–6 and 77 n. 47.

[74] Council of Béziers, canon 5, in Mansi, *Concilia*, xxiii. 271: *ut sacerdotes erga omnes suspectos de haeresi, quos per scripturam et ex nomine cognoscere debent.* The date of the council (1232) is often incorrectly given as 1233; see Y. Dossat, *Les Crises de l'Inquisition Toulousaine au XIIIe siècle* (Bordeaux, 1959), p. 109. Canon 25 of the synod of Albi (1230) provided for a register of those who had confessed and taken communion, those who had not, and the excommunicate, *Les Statuts Synodaux Français du XIIIe siècle*, ii. *Les Statuts de 1230 à 1260*, ed. O. Pontal (Paris, 1983), p. 24. Names of the excommunicate are to be inscribed on *rotuli* in a post-1255 addition to the Albi statutes, ibid., p. 468, and the names of those making annual confession on *chartularia* in canon 19 of the council of Arles, *c.*1275, Mansi, *Concilia*, xxiii. 152–3.

[75] Dossat, *Crises de l'Inquisition*, pp. 232, 233–4. The parallel has been suggested by Kolmer, *Ad Capiendas Vulpes*, p. 77.

[76] Robert Grosseteste's sermon *Ego sum pastor bonus* heavily emphasizes the need to know

a Cologne parish priest complaining about Dominicans hearing confessions in his parish, Thomas of Chantimpré inserts the following crisp exchange between the legate Conrad and the parish priest. 'Conrad: "What is the number of the men subject to you in your parish?" And he [the parish priest] said, "Nine thousand"' (*Conradus: Quis est numerus hominum in parochia tibi subditorum? Et ille, novem millia, inquit*).[77] Another one, given by another Dominican, Stephen of Bourbon, has the archbishop of Lyons shipwrecked, and coming across a poorly dressed figure writing and reading. The humble figure is the bishop of a tiny see, and he is zealously entering and examining details of his flock, whose names and deeds he knows, as well as their number, about forty. The archbishop on the other hand was embarrassed not to know the vast numbers of his large diocese, for which omission he was warned he would suffer the torments of God. Stephen is using the polarity forty: innumerable to give an exaggerated version of the stark contrast between large French archdioceses and the very numerous and often minute dioceses of Italy, Corsica, Sardinia, and Sicily.[78] What is relevant to us is that some sort of register is being envisaged in a tiny southern diocese in the late twelfth century—the Lyons archbishop is John Whitehands, whose episcopate ran from 1181–93—and that two Dominicans compiling *exempla* in the mid-thirteenth century produce stories in which there is dialogue of question and answer about numbers in a parish or diocese. In the ideal register envisaged by Stephen's *exemplum* and the registers commanded by Languedocian conciliar and synodal legislation, would names have been ordered under males, then females? This seems likely, but nothing helps us to answer the question 'would they then have begun to suggest a ratio?'

A third scrap of evidence can be put alongside Stephen's Mediterranean bishop and Thomas's parish priest of Cologne. In Chapter 3 we saw William of Auvergne as bishop of Paris running his diocese tightly, and through concern for the size of his parishes applying to the pope for leave to divide them. It was from a man who was one of his three archdeacons in 1239 that we had a figure quoted, 43,000, for the souls living in an enormous Paris parish which stretched far into the countryside, St Germain-L'Auxerrois. Does this emerge from wider attempts to list or measure, subsequently lost? All we can note is the extraordinary coincidence of this remarkable survival and the bishop in whose diocese this parish fell having

parishioners by name, ed. O. Gratius, *Appendix ad fasciculum rerum expetendarum* (London, 1690), pp. 260–3 (p. 262).

[77] Thomas of Chantimpré, *Bonum Universale de Apibus*, I. ix (Douai, 1627), p. 33.

[78] The story is given twice in Stephen of Bourbon, *Tractatus*, nos. 400 and 496, pp. 351–2, 427–8. Here is the second: *viderunt unum hominem . . . scribentem in quadam tabula et studentem in ea . . . respiciebat numera parrochianorum suorum, et studebat circa statum et salutem eorum, de quibus eum oportebat reddere rationem. Et cum quererent si sciret quot essent, et responderet quod circa quadraginta, cum magis super hoc stuperent, quesivit ab archiepiscopo dicto quis esset: 'Transmarinus episcopus sum', ait. Et ille: 'Et tu, quot habes animas?' Respondit: 'Nescio, nisi quod inumerabiles habeo, quas ego non cognosco'.* Stephen says he was told the story by Aimon, who was with John on this journey and later became bishop of Mâcon (1219–42). On the large number and tiny size of Italian dioceses see R. Brentano, *Two Churches: England and Italy in the Thirteenth Century* (Princeton, 1968), pp. 62–4.

such an acute awareness both of the density of population and also the ramifications of the theme of sex-ratio at birth and in the population.

There is a southward pull in Stephen of Bourbon's story; Archbishop John was journeying towards Rome. It is also in the south, in Florence, that we find the idea of sex-ratio attested best, as we shall see further in Chapter 14. There may not even have been a phrase for the 'sex-ratio' before the thirteenth century. Theological discussion had been sparked by scientific material on sex-determination, and (probably) by experience of ratio among the religious and (possibly) by observation of ratio among the laity. A new thought had emerged, in the second quarter of the thirteenth century. By 1250 the concept was being extensively discussed, and for some unknown number of years before 1338 in one Tuscan city there was a regular attempt to measure numerically the ratio at baptism.

5

THE PRECEPT OF MARRIAGE AND SUFFICIENT MULTIPLICATION

Peter Brown's *The Body and Society* delineates the ideal of sexual renunciation in early Christianity, traced through the writings of the Greek and Latin fathers. Interwoven with this theme is the human race in biblical and post-biblical history. In the beginning there was the injunction to multiply. After expansion there was reduction to Noah and his wife, and then after the flood expansion again. Now that the world is sufficiently populated, the injunction to multiply no longer binds, and celibacy and virginity have become more praiseworthy than marriage. Brown quotes passages from Jerome, Augustine, and others which express their sense of a world packed and teeming with people. In Brown's subtle account this sense is not an alternative to meditation on the end of time and the completion of the number of the elect. It goes hand in hand with these themes, intertwines with the practice of celibacy, and is set in a specific demographic context. The celibacy of the Encratite communities is evoked against a background of the mountainous areas of Syria and Asia Minor, where 'the population always exceeded the scarce resources of the highlands' and John Chrysostom's praise of virginity is set against the quarter of a million inhabitants and three thousand widows and virgins who were under the Church's protection in late fourth-century Antioch.[1]

Similar texts and themes are addressed in this chapter.[2] Historical demographers cite evidence from many different parts of western Europe showing very high population in the years around 1300. Take cities at opposite ends of Europe. Expanding city walls of Italian cities constitute one sort of indirect evidence,[3]

[1] P. Brown, *The Body and Society: Men, Women and Sexual Renunciation in Early Christianity* (London, 1989), pp. 101, 306, and 310.

[2] The following is based on L. Génicot, 'On the Evidence of Growth of Population in the West from the Eleventh to the Thirteenth Century', in *Change in Medieval Society: Europe North of the Alps, 1050–1500*, ed. S. Thrupp (London, 1965), pp. 14–29; J. Z. Titow, 'Some differences between manors and their effects on the conditions of the peasantry in the thirteenth century', *Agricultural History Review* 10 (1962), 113–28; R. M. Smith, 'Human Resources', in *The Countryside of Medieval England*, ed. G. Astill and A. Grant (Oxford, 1988), pp. 188–212; B. F. Harvey, 'The population trend in England between 1300 and 1348', *TRHS*, 5th ser. 16 (1966), 23–42; ead., 'Introduction: the "crisis" of the early fourteenth century', in *Before the Black Death: Studies in the 'Crisis' of the Early Fourteenth Century*, ed. B. M. S. Campbell (Manchester and New York, 1991), pp. 1–24 (see there, p. 4 n. 6 for references to Postan's works); R. M. Smith, 'Demographic developments in rural England, 1300–48: a survey', ibid., pp. 25–77; W. C. Jordan, *The Great Famine: Northern Europe in the Early Fourteenth Century* (Princeton, 1996).

[3] See Ch. 14 below.

while 'property values and building density in Cheapside' provide the basis of a population estimate for London around 1300 of *c.*80–100,000.[4] England has been attractive for study, because of the evidence of Domesday Book (1086), the Poll Tax returns of 1377, and quite a few smaller collections of data. If we take a stand in 1300 and look about us, we see a few clear patches in the mist. We can look backwards, hypothesizing population growth over several centuries.[5] Individual figures for particular areas may point in broadly the same direction. The villages of Moulton and Weston in 1086 had 77 households, but by 1259/60 had 389; figures relating to Taunton show 506 males in 1209, 1359 in 1311. However, Richard Smith emphasizes regional variation—the examples just quoted will represent but two among several possible demographic chronologies—and warns about the extraordinarily high levels of possible error in conjectured overall aggregates. Smith is prepared to say that the population around 1300 will have been at least twice as high as the highest estimates of population in 1086. He goes further to state the '*probable* higher population equilibrium of 1300 compared with that of 1600 or 1650', and that a 'possibility' which has to be 'seriously . . . entertained' is that population in 1300 was a million greater than the 5.2 million of the 1650s.

It is generally agreed that population was pressing upon resources in 1300, although with marked local and wider regional variation. The largest 'regional variation' was Spain. There, although population is agreed to have been growing much as in the rest of western Europe, reconquest kept on throwing open vast territories for resettlement. The pace of this was such as to provoke policies to encourage expansion of population. In other areas, however, we can usually point to overpopulation. Coupled with historical demographers' knowledge of short-term disasters in the early fourteenth century, especially the famines of 1315–17, as well as a decline in population which seems to have been well under way before the Black Death, this has long produced the term 'crisis' to describe the period. In recent years there has been much debate about the nature of this crisis, and further demographic research which has been marked by a wider range of approaches and more refinement in the uses of sources. At the core of the debate has been the search for the underlying causes of population decline, and a fundamental divide between those who rely on one sort of 'check' and those who emphasize another. The older view, eloquently and persuasively urged by Michael Postan, ultimately relied on the 'positive check': high death-rates. In a fundamental article published in 1966, Barbara Harvey suggested that the death-rate was not the more profound influence on the population trend, and invited the renewal of speculation about the influence of the birth-rate. While followers of Postan continued to emphasize mortality, Smith and Harvey have continued to point to its difficulties—the need, for example, to postulate death-rates which look implausibly high when compared to population declines and death-rates in later and

[4] Smith, 'Demographic developments', p. 50.

[5] See further Ch. 9 below, and the question of 'overpopulation' revealed in isolated islands of habitation in ninth-century polyptychs.

more measurable populations. Both Harvey and Smith concentrate their attention on surveying 'preventive checks': patterns of inheritance and delay of marriage; numbers of adults remaining single; fluctuations in the remarriage of widows; even the attempt to limit conception inside marriage. As we shall see in Chapters 6–8, nothing firmer than extensive clerical comment provides evidence for this last practice, and it may have been the least demographically significant among the 'preventive checks'.

To recapitulate: in the best documented and studied part of north-western Europe, England, there had been rapid population growth in the thirteenth century, varying regionally. In some parts the sharpest increase was in the first half of the thirteenth century,[6] and there is evidence of increasingly intense pressure on resources by the later thirteenth century. Although there is a general picture of earlier expansion, rapid thirteenth-century growth should not be projected back into the twelfth. There is even suggestion of some demographic retrenchment in the mid-twelfth century.[7]

Latin Christendom also possessed large and increasing numbers of religious celibates, and its generalizing thinkers were mainly theologians, themselves celibate. Like the early fathers they handled a biblical account of the origins and spread of God's people, and to this was added much of the fathers' own writings, in particular, those selected to enter Peter the Lombard's *Sentences.* How far did they develop this material? How far did they use it for populationist thought? And how far was it a vehicle for reactions to varying populousness in Latin Christendom?

The two histories of people contained in the *Sentences* need to be recalled here. There are the beginning with God's creation of Adam and Eve and the ending with the completion of the number of the elect, the last things, and the resurrection. Within this is set the schematic history of the Jews and the Christians. The principal general historical treatments are in distinctions 26 and 33 of the fourth book of the *Sentences.*

Distinction 26 deals with the double institution of marriage and the repeated injunction, 'Increase and multiply', which was given to the first two people and again given after the flood, when 'virtually the whole human race was wiped out'. After both these injunctions all people were 'bound' to marry, 'under precept'. The precept bound 'until multiplication happened', until the point when 'man had in fact multiplied' (*usquequo facta est multiplicatio, multiplicato vero homine*). Afterwards marriage was not under precept but was 'indulged': 'granted', 'allowed', or 'tolerated'.[8]

The explicit theme of distinction 33 was the 'variety of laws' of marriage, principally variety through time. Along with a more precise historical theme (permission of divorce in the Old Testament), the two large themes were (1) plurality of

[6] See Ch. 3 above for William of Auvergne's involvement in one by-product of Paris's population growth, the sub-division of parishes.

[7] Smith, 'Human Resources', p. 196.

[8] Peter the Lombard, *Sententiae*, IV. xxvi. 3; ii. 418.

wives and permission of concubines and (2) the relation of marriage to virginity. Why was plurality of wives permitted in the Old Testament? At the beginning there were only two people, and their sons and daughters had to marry. Following this there were still few people in the cult of God. Therefore these few men had to unite to marry many women, lest with the failing of their few numbers the cult of God should also fail. They sought the multiplication of the people of God through the fertility of many women, because then the succession of religion was through succession of blood. In these 'olden times', *antiquis temporibus* in Ambrose's words, there was such emphasis on this sort of multiplication that the 'sterile [man] who did not leave his seed upon the earth was cursed' and priests had to marry. Marriage and virginity are compared, for their value varies according to time and circumstance. People militate for Christ according to the 'distribution of times'. 'Just as earlier Abraham pleased [God] in marriage, so virgins please in chastity now. He served the law and his time, we serve the law and our time, "upon whom the ends of the world are come".' A return to the theme of plurality brings the next part of history. When the grace of Christ [people of God] had spread everywhere, the law of marriage was restored to its earlier worthy institution [monogamy]. Not succession [spread of the faith through larger numbers of people] but perfection of life was sought. Virginity was put above chastity, and continence was appointed for priests.[9]

This is a text to be seen, first of all, as a product of its own time: the late 1150s. Different dispensations for different times are presented, with emphasis on fertility in the remote past. The present, however, was not directly addressed. Although the Lombard followed the fathers in putting virginity above marriage, he did this with no special emphasis. He did not state that the earth is full, nor did he quote 'the earth is full' texts of Jerome, Augustine, and others. These nuances do not stand out in this apparently bland text, when it is read in isolation, but strong light and shadow plays upon them when they are compared with the emphases found in commentaries written a century later. While developments in the forms and techniques of teaching and discussion in the schools explain some of the differences, it is also the case that the Lombard was writing at a time when north-western Europe was not as densely populated as a century later, and when parts of it may even have been experiencing some contraction.

Before looking at the Lombard's later commentators, we need to address his text's limitations as a vehicle for thought about population. It was eschatological, and it concerned the relative spiritual merits of virginity and marriage. It dealt with God's people. It dealt only with the few or the many. How far were these real, how far only apparent restrictions?

First, eschatology cast a long shadow. Our writers were theologians, were they not? Surely men more interested in the completion of the numbers of the elect at the end of time, rather than (in modern terms) the contemporary demographic situation? Consider the Franciscan Peter of John Olivi. In one text which was

[9] Peter the Lombard, *Sententiae*, IV. xxxiii; ii. 456–62.

written about 1276, and examined for its orthodoxy in 1282, he asked 'Whether virginity or the chastity which abstains from all sex is absolutely better than marriage'. Although contained within a series of questions *De perfectione evangelica*, this was written with knowledge of and within the tradition of commentaries on this theme in distinction 33 of the fourth book of the *Sentences*. In a long,[10] rich, and complex piece of writing Olivi launched an extraordinary attack on marriage and the production of children. He came near to denying (so it seemed to some) that marriage was a sacrament.[11] Although the current level of population and the common good of the human race did enter the discussion, it was the cessation of marriage in relation to the imminent end of time which drove this powerful and passionate invective. Eschatology, not the current demographic situation.

Although a few theologians were like Olivi, in fact, as we shall see, most mainstream commentators looked at *both* topics: at eschatology *and* at the 'condition of the time'. Consider Albert the Great commenting on distinction 33, asking whether the saints [fathers] were correct in asserting that all men should be virgins, and parading the two contrary texts, Jerome on different times (Abraham and marriage serving his time, virginity serving ours) and Paul's 'I wish all to be like me'. Referring to this last text, Albert wrote that 'it seems to be awkward, because if all were chaste the world would be destroyed'. He goes on: 'Some say that it was revealed to the saints, who spoke thus, that if living men remained chaste the number of the elect would be filled. . . . It could be said otherwise, as Jerome implied here, that the Apostle spoke according to the condition of the time. Hence the meaning of "I wish all, etc." [is] "insofar as the time is opportune". So Jerome says, "just as they [served] their time, so we [serve] ours".'[12] Two approaches are juxtaposed and clearly distinguished. One is the completion of the number of the elect and the end of time, and the other is the 'condition of a time'—the condition of a particular period in ordinary historical time, where

[10] Peter of John Olivi, *De perfectione evangelica*, Qu. 6, *An virginitas sit simpliciter melior matrimonio*, ed. in A. Emmen, 'Verginità e matrimonio nella valutazione dell' Olivi', *Studi francescani*, 64 (1967), 11–57 (pp. 21–57). The question takes about 12,000 words.

[11] In general in this chapter I have been suggesting that theologians used one of the principal even if clumsy tools for demographic thought at their disposal, *Sentences* commentaries, to remark on the current large size of population and the expediency within this of less marriage or remarriage. The editor of Olivi's question has traced the influence of Olivi's downgrading of marriage, principally in the later tradition of statements minimizing the grace conferred by marriage, which can be found in the *Sentences* commentaries of Olivi's Franciscan follower Peter de Trabibus, in Florence around 1295, and in modified form among a couple of early fourteenth-century Dominicans (Emmen, 'Verginità e matrimonio', pp. 15–20). This suggests an additional and more complex hypothesis. If we had the evidence to reconstruct something nearer 'total history' of the west around 1300, its web might well contain some tangled and indirect threads connecting overpopulation and an odd but distinct trend among theologians to erode one element of marriage as a sacrament.

[12] Albert, *In sententias*, IV. xxxiii. 22; xxx. 316a–b: *Videtur autem hoc esse inconveniens: quia omnis existentibus castis, mundus dissolveretur. . . . Quidam dicunt, quod sanctis taliter loquentibus revelatum fuit, quod ex praesentibus si casti remanerent, numerus electorum impleretur. . . . Aliter potest dici sicut hic innuit Hieronymus, quod Apostolus hoc vult secundum conditionem temporis. Unde sensus est,* Volo omnes *etc.*, *quantum opportunum est tempori. Et tamen dicit Hieronymus, quod sicut illi fuerunt tempore suo, ita nos nostro.*

'condition' meant few or many people, and virginity was inopportune or opportune in relation to these numbers. Worth noting is what Albert displays in another passage, when glossing those who are in 'virginity'. Those in 'virginity', writes Albert, are those in a 'single state' (*individuitas*).[13] His interest is not in their spiritual status, nor is he being technical about physical integrity. Rather, his gloss shows that what concerns him is defining them as members of a population.

While looking at the 'condition of time', the theologians' primary concern was to debate what they were supposed to be debating, the alternation of God's precepts and marriage versus virginity, rather than to use a theological topic to write about population. They were indeed led on by the theological topics to write about population, but we must keep in mind that this theme was secondary.

Secondly, was not the focus on God's people rather than all human population? Both God's people and broader human population were in the fourth book of the *Sentences*, in which distinction 33 talked mainly of the first category while distinction 26 in part leant towards the second, dealing with 'men', 'the first men', 'the human race' (*homines, primi homines, genus humanum*). The distinctness of the categories was too self-evident to attract direct discussion, and it is revealed casually in a commentator's passing comments. Discussing suspension of the law of monogamy, Hugh de Novo Castro wrote 'if anyone can change this law this will either be for the multitude of people absolutely, or for the multitude of the Christian people; or perhaps one could not wish [both] to amplify the increase of the faithful or [*correctly*: and] the whole human race'.[14]

When turning to the contemporary or near-contemporary world, the commentators may not flag the distinction. But they assume it, and it is clear. Consider three examples.

(i) Alexander of Hales asked in one of his questions, 'If someone has espoused a wife, is it better to take her rather than receive the cross? . . . to fight against the infidels?' In contrast to the period and conditions when it was necessary for the faithful to be multiplied, 'now however he may well take up the cross, for the multiplication of the faithful is not necessary now; in fact it is more necessary to multiply the faith [amplify the faith by conversion and crusade] than to multiply the faithful [= for the numbers of faithful to grow through their fertility]'.[15]

(ii) Albert's discussion of plurality of wives brings in Muslims named as 'Arabs'.[16]

(iii) When discussing possible dispensation of the law of monogamy in a case of necessity, Peter of la Palud alludes to the possible suggestion of doing this in 'Outremer', in the Holy Land, 'to multiply [Christian] inhabitants there'.[17]

[13] Albert, IV. xxvi. 10; xxx. 111b: *in virginitate, scilicet in individuitate.*

[14] Hugo de Novo Castro, [*Quaestio super distinctionem 33, Utrum fuerit licitum antiquis patribus habere plures uxores*], Vatican, MS Chigi B.VI.96, fol. 91va: *si quis potest hanc legem immutare, vel hoc erit propter multitudinem populi absolute, vel propter multitudinem populi christiani, sed forte posset non velle plurificacionem fidelium amplificare vel tocius humani generis.* Hugh, a Franciscan and follower of Duns Scotus, was writing between 1305 and 1317.

[15] Alexander of Hales, *Quaestiones*, LIX. v; ii. 1175.

[16] Albert, *In sententias*, IV. xxxiii. 2; xxx. 291b.

[17] See below Ch. 9 n. 115.

In all three instances there is casual implication of something which is a commonplace, the omnipresence of an elementary map of populations and faith: there (outside Latin Christianity), pagans, Arabs, possible colonies of Latin Christians; and here, people living in Latin Christendom.

Peter the Lombard had left the 'few' past faithful in a population vacuum, which gets filled up by later writers—for instance by William of Auxerre, writing that 'there were few worshippers, virtually the whole world was under idolatry', or by Albert writing that then 'there was a multitude dragging [people] to idolatry, and [only] few worshipping God'.[18] The phrase becomes the careful 'the multiplication of the people of God *and* of the human race'. If we find only haziness beyond this point, it is to be attributed to caution about orthodoxy, not lack of awareness. Noted in Chapter 2 above was the incorporation into the commentaries of Cicero's text on the earliest men—forest-dwellers who knew no marriages—and the condemnation in Paris in 1277 of the notion 'That there was not a first man, nor will there be a last man, in fact there always was and always will be generation of man by man'. If these are traces of the danger of a view of the distant early population which was not immediately and explicitly set in Genesis, they are also traces of people thinking this thought.[19]

Thirdly, the Lombard and his commentators talked about numbers of people only in very broad terms, and this elementariness seems to be another limitation. In the Lombard's text population is either there or not there, with hardly a gradation in sight. Men are multiplied or not multiplied. They are few or many. There is just one use of a more qualified term, borrowed from Ambrose: 'rarity in the human race'. Similar are the historical periods, which can be simplified and reduced, ultimately, to the ante- and post-diluvian stages of the old Law of the Old Testament and the third and continuing stage following the coming of Christ. In such simple schemata, what place is there for more qualified demographic movements, taking place in shorter and more specific historical periods?

In fact, although the phrases expressing elementary dichotomies of 'few' or 'many' and broad stages in history remained, they came to be overlaid by more varied categories. There could be phrases for size or degree of increase of population: 'a moderate number', 'a great multiplication', 'a greater multiplication', 'a very great multiplication', 'strongly multiplied' (*modicus numerus, magna/maior/maxima multiplicatio, valde multiplicatus*). Times past are more qualified, perhaps to be vaguer and thereby escape the explicit confines of Old Testament time: 'in olden times', 'sometimes' (*antiquitus, quandoque*). The strait-jacket of combining pairs such as 'few/many' with theologico-historical periodization could be cut through. Thus Thomas of Strasbourg will write, on the period after Abel, 'afterwards men were *always more* multiplied'.[20] Commentators

[18] Albert, *In sententias*, IV. xxxiii. 7; xxx. 299a: *instabat multitudo pertrahentium ad idolatriam, et paucitas Deum colentium.*

[19] See above Ch. 2 and n. 156.

[20] Thomas of Strasbourg, *In sententias*, IV. xxvi. art. 3; ii. 146ra: *semper homines postea fuerunt magis multiplicati.*

raise questions about, or look at, more specific periods. Thus, for example, the fewness of the faithful which justified plurality of wives: were there not other times when the faithful were few? So Peter of Tarentaise raised for debate and refutation the point that the multiplication which was the cause of dispensing [monogamy] with the fathers was just as necessary in the primitive church.[21]

We need to avoid a forced, modernizing reading of these texts, and to acknowledge the long forward shadow cast by the Lombard. The genre remained conservative. Commentary on this particular text and on these particular words meant the continuing presence of the Lombard's cumbersome categories, from which the commentators' thoughts about population never entirely escaped. Nor did these thoughts ever acquire complete transparency and, while there are important developments, there is no breakthrough comparable to the invention of the idea of sex-ratio. We need also to avoid being blind to the degree to which theologians did in fact write about population and articulate notions of variation, sufficiency, and the marriage-rate. The distinctions discussed in this chapter experienced the general sea-change undergone by *Sentences* commentaries, which was described in Chapter 2 above, with flesh being put on bare bones, as things were expanded and spelled out. And, as we shall see (in section 4 below) similitudes played an important role in quickening the texts and supplying them with realistic colour: comparisons of population with the family, almsgiving, and an army.

5.1 *The precept to marry*

One of the busiest and most influential periods in the production of later commentaries was the decade beginning in 1249, which saw those of Albert the Great, Bonaventure, Thomas Aquinas, and Peter of Tarentaise. Aquinas used much of Albert, and Peter of Tarentaise used both Bonaventure and Albert while also striking out independently. Ninety years after the Lombard much has changed. A theme has been turned into a question, which is treated formally, with statement of question, pro and con arguments, reply, and replies to the specific arguments on the losing side. This form is permitting and encouraging systematic examination of central ideas such as 'precept' and new ideas or themes, such as the relation of individual good to common good and the distinction between what binds every individual and what has to be fulfilled by some but not all. Shared by all four, this form is still found, only slightly changed, in the early fourteenth century.

Questions have been emerging, in distinction 33 on whether plurality of wives was ever licit, or whether virginity is licit or is preferable to marriage, and in

[21] Peter of Tarentaise, *In sententias*, IV. xxxiii. Q. 1 art. 2; iv. 334b. He was followed in this by the commentary of the Franciscan Walter of Bruges on book 4, distinction 33, on the question of the dispensation of plurality of wives in the Old Testament, Vatican, MS Chigi B.VI.94, fol. 169r: *in primitiva ecclesia maior fuit raritas colencium Deum quam in tempore legis scripte, sed tunc non fuit dispensatum.* The commentary is postdated by its citation of Aristotle's *Politics.*

distinction 26 on marriage as a precept. When and how did precept emerge as a question? Writing between 1160 and 1170, Gandulph of Bologna wrote under a heading which suggests it: 'Until when marriage was a precept' (*Quousque fuit praeceptum matrimonium*).[22] But Peter of Poitiers simply repeated the succession of precept and indulgence,[23] and the question is not present in the questions of Simon of Tournai (d. 1203). William of Auxerre (writing probably post-1218) raised 'the condition of marriage in the first state [of man]' as a question—and his emphatic comment on the current cessation of the precept will be quoted later—but the precept is still not made into a question.[24] Alexander of Hales's gloss on the *Sentences* (between 1223 and 1227) draws near. In commentary on book 2 he says that Peter the Lombard 'deals here with precept concerning generative power.... Through this precept, "Increase and multiply", it seems that virginal chastity is forbidden ...'[25] He is very brief, and in commentary on book 4 he says, 'One asks if it [marriage] was in precept and when' and then refers back to his few words in book 2.[26] So Alexander states the question, but does not deal with it as a question. In the manuscript Douai 434, which preserves 572 theological questions from Paris in the 1230s, the questions on marriage do not include the precept. It seems, then, that precept emerged as a fully-fledged and treatable question some time between Alexander in the 1220s and Albert in 1249.

Albert asked only whether in its first institution marriage was under precept, although he included the question of its possible return, a theme which was not taken up again for several decades.[27] While Bonaventure is still confined to 'Will the institution of marriage have been under precept?',[28] Thomas breaks the mould. He formulates only one question, one which turns the spotlight onto *now*: 'Does marriage *still* remain under precept?'[29] There is then a comprehensive alignment of approaches by Peter of Tarentaise, who devotes one question to 'The obligation of marriage', and breaks it down into three articles, each of which is a question. 'First, was it instituted under precept before sin? Second, was it instituted under precept after sin? Third, does this precept still remain?'[30]

Paths then diverge. Richard of Middleton follows Peter of Tarentaise's triad, while many later Dominicans, such as Vidal de Four, Durand of St Pourçain, and

[22] Gandulph of Bologna, *Sententiarum libri quatuor*, IV. ccxvii, ed. J. De Walter (Vienna and Wrocław, 1924), p. 507. On Gandulph see also Landgraf, *Scolastique naissante*, p. 139.

[23] Peter of Poitiers, *Sententiarum libri quinque*, V. xv; *PL* 211, 1258. Peter was writing before 1170, Langraf, *Scolastique naissante*, p. 142.

[24] William of Auxerre, *Summa aurea*, II. ix. 2 Qu. 4; XVII, 252–3.

[25] Alexander of Hales, *In sententias*, II. xx. 1; ii. 174.

[26] Ibid., IV. xxvi. 6; iv. 457.

[27] Albert, *In sententias*, IV. xxvi. art. 10; xxx. 111a–13a: *An prima institutio matrimonii habuit praeceptum*. Albert's sixth contra argument is that the precept still (*adhuc*) seems to bind everyone.

[28] Bonaventure, *In sententias*, IV. xxvi art. 1 Qu. 3; iv. 664a–5b: *Utrum institutio matrimonii fuerit sub praecepto* (awkward Latin—it is not the *institution* of marriage which was under precept but marrying itself).

[29] Aquinas, *In sententias*, IV. xxvi. Qu. 1 art. 2; viii. 918b–9a: *Utrum matrimonium adhuc maneat sub praecepto.*

[30] Peter of Tarentaise, *In sententias*, IV. xxvi. Q. 2; iv. 284b–86b: *An matrimonium fuerit in praecepto ante peccatum; An matrimonium fuerit in praecepto post peccatum; An matrimonium sit adhuc in praecepto.*

Peter of la Palud follow Aquinas with a question which is in the present tense, even if it does not contain 'still' (*adhuc*). There is proliferation, as the question of precept turns up in many other settings.[31] For the sake of economy and control the current chapter is confined mainly to its appearance in distinction 26.

While the emergence of formal questions is a constituent element of the history of scholastic method, it is not only this. One question emerges while another does not. One question which emerged about marriage and precept was contemporary, and it directed enquiry *against* rather than for marriage and fertility. 'Is it still under precept?' By the first half of the fourteenth century there had been one further development, in which an older theme (marriage binding on all or only some) became a question. It is exemplified by an anonymous commentator, in an Erfurt manuscript, asking 'whether *all* are bound to marry',[32] and likewise Thomas of Strasbourg writing 'about its obligation, that is, whether *each* man is bound by the necessity of this precept to marry?'[33]

'Increase and multiply'. Does the precept to marry still bind? Investigation of the nature of precepts led the way. There are affirmative and negative precepts: 'Thou shalt . . .' and 'Thou shalt not . . .' . An affirmative precept binds only according to place, time, and circumstances.[34] Here is Peter of Tarentaise writing on this point. 'An affirmative [precept] binds always but not for always (*semper sed non ad semper*), in fact [only] in an appropriate place and a necessary time. The precept of marriage as a task (*officium*) was affirmative, not negative. So it did not bind for always but only according to appropriateness and necessity. As long as there was necessity of multiplication'. And he goes on to spell out this necessity.

The question about the licitness of virginity led to the same point via a slightly different road. Virginity was against the precept of marriage, as also against Old Testament hostility to sterility. A virtue, however, relates to 'circumstances'. In Aquinas's words, we should look to 'the mean of virtue [which is] taken as according to the proportion of circumstances in the light of right reason'. 'Time', meaning the conditions of a period, is a 'circumstance'. If the precept of marriage is being carried out in some other way, then virginity is measured according to circumstance. Whether marriage or virginity is higher depends on the condition of the time.[35]

31 In commentary on book 2 of the *Sentences* the theme can turn up with the institution of marriage in paradise—would the first pair have sinned in not having sex, and thus going against the precept? On book 4 and distinction 26 the precept may turn up under a broader question on marriage and natural law. In distinction 33 the treatment of virginity as a virtue introduces the further question 'Is it licit?', in part because of its going against the precept 'Increase and multiply', and in this way it can crop up in quodlibetic questions on virginity.

32 Erfurt, StadtBibliothek, MS Fol. 108, fol. 188rb: *utrum omnes obligentur ad matrimonium.* See Stegmüller, *Repertorium,* no. 990.

33 Thomas of Strasbourg, *In sententias,* IV. xxvi; ii. 44va: *de eius obligatione, puta, utrum quilibet homo de necessitate praecepti teneatur ad contrahendum matrimonium?*

34 Alexander of Hales, *Summa,* II. i, Inq. IV, Tract. III, Q. 2, c. IV; ii. 710.

35 Aquinas, *In sententias,* IV. xxxiii. Qu. 3 art. 2; viii. 978b: *medium virtutis accipitur secundum proportionem circumstantiarum ad rationem rectam; et . . . tempus est una de circumstantiis.*

The questions about the precept of marriage and the relative worth of marriage and virginity both pointed to time and place, and 'necessity' or 'opportuneness' in a particular time and place. The elementary point about multitude was omnipresent: precept for multiplication; precept ceasing when man has multiplied. Much discussion related to the past. When has the precept been revoked in the past? The answer could be elementary, just the supersession of the fertility of the old Law by the praise of virginity in the new, or it could be several times, in a varied and detailed theological history of the multitude. If the precept was revoked because its cause, multiplication, ceased, could it return if the cause, need for multiplication, returned? And could it thus bind again in some future time? Here, as we shall see later in this chapter, minds were freer than usual when spelling out the pre-condition, decline in the multitude. The temporal framework, which was provided by speculations about the relationship between precept and multitude in the past and possible future, suggests heightened awareness in a commentator about what he was doing when he turned to ask about 'time', 'place', 'opportuneness' and 'necessity' in the present: now.

5.2 *The common good of the multitude*

The analysis of the precept to marry as a member of the group 'precepts' threw up a further question. Some precepts bind every single person in a multitude. Other precepts are of the sort which do not bind each and every person. If these precepts are being obeyed by some people, others are not bound. How did this point apply to the precept about marriage?

One impulse towards the obvious answer to this, that the precept did not bind everyone, came from the development of the notion of the 'common good', its incorporation into discussions of marriage and virginity, and its application to the particular case of the human race regarded as a multitude. Although no treatise specifically devoted to the common good was written until the Florentine Dominican Remigio dei Girolami's *De Bono communi* around 1300, the theme had long had a strong presence in western thought.[36] John of Salisbury is one mid-twelfth-century figure who played with it, drawing upon patristic texts, works by Cicero and Seneca, and Roman Law. Vocabulary included 'the useful', 'common utility', 'public good', 'the state' (*res publica*), and the 'common good'. There were two important accretions in the mid-thirteenth century: a Roman Law gloss by Accursius which conveniently gathered together the principal Roman legal references to the theme of the common good, and the availability and reading of Aristotle's *Ethics*, whose language of common and private goods was added to and became pre-eminent in an area of thought which had a long patristic and Roman tradition.

[36] M. S. Kempshall, *The Common Good in Late Medieval Political Thought* (Oxford, 1999), pp. 14–25.

'Good' had had a long existence in theological discussion of marriage, which was dominated by Augustine's trio of goods, faith, offspring, and sacrament. The 'good of offspring' was the fertility of any two individuals marrying. Had Adam and Eve not sinned it would have been the good of multiplication until the completion of the numbers of the elect. The notion of the common good intruded into discussion the notion of an intermediate good, the good of the multitude in the existing world, now, and not under the shadow of the end of time. This intermediate good has a near neighbour in marriage and a 'social' good, that is to say, a good concerning relations. One of its goods or worthy causes was, as formulated by Peter the Lombard but in Walter of Mortagne's words, 'the reconciliation of enemies and the reintegration of peace', and, as expanded by William of Auxerre, 'the spreading of charity, the reconciliation of enemies, the settling of wars, the pacification of realms, and suchlike'.[37] Even before the translation of the *Politics* there was a broader view of another good of marriages, as building-blocks in kingdoms, as we have seen in William of Auvergne, and after the introduction of the *Politics* this good was presented more systematically. Thus Vidal du Four: 'according to positive or civil law marriage is for the preservation of realms. For through marriage the household is generated, consequently villages, consequently towns, consequently the realm. Kings and emperors therefore have dealt with marriage insofar as the preservation of the realm is their [concern]. For the realm over which the legislator presides could not be preserved without men multiplying, in fact it would perish through the death of men.'[38] While relating marriage as a whole to a good of social relations or a wider good, theologians also did the same to particular aspects of marriage regulation, present or past. Prohibited degrees of marriage forced people to marry outside their kin,[39] and thus extended links of friendship and marriage, while divorce in the Old Testament, preventing uxoricide or worse, was permitted, in Alexander of Hales's words, 'to keep the community standing' (*ut stet communitas*).[40]

The consideration of marriage and good in these neighbouring areas had encouraged two things. One was a sense of marriage as an institution or

[37] Peter the Lombard, *Sententiae*, IV. xxx. 3; ii. 441; William of Auxerre, *Summa aurea*, IV. xvii. 2; XIX, 383.

[38] In a *reportatio* of questions on the fourth book of the *Sentences* from Montpellier, 1295/6, Vatican, MS Vat. Lat. 1095, fol. 43ra: *Matrimonium autem, ut est de dictamine legis civilis sive iuris positivo* [sic] *est ad conservacionem regnorum. Per matrimonium autem generatur familia, per consequens vicus, per consequens villa, per consequens regnum. Reges ergo et imperatores sic de matrimonio tractaverunt in quantum suus eius* [blotted; could be: *cuius*] *est conservacio regni. Regnum enim, cui preest legislator, conservari non posset nisi homines multiplicarentur, ymo periret per mortem hominum.* For an example of language fusing Augustinian and Aristotelian goods, see Peter Aureoli, citing the advocacy of community of wives and property in the third book of the *Politics* and writing that this was *contra bonum prolis, contra bonum familie, et contra bonum civitatis*; *In sententias*, IV. xxvi–xxvii. 2, in the (falsely attributed) Peter of Aquila, *Quaestiones in quatuor libros sententiarum* (Speyer, before 1487, unfoliated).

[39] In some authors the history of fewer degrees of prohibition (in early population), then more degrees of prohibition, and then again fewer degrees of prohibition with the Lateran Council of 1215, becomes an intertwined history of population, waxing and waning degrees of charity in the human race, and the regulation of marriage.

[40] Alexander of Hales, *Quaestiones*, LIX. i; iii. 1161.

system within a general community, which is in turn affected by the precise characteristics of the marriage system, and the other was some autonomy in the discussion of marriage and such other goods. There are parallels when we turn to the specific theme of marriage and the common good of humans considered as a multitude, whose vocabulary was emerging in the early thirteenth century. In his questions (pre-1236) Alexander of Hales divided goods into 'worthy', 'expedient', and 'pleasurable' (*honesta, expedientia, delectabilia*). Multiplying was an expedient good. When comparing marriage and virginity he used definitions taken from Seneca to consider a worthy good, that which was arduous, commodious (or expedient), and secure. His conclusion was that both virginity and marriage possessed expedient and worthy goods, but when compared and examined under the headings of single goods, marriage had more of expedient good and virginity more of worthy good. 'However, if "worthy" is understood in the way that it is when peace in the city is called "worthy", then marriage has more . . . because in marriage there is love, which is the glue which sticks spouses together.'[41] Alexander's approach to this wider good is cumbersome and indirect, and though by 'expedient' good he presumably means the preservation of the human race, he does not spell this out. Another early text is crisper. William of Auxerre refers briefly to what is 'not more fruitful or useful to the state (*utile rei publicae*), or to the Church militant, or to the Church triumphant'.[42] The language is more advanced, as is also the separateness of the three spheres in which what is 'useful' is to be weighed, the civil community and the Church in this world in the first two categories, and in the third the completion of the numbers of the elect.

When we turn to Albert's presentation of the question of the precept of marriage, we see reference to Aristotle's *Ethics*, the hierarchy of common and personal goods, and 'common good' as the good of human beings considered as a multitude.[43] All of this is repeated and becomes commonplace, handed down through Aquinas. Another 1250s commentator, Peter of Tarentaise, also produced formulations which were to become commonplace, writing that marriage in the post-lapsarian state was for 'the preservation and multiplication of human nature', a matter which 'is common [necessity] relating to common utility, not the necessity of a person', and, in relation to the continuing precept of marriage, that 'the good of the species is greater and more necessary than the good of the individual'.[44]

[41] Alexander of Hales, *Quaestiones*, LVII. ii; iii. 1123–4: *Si tamen honestum dicitur secundum quod pax in civitate dicitur honestum, sic coniugium . . . quia in coniugio est amor, qui est glutinum coniugum ad invicem.*

[42] William of Auxerre, *Summa aurea*, III. xxiii. 2 Qu. 6; XVIIIa, 436.

[43] Albert, *In sententias*, IV. xxvi, art. 10; xxx. 112a–b: *Ponderatio* [see Ecclesiasticus 26: 20] *boni communis praeponderat quantumcumque bono personali, praecipue tale bonum quale est salus speciei humanae. Et hoc est quod dicit Aristoteles quod si bonum est bonum hominis, melius erit quod civitatis, et maximum bonum quod gentis* (The 'price' of the common good outweighs any personal good—especially such a good as the preservation of the human species. And this is what Aristotle says, that if a good is a good of man, [the good] of the city will be better, and the greatest good [will be the good] of a people'). See Aristotle, *Ethics* I. i, 1094^{b}6–11; AL xxvi. 1–3, p. 142.

[44] Peter of Tarentaise, *In sententias*, IV. xxvi. Q. 2 art. 2; iv. 285b: *naturae humanae conservatio et*

Let us move on swiftly in time, to after 1300. Robert Cowton: 'The fruit of offspring is ordained to the common good of the city or the common good, virginal good however to a particular good and [a good] of the private person';[45] Guiraud d'Ot: 'the community of men is bound to the procuration of offspring' and the act for the preservation of the species is by natural law;[46] the Erfurt anonymous: 'the multitude of the human race is one of the goods which pertains to the community . . . The common good of the multitude as a multitude is everywhere to be found.' The Erfurt anonymous continued thus:

> Since the multitude of the human race is one of the goods which pertains to the community, it is not necessary for each person always to be bound [to marry]. But there are different commandments according to the diversification of circumstances. So, it was under precept in the beginning and [also] after the flood, when there were few men and the human race could not otherwise be multiplied . . . since there is not [now] this necessity, and the good of contemplation is a good of the community and also the individual . . . men are not bound. If, however, that which existed in some state [were to return]—that there were few men, as there were [once]—each person would be bound to marry.[47]

This slightly clumsy prose contains the three main developments which were brought about by systematic analysis of the precept to marry and the intrusion of the common good of the multitude. First, there was the notion of the good of the preservation of the species being carried out by some but not all of the community. Secondly, there was comment on current necessity. Thirdly, through speculation about the relation of marriage and virginity to specific conditions, alongside past revocations and possible future return of the precept to marry, the notion of proportions marrying as response to degrees of populousness slowly acquired greater prominence and clarity.

5.3 *Diversification of tasks in the multitude*

'Although it is a greater good, this good can be sufficiently preserved by others':[48] so Peter of Tarentaise on the good of preservation of the species.

There was a tradition of interpreting particular Old Testament figures as representing rulers in the Church, religious celibates, and the married, while the

multiplicatio . . . communis respiciens utilitatem communem, non necessitatem personae; IV. xxvi, Q. 2 art. 3; IV, 286a: *maius est bonum speciei et magis necessarium quam bonum individui.*

[45] See n. 79 below.

[46] Paris, BN, MS Lat. 3068, fol. 58va: *communitas hominum obligatur ad procuracionem prolis.*

[47] Erfurt, Stadtbibliothek, MS Fol 108, fol. 188rb: *cum multitudo generis humani sit de bonis que pertinent ad communitatem, non oportet quod quilibet semper obligetur, sed secundum diversificacionem circumstanciarum sunt diversa mandata. Unde cum a principio, cum essent homines pauci et non posset aliter muliplicari genus humanum, fuit in precepto et post diluvium . . . cum non sit necessitas huius, et bonum contemplacionis est bonum communitatis et eciam individui . . . ideo non obligantur. Si tamen rediret illud quod in aliquo statu fuit, quod essent pauci homines sicut erant, omnis matrimonio teneretur.*

[48] Peter of Tarentaise, *In sententias*, IV. xxvi. Q. 2 art. 3; iv. 286a: *Quamvis sit maius bonum, tamen illud bonum sufficienter per alios conservari potest.*

varying fruits of virginity, widowhood and marriage, and the theme of comparison of virginity and marriage were patristic commonplaces. To a reader who lifted his eyes from these topics and looked out onto the world of living clerical and religious celibates on the one hand and married people on the other, one thing must have been self-evident, the division into one group of those who in principle did not generate and another of those who in principle did. Nevertheless, it would be anachronistic to take as already given what is coming into clear light only now: the formal statement of diversification of tasks in the multitude, generating or not generating, and the presentation of this in these terms as a theme for examination and discussion. It took time.

The theme has come to be stated in these terms and with transparent clarity by the mid-thirteenth century, and it is elaborated. Albert distinguished tasks under precept which could only be carried out by each individual, such as eating, and those which need to be carried out only by some, such as preservation of the species.[49] Aquinas's reply smoothly expands Albert's spare statement, distinguishing the obligation to perfect the individual from the obligation to perfect the multitude. Each binds in different ways. 'Not every single man is obliged by way of precept [to those things which pertain to the multitude]. Otherwise each man would be obliged to engage in farming and building and tasks of that sort which are necessary to the human community. But the inclination of nature is satisfied when diverse things are done by diverse people.'[50] He expands the theme of diversity. 'Human nature commonly inclines [people] to different jobs and actions... It inclines one person more to one of these jobs, another to another. And from this diversity together with divine providence, which moderates all things, it happens that one person chooses one job, like farming, while another [chooses] another [job]. And so it also happens that some choose married life, others contemplative [life]. And from this no danger threatens.'[51]

In the old schema of three orders of men in the world, those who fight, those who pray, and those who till the soil, diversity of task implied complementariness: soldiers defended everyone, monks prayed for everyone, and peasants supplied the food. Whereas the accent in Aquinas's *Sentences* commentary is on diversity and complementariness is only implicit, in the amplification of the theme in his later *Summa theologiae* both are explicit. Some generate for all, others procure spiritual advance for all.[52] Given the usually colourless character of *Sentences* commentaries, the penchant for similitudes which was displayed by theologians

[49] Albert, *In sententias*, IV. xxvi. art. 10; xxx. 111a.

[50] Aquinas, *In sententias*, IV. xxvi. Qu. 1 art. 2; viii. 919a: *Non obligatur quilibet homo per modum praecepti; alias quilibet homo obligaretur ad agriculturam et aedificatoriam, et hujusmodi officia, quae sunt necessaria communitati humanae: sed inclinationi naturae satisfit cum per diversos diversa complentur.*

[51] Ibid.: *natura humana communiter communiter ad diversa officia et actus inclinat... unum magis inclinat ad unum illorum officiorum, alium ad aliud. Et ex hac diversitate simul cum divina providentia, quae omnia moderatur, contingit quod unus eligit unum officium, ut agriculturam, alius aliud; et sic etiam contingit quod quidam eligunt matrimonialem vitam, et quidam contemplativam. Unde nullum periculum imminet.*

[52] The text is quoted below.

when they came to address the diversity of tasks of those generating and those not generating is remarkable. The images or similitudes take three forms. A rich stream of images in the Old Testament and the writings of the fathers, on the one hand, and surrounding agriculture on the other, would always suggest one fundamental group of metaphors or similitudes for marriage and virginity,[53] and it is unsurprising to see the fertile field as marriage and the sterile field as virginity appearing in Bonaventure[54] and Peter of Tarentaise, and in those who copied them. Farming has already been seen in Aquinas's commentary on the *Sentences*, quoted above. Comparing the harder work of marriage to the lighter work of virginity, for example, Robert of Melun had used the analogy of peasants and farmers, who work harder than contemplative men.[55] It is used thus by Peter of Tarentaise to illustrate diversity. 'One can say that no one is bound . . . because the necessity [for every individual to generate] does not occur, since it is sufficiently supplied by others. Similarly, if there were no other workers on the land, even bishops would be bound to dig the land. [But], since others now suffice [to dig the land], [bishops] are better occupied in more useful things.'[56]

The second similitude is military, and it appears in Aquinas's *Summa theologiae*, where in his treatment of diversity of tasks he expanded what he had written in his earlier *Sentences* commentary:

> A duty can be in two ways. One way, that it has to be carried out by one person: and this duty cannot be passed over without sin. Another, however, is a duty which has to be carried out by the multitude. And not each person from the multitude is bound to carry out this duty. There are many things necessary for the community where one person is not enough to carry them out, but they are carried out when one does this [and] another does that. The precept of the law of nature given to man about eating necessarily must be carried out by each person: otherwise the individual cannot be preserved. But the precept given about generation relates to the whole multitude of men: to whom it is necessary not only that they should multiply physically but also that they should advance spiritually. And therefore there is sufficient provision for the human multitude when some devote themselves to physical generation: some, however, abstaining from this, devote themselves to contemplation of divine things, for the beauty and salvation of the whole human race.

The point is immediately hammered home with a similitude. 'Just as in an army some guard the castles, some bear the standards, some fight with swords: all of these are duties for the multitude, but they cannot be carried out by one person [alone].'[57] Castles framed the life of Thomas Aquinas, who had been born (probably)

[53] In the case of William of Auvergne the agricultural imagery came from the Koran.

[54] Bonaventure, *In sententias*, IV. xxxiii. art. 2 Qu. 3; iv. 755a.

[55] Robert de Melun, *Questiones [theologice] de Epistolis Pauli*, ed. R. M. Martin, Spicilegium Sacrum Lovaniense 18 (Louvain, 1938), p. 200: *rustici et agricultores gloriosiores essent viris contemplativis, quia magis laborant.* Martin says the work was written between 1145 and 1155, ibid., p. lviii.

[56] Peter of Tarentaise, *In sententias*, IV. xxvi. Q. 2 art. 3; iv. 286a–b: *Potest dici quod nullus tenetur . . . quia necessitas non occurit, cum per alios sufficienter suppleatur. Sicut etiamsi non essent alii laboratores terrarum, etiam episcopi terras fodere tenerentur, nunc vero cum alii sufficiant, melius in utilioribus occupantur.*

[57] Aquinas, *Summa theologiae*, IIaIIae, Qu. 152 art. 2; Blackfriars edn., xliii. 174–7. When commenting on the injunction to multiply in Genesis, later Dominicans copied Aquinas's castle image—examples are

in the Aquino castle of Roccasecca and who was to spend his penultimate days in his sister's castle at Maenza. While the image is pictorial and colourful it is also very general. It carries a hint of the use of the image of swords in generalizing thought about authority and power, whether the spiritual and temporal swords or the sword wielded by the prince in battle and justice, and in so doing it exemplifies the stylistic proximity of demographic and political thought.

The third similitude is a family. In particular, it is of parents, represented by the father, children, and children's duty to their parents. Two parallels suggested this: a duty which is under precept; and a duty where necessity had to be supplied. The fourth commandment, 'Honour thy father', was usually seen as including children's duty to 'minister necessities' to parents,[58] and tricky aspects of the precise mode of this material support were a standard theme in later thirteenth-century quodlibetic questions.[59] The analogy with the duty to support a father appeared in Peter of Tarentaise. 'Therefore as long as there was the necessity for multiplication, it [the precept] bound. Now, however, it does not bind, because now the human race has sufficiently multiplied, and there are many through whom the necessity can be supplied: just as I am not bound to supply the necessity of [my] father, when he does not have necessity, or when another sufficiently supplies his necessity.'[60] By the time of the commentary of an early Cistercian master, possibly Guy de l'Aumône (probably mid-1260s), the image is spelled out in more detail. Addressing the question whether the precept to marry was still binding, he wrote thus: 'An affirmative precept does not bind forever but only for time and place. Whence if a father has twelve children and one [child] sufficiently "honours" his father giving [him] necessities [of life], the other [children] are not bound to give to him but can spend [their money] on other legitimate uses.'[61]

The image persisted. Where Peter of Tarentaise included two elements, when there is need, and the possibility of others supplying, Thomas of Strasbourg emphasized *when.* 'In modern times', he wrote, 'because things are as they are now, no one is bound or obliged de facto to contract marriage. For, just as we have an affirmative precept about helping parents, . . . nevertheless when the father is

Dominic Grima (BN, MS Lat. 362, fol. 25va) and Peter of la Palud (Naples, Biblioteca Nazionale, MS VI. D. 74, fol. 59va).

[58] This would be found in comment on the repetitions of the fourth commandment in Eccles. 3: 9 and Eph. 6: 2.

[59] Examples are Thomas (1266), the use of a dowry gained through marriage to support a father one could not otherwise support; with Gérard of Abbeville (between 1270 and 1272), the binding nature of the precept when it meant materially supporting an evil-doing father; with Henry of Ghent (1287) and Godfrey of Fontaines (1292), a Christian son's duty materially to support an infidel father.

[60] Peter of Tarentaise, *In sententias*, IV. xxvi. Q. 2 art. 3; iv. 286a: *Quamdiu ergo fuit necessitas multiplicationis, obligavit, nunc vero non obligat quia iam sufficienter multiplicatum est genus humanum, et sunt multi per quos necessitas potest suppleri: sicut etiam non teneor supplere necessitatem patris, quando non habet necessitatem, vel quando alius sufficienter supplet eius necessitatem.*

[61] Paris, BN, MS Lat. 14911, fol. 100rb: *si aliquis pater habeat xii filios et unus sufficienter honoret patrem danda necessaria, alii non tenentur ei dare sed possunt in alios licitos usus expandare* [sic]. The commentary is on a question raised in relation to book 2, distinction 20, whether the first parents would have sinned in not having sex and thus going against the precept.

not in need, a son is not bound to help his father.'[62] Another writer, Peter of la Palud, moved away from the broader and less extreme case of a general duty to support parents, and turned to the more extreme case of material support of those who are not defined by physical relationship but only by need: alms-giving to the indigent. He produced the comparison when dealing with a question of revocation of the precept to marry before the flood. 'It is like this. If no one is indigent the precept about giving alms is not for this reason revoked. But for a while no one is bound [by it]. When necessity returns, however, anyone who sees [necessity] and can help is bound [to help].'[63] Here in the first half of the fourteenth century we see imagery becoming more urgent, with this emphasis on *when* and Peter's turning to an exclusively economic similitude.

5.4 *Sufficient preservation of the multitude*

When analysing marriage theologians repeated Augustine's 'good of offspring'. While their 'procreationism' can be overemphasized by anyone who only reads this and does not go on to read the same theologians writing in an understanding way about the problems of rearing many children, it would be idle to deny that this good is a good of fertility. Also not to be ignored is an older sentiment which was expressed in the Old Testament, 'In the multitude of the people is the dignity of the king: and in the small number of people the dishonour of the prince' (Prov. 14: 28). This is found as a commonplace in the genre of 'praise of the city' for its populousness,[64] for example, or in the passage about a realm's need for men written by Vidal du Four (above, p. 122). However, the Augustinian good was the good of individual marriages, not of many marriages in relation to the multitude, and the text from Proverbs and its descendants are thoughts in a neighbouring area, about political communities and their power, prestige, and military resources. Neither are about the multitude viewed as multitude. And in thought about the multitude as multitude we find a different note.

Let us recapitulate. The precept applies according to opportuneness and necessity of time and place. Past revocations of the precept with necessity ceasing, and possible future return with necessity re-appearing, are combining to turn the spotlight on the time between the past and the future. Formerly that intervening time was vaguely and broadly post-Old Testament, but increasingly it is 'now', 'modern times', 'things as they are now'. The common good of the human race considered as a multitude is now considered. What was this common good? It was the *salus* of the human race: its preservation. 'Preservation' here meant

[62] See n. 78 below.

[63] Peter of la Palud, *In sententias*, IV. xxvi Qu. 3; 140va: *sicut si nullus indigeat preceptum de elemosina non propter hoc est revocatum sed interim nullus obligatur. Superveniente autem necessitate obligatur quicunque qui videt eam et potest subvenire.*

[64] See Remigio dei' Girolami on Florence's population, in Ch. 14 below.

continuation, not expansion, and it was hedged about with qualifications which emphasized this, and emphasized it in contemporary circumstances. The different note is struck by the coming together of one old theme—that once there has been multiplication the precept ceases—and the increasing use of two phrases: 'sufficient multiplication' and the implicitly critical 'there is a great multiplication'. There is a stark contrast between the text which the Lombard put together in the late 1150s and the most popular and influential of the theological treatises being written in Paris in the early thirteenth century, William of Auxerre's, *Summa aurea*. Where the former was bland, not focused on present time, and devoid of 'the world is full', this is how William wrote, when discussing both the cessation of the precept and the supersession of the pre-eminence of marriage: 'Now, however, marriage is by way of remedy, not precept, rather by permission. For now the people of God is increased throughout the whole world, and everywhere innumerable marriages sufficiently generate children of God' (*Modo vero matrimonium magis est ad remedium nec est in precepto, sed potius in permissione, quoniam modo populus Dei augmentatus est per totum mundum, et innumerabiles nuptie ubique modo generant filios Dei ad sufficientiam*).[65]

In William the subject was still the people of God, and the repeated 'now' was simply laid over the elementary two-stage theological history of precept-remedy. With Peter of Tarentaise the human species takes centre stage, and there enters a distinction between expansion and continuation of the multitude. In the first of his three articles on the obligation of marriage, dealing with the first institution of marriage, he spells this out. 'Marriage was first instituted not just for the preservation but also for the multiplication of the species.' This is repeated in the next article, on marriage's second institution after sin. 'There is a double necessity for using marriage after sin, the first being the preservation and multiplication of human nature, the other the avoidance of fornication. The first is common, relating to common utility.' But at a certain point, he indicates, 'preservation' continues but 'multiplication' ceases, for he continues immediately: 'as far as this first cause was concerned, marriage was under precept until sufficient multiplication had come about.' This is repeated: 'a precept until the time of sufficient multiplication'. The third article, on whether the precept still binds, serves to apply the description of sufficient multiplication to 'now'. 'As long as there was necessity of multiplication [the precept to marry] bound, now however it does not bind, because now the human race has multiplied sufficiently.'[66]

'Multiplication' is *expansion* of the multitude, while its 'preservation' (*conservatio*) is its *continuation*. As distinct from expansion, 'preservation' has become

[65] William of Auxerre, *Summa aurea*, II. ix. 2 Qu. 4; XVII, 253.

[66] Peter of Tarentaise, *In sententias*, IV. xxvi. Q. 2 art. 1; iv. 285a: *Non tantum institutum est propter conservationem sed etiam propter multiplicationem speciei*; art. 2; iv. 285b: *Duplex est necessitas utendi matrimonium post peccatum, una est naturae humanae conservatio et multiplicatio, altera fornicationis evitatio. Prima est communis respiciens utilitatem communem, non necessitatem communem. Ideo quoad primam fuit matrimonium in praecepto, usquequo facta est sufficiens multiplicatio . . . praeceptum usque ad tempus multiplicationis sufficientis.* Article 3 is quoted in n. 60 above.

an elementary form of the modern phrase 'stable population'. The word 'sufficient' saturates Peter of Tarentaise's articles on the precept:[67] 'until sufficient multiplication had occurred', 'until the time of sufficient multiplication', 'because now the human race has been multiplied sufficiently', 'when someone else supplies his necessity sufficiently', 'this necessity is supplied sufficiently by others', 'this good can be preserved sufficiently by others', 'since this is supplied efficiently by others' and 'since others suffice'. Unspecific though Peter of Tarentaise's notion of 'sufficient' multitude may be, it unmistakably leans towards moderation. And this word 'sufficient', as adjective or adverb, is what crops up most frequently in later thirteenth- or early fourteenth-century *Sentences* commentary discussions of the precept. There were two further developments: greater emphasis on contemporary conditions; and the notion of the expedience in these conditions of not marrying.

Both are found in Richard of Middleton, who preferred referring to God's people than to the human race. He projects both into the past as well as describing them in the present. On precept after sin he begins by following Peter of Tarentaise: 'it was under precept even after sin, until sufficient multiplication of men had come about.' In what immediately follows Richard went further than Peter. 'And there were so many devoting themselves to this work that it was better for some to remain in virginal or widows' chastity than for all to aim at matrimonial union.'[68] Adjectives used for quantity are now more shaded, and Richard continues with expediency when he turns to *now*. 'While there was a moderate number of men worshipping God, this precept obliged. Its cause now ceases. For there is a *great* multiplication of men worshipping God, and there are so many devoting themselves to matrimonial union, that it is expedient for many to remain in virginal or widows' continence.'[69]

Later, with Thomas of Strasbourg, the contemporary emphasis is even more marked. 'In modern times, because things are as they are now, no one is bound or obliged de facto to contract marriage. . . . there are now so many men who willingly contract marriage that the world is virtually filled up with men. Therefore those who wish to abstain are not bound to contract. I say this specifically about now or about [a time when] things are as they are now.'[70]

[67] His second and third articles, that is to say, on whether marriage was under precept after sin, and whether it is still under precept.

[68] Richard, *In sententias*, IV. xxvi. art. 3 Qu. 2; iv. 406b: *fuit in praecepto etiam post peccatum, quousque facta fuit sufficiens multiplicatio hominum ad cultum divinum, et quod tot fuerunt vacantes illi operi, quod melius erat aliquos manere in castitate virginali, vel viduali, quam omnes copulae matrioniali intendere.*

[69] Ibid., *In sententias*, IV. xxvi. art. 3 Qu. 3; iv. 407a: *quandiu fuit modicus numerus hominum Deum colentium, illud praeceptum obligavit. Quae causa modo cessat, quia magna est multiplicatio hominum Deum colentium, et tot sunt vacantes copulae matrimoniali, quod expediens est ut multi maneant in continentia viduali et virginali.*

[70] See n. 78 below.

5.5 *Future decrease in the multitude*

The precept had ceased with the cessation of the cause: the cessation, that is, of the necessity to multiply. What if the necessity returned? Although Albert had briefly alluded to this, saying that 'notwithstanding any vow, every man would be bound [by the precept to marry] if there were to be similar conditions [again]',[71] the theme did not attract particular attention in mid-century. Bonaventure, Aquinas, and Peter of Tarentaise did not examine this question, and I have not yet seen it in lesser figures of this period.

It enters with—or has already entered by the time of—Richard of Middleton. Discussing the diversification of tasks, some helping to preserve the human race while others remain in the continence of virginity or widowhood, Richard goes on to a further possibility. 'If however', he writes, 'the world were to be reduced to such a small number of men that while some observed chastity the others did not suffice for sufficient multiplication of men for divine cult, then matrimonial union would be a [matter of] precept for all able to engage in this act.'[72] He then proceeds to quote Augustine on completing the numbers of the elect. Here in the mid-1290s is Peter de Trabibus on the same theme:

> But suppose that men were wiped out from the world either through plague or mutual destruction and very few remained, and these perhaps votive [vowed to continence]. In such an eventuality, could not the votive man and votive woman contract [marriage]? Some say 'yes', and that they not only could but ought to. Since the precept about marriage, 'Increase and multiply', is affirmative and has not been revoked by God, it still always binds according to time and place. And because in such an eventuality there would be the place and time for multiplying the human race, even votive men could and should accede to marriage.[73]

The focus on religious celibates has an extra sharpness here, and Peter—a follower of Olivi—ends up arguing against the return of the precept in such a case.

By this time wide discussion is attested not only by the implication of Peter's reference to variety of opinion, but also by the number of those in whose commentaries we can find it, especially among Franciscans. The specification of causes of possible future reduction of the multitude shows increasing precision, as here in Peter de Trabibus and also in Duns Scotus. In Duns' view the precept would still oblige 'if paucity in children should happen through some reason,

[71] Albert, *In sententias*, IV. xxvi. art. 10; xxx. 112: *nullo voto obstante omnis homo teneretur si similis esset casus.*

[72] Richard, *In sententias*, IV. xxvi. art. 3 Qu. 3; iv. 407b: *Si tamen redigeretur mundus ad ita parvum numerum hominum, quod quibusdam castitatem servantibus aliis [alii] non sufficerent ad sufficientem multiplicationem hominum ad cultum divinum, tunc matrimonialis copula omnibus illi actui vacare potentibus esset praeceptum.*

[73] [*In sententias*], II. xx: *Sed pone quod homines deleantur de mundo, sive per pestilentiam sive per cedem mutuam, et remaneant homines paucissimi et forte votivi. Numquid votivus et votiva in tali casu contrahere possunt? Dicunt aliqui quod sic, et non solum contrahere possunt, immo debent. Cum enim preceptum de matrimonio, 'Crescite et multiplicare', sit affirmativum et non sit a Deo revocatum, adhuc semper obligat pro loco et tempore. Et quia in tali casu esset locus et tempus multiplicandi genus humanum, possent et deberent homines, eciam votivi, accedere ad matrimonium*; Leipzig, Universitätsbibliothek MS 524, fol. 134v.

such as war, disease, disaster or suchlike'.[74] Duns is also more thorough in projecting the past onto the future, looking not only at the past of marriage as a precept but also the former divine permission of a plurality of wives for greater multiplication. The 'subtle doctor' also lived up to his name in his envisaging of a partial future decline, which altered the numerical balance of the sexes. After repeating God's dispensation of a plurality for the greater good, multiplying the faithful when there were few worshippers, he proceeds thus. 'It (bigamy) is now illicit because its principal end is not necessary, because many devote themselves to the generation of the faithful, because faith has multiplied. . . . If however the case were to come about, either through war, or disaster or disease, that the multitude of men fell and the multitude of women remained, bigamy could then be licit . . .'.[75]

Debate is also indicated in Peter of la Palud: 'according to some, if the world were to be failing [in numbers] someone [= anyone] who vowed virginity would be obliged to contract marriage.'[76] The influence of the *Politics* is discernible in Peter Aureoli, who raises the question of the legislator compelling people to marry.[77] Most advanced in thought is the latest author writing on this, Thomas of Strasbourg. After saying that in 'modern times, things being as they are now . . . the world is virtually full of men, [and] therefore as far as now [is concerned] those who wish to abstain are not bound to contract', he continues thus: 'However, I am saying emphatically "as far as now [is concerned]" or "things being as they are now" (*Dico autem notanter, pro nunc, vel rebus se habentibus, ut nunc*). Because such a great mortality of men could happen that those few who were left living would be bound to marry for the preservation of the species or for some other imminent necessity, provided that they were persons who could legitimately contract [marriage].'[78] 'Legitimate persons' for contracting marriage were those not barred by vow of continence, Holy Orders, kinship, disparity of cult and so on. Thomas has opened up the theme. Previously a narrow balancing of the married and those vowed to celibacy, the theme now seems to concern the

[74] Duns Scotus, *In sententias*, IV. xxvi; ix. 599: *adhuc videtur eodem modo obligare, si paucitas in filiis ex aliqua causa accideret, puta ex bello, peste, vel clade et huiusmodi.*

[75] Ibid., IV. xxxiii. Qu. 1; ix. 705–6: *est illicita, quia nunc non est necessarius ille finis principalis, eo quod multi vacant generationi fidelium, quia fides multiplicata est. . . . Si tamen contingeret casus per bellum, vel cladem, vel pestem, quod multitudo virorum caderet, et multitudo mulierum remaneret, posset tunc bigamia esse licita.*

[76] Peter of la Palud, *In sententias*, IV. xxvi. Qu. 3; 140va: *Si autem mundus deficeret qui virginitatem vovit secundum quosdam contrahere deberet.*

[77] See above, Ch. 2, p. 51 and n. 149.

[78] Thomas of Strasbourg, *In sententias*, IV. xxvi. art. 3; ii. 146ra: *Conclusio secunda est, quod modernis temporibus rebus se habentibus ut nunc, nullus tenetur, seu obligatur, ut de facto contrahat matrimonium. Quia sicut de subventione parentum habemus praeceptum affirmativum, et nihilominus eo tempore, quo pater non indiget, filius non tenetur de facto patri subvenire, sic quamvis de hominum multiplicatione, et per consequens de contrahendo matrimonio Deus dederit praeceptum affirmativum, tamen quia pro nunc tot homines sunt, qui voluntarie matrimonium contrahunt, quod mundus quasi repletus est hominibus: ideo illi, qui volunt abstinere, pro nunc non tenetur contrahere. Dico autem notanter 'pro nunc' vel 'rebus se habentibus ut nunc', quia posset contingere tanta mortalitas hominum, quod illi pauci, qui vivi manerent, propter conservationem humanae speciei vel propter aliquam aliam imminentem necessitatem, tenerentur contrahere matrimonium, supposito quod essent personae legitime ad contrahendum.*

applicability of the precept to marry to all who may lawfully marry. This may embrace either those not yet vowed to celibacy, or simply those who are adult and lay but single. Some secularization of this branch of thought about population is discernible.

If there were correlations between the development of these *Sentences* commentaries and population conditions, they will usually have been relatively broad. The point has already been made about the demographically different worlds of Peter Lombard on the one hand and William of Auxerre and the *c.*1250 commentators on the other, who emphasized the world's fullness and the theme of sufficiency. Perhaps there could also be some more precise intrusion of direct experience of current population. Thomas of Strasbourg underlines current conditions as emphatically as he can. Now, this northern European, an Augustinian friar who read the *Sentences* in Paris between 1335 and 1337, and was to die in Vienna in 1357, was presumably born near the turn of the century, or a little before, and he will have been a young man (or perhaps early middle-aged) during the terrible famines of 1315–17. It is not difficult to see the possibility of this experience sharpening the words of a man who would write about 'such a great mortality of men' and deepening his thought in the way we have just seen.

It is a commonplace of modern accounts of 'real' population in the mid-fourteenth century that population responded flexibly to the disaster of the Black Death. The marriage-rate went up, as can be seen in the tiny example of the famous surviving marriage register of the Burgundian village of Givry. We have seen theologians handling a narrow theme of varying dispensations in the precept to marriage and the preference of marriage or virginity. As they have developed this theme, applied it more directly to contemporary conditions, and envisaged more precisely future conditions, an area of thought slowly emerged. It is expressed in old and theological language, and is still near the primitive stage of 'either:or'. But it is an ancestor of the thought which is implied now when a historical demographer talks about increased marriage-rate as a demographic response.

5.6 *Caveats*

When radical Franciscans like Olivi or Peter de Trabibus turned to the precept of marriage, it was obvious that they would write within the tradition of discussion of the subject, and since multitude loomed large in this tradition they would talk about multitude. This did not mean that they were interested in what this book calls *demographic thought.* Their preoccupation was evangelical perfection and its component, religious celibacy, and here it was driving them to whittle away at marriage and to deal with all the usual arguments. Their words should not be twisted and modernized, and their lack of interest needs to be recalled alongside the very different outlook displayed by other commentators who have been examined in this chapter, especially the last, Thomas of Strasbourg, whose intruding of demographic interests into theological language is patent.

There is a final caveat, and the peg upon which I shall hang it is the *Sentences* commentary of the Franciscan Robert Cowton, which comes from Oxford before 1311/12.[79] 'The fruit of offspring is ordained to the common good of the city or the common good, virginal good however to a particular good and [a good] of the private person', wrote Cowton. 'I argue that the virginal condition is more perfect, firstly thus. That which has its goodness from the circumstances of necessity and indigence is not good absolutely, because such a good ceases when necessity and indigence cease. For example, throwing goods into the sea is the sort of good that receives its goodness from the circumstance of necessity and indigence. Therefore it is not a good absolutely. But all [its] good ceases when the necessity ceases. But the condition of marriage is a condition which receives its goodness from the circumstance of necessity and need . . . marriage was invented for this reason, so that the multitude of the human race should come about, for such a species cannot be preserved in one individual.' So far Cowton is vividly expressing the conventional view. Then he turns away from the good of population to eschatology, continuing thus. 'Therefore the condition of marriage is not a good absolutely, and with the necessity removed the condition of marriage will cease, as will be the case when the number of the elect will be complete.' If eschatology is Cowton's principal thought, current population is also there. 'And even now', he continues, 'in the church militant, as far as many are concerned [and] in this necessity [= in current conditions] it [the condition of marriage] could be taken away.'[80]

It is an aside. A passing allusion to contemporary extreme overpopulation. What is worth dwelling on is not the statement itself but the fact that it is made in a throw-away remark. Glimpsed momentarily is the gulf between the modern scholar, extracting blood from the stone of the surviving texts, and the casual and informal thoughts about population in the minds of men of Cowton's time. Usually such thoughts were not set down in writing.

[79] H. Theissing, *Glaube und Theologie bei Robert Cowton OFM*, BGPTM 42(3) (Münster, 1970), p. 12.

[80] Oxford, Merton College, MS 117, fol. 251rb: *Bonitas prolis ordinatur ad bonum civitatis sive ad bonum commune, bonitas autem virginalis ordinatur ad particulare bonum et persone private. . . . Quod autem status virginalis sit perfectior arguo, primo sic. Illud quod bonitatem suam habet ex circumstancia necessitatis et indigencie non est bonum simpliciter, quia cessante necessitate et indigencia cessat tale bonum. Verbi gracia proicere merces in mare est tale bonum quod bonitatem suam recipit ex circumstancia necessitatis et indigencie. Ideo non est bonum simpliciter sed condicionatum* [perhaps] *et cessante necessitate cessat omne bonum. Sed status coniugale est status qui bonitatem suam recipit ex circumstancia necessitatis et indigencie, quod patet etc per commentatorem, qui dicit quod ideo matrimonium inventum fuit ut multitudinem* [recte: *multitudo*] *generis humani fieret, quia talis species non potest salvari in uno individuo. Ergo status coniugale non est bonum simpliciter, et ablata ista necessitate sicud erit cum completus erit numerus electorum—et eciam modo in ecclesia militante potest quoad multos ista necessitate* [recte: *necessitas*] *auferri—cessabit status coniugale.*

6

AVOIDANCE OF OFFSPRING (I): THE GENERAL PICTURE

If you can't be good, be careful[1]

Part 1's account of demographic thought within medieval theology concludes with avoidance of offspring. The theme is direct action, either in avoiding conceiving or aborting, not the control identified by modern historical demographers as having most significance, namely late marriage. In order to provide one example of the complex threads connecting many individual human acts and theologians' generalizing thought about them, I am treating this theme at length, in three chapters. 'Reality' is dealt with here, in Chapter 6, which looks at some individuals avoiding conception and sketches medicine, suggesting some developments around 1300. Chapters 7–8 describe thought inside the Church, Chapter 7 examines the large collections of canon lawyers and the *Sentences* commentaries of the academic theologians, and Chapter 8 the larger confessors' treatises, and the tiny common-or-garden pastoral books. These texts are treated independently but side by side in order to suggest both interconnections and also differences. In particular, some may show little change, others may be more responsive. Enormous texts may be compendious, while tiny pamphlets may contain only what authors and pastors thought important. Some may be more immediately connected to the contemporary and ordinary Catholic Christians who were their concern, some less so. In the decades around 1300 these texts change in character. There is more concentration on the subject, the intrusion of new language, medicalization, and early signs and growth of *generalization* about the subject.

A commonplace of medieval confessors' manuals is care in questions about sex, care lest too precise questions pass on knowledge to an innocently ignorant person. If intimate sexual matters were dealt with and referred to with a mixture of obscurity and openness, so also were abortions panicky and desperate deeds done in secret. Dark territory for the later historian, this area is peculiarly vulnerable to modern distortions, against which the scant evidence available affords little defence. The account provided in these three chapters is often an implicit

[1] In spirit this is the closest equivalent of the medieval catch-phrase *si non caste tamen caute*, 'if not chastely at least carefully', first attested in the eleventh century. See P. Biller, 'Birth-control in the West in the Thirteenth and Early Fourteenth Centuries', *Past and Present* 94 (1982), 3–26 (p. 17 and nn. 56–9).

criticism of other modern accounts of medieval birth-control, whose main concerns are recapitulated here.

First, some modern accounts have pushed primitive mentality into the vacant ground, on the one hand arguing that 'birth-control' was 'unthinkable' by the medieval mind,[2] and on the other hand that the thought and desire are universal in mankind but that methods were quaint and bizarre.[3] Here academic works have been closer than they usually are to the outlook of most non-academics, which is, on this subject, incredulity: 'What? Really? *Then?*'

Secondly, the interest in birth-control taken by liberal Catholicism around the time of the second Vatican Council shone the spotlight on the history of the Church's teaching. If one could show that this teaching had varied, then the modern Church's ban on birth-control might look more vulnerable—or vice versa. Writing at this time, one fine and learned historian, John Noonan, decided to present the medieval Church's thought as challenge and response: challenged by Catharism, a heresy which condemned procreation, the Church responded with greater emphasis on procreation and hence severe condemnation of contraception.[4] Not only was this heresy less significant than Noonan thought it was, and not, as he suggested, an advocate of birth-control. But, and more importantly, Noonan's interest in it displaced what should have been centre-stage, removing what was the real and principal concern of the medieval Church: the morality of the sex lives of millions of ordinary Catholic Christians. Further, the proportions of Noonan's writings reflected modern liberal Catholic campaigning concerns: much on birth-control, less on abortion.[5] For a long time abortion was underwritten.[6] Dimly discernible are other pressures helping to minimize the attention given to abortion: greater interest in the earlier twentieth century in propaganda to extend the practice of birth-control; reluctance by historical demographers to accord significance to abortion; and simple repugnance.

Thirdly and more recently, drug companies' investment in research into herbal medicines and also the history of medicine has helped produce the work of John Riddle, whose writing has swung the pendulum away from the quaintness of ancient medicine and over to the other extreme: the efficacy of ancient drugs.[7] We

[2] See Biller, 'Birth-control', pp. 3–5, on these arguments in Philippe Ariès and Keith Hopkins.

[3] The approach of N. E. Himes, *A Medical History of Contraception* (Baltimore, 1936); see pp. xxxiii–xxxvi.

[4] J. T. Noonan, *Contraception: A History of its Treatment by the Catholic Theologians and Canonists* (Cambridge, Mass., 1966), Ch. 6; Biller, 'Birth-control', pp. 8–12; see also J.-L. Flandrin's review of the French translation of Noonan, *Annales de Démographie Historique 1969* (1970), 337–59 (pp. 346–7). The pagination and contents of the 1966 and 1986 editions of Noonan's *Contraception* are the same, the later edition having the addition only of an appendix (pp. 535–54) on papal encyclicals.

[5] His account of abortion is in 'An Absolute Value in History', in *The Morality of Abortion* (Cambridge, Mass., 1970), ed. J. T. Noonan, pp. 1–59.

[6] Examples of modern treatment: J. C. Bologne, *La naissance interdite: Stérilité, avortement, contraception au Moyen Âge* (Paris, 1988), pp. 165–77; S. Laurent, *Naître au Moyen Âge. De la conception à la naissance: la grossesse et l'accouchement (XIIe–XVe siècle)* (Paris, 1989), pp. 145–55.

[7] J. M. Riddle, *Contraception and Abortion from the Ancient World to the Renaissance* (Cambridge, Mass., London, 1992); *Eve's Herbs: A History of Contraception and Abortion in the West* (Cambridge,

need to note the dangers of uncritical enthusiasm, and Riddle's ignoring of the distinctions which were made in the ancient texts, between drugs which induced menses (emmenenagogues), drugs which produced abortions, and drugs which impeded conception.[8] Riddle does not set the drugs within their immediate context, the development of medicine and the apothecaries' profession and texts in the middle ages, and he does not carefully juxtapose their use to other ways of avoiding offspring.

A final distortion comes through the language in which these modern accounts are written. The *Oxford English Dictionary* provides the elementary materials of a history of such words and phrases as *preventive, preventative, Malthusian check, birth-control, contraception, contraceptive, coitus interruptus*, and the thought-world in which they are embedded. Providing its first entry for *birth-control*, in *The Birth Control League* (1914), the *Oxford English Dictionary* reminds us of both the newness of the phrase itself and its associations: campaigning polemic, government policies, the world population problem. When used in modern histories of past peoples, these words insidiously imply past possession of these categories, past capacity to think similarly. Now, it is part of the case here that there was much such thought, and also development in it. But if this medieval 'thought' is to be delineated precisely, medieval texts need to be expounded as far as possible literally in their own terms and without the use of such dangerous modern vocabulary.[9]

6.1 *Individuals and modern demographic conjecture*

The volume of surviving evidence grows in the central middle ages. Traces of a few individuals avoiding offspring then begin to appear.

The first kind of evidence is the writings of monks interested in details about élite families. Making up the immediate audience for a chronicle written by a monk were his fellow monks: men from noble families who liked to hear about the marriages of their relatives. An example is Orderic Vitalis, writing in the early twelfth century in the Norman monastery of Évroult. For fellow monks, descended from and related to patrons and noble families of the area, Orderic's history contained the equivalent of a modern newspaper's marriage column. There were entries such as 'N, son of count M, married so-and-so, a beautiful girl of noble birth, and engendered by her X and Y', and there could be the occasional further detail about individual noble marriages. In Orderic there can be a snatch

Mass., London, 1997); see the review of this by Monica Green, *Bulletin of the History of Medicine* 73 (1999), 308–11, and above, Ch. 1 n. 13. I am grateful to Professor Philip Stell for examining the scientific articles cited by Riddle in his 1992 book. Another account of herbs is provided in Bologne, *Naissance interdite*, pp. 157–64.

[8] I am grateful to Monica Green for comment on this point.

[9] In these three chapters an exception is made for coitus interruptus, whose paraphrase would be cumbersome. Ch. 7 below shows how in the early fourteenth century theologian's language was describing what we mean by coitus interruptus with increasing precision.

of conversation between a husband and wife, or an elaborate portrait of an ideal, prayerful, ascetic, and charitable married pair, while elsewhere among other monastic writers of this period intimate matters occur. One monk writes about his father's long drawn-out impotence,[10] while another provides the names of the two Italian physicians who attended Henry I's first wife, Matilda, when she was giving birth.[11]

Avoiding offspring was also described. The west-country monk William of Malmesbury, writing about 1125 about Henry I's first wife, Matilda, refers to her stopping having children after having the first two. Her deliberateness is the central point of his brief words. 'She, therefore, content with these offspring, one of each sex, from now on left off conceiving and giving birth' (*Haec igitur duobus partubus, alter alterius sexus, contenta, in posterum et parere et parturire destitit*). A goodbye to the royal court and a tactful reference to her husband's 'attention being elsewhere' (*rege alias intento*) indicate clearly William's view that this convent-educated girl achieved her purpose by abstinence.[12]

A different method seems to have been employed by the wife of a cousin of Henry I's, Robert II of Flanders. Her actions were described by Hermann, a knight's son, who had entered the abbey of St Martin of Tournai in 1092 and was an old man when writing from about 1143 and drawing on his memory to describe his father's world of around 1100, and in particular the families of the counts of Flanders.[13] Robert II's wife, Clémence, was the daughter of the count of Burgundy and sister of the archbishop of Vienne. She had three children by Robert in a short space of time, and then desisted for dynastic political reasons, to avoid the divisiveness which might result from many heirs. 'This Clémence, however, when she had given birth to three sons by her husband Count Robert, [and these] within three years, was afraid if she still gave birth to more, that they would fight among themselves about Flanders.' What she did and how she did it aroused the hostility of Hermann, who goes on to describe divine revenge on her for her actions. All her three sons died before she did, and in her widowhood she lived to see other men as counts of Flanders. 'She acted with womanly skill', wrote Hermann, 'in order not to give birth any more' (*Haec vero Clementia cum de viro suo Roberto genuisset tres filios infra tres annos, timens ne, si plures adhuc generaret, inter se de Flandria contendererent, arte muliebri egit ne ultra parerent*). Where the word *ars* meant 'technical skill', as in such phrases as 'the art of the mason' or 'the art of a versifier', the nearest sense of *ars muliebris* here is this: 'a woman's technical skill' or 'a technique practised by women', directed here 'to avoid giving birth to any more children'.[14] A first? It is worth noting that Clémence came from and

[10] Guibert de Nogent, *Autobiographie*, I. xii, ed. E.-R. Labande (Paris, 1981), pp. 76–9.

[11] E. J. Kealey, *Medieval Medicus: A Social History of Anglo-Norman Medicine* (Baltimore and London, 1981), p. 67; pp. 65–72 on the physicians in question.

[12] William of Malmesbury, *De gestis regum Anglorum*, ed. W. Stubbs, 2 vols., RS 90, ii. 494.

[13] See on Hermann (d. probably *c.*1147) J. Pycke, 'Heriman de Tournai', *Dictionnaire d'Histoire et de Géographie Ecclésiastiques*, xxiii. 1453–8.

[14] Hermann of Tournai, *De restauratione abbatiae Sancti Martini Tornacensis*, XVIII, *PL* 180, 54. See comment in J. Verdon, 'La gynécologie et l'obstétrique aux IXe et Xe siècles', *Revue française de*

lived in an area whose precociously developing towns were to be in the vanguard of medical developments: hospitals, numbers of doctors, and an effort in the next century to disseminate (ultimately Greek) obstetric techniques for the manual rectification of non-natural presentations of the foetus. If Clémence was the medieval west's first identifiable 'birth-controlling' woman, there is also an irony: for her brother was to become Pope, as Calixtus II.

By around 1200, records of legal proceedings begin to survive in quite large quantities, and there is now, therefore, the possibility of writing old 'history of daily life' and modern 'history from below'. One set of records begins in the late 1230s: inquisitors asking people about their faith. By the early fourteenth century there were so few suspects of heresy left in Languedoc that a curious inquisitor could spend many days squeezing the last detail from a suspect on many extraneous matters, and it is thus that the most detailed evidence about a named individual trying to avoid conception survives. The milieu now is not the advanced towns of Flanders but a remote village high up in Pyrenees. On one day during her long interrogations in Pamiers, a woman recalled one of her love affairs. Béatrice de Planisolles was a young girl (*puella*) six years before her marriage to her first husband. By 1294 she was already married, had already had children, and was pregnant again, and in 1295 she was 'not long risen from childbirth'. Four daughters are known. Her first husband died about 1298, and, after a rape, from which no conception is reported, she started an affair, on 6 July 1300.[15]

It lasted for a year and a half, or perhaps two years, with the lovers meeting two or three times a week. Given marriage probably in her mid- to late teens, the subsequent bearing of four daughters and finally her first widowhood, it is probable that Béatrice was in her late twenties. The risk of conception was her first thought at the beginning of the affair. One reason, she said, was that her father, Philip, would have found this very shameful. 'At the beginning, when the said priest had first known her carnally, she said to the said priest, "And what shall I do if I'm made pregnant by you? I shall be confused and lost". The said parish priest replied to her that he had a certain herb, and if a man wore this when he had sex with a

Gynécologie, 71 (1976), 39–47 (p. 44); T. de Hemptinne, 'Les épouses des croisés et pèlerins flamands au XIe et XIIe siècles: L'exemple des comtesses de Flandre Clémence et Sibylle', in *Autour de la première croisade*, ed. M. Balard, Série Byzantina Sorbonensia 14 (Paris, 1996), pp. 83–95.

[15] The affair is recounted in *Le registre d'inquisition de Jacques Fournier, évêque de Pamiers (1318–1325): Manuscrit no. Vat. Latin 4030 de la Bibliothèque Vaticane*, ed. J. Duvernoy, 3 vols., Bibliothèque Méridionale 2nd series, 41 (Toulouse, 1965), i. 243–4, and in French trans., *Le registre d'inquisition de Jacques Fournier, évêque de Pamiers (1318–1325)*, ed. and trans. J. Duvernoy, intr. E. Le Roy Ladurie, 3 vols., École des Hautes Études en Sciences Sociales, Centre de Recherches Historiques, Civilisations et Sociétés, 43 (Paris, Hague, and New York, 1978), i. 280–1. The text has often been used to illustrate medieval contraception. See e.g. E. Le Roy Ladurie, *Montaillou, village occitan de 1294 à 1324* (Paris, 1975), pp. 248–9 (*Montaillou: Cathars and Catholics in a French village 1294–1324* (London, 1978), pp. 172–3); Laurent, *Naître au Moyen Âge*, p. 32; Riddle, *Eve's Herbs*, ch. 1. Duvernoy's original edition contained many mistranscriptions, some of which were pointed out in a review in *Revue de l'histoire des Religions* 178 (1970), pp. 49–56, and Duvernoy accepted this criticism, applied himself again to the manuscript, and published a 48-page list of corrections: J. Duvernoy, *Le registre d'inquisition de Jacques Fournier, évèque de Pamiers (1318–1325): Corrections* (Toulouse, 1972). Riddle's claim that Ladurie used only the French translation (*Eve's Herbs*, p. 23) is inaccurate; Ladurie used the Latin text, and was aware of Duvernoy's *Corrections*.

woman, the man could not generate nor the woman conceive. She replied to him, "And what sort of herb is that?"'. This herb was 'wrapped up and bound in a piece of linen cloth, the size and length of an inch, or the first joint of her little finger', attached to a long cord, and was put around her neck before they made love. It would hang down between her breasts to the 'orifice of her stomach'. Sometimes they would make love twice or more in a night, and each time before they made love 'the priest would take the said herb and place it on the orifice of her stomach'.[16] He was persistent: 'he would have sex with her this way and not otherwise'. After her father's death Béatrice 'would have very much liked to have been impregnated him [her lover]'. His will seems to have prevailed. So, several times a week for a year and a half Béatrice made love to a man who insisted every time on placing on her a herb to avoid conceiving, and she did not conceive.

Traces of a few other individuals appear in other later medieval archives. Another instance of a named individual woman perhaps making love and practising birth-control survives in a late fifteenth-century York marriage case. The woman was Joan Leek and the man John Dowson, 'who was and is now a capital enemy, in fact a diffamer of the same Joan'.[17] He defamed her, in these words: 'Thow berist stuff must or theyr uppon the to thentent thow shalnot be gotten wth child when thow japys or lyeth wth men.' Dowson is putting together Joan's (alleged) promiscuity and the fact that it did not lead to pregnancy to produce the defaming allegation that she must be avoiding conceiving by 'bearing stuff or thereupon her'—perhaps a pessary. The fact that this was said *in a world where it could have been true* is more significant than whether or not Dowson was a liar in this particular case.

Individual abortions occasionally appear in episcopal visitation records, and in judicial records—presumably more so the later the termination. Among French

[16] Readings in square brackets are from Duvernoy's *Corrections* unless otherwise noted. *Ipsa dixit dicto sacerdoti: 'Et quid ego faciam si inpregner a vobis? Ero confusa et perdita.' Cui dictus rector respondit quod ipse habebat quamdam herbam quam si homo defferret quando comiscebatur cum muliere, vir generare non posset nec mulier concipere, cui ipsa respondit: 'Et cuiusmodi erba est illa? Estne illa quam vaquerii ponunt super ollam lactis in quo lacte posuerunt coagulam, que herba non permittit quod lac coaguletur, quamdiu stat super* [*dictam*] *ollam lactis?' Et ipse respondit quod non curaret que herba erat, sed, ut dixit, quedam herba erat, que predictam virtutem habebat, quam herbam ipse, ut dixit, habebat. Et ex tunc quando volebat ipsam que loquitur carnaliter cognoscere, portabat quamdam rem involutam et ligatam panno lineo, grossitudinis et longitudinis oncie, vel* [*iniunc*]*-ture primi digitis minoris manus ipsius que loquitur, et habebat quemdam filum longum quem ponebat in collo ipsius dum commiscebatur cum ea, et dicta res quem dicebat erbam pendens in filo descendebat inter mamillas eius, et stabat in orificio stomachi* [original edn: *stomachis*] *ipsius que loquitur, et dictam rem semper sic ponebat quando eam carnaliter cognoscere volebat, que manebat in collo ipsius que loquitur, quousque dictus sacerdos surgere volebat, et dum volebat surgere, dictam rem de eius collo dictus sacerdos accipiebat. Et, ut dixit, si aliquando in una nocte bis vel plur*[*i*]*es ipsam carnaliter cognoscere vellet, dictus sacerdos petebat ab ea, antequam ei coniungeretur, ubi dicta erba erat, quam ipsa accipiens, inventam per cordam quam habebat in collo, ponebat in manu eius, et dictus sacerdos accipiens dictam herbam* [original edn: *erbam*] *ponebat eam in orificio stomachi* [original edn: *stomachis*] *ipsius que loquitur, transeunte corda predicta inter mamillas eius, et sic se coniungebat carnaliter cum ea, et non aliter.* See below and n. 93 on this method in contemporary medicine.

[17] York, Borthwick Institute of Historical Research, Cause Paper F. 261, article 5: *Johannes Dowson fuit et est dicte Johanne Leek modum inimicus capitalis verum etiam diffamator.* I am grateful to Jeremy Goldberg for reference to this.

judicial records, there is a certain Jeanette in 1398, pregnant, who took abortifacients but aborted much later. She obtained 'some herbs' and 'ate [them] just once, and about two months afterwards through illness or otherwise she put out of her body a baby which was not larger than an apple, and it had life, so it seemed to her': a case where the witness is suggesting that the much earlier herbal abortifacients had failed? She extinguished its life and was prosecuted for this. In 1453 an 18-year-old girl whose father had had sex with her gave birth to a dead baby after drinking abortifacient herbs.[18] In England there are cases in the act-books of ecclesiastical courts. For example, there is the case of a Joan, unsurnamed, servant of Joan Gibbes of the parish of Deal, about whom it is stated in a Canterbury Act book, in 1469, that 'she recently killed the baby in her womb with herbs and medicines'. There is also the case of a George Hemery. The judge in consistory court in Rochester in 1493 states that George 'administers medicines in a drink [to a woman] to destroy the child he has procreated'.[19]

While Clémence and the others may help us to imagine past reality, they are dangerous friends. Early monastic sources tell us only about the noble few. It is patently *evidence* which has begun to survive, not *practice* which has started; and only an infinitesimally tiny fraction of past practitioners who appear in this evidence, not a fair and clearly representative sample. How, then, can we generalize about practice?

Modern historical demography can produce conjectures. One is regional, and its implications are spelled out here in their simplest form. Clémence came from north-western Europe, one part of which, England, has been established as a region in which already by the mid-thirteenth century large numbers of adults in the population did not marry, and girls usually married for the first time quite a few years after adolescence, when they were in their twenties.[20] Despite some illegitimate births, both features would have restricted birth: substantial numbers of adults not conceiving because they remained single, and girls not conceiving for the first five or ten years in which they could have conceived, because they were delaying marriage. Further slight restriction could have come through extended periods of breast-feeding. Hammered over from the pulpit were recommendations to mothers to breast-feed their own babies, and this may have been also a lay ideal, and to some degree followed. What of the southern Europe in which Béatrice lived? In Tuscan families a higher proportion of the adults in the population were married, and girls married in their mid-teens, not long after the onset of puberty. Both should have had the opposite effect on conceptions, with more adults married and girls not having their early fertile years shut off. In comfortably placed families there was extensive use of wet-nurses for little children.

[18] R. Vaultier, *Le folklore pendant la guerre de Cent ans d'après les lettres de rémission du Trésor des Chartes* (Paris, 1965), pp. 227 and 229.

[19] R. H. Helmholz, *Canon Law and the Law of England* (London and Ronceverte, 1987), p. 159 and nn. 12–13. See also examples from 1530 in *Women in Medieval England c.1275–1525*, ed. P. J. P. Goldberg (Manchester, 1995), pp. 122–3, no. 32(c) and (e).

[20] See Ch. 12 below.

Thus removed, for some at least, was one practice which slightly restricted conception.

In contrast with the individuals of the previous paragraphs, these statements are speculative, general and suggestive. In north-western Europe (or parts of it) avoiding offspring by more direct methods would have been attempted against a background of other habits and practices which brought with them fewer conceptions, and at the same time a different outlook or climate of thought. And there would have been the opposite in the south. Conception is already more a matter of fate if it is what happens to you just after puberty. It is also less a matter of fate, if you are a girl, if you earn money, and if you take your own decision about marriage when you are 22. We should therefore be alert to hints of regional patterns of practice.

A second conjecture is based on the findings of economic and demographic study combined. Chapter 5 above alluded to the sharp population growth of the thirteenth century. The possibilities of feeding more through taking more land under cultivation or cultivating more intensively became thinner as western Europe reached the closing decades of the thirteenth century. The harsh reality appears dramatically in figures from the west of England. In the village of Taunton population more than doubled between 1209 and 1311, and land per person decreased from 3.3 acres in 1248 to 2.5 acres in 1311. The prospect of hunger if a couple conceived, or conceived more, would have pressed them to try to avoid conceiving: if they thought in those terms, and if they could think of techniques.

The iceberg best represents our knowledge of what they thought and did. There are medical texts, and therefore we must look at them (as we do in the next section). However, this visible tip is only a fraction, while the other seven-eighths of past thought and practice remain hidden, and are permitted here no more than one entirely conjectural paragraph. *The Good Wife Taught her Daughter* was both the title of a middle-English text and the theme of an Italian mother's advice to her daughter.[21] Did mothers pass on to their daughters Clémence's *ars muliebris*? A commonplace of pastoral manuals, which ask about ways of men spilling seed, is that priests should not ask questions which teach men how to sin. Bad priests from southern Germany are censured in a text of *c.*1260/6 for advising their parishioners to go 'if not chastely, at least with precaution' (*si non caste, tamen caute*): near to 'if you can't be good, be careful'.[22] Were men being taught to avoid conceiving when making love, by withdrawing and 'spilling seed', and are these last texts faint survivals of a world *part of which* was nudge and wink knowledge of this sort of thing? In 1409 the midwife Adelheit of Stutgarten was expelled from Sélestat for providing abortions.[23] Was a midwife the usual source of abortifacients or knowledge about them? Or is Adelheit a 'dangerous friend', an isolated individual insidiously and misleadingly suggesting a broader trend?

[21] Biller, 'Birth-control', p. 19. [22] Ibid., p. 17.

[23] E. Wickersheimer, *Dictionnaire biographique des médecins en France au moyen âge*, 2 vols. (Paris, 1936, repr. Geneva and Paris, 1979), i. 9.

A little more will be said later. For some of the changes in pastoral literature and theological commentary around 1300, which are surveyed in Chapters 7 and 8, seem to be rooted in observation of the thought and practice of ordinary people.

6.2.1 *Medicine (i) Apothecaries and herbals*

One of the masterpieces of modern scholarship is Michael McVaugh's reconstruction of medical practice in Aragon and Valencia in the decades around 1300.[24] It is of extraordinary concrete detail and variety, and I have used it in this chapter to suggest a denser context for apothecaries and the provision of drugs. Another masterpiece in the course of construction is resulting from the combination of meticulous scholarship, historiographical criticism, and the concerns both of medical and social history which Monica Green has been bringing to bear on women's medical practice, women's health-care, and the treatment of the latter in 'Trotula' treatises.[25] Writing while her studies are appearing, I have confined the sketch which I give in the next section to one well-known general medical text, Avicenna's *Canon*.

Let us look at apothecaries and their activities in parts of southern Europe around 1300, through McVaugh's book,[26] a herbal from Genoa, and some Church legislation from south-eastern France.

McVaugh sets various medical practitioners in relation both to overall population and cities, towns, and countryside. 'Figures indicate a likely base level for existence everywhere in the pre-plague west—a level that, in the large urban centres, was already approaching early modern levels and was perhaps not too different from what one might observe today in Spanish towns of comparable size'.[27] Doctors worked in collaboration with the specialist suppliers, apothecaries, even on occasion with an exclusive contract for supply of medicines. The names of many apothecaries survive; those in Barcelona tended to live in one street, and to intermarry: the Barcelona apothecary Pere de Berga married an apothecary's daughter, whose sister also married an apothecary. A contract shows a doctor of

[24] M. R. McVaugh, *Medicine before the Plague: Practitioners and their Patients in the Crown of Aragon, 1285–1345* (Cambridge, 1993).

[25] Two major works are forthcoming: the monograph *Women and Literate Medicine in Medieval Europe: Trota and the 'Trotula'*, and the translation *'The Diseases of Women According to Trotula': A Medieval Compendium of Women's Medicine.* Green's account is accessible in M. H. Green and M. Schleissner, 'Trotula (Trota), "Trotula"', *Die deutsche Literatur des Mittelalters: Verfasserlexikon*, ed. K. Ruh (Berlin and New York, 1978–), ix (1996), 1083–8, and M. H. Green, 'The Development of the *Trotula*', *Revue d'Histoire des Textes* 26 (1996), 119–203 . In her 'Women's Medical Practice and Health Care in Medieval Europe', in *Sisters and Workers in the Middle Ages*, ed. J. Bennett *et al.* (Chicago, 1989), pp. 39–78, Green comments on the historiography of the subject. See n. 28 below.

[26] McVaugh, *Medicine before the Plague*, pp. 7, 32, 111 n. 15, 38–9, 42–67, 76, 104, 116–23, 129, 154–7, 193, 197, and 199; L. García-Ballester, M. R. McVaugh, and A. Rubio-Vela, *Medical Licensing and Learning in Fourteenth-Century Valencia*, Transactions of the American Philosophical Society, 79, Part 6 (Philadelphia, 1989), pp. 6, 19–20, 37–9, and 66–7.

[27] Ibid., *Medicine before the Plague*, p. 67.

Santa Coloma binding himself for five years to direct all custom generated by his practice towards the shop of one apothecary, Ramon Roqueta, while the inventory of a Valencian apothecary who was active in the 1320s lists the around fifty compound and simple medicines found in his shop, together with his paper book called *Antidotar*. This last was probably the standard *Antidotarium Nicolai.* Yet another document shows an apothecary at Manresa recording details of 230 prescriptions in Lent 1348. There is one glimpse of an apothecary's widow at Puigcerdà hiring another apothecary to run the shop, but then together with her sons running what she called 'our' or 'my' shop. She is one representative only of the many women who practised as apothecaries, most of whom, however, will have escaped record because they only practised medicine intermittently and because women were usually not defined by profession in medieval records.[28]

McVaugh shows that there was widespread demand for medical provision, and that the alliance of the dense presence of these practitioners and public demand was leading to the 'medicalization' of various areas of life. For example, medical testimony was entering trials, as the 'medical expert' arrived in the court-room. There was increasing royal and municipal regulation. Apothecaries' capacity to understand was the concern of one of seven provisions in Valencian legislation of 1329, that 'Practitioners, both physicians and surgeons, shall give prescriptions for medicines in the vulgar tongue, naming herbs and other medicinal things by their common or popular names'. By 1350 there is provision for two apothecaries who were 'knowledgeable in the art' formally to examine new apothecaries, in legislation which uses the language of concern for public health. 'It is a dangerous thing for them to practice without such examination, and likewise the said apothecaries at times engage in giving an herb for this or an herb for that without being acquainted with the said herbs or medical things. . . . The council . . . appointed Antoni Pautrer and Guillem Caner, who . . . shall inspect and examine them and the medicines they have in their shops or houses; and whenever they discover anything incorrect, they may destroy it.'[29]

'I did not see this [herb] written down, but I saw it in the city of Bologna, that the herbalists (*herbolarii*) brought it to the apothecaries (*ypothecarii*), who put it in cold syrups'.[30] The comment is from Rufinus, the author of a herbal written after 1287 and probably before 1300. Although there is singularity here, in a work which only survives in one manuscript and an author who seems to have been a monk, an episcopal penitentiary, a botanical observer, and a medical practitioner, a window is opened onto something more general. Herbs are listed alphabetically, and they and their medical uses are carefully described. Rufinus does this in part

[28] Here I am following M. Green, 'Documenting medieval women's medical practice', in *Practical Medicine from Salerno to the Black Death*, ed. L. García-Ballester *et al.* (Cambridge, 1994), pp. 322–52.

[29] García-Ballester, *Medical Licensing and Learning*, pp. 61 and 67–8.

[30] *The Herbal of Rufinus*, ed. L. Thorndike (Chicago, 1945), p. 19 (fol. 21va), A28. Here the reference is (1) to the modern page number in Thorndike's edition, (2) to the folio no. in the manuscript (entries in Thorndike's modern index refer to folio nos.), and (3) to the initial number and letter of the herb (Thorndike prints the manuscript's index, which lists the herbs alphabetically and then, under each letter, numerically). The reference in this case is to the twenty-eighth herb whose name begins with *A*.

through a careful anthology from standard texts, including a commentary on the *Antodotarium Nicolai*, while adding comments from his own experience and observation.[31] A window, then, is opened onto common texts, and also a late thirteenth-century world of practice, and the connection of the two is implied throughout. Let us turn first to those texts which spell out the medical applications of herbs to menstruation, miscarriages, abortion, and conception. Use and purpose are spelled out directly, and with discrimination. Rufinus's medical world knew as commonplaces a relation between woman's health and menstruation, the need to remove a dead foetus, the need to expel the afterbirth, and so on, and these are distinct purposes in the texts quoted. There are many herbs which 'provoke menses', quite a few which 'drive out a dead foetus', a few where abortion follows, and one which stops conception. These are the herbs in the last two categories.

Herbs which bring about abortions:

Nepita (cat-mint, dead nettle, calamint): 'if a pregnant woman drinks this or applies [it] ground up, she aborts' (*Si bibit hanc pregnans aut tritam subdit, abortit*);[32]

Pulegium (pennyroyal, wild thyme): 'if a pregnant woman takes this herb often, she aborts' (*Sepius hanc herbam si pregnans sumit, abortit*);[33]

Malva (mallow): 'the Theban Olympias wrote that this [herb] was abortive . . . and thus it is applied as pessaries are to the vulva' (*Scripsit abortivam Thebana Olympias illam . . . Et sic subdantur veluti pessaria vulve*);[34]

Anabula (spurge, stinking camomile, mayweeed): 'ancient doctors instruct that this should be . . . and it brings about abortion. It often happens that the woman dies. For God's sake be careful not to give it to a pregnant woman' (*precipiunt antiqui medici ut . . . et abortum facit. Sepe evenit ut mulier moriatur. Cave per Deum ne mulieri pregnanti dederis*).[35]

Some herbs are not listed here, because the line being drawn *in the text* between deliberate abortion and expelling after a miscarriage needs more study—such are *ruta* (rue), which 'expels the foetus' (*expellit partum*), and *salvia*, which 'drives out the abortive' (*pellit abortivum*).[36]

Herb against conception:

Menta romana (wild mint, Roman mint): 'if the juice of this is applied before intercourse, the woman does not conceive from this [viz. from this intercourse]' (*sucus si subditur illius antequam fiat coytus, mulier non concipit inde*).[37]

Notable, again, is discrimination and clarity in these texts, and the range, from implicit recommendation to dire warnings. Apart from *anabula*, these are all quotations from Macer Floridus's *Liber de viribus herbarum*.[38] Rufinus is not being original.

[31] Ibid., pp. xvi–xvii. [32] Ibid., p. 205 (fol. 73vb), N8. [33] Ibid., p. 256 (fol. 89vb), P38.
[34] Ibid., p. 177 (fol. 66rb), M2. [35] Ibid., p. 25 (fol. 23ra), A42.
[36] Ibid., p. 275 (fol. 96ra), R14, and p. 284 (fol. 98vb), S10. [37] Ibid., p. 187 (fol. 68vb), M14.
[38] Ibid., p. xxix on Rufinus's use of Macer, and P. Diepgen, *Frau und Frauenheilkunde in der Kultur des Mittelalters* (Stuttgart, 1963), pp. 72–3, on women's medicine in Macer. The author is thought to be Odo

Rufinus's work is rooted in a world of practice. Geographically it consists of Genoa and other Ligurian towns, Piacenza, Verona, Bologna, Tuscany, and Naples.[39] Herbalists supply apothecaries, as we have seen. The coarser kind of one herb is brought from Verona, the finer variety is found in the diocese of Bologna,[40] while a physician tells Rufinus of the location, in Rapallo, of another herb.[41] 'The herbalists of Bologna and Naples' say this or that about the properties of particular herbs.[42] Rufinus notes his own grinding and preparation of a medicine from herbs, often refers to a physician, and occasionally mentions a particular woman preparing and using.[43] A few times a patient is named: a fortunate John of Pino recovered from his foot and leg problems, but Master Matheus of Genoa is noted for giving Raymond Conrad a concoction which turned out to be lethal.[44] A note on the use of a preparation is given in the first person—'If we have given [this] to women, it moves the menses'.[45] This may mislead at one level, in that it may be Rufinus copying another source, as he does four-fifths of the time, but not at another level, insofar as it suggests practice. Rufinus himself treated both sexes. He claimed to have treated more than sixty-five men and women between Easter and September 1287, noting that the illness in question affected women more than men that year. He makes a note about the duration of illness of one particular woman.[46] This was for flux of blood, and the attention paid to gynaecological matters in Rufinus's text writing seems to have had a counterpart in Rufinus's personal attention. When turning to one herb and one medical preparation which may be used, he writes as himself, Rufinus. 'One should know that there is a certain illness which is generated among women through the retention of menses . . . And many ladies [who are] widows and also virgins [who are] nuns, who have kept themselves with all care in order to avoid offending their creator have fallen into this illness, and have met with opprobrium and derision from the ignorant.'[47] Observation is implied, and there is apparent sympathy. Rufinus thought carefully about the texts he anthologized, not only adding but also pointing out contradictions, for example, here 'there is the greatest diversity among the wise'.[48] Macer Floridus was not, then, being anthologized by a passive, ignorant or academic compiler, but by an independently-minded practitioner.

Macer's was among the most widely known of herbals, perhaps even the most widely known, both in itself and through its anthologizing and translation. We can see it on the one hand being drawn into one of the massive Latin volumes of

of Meung, who lived in the first half of the eleventh century; see *A Middle English Translation of Macer Floridus de Viribus Herbarum*, ed. G. Frisk (Uppsala, Copenhagen and Cambridge, Mass., 1949), pp. 13–17.

[39] *Rufinus*, ed. Thorndike, pp. xxiv–xxvi.

[40] Ibid., p. 147 (fol. 58ra), G7.

[41] Ibid., p. 191 (fol. 70ra), M21.

[42] Ibid., p. 79 (fol. 38va), C36; p. 115 (fol. 49ra), D7. Bologna: p. 152 (fol. 59rb), H2; p. 185 (fol. 68ra), M11; p. 194 (fol. 71ra), M26; p. 208 (fol. 75ra), O1. Rufinus had studied in both cities: ibid., p. 1 (fol. 17ra).

[43] Ibid., p. 19 (fol. 21rb), A27, a Lady (Domina) successfully curing frenetics; p. 117 (fol. 49vb), E4, a little old woman (pejorative *vetula*) being executed in Bologna for her attempt to cure tertian fever leading to the patient's death.

[44] Ibid., p. 352 (fol. 118ra), Z4.

[45] Ibid., p. 311(fol. 106rb), T1.

[46] Ibid., p. 227 (fol. 81ra), P1.

[47] Ibid., p. 76 (fol. 37va), C34.

[48] Ibid., p. 69 (fol. 35va), C15.

the Dominican Vincent of Beauvais' encyclopaedia,[49] where these passages from Macer (with the exception of *malva*) are simply repeated, while on the other we see it going into vernacular middle-English and language of startling bluntness. Thus mint: 'Mint iuus underput to þe matrice a-fore þe cunte makeþ þat þe woman shal nat conceyve at þat tyme'.[50] Macer's text was standard in both Latin and vernacular, and it was at home in Rufinus's herbal, in a work which was steeped in the practice of procuring, preparing, and supplying drugs among late thirteenth-century apothecaries.

These apothecaries who have been glimpsed through Rufinus were active principally in north-western Italy, in the region of Genoa. To the east and north-west we find in these decades some repressive synodal legislation, in Reggio (north-eastern Italy) in 1285 and again in Avignon in 1326, dealing with apothecaries and also the selling of a poison or abortifacient (*abortivum*): attempted repression which is itself evidence of practice?[51]

Let us stand back from this cluster of relatively dense data around 1300 and consider a long span, from the ninth to the fifteenth centuries. The long history of the supply of abortifacient drugs in itself, the professional category of the druggist, and the gender of those engaged in this business are all problematic. In one set of statutes (802–5) of Gerbald, bishop of Liège, the person in question is the 'poisoner', female (*venefica*),[52] a word present in earlier church material which does not specify profession. The choice of word reflects Gerbald's preference for a moral rather than professional category, not the absence of a profession, for very near to him in time and place was Halitgar, bishop of Cambrai (d. 831), who chose to incorporate into one of his works a penitential in which the professional term, 'herbalist' (*herbarius*), is specified. We can move from this to the usual central-medieval terms which we have seen in Rufinus, apothecaries and herbalists, to the spice-dealers or druggists (*aromatarii*) described by Antoninus of Florence in the fifteenth century, at which time, according to him 'well-ordered cities are accustomed to provide that some of them keep their shops open [on feast-days]'.[53] Antoninus specified in his *Confessionale* that they were to be asked in confession, 'If they instruct [in the use of] or sell those things which bring about abortion'.[54]

[49] Vincent, *Speculum naturale*, X. xcv, 734 (*menta*); X. ci, 738 (*nepita*); X. cxxii, 753 (*pulegium*); X. cxxxix, 767 (*ruta*); X. cxl, 768 (*salvia*). In the still useful survey of Macer, M. Manitius, *Geschichte der lateinischen Literatur des Mittelalters*, 2 vols. (Munich, 1911–23), ii. 539–47, see p. 546 on Vincent's use of Macer. Noonan's comment (*Contraception*, p. 211 n. 20) on Vincent's reticence on such matters is misplaced.

[50] *Middle English Translation of Macer Floridus*, ed. Frisk, p. 128. On linguistic grounds Frisk attributes it to the late fourteenth century (p. 55).

[51] Mansi, *Concilia*, xxiv. 580–1, and xxv. 754; in both cases adjacent canons deal with apothecaries and the provision of such drugs.

[52] *Capitula Episcoporum*, ed. P. Brommer, MGH, 1- (Hanover, 1984–), I, 29: *veneficas, id est, mulieres, quae potiones aliquas donant, ut partus excutiant.*

[53] Antoninus, *Theologia moralis*, I. viii. 6, ed. P. Ballerini, 4 vols. (Verona, 1740), iii. 317: *super quo* (selling on feastdays) *inde civitates bene ordinatae, sicut Florentia, solent providere ut aliqui ex eis teneant apothecas apertas, puta unam per quarterio, et hujusmodi.*

[54] Antoninus, *Confessionale*, III (Cologne, *c.*1470): *Circa aromatarios . . . Si docent vel vendunt ea que*

Over six centuries earlier Halitgar had put in apposition to his herbalists the phrase 'baby-killers' (*interfectores infantum*)—'herbalists, baby-killers': a pair of phrases here expressing, undoubtedly, a moralist's rage, but also suggesting that the pairing was familiar, the ordinary early medieval equivalent of 'chemist abortionists'. These apothecary baby-killers were of both sexes. Gerbald of Liège indicated clearly that he envisaged female 'poisoners', providing abortifacients, while the phrasing in the penitential adopted by Halitgar indicates profession and both sexes: 'herbalist man or [herbalist] woman, baby-killers' (*Herbarius vir aut mulier, interfectores infantum*).[55] Green has pointed out that legislation in Paris in 1271 regulating medical practice envisaged both male apothecary and female (*apothecaria*),[56] and legislation from Avignon against the giving or selling of abortifacients envisaged apothecaries of any sex or condition.

Are the gaps in the evidence only that, gaps in the *direct traces* of an increasingly regulated profession which in reality continued over many centuries to be the main supplier of abortifacient drugs? Since the few surviving traces concern repression, they do also suggest that there may have been cycles of repression and laissez-faire whose history has now been lost.

6.2.2 *Medicine (ii) doctors and learned medical texts*

Over one million words long, Avicenna's *Canon of Medicine* had been translated into Latin by Gerard of Cremona (d. 1187).[57] Parts of it became standard texts to be read in medical faculties, and, although it did not displace the short Salernitan anthology which later bore the name *Articella*, it achieved such a position among medical men that Arnau de Vilanova was driven to attack excessive veneration for it. At this time, around 1300, we can look to the great university of the city of Bologna and the circle of advanced medical writers around Taddeo Alderotti, who are writing commentaries on the *Canon*.[58] At the same time we turn to a remote place, looking at Vic, a little town of perhaps four thousand inhabitants which was on a high plain surrounded by mountains about sixty kilometres north of Barcelona. Living there between 1297 and 1324 was the doctor Guillem Galaubi, and through his possession of an *Evincena* we know of the presence in Vic in this period of Avicenna's *Canon of Medicine*.[59]

procurant aborsum. On the apothecaries of Florence during the period when Antoninus was archbishop, see K. Park, *Doctors and Medicine in Early Renaissance Florence* (Princeton, 1985).

[55] *Poenitentiale Pseudo-Romanum*, XI. xxiii, ed. F. W. H. Wasserschleben, *Die Bußordnungen der abendländischen Kirche* (Halle, 1851), p. 375; on the work, see R. Meens, *Het tripartite boeteboek: Overlevering en betekenis van vroegmiddeleeuwse biechtvoorschriften (met editie en vertaling van vier tripartita)* (Hilversum, 1994), pp. 51–2.

[56] Green, 'Women's Medical Practice', p. 53 and n. 42.

[57] R. Le May, 'Gerard of Cremona', *Dictionary of Scientific Biography*, xv (New York, 1978), 173–92 (p. 185); Jacquart and Micheau, pp. 147–65.

[58] Siraisi, *Taddeo*, esp. Ch. 4.

[59] McVaugh, *Medicine before the Plague*, p. 87.

Because it was standard and eventually so widely diffused, Avicenna's *Canon of Medicine* will be used here as a peg upon which to hang a sketch of the presence of avoidance of offspring in learned medical books owned by doctors.[60]

The *Canon* was a large work, divided and subdivided according to a very clear scheme, in which a monographically treated topic was easy for a reader to find.[61] A reader would go to the third book, which contained a treatment of illnesses in the standard head-to-toe order, then proceed to fens[62] 20 and 21, devoted successively to male and female generative organs, and, bypassing the incidental treatments of sterility in the section on male organs, go quickly to treatise number 1, chapters 8–10, and treatise 3, 15, and 17. Here the material of particular chapters was clearly labelled: 'On sterility and difficulty of impregnation';[63] 'On signs of sterility;[64] "On the regimen and cure" of sterility';[65] 'On abortion' (= miscarrying);[66] 'On preserving the embryo and precaution against abortion';[67] 'On the regimen of abortion [= inducing abortion] and extraction of the dead foetus';[68] 'On the instrument whereby there is injection into the womb'[69] to induce abortion; 'On the preventing of impregnation'.[70] This is a direct and quite large treatment, in which deliberate abortion gets three times the space allocated to avoiding conception. The vocabulary is distinct and precise: 'sterility', 'abortion', and 'preventing impregnation' or 'conception', where I am using 'prevent' to translate

[60] Notable previous accounts are Noonan, *Contraception*, pp. 201–3 and 210, and B. F. Musallam, *Sex and Society in Islam: Birth Control before the Nineteenth Century* (Cambridge, 1983), pp. 65, 67–8, 69, 72, 84, and 88.

[61] N. Siraisi, *Avicenna in Renaissance Italy: The Canon and Medical Teaching in English Universities after 1500* (Princeton, 1987), p. 22. On the edition used here, see ibid., pp. 133–4, 166–7, and 334. I have compared the chapters on abortion and contraception in this edition and a fourteenth-century manuscript of the *Canon*, BL, MS Royal 12.G.6, fols. 394vb–400vb. The comparison makes it clear that Renaissance revisions had not affected the text in these sections, which is nearly always identical. There is some fluidity with the rubrics of the chapters—there are some variations in the placing of titles, and there are some discrepancies *within* the manuscript between the listing of chapters in the contents list (fols. 186vb–9ra) and the correlative chapters—but they are very similar to the numbers in the printed edition; see nn. 63–70 below. Shorn of its marginal annotations, this edition gives a very good general idea of a medieval manuscript version of the *Canon*. In the following references to the *Canon*, Ed. = printed edition, and the numbers correspond, successively to the *Canon*'s divisions Liber, Fen (not where the reference is to Liber 2), Tractatus and Capitulum, while MS = BL, MS Royal 12.G.6.

[62] Name of a part of Avicenna's *Canon*, similar to such words as section, part, and division.

[63] Ed., III. xxi. 1. 8; 287vb: *De sterilitate et difficultate impregnationis*; MS, fol. 394vb: *Signa sigccitatis* [*sic*] *de sterilitate et difficultate impregnacionis.*

[64] Ed., III. xxi. 1. 9; 288rb: *De signis sterilitatis*; MS, fol. 395rb: *Signa eius.*

[65] Ed., III. xxi. 1. 10; 288va: *De regimine et cura*; MS, fol. 395va: *Regimen et curatio.*

[66] Ed., III. xxi. 2. 8; 290vb: *De abortu*; MS, fol. 398rb: *De aborsu.*

[67] Ed., III. xxi. 2. 10; 291rb: *De conservatione embryonis et cautella abortus*; MS, fol. 399ra: *De conservacione embrionis* [*et*] *cautela aborsus.*

[68] Ed., III. xxi. 2. 12; 291va: *De regimine abortus et extractione fetus mortui*; MS, fol. 399va: *De regimine aborsus et extractione fetus mortui.*

[69] Ed., III. xxi. 2. 13; 292ra: *De instrumento quo iniectio fit in matrice*; MS, fol. 399vb: *De instrumento quo iniectio fit in matrice.* See Diepgen, *Frau und Frauenheilkunde*, p. 32, on injection in Rasis' *Liber divisionum continens*—the work translated by Gerard of Cremona and not to be confused with the same author's *Liber continens.*

[70] Ed., III. xxi. 2. 17; 292vb: *De prohibitione impregnationis*; MS, fol. 400vb: *De prohibitione impregnacionis.*

prohibeo. One word, *abortus*, is used in relation to both unintended and intended termination, where it is always clear from context whether 'miscarriage' or 'induced abortion' is intended.

The implied reader is a doctor, he is envisaged as having a duty to do something ('it is necessary for the doctor to . . .'), and he is also seen as giving advice to a patient: 'you should instruct that . . .'. The remarks which introduce both deliberate abortion and avoiding conception provide the doctor with a firm medical-ethical rationale for his actions. Danger to the life of the mother in childbirth is the justification, and a duty falls upon the doctor. Thus, 'sometimes abortion . . . is necessary . . . when the pregnant person is a girl, small, whose death from childbirth is feared'[71] and 'it is sometimes necessary for the doctor to prevent impregnation in a small woman, whose death from childbirth is feared, and in a woman with illness in her womb, and in a woman with weakness in her bladder'.[72] These can be juxtaposed to generalizing comments on the broader relation between child-bearing and not child-bearing and women's health and longevity. 'A woman who bears children and is impregnated is less ill than a sterile woman, however she has a weaker body than her and ages quicker. But a sterile woman is full of illnesses and [her] old age is delayed and she is like a young [woman] for most of her life'.[73]

Abortion occupies three times as much space as prevention. Inducing abortion begins with motion, and proceeds to medicines to be drunk, such as water of rue, or medicines to be applied in pessaries, with Avicenna describing them and also referring the reader to tables of simple medicines and the antidotary with composite medicines to be found elsewhere in the *Canon*.[74] This chapter and the following one also include mechanical means, the insertion into the mouth of the womb of a lint scroll or a bitter and scraped herb the length of a feather, and also an 'instrument for injection into the mouth of the womb'.[75] In the chapter on preventing impregnation, after the advice on avoiding the impregnating mode (to which we shall return), there is instruction on movements after intercourse, such as jumping by the woman, to dislodge seed,[76] and there is instruction on

[71] Ed., III. xxi. 2. 12; 291va: *Quandoque abortus . . . necessarius est . . . qum pregnans est puella, parva, supra quam timetur mors ex partu.*

[72] Ed., III. xxi. 2. 17; 292vb: *Medico quandoque necessarium est prohibere impregnationem in parva, supra quam timetur de partu; et in ea in cuius matrice est egritudo; et in ea in cuius vesica est debilitas.*

[73] Ed., III. xxi. 1. 8; 288rb: *mulier que parit et impregnatur minus infirma est quam sterilis, verumtamen est debilioris corporis quam ipsa et velocius fit anus. Sterilis vero est plurium egritudinum et tardatur eius senectus.*

[74] Ed., III. xxi. 2. 12; 291vb: *singulares quidem iam diximus in tabulis medicinarum singularium, et compositas in antidotario.*

[75] Ed., III. xxi. 2. 12; 291vb: *intromittatur in os matricis pregnantis charta facta licinium aut penna aut herba amara vel abrasa cum mensura quantitatis penne.* My paraphrase is a provisional version of this text, whose variant readings need collection; compare the translation from the Arabic text in Musallam, *Sex and Society*, p. 69. See below Ch. 8 n. 139 for Alvaro Pelayo's reference to women procuring sterility 'with the reedy stick of the doctors'. There is a brief discussion in G. Devereux, *A Study of Abortion in Primitive Societies* (London, 1960), p. 36.

[76] Ed., III. xxi. 2. 17; 292vb: *et precipue ut elevetur mulier cum complemento coitus, et saliat ad posteriora, usque ad vii et ix saltus; fortasse enim egredietur sperma.* Note the caution of *fortasse*, 'perhaps'.

medicines to be 'applied underneath' (in the case of the woman) or 'anointed' (in the case of the man), and on medicine to be taken in drink. Elsewhere in the *Canon* many medicines are listed, which have been studied by Noonan and Musallam. On the most important herbs, the *Canon* overlaps with what we have already seen in herbals, for example: 'Mint: when it is placed under before the time of intercourse, it prevents impregnation.'[77] Avicenna's words play variations on a theme of effectiveness. On the one hand some phrases indicate possible doubt: 'it is thought [that it blocks impregnation]', 'it is said', and 'some believe'. An example is 'Scolopendria . . . And it is said that [when] hung from the neck it prevents impregnation.'[78] On the other hand the simple 'it prevents' implies the confident 'it does'.

A reader's understanding of Avicenna's central statements about the timing and mode of intercourse will have been shaped by the elaborate and interlocking structure of the chapters in which they appear. There is system. The description of causes of sterility is mounted with a listing and divisions and subdivisions into 'either/or'. Thus there is either inherent defect (implied) *or* contingent defect; inherent defect either in the man's seed, *or* in the woman's, either in the female member *or* in the male; *or* there is contingent defect, and contingent defect is either in sexual intercourse (during it) *or* after it. This mode seems to encourage exhaustive listing, and with intercourse itself it seems to encourage an analysing approach, an example of which will be given in a moment. Dominant in the system are opposites: trying to avoid *or* induce abortion, trying to bring about *or* avoid pregnancy. These are underlined by the juxtaposition of the chapters; by repetition of the same material reversed, 'do this' *or* 'avoid this'; and by Avicenna's explicit reference backwards, 'as we have said'. The chapter on regimen and cure of sterility reverses the order of causes, beginning with remedying contingent defect, in other words providing instruction on how to have intercourse in a way which will lead to impregnation, and then proceeding to remedies for intrinsic defects. Linked with this, as its opposite, is the chapter on preventing pregnancy, which begins its advice with *avoiding* the impregnating mode of intercourse which has been specified earlier. Chapters on avoiding and inducing abortion are similarly linked by their advice, in opposite directions, on avoiding *or* engaging in sudden and violent motion. When looking at a particular chapter, then, a reader will have thought both about what it said should be done to *achieve* a particular result, and what this implied should be done to *avoid* the same result.

In the case of *mode* of intercourse, the opposite is spelled out. Avicenna (1) describes the defect in mode of intercourse which produces sterility and (2) the

[77] Ed., II. ii. 496; 111va: *quando supponitur ante horam coitus, prohibet impregnationem.* Mint is very widely attested—see e.g. Pietro d'Abano, *Conciliator*, Differentia 149; 207va: *quae quidem ante horam coitus supposita prohibet impregnationem*; John of Gaddesden, *Rosa Anglica*, on sterility, and on the causes on the part of the woman (Venice, 1516), 75rb: *succum mente in[i]ectum in matrice* (mint juice injected into the womb). While Riddle has the merit of drawing attention to the possible part-efficacy of such drugs (see the index-entries under 'mint' in the works cited in n. 7 above), further enquiry will need to bring together more carefully history and modern laboratory study.

[78] Ed., II. ii. 637; 124ra: *Et dicitur quod suspensa ad collum prohibet impregnationem.*

mode which is most conducive to impregnation, and then (3), under 'preventing impregnation', he says, 'you should instruct that, at the hour [when] intercourse [takes place], the impregnating mode, which we have stated [= described], should be avoided' (*precipias in hora coitus, ut caveatur forma impregnativa, quam diximus*).[79] In the case of *timing* the opposite is not spelled out. While advising how to remedy sterility, Avicenna recommends having intercourse 'at the end of menstruation'. Here the thought was left dangling, encouraged by the other pairs of thoughts: that if one could procreate by having intercourse at a particular time in relation to menstruation, one could have intercourse but avoid procreation by doing it at another time.

In both cases there was a paradox in practice, seen when this material is subjected to the crude light of modern knowledge, for anyone following this either/or thought about timing would have been trying to procreate at an infertile period, and trying to avoid procreation by having intercourse at a more probably fertile point in a woman's cycle. This point probably also applies to mode. The modern reader of the advice quoted at the beginning of the previous paragraph will have in mind the simplest of methods, where the man withdraws and emits seed outside: coitus interruptus. The clarity of Avicenna's description provides important encouragement in this direction, as does also the emphasis on emission of seed and the man and woman's 'separation with speed' after intercourse. This point should not be submerged by the larger and well-known point, namely Avicenna's subscription to the two-seed theory of conception, and its consequence here. Avicenna held that the emission of seed by both man and woman was necessary for conception. Hence his advice on encouraging impregnation was, in effect, on techniques of love-making which would encourage the woman to 'emit seed'. Simultaneous emission and staying together for a while was best. The counterpart, causes of sterility, spelled this out. 'A contingent error is when there is emission of seed before completion or after completion. Before completion when seed is emitted—[this] is when the woman and man are different in the time of intercourse and emission of seed, leading to one always preceding the other in emission of seed. If therefore there is anticipation by the man, he may leave her, and [she] may not emit seed. And if there is anticipation by the woman, the man will emit after the woman has emitted'.[80] No more detail is needed. Given (*a*) the centrality of the notion that emission of the woman's seed is also needed for conception, and (*b*) the logic of opposites which Avicenna's text encouraged, doctors reading this could have been led to give the advice that couples would be preventing impregnation when having intercourse in a way where the man emitted seed but the woman did not. This is the immediate message, again one which in

[79] Ed., III. xxi. 2. 17; 292vb.

[80] Ed., III. xxi. 1. 8; 288rb: *Error autem accidens est cum spermatis sit emissio ante complementum aut post complementum. Ante complementum vero cum sperma emittitur est ut sint mulier et vir diversi in tempore coitus, quare non cessat unus eorum antecedere cum emissione spermatis. Si ergo fuerit antecessio viri, dimittat eam et non emittat spermam. Et si fuerit antecessio mulieris, emittet vir postquam emiserit* [*mulier*].

the light of modern knowledge would have been counter-productive. We could suggest that Avicenna's text contains two strata, where two-seed theory is one stratum which is imposed on another stratum of common-sense knowledge about intercourse and conception, and that readers looking for practical advice would have ignored the upper stratum. But I can see no evidence to support such a conjecture.

The *Canon*'s translation was being read by the second quarter of the thirteenth century. What does the picture look like when we move on to the decades around 1300?

Although some texts may have been deliberately silent about health grounds for abortion or avoiding conception, the 'Trotula' tradition was not. One Trotula text cited Galen as commenting on the danger to women who are narrow—'they ought not to use men, lest they conceive and die; but since not all of these can abstain, they need our help' to avoid conceiving.[81] Rasis's *Continens* used very emphatic language on the need to abort, especially when there is the first pregnancy of a girl who has conceived when she was 'small'.[82] This text was translated into Latin in 1278,[83] and its spread needs to be set alongside the rise of commentaries on the *Canon* as part of the background to a remarkable phenomenon, the considerable attention which is soon to be paid in Italian learned medicine to the ethics of this area, by Mondino de' Liuzzi (d. 1326), Dino del Garbo (d. 1327), and Gentile da Foligno (d. 1348). Siraisi discovered a '*consilium* for preventing pregnancy', attributed to Mondino, which repeats but also broadens the justification for a doctor providing instruction to help avoiding conception. Here is a translation of the text, provisional and literal because the Latin is not always clear:

In the *ars* of medicine it is plain that it is not only necessary to make known those things which induce pregnancy and [help to] make it strong, but also to *constrare* [*perhaps*: make clear] those things which oppose impregnation, so that they [impregnations] are avoided.... So that impregnation is prevented [in those women], who are by [their] natural disposition unsuitable for conception, such as girls and small women in whom impregnation is a matter of fear because of dangerous childbirth, or in those who are unsuitable for conception because of [their] contingent disposition, such as those who have either ulcers or other suffering in their bladders or other members, such as the womb. And also that impregnation should be prevented for those who have intercourse illicitly, or are forced by nature and [are so] troubled [that they are driven] to have intercourse. And [since these are women] who ought not to be impregnated, for this reason, although it may be a sin to prevent conception in them, nevertheless [preventing conception] is less evil than aborting a conceived foetus.[84]

[81] Treatise *Cum auctor*, xi, ed. I. Spach, *Gynaeciorum sive de mulierum tam communibus tam gravidorum, parientium et puerporum affectibus et morbis* (Strasbourg, 1597), p. 47: *Nota, dicit Galienus, quod mulieres, quae habent vulvas angustas, et matrices strictas, non debent viris uti, ne concipientes moriantur. Sed cum non omnes illae possent abstinere, indigent nostro auxilio.* On the edition, see M. Green, 'The Development of the *Trotula*', *Revue d'Histoire des Textes* 26 (1996), 119–203 (pp. 121–2 n. 7), and on *Cum auctor*, ibid., pp. 130–5.

[82] Rasis, *Continens*, XXII. vii. 2 (Venice, 1542), 236rb.

[83] Jacquart and Micheau, p. 207.

[84] The Latin text is edited by Siraisi, *Taddeo*, p. 283 n. 61; see her comments (pp. 282–3).

When Gentile came to raise and discuss formally the question 'whether it is licit to induce abortion', he cited earlier response by Dino del Garbo to the same question.[85] Here, then, we have a concentration of discussions among early fourteenth-century learned Italian doctors, and this seems to be the intelligible background to a quodlibetic theological question we shall see later, responded to by an early fourteenth-century Italian Dominican, on the licitness of inducing abortion.

'More' is the reader's main conclusion when moving to other features of Avicenna's text and comparing them to material from around 1300. There are now more monographic treatises on conception and sterility, which seem to have been an area of special concern in the school of Montpellier around and just after 1300. When juxtaposed to the relevant sections in more general treatises, these provide the impression of greater wealth and variety of method. In their formal internal structure, Avicenna's chapters seem to be earlier points in an upward line which leads to the schematic divisions and sub-divisions of the *De sterilitate* of the Anonymous of Montpellier and the *Compilacio de conceptione* attributed to Arnau de Vilanova.[86] The latter's breaks down reasons for failure to conceive, and thus by implication their opposites. 'We should say that this fault occurs either before intercourse, or during intercourse, or after intercourse' (*dicamus quod illud peccatum aut ante commixtionem aut in commixtione occurrit aut postea*). The author goes on to say that 'we shall gather all the kinds of preventive causes in one table' (*omnes species causarum prohibentium in una tabula congregamus*). The resulting tables, in both the manuscripts and the Renaissance editions of this work, provide startling witness to the author's concern for graphic clarity.[87] At the same time a doctor's practice and experience have a stronger textual presence. Rasis's *Continens* shows the claim to experience held up by the translated Arabic texts: 'I say, this pessary is wonderful' (*Dico, hoc est pessarium mirabile*), and 'pregnant women have told me that . . .' (*Recitaverunt mihi pregnantes quod . . .*).[88] So John of Gaddesden claims that something works for inducing menses 'as I have proved often by experience', or says that a 'suppository [is] very good, and tried out by me'.[89] Given the great difficulty here of distinguishing literary topos and

[85] *An sit licitum provocare aborsum*, ed. R. J. Schaefer in his 'Gentile da Foligno über die Zulässigkeit des artifiziellen Abortes (ca. 1340)', *Archiv für die Geschichte der Naturwissenschaften und der Technik* 6 (1913), 321–8 (pp. 325–6). On Dino (d. 1327), see Siraisi, *Taddeo*, pp. 55–64.

[86] *Tractatus de sterilitate: Anónimo de Montpellier (s. XIV) (Atribuido a A. De Vilanova, R. De Moleriis y J. De Turre)*, ed. E. M. Cartelle, Lingüística y Filología 16 (Valladolid, 1993). On the proliferation of sex treatises at Montpellier in this period, see ibid., pp. 18–19, and L. E. Demaitre, *Doctor Bernard de Gordon: Professor and Practitioner*, Studies and Texts 51 (Toronto, 1980), pp. 85–6.

[87] Arnau de Vilanova, *Opera nuperrime revisa* (Lyons, 1332), 213va–314ra; Munich, Bayerische Staatsbibliothek, MS CLM 7576, fol. 97va; BN, MS Lat. 6971, fol. 70r–v. I am grateful to Michael McVaugh for supplying photostats of these manuscripts. I have not seen the manuscript from Fritzlar listed in L. Thorndike and P. Kibre, *A Catalogue of Incipits of Medieval Writings in Latin* (London, 1963), col. 849.

[88] Rasis, *Continens*, XXII. vi and XXII. vii. 2; 229vb and 236rb.

[89] John of Gaddesden, *Rosa anglica*, 79ra and 80ra: *saturgia bibita optima est in provocatione menstruorum sicut expertus sum frequenter*; *optimum suppositorium et a me probatum.* See *Breviarium*, III. v, in Arnau de Villanova, *Opera nuperrime revisa*, 189v: *Et ego hoc suppositorium feci et probavi in quadam patiente molam et statim eam liberavi.*

straight reporting, the language of 'construction' is unusually apt. These texts increasingly construct a world in which doctors actively intervene in these areas.[90]

There is further, around 1300, a drawing near of medical texts to both theological, pastoral, and deposition material. A woman's quick or violent jumping up in an attempt to dislodge seed, present in the *Canon* and richly present in other medical treatises of around 1300, is something we will see spelled out and emphasized in a confessor's manual of this period.[91] Although *prohibere* is still there, Arnau de Vilanova is using *impedire* for an action to 'impede' conception, and this word comes into confessors' manuals at this period. To add to the apparently magical hanging of something around the woman's neck, seen for example in the *Canon* and also in a text in the 'Trotula' tradition,[92] is the spelling out in a work (attributed to Arnau de Vilanova) of something to be 'wrapped in a piece of cloth and borne on the navel', which recalls quite closely the method advocated to Béatrice de Planisolles by Pierre Clergue.[93] The theological example is given below.

In three areas there seem to me to be changes of substance. First, translations were presenting the theme of women not conceiving while breastfeeding. As we shall see in Chapter 10, a translation of one of Aristotle's works, around 1260, aired this theme, which had been omitted from an earlier translation, and Averroes' *Colliget*, translated into Latin in 1285 or earlier, ventilated it further. 'There are some women', wrote Averroes, 'who cannot be impregnated while they produce milk' (*sunt alique mulieres que non possunt impregnari dum lactant*).[94]

Secondly, there was the well-known Aristotle versus Galen match. There was much philosophical and medical discussion of the opposition between the one-seed and the two-seed theories of conception, one of which laid down that emission of seed by both male and female was necessary for conception (as we saw above with Avicenna) and the other of which, Aristotle's, envisaged only the male seed as necessary.[95] Entering this field in the later thirteenth century was the

[90] See Jacquart and Micheau, p. 208, on the late thirteenth-century translations of Arabic treatises encouraging the recounting of examples of one's medical practice.

[91] *Tractatus de sterilitate*, I, ed. Cartelle, p. 72. For other examples from this period, see Bernard de Gordon, *Lilium medicinae*, VII. xiv (Lyons, 1574), p. 618: '[Sterility] occurs when she jumps after coitus, or moves too quickly' ([Sterilitas] *accidit quando post coitum saltat, aut nimis velociter movetur*); and the *Compilatio de conceptione*, Arnau de Vilanova, *Opera nuperrime revisa*, 214ra: 'Sudden rising up of the woman. Big jump' (*Subita erectio mulieris. Saltus magnus*). The suggestion being made here is of wider diffusion of the idea, not novelty.

[92] See n. 78 above, and *Cum auctor*, xi, ed. Spach, p. 47.

[93] *Breviarium*, III, in Arnau de Vilanova, *Opera nuperrime revisa*, 189va: *in pecia lini involvatur et supra umbilicum imponatur et portetur, quia quot diebus portat supra umbilicum tot mensibus stat mulier quod non concipiet.* See above, the method urged upon Béatrice de Planisolles by Pierre Clergue. *Pecia lini involvatur* seems similar to *involutam et ligatam panno lineo*, and *in orificio stomachi* similar to *supra umbilicum*, when it is recalled that Latin *in* can mean *on* or *above* as well as *in*.

[94] Averroes, *Colliget*, II. x (Venice, 1497), 51rb. On the date of translation, see Jacquart and Micheau, p. 182 n. 30. According to V. Fildes, *Wet Nursing: A History from Antiquity to the Present* (Oxford, 1988), p. 8, 'the contraceptive advantages of lactation . . . were well known to all women in all societies in all periods'; see further ibid., pp. 8 n. 16, 16, 34, 57 and n. 21.

[95] See Hewson, *Giles of Rome*, pp. 67–94; L. Demaitre and A. A. Travill, 'Human Embryology and Development in the Works of Albertus Magnus', in *Albertus and the Sciences*, pp. 405–40 (pp. 414–19); Siraisi, *Taddeo*, pp. 187 and 195–201; D. Jacquart and C. Thomasset, *Sexuality and Medicine in the Middle*

Colliget. The lack of need for woman's seed in generation, wrote Averroes, 'is manifest to sense and known through argument. Through sense [observation] because one sees that a woman is impregnated without her emitting seed. And after I read the books of Aristotle I asked many women about this, and they replied that many [women] were impregnated without emitting seed: and even if intercourse did not give them pleasure. And I saw many who had been raped by males [who were nevertheless] impregnated by them'.[96] The assumption in the last is this: women were raped, that is to say, they experienced a form of sex which did not give the pleasure [= they did not emit seed], but they did conceive, which means that women do not need to emit seed in order to conceive. This had been preceded by Albert the Great's reporting of what 'some women say, that they were impregnated from sex in which they did not have pleasure through emissions of seed',[97] but it was the *Colliget* which came to be quoted.[98]

These texts are well-known to the abundant modern scholarship on this topic, the history of the struggle of these two theories is long and complex, and it did not have a decisive outcome in our period. Despite this, I would like to draw attention to the sheer bluntness of the attack in Averroes and the power of its appeal to experience, and also to raise a question. Once a text of such force was in play, could there have been a shifting of balance in the medical texts? Continuing academic debate and confusion, but increasing doubt about the role played in reality by the emission (or not) of female seed? Allied to the emphasis in medical texts on an 'apt mode' of intercourse for conception, and avoiding the 'apt mode' in order to avoid conception, increasing doubt would have helped to clear the path for medicine to suggest and underwrite avoidance of conception by the man—and the man only—avoiding emitting seed inside a woman in order to avoid the woman conceiving. To clear the path, in other words, for the implicit presence in medical texts of coitus interruptus. I write 'underwrite' and 'in medical texts', because the practice was described differently in the Bible, and perhaps practised differently, as we shall note below. There is no warrant to assume that learned medicine had been the dominant element in a mix of thought and practice in which western women's and men's experience *may* already have been in opposition to medicine. My question is put hesitantly, and I must emphasize that in the philosophical and medical texts two-seed theory continued for long to co-exist with one-seed theory, and thus to be a potential source of misinformation.

Ages, trans. M. Adamson (Oxford, 1988), pp. 61–78; J. Cadden, *Meanings of Sex Difference in the Middle Ages: Medicine, Science and Culture* (Cambridge, 1993), pp. 117–30.

[96] Averroes, *Colliget*, II. x; 50vb: *manifestatur sensu et cognoscitur per argumentum. Per sensum quia homo vidit quod mulier impregnatur absque eo quod spermatizet. Et postquam legi libros Aristotelis ego quesivi a multis mulieribus de hoc, et responderunt quod plures impregnate fuerunt absque spermatizatione, et etiam si displicuisset eis coitus. Et etiam vidi quamplures ex istis impregnatas que fuerant a masculis violate.* See Hewson, *Giles of Rome*, pp. 87–8.

[97] Albert, *De animalibus*, XV. ii. 11; ii. 1056: *quaedam mulieres dicunt se impraegnatas a coitu in quo non habuerunt delectationem per emissiones spermatis.* See comment by Jacquart and Thomasset, p. 68, and Cadden, *Sex Difference*, p. 126.

[98] Hewson, *Giles of Rome*, p. 72; John of Gaddesden, *Rosa anglica*, 75ra (John also refers to Giles). But among the Bologna doctors, only Dino used the *Colliget*: Siraisi, *Taddeo*, pp. 195 and 201.

The 'fertile' and 'infertile period' is the final theme. I put the phrases in quotation marks in order to avoid implying that the authors we are studying necessarily thought in these terms. What we find clearly in medical texts is advice to have sex at such and such a time *in order to conceive*, and, if the logic of opposites which we have seen so clearly in Avicenna prevailed here, this brought in its wake the thought 'do not have sex at such and such a time if you want to avoid conceiving'. I am not aware that the history of medieval thought on the times thought to be conducive to conception has been written.[99] Such a history would be complex. While the *Canon*, as we have seen, recommended intercourse at the end of menstruation,[100] advice which was both good and bad (in modern terms) could be found elsewhere.[101] Set against a confusing background, but one in which there seems to have been more (and in modern terms misguided) emphasis on intercourse at the end of menstruation, are two things from around 1300. One is a more probably (again in modern terms) effective note which is struck by the Anonymous of Montpellier's *De sterilitate*, which recommends abstaining for five days or more before menstruation, and also for four or five days after, and then starting to have intercourse.[102] The older advice was still abundantly present,[103] and the question put forward here is again tentative: might further research show a shifting of balance in the texts? The other is one remarkable early fourteenth-century *Sentences* commentary which, as we shall see in the next chapter, is another example of medicine and theology drawing nearer to each other. It suggests that couples are using experience of times of fertility or infertility to avoid conception.

[99] See Bologne, *Naissance interdite*, pp. 155–6, on the ineffectiveness of the period method before the twentieth century.

[100] See also Rasis, *Liber ad Almansorem*, V. lxxii (Venice, 1497); 27ra: (on things helping impregnation) *Et fit coitus post menstruorum purgationem. Epistola de anatomia* attributed to Hippocrates and quoted thus by Vincent de Beauvais, *Speculum naturale*, XXXI. xxvii; 2313: *Neque vero quoties coitus fit, mulier concipit, sed tantummodo certo tempore, sc[ilicet] aut in initio purgationis, aut in fine.* Avicenna, *De animalibus*, IX. i; 40vb: *quando menstruatur mulier complete post erit tempus naturale impregnationis, et aliquando impregnatur mulier tempore menstruorum.*

[101] *Cum auctor*, XI, ed. Spach, p. 46, recommends starting to have intercourse seven days after the end of menstruation, and repeatedly in the following week, but later in the same chapter (p. 47) recommends intercourse at the end of menstruation in order to conceive a male.

[102] *Tractatus de sterilitate*, IX, ed. Cartelle, p. 150: 'Moreover, it helps with conception if the man and woman abstain from coitus and embraces for five days or more before menstruation, and throughout the whole time of the flow of menstruation, and, after this menstruation, for three or four days and nights' (*Confert autem ad conceptum si vir et mulier abstineant a coytu et amplexibus per V dies vel amplius ante menstrua et toto tempore fluxus menstrorum et post ipsa menstrua III vel IIIIor diebus et illis noctibus*).

[103] See e.g. Taddeo Alderotti, *I 'Consilia'*, 13, ed. G. M. Nardi (Turin, 1937), p. 33, in the course of advice on how to achieve conception: 'And also that there should be coitus when the menses have not been got rid of' (*Et etiam quod coytus fiat menstruis non evacuatis*).

7

AVOIDANCE OF OFFSPRING (II): CANON LAW AND *SENTENCES* COMMENTARIES

In marriage there is often the procuring of sterility[1]

7.1 *Canon law*[2]

Canon-law books were used in the schools of canon law, where they were the subject matter of lectures and the object of glosses and commentaries. These books had been studied and learnt by the practising lawyers, and they were supposed to be consulted by judges in marriage courts, alongside 'men learned in law'. The milestones among these books were Gratian's *Decretum* of around 1140 and Gregory IX's *Five Books of the Decretals* of 1234.

The collection made by Ivo, bishop of Chartres, around 1094, firmly belongs to an earlier world. Measures of avoidance are not yet subordinated to or set within a theological view of marriage, and there is no mark of use in the schools. There is no raising of questions, and no running commentary other than that which is quietly suggested by a succession of rubrics on connected themes. Ivo's *Decretum* is a clear and practical work, drawn up by an experienced bishop who knew much about the application of canon law to marriage cases. The structure is plain. The work is divided into seventeen sections, each with a theme, and our material is distributed among three of these sections,[3] one on marriages, one on sexual sins, and one on homicide. In each section there is simply a series of chapters, each of

[1] Anonymous commentary on *Sentences*, IV. xxxi, BN, MS Lat. 14308, fol. 266rb: *sepe enim in matrimonio est sterilitatis procuracio.*

[2] All later work has been indebted to the fundamental account in J. T. Noonan's *Contraception: A History of its Treatment by the Catholic Theologians and Canonists* (Cambridge, Mass., 1966), and mine is no exception. Referring to every point of coincidence or divergence would be tedious and long, and here I confine myself to recommending his fine work, and to summarizing the principal differences between us. Noonan's account is longer, it does not discuss some crucial texts, such as *Solet queri* (cited in n. 5 below) and *Concubitum qui non fit causa prolis*, and it antedates much important scholarship which is exploited here, for example Zeimentz's and Reinhardt's accounts of the theology of marriage in the school of Laon, and Weigand's history of the canon-law of pre-marital conditions. See further Ch. 6 above and n. 4.

[3] Sections 8–10.

which has a brief rubric, such as 'On women who fornicate and kill their foetuses' (*De mulieribus quae fornicatae partus suos necant*),[4] followed by an authoritative text.

In its selection of material, however, Ivo's *Decretum* is a half-way house. It continues to include older material, such as the council of Ancyra on abortion, that had been contained in the works of Burchard of Worms (d. 1025) and Regino of Prüm (*c*.906). However, Ivo also incorporates patristic theological texts, in particular from Augustine—most significantly *Solet queri*,[5] *Aliquando*,[6] and three texts distinguishing early and late abortion, *Quod non formatum*, *Moyses tradidit*, and *Sicuti semina*.[7] The avoidance texts are slightly bigger. Included was a sixth-century expansion of a canon of the Council of Ancyra, added parts indicated here in italics: 'If some woman has fornicated and killed the baby which was born from this, or has applied herself to bringing about an abortion and killing what has been conceived, *or [has applied herself] to taking care that she does not conceive* . . .'[8] Including *Aliquando* represented a similar shift, for it also covered both abortion and avoiding conceiving. In both cases, however, the rubric draws attention only to abortion: 'On women who fornicate and have abortions', and 'On those who kill the foetus in the womb'.[9] The rubric to *Solet queri* does not draw attention to what the text says about procreation or avoidance.[10]

In Gratian's *Decretum* the theme acquires autonomous and separate treatment,[11] a theological setting, and dialectical presentation. This last meant a textual debate: the statement of motions for and against, each with its suppporting authorities. The thesis for this: 'it seems that one can prove that [a woman] who is married only for incontinence is not a wife, in this way: marriage was instituted by God for the sake of propagation, not the sating of lust. For this was the blessing on marriage: "Increase and multiply".' The thesis against is based in part on the double institution of marriage, where the second institution included remedying incontinence. 'Marriages are not for this reason [remedying incontinence] adjudged evil', Gratian continues. 'What happens beyond the intention of generating is not an evil of marriages, but venial, because of the good of marriage, which is threefold.' Augustine follows, on 'immoderate use of the married' being only venial.

Pro and con have formed parts one and two of the question, and after a third part which goes off in another direction,[12] Gratian returns in parts 4–5 to the theme of marrying for incontinence. His own comments and the rubrics show his intention of going through three possibilities. The first is marrying only for incontinence while not avoiding conceiving or having abortions [1]. The second

[4] Ivo of Chartres, *Decretum*, VIII. cccxix; *PL* 161, 652.

[5] Ibid., VIII. lxv; 597–8. [6] Ibid., X. lv; 706. [7] Ibid., X. lvi–lviii; 706–7.

[8] Ibid., VIII. cccxxxi; 655: *aut certe ne concipiat elaborare.*

[9] Ibid.: *De mulieribus fornicariis, et abortum facientibus*; X. lv; 706: *De illis qui fetus in utero occidunt.*

[10] Ibid., VIII. lxv; 597. The rubric indicates how semi-marriage arises from someone using a concubine in such a way that he neither has nor desires to have another woman.

[11] C. 23 q. 2 c. 1–11; Friedberg, i. 1119–23.

[12] The absence of the Holy Spirit during conjugal acts.

is marrying only for incontinence, and avoiding conceiving [2]. The third is having abortions, which Gratian divides into early and late [3].

[1] He begins part 4 thus:

This is to be understood about those who are joined in conjugal affection: even though they come together not for the sake of procreating children but for satiating lust, they are not therefore called fornicators but married people. This is proved by the authority of St Augustine in the book *On conjugal good.* [Rubric:] Those who are joined together only for the sake of incontinence are married people. [The supporting authority, Augustine's *Solet queri,* is then quoted] '*One is accustomed to ask*... [This can be called marriage] even if they have not united for this reason, so long as they have not avoided the generation of children, in such a way that they do not want children to be born, or do some evil thing so that children are not born...'

[2] The next rubric is 'Those who procure poisons of sterility are fornicators, not married people', and the supporting authority is Augustine's *Aliquando.* There is a shift. Whereas in Ivo's *Decretum* a text which fact covers both avoiding conceiving and abortion was rubricated to refer to abortion, in Gratian's *Decretum* it is rubricated to refer to those who use 'poisons of sterility' to avoid conceiving.

[3] *Aliquando*'s reference *also* to abortion enables a useful connection with what immediately follows in part 5, which Gratian introduces thus. 'About those who procure abortion—the question is raised, whether or not they should be adjudged homicides?' Gratian then uses texts from Augustine—the three texts already used by Ivo—to distinguish between a foetus not yet animated (whose abortion is not homicide) and after animation (homicide).

Much of the contrast with Ivo's *Decretum* is pedagogic. Gratian's union of theology and canon law is up to the minute, and the dialectic, the raising of questions, and the parade of relevant authorities are appropriate for lawyers' classrooms, as also the style. Gratian's schematicism smells of the textbook and the classroom. First, marriage: for procreation or incontinence? Second, incontinence: with or without deliberate avoiding? Third, deliberate avoiding: avoiding conception or abortion? Fourth, abortion: early or late? Lawyer's limpidity here is offset by the highly charged and sometimes opaque prose of the texts from Augustine. Rapidly the *Decretum* became a standard text in Bologna and Paris, and in less well-known Rhineland and Anglo-Norman schools. Gratian's treatment was also appropriated by academic theology, as we shall see, and its categories and vocabulary therefore acquired extraordinary diffusion. The sharpest example of this is 'procure poisons of sterility' (*venena sterilitatis procurare*), which is transmitted by the appearance of *Aliquando* in the *Decretum* and is consequently and subsequently found in any sort of Church text as the phrase for avoiding conception. When we encounter clerical writers choosing another phrase, we should always suspect that they are showing the awareness of the tension between a phrase which, if taken literally and narrowly, may only refer to medicines taken as drinks, and the variety of practice and vocabulary in the real world.

The great collection issued by Gregory IX in 1234, the *Five Books of the Decretals*, had only one item of significance to add to this, a decretal on prior conditions attached to a marriage contract, where the stipulation of avoiding offspring would nullify the contract. About sixty years of writing and debate lay behind this.[13] In the late 1170s treatises from French and German schools of canon law as well as Bologna had turned their attention to conditions 'against the substance of marriage',[14] without spelling out precisely what an 'illicit pact'(*illicita pactio*) might be.[15] Around 1186 a treatise from the Anglo-Norman school referred to *Solet queri*[16] to exemplify such a condition,[17] and then comes the first work to spell out an anti-procreative condition, albeit awkwardly. 'If however it is contracted with a condition [about something] without which there cannot be marriage, such as "that there is never intercourse" or "that they procreate miscarriage" [*sic*], nothing is effected.' By now there is debate. For, after referring to *Solet queri*, the anonymous continues, 'However, some are doubtful on this [point].'[18]

Bologna produced the most substantial early treatment, in Huguccio's *Summa decretorum*.[19] A condition is either worthy or unworthy (*honesta, inhonesta*). If unworthy it is against the substance of marriage, or it is not. A condition which is against the substance of marriage is, for example, a condition 'about extinguishing offspring or about avoiding [offspring] or about [offspring] not being born (*puta de exstinguenda prole uel de uitanda uel de non nascitura*) or about not consenting to fleshly union or suchlike'. Huguccio refers not only to the more general *Solet queri* but also to the more specific *Aliquando*, and he returns to the subject, spelling out the condition in different terms: 'a condition . . . which contains an agreement about not procreating children or suffocating those who have been procreated' (*conditio . . . que continet conuentionem de liberis non procreandis uel procreatis suffocandis*). Huguccio distinguishes finely between having the *will not* to have children and *not having* the will to have children. 'Similarly it is impeded if they have the will of avoiding or killing offspring (*si habent uoluntatem uitandi uel necandi prolem*). If therefore they contract thus—that they *will* not to have—marriage is impeded. If however they contract [thus]—that they do not have the will to have—it is not impeded.'

Between Huguccio and 1234 many canon lawyer writers continued to examine such conditions,[20] now usually referring both to *Solet queri* and *Aliquando*, and sometimes expressly indicating that there was debate on these issues. Although the theme has become standard, there was still variation in the way the condition was exemplified. 'Extinguishing' or 'killing offspring' continued, paired with

[13] The following account is based on R. Weigand, *Die bedingte Eheschliessung im kanonischen Recht: Ein Beitrag zur Geschichte der Kanonistik von Gratian bis Gregor IX* (Munich, 1963).

[14] The *Summa Monacensis* (1175 × 1178) was the first to order conditions under the category 'against the substance of marriage', Weigand, p. 164.

[15] Phrase used in the *Summa* on the *Decretum* of Simon of Bisignano (1177 × 1179), Weigand, p. 171.

[16] See Gratian [1] above. [17] The *Summa Lipsiensis* (*c.*1186), Weigand, p. 187.

[18] *Summa* 'De iure canonico tractaturus', Weigand, p. 190: *Si autem contrahatur cum condicione sine qua non possit esse matrimonium, puta: 'ut nunquam coetur' vel 'ut abortum procrearent' nihil agitur, ut infra xxxii q. ii. Solet. De hoc tamen quidam dubitant.*

[19] See Weigand, p. 203 n. 13, on this: written from 1178 and finally published 1188 × 1190.

[20] Weigand examines sixteen from this period.

avoiding conceiving.[21] While the phrase 'procuring poisons of sterility', derived from *Aliquando*, continued, there appeared alongside it the neat phrase 'avoidance of offspring' (*vitatio prolis*),[22] and this was to acquire great diffusion through its appearance in the 'ordinary' gloss to Gratian's *Decretum*, written by John the German around 1215.[23]

Then came the important moment, in 1234, when Gregory IX sent out the official new decretal collection to Paris and Bologna, to be taught there and regarded as the official law of the Church. The culmination of sixty years of thought about conditions was the selection of one of Gregory IX's own decretals, *Si conditiones*. 'If conditions against the substance of marriage are inserted . . . the matrimonial contract lacks effect'.[24] The first of the three stated conditions[25] was against generation. Now, as we have seen, the earlier texts had used various phrases: more or less specific, sometimes holdalls, and sometimes stretching as far as infanticide. A condition restricted to abortion had even put in a brief appearance in the first decade of the thirteenth century in two texts produced in France: 'I contract with you if you procure abortion' (*contraho tecum si procuraveris abortum*).[26] This had not reappeared, and now there seems to be a distinct shift of emphasis. The example given in the decretal chosen for inclusion in this most important collection is specifically avoiding conceiving, not abortion. And the preferred phrase was not the technically narrow Augustinian phrase, 'procure poisons of sterility', but a broader phrase which harks back to the *vitatio prolis* of the ordinary gloss on the *Decretum*. The example spelled out in *Si conditiones* is this: 'I contract with you if you avoid generation of offspring' (*contraho tecum si generationem prolis evites*).

Let us stand back and survey these canon-legal collections, treatises and commentaries.[27] In the first instance they are all evidence of vocabulary, thought, and debate among canon lawyers. The treatises show the theme's presence in various schools of canon law, and argument about it: 'some . . . are doubtful on this point'. A question in one treatise, beginning 'A question was raised about conditions', goes on like this. 'Item, "I consent to you if you give me 100 [of a particular currency] or procure poisons of sterility". The question is raised, whether [this] is a marriage.' Support comes first: 'It seems that it is . . .'[28] Here we glimpse

[21] The *Summa Reginensis*, written possibly by Peter of Benevento and contemporaneous with Huguccio, has 'extinguishing offspring' (*de extinguenda prole*), while another Bologna lawyer, Bernard of Pavia, in his *Summa Decretalium* (1191 × 1198) has if 'you avoid children by evil arts' (*filios malis artibus evitaveris*); Weigand, pp. 218 and 253.

[22] In the *Glossa Palatina* of the early thirteenth-century Bologna master, Laurentius Hispanus; Weigand, p. 334.

[23] Weigand, p. 379.

[24] X 4.5.7; Friedberg, ii. 684.

[25] The others were 'until I find a woman worthier than you in honour or means' and 'if you give yourself over to adultery for profit'.

[26] The gloss apparatuses *Ecce vicit leo* and *Animal est substantia*, which were produced in France (respectively 1202 × 1210 and 1206 × 1210); Weigand, pp. 295 and 299.

[27] The history of the treatment of the texts in Gratian and *Si conditiones* in subsequent canon-legal commentaries and treatises is not traced here.

[28] *Summa quaestionum* 'Quesitum est de condicionibus', Weigand, p. 323: *Item, 'consencio in te si dederis centum vel venena sterilitatis procuraveris'. Queritur utrum sit matrimonium. Videtur quod sic . . .*

formal academic debate taking place in some French school of canon law, just before 1210.

The surviving records of marriage cases, from Canterbury, York, Rochester, and Hereford in England, Cerisy and Paris in France, and Augsburg and Regensburg in Germany, throw up an awkward question about the relation between such discussions and the real world. Some cases contain a pre-nuptial condition, such as these from late fifteenth-century Regensburg. Wolfgang Clothcutter said to Magdalene, 'If I wanted to marry, I would marry no one but you.' Andrew said to Elizabeth, 'If you let me sleep with you, I'll then serve you in everything, that is, marriage.' Ulrich said to Margaret, 'If you become pregnant by me, I'll marry you.' John Drosching said to Elizabeth, 'If you're really a virgin, I'll marry you.'[29] And so they go on. Now, among these *no* case has yet been found in which the condition at issue is avoiding conception or having abortions.[30] Were the lawyers, who wrote about such pre-nuptial agreements, simply engaging in an academic exercise? An academic lawyer *could* have been exploring the consequences 'if someone does something' simply in order to explore the coherence of a principle, not because people in fact did such things. Academic commentaries which explicate difficulties do use the indicative: 'some people do this.' Augustine's *Aliquando* provided a model for saying that 'sometimes' they did this, and the use of the present tense in the standard gloss on this text in the *Decretum* implies the continuation of this into the world which is contemporary to its author, that is to say, the early thirteenth century: 'Some married people act so that they do not conceive a foetus, or so that a conceived foetus is cast out, or a formed foetus is extinguished.'[31]

Let us look the discussion by the leading Bolognese lawyer of the mid-thirteenth century, Henry of Susa (Hostiensis).[32] Conditions are 'worthy' or 'unworthy', and 'possible' or 'impossible'. An example of unworthy and impossible is 'if he says to the woman, "I contract with you, if you celebrate mass today"', while worthy and impossible is 'I contract with you, if you give me the Empire or if you touch the sky with your finger'. When Henry moves to examples of worthy and possible, he chooses 'I contract with you if you give me 100 [of some currency]', or 'if your father or paternal uncle consent'. For unworthy and possible Henry chooses 'I contract with you if you avoid offspring, [or] if you give yourself over to committing adultery, [or] if I can't find a better [person]'. Other canon lawyers exemplified conditions similarly. When they wanted to remove their

[29] *'Si ego voluero ducere uxorem tunc nullam ducam nisi te'; 'Si me permiseris tecum dormire tunc te omnino servabo, hec est ad matrimonium'; 'Si pregnans ex me futura eris, ego ducam te in uxorem'; 'Si es virgo ego vere volo ducere te'*; R. Weigand, 'Die Rechtsprechung des Regensburger Gerichts in Ehesachen unter besonderer Berücksichtigung der bedingten Eheschließung nach Gerichtsbüchern aus dem Ende des 15. Jahrhunderts', reprinted in his *Liebe und Ehe im Mittelalter*, Bibliotheca Eruditorum, 7 (Goldback, 1993), pp. 245–305 (pp. 283, 285, 287, and 290).

[30] I am grateful to Richard Helmholz for confirming this point.

[31] *Coniugati quidam operantur ne fetus concipiant, aut ut fetus conceptus fundatur, aut formatus extinguatur*, in *Glossa ordinaria* on Gratian, *Decretum*, C. 32 q. 2. C. 7, in *Decretum divi Gratiani . . . unacum variis scribentium glossis et expositionibus* (Lyons, 1560), col. 1572.

[32] Henry of Susa, *Summa aurea*, IV, *De conditionibus appositis* (Venice, 1574, repr. Turin, 1963), pp. 1301–4. The *Summa* was written in 1253.

speculations from the real world, they went to town in their choice of unreal conditions, with women celebrating mass, and people handing over the Empire or touching the sky. When Henry chose possible and worthy, he chose two conditions which were frequently encountered in the courts: a girl making marriage conditional upon parental or kin consent, and a man making marriage conditional upon payment of a dowry.[33] In other words, Henry represented possible by what was utterly everyday. While pre-nuptial agreement to avoid offspring or procure abortion did not get into the courts, we have every reason to suppose that Henry was continuing to think about what was *very plausible* in the real world.

The question needs to be reformulated. It is not, 'Were people doing these things?' but 'Is it surprising that these conditions did not get to court?' These were 'unworthy' conditions, and there would be severe consequences for anyone who admitted them. These would be the penalties of public law for a man who married on the condition that his wife would act as a prostitute ('if you give yourself over to committing adultery'), or a man or woman whose condition was engaging to kill what was conceived. Given the severity of confessors on this matter, it would have been extraordinary for one or two parties to attempt annulling marriage by claiming in a church court that there had been a pre-marital pact to avoid conception. There were, further, problems of proof. Whereas a pact involving a condition of parental consent or dowry was very much part of respectable actions and discussions among respectable people and respectable families, and might well be witnessed, a pact to avoid offspring was disreputable, likely to involve only the two in question, and very unlikely to be witnessed. Canonists and judges restricted as far as possible the rule which allowed annulling of marriages, and the law was further tightened in this particular case.[34] Here is Innocent IV on *Si conditiones.* 'Unless *both* consent, marriage is not impeded. If one says, "I contract with you if you avoid offspring, or until I find a more handsome [person]", but the other speaks against [this], there is a marriage. But if the other person keeps silent, [the effect is] the same, because [the other person] is presumed to speak against [it], in favour of marriage.'[35] Pre-marital contracts to avoid conception or commit abortions were highly unlikely ever to be brought to court.

If canon lawyers devoted so much effort to elaborating law in this area, between the 1170s and 1234, despite silence in the marriage courts, this was because it was such a fact of life among contemporary couples that it could not be ignored. If this large legal development had such a counterpart in the contemporary world, then we should reflect upon two facts. One is that after toying with various measures

[33] J.-P. Lévy, 'L'officialité de Paris et les questions familiales à la fin du XIVe siècle', in *Études d'histoire du droit canonique dédiées à Gabriel Le Bras*, 2 vols. (Paris, 1965), ii. 1265–94 (p. 1269); Weigand, 'Rechtsprechung des Regensburger Gerichts', pp. 45–3. See the fine general discussion in R. H. Helmholz, *Marriage Litigation in Medieval England* (Cambridge, 1974), pp. 47–57.

[34] A. Esmein, *Le mariage en droit canonique*, 2nd edn., 2 vols. (Paris, 1929), i. 198.

[35] *Nisi ambo consentiant, non impeditur matrimonium. Si unus dicat, 'Contraho tecum si generationem prolis evites', vel 'quousque pulchriorem aliam inveniam', sed alius contradicat, matrimonium est; sed si taceat, idem, quia praesumitur contradicere in favorem matrimonii*; quoted Esmein, *Mariage en droit canonique*, i. 198 n. 1.

directed against offspring, with abortion on its own, and with narrowly technical words for one method of procuring sterility, canon law decided to concentrate on avoiding conceiving, and a technically catch-all formulation, 'avoid generation of offspring' or simply 'avoidance of offspring'. The second is that the *precise* chronology of this development is in the first instance the internal chronology of the development of law schools and their texts. 1234 is a date in the history of canon law rather than of contraceptive practice.

Although the pre-nuptial pact did not come before the courts, in fact courts concerned with another area of law did sometimes enquire about one form of sex which may have been one of the commonest of ways of avoiding conceiving. The relationship of affinity was an impediment to marriage. Affinity arose out of an earlier marriage: between, say, a man and a relative of the woman he was going to marry. It also arose through illicit sexual relations with the relative. Here is how Ivo of Chartres begins a letter to the archbishop of Sens about such a case: 'about the knight who, before lawful marriage, slept with the sister of his [future] wife'. This notion of affinity caused not only by marriage but by illicit sexual union was already broadly accepted in the ninth century.[36] At the heart of it was the notion of a man and a woman becoming 'one flesh'. Except where there was a specific allegation that a marriage had not been consummated, it was assumed that man and woman became one flesh in marriage, and courts would not enquire further about the details of their sexual activity. But this assumption was not made about illicit sexual union, which could have been only on one occasion, in various forms, and in a manner which fell short of the two becoming 'one flesh'. Illicitness encouraged forms of sex which did not lead to conceiving: incomplete acts. Accordingly, there was concern both in written law and in the courts to define and establish the boundaries between sex which did or did not constitute becoming one flesh. Gratian presented two texts,[37] the first establishing that 'No one is to marry a woman [who has been] known by a blood-relative, or stained with some pollution [by the relative]'. Gratian qualifies 'Known, or stained' as 'according to the order of nature; if extraordinarily (*extraordinarie*), not so [viz. the woman is not stained and there is no impediment]'. His next text, *Extraordinaria pollutio*, an extract from a late eleventh-century decretal,[38] states this a little obscurely, but there is progressive clarity and explicitness in subsequent glosses. For example, around 1190, Bernard of Pavia: 'Concerning extraordinary pollution, I say that every pollution which is not done inside the vessel which is by nature appropriate, that is to say the vulva, whether this takes place inside another vessel, or outside, does not bring about mixing of seeds or union of flesh, and therefore does not induce affinity or impede marriage.'[39] And more precise discrimination in a text

[36] Esmein, i. 420. [37] C. 35 q. 2 and 3 c. 10–11; Friedberg, i. 1266–7.

[38] Urban II to Hugh, bishop of Grenoble, between 1088 and 1099.

[39] Bernard of Pavia, *Summa decretalium*, IV. xiv. 17, ed. E. T. A. Laspeyres (Regensburg, 1860, repr. Graz, 1956), p. 173: *De extraordinaria pollutione dico quod omnis pollutio, quae non est facta intra vas aptum naturae, i.e. intra vulvam, sive fiat intra aliud vas sive extra, non facit seminis commixtionem nec carnis unionem, ideoque non inducit affinitatem nec impedit matrimonium.* Preceding this, a little before 1170,

produced between 1210 and 1214:[40] 'Such pollution as takes places outside the vulva does not bring about mixing of blood or unity of flesh. But what if someone breaks through into the gate of modesty, but does not emit seed there, or not [together] with her? I say with H[uguccio] that neither unity of flesh nor mixing of blood are brought about through such sex.' Intromission without ejaculation inside, therefore, did not impede marriage.

Where cases came up, then, a defence would be that the sex in question lay anywhere between groping and (in modern terms) coitus interruptus: sex which almost made the two one flesh, but not quite. The courts enquired. We already get glimpses of this through Ivo of Chartres's letters in the years around 1100. Writing to Hildebert, bishop of Le Mans, he deals with the case which has been raised by Hildebert. It concerns 'a man who, before he married his wife, stained his wife's mother around the marital places with exterior pollution' (*circa maritalia loca . . . exteriori pollutione maculavit*). He recalls the case which was dealt with by Urban II in his letter to the bishop of Grenoble. Urban II 'advised that enquiry should be made, with very diligent and sharp questioning, whether in this shamefulness there was some mingling of flesh, by which through the mixing of seeds they would become one flesh'. And Ivo reports hearing the result of this case, the man's successful purging and denial.[41]

Contraceptive intent was not here a concern of the courts. But because illicit sex and intent to avoid go hand in hand, and coitus interruptus did not make couples one flesh according to canon law, courts found themselves in practice enquiring about coitus interruptus, along with other forms of sex which fell short of this.

7.2 Sentences *commentaries*

As the theology of the schools emerges in the early twelfth century the theme is already there. Compiled around 1120, the *Sententie Magistri A* contains a selection of passages from Augustine forming the links in a chain of reflections on the theology of marriage, and its three goods, including offspring. Augustine's *Concubitum qui non fit causa prolis* brings together procreative purpose (or its opposite) and 'unnatural' forms of sex: 'marriages . . . procure pardon for sex which is not for the sake of offspring, so long as . . . it [the sex] is not changed into that use which is against nature' (*Concubitum qui non fit causa prolis, nuptie . . . imperant ignosci, si tamen non . . . immutetur in eum usum, qui contra naturam est*). This is

the comment of the *Summa Parisiensis on the Decretum Gratiani*, ed. T. P. McLaughlin (Toronto, 1952), 'if she was known by him in the natural members according to the order of nature' (*si tamen ordine naturae in membris naturalibus fuerit ab eo cognita*), is scarcely in advance of Gratian.

[40] *Glossa palatina*, quoted by J. A. Brundage, *Law, Sex and Christian Society in Medieval Europe* (Chicago, 1987), p. 356 n. 156: *Talis enim pollutio que fit extra vulvam non facit sanguinis commixtionem nec carnis unitatem; sed quid si quis frangit claustrum pudoris, sed non spermatizat ibi uel si spermatizat, non cum ipsa? Dico cum h. per talem coitum unitatem carnis non fieri nec sanguinis commixtionem.*

[41] Ivo of Chartres, *Epistola* 232, *PL* 162, 235.

followed by *Solet queri*,[42] which, as we have seen, presents the theme of couples who marry not to procreate but for incontinence, who are to be regarded as married so long as they have not avoided, or wished to avoid, or acted evilly to prevent offspring. The overlap with Ivo's *Decretum* is slight. Ivo had included *Solet queri*, but in relation to concubinage as a form of marriage, and had not used *Concubitum qui non fit causa prolis*. *Aliquando*, a text most conveniently found at this time under the treatment of 'Killing' in Ivo's *Decretum*, was absent from the *Sententie Magistri A*, perhaps because it would have struck a jarring note in this often high-flown piece of marriage theology.

The *Sententie Magistri A* preceded and influenced other theological treatments of marriage from Laon and Paris.[43] The absence of *Aliquando* meant freedom from the vocabulary which *Aliquando* imposed on later academic theology, in particular 'poisons of sterility'. The simple and direct phrase *vitatio prolis*, 'avoidance of offspring', was used in these early theological texts. Here the anonymous *Decretum Dei fuit* abbreviates *Solet queri*—'if they neither avoid nor impede offspring' (*si nec vitent nec impediant prolem*)[44]—while in two other works, the *Sententie* [*Pseudo-*] *Anselmi* and *De coniugio*, the summarized theme becomes an important part of the general definition of marriage. 'Marriage is the consent of male and female that preserves their individual custom of life, that is to say, [consent] individually to live together and mix carnally, *without avoidance of offspring*' (*absque prolis vitatione*).[45] These theological compilations were very short, and through the requisite succinctness the theme acquired startling prominence.

During these same years one fundamental textbook was being elaborated, much of it by Anselm of Laon (d. 1117) but much also by others between about 1100 and 1130: the 'ordinary gloss' on all the books of the Bible. This tackled Onan in Genesis 38: 'He knowing that the children should not be his, when he went in to his brother's wife, spilled his seed upon the ground, lest children should be born in his brother's name.' Anselm—or someone else—glossed this passage straightforwardly and literally: 'he spilled seed on the ground in order not to make Thamar fertile' (*fundebat semen in terram, ne foecundaret Thamar*).[46] The reader of both text and gloss was presented, then, with Onan going into his brother's wife, and then spilling seed on the ground in order to avoid the conception of chidren. Present, then, in early twelfth-century theological treatment of marriage was prominent and direct treatment of 'avoidance of offspring', and in the standard gloss a straightforward and literal interpretation of the Bible's description of the first identified individual in history avoiding conceiving and doing this by withdrawal.

[42] *Sententie Magistri A*, nos. 44 and 63, ed. Reinhardt, *Anselm von Laon*, pp. 179 and 186.

[43] See Ch. 2.3 above. Hugh of St Victor was to repeat all of *Concubitum qui non fit causa prolis*.

[44] *Das Schrifttum der Schule Anselms von Laon und Wilhelms von Champeaux in deutschen Bibliotheken*, ed. H. Weisweiler, BGPTM 33, 2 vols. (1936), i. 361–79 (p. 363).

[45] *Anselms von Laon systematische Sentenzen*, ed. F. Bliemetzrieder, BGPTM 18, parts 2–3 (1919), p. 141; ed. F. Bliemetzrieder in his 'Théologie et théologiens de l'école épiscopale de Paris avant Pierre Lombard', *RTAM* 5 (1931), 272–91 (p. 279).

[46] *Biblia sacra cum glossis*, 6 vols. (Lyons, 1545), i. 104r. See P. Biller, 'Birth-control in the West in the Thirteenth and Early Fourteenth Centuries', *Past and Present* 94 (1982), 3–26 (pp. 5–6 and n. 14).

When Peter the Lombard came to compile the distinction in which he dealt with avoidance of offspring and abortion (book 4, distinction 31),[47] he had behind him what we have been surveying: the plain words of early twelfth-century theology, the gloss on the Bible, and the new shape and dialectic which had been given to the theme by Gratian. While he did not quote the gloss or Genesis 38, Peter combined the other two traditions. Essentially what he did was this: he appropriated Gratian, and inserted a mildly adapted version of him into a theological framework. Since Peter's work provided all later medieval academic theologians with their standard material, we must describe this in more detail.

The theological setting is provided by a recapitulation of the three goods of marriage in chapter 1 of the distinction. While the first three paragraphs of chapter 2 deal with the 'good' of the 'sacrament',[48] the fourth paragraph introduces the existence of marriage even when a 'good' is lacking:

> The good of offspring (*bonum prolis*) is not present in all marriages. For some with an equal vow [= a vow taken by both the man and woman] observe continence. Others cannot generate through defect of age or some other cause. Nor do all who have offspring have the good of offspring. For the 'good of offspring' is not said to be offspring themselves or that hope of offspring which relates not to religion but rather to hereditary succession, as when someone desires to have heirs to his earthly property. Rather [it is said to be] the hope and desire with which offspring are sought, [when they are sought] so that they can be brought up in religion.

Peter the Lombard thus prepares the way for the next paragraph, which explores 'lack of the good of offspring' among those who are married not for the sake of offspring but for lust. Here begins the appropriation both of Gratian's schematization and his selection of material. (Numbers in square brackets are used here to ease comparison with my earlier summary of Gratian.)

[1] In the last paragraph of chapter 2, *Solet queri* provides the general category of couples joined only for lust, to be regarded as married so long as they do not avoid.

[2] Immediately following, in chapter 3, *Aliquando* spells out the sub-category of those who avoid, those who procure poisons of sterility, or those who extinguish the foetus.

[3] Immediately following this, in chapter 4, come the texts—again from Gratian—which deal with the sub-categories of those who extinguish the foetus: murderers when abortion is late but not when it is early.

The Lombard helps the reader who needs to be informed quickly, providing rubrics[49]—for example, the following for chapters 3 and 4: 'On those who procure poisons of sterility' (*De his qui procurant venena sterilitatis*), and 'When those who procure abortions are homicides' (*Quando sunt homicidae qui procurant abortum*). With *Solet queri* Peter Lombard follows the quotation with a repetition, whose effect is to underline it. 'So', he writes, 'they are called "married", who unite

[47] Peter the Lombard, *Sententiae*, IV. xxxi. 2–4; ii. 443–6.
[48] Meaning indissolubility.
[49] On Peter's authorship of the *Sentences*' rubrics, see Brady, *Prolegomena*, pp. 138*–41*.

only for sex, so long as they do not avoid the generation of offspring through some evil artifice' (*Ecce coniuges dicuntur, qui solius concubitus causa conveniunt, si tamen prolis generationem aliquo malo dolo non vitent*).

After Peter's incorporation and mild adaptation of Gratian, he proceeds in the remaining chapters of the distinction to further theological analysis of the sexual act in marriage,[50] which has attracted much attention in modern Christian, feminist, and gender scholarship. Relevant to our concern is that at one point, in chapter 7, Peter followed Hugh of St Victor and earlier twelfth-century theology in quoting Augustine's *Concubitum qui non fit causa prolis*, parading thereby a juxtaposition of absence of procreative purpose and 'unnatural' intercourse. The reader could thereby be reminded of one possible technique available to the person who is actively avoiding conception. The reader could also be reminded of the same thing by the comment on 'unnatural' sex between man and wife in another Augustine text, *Adulterii malum*. However, this was oddly placed in Peter Lombard's *Sentences*, in a distinction which was devoted to vows, and consequently readers interested in avoidance of offspring were more likely to miss this one.[51]

As with the *Decretum* in canon law, the first point about the Lombard's work was that it constituted a pedagogic advance in theology. Gratian's already clearly organized material is now inserted into a theological framework, forming a separate part, a 'distinction', and this in turn is crisply organized, with titles and comments which highlight principal themes. Through the incorporation of *Aliquando* and its rubric, Peter the Lombard adds to the encouragement, which was already coming from the *Decretum*, for the phrase 'procuring poisons of sterility' to be used as a blanket-term for avoidance of conception. This was a development in the vocabulary favoured by academics, rather than out there, in the real world. Peter did not attempt to incorporate the 'ordinary gloss' on Genesis, and there was no reason for him to do so. The 'ordinary gloss' was fairly recent, the most standard work after the Bible itself, and to be found everywhere. Peter the Lombard and his readers will have taken for granted Onan's avoiding conceiving by entering into Thamar and then withdrawing, to spill his seed on the ground, as the best-known such act in all human history. Reference to it was unnecessary. The second point concerns the contemporary world, which directly though briefly was evoked in chapter 6 where, after citing Paul's concession of marriage as 'indulgence', Peter the Lombard wrote, 'To what is grace granted, if not to [something which bears] guilt? Also, through this [dictum] some want to

[50] Summarily, they are as follows. Ch. 5 (i), 'On the excuse of sex through the goods': when married couples come together for the sake of offspring, this act has no sin; where the 'good of offspring' is lacking and they come together only for incontinence, this is not so far excused as to be without guilt, but the guilt is venial. Ch. 5 (ii): the too ardent lover of his wife is an adulterer. Ch. 6: 'On St Paul's indulgence, how it is to be understood'—the meaning of 'indulgence' in St Paul's reference to marriage, 'But I speak this by way of indulgence' (1 Cor. 7: 6). 'Through this some want to prove that marriage is a sin'. Ch. 7 ventilates the subtle problem of the precise evil of incontinence, which is made venial through the 'good' of marriage, and this leads to further discussion in Ch. 9, which discusses whether all fleshly pleasure is sinful, and whether sex can be sinless.

[51] Peter the Lombard, *Sententiae*, IV. xxxviii. 2; ii. 481–2.

prove that marriages are a sin.'[52] Here the 'some' are almost certainly the Cathar heretics, strongly entrenched at this time in northern France and the Rhineland, who taught that marriage was utterly sinful.[53] The Cathars did not put in any further appearance in the Lombard's text, as opponents of procreation (which they were) or as advocates of avoidance or abortion (which they were not). Like earlier theologians and canon lawyers, the Lombard had no need to spell out what was self-evident: that the counterpart to his discussion in the outside world was the sinfulness of ordinary Christian folk.

In the rest of this chapter we shall look at how the Lombard's basic text was being handled in two later periods: in the 1250s, and in the early 1300s. Each of the classic commentaries of the 1250s, those of Bonaventure, Thomas Aquinas, and Peter of Tarentaise, had three elements, two of which were brief and technical—a formal summary of the distinction, and comment on particular problems in its literal interpretation, which Bonaventure entitled 'doubtful things in the letter [of the text]'. The other element was by far the longest: the lengthy, formal, and elaborately sub-divided questions which were raised upon matters of substance. When we look for our theme we find a sharp contrast. It is present in the two brief technical sections, and in one of these, it is put forward with notable crispness, witness Aquinas. With *Solet queri*, writes Aquinas,

> he [Peter the Lombard] does three things. First he determines about marriage in which the good of offspring is not intended. Secondly, [he determines] about [marriage] in which the good of offspring is not only not intended but is also impeded, there [where he writes], 'Those who procure poisons of sterility are not spouses but fornicators.' Thirdly, he determines a certain question which arises, 'Here one usually asks about those who procure abortion'.[54]

But the theme does not occur as a subject of the large formal questions. Instead, they treat the general themes of the definition, number, and necessity of the three goods of marriage, and the particular themes of chapters 5 to 9 in the distinction, the possible excusing of sex in marriage through these goods.

However, though not the direct subject, the theme of avoidance still slipped in. Over and over again these questions bring up the two broadest categories, sex 'for offspring' and sex 'beyond the necessity of procreating children'. The second will have always reminded those readers, who had been looking closely at the text, of the more sinful sub-category of active avoiders and procurers of abortion, which had been discussed in chapters 2–4 of the distinction. In addition, attention to the precise meaning of 'the good of offspring' brought with it a crucial point which is adjacent to avoiding conceiving: the possibility of questioning this good or eroding it.[55] There was always the possibility of avoidance cropping up incidentally,

[52] Peter the Lombard, *Sententiae*, IV. xxxi. 6; ii. 447.

[53] See my 'Northern Cathars and Higher Learning', in *The Medieval Church: Universities, Heresy and the Religious Life: Essays in Honour of Gordon Leff*, ed. P. Biller and [R.] B. Dobson, SCH, Subsidia 11 (Woodbridge, 1999), pp. 25–53.

[54] Aquinas, *In sententias*, IV. xxxi, *Divisio textus*; iii. 953.

[55] In Bonaventure's 'doubtful matters', for example, questioning its meaning leads to a triple

especially in a question debating 'Whether [all] three goods are necessary in marriage' and consequently 'Whether where one of these goods fails marriage fails'. Thus, in Peter of Tarentaise's handling of this the lack of the good of offspring raises the theme of two different categories, sterile couples' 'despair of offspring' and other couples' deliberate 'avoidance of offspring': *desperatio* against *evitatio*.[56] Finally, it is likely that nominal absence of the theme from the subjects of the formal questions forced some material into the section where literal problems were tackled, where the theme lived on, and had some slight further emphasis and development.[57]

Why was the theme not the subject of the large formal questions? The first reason is large and elementary. The Augustinian text which had introduced the theme, *Solet queri*, had been unclear on the marriage of those who do not unite for offspring. Those who avoided or aborted: were they doing this *before* or *during* marriage? Eventually clarity was to come with the attention which canon lawyers devoted to conditions attached to the contract, and with their fundamental distinction between an agreement to do such things as a condition, before marrying, and practice after marrying. But only eventually. If we turn to the Paris of the 1220s and Alexander of Hales's gloss on distinction 31 we see a lot of attention being paid to the relation between contracting marriage and procuring sterility. In question are not only those couples who make procuring sterility a prior condition, but also those who are procuring sterility when contracting marriage, without continuation of this being made a prior condition, and also those who procure sterility subsequent to marriage.[58] Alexander's gloss looks fussy and confused, but then the confusion was soon to be dispelled, at a stroke, with the adoption of *Si conditiones* in 1234. With the passing of several decades, it would have become elementary that the questioning of marriage in *Solet queri* really only applies to a condition attached to the contract, and that the proper place for commentary on this is an earlier distinction in the Lombard, where the consent which forms marriage is debated. In the 1250s, then, Bonaventure and Peter of Tarentaise insert material on this and reference to attached conditions into distinction 28, and into a general question about conditional marriage contracts.

distinction of intentions in seeking offspring. 'The first is for offspring to be educated in the cult of God. The second is for offspring to succeed in [one's] inheritance. The third is so that someone can appear glorious through the multitude and beauty of their offspring (*ut quis in prolis multitudine et pulcritudine gloriosus appareat*).The first is a good by reason of the good, the second by reason of what is indifferent, [and] the third is a deformed good, or [a good which has been] converted into evil'; *In sententias*, IV. xxxi, *Dubia circa litteram*, i; iv. 727. Apart from parallels to this in other discussions of the good of offspring, we should remember earlier discussion in Paris, by William of Auvergne, of appropriate sizes of family.

[56] Peter of Tarentaise, *In sententias*, IV. xxxi. Q. 2 art. 2: iv. 322. The theme is already present in Alexander of Hales, *In sententias*, IV. xxxi (iv. 499), as also the opposed categories: *Aliud enim vitatio prolis, aliud desperatio.*

[57] Thus Thomas Aquinas crams his *Exposition of the text*, with problems about the texts on avoidance of offspring and abortion, *In sententias*, IV. xxxi, *Expositio textus*; iii. 958.

[58] Alexander of Hales, *In sententias*, IV. xxxi; iv. 490–1.

While absence from distinction 31 is partly a matter of displacement, I would also suggest that the relation between avoidance of offspring and the existence or otherwise of a marriage had become so clear that there was little intellectual fizz in debating it. The same point can be applied to the comprehending of Peter Lombard on those avoiding generation and abortion. There was no evident confusion of definition and distinction between these, or about early and late abortion, and these were primarily practical matters, pertaining to canon-law and penance. By contrast gradations of licitness of the sexual act in marriage constituted a more difficult theme, and one more productive of general theological speculation. *Sentences* commentators in the 1250s, then, looked briefly and sharply at avoidance and abortion, but did not see these as supplying debating subjects for the large formal questions.

Tentatively I would suggest another reason. In the late twelfth century a large number of concrete pastoral cases survive as brief questions in the works of Peter the Chanter and others, while from the mid-thirteenth to the early fourteenth centuries these appear in a substantial minority of formal quodlibets. A hiatus? If so, was this a hiatus in the phenomenon itself, *or* only a hiatus in the survival of evidence and in modern study of Paris theology between about 1215 and 1250? There may have been a more continuous tradition of discussion of such questions. Now, these pastoral questions were often about sex, and sometimes of startling precision. Under the question 'Should one confess all sins?', Peter the Chanter envisages confessing to a simple priest, whom one has a duty not to corrupt by confessing 'the thousand ways of having sex',[59] while in the mid-thirteenth century Robert de Sorbon concerned himself with special modes of kissing[60]—whether solemnly or humorously it is difficult at this distance to gauge. There was, one hopes, only seriousness in one area, however, the relation between conception and danger to the life of a woman, and the consideration of avoidance for this reason. This was discussed by Peter the Chanter:

> Someone's wife has an umbilical rupture, [caused] by frequent childbirth. The doctors tell her that if she gives birth again she will die. Nevertheless, the man demands the [marital] debt. Is she bound to pay it, when she knows for certain that she will die if she conceives? She knows that if she returns the debt she will conceive, because she is still a young woman. Item. The question is asked, whether she can procure sterility for herself, not primarily in order to impede [the conception of] the foetus [for its own sake], but [to impede conception] in order not to die in childbirth. In no way would I advise this last, because this would be to procure the poison of sterility, which in every case is forbidden. [But] about the first I would doubt [that she would be so bound].[61]

[59] Chanter, *Summa*, II, 310: *in mille modis coeundi.*

[60] Robert de Sorbon, *De confessione*, in *Maxima Bibliotheca Veterum Patrum*, ed. M. de La Bigne, 28 vols. (Lyons, Geneva, 1677, 1707), xxv. 355: *Hic caveat sibi, confessor, ne descendat ad speciales modos osculandi.*

[61] Chanter, *Summa*, III, 463: *Uxor alicuius ex crebro partu rupta est in umbilico. Dicunt ei medici quod si iterum peperit morietur. Vir nihilominus petit debitum. Tenetur ne ipsa reddere, cum pro certo sciat se morituram si conceperit? Scit quod si reddit debitum concipiet, quia adhuc iuvencula est. Item. Queritur an ipsa possit procurare sibi sterilitatem, non principaliter ut impediat partum, sed ne moriatur in partu. Istud*

Presumably the original school discussion was longer and more detailed. A second formal debate, a quodlibet about the licitness of abortion where the mother will die if the foetus is not aborted, was to be held by the Dominican John of Naples, who is likely to have responded to it either in Paris, where he taught in 1315–17, or Naples or Avignon—he is discussed later. My suggestion is that the line of concrete pastoral-theological questions which goes from Peter the Chanter's cases to the quodlibets of the later thirteenth and early fourteenth centuries may sometimes have attracted, and therefore deflected from *Sentences* commentaries, debate about these themes. There may have been a penumbra of more informal discussions of them in the convents where the pastoral experts, mendicants, were gathered.

To recapitulate the scene in Paris in the 1250s. The subject was present in the epitomes and 'knotty points' sections of commentaries on Peter the Lombard's distinction 31, and in these the subject loomed large. It is a theme also in distinction 28, on conditional marriage, while forms of sex which avoided conception were held in mind through texts in distinctions 28, 38 and also, incidentally, 41, which dealt with forms of sex which did or did not form the full union which constituted the impediment of affinity. Though it was rare for theologians to import Onan and Genesis 38,[62] no theologian could have been unaware of this fundamental text on avoiding conception through coitus interruptus. Other treatises on the sacrament of marriage were written and read in Paris, and, as we saw in Chapter 3, William of Auvergne's treatise discussed size of family and avoiding conception; this text was read and used by Guillaume Peyraut, possibly first in Paris. Finally, there had been case-discussions in Peter the Chanter's circle, although continuity between these and mid-thirteenth-century Paris is only surmise.

Let us move on to the years around and after 1300. Although by this date many commentaries on the sacraments in book 4 of the *Sentences* were just using these distinctions as pegs upon which to hang abstract philosophical and theological discussions, in the more conservative and pastoral commentaries on distinction 31 there was a continuing domination of the classic questions of the 1250s, the three goods and how they excuse sex in marriage. Continuing also in the interstices of this and other distinctions was material on generation and avoiding conception. In this material there is much that is new. Here is the best-known passage from commentaries of this period, Peter of la Palud, discussing those cases in which sex in marriage is sinful:

> The man, however, who knowingly spills his seed outside in order not to have more children than he can feed—[he does] a detestable thing, as did the son of Juda [Onan], Gen. 38. If, however, before the completion of the act he withdraws and does not emit seed with the same intention [= does not emit seed outside with the intention of avoiding], he does not seem to

ultimum nullatenus consulerem, quia hoc esset procurare venenum sterilitatis, quod in omni casu prohibitum est. De primo dubitarem. See J. W. Baldwin, *The Language of Sex: Five Voices from Northern France around 1200* (Chicago, 1994), p. 319 n. 17, for an earlier version of this text.

[62] An exception: Alexander of Hales, *In sententias*, IV. xxxviii; iv. 577.

sin mortally, unless through this the woman is provoked to seminate [= emit seed]. Similarly, if on account of this he avoids knowing his wife and [he does this] with common consent [of the two of them] and does not deny the [marital] debt [= does not refuse to have sex if his wife asks him to]: [in this case] it does not seem that he sins, even venially. For, even if they longed to have more children than he could feed, he is neither under an obligation to seek the debt nor to finish the act unless his wife asks [him to do so].[63]

This is longer and more detailed than anything found earlier. It is more precise on what is involved physically. And the moralists' concern with the relation between existing numbers of children and the ability of a particular couple to feed them has a psychological twist: the couple's longing for children despite adverse conditions. The reader seems in a world in which the quantitative changes have reached a point where they have precipitated a qualitative change in text and thought.

Let us survey the changes. Any reader of Peter of la Palud who sits down to read his section on marriage from beginning to end will be astonished by the sheer quantity of material bearing upon this theme. To illustrate the qualitative changes on particular topics which are found in Peter and in other commentators, let us look first at treatment of the pre-marital pact to avoid offspring. The examples of such pacts are ever more specific. Duns Scotus envisages *either* sex procuring: 'I take you [female] if you procure poisons of sterility or if you consent with me [male is implied] in the procuring of such poisons.'[64] Avoiding conception is something done with assiduity: 'sedulously [*studiose*] procuring that offspring do not result'. Vidal de Four envisages the taking of the potion: 'I take you, if you *drink* poison to be sterile.'[65] Peter of la Palud is characteristically copious and detailed. In one remarkable case he envisages a widower, who already has too many children, bargaining with a girl's parent. 'I take, or I shall take, your daughter, who has procured poisons of sterility, or who is sterile. For I have too many children, and therefore I do not seek offspring but only [desire marriage] in order to avoid [falling into] fornication.' In another example, a case is produced through subtle analysis of a condition about the present or past which would affect the future, such as 'if you have [already] found or have poisons of sterility to use in our marriage'.[66] Elsewhere, discussing unworthy intentions when

[63] Peter of la Palud, *In sententias*, IV. xxxi. 3: 161ra: *Qui autem ideo semen extra fundit ne habeat plures filios quos nutrire non possit, detestabilem rem cum filio Iude operatur, Genes*[*is*] *38. Si autem ante completionem actus se retrahit nec semen emittit eadem intentione non videtur mortaliter peccare nisi ex hoc forte mulier ad seminandum provocaret. Similiter si propter hoc omittit cognoscere uxorem et ex communi consensu negat debitum, non videtur quod peccet etiam venialiter, quia licet appeterent habere plures filios quam possit nutrire, nec ipse tenetur debitum petere nec incohatum* [sic] *actum consumare nisi uxore petente.* See Noonan, *Contraception*, p. 298.

[64] Duns Scotus, *In sententias*, IV. xxxi: v. 672: '*accipio te in meam, si procuraveris venena sterilitatis, vel consentias mecum in procuratione talium venenorum.*' One anonymous commentary has 'if the woman says, "I consent if you procure sterility for me"' (*si dicat mulier, consentio si procures mihi sterilitatem*); Vatican MS Vat. Lat. 782, fol. 170rb.

[65] Vidal de Four, *In sententias*, IV. xxviii–xxix; Vatican MS Vat. Lat. 1095, fol. 37rb: '*contraho tecum si biberis venenum quod sit sterilis.*'

[66] Peter of la Palud, *In sententias*, IV. xxix. 2; 154vb: '*Accipio vel accipiam filiam tuam que procuravit venena sterilitatis vel que est sterilis, quia habeo nimis multos filios. Unde non quero prolem, sed solum vitare fornicationem*'; 155rb: '*si invenisti vel habes venena sterilitatis ad utendum in matrimonio nostro*'.

contracting marriage, he specifies two methods alongside each other: if 'one intends to procure poisons of sterility, or to spill seed'.[67] Thomas of Strasbourg's condition is this. 'I contract with you if you promise that you will always procure an impediment against conception, or some poison of sterility.'[68] Apart from the detail of a promise for *always*, Thomas is using the word 'impediment', which we will see by around 1300 coming into pastoral manuals. And, like Peter of la Palud, he seems to be envisaging at least two methods, albeit not the same ones. In Thomas's case, since the person procuring is the addressee, a woman, what is linked to a potion but precedes and is an alternative to it is presumably a pessary.

Precision about sex itself is advancing during the early 1300s. Already seen in Peter of la Palud, this is not confined to him. Compare, for example, Richard of Middleton and Thomas of Strasbourg on the form of sex which induces affinity. Richard begins his description of when this happens by writing that it is incurred, 'by every [act of] sexual intercourse by which man and woman are said to be one flesh . . . and man and woman are not made one flesh by physical pollution which does not occur naturally in the appropriate vessel but outside . . .'[69] About forty years later (1337 or shortly before), there is Thomas's slightly different definition, 'by sexual intercourse, so long as it is natural and complete', after which he continues thus. 'I said particularly, "so long as it is natural and complete", because if the man with his body [= penis] has reached inside the body of the woman, and yet desists from the act, before manly seed has proceeded from him, no affinity is generated by this . . . [nor is it] even if seed does proceed from the man, provided that it [= the seed] is not received in the natural place of the woman.'[70] The combination of brevity and slight circumlocution has given way to what is almost clinical precision.

The anachronistic 'clinical' is used here to recall the learned medical texts of this period. Their presence in Thomas of Strasbourg's mind is not spelled out directly, but it is explicit in one remarkable passage in Peter of la Palud which brings together theology, learned medicine, the experience-based knowledge of married couples, and avoiding conception. It occurs in Peter's commentary on distinction 32. Dealing with the 'return of the [marital] debt', this distinction examined the return at certain times, including menstruation.[71] When we turn to

[67] Ibid., IV. xxvi. 2; 140rb: *'si intendat procurare venena sterilitatis, semen fundere, aut pro questu uxorem exponere'*. In the edition used here, 140 mistakenly bears the number 146.

[68] Thomas of Strasbourg, *In sententias*, IV. xxvii–xxviii; ii. 149rb: *'Ego contraham tecum, si promiseris quod semper procures impedimentum contra partum, vel aliquod sterilitatis venenum.'*

[69] Richard, *In sententias*, IV. lxi; iv. 538: *per omnem carnalem copulam per quam vir et mulier dicuntur effici uno caro . . . et quia per carnalem pollutionem factam non in vase naturaliter ad illum usum ordinato sed extra . . . non efficiuntur vir et mulier una caro.*

[70] Thomas of Strasbourg, *In sententias*, IV. xli; ii. 166va: *Dixi etiam notanter, 'dummodo fuerit naturalis et completa', quia si vir cum corpore suo attingeret infra corpus mulieris et tamen ab actu illo desisteret, antequam semen virile ab eo procederet nulla ex hoc generaretur affinitas . . . etiam dato quod semen a viro procedat, si tamen non recipitur in loco naturali ipsius mulieris.*

[71] Earlier commentaries accepted that if menstruation was normal conception could occur then, e.g. Bonaventure, *In sententias*, IV. xxxii art. 3 Q. 1; iv. 737: *Si* [*tempus menstruorum est*] *secundum naturam semel in mense . . . tunc possibile est filios generare.*

Peter de la Palud, we find the following. He indicates that there is uncertainty about 'the menstrual time . . . then, according to some, a woman cannot conceive . . . it is not certain whether a woman conceives then' (. . . *de tempore menstruorum . . . Tunc etiam mulier concipere non potest, secundum quosdam . . . non est certum utrum tunc concipiat*). Here he is probably reflecting his knowledge of changing opinion in learned medicine, noted in Chapter 6 above. When summarizing, he describes a man having sex with his menstruating wife, and 'knowing that there will be no generation, or believing that there will probably be none, either because she is sterile or because she is not wont to conceive then. For husbands know the conditions of their wives better through experience, and vice versa' (*sciens non generari vel probabiliter credens, vel quia sterilis, vel quia non consuevit tunc concipere: quia viri cognoscunt melius conditiones uxorum et econverso per experientiam*). Given the topic, menstruation, 'vice versa' here does not mean wives knowing the conditions of their husbands but knowing their own conditions.

Here Peter may be reflecting, in the first instance, the sort of recent medical statement we have seen in the Anonymous of Montpellier's *De sterilitate*, as well as discrepancy in medical texts: 'according to *some*'. He is then, secondly, referring to husbands' and wives' knowledge that a woman will not conceive, either through sterility or because they know her 'conditions'. They know them 'better': that she will not *then* conceive. There is a moral consequence. 'Then, according to some', he writes, 'a woman cannot conceive, and therefore there is no fear of offspring. It is therefore a venial sin to seek [the debt] then, since offspring are not hoped for' (*Tunc etiam mulier concipere non potest, secundum quosdam, unde non timetur proli, unde tunc est veniale petere cum non speretur proles*).[72] Peter is not only attesting lay people's empirically based knowledge of times when a woman will not conceive. Through his reflection on its moral consequences, he is also revealing that couples are trying to avoid conceiving through having sex during what couples regard as those times.

Here, as elsewhere, Peter's text is one of the best examples of the extraordinary capacity which is being shown by some early fourteenth-century academic theology to bring into the text the couples themselves, engaging in pacts, too poor to have more children, and using coitus interruptus, infertile times, or potions. The practice of doctors rather than couples is what predominates, however, in the interests of a fellow-Dominican of Peter's, whom he knew at the convent in Paris and with whom, on occasion, he collaborated: John of Naples. It is not quite clear when and where John's remarkable quodlibetic question on abortion was raised. He had been a student in the convent of St Dominic in Bologna (1298–1300), taught in the Dominican studium at Naples and then at Paris, where he was a regent master in theology (1315–17), and then he was back again in Naples as regent master from 1317 onwards, and is noted as Papal chaplain in 1347. Paris, Naples and Avignon are the possibilities. John responded to several quodlibets on

[72] Peter of la Palud, *In sententias*, IV. xxxii: 162vb–3ra. See also John de Burgo on this, quoted in Ch. 8 below, n. 107.

the ethical problems of doctors,[73] and among these there is found the remarkable 'Whether a *medicus* ought to give to a pregnant woman medicine from which would follow the death of [her] child, and if he did not give it the death of both would follow'.[74] The intelligible context is the marked interest taken by early fourteenth-century Italian learned medicine in the ethics of providing help in procuring abortion and avoiding conceiving, discussed in Chapter 6 above, and together with Peter's discussion of infertile times, it demonstrates remarkably the convergence in this period of the precise concerns of theology and learned medicine.

Finally, among the *Sentences* commentators there are small signs of a move of extraordinary importance, towards generalization about their theme, and we shall return to this at the end of the next chapter.

[73] e.g. 'Whether a *medicus* who foresees the death of an ill man in his care ought to reveal it to him'; see P. Biller, 'John of Naples, Quodlibets and Medieval Theological Conncern with the Body', in *Medieval Theology and the Natural Body*, ed. P. Biller and A. J. Minnis, York Studies in Medieval Theology 1 (York, 1997), pp. 3–12 (pp. 6–9).

[74] *Utrum medicus debeat dare medicinam mulieri praegnanti ex qua sequeretur mors filii, et si non daret eam sequeretur mors utriusque.*

8

AVOIDANCE OF OFFSPRING (III): THE PASTORAL PICTURE

Unhappy the man of large brood and little bread[1]

We now turn to those texts which are traces of priests dealing with ordinary people, looking at some examples from three periods, around 900, 1200, and 1300.

8.1 Regino and the Rhineland around 900

The *Two books on synodal cases and ecclesiastical disciplines*[2] was written in 906 by a Rhinelander, Regino of Prüm. Let us see how Regino envisaged a priest dealing with the avoidance or suppression of offspring.

Regino approaches pastoral activities in several ways. He supplies questions for 'what a bishop or his ministers in a synod ought carefully to enquire, through the settled communities (*vici*) or estates (*villae*) or parishes of his diocese', about the church and how the priest carries out his parochial duties.[3] Using 'parish' to translate *parochia*, I leave aside the question what a parish meant at this period,

[1] See n. 144 below.

[2] Regino of Prüm, *Libri duo de synodalibus causis et disciplinis ecclesiasticis*, ed. F. G. A. Wasserschleben (Leipzig, 1840, reprint Graz, 1964). Regino was born at Altrip on the Rhine, was abbot of Prüm 892–9, and went from there to the monastery of St Maximinus in Trier, where he wrote works which included a treatise on music, two books of chronicles, and some letters, and the *Libri duo de synodalibus causis*. He died in 915. On Regino and this work see Wasserschleben's introduction; P. Fournier and G. Le Bras, *Histoires des collections canoniques en Occident depuis les Fausses Décrétales jusqu'au Décret de Gratien*, 2 vols. (Paris, 1931–2), i. 244–68. On Regino's use of the Pseudo-Bede 'double' or 'mixed' penitential, which was edited by F. W. H. Wasserschleben, *Die Bußordnungen der abendländischen Kirche* (Halle, 1851), pp. 248–82, see R. Haggenmüller, 'Zur Rezeption der Beda und Egbert zugeschriebenen Bußbücher', in *Aus Archiven und Bibliotheken: Festschrift für Raymond Kottje zum 65. Geburtstag*, ed. H. Mordek, Freiburger Beiträge zur mittelalterlichen Geschichte 3 (Frankfurt, Berne, New York, and Paris, 1992), pp. 149–59 (pp. 155–6). On avoidance of generation in the penitentials, see P. S. Callewaert, 'Les pénitentiels du moyen âge et les pratiques anticonceptionelles', *La Vie Spirituelle* 74, Supplement (1965), 339–66; J. T. Noonan, *Contraception: A History of its Treatment by the Catholic Theologians and Canonists* (Cambridge, Mass., 1966), pp. 152–70; P. J. Payer, 'Early Medieval Regulations Concerning Marital Sexual Relations', *Journal of Medieval History* 6 (1980), 353–76 (pp. 358–60); id., *Sex and the Penitentials: The Development of a Sexual Code, 550–1150* (Toronto, 1984), pp. 33–4, 57, and 89. On abortion in early canon law and the penitentials, see E. Nardi, *Procurato aborto nel mondo greco romano* (Milan, 1971), pp. 669–79.

[3] Regino, *De synodalibus causis*, I, *Notitia*; pp. 19–26.

merely warning the reader against assuming something like a later medieval or modern parish.

Regino prescribes how priests should perform their duties, which included inviting their flock to confession each year before Lent, and taking the lay penitent through questions about sin which were provided in an *Order for Giving Penance.*[4] The questions put in confession covered various forms of sexual sin, and abortion, infanticide, and 'overlaying' of babies. There is also this: 'Have you drunk any *maleficium* [maleficent magic], that is to say, herbs or other things, so that you could not have babies, or given [them] to another person?', which continues, without a break, 'or wanted to kill a man through a lethal potion, or instructed someone else to do this?'[5] It not clear whether 'instructed' covers only murder by poison, or both this and the use of 'contraceptive' potions.

Regino also provides forms for an enquiry in front of a bishop presiding in a synod. One or two days before the episcopal visitation, an archdeacon or archpriest goes round parishes, announcing the visit and summoning people to the synod. At the synod seven or so worthy and truth-telling men take a solemn oath on holy relics, to tell the truth about what had gone on in the parish. Eighty-nine questions are then put to them. Following their replies there are further enquiries by the visiting bishop or his official, the giving of judgement on sinners in the synod, and the public imposition of penance.

Among the eighty-nine questions put to the worthy men the first fourteen questions are about homicide, and four of these deal with foetuses or babies:[6]

4. Is there any man or woman who has put down their own baby? Or suffocated it with the weight of clothes? And, if this has happened, before or after baptism? Or, if the baby became ill through a parent's negligence, did it die without baptism?
5. Is there a man or a woman who struck out the foetus (*partus*) of another woman? Or, did a woman herself [and] of her own will strike out her own foetus and bring about [its] abortion?[7]
6. (Question on infanticide—quoted later)
9. (I refer to this below as *Est aliquis.*) Is there a man or a woman who has done this or taught another person how to do it: [to bring it about] that a [*or* the] man cannot generate nor a [*or* the] woman conceive?' (*Est aliquis vel aliqua, qui hoc fecerit, vel alium facere docuerit, ut vir non possit generare aut femina concipere?*).

Following immediately an item about the use of 'poisonous herbs and lethal potions' in order to kill, this would seem to mean sterilizing herbs and potions. Translation is difficult, because of the impact of using *a* or *the.* The individuals in

[4] *Ordo ad dandam poenitentiam*, ibid., I. ccciv; pp. 141–8.

[5] Ibid., I. ccciv; p. 145: *Bibisti ullum maleficium, id est, herbas vel alias causas, ut non potuisses infantes habere, aut alii* [*sic*] *donatisti, aut hominem per mortiferam potionem occidere voluisti, aut alium hoc facere docuisti?* Copied from the Pseudo-Bede 'double' or 'mixed' penitential, Wasserschleben, p. 255 no. 30; see Noonan, *Contraception*, pp. 156–7.

[6] Regino, *De synodalibus causis*, II. v. 4–6 and 9; p. 209.

[7] *Est aliquis vel aliqua, qui alterius partum excusserit, vel, si ipsa femina propria voluntate suum partum excusserit, et abortivum fecerit?*

a couple themselves are suggested by 'nor *the* woman conceive', injury to a third party by 'nor *a* woman conceive'.

Later in the work Regino lists penances for homicides, and care and negligence of babies constitute a large theme. There is the guilt of a mother leaving a baby near a hearth, where the baby is killed through someone spilling boiling water on it; the accidental killing of a child; and the putting down of babies. The last theme occupies the first two of a group of eleven chapters which bring together various protective provisions.[8] Abortions crop up in the following three chapters, followed by mothers who conceive in fornication and dash out their own foetuses, and then a chapter on infanticide, which envisages adulterous conceptions and also includes abortion which has been induced by potions.[9] Another chapter specifies that in abortion there is a great difference between the guilt of a poor woman and a fornicating woman. The next chapter is on killing babies conceived in fornication, by burying them or throwing them into water, and the following three chapters deal with the abandonment of babies.

Finally, there is an isolated chapter, *Si aliquis*, which is the counterpart to the ninth synodal question, *Est aliquis*.

If someone to sate his [or her] lust or out of deliberate hatred has done something to a [*or* the] man or a [*or* the] woman, so that children are not born of him [or her], or has given [one of them] to drink, so that he [or she] cannot conceive or generate, he [or she] is to be regarded as a murderer (*Si aliquis causa explendae libidinis vel odii meditatione, ut non ex eo soboles nascatur, homini aut muieri aliquid fecerit, vel ad potandum dederit, ut non possit generare aut concipere, ut homicida teneatur*).[10]

The two categories of motive, sating one's own lust, and deliberate hatred, indicate that *Si aliquis* is a hold-all, that is to say, it contains both individuals in a pair (doing to self or themselves) and also malicious action to bring infertility in others. Two methods are indicated, with the second, the 'drink', clearly a 'contraceptive' herbal potion. The first ('done something') could be maleficent magic, as Noonan suggests, or a hold-all for any method other than a potion. If the precise setting is suggestive—the preceding chapter is on castration and the succeeding one on circumcision—precisely what is suggested is not clear. Perhaps damage to either man or woman which makes generation or conception henceforth impossible? Notable is some contrast with the question in private confession. This is very clear when it underlines an action concerning oneself ('Have you drunk . . . potions or herbs so that you could not have children?'), and when it spells out action relating to others: 'Have you given to another?' and 'Have you taught another to do this?'

In the pastoral world which is evoked in Regino's work the priest and a local Church have no role in the ceremony of marriage, and there is no theology, no mention of a sacrament.[11] In the priest's public preaching, admonition, and

[8] Regino, *De synodalibus causis*, II. xix (pp. 221–2); II. xxi (p. 222); II. lx–lxx (pp. 237–42).

[9] Ibid., II. lxiii (p. 239).

[10] Regino, *De synodalibus causis*, II. lxxxviii; p. 248. See Noonan, *Contraception*, pp. 168–9.

[11] For rare glimpses of the theology of marriage and its procreative purpose in other texts from this

instruction there is only one reference to sexual activity. 'Does he also remind [the people] of this, at what times married men ought to abstain from their own wives?'[12]

There is, however, a great deal of intervention in sexual activity through private annual confession and public enquiry, and in the former there is the use of guides called 'penitentials', two of which Regino named when specifying that a priest should be asked whether he owned 'the Roman penitential, either the one issued by bishop Theodore or the one issued by the venerable Bede'.[13] These books, short and small in size, and containing lists of sins and tariffs of the penances to be applied, went back to the sixth century. Produced first in Ireland, and then in Anglo-Saxon England and the continent, for several centuries they dominated the handbook market for priests' guides in how to handle sin.[14] Regino's roots in these works suggest long duration of more or less the same thing, from the sixth to the tenth centuries. As far as sexual relations inside marriage are concerned, there is the long dominance of a theme which we also see in Regino. Dinned in Sunday after Sunday by priests to men who are married: abstain. Abstain from using your wives. Abstain during many times in the Church calendar. And abstain during the menstruating and post-childbirth calendar of their bodies.[15] Offspring? There is the saturation of both the penitentials and Regino's work with provisions about infanticide[16] and abortion, unvarying over these centuries.

Unvarying? Not quite. Some chronological patterns are discernible, and some new developments. I begin with the less certain one, some slight shift from infanticide to abortion. The latest of the penitentials attributed to Bede—the 'double' or 'mixed' Pseudo-Bede penitential, whose earliest manuscript dates from the second quarter of the ninth century[17]—shifts the topic of the lesser guilt of the poor woman from her commission of infanticide to her commission of abortion, and this is repeated in Regino.[18] This is suggestive, especially when set against the background of other examples of sharp attention to abortionists in the early ninth century.[19]

More certain is the intrusion of 'contraception'. The sequence is this. Such material is *entirely* absent from the earlier penitentials.[20] The dog not barking in

period, see R. Kottje, 'Ehe und Eheverständnis in den vorgratianischen Buβbüchern', in *Love and Marriage in the Twelfth Century*, ed. W. Van Hoecke and A. Welkenhuysen, Mediaevalia Lovaniensia, Series 1, Studia 8 (Louvain, 1981), pp. 41–58 (pp. 32–3 n. 56).

[12] Regino, *De synodalibus causis*, I, *Notitia*, LXI; p. 24.

[13] Ibid., I, *Notitia*, XCVI; p. 26.

[14] For opposing views of the real extent of the use of penitentials, see A. Murray, 'Confession before 1215', *TRHS* 6th ser. 3 (1993), 51–81, and R. Meens, 'The Frequency and Nature of Early Medieval Penance', in *Handling Sin*, pp. 35–61.

[15] The utter dominance of this theme is argued by Payer, 'Early Medieval Regulations', pp. 362–76.

[16] Among the seven (or eight) penitential letters probably collected by Wulfstan, archbishop of York, some of which were issued while he was bishop of London (996–1002), in no less than three the sin is killing of offspring; *Councils & Synods I*, i. 234–7, nos. ii, v, and viii.

[17] Haggenmüller, 'Beda und Egbert zugeschriebenen Buβbücher', p. 155 n. 24.

[18] Regino, *De synodalibus causis*, II. lxv; p. 240. See Noonan, *Contraception*, pp. 159–60.

[19] See Gerbald and Halitgar, cited in Ch. 6 and nn. 52 and 55.

[20] I am ignoring many bizarre sexual sins described in them. Although they could not result in

the night really is significant, given that the penitentials were preoccupied with virtually every form of sex under the sun. Then, with the 'double' Pseudo-Bede penitential there enters the first text which can be directly and clearly construed 'contraceptively'. 'Have you drunk any *maleficium*, that is to say, herbs or potions, so that you could not have babies?' We saw Regino copying this. Then another text enters the field, in the St Hubert penitential. Headed *De potionibus mulierum* (*On the potions of women*), it goes like this:

If anyone has taken potions, so that woman does not conceive, or has killed [aborted] the conceived, or if the man has spilled his seed from sex with the woman, in order not to conceive, as the sons of Judah did in Thamar (*Si quis potiones acceperit, ut mulier non concipiat, aut conceptos occiderit, aut vir semen effuderit a coitu mulieris, ut non concipiat, sicut filii Judae fecerunt in Thamar*).[21]

This spells out very clearly a range of measures against birth: potions for a woman not to conceive; potions for abortion; and not conceiving by withdrawal. Genesis has been read carefully, for withdrawal is ascribed to both sons, not only to Onan. The penitential containing this certainly postdates 829, and is usually dated around 850. Finally there comes a third text, *Si aliquis*, attested for the first time in Regino's work.

The chronology is clear: silence earlier on and then very strong presence, attested in three texts whose firm dates go from *c*.825–850[22] to 906. What lies behind this?

The first important point is that in the case of Regino's text, at least, we know that we are dealing with a self-consciously selective work, which was shaped by and intended for a particular milieu.[23] It was produced at the command and with the encouragement of archbishop Rathbod of Trier, and a copy was being sent to the archbishop of Mainz. Regino writes that he has not thoughtlessly decided that the archbishop's chests lack an abundance of books. However, 'it is probably burdensome for many volumes of councils [conciliar decrees] to be carried around far and wide' with the archbishop while he is 'engaged in assiduously administering public matters'. Regino has therefore 'brought together and united' material

conception, these acts would only be relevant to my theme if there was a hint that avoiding conception was the intention. On earlier absence, see Callewaert ('Pratiques anticonceptionelles', p. 357), who sees distinct and clear reference to contraception in continental penitentials only from the ninth century. This opinion is shared by Payer, *Sex and the Penitentials*, p. 34. Noonan (*Contraception*, p. 155) sees 'indisputable reference . . . not earlier than the eighth century', basing this date on penitentials usually attributed to the ninth century which he, however, attributes to the eighth.

[21] *Poenitentiale Hubertense* 56, ed. Wasserschleben, *Bußordnungen*, p. 385. For details of the editions, studies and conjectured date of the St Hubert penitential, see C. Vogel, *Les 'Libri paenitentiales'* Typologie des sources du moyen âge occidental 27 (Turnholt, 1978), pp. 75–6; the revision of this, A. J. Frantzen, *Mise à jour du fascicule no. 27* (Turnholt, 1985), p. 30; R. Meens, *Het tripartite boeteboek: Overlevering en betekenis van vroegmiddeleeuwse biechtvoorschriften (met editie en vertaling van vier tripartita)* (Hilversum, 1994), pp. 39–40 and nn. 75–6. Cf. Noonan, *Contraception*, pp. 162 (the earlier date given on p. 164 is an aberration). Excluded from discussion here is the second diocesan statute (post-813) of Theodulf, bishop of Orléans (*c*.750–821), whose use of the Genesis text concerns only unnaturalness, not avoidance of conception; it is quoted in Payer, *Sex and the Penitentials*, p. 57.

[22] This is only the date of the earliest extant manuscript *copy* of the 'double' penitential.

[23] The following is based on Regino's preface, *De synodalibus causis*, pp. 1–2.

from various councils and decrees, all into one book which he describes as a 'hand codex' (*manualis codicilis*) or 'thing to hold in one's hand' (*enkyridion*) for those times when a 'plenitude of books' is not available. It envisaged this archdiocese. In his preface Regino made it very clear that he saw pastoral needs as varying by time and place. 'If anyone is moved to ask why I have used more frequent examples from the councils of Gaul and Germany, let him accept [this] reply.' In what follows Regino states that things that are done vary through time: there are crimes committed these days which were unheard of in earlier times. And things vary regionally and according to peoples: 'diverse nations of peoples differ in kind, morals, language, laws.' Similarly, the universal Church may be united in faith, but varies locally in ecclesiastical customs. Regino reflects this linguistically, writing in Latin but occasionally allowing in a German word. The Church's varying response to varying needs justifies Regino's selection. 'Let him accept [this] reply', and he continues: 'let him know that I have taken care to insert those things especially which I knew were more needed in our dangerous times and which seemed to be relevant to the matter in hand.'

Study of Regino's sources has in fact shown his selectiveness.[24] For example, he made heavier use of what was chronologically and geographically nearer to him, in particular canons from a council held only a decade before (Tribur, 895) and presided over by his work's dedicatee, Hatto. And he included some new material. Oaths were to be taken to the archbishop of Trier. What Regino's work represents, then, is his view of what was needed in Rhineland parishes around 900, together with the unknown pastoral experts who lay behind the practices of the archdiocese of Trier upon which Regino seems to have drawn.[25]

One caveat before further speculations. In imposing upon us a view—pastors trying to repress sin—Regino's text insidiously encourages a one-way view of pressure exercised on sinning lay people, and of discrepancy between the views of clergy and people. Distance is implied, mistakenly in my view. Take one of Regino's questions, shortly before *Est aliquis*, on infanticide. 'Is there a woman who conceived in fornication and was frightened that she would be discovered, and [therefore] threw her own baby into the water or hid it in the earth—which they call "murder"?' (*Est aliqua femina, quae in fornicatione concipiens, timens, ne manifestaretur, infantem proprium aut in aquam proiecerit, aut in terra occultaverit, quod 'morth' dicunt*).[26] Regino intrudes a vernacular word which expresses what 'they', the people 'say' and think, calling this deed *morth*, and his text finds its counterpart and incidental confirmation in a famous story which is preserved

[24] Fournier and Le Bras, *Histoires des collections canoniques*, i. 248–50.

[25] The surviving manuscripts suggest that in the tenth and eleventh centuries Regino found a reasonable market in part of north-western Europe, particularly the Rhineland, among people who found his writing handy and practical for their work. Wasserschleben knew of ten manuscripts, describing six of these, three tenth-century, one tenth/eleventh, two eleventh-century, and he gave locations at *some* date for three of these: one was once in Trier, one in Rheims, one in the monastery of St James in Mainz; Regino, *De synodalibus causis*, pp. xx–xxi. An eleventh-century copy which was once at the abbey of St Vaast was added by Fournier and Le Bras, *Histoires des collections canoniques*, i. 245 n. 2.

[26] Regino, *De synodalibus causis*, II. v. 6: p. 209.

in the life of St Leoba,[27] where there is anger in a village when a dead baby is found which has been drowned in a pool by the river. If Regino's text draws close to real people here, so it does also on the abandonment of babies. Any woman who has conceived and given birth secretly should leave the baby at the doors of the church, rather than killing it; left with the priest, it can be taken over and brought up by someone else.[28] Making use of a solid building and a local figure of authority, it looks sensible, and it involved several co-operating parties.

In Regino's specification of the questions to be put in the enquiry about a church and its priest's life and ministry, one question about the church asked for a number, 'How many manses does it have . . . from which tithes are rendered?'[29] One of the types of documents to survive from Regino's world, the one which gives us the largest window onto the number and lives of ordinary people, is the polyptych, which surveyed estates, counting manses and inhabitants on them. In Georges Duby's classic account of medieval rural economy and his demographic analysis of ninth-century Carolingian estate surveys, use was made of a polyptych of the abbey of Prüm. This polyptych surveys the abbey's estates, which were very widely spread over the northern part of the kingdom of Lotharingia. Dated 892–3, this survey overlaps with the beginning of Regino's abbacy (892–9), in other words his administration of the abbey of Prüm and its possessions. Regino will have had to occupy himself with this, and one odd detail in Regino's *Two books on synodal cases* appears to confirm this. When detailing partners in illicit sexual encounters in a question to be put in confession, Regino copies the categories of an earlier penitential—another man's wife or betrothed, virgin, and nun or woman dedicated to God[30]—and then he adds two more. One is 'a woman not tied, that is to say, without a husband' (*absoluta femina, id est, sine marito*), referred to later in the same passage as an 'unoccupied woman' (*femina vacans*), the other a man's 'own slave' (*propria ancilla*). Both could easily have been suggested by the categorizations of people in a polyptych's list of people on estates.

The norm was for a manse to support one family. But the Prüm estates in the Ardennes (in today's Belgium and Luxembourg) contained, according to the polyptych, 116 families established on 35 manses, 88 of them on 22 manses. Duby remarked on these numbers, while also looking at eight villages near Paris. In the demographically favourable conditions of the eighteenth century these villages were to number 5,700, but according to the polyptych of St Germain-des-Prés they already had extraordinary numbers of inhabitants in the early ninth century: 4,100 people. Duby attempts to reconcile these with the notion of low *overall* population in north-western Europe at this time. On the one hand there were 'ocean-like stretches of country where farming was well-nigh impossible', where

[27] Abbess of Bischoffsheim in the diocese of Mainz until her death in 779. The story is given in translation in C. H. Talbot, *The Anglo-Saxon Missionaries in Germany* (London, 1954), pp. 216–18. See comment on it by R. A. Fletcher, *The Conversion of Europe: From Paganism to Christianity 371–1386 AD* (London, 1997), pp. 286–8.

[28] Regino, *De synodalibus causis*, II. lxviii; p. 241.

[29] Ibid., I, *Notitia*, XV; p. 20.

[30] Wasserschleben, *Bußordnungen*, p. 253.

population was virtually nil. On the other hand, while citing St Germain and the abbey of Prüm's estate in the Ardennes, he writes of 'overpopulation':[31] 'over-populated islands, where biological increase stimulated by agrarian prosperity pushed men to the verge of scarcity'.

Noonan did not read polyptychs, and Duby did not read these penitentials. When brought together, however, these texts show a remarkable coincidence. While the Prüm polyptych shows over-population in the Ardennes, it is an abbot of Prüm, who knew this survey, who is also the first person to record one remarkable text on avoiding offspring, *Si aliquis*, and it is a manuscript from the Ardennes which is the earliest of the two manuscripts of a penitential which, uniquely among such texts, unambiguously spelled out 'contraceptive' withdrawal. The chronological and geographical coincidences are so remarkable that they look almost too neat. For it is clear that they support the hypothesis that the pastoral concern with avoiding conception, which emerged and then intensified between the early ninth century and around 900, was an alert response to patterns of sin among the flock: one sin was being committed more than it had been, in an area suffering what we call over-population. If this is so, we must be careful about the patronizing assumptions implied in an account of demographic thought much of which is progressive, that is to say, a history which shows it advancing. Regino may not have had at his disposal a literary and intellectual tradition which would have encouraged him to articulate in *writing* and to generalize about this theme. But the pastoral response of *Est aliquis* and *Si aliquis* and the St Hubert penitential shows that there may well have been behind this response, inside the minds of Regino and other pastoral experts of this period, the *awareness* and *thought* of 'many people', 'they are poor', and 'they are avoiding conceiving'.

8.2 The decades around 1200

These years were a pastoral watershed. In England and France synodal statutes emerged as a means of educating the clergy. Reforming legislation started in the early thirteenth century, and continued for a century. All parish priests were required to have copies of the statutes, cheap and little books, containing brief instructions in their duties, what to tell their parishioners and how to administer the sacraments. Copies of synodal legislation did not monopolize a market for works of instruction, an expanding and changing market. Monographic treatises for confessors began to be produced, in a line which can be taken to start with

[31] G. Duby, *Rural Economy and Country Life in the Medieval West* (London, 1968), pp. 12–14. C.-E. Perrin had studied the polyptych of Prüm in his *Recherches sur la seigneurie rurale en Lorraine d'après les plus anciens censiers (IXe–XIe siècle)*, Publications de la Faculté des Lettres de l'Université de Strasbourg 71 (Paris, 1935), pp. 1–98. He analysed its data in 'Le manse dans le Polyptyque de l'abbaye de Prüm à la fin du IXe siècle', *Études historiques à la mémoire de Noël Didier* (Paris, 1960), pp. 245–58, discussing the 'surpeuplement' of the domains of the abbey of St Germain-des-Près and the Ardennes estates of the abbey of Prüm, pp. 252–3 and 258.

those written by Alain de Lille[32] around 1200, Robert of Flamborough (between 1208 and 1213),[33] and Peter of Poitiers[34] and Thomas of Chobham[35] around or just after 1216. This genre was then widened and enriched in the following decades through the most fundamental pastoral development of the early thirteenth century, the rise of the mendicant Orders, in particular the Dominican, and their rapid spread through the cities and towns of Latin Christendom. The professional specialist activities of the friars, preaching and confession, required equally specialized works of instruction. These were being produced by the 1220s,[36] and from this time on works on confession by seculars were accompanied by an ever-growing stream of works written by mendicants, forming now a market of many tiers. This last point can be seen in the size and selectivity of an instruction work. It could be a few paragraphs in the booklet of synodal statutes. After a few decades the paragraphs were being replaced by mini-tracts on confession in some English and French sets of synodal statutes. The monographic treatises were longer, some of them, like those written by Thomas of Chobham and the Dominican Raymond of Peñafort, much longer. Thomas's would find its way into the book-chests of an élite of wealthier and more educated clergy, Raymond's would be chained up in convent libraries. The Dominicans also had their equivalent of the priests' copy of the statutes, a tiny booklet to fit in a pocket.

In the statutes, the section on marriage had the parish priest playing a large role. In some statutes he commended marriage and put over to parishioners its elementary theology. Priests published banns, and the new legislation of the fourth Lateran Council of 1215 on prohibited degrees of relationship quickly came to be spelled out. The priest was instructed how to take penitents through sins they might have committed, and the statutes reflected new developments in the handling of sin. The intense concern of the late twelfth-century Paris theologians with practical analysis of sin trickled through, with synodal statutes having a parish priest concerned with 'circumstances' of sin and sinner. Elsewhere in the statutes a list of specially big sins, which are 'reserved' and have to be remitted to

[32] Michaud-Quantin, *Sommes*, pp. 16–19; Baldwin, *Peter the Chanter*, i. 43; Alain de Lille, *Liber poenitentialis*, ed. J. Longère, 2 vols., AMN 17–18 (1965); Alain de Lille, '*Liber poenitentialis*: les traditions moyenne et courte', ed. J. Longère, *AHDLMA* 32 (1966), 169–242.

[33] Michaud-Quantin, *Sommes*, pp. 21–4; Baldwin, *Peter the Chanter*, i. 32–3; Robert of Flamborough, *Liber poenitentialis*, ed. J. J. F. Firth, Studies and Texts 18 (Toronto, 1971).

[34] Baldwin, *Peter the Chanter*, i. 33–4; Peter of Poitiers [*Summa de confessione*] *Compilatio praesens*, ed. J. Longère, CCCM 51 (1980).

[35] Michaud-Quantin, *Sommes*, pp. 21–4; Baldwin, *Peter the Chanter*, i. 34–6; Chobham, *Summa confessorum*. One suggestion by the editor of Robert of Flamborough is that identified medieval ownership represents a late stage in a principally one-way flow, with secular priests who owned copies of Flamborough holding them as valuable objects and tending to bequeath them to religious houses, not the other way round; Robert, *Liber poenitentialis*, p. 18 n. 100. This suggestion probably applies to other long manuals, such as Thomas's—that is, that the usually unidentified earlier stage is wide ownership among parish priests. Despite its cost (it was about 120,000 words) Thomas's treatise was very popular. It survives in over one hundred copies, and among the twenty described in Broomfield's edition (Thomas, *Summa confessorum*, pp. lxxvii–lxxxi), two had belonged to parish priests.

[36] By around 1221 Paul of Hungary had produced the earliest penitential work written by a Dominican for Dominicans.

the penitentiary, reflected a new development on the ground, the rise of the bishop's specialist in sin. Seen in the diocese of York in 1195, the specialist was acquiring the name 'penitentiary' in the opening years of the thirteenth century.

Similarly the monographic treatises for confessors were new in themselves and reflected recent developments. At the core of this was the development of a less schematic and rigid approach to confession. Confessors were to look carefully at a sinner and his or her 'circumstances'—for example, gender, profession, age—and weigh up the penance accordingly. A reader who passes immediately from a work on sin and penance composed for priests by a bishop of Exeter, Bartholomew, between 1150 and 1170[37] to the instructional work written for confessors by Thomas of Chobham, official of the bishop of Salisbury, around 1216, crosses from one world to another. The former is called by its modern editor his 'penitential', accurately so, for, although its author is affected by theological and legal developments of the time, the work remains in substance and spirit a collection of old penitential canons: a lists of sins and the penances. It feels old. Thomas's work feels new. It breathes throughout the observant and practical air of an author who declared in the preface that his intention was to 'put aside subtleties and theoretical questions and carefully follow the practical actions and considerations which are necessary to priests when hearing confessions'.[38] It is not just that circumstances of sin and sinner are there, but that concern with circumstances frequently leads to lively comments, case-studies, vignettes, much quotation of things from recent decades, and, of course and above all, a large slice of the remarkably concrete and observant discussions of sin in Peter the Chanter's Paris. Addressing sex in marriage, a treatise for confessors now discriminated carefully, calibrating it according to different motives and Augustine's three goods of marriage. Such sex, according to Thomas, is *licit* or *fragile* or *impetuous*.[39] Where there had once been penitential silence on sex in marriage, or only crude concern about the external matter of the 'naturalness' of the physical actions, there was now steady and subtle attention directed towards internal disposition. And the human behaviour discriminated in this fashion was now systematically related to theology.

Henceforth what is commonplace in works of instruction for confessors is the intrusion of theology and three thoughts in a sequence: theological legitimation of sex in marriage through the intent to procreate; the lack of intent to procreate; and the thought which is encouraged by the first two, active steps to avoid procreating. If the first is Thomas's *licit* category and the second *fragile*, *impetuous* does not bring in avoidance or prevention of generation as a subject on its own. It does appear, but only secondarily, as the result of other actions which are being condemned.

[37] Edited in A. Morey, *Bartholomew of Exeter, Bishop and Canonist: A Study in the Twelfth Century* (Cambridge, 1937), pp. 175–300.

[38] Thomas of Chobham, *Summa confessorum, Proemium*, p. 3.

[39] Ibid., VII. ii. Q. 2a (p. 333 and n. 1), which notes the distinction in earlier theology, including a gloss on the *Sentences*.

There are four sorts, (i) extraordinarily excessive lust, (ii) 'use of a member not deputed for this', (iii) sex at a prohibited time, (iv) sex with a pregnant woman who is near to childbirth, menstruating, or in childbirth. Under (iv) Thomas is in line with Robert of Flamborough—such sex is 'impetuous because it happens often that a woman weighed down in this way aborts'[40]—but under (ii) he goes further than earlier writers. '"Use of a member not deputed for this" is not very different from the sin against nature, for there is present there also a falling and loss of the *partus* [possible conception], as is said below.' This phrase from Augustine's *Adulterii malum,* familiar through its presentation by Peter the Lombard, Gratian, and Bartholomew of Exeter, now attracts further exposition. When Thomas turns to it 'below' (in the section on *sin against nature*) he defines it more precisely. 'Some', he writes, 'abuse women, either *not* in the place *deputed for this*'. 'In the place deputed' is Thomas's addition, specifying that it means what we call anal intercourse. He then adds to it a second form of men's abuse of women. 'Or', he continues, 'without observing the order of nature' (*ordine nature non observato*).[41] Although *without observing the order of nature* could in principle cover much, its juxtaposition, as an alternative, to a quite precise phrase for a precise action (anal intercourse), suggests that Thomas is writing these words to denote a particular additional, and alternative, proscribed action. The fundamental and oldest senses of *order* (*ordo*) stress things happening in an orderly sequence or series, and here orderly sequence would be intromission followed by emission of seed; such a sequence would coincide with *order* as the conventional view of 'what nature has *ordained*'. *Not observing the order of nature* seems to be an early equivalent of our phrases *withdrawal* and *coitus interruptus.* It is an awkward phrase, like *use of a member not deputed for this,* and it is less transparently precise than the modern phrases. It leaves open the possibility of ambiguity recurring in its use by other writers, because of the hold-all capacity of any negative definition, such as 'that which is not something or other'; here, 'that which does not observe the order of nature'.

Thomas is the first of the authors examined here to include avoidance as an illustration of nullifying conditions attached to a marriage contract, thoughtfully specifying the speaker as either female or male: 'I take you [female] as mine or I take you [male] as mine with this condition, that we procure sterility so that we never generate offspring.'[42] Henceforth a pre-marital pact against conception will be commonplace in any works for confessors which also deal with the contracting of marriage.

Both here and in his treatment of sex in marriage avoidance comes up

[40] Thomas of Chobham, VII. ii. Q. 2a. 3; pp. 338; Robert of Flamborough, *Liber poenitentialis,* IV. viii; p. 197 no. 226.

[41] Thomas of Chobham, *Summa confessorum,* VII. ii. Q. 2a. 3 (p. 336); VII. ii. Q. 18a. 1 (p. 398).

[42] Ibid., IV. ii. Q. 7a. 4; p. 148. Compare this with another work produced in the circle of Paris's Peter the Chanter, Robert of Courson's *Summa,* written between 1208 and 1212/13 (Baldwin, *Chanter,* i. 23), where the condition given is 'I contract with you if you procure for us that children are not born, either through poisons of sterility or some other way' (*Ego contraho tecum si procures nobis non nasci filios per venena sterilitatis vel alio modo*); BN, MS Lat. 14524, fol. 140vb.

secondarily, but it is treated in its own right in a long section entitled *Concerning those who kill their own offspring*:[43]

Further to be noted is another very shameful type of homicide, mothers killing what they bear [*partus*, which covers a range from embryo to a baby after birth]. And this happens five ways, that is to say: (i) when poisons of sterility are procured; or (ii) when after conception the foetus is forced out with violence; or (iii) when after childbirth [the baby] is separated from the [mother's] own breasts; or (iv) when it is cast out and exposed; or (v) when through negligence it is stifled in the bed of the sleeping mother.
(i) To procure sterility through potions or spells [*incantationes*] is a great sin, for the propagation of the human race is thereby hampered. Some women do this so that they can be allowed to engage in the pleasure of lust and not to be found out through a *partus* following [upon this]. Others also do the same thing in order to avoid the pain of giving birth. To do this, however, is a great sin.
(ii) A more serious and greater sin is the second [way], when the *partus* is cast out by a potion or in another way. But then there is a distinction, whether the infant [*puerperium*] was formed or unformed. For when the infant is formed it is infused with a soul, and then [abortion] is full homicide and very damnable, because [the infant] is killed in body and soul. And the woman who begrudges her foetus [*fetui*] eternal life and cannot bear her foetus to be born [and receive] baptism is very cruel. To this end [this] is written in the law of Moses: '*if someone strikes a woman* who has [a foetus] in her womb, *and she aborts*, if the infant was formed, *he shall render life for a life*' [Exod. 21: 22–3]; if however it was not formed, he shall be punished with a fine [all of this is a text of Ambrosiaster present in Gratian and Peter Lombard]. From these [words] it is clear how much more serious a sin it is to cast out a formed infant than to cast out an unformed [one].

Priests therefore ought to charge women, who are pregnant and have a *partus*, not to press on with heavy work after conception. For doctors say that [even] with light work the foetus is cast out from the womb after the birth [= onset] of conception. One reads about a certain woman who wanted to cast out her *partus*. She gave three jumps from a bench to the ground, and on the third jump the foetus fell out to the ground, wrapped round in a little skin. It is clear from this that women who have not been instructed about this often eject some conceived foetus, either through work or exertion.
(iii) The fact that separating a baby from the [mother's] own breasts pertains to killing is clear from the writings of the saints [= fathers], who say that no milk is so suitable for nursing a child as maternal milk. Therefore a [baby] often perishes when it is nursed with strange milk, with, so to speak, a contrary nutriment. This can happen because the complexion of the nurse is contrary to the baby's complexion, and thus the baby contracts some corruption from milk

[43] Ibid., VII. iv. Q. 9a. 15; pp. 463–5. See earlier comment by J. W. Baldwin, *The Language of Sex: Five Voices from Northern France around 1200* (Chicago, 1994), pp. 212–13.

which is contrary to it. . . . A woman who disdains to nurse the offspring she has conceived is crueller than any beast. She fed it in her womb with menstrual blood and now she neglects to nurse it with God-given milk. For God gave woman breasts and commanded milk to grow in them so that she could rear her offspring thus. Now, however, there are kinds of women who try to invalidate God's work and nullify the milk which God created for use. Priests should rebuke such women and impose heavy penance for disdaining to feed their babies according to nature's use. If the woman is delicate and says she cannot bear such labour, was she not so delicate when she bore intercourse and the labour of giving birth? If she truly cannot bear the labour, she should at least feed and wash the baby when she can, to avoid appearing to overturn nature through never deigning to approach her offspring.

(iv) Sufficient was said above about those [women] who hold their little babies in contempt, and therefore one ought not to repeat it here. [a. There had been reference under baptism: 'About abandoned little babies, where there is doubt about whether they have been baptised or not, there is a specific form' 'for baptising'. b. There had been another reference in a miscellany of comments towards the end of the section on reserved cases: 'Item, if a woman exposes her little baby and abandons him totally and the Church collects the baby, the woman cannot subsequently reclaim her child, for when she exposed the child she forfeited whatever [rights] in law she had in him.']

(v) The priest should attend carefully to those who stifle their own foetuses [*fetus* but should be babies]. He should forbid his parishioners from bringing together their little babies in one bed, because a baby is easily stifled if its mouth is covered by some cloth for a little while. There is a custom for all such people—who have stifled or put down their little babies through negligence—to come on Ash Wednesday to confess to the bishop, although public penance should not be imposed upon them if the sin is secret. But priests ought to enquire carefully whether it was gross or small negligence, and in the light of this they should make the penance heavier or lighter. For parents ought to take great care in bringing up their little babies, for after baptism they have these [children] commended to their care until the end of the seventh year. Thus, if they perish while in their custody, [the parents] have to respond [for this] to God and the Church.

This was to be very influential, both through the great popularity of Thomas's work, which is still extant in over a hundred manuscripts, and also by way of its adaptation in the next century, as we shall see later. Notable is the way the text completes one recent development. Bartholomew of Exeter had shunted together texts on avoiding conception and abortion, one the Council of Anycra text (which is exclusively on abortion), and *Si aliquis* (which deals with both), putting them both under the rubric *Those who perpetrate abortion.*[44] Taking over both texts from Bartholomew and in the same sequence, Robert of Flamborough had made

[44] Bartholomew, *Penitential*, LVI, p. 222: *De perpetrantibus abortum.*

two chapters of them, putting Ancyra under *On women who fornicate and kill their foetuses* (abortion), and *Si aliquis* under *On those who impede the conceptus* (both conception and that which is conceived),[45] thereby moving towards a stronger demarcation between abortion and impeding conception. Finally Thomas brings complete clarity to the distinction between the two of them, numbered (i) and (ii). Motive also attracts Thomas's attention: avoiding detection of sexual sin which arises through pregnancy, and fear of the pain of childbirth. In this section methods are 'potions or incantations'. Perhaps this is method, singular, rather than method*s*. For Thomas has a long independent section on various forms of sorcery and superstitions, in none of which there is any mention of maleficence and spells to impede generation.[46] However, Thomas does write against the use of incantations when collecting and using herbs, as though this conferred on them power beyond what they had according to nature.[47] Fused here are, perhaps, two different campaigns of Thomas, one against herbal contraceptive potions, the other against the element of superstition, added to what was natural, in the use of herbs.

There is a great deal that is new in Thomas, but what does it signify? There is new canon law. There is reflection of late twelfth-century Paris. The brief but precise question about the delicate woman may well have been first a question raised in Paris by Peter the Chanter, like much in Thomas, for it is reminiscent of Peter's discussion of therapeutic abortion, which we quoted in Chapter 7. *Complexio*[48] and *contrarium nutrimentum* hark back to natural philosophy or medical textbooks, as also the abortifacient leaps.[49] The schematic clarity of Thomas's five ways is all of a piece with an intellectual world which in these years was giving chapter divisions to books of the Bible and introducing such things as contents lists and indexes.

If Thomas's work was a product of new developments in confession, the literature of confession, and developments in the schools of Bologna and Paris, it is not quite so clear what new observation and pastoral concerns were influencing it. Most remarkable in the long passage quoted above is the dominance of a spectrum of care, running from conception through to feeding, and the heavy emphasis on this care, whether preventive care of a pregnant woman or of a baby breast-fed and, at the very least, washed and dealt with by its own mother. Thomas has taken a canon-legal and penitential tradition, linking measures against conception or the foetus and accidental or deliberate stifling, and adding newer canon law, for example, Gratian's inclusion of a text distinguishing stages

[45] Robert of Flamborough, *Liber poenitentialis*, V. ii. vi–vii; pp. 222–3: *De mulieribus quae fornicantur et partus suos necant*; *De impedientibus conceptum*. In the first case Robert is simply using the opening words of the quoted text as its rubric.

[46] Thomas of Chobham, *Summa confessorum*, VII. v; pp. 466–87.

[47] Ibid., VII. v. Q. 9a; pp. 480–1.

[48] See a parallel in Alain de Lille, '*Liber poenitentialis*: les traditions moyenne et courte', ed. Longère, p. 194, where *complexio* is a 'circumstance' of a sinner, particular complexions inclining more to one sin or another.

[49] See Baldwin, *Language of Sex*, p. 215.

of abortion.[50] The emphasis on baby-care has its counterpart in thirteenth-century English synodal statutes:[51] we are encountering something whose concentrated concern is distinctive to England and, perhaps, northwestern Europe.

Avoidance? Presented clearly, yes; linked to new theology, yes. But there is little that suggests change in *pastoral* concern about it. In their specification of what priests should say on Sundays, the synodal statutes being produced in the three or four years just after Thomas's work, such as Angers (between 1216 and 1219) and Salisbury (between 1217 and 1219), show clearly a parish priest's principal concern about marriage. Commend marriage, and condemn all sex outside it. Avoidance is not a theme for Sunday instruction, and it is not a matter of special or new emphasis in the instructions on confession.

A similar impression is given by other works intended for confessors, the earlier treatises written by Alain de Lille, Peter of Poitiers, and Robert of Flamborough, and the ones that were about to appear from the new specialists, the Dominicans. The Dominican's most important large and inclusive work, comparable in size to Thomas of Chobham's, was Raymond of Peñafort's *Summa of Cases* or *Summa of Penance* (*Summa de casibus* or *de poenitentia*), whose first recension in three books is from 1224–6.[52] Raymond went through cases, and here he is on avoidance and abortion:

> What if (i) someone strikes a pregnant woman, or (ii) gives her poison, or (iii) she herself receives [poison], in order to commit abortion, or (iv) [someone gives her poison or (v) she receives poison] so that she does not conceive, should not such a person be adjudged a homicide, or irregular? Reply. If the infant was already formed or animated, it is rightly [adjudged to be] homicide, if the woman has committed abortion through this hitting or drinking, because she has killed a man. If it was not yet animated, this is not called homicide, as far as irregularity is concerned, but it will be held to be like homicide as far as penance is concerned. And the same [applies] to the person who gives or receives poison, or [does something] similar, in order that generation or conception should not take place. 32 q. 2 *Quod non formatum puerperium* and *Moyses*; supplementary on the same, *Si aliquis* and *Sicut ex littterarum*.[53]

Avoidance and abortion are taken together but carefully distinguished. There is a significant negative: *maleficium* or *incantationes* are absent from methods, as they usually are henceforth. Positively, abortion is from violence or 'poison', avoidance

[50] Also in Robert of Flamborough, under irregularity.

[51] P. Biller, 'Marriage Patterns and Women's Lives: A Sketch of a Pastoral Geography', in *Woman is a Worthy Wight: Women in English Society c.1200–1500*, ed. P. J. P. Goldberg (Stroud, 1992), pp. 60–107 (pp. 79–80).

[52] On Raymond's work, see Michaud-Quantin, *Sommes*, pp. 34–42, and *SOPMA* iii. 285. The second recension, adding the fourth book on marriage, was in 1234. Humbert de Romans specified Raymond's book for the convent library, listing it immediately after glossed and unglossed bibles; the English Dominican Simon of Hinton (writing between 1240 and 1250) said that Raymond's work was universally 'had' among the friars; and the Dominican education-commission of 1259 envisaged convent teaching on it. In the edition used here, Raymond of Peñafort, *Summa de poenitentia et matrimonio, cum glossis Ioannis de Friburgo* (Rome, 1603, repr. Farnborough, 1967), the glosses attributed to John of Freiburg are in fact by William of Rennes.

[53] Raymond, *Summa de poenitentia*, II. i. 6; p. 153.

of conception from 'poison' or something 'similar'. Something similar to a herbal decoction taken as a drink would be a pessary soaked in a herbal decoction.

It is Raymond's jurist's outlook and clarity of mind that are on display here, in the careful distinctions and the canon-legal references. At one point in the fourth book on marriage, Raymond asks if a marriage holds when contracted for such secondary unworthy causes as beauty and riches. In his answer he refers to but does not quote *Solet queri.* Raymond *omits* from Gratian—either Gratian's own words or texts cited by him—anything concerning procreation or its avoidance, concentrating instead on Old Testament texts on seeing a beautiful woman, loving her passionately and wishing to marry.[54] There seems no special interest in avoidance of generation.

What of the booklets that could go into the pocket of a travelling Dominican friar? The *Summa penitentie fratrum predicatorum* was one of the earliest of these extremely brief little manuals, probably just pre-dating Raymond and written by a northern European (but not French) Dominican. It was very popular.[55] There are questions under the ten commandments, where fifteen of the forty-nine brief words under 'Thou shalt not kill' are these: 'or if the [penitent] killed the foetus of a woman, or taught [someone] how to kill it, or did something so that a woman would not conceive'.[56] There is nothing elsewhere on the theme. The author is direct and more interested than Raymond. However, what there is on avoidance or abortion is traditional, given no special spin by new pastoral concern, and it is brief. Elsewhere in the booklet opportunities to underline interest by repetition are not taken. Questions go through the seven deadly sins, where fairly detailed questions under 'lust' do *not* include avoidance of conception. Where the confessor is envisaged as addressing *circumstances* of sin, the *circumstance* of *mode* leads only to positions adopted in (otherwise legitimate) sex.

8.3 *The decades around 1300*

Spotting the differences between the texts of around 1200 and those of around 1300 is made easier through the underlying continuity of the pastoral texts.

Although there was expansion of activity in the universities in the intervening period, there was no watershed or revolution in the theology of penance or marriage or the literary genres of pastoral literature. The later texts develop in an unbroken line from the earlier. Reforming and educational synodal legislation continues, and there are quite precise equivalents of the earlier monographic

[54] Ibid., IV. ii. 6; p. 514.

[55] It is edited and studied in J. Goering and P. J. Payer, 'The "Summa penitentie fratrum predicatorum": A Thirteenth-Century Confessional Formulary', *MS* 55 (1993), 1–50. Despite the fact that its brevity must have made many of its copies ephemeral (it is less than 3000 words), it still survives in twenty-nine copies, all but one (a Vatican copy) currently in libraries north of the Alps, especially Germany.

[56] 'Summa penitentie fratrum predicatorum', p. 36: *si conceptum mulieris interemit vel interimere docuit, vel si fecit aliquid ne mulier conciperet.*

treatises. Among the Dominicans two treatises by John of Freiburg are the counterparts of the earlier treatises we examined, for John's long *Summa confessorum* incorporated and extended Raymond of Peñafort's *Summa of Cases*, serving as the large reference work for the convent library, while his brief *Confessionale* was the Dominican pocket-book, comparable to early booklets like the *Summa penitentie fratrum predicatorum*. At the same time William of Pagula's priests' manual, the *Oculus sacerdotis*, was an outcrop both of the increasingly lengthy instructional elements of synodal statutes and of Thomas of Chobham's treatise, upon which it drew heavily. Speculation about the significance of changes becomes less dangerous. The variables are fewer.

We begin with John of Freiburg.[57] His writings are almost entirely on confession, and they fall into two groups. One group is essentially an extension to Raymond of Peñafort's treatise and William of Rennes' gloss on it.[58] John composed an index and an addition to these,[59] and then, finally, in 1297–8, a *Summa confessorum*[60] which broadly incorporates Raymond and William as well as commenting upon them and adding to them.[61] The other group consists of a *Manuale confessorum*,[62] and the *Confessionale*, whose cross-references to the *Summa confessorum* of 1298 presumably indicate a slightly later date of composition.

The *Summa confessorum* is still extant wholly or in part in 176 manuscripts.[63] It is likely that many of these and the other now lost earlier manuscripts did not differ greatly in their essential characteristics from the early printed editions which modern scholars usually consult: large in size, very expensive, and located in a library. The reader can quickly size up the *Summa confessorum* by looking at abortion. He finds that while abortion was the sixth topic or question under 'homicide' for Raymond, John has added so much more material that for him it is the twenty-ninth!

Here for example is John copying Raymond, Raymond in Roman, John's additions in italics. 'What if someone strikes a pregnant woman, or gives her poison, or she receives [poison], *which is prepared by another person, or* [she receives poison] *with the advice of someone else*, in order to commit abortion . . .'[64] The text

[57] Born in Freiburg-im-Breisgau (*c.* mid-thirteenth century), he joined the Dominicans there, and studied in Strasbourg and perhaps also Paris. He spent most of his life, as far as we know, in the Dominican convent in Freiburg, dying perhaps in 1314. At the convent he had become lector in 1280, giving lectures to Dominicans in the convent and local clergy if they wanted to attend. See M. Hamm, 'Johannes von Freiburg', *Vf* iv. 605–11.

[58] Around 1240–5, according to Michaud-Quantin, *Sommes*, pp. 40–1; around 1241 according to *SOPMA* ii. 156.

[59] Boyle, *Pastoral Care*, III, pp. 247–8; *SOPMA* ii. 428–9.

[60] Michaud-Quantin, *Sommes*, pp. 44–8; Boyle, *Pastoral Care*, III; Boyle, '*Summae confessorum*', pp. 236–7; *SOPMA* ii. 430–3.

[61] This work is well-known through the magnificent analysis of its sources in Boyle, *Pastoral Care*, II–III, and through its use in T. N. Tentler, *Sin and Confession on the Eve of the Reformation* (Princeton, 1977).

[62] Michaud-Quantin, *Sommes*, p. 44; Boyle, '*Summa confessorum*', p. 237 and n. 13.

[63] *SOPMA* ii. 430–3, and iv. 151–2.

[64] Raymond, *Summa de poenitentia*, II. i. 6 (p. 153), and John of Freiburg, *Summa confessorum*, II. i. Q. 29 (Augsburg, 1470, unfoliated): *Quid si aliquis percutit mulierem praegnantem, vel dat ei venenum, vel ipsamet accipit quod ab alio paratum est vel ad consilium eius, ut abortivum faciat, vel ut non concipiat.*

continues to follow Raymond, while adding references to theological works by Albert the Great and Thomas Aquinas and canon-legal works by Innocent IV and Geoffrey of Trani. John then proceeds to the next question, number 30, which refers to William's gloss on this passage in Raymond, and copies it out. This pattern can be seen throughout the work: incorporation of all of Raymond and most of William, along with much recent canon law and practical pastoral theology, especially from Paris.

When dealing with abortion and avoidance of conception, John includes all of Raymond and some of William's extras.[65] Apart from the minor additions to the abortion passage quoted above, there is virtually no development of our theme apart from a concluding and approving point about the customary mode of intercourse: 'and thus women more easily conceive unless contingently [conception] is impeded'.[66] John does not cross-refer back to his abortion and avoidance passage, nor does his massive treatment of the sexual act in marriage contain the intention to avoid offspring as an independent theme. John's *Summa* reflects inflation, not changes in pastoral concern about avoidance.

Against the over 300,000 words of his *Summa confessorum*, John's *Confessionale*[67] takes up less than 20,000 words. One hundred and sixty-four manuscripts[68] of it are still extant. We may conjecture that there were once many more copies, with its lesser size and cost leading to proportionately greater losses. An idea of the characteristics of these booklets is given by Munich, Bayrische Staatsbibliothek MS CLM 28427.[69] This is 21 by 15 cm. in size, and contains the *Confessionale* in the first thirty leaves, and a few confessional formulae and two letters of penance from the diocese of Augsburg in the final four leaves: a small, easily portable and relatively inexpensive book intended for everyday use in the administration of confession and penance.[70]

In writing the gigantic *Summa confessorum* and the tiny *Confessionale* John puts himself forward as a writer making deliberate choices, for two different audiences. John opens the *Confessionale* with words which introduce himself as an author with one audience in mind, 'Desiring to instruct the simpler and less expert confessors about the way to hear confessions' (*Simpliciores et minus expertos confessores de modo audiendi confessiones informare cupiens*).[71] The author of a

[65] Excluded are his additions on the pre-marital pact to avoid offspring, included are his additions on affinity.

[66] John, *Summa confessorum*, III. ii. Q. 47: *sic etiam facilius concipiunt mulieres nisi per accedens* [*sic*] *impediatur.*

[67] Michaud-Quantin, *Sommes*, pp. 49–50; Boyle, '*Summae confessorum*', p. 237.

[68] *SOPMA* ii. 433–6, and iv. 152.

[69] G. Glaucke, *Cod. Lat. 28255–28460*, in C. Halm *et al.*, *Catalogus codicum manuscriptorum Bibliothecae Regiae Monacensis*, I- (Munich, Wiesbaden, 1868–), IV, part 8, 258–60.

[70] Even more portable would have been a copy now in Trier, which measures 9.5 by 13.3 cm.; M. Keuffer, G. Kentenich, *et al.*, *Beschreibendes Verzeichnis der Handschriften der Stadtbibliothek zu Trier*, 10 parts (Trier, 1888–1931), V, 27–8, no. 564. Another manuscript, Stuttgart, Württembergische Landesbibliothek MS HB I 60, from Weingarten, contains the *Confessionale* in 66 leaves of a manuscript measuring 21.5 by 15 cm., J. Autenrieth *et al.*, *Die Handschriften der ehemaligen Hofbibliothek Stuttgart* (Stuttgart, Wiesbaden, 1963–), I, part 1, 95–6.

[71] Oxford, Bodleian Library, MS Laud Misc. 278, fol. 354ra.

comparable short tract, *In primis debet* wrote, he said, for 'priests who have no knowledge [about confession]'.[72] Formulaic though these phrases may be, there is a useful approximation between what they suggest and our modern phrase 'idiot guides'.

Where there is a pair of opposites in John's picture of two sets of readers—the *periti*, the learned, who read the *Summa confessorum*, and the *inperiti*, the simple, who read the idiot-guide called the *Confessionale*—there is also a pair of opposites in the selection or non-selection of contents. On the one hand, material in the large *Summa* was in one way deliberately unselective. It tried to cover all possible eventualities, regardless of their frequency or rarity. When 'rare and difficult problems come up', writes John, the confessor who has the *Confessionale* needs to go off to the comprehensive texts. 'Read [about them]', writes John, 'in the *Summa* of the blessed Raymond, in the *Book of Case-questions* and specially and more fully in the *Summa of Confessors*'[73]—the second and third references here being to two of John's own works.

On the other hand, when writing the *Confessionale*, John was like someone writing an exam essay and with a word-limit. He had to select severely and stick to his theme. The theme is the *more common* sins. This is spelled out straightforwardly and simply in his preamble. 'I have divided this treatise into two parts . . . In the second part, on the questioning which should be done with certain people, [people] of various dignities, estates and occupations, I have given special instruction according to the sins which are *more frequently* committed by *such* people.'[74] John opens the second part by repeating this formula, underlining it by spelling out the contrast with the questions which have just been paraded, in the first part, under the heading of the seven deadly sins. 'After instruction on questioning about those sins which for the most part can be found commonly among men [people][75] of any estate, I have judged it useful to provide some things on the enquiries which should be made about some particular sins which are more frequently committed by people of various dignities, estates and occupations.'[76]

This is a particularly sharp expression of a development which was rooted in confessional concern with circumstances. It had found fundamental early expression in Raymond of Peñafort's account, in his *Summa*, of how interrogations should address the sins of the group to which the confessing sinner belonged:

[72] The text is quoted more fully below.

[73] . . . *erga rara et dubia, cum occurrerint, lege in summa fratris Raymundi et in libello questionum casualium, specialiter autem et plenius in summa confessorum*; MS Laud Misc. 278, fol. 354ra.

[74] MS Laud Misc. 278, fol. 354ra: *Hunc autem tractatum in duas partes distinxi . . . Secundo autem de interrogacionibus faciendis circa quasdam personas diversarum dignitatum, statuum et officiorum instructionem specialem tradidi secundum peccata que a talibus frequencius committuntur.*

[75] 'Men' (*homines*) is intended here to cover both sexes.

[76] MS Laud Misc. 278, fol. 358va: *Post instructionem de interrogationibus eorum peccatorum que ut plurimum inveniri possunt in hominibus cuiuscunque status communiter, utiliter iudicavi aliqua tradere de inquisitionibus faciendis de aliquibus peccatis specialibus que a quibusdam personis diversarum dignitatum, statuum et officiorum frequencius committuntur.*

Item, with princes [ask] about [the mal-administration] of justice. With knights, [ask] about pillage. With merchants, and officials, [and those] practising the mechanical arts, [ask] about perjury, lying, theft, fraud, and suchlike. With burgesses and citizens generally, [ask] about usuries and securities. With peasants, [ask] about envy, theft—especially about tithes, first-fruits, dues, and taxes.[77]

In the mid-thirteenth century works written by two Bolognese canonists, Johannes de Deo[78] and Henry of Susa (Hostiensis),[79] had listed many more groups and many more questions to be put to each of them, and these treatises, in turn, had influenced the elaborate interrogatories for various ranks, estates and professions which were provided in the *Confessionale.*[80] Later they would also shape the *De planctu ecclesie* written in 1332 by another expert in confession, the papal penitentiary Alvarus Pelagius,[81] and in England a manual of the 1340s, William Doune's *Memoriale presbiterorum.*[82] There are several assumptions in these lists of sins, always implicit and sometimes spelled out. In the case of necessarily illicit or dubious professions, such as those of people who fight for hire, beggars, and prostitutes, the sins are those which are implicated in the job itself. In the case of other professions, the sins are those which the job's exercise provides the opportunity to commit—which, therefore, *may* be committed. *May* shades into *often*, and by the time of John of Freiburg this has led to the notion of 'the sins which are more frequently committed' by a particular group. 'Ascribing patterns of behaviour to social groups' slightly misleads through semantic-conceptual anachronism, but it roughly describes what is being done in John's interrogatories.[83]

As we then read John listing clergy and religious, judges, lawyers, doctors, teachers, nobles, and so on and ascribing typical sins to them, we can see someone who is writing in this tradition, looking over his shoulder at the large, learned, and unselective *summae*, to which he provides handy cross-references, and gazing out at his contemporary world. This was the world in and near Freiburg, the other friars and clergy whom he taught and for whom he wrote, and beyond them the German-speaking men and women of whose more frequent sins he was trying to

[77] Raymond, *Summa de poenitentia*, III. xxxiv. 33; p. 467a–b; see M. Haren, 'Social Ideas in the Pastoral Literature of Fourteenth-Century England', in *Religious Belief and Ecclesiastical Careers in Late-Medieval England: Proceedings of the Conference held at Strawberry Hill, Easter 1989*, ed. C. Harper-Bill, Studies in the History of Medieval Religion 3 (Woodbridge, 1991), pp. 43–57 (p. 46). On Raymond's work, see Michaud-Quantin, *Sommes*, pp. 34–42, and *SOPMA* iii. 285.

[78] See Haren, 'Social Ideas', p. 47; Michaud-Quantin, pp. 26–7.

[79] See Haren, 'Social Ideas', pp. 47 and 50–1.

[80] Haren, 'Social Ideas', p. 49; Michaud-Quantin, *Sommes*, p. 50.

[81] Haren, 'Social Ideas', p. 49; N. Iung, *Un franciscain, théologien du pouvoir pontifical au XIVe siècle: Alvaro Pelayo, évèque et pénitencier de Jean XXII* (Paris, 1931), pp. 23 and 52–5.

[82] Haren, 'Social Ideas', pp. 49–51; M. Haren, 'The Interrogatories for Officials, Lawyers and Secular Estates of the *Memoriale presbiterorum*', in *Handling Sin*, ed. Biller and Minnis, pp. 123–63.

[83] Perhaps less significant, but still striking, is that these lists have now become the umbrella for much miscellaneous 'social' comment, as when Alvarus Pelagius uses a vast list of the sins of one estate, women, as an excuse to comment on Florentine mothers spoiling their children. Alvarus Pelagius, *De planctu ecclesie*, II. xlv (Venice, 1560): *Nimis delicate nutriunt filios, quos carnaliter diligunt, sicut domine Florentine* ('Like Florentine ladies they [= some women] bring up their children, whom they love physically [rather than spiritually], with excessive indulgence').

provide a brief 'sociography'. Thus, John writes, under the questions to be put to 'peasants and farmers', such a person should be asked, 'whether he has moved [*or* altered] field-boundaries, which in German are called "Markstein"'.[84] A pub-landlord (*tabernarius*) is to be asked about misleading customers over wine, selling wine purporting to come from one country or estate when in fact it came from another.[85]

In the first part of the *Confessionale*, sex between men and women crops up under 'Lust'. Most of this is as usual. The confessor is to ask the penitent 'if he lay with a woman not in the right way. But one must ask carefully about this, and only in general. And if the person confessing has declared some irregular way, he should be asked further if he has committed any other irregularity. And nothing is to be made specific to him, to avoid him learning evil. On this theme, at the beginning one can question in a general way, thus in Latin, "Did you have any irregular gestures with women?"'. The only new point here is John providing the (German) vernacular for the question—the only occasion of this in the interrogations—*Hetest du iede heme geberde mit vrowen die niht zimelich waren*?[86]

John focuses on the theme in the estates-sins questions addressed to those who are married, *Ad coniugatos.* Canon law is there, with John's cross-references, and a selection of sins based on John's observation of the married: mutual relations, adulterous conception and inheritance, and the handling of property are the hardnosed questions. The questions are rounded off thus. 'Item, did the wife effect some impediment to conceiving? And the same [question] about the man, [did he effect some impediment to conceiving?]. Or did she procure an abortion?' (*Item, si mulier aliquod impedimentum fecit ne conciperet; et idem de viro; vel si aborsum procuravit*).[87] The abortion question is not repeated for the man.

Clearly the condition of being married or not married had always been fundamental, in that *not* being married had always defined some acts as sinful, and all the attention paid to the varying degrees of licitness of the sexual act were to do with it inside marriage. What is implied here then comes to be spelled out through the growing emphasis on the *circumstance* of estate or condition, which laid its foundation. Now the married are being listed as an estate, in the *Confessionale* and other manuals.[88] This is the first significance of John's list. Positive steps to avoid

[84] *Ad rusticos et agricolas . . . si mutavit terminos agrorum, qui dicuntur teutonice Markstein*; MS Laud. Misc. 278, fol. 362va. In the photographic reproduction of this manuscript which I am using, *mutavit* appears to have been written *mutitavit*, with *it* partly erased.

[85] Ibid., fol. 362rb.

[86] Ibid., fol. 355ra. *Geberde* is preceded in the manuscript by *geb* which appears, in the photographic reproduction I am using, to be partly erased. Cf. BN, MS Lat. 3532, fol. 367ra: *Teuthonice, hattest du iede heme geberde mit vrowen die niht zimelich wearen. Inordinatos gestus* is a hold-all question, which could embrace positions and the question of 'unnaturalness' per se, but, given John's preoccupation with avoidance of offspring, withdrawal to avoid conception was probably the principal concern.

[87] MS Laud. Misc. 278, fol. 361va.

[88] One which was roughly contemporary was the anonymous *Sacerdos igitur*, where there is to be enquiry *A coniugatis et matrimonio copulatis*, beginning with the question whether they contracted marriage with the intention of having offspring to bring up in the praise of God, or with the intention of sating their lust; Vatican MS Pal. Lat. 719, fol. 18va. On the work, see Michaud-Quantin, *Sommes*, p. 85.

conception or abort are spelled out,[89] and these have moved into questions for the married. Avoiding conception comes first, before abortion, whereas in the more remote, academic, and legal *Summa confessorum* abortion comes first. Both husband and wife are alternatives: either impedes conception. There is John's choice of words. He avoids the Augustinian phrases, 'avoid generation of offspring', 'procure poisons of sterility', and 'act with some evil work so that they are not born', which had been so widely spread by *Solet queri* and *Aliquando.* In the decades around 1300 forms of the word *impedire* (impede) are coming into use, *impeditive, impediment,*[90] and John is part of this fashion when writing, 'effect an impediment to conceiving'. Again, the old Augustinian phrases are shuffled off, and replaced by something terse and direct. Finally, there is selectivity—selection of a more frequent sin of a particular group—as well as selection of something important enough to go into the idiot-guide pocketbook.

Let us compare the *Confessionale* to another confessional booklet from the same period, the *In primis debet sacerdos,* which may have been written by Bérenger Frédol the Older.[91] It was also a short idiot's guide, and a very popular one.[92] Because it does not use an estates list there is not such a sharp sense of 'sociography' of sin, although the author does show a pastoral expert's and canonist's interest in generalization, writing—in reference to matrimonial matters and questions—that these are things which occur frequently.[93]

Where estates dominate the *Confessionale,* the ten commandments dominate *In primis debet sacerdos.* Given the heading 'Thou shalt not kill', abortion comes first. There is a mixture of questions and description:

[89] Compare the question around 1200 in Alain de Lille, '*Liber poenitentialis*: les traditions moyenne et courte', ed. Longère, p. 195, where, after the question whether sex was with one's wife or not, there follows the question, if it was with one's wife, was it with hope of offspring, to remedy incontinence, or to sate lust—standard categories which do not spell out positive measures to avoid.

[90] Peter of John Olivi, [Quaestiones de matrimonio], Vatican MS Vat. Lat. 4986, fol. 110r: *Queritur an exercens opus coniugale propter voluntatem solam aut principalius* [*sic*] *propter illam, sic tamen quod nullo modo hoc faceret nisi cum leggitime sua, nec modo aliquo modo innaturali aut proli procurando impeditivo, peccet aut peccatum commitat mortaliter*; probably written about 1276. Astesanus of Asti, *Summa de casibus conscientiae,* VIII. ix (pre-1479, place unknown; copy used is Oxford Bodley Auct. 4.Q.116): *procurando impedimentum aliquod prolis*; written around 1317. For Thomas of Strasbourg's use of the phrase *impedimentum contra partum,* see Ch. 7 above and n. 68.

[91] Michaud-Quantin, *Sommes,* pp. 50–1, and 'La "Summula in foro poenitentiali" ', *Studia Gratiana* 11 (1967), 145–67 (p. 162 on date). Bérenger originated in the Montpellier region, and studied in Paris and Bologna, where he became a noted canon lawyer. He was bishop of Béziers (1294–1305) and from 1305 cardinal and grand penitentiary in Avignon, dying in 1323. See P. Viollet, 'Bérenger Frédol, canoniste', *Histoire littéraire de la France* 34 (1914), 62–178. He appears often in B. Guillemain's *La cour pontificale d'Avignon, 1309–1376: Étude d'une société* (Paris, 1966).

[92] It has a perversely long title—a self-referring joke?—'Short and useful little summa for the forum of penance, and very useful to priests, especially those who have no knowledge in this area' (*Summula in foro poenitentiali brevis et utilis valdeque necessaria sacerdotibus, maxime super hoc notitiam non habentibus*); Michaud-Quantin, 'Summula', p. 149. Michaud-Quantin, 'Summula', pp. 166–7, provides a provisional list of fifty-eight manuscripts. Michaud-Quantin's comments on the appearance of the manuscripts (often produced with care, by professional scribes) may indicate a little distance between this work and the commonest and roughest little confessors' manuals.

[93] BN, MS Lat. 3265, fol. 69v: *Quoniam in foro penitentiali sepe occurrunt casus et questiones matrimoniales atque dubia, ideo breviter intendo super hiis aliqua notare.*

Whether he/she brought about the loss of the foetus; or taught how it [could be] killed; or acted in some way in order not to conceive. For women who have many children, more than they would want, do not pay the debt and they keep themselves away from their husbands. Item, they do worse than this, because after their husbands have made use of them, they rise up or move around in another way, in order not to conceive. Therefore there should be careful questioning of them, whether they do anything to avoid conceiving, either before or after carnal intercourse, or whether they have taken some potion of herbs or some other thing for the same reason.[94]

Since the author of *In primis debet sacerdos* questions under the heading of a commandment rather than of the estate of the married, he is, self-evidently, not excluding the unmarried and avoidance of conception outside marriage. The fact that he is not specifically directed by the estate-category of the married only lends more significance, then, to his passing reference to husbands. He is thinking mainly about the married avoiding conception.[95] At last, with both of our tracts, the centuries-long tradition of pastoral penitential emphasis on this sin *in general* or *outside marriage* has moved *inside marriage*. Like John, the author avoids 'poisons of sterility', unlike John he provides a 'catch-all' phrase, 'do something not to conceive', and also various methods, ranging from wives repelling their husbands to post-coital movements and the drinking before or after sex of herbal drugs directed against conceiving. The post-coital movements recall a (slighter) medical element in Thomas of Chobham. More directly they echo the language and contents of Avicenna's *Canon* and the Montpellier sex-treatises of around 1300, examined in Chapter 6 above. Finally, the author of *In primis debet sacerdos* differs from John of Freiburg in placing more emphasis on a wife's actions, and he more than makes up for the lack of an estates category by briefly establishing a distinct group of wives. This is the mothers with more children than they would want, who therefore try to keep their husbands at bay: lay off sex.

If Dominican products of the first half of the thirteenth century were updated and superseded by John of Freiburg's works, then the northern European and in particular English secular tradition was updated and superseded by William of Pagula's *Oculus sacerdotis*. Written between 1320 and 1327, this text could be copied in medium-sized script on about 150 folios of a medium-sized book. Coming from Paull, near Hull, William was a canon lawyer, who probably went up to Oxford in 1314.[96] He was also a man of extensive pastoral experience. He was vicar of Winkfield, about three miles south-west of Windsor. One glimpse of his outlook is provided in a letter he wrote to the king complaining about depredations

[94] Fol. 36v: *Si conceptum mulieris perdidit, vel occidi docuit, vel fecit aliquo modo quod non conciperet. Et quia mulieres habentes multos filios, plures quam vellent, non reddant debitum et deffendunt se a maritis. Item, faciunt peius, quia postquam cum eis viri usi fuerint, surgunt vel aliter se movent ne concipiant. Unde caute queratur ab eis, si faciunt aliquid ne concipiant, sive ante carnale copulam sive postea, vel si sumpserint aliquam potionem herbarum, vel alicuius alterius rei propter illam causam.*

[95] There is an allusion to withdrawal elsewhere in the treatise, where a husband's making love to his wife in an unnatural position is allowed *dummodo faciat in vase debito et non effundat semen extra scienter*; ibid., fol. 71r.

[96] The following is based on L. Boyle, *Pastoral Care*, III, pp. 262–3, IV, IX, p. 21, and XV, pp. 418–19 n. 20 and 432–4.

in the Forest of Windsor, 'on account of [which] diabolical deeds poor men's land is not being tilled or sowed, nor do poor men have any goods with which to bear these burdens'.[97] William went on to provide precise figures for forced prices, for example one penny for a cock worth two, and to discuss measures and prices prevailing in London. Clearly he had an eye for the hard material facts of life, and what he learnt as a parish priest will have been extended in very particular areas by his further experience as a penitentiary. He is noted as a penitentiary in the deanery of Reading in 1321, and his power was later extended throughout the archdeanery of Berkshire. Patterns of reserved sins in these areas will have been known to him, and his invocation of what 'penitentiaries say' shows that discussion with other penitentiaries (or perhaps only one)[98] was another source of his knowledge about the commission of sins. The work reflects its author's England in various ways, and snatches from the vernacular and problems from marriage courts enter it, all exemplifying the sharpness of pastoral observation which is advertised by its title, *Eye of the Priest*.

At several points William turns to sex between men and women and action to avoid generation. In part 1, on confession, the interrogations proceed partly by the seven deadly sins, and the last sin, lust, provides several questions about the spilling of seed. In part 2 there is a list of things which the priest ought to tell his parishioners. This includes warning them against doing anything to impede conception, followed by a warning against sin against nature. 'Sin against nature' is later discussed. And there is a discussion of a husband's four motives for knowing a wife, procreating offspring, returning the debt, as a remedy against incontinence, and to satiate lust, which is by now a commonplace of pastoral manuals.

Let us see first what William was doing with his English manualist and legislative traditions, beginning with Thomas of Chobham. For over a century Thomas had provided readers with the extraordinary passage, quoted in full above, which described a spectrum from (i) 'contraception' through (ii) abortion, (iii) care of the pregnant woman, and (iv) breast-feeding, and ending with (v) baby care. William preserved much of this, but also broke it up and omitted part of it. He decided to put his largest quotation in part 1, under confession and after dealing with imposing penance. There is Thomas's section (iii), 'The priest ought to impose on the pregnant woman . . .', mainly verbatim, though the story about abortion after jumps is omitted. There then comes, again mainly verbatim, section (iv), beginning 'Item, a mother ought not to separate her own child from her breasts'.[99] So far William is following Thomas, but now he alters, in the first place mainly by location. Thomas's sections (i) and (v) are transferred to part 2 of the *Oculus sacerdotis*, and by this move they become matters for public preaching rather than private confession.

[97] J. Moisant, *De speculo regis Edwardi III* (Paris, 1891), p. 100.

[98] As with *aliqui dicunt* in academic texts, the plural can mean *one* person who is being rhetorically multiplied into '*some*' say.

[99] Oxford, Bodley, MS Rawlinson A.361, fols. 11vb–12ra, and Rawlinson A.370, fols. 12v–13r: *Sacerdos debet iniungere mulieri pregnanti . . . Item, mater non debet separare proprium filium a suis mammis.*

Here, while Thomas's sections partly provide the thematic tradition, it is English provincial and synodal legislation which provides the principal precedent for the form. There had been much provision for 'frequent preaching', or preaching every Sunday: hence the first and main section of part 2 of the *Oculus sacerdotis*, which specified the things which the priest needed to get over from the pulpit to the public. In bringing one of Thomas's sections under this heading William was breaking up Thomas but not innovating, for as we noted earlier English synodal statutes had been saturated with equivalents of (v), baby care.

The conservatism William displayed up to this point underlines the novelty of his treatment of Thomas's other two sections. The second section, abortion, has to appear in William's list of reserved cases, but otherwise it is prominent by its absence. It has less attention than in any other pastoral manual I have read. On the other hand, avoidance of conception is given extraordinary prominence. The line of development in what a priest was instructed to put across from the pulpit goes like this. In early thirteenth-century synodal statutes the priest had to get over the simple message that all sex between man and woman not excused by marriage was unlawful. In other words all sex *outside* marriage was unlawful.[100] Then, with Archbishop John Peckham and the Council of Lambeth (1281), the priest was asked to expound the commandments in the vernacular four times a year, and this was what the canon prescribed under the sixth commandment: 'In this adultery is explicitly prohibited, and also implicitly fornication . . . Prohibited also in the same commandment is *every mixing of man and woman which the goods of marriage do not excuse*; also every voluntary pollution in whatever way deliberately and voluntarily brought about.' The condemnation of all sex outside marriage continues, but now there is also surveillance of sex *within* marriage.[101] Now came the third stage, with an experienced manualist who is acutely aware of this earlier tradition deciding that a priest should issue *public* warnings about *avoidance of conception*, principally within marriage.

This is immediately followed by what the priest should tack on—'He ought also to say to his parishioners . . .' This is a long and roundabout statement about emitting seed. It needs to be set in context by William's earlier questions, in part 1;

[100] Statutes of Salisbury (1217 × 219), no. 35, *Councils & Synods II*, i. 72: *In confessionibus et predicationibus sepius laicis inculcetur . . . quod omnis commixtio maris et femine, nisi per matrimonium excusetur, est mortale peccatum.*

[101] *Councils & Synods II*, ii. 902–3. There may have been careful thought behind this addition. 'We are adding things which seem to us necessary to be ordained' (ibid., ii. 894), says the preamble to the canons of a Council which came after two years of meetings with the clergy. Whatever pastoral observations such discussions produced, they came to the ears of a man who was acute on this theme. In one of his theological works, Peckham chose marital sex to illustrate the point that renouncing everything can be easier than renouncing less, invoking Augustine on the particular point, and observation or 'experience' in general. 'Among many people counsels are observed before precepts . . . As Augustine says about some [who live] in chastity, [in his] *On the Conjugal Good*: "Today many people abstain for the whole of their lives from all sexual intercourse more easily than [other people] stick to not having sex except only for the sake of [procreating] offspring". This is also clear from one's experience (*experimentis*), for there are many in the world who cannot—so they say—abstain from sin. [But] when they come to the state of counsels [= take religious vows] they easily avoid all mortal sin'; J. Peckham, *Quodlibeta quatuor*, I. xx, ed. J. Etzkorn, Bibliotheca Franciscana Scholastica Medii Aevi 25 (Grottaferrata, 1989), p. 49.

by its location here; and by a later statement about the 'sin against nature' drawn from Guillaume Peyraut. The earlier treatment had come while William went through interrogations under the seven deadly sins, proceeding through pride, wrath, envy, avarice, and gluttony. Sloth was penultimate, where, as with most sins, William could be precise and direct—for example, 'If a man has not maintained his wife sufficiently'. Lust comes last: 'If (i) he has spread his seed outside the right vessel, and how. Item (ii), one should ask about sodomitic vice . . . The priest can talk thus to the penitent, "Brother, everyone ought to know that if he has ever knowingly and while awake emitted seed, other than naturally with his wife, he sins gravely, however it happened".'[102] Here William juxtaposes while distinguishing (i) men wasting seed while having sex with women from (ii) men doing this with men. However, where under (ii) a catch-all statement is put into the confessor's mouth, William follows a pastoral tradition. However sharply heterosexual and homosexual acts are being distinguished and however vast the difference of opinion about them in the outside world, there is some diffuseness in the language used about the acts in question, and there is among the pastoral theologians a polemical attempt to pull the heterosexual 'contraceptive' act into the category 'unnatural'. Spreading opprobrium is the game.

In part 2 William has a priest warning the married (and others) against doing anything when making love 'on account of which the conception of a foetus is impeded'. Like John of Freiburg William abandons the old vocabulary of Augustine and adopts the currency of the years around 1300, 'impede' or 'impediment'. Like John of Freiburg he very explicitly puts the point with regard to actions by both husband and wife. Unlike John of Freiburg he puts the husband's action first, and the wife's as the second and alternative action. And unlike John of Freiburg he asks the priest to tack on a warning against emission of seed.

This added warning is long and follows tradition in being catch-all. Here is the admonition against the impeding of conception, and most of the added warning (most of my omissions are canon-legal references).

Item, he [the priest] ought frequently to make public that a man when carnally knowing his wife, or another woman, ought to do nothing, nor should his wife [do anything] on account of which conception of a foetus is impeded.

He ought also to tell his parishioners that because human nature is always inclined to evil . . . Some men, and even women, emit seed in various ways, when asleep and also [when] awake . . . Therefore anyone to whom this has happened either when asleep or awake is bound to say to his confessor how he did this, with what intention and what pleasure, since this can happen in many and varied ways. [I have omitted putting 'her' and 'she' as alternatives in square brackets, since the earlier 'even women' suggests William was going on to consider only men.] Then the confessor should say to the one who is confessing that this is a grave and detestable sin . . . The priest is not to state to anyone a way by which one can sin against nature, unless the sinner has expressed it to him in confession. And it is necessary to make

[102] Oxford, Bodley, MS Rawlinson A.361, fol. 7rb–va: *si extra vas semen fundit quomodo. Item, querendum est de vicio sodomitico . . . Et potest sacerdos sic dicere penitenti, 'Frater, unusquisque debet scire si unquam semen coytus emiserit sciens vel vigilans aliter quam naturaliter cum uxore sua quocunque modo fuerit graviter peccat.'*

this public in churches, as bishops' penitentiaries know very well, because there are many men these days who believe that in many cases the sin against nature is not a sin, which is to be deplored. And therefore the priest can safely say among his parishioners, 'You ought to know that if anyone has emitted the seed of coitus other than naturally with his wife, in whatever way he has done it, he ought to tell [this] to his confessor.'[103]

The tension crackles between the need to be obscure about the mode, because one might instruct, and the need to make public statements because so many men think that in many cases spilling seed is not a sin. And the desire to make the sin as detestable as possible once again pulls it under 'sin against nature'. William proceeds later to a discussion of 'sin against nature' in which he reproduces an earlier text, probably copying Guillaume Peyraut:

Those labouring in this vice and murder are spiritually the enemies of God and the human race. For in what they do they are saying to God, 'You created man and woman to multiply. We are applying ourselves to make them diminish.' Whence it is read in Genesis 38 [that] Onan, when knowing his wife, poured his seed on the ground, depriving her of [the opportunity to have a] foetus, and for this reason the Lord struck him and he died.[104]

From William of Pagula's England let us look in two directions, at later England and contemporary southern Europe. This side of 1348 there is repetition of William's public warnings. The whole section is taken over verbatim in the anonymous *Regimen animarum* of 1343.[105] In the *Speculum curatorum*, ascribed to Ranulph Higden and 1340, under 'What and what sort of things a priest ought to declare on Sundays and feast-days', there is this. 'Item, he should declare that in carnal intercourse nothing should be done whereby conception can be impeded':[106] it is a shorter version of William.

When we look beyond 1348, a divide both real and symbolic, we see in 1384 something very different. This is John de Burgo's *Pupilla oculi*. It is a second edition of the *Oculus sacerdotis*, rearranged for clarity: but perhaps also changed in relation to changing circumstances and the passage of time? Perhaps time-lag is discernible in the intrusion of medical opinion on fertility, where sex during menstruation is at issue: 'for according to what some say', writes John (perhaps having read Peter de la Palud?), 'a woman in that condition cannot conceive.'[107] There is accretion, with more complex moral cases being considered—for example, under 'adultery', the case of a man, whose wife cannot conceive by him but

[103] See the appendix to this chapter.

[104] Oxford, Bodley, MS Rawlinson A.361, fol. 89ra: *Item, laborantes hoc vicio et homicidio spiritualiter sunt hostes Dei et generis humani. Facto enim dicunt Deo, 'Masculum et feminam tu creasti ut multiplicarentur, nos operam dabimus ut minuantur'. Unde legitur gen. xxxviii* [*quod*] *Iona* [Onan] *in cognoscendo uxorem suam privans ea conceptu semen fundebat in terram, et ideo percussit eum Dominus et mortuus est.* This seems to be from Guillaume Peyraut, *Summa de vitiis et virtutibus*, II. iii. 2. 3; 2 vols. (Antwerp, 1571), ii. 4r. Peyraut's source was probably Peter the Chanter, *Verbum abbreviatum*, either the short version, *PL* 205, 334–5, or the long version, edited in Baldwin, *Language of Sex*, p. 248.

[105] Oxford, Bodley, MS Hatton 11, fol. 57ra–b.

[106] Cambridge University Library, MS MM.i.20, fol. 118v: *Item, proponatur quod in copula carnali nil fiat unde conceptus posset impediri.*

[107] John de Burgo, *Pupilla oculi*, VIII. v (Strasbourg, 1518), 129ra: *quia mulier in statu tali concipere non potest, ut dicunt quidam.*

can by others, who accepts her conceiving by another.[108] And there seems to be the capacity to respond to changes, an example of which is the Hundred Years War and the additional attention John pays to themes such as war expenses, propaganda, giving advice about machines, and commanding ships. There is also subtraction. John leaves out the opening part of the second section of the *Oculus sacerdotis*—the things a priest is to put over to his parishioners. Thereby public warnings about avoiding conception drop away.

How far is this only a matter of rearrangement? Other things emphasized by William survive—obviously best if they had originally been treated elsewhere in the *Oculus.* Thus emphasis on breast-feeding in William, who reworked Thomas, survives in abbreviated form in John, in the correlative section on enjoining penance. Telling parishioners the vernacular form of baptism was part of William's list: in this form it may have disappeared, but the vernacular forms are still there in the section on baptism. We cannot see further into the mind of John when he decided to omit this section, and ultimately we can do no more than stand back and look at William and John from middle distance. Their two texts from the 1320s and 1384 can be seen as standards. The earlier appeared towards the end (or just after the end) of a long period of intense pressure of expanding population, and contained the specification that parish priests should frequently publish warnings against the married (and others) avoiding conception. The second edition was made during a period of great population decline, and while heavily overlapping in nearly everything with the earlier text, it omitted the warnings about avoidance of conception. Was this absence in 1384 based in part on a conscious pastoral observation, that there was not now the problem that there had been in the 1320s? And therefore it no longer needed denunciation from the pulpit every Sunday?[109]

The treatises we have been examining around 1200 and 1300 have come principally from England, France, and Germany. What of southern Europe? Raymond of Peñafort and the man who glossed him, William of Rennes, can be taken together as southerner and northerner. Raymond was a Catalan who taught in Barcelona, studied and taught law at Bologna, and then returned to Barcelona, where he was canon (and perhaps penitentiary) before entering the Dominican Order. William of Rennes had been a canonist and official of the churches of Sens, Rheims, and Tours, before entering the Dominicans at Orléans, where he became lector: a northern Frenchman. The regional contrasts that exist on some other issues raise a question about the contrast that is discernible on avoidance.[110] William insists on the theme more than Raymond. Where we saw Raymond referring to but not citing Gratian's *Solet queri*, and omitting in this section anything

[108] Ibid., V. xii; 55vb.

[109] See a parallel in Ch. 9, pp. 229 and n. 44, where an Englishman translating in 1398 a text written in the mid-thirteenth century alters the description of one region in Germany from 'too populous' to 'populous'.

[110] See e.g. the references in William's glosses to regional customs in dowries, 'Gallican custom' Britanny, sterling etc., Raymond, *Summa de poenitentia*, pp. 178, 229, 252, and 253.

that concerned procreation or its avoidance, William seizes upon 'suffices', in Raymond's proposition that such a less worthy cause 'suffices', and then adds, introducing the avoiding and abortive elements from *Solet queri*.[111] Discussing whether marriage still holds when one of its goods is present Raymond refers to his later discussion of conditions, where he briefly supplies 'I contract with you, if you avoid the generation of offspring' as one of several conditions against the substance of marriage, and he provides no further comment. William, on the other hand, delves into the subject immediately, under goods of marriage and Raymond's reference to condition, and produces a long disquisition about conditions, with much material about the pact to avoid which he draws from Huguccio.[112] Raymond was a heavy user of Huguccio, but he had not thought worth including, as William did, Huguccio's fundamental distinction between the absence of intention to have and the presence of intention to avoid. William's insistence is observable elsewhere. William comments further than Raymond does on marital sex according to motive and mode, and through including *order of nature being observed* and *knowingly emit seed outside* his gloss provides one category which denotes and another which includes withdrawal.[113] A context of richer medical knowledge is implied, and in particular the medical notion of a potentially procreative act, in an addition he makes to Raymond on forms of sex which entail affinity: the case where a man emits seed but the woman does not.[114]

What of the texts from around 1300? One candidate for comparison with John's *Confessionale* is a work written by the Italian Franciscan Marchesino of Reggio Emilia a few years before 1315.[115] It has the same title, *Confessionale*, its length is comparable, about 18,000 words, and there is a similar intention to provide a rudimentary guide.[116] Marchesino has only a question about abortion, none about avoiding conceiving: 'if he [*or* she] killed, hampering the foetus or procuring an abortion, [even] though perhaps the effect of this sort of thing did not follow' (*si occidit, conceptum praepediendo, vel abortum procurando, licet fortassis effectus in hujusmodi non fuerit subsecutus*).[117]

An obvious candidate for comparison with William of Pagula's *Oculus sacerdotis* is the priests' manual written in the next decade by a Spaniard, Guido of Monte Roterio, who at the time of the work's dedication, in 1333, was a parish priest in Teruel in Aragon. Like the *Oculus* Guido's *Manipulus curatorum* dealt with a whole range of the parish priest's duties, not just penance, it is of similar length, it

[111] Gloss on Raymond, *Summa de poenitentia*, IV. ii. 6; p. 514. [112] Ibid., IV. ii. 12; p. 518.

[113] Ibid., IV. ii. 13; p. 520. [114] Ibid., IV. xv. 5; p. 558.

[115] On the work, see Michaud-Quantin, *Sommes*, pp. 55–6 and 118; on manuscripts see also M. W. Bloomfield *et al.*, *Incipits of Latin Works on the Virtues and Vices, 1100–1500 AD* (Cambridge, Mass., 1979), pp. 223, no. 257, and 500, no. 5782. It is found printed among Bonaventure's works, and the edition used here is Bonaventure, *Opera omnia*, ed. A. C. Peltier, 15 vols. (Paris, 1864–71), viii. 359–92.

[116] The author states his aim with a verbal frivolity which would have been alien to John, presenting himself as *simplex simplicibus simplicia scribens simpliciter* ('a simple man writing simply things simply for simple men'); Marchesino, *Confessionale*, Preface; viii. 359b.

[117] Ibid., II. xiii; viii. 364b.

achieved extraordinary popularity, and, although it is the drier of the two works, it does permit entry to something of its Spanish milieu.[118]

How are measures against generation tackled? Dealing with marriage in part 1, Guido addresses the three goods of marriage, including a pre-marital pact to avoid offspring. In the second part of the book, on confession, questions to be put to the penitent are organized under the seven deadly sins, not by estates, and under lust there is a large treatment of sex between man and wife. The questions are conventional, three motives for a man knowing his wife, and the possibility of a man sinning in various ways listed in the familiar mnemonic, *time, mind, place, condition, mode*. There is one notable cross-reference, when detailing one of the three ways of knowing a wife: 'by *condition*, that is to say, if he knows her with an unworthy or illicit condition, as was examined above in the treatment of marriage'.[119] The section referred to here, dealing with 'unworthy condition', discussed the pre-marital condition where he said he would marry her if she procured poisons of sterility[120] or committed adultery for money, or was marrying her temporarily, until he found another and prettier woman. The reader would already have found this pre-marital pact. This one direct reference to avoidance of conception, then, comes amidst a catch-all about 'unworthy pre-marital conditions', and in principle it is confined to sexual relations within marriages which have been contracted in that way. Abortion is only present implicitly under homicide, in Guido's references to reserved cases. In the third part the ten commandments provide obvious opportunities to deal with abortion and avoiding conception, but Guido does not take them.

How do the manuals compare? Apart from the question in confession about knowing with an unworthy condition, Guido is silent. There is no other reference to avoiding conception, no reference to withdrawal,[121] and above all there are no public admonitions. English parish priests after the 1320s were to issue public warnings about avoiding conception, but there is no counterpart for the many parish priests who owned and read a manual composed in northern Spain in 1333, a manual which is still extant in over one hundred and eighty manuscripts.[122] If one was virtually parish furniture[123] in England in the later middle ages, the other was parish furniture in southern Europe. The contrast is striking.

[118] See Biller, 'Pastoral Geography', pp. 64, 69, and 77, and comments on Spanish boys and sodomy and women's use of a word for it (*castella*) in Guido of Monte Roterio, *Manipulus curatorum*, II. iv. 5 (Albi, *c.*1475, unfoliated).

[119] Guido, II. iii. 9: *conditione, id est si cognoscat eam conditione inhonesta vel etiam illicita sicut visum fuit supra quando agebatur de matrimonio.*

[120] Ibid., I. vii. 2: *contraham tecum si procures tibi venena sterilitatis.* Here, where Guido is Augustinian, William has the more up to date *si generationem prolis evites*, Oxford, Bodley, MS Rawlinson A.361, fol. 143ra.

[121] Apart from what is implied in canon-legal discussion of the modes of sex by which affinity was contracted.

[122] Biller, 'Pastoral Geography', p. 97.

[123] Boyle, *Pastoral Care*, IV, p. 94. See my earlier comment, 'Pastoral Geography', p. 96, on the influence of these manuals.

8.4 Conclusions

Three chapters here have surveyed the textual survivals of thought, the expression of thought in words, and actions. Separated thus, we can see differences and overlaps between the acts of a few identifiable individuals, medical texts, academic theology and canon law, and pastoral observation. The thought of countless past individuals is like a pyramid, where we know virtually nothing of the base but nearly all of the tip: pastoral observation. What can we say about this tip?

There is a correlation between increasing concern by pastoral observers and times when modern historical demographers have discerned intense pressure of population, both in some isolated areas of the late Carolingian world and more broadly around 1300. There is a regional emphasis, for we find most concern about avoidance among north-west European pastoral experts, and perhaps more about apothecaries and abortion in southern Europe.

By 1300 the historians' evidence is rich and varied: medical texts, academic texts, pastoral texts, and texts bearing upon individuals. These now overlap. Béatrice de Planisolles' method was *also* in medical texts. Another method detailed in medical texts was *also* in a confessor's manual, *In primis debet sacerdos.* A method described in a work of academic theology, Peter of la Palud's, is connected both to medicine and the experience and actions of the married.

There is a more precise contrast between a Regino and a William of Pagula. However sharply and more generally Regino *thought*, what was expressible in texts was constrained. By 1300 authors are beginning to generalize, and we can see in the years after 1300 a welling up of this type of thought. Among the *Sentences* commentators Peter of la Palud's point about poverty concerned an individual poor man, who has more children than he can feed, but with the Franciscan Minister-General Guiraud d'Ot the point moves from the individual to the group: 'Some who have offsping but do not gratefully receive them, such as the many poor men who do not have the wherewithal to feed them'.[124]

Take two examples. First, in the late twelfth century we have an early example of generalization in the area of fertility and its avoidance. A point about sin is applied to a particular estate. Peter the Chanter is talking of noble girls, perhaps from the Beauvaisis nobles among whom his own family lived. 'Some noble girls . . . stifle their offspring . . . and they are so ashamed . . .'[125]

The other example comes a century and a half later, in the long list of estates and detailed interrogatories and penances of the *Memoriale presbiterorum*,[126] which by this date (1344) amounts to an estates-map of sexual sins.[127] Knights are

[124] [*In sententias*], IV. xxxi; BN, MS Lat. 3068, fol. 62v: *aliqui qui prolem habent sed non gratanter acceptant, sicud multi pauperes qui non habent unde nutriant eam.*

[125] Chanter, *Summa*, III, p. 280: *Quedam nobiles puelle . . . suffocant partus suos . . . ita verecunde sunt.*

[126] Written by William Doune, registrar to bishop Grandisson of Exeter. On text and author, see M. Haren, 'Confession, Social Ethics and Social Discipline in the Memoriale Presbiterorum', in *Handling Sin*, ed. Biller and Minnis, pp. 109–22.

[127] Some of the interrogatories are edited and translated in M. Haren, 'The Interrogatories for Officials, Lawyers and Secular Estates of the *Memoriale Presbiterorum*', ibid., pp. 123–63.

to be questioned about adultery, lust, and putting away their wives.[128] Prostitutes feature in a wide range of inquiries—the brothel-keeper (in a discussion of penances on pimping),[129] houses (with a question to townsmen about letting houses to prostitutes), clients (with an allusion to sailors consorting with them),[130] and ages (with discrimination about the old and decrepit former prostitute).[131] The married woman is interrogated about avoidance of offspring and abortion:

Item, if she ever drank, or gave others to drink, potions or the juice of herbs in order not to conceive by someone. Or did she give [to others] or did she [herself] drink [potions or the juice of herbs] to bring about abortion, that is to say, to kill the foetus or embryo [conceptum] in her womb, because she has, perhaps, secretly conceived through having illicit sex? And in this case you ought to enquire carefully whether the foetus [partus] was vivified in the womb or not, because the penance which is to be inflicted should be moderated according to this.[132]

'Adulteress' is even used in cases of primitive conception by donor, where a woman has sex with another man in order to conceive, because she cannot conceive by her husband.[133] In all of this, selection of the sin for the interrogatory of a particular group *implies* 'they frequently do this', but 'they do this' is also explicit. Sailors are described as contracting *de facto* marriages with different women in different countries,[134] while alienating husband's goods in relation to a love-affair is said to be something done by 'many great ladies ansd especially [rich] townswomen'.[135] And against the background of *that* sort of generalization we are just beginning to find observations that move towards the demographic: 'many women hold their husbands in contempt and leave them, going away to live on their own.'[136]

What of our theme, avoidance of offspring? Its *frequency* as a sin committed by the married is the direct implication of John of Freiburg's *Confessionale.* With the *De planctu ecclesiae* written (first recension 1330–2) by an Iberian and papal penitentiary, Alvaro Pelayo, there is more.[137] Peasants (*rustici*): 'They often abstain from sex with their wives, in order not to generate children, fearing they cannot feed so many [on] the pretext of poverty.'[138] Women: some 'procure their sterility with the juices of herbs, and other old women's spells, and with the reedy stick of the doctors.'[139] 'Often in their madness they kill them [their babies], sometimes

[128] Ibid., p. 140.

[129] Cambridge, Corpus Christi College, MS. 148, fols. 42vb–3rb: *Penitencia pro lenocinio.*

[130] Haren, 'Interrogatories', pp. 148 and 150.

[131] Biller, 'Pastoral Geography', pp. 88 and 105 n. 140.

[132] Haren, 'Interrogatories', p. 158.

[133] Cambridge, Corpus Christi College, MS. 148, fol. 48va: *Item, si uxor alicuius fateatur quod filium concepit de adulterio, forsan quia non potuit concipere de marito suo.*

[134] Haren, 'Interrogatories', p. 150. [135] Ibid., p. 158.

[136] Ibid., pp. 156 and 158: *multe contempnunt maritos suos, et ab eis recedunt, seorsum commorando.* See speculative comment in Biller, 'Pastoral Geography', p. 85.

[137] I use the edition printed in Venice, 1560.

[138] Alvaro, *De planctu ecclesie*, II. lxiii. 14; 147rb: *abstinent sepe a coitu uxorum, ne filios generent, timentes non posse tot alere paupertatis pretextum* [recte *pretextu*].

[139] Ibid., II. lxv. 79; 149rb: *procurant cum succis herbarum et aliis carminibus vetularum et baculo*

married women [do this] to cover their adultery or virgins their loss of virginity. Or other single women procure abortion [to cover] their fornication. Frequently with their cursed herbs or drinks, which they drink, they kill the foetus . . . Some women do not receive the seed of the man in their vessel, in order not to conceive, about whom [the text] *Aliquando* [applies], xxxii, q.ii. On account of this vice the Lord struck Onan, the son of Judah, Gen. xxxviii, where it is said about Onan that he spilled seed on the ground lest children be born in his brother's name.'[140] Southern people are often in question—Alvaro remarks on prostitutes at the courts of Spanish kings, and Florentine ladies bringing up their children too delicately[141]—and Alvaro's greater concern with abortion and doctors' intervention may also strike a distinctively southern note. But what is most significant is the varied and panoramic view. If the *Memoriale* provides an estates-map of sexual sin, *De planctu ecclesiae* provides parts of an estates-map of avoidance.

William of Pagula wrote that penitentiaries knew that there were 'many' who in many cases thought that spilling seed was not a sin. Who constituted William of Pagula's plural, 'penitentiaries', at the period when he was writing, in the 1320s? He himself was one, and another well-known penitentiary to the west of William, in the diocese of Hereford in 1326, was John Bromyard.[142] Did penitentiaries meet and discuss sin?

John Bromyard's massive *summa* for preachers shows him a man who thought very readily in terms of numbers of people, ages, life-span, procreation and economic reality, and the relation between numbers and land. When talking of different ages at which people die he brings in various illnesses, and produces an estimate, the fraction of those who are born who do not reach eighty; that it is absurdly low (one tenth) should not blind us to its significance, the cast of mind it reveals.[143] He adverts twice to marriage or procreation and poverty, once under 'Lechery' where he has one group of men saying they are poor and therefore cannot marry, and once under 'marriage' where he alludes to 'the poor man who has a wife who bears many offspring and does not have the wherewithal to feed them, and according to the old saying "It is awful to have a lot of children and not much bread" '.[144] Significantly for us, he is very ready to raise the game, leaving the

arundineo . . . medicorum sterilitatem suam. See Ch. 6 above, n. 75, on mechanical intervention to produce abortion in Avicenna's *Canon.*

140 Alvaro, *De planctu ecclesie*, II. lxv. 81; 149rb: *sepe ex furore eos occidunt, aliquotiens ut cooperiant adulterium coniugate, vel alie solute suam fornicationem aborsum procurant; cum suis maledictis herbis vel potibus quas comedunt fetus frequenter occidunt.* II. lxv. 82; 149rb–va: *Alique non recipiunt semen viri in vas suum ut non concipiant, de quibus xxxii q.ii* Aliquando. *Propter hoc vitium percussit dominus Onam filium Iude, Gene. xxxviii, ubi dicitur de Onan quod semen fundebat in terram ne liberi fratris nomine nascerentur.*

141 Ibid., II. xxx. 31 and II. lxv. 96; 138ra and 149vb.

142 On John and his treatise, see L. E. Boyle, 'The date of the *Summa praedicantium* of John Bromyard', *Speculum* 48 (1973), 533–7, and P. Binkley, 'John Bromyard and the Hereford Dominicans', in *Centres of Learning: Learning and Location in Pre-Modern Europe and the Near East,* ed. J. W. Drijvers and A. A. MacDonald (Leyden, New York, and Cologne, 1995), pp. 255–64.

143 See below, Ch. 10 n. 212.

144 John Bromyard, *Summa Praedicantium*, 2 vols. (Venice, 1586),—Luxuria, i. 462; *Matrimonium*, ii. 15va: *Quia si pauper sit, et uxorem habeat magnam prolem parientem, non habet unde eos nutriat, et secun-*

individual and going on to envisage the multitude. Thus his image for the numbers of the needy in purgatory is the numbers of the sick and needy in all the hospitals in the world, brought together into one enormous hospital. Elsewhere he uses an artificial biblical theme about longevity, early great length of life and modern abbreviation of life. He correlates the first with the world at the beginning, when the earth or earthly possession was ampler for inhabitants, because there were fewer inhabitants. This sets the stage for what he wants to observe in the world now. 'In modern times, however', he writes, 'the boundaries of lands and possessions are straitened, because possessors and inhabitants are multiplied, [and thus] land scarcely suffices for them.'[145]

This penitentiary, then, was a sharp observer of the contemporary relation between population and quantity of land, and at one point he turned his eye towards lack of offspring in marriage. 'Some wonder and many are worried that many people who are married lack offspring . . . looking at the abuse of the act which they practise in marriage, which displeases God, it is not to be wondered at that they are deprived of the due end and reward of offspring.'[146]

With Alvaro generalization was linked to estate, but now, at last, it is about the multitude: contemporary population. Both William and John use 'many' (many thinking something not a sin, many marriages), in one case time is specified ('these days'), and action is connected with results ('abuse of the act', and therefore 'many lack offspring'). In William's manual, a text was included which allows a move from individuals to population at its widest level: from Onan to attempting to diminish the multitude. In John's *Summa*, amidst lively interest in population themes, there is a clear view both of procreation and poverty and the limits of land and large numbers of population. It seems that William's penitentiaries, who know about people not thinking, in many cases, that emitting seed is a sin, and John's 'many', who are worried about the married lacking offspring through abuse of the act in marriage, are overlapping groups: and that the penitentiaries of the 1320s, William and John, were themselves leading figures among these people 'who knew and were worried'. Avoidance of offspring, and one way to do it, withdrawal, were centre-stage in the pastoral 'eye' of England in the first half of the fourteenth century. They were being observed, causing worry, and being written about.

The pressure of population on resources, the behaviour of married people, and the increasing presence and variety of relevant medicine were all exercising pressure, stimulating thought and making it more complex, while it was being coaxed

dum antiquum proverbium tediosum est magnam habere prolem et modicum panem. In the parts of Bromyard which I have read I have found no significant variation between this Venice edition and BL, MS Royal VII.E.4.

[145] Ibid., *Mors*, ii. 71rb: *Moderno vero tempore . . . terrarum termini et possessiones arctantur, quia possessores et inhabitatores multiplicantur, quibus terra vix sufficit.*

[146] Ibid., *Matrimonium*, ii, 16rb–va: *nonnulli mirantur et plures gravantur, quod multi matrimonialiter copulati prole carent . . . habendo eciam respectum ad operis abusum, quem in matrimonio exercent, qui Deo displicet, non est mirabile quod fine debito et prolis frustrantur mercede.*

into a generalizing mode both by the growth of pastoral 'sociography', which we have been describing, and increasing familarity with book 7 of Aristotle's *Politics*, which we shall discuss in Chapter 13 below. *Birth-control* is anachronistic, certainly. But the gap between the modern phrase and medieval thought was narrowing markedly around 1300.

Appendix to Chapter 8
William of Pagula, Oculus sacerdotis

I provide here the text of William of Pagula's instruction to parish priests on what to preach about avoiding conception, using Oxford, Bodley, MS Rawlinson A.370, fol. 50r–v, which I have checked with MS Rawlinson A.361, fol. 53va–b, and BL, MS Royal VI.E.1, fol. 25va. I have also compared it with the single extant manuscript (the early fifteenth-century Oxford, Merton College, MS 217, unfoliated) of William's *Speculum Prelatorum ac religiosorum et parochialium sacerdotum*, where the same passage occurs in pars II, titulus XVII. According to Leonard Boyle, William had composed this by 1319/20. The only significant difference is that where the text of the *Speculum prelatorum* have *De hoc nota supra, in prima parte* . . ., the text of the *Oculus sacerdotis* cross-refers, thus: *De hoc nota in* Speculo prelatorum, *in prima parte* . . .

The text of the *Oculus sacerdotis*:

Item, frequenter publicare debet quod vir cognoscendo uxorem suam vel aliam mulierem carnaliter nihil faciat neque uxor eius per quod impediatur concepcio partus, quod si fecerit gravius peccat quam si cognosceret aliam mulierem carnaliter, xxxii q. ii. Aliquando [C. 22 q. 2 c. 7; Friedberg, i. 1121–2] *et q. vii* Adulterii [C. 32 q. 7 c. 11; Friedberg, ii. 1143].

Dicere eciam debet parochianis suis quod quia humana natura prona *semper* est in malum, *xii q. i.* Omnis etas [C. 11 q. 1 c. 1; Friedberg, i. 676], *et omnis creatura sub vinculo est, de pe. di. ii. c.* Caritas *ad finem di* [D. 2 de pen. c. 5; Friedberg, i. 1191], *ac* proclivus *est* hominum cursus ad voluptatem et natura est invitatrix viciorum, *xx q. ii.* Proclivus [C. 20 q. 3 c. 2; Friedberg, i. 849], *quidam viri et eciam mulieres diversimode semen seu sperma emittunt dormiendo et eciam vigilando, vi. d.* Testamentum [D. 6 c. 1; Friedberg, i. 9–10]. *Igitur quilibet cui hoc accidit dormiendo sive vigilando dicere tenetur in confessione confessori suo qualiter, qua voluntate et qua delectacione hoc fecerit, cum multis et variis modis hoc accidere potest.*

Et tunc confessor suus dicet ipsi confitenti quam grave et quam detestabile sit istud peccatum, quia potest quibusdam modis sperma vel semen emittere, quod tunc gravius peccaret quam si matrem et sororem suam carnaliter cognosceret, xxxii. q. vii. Flagicia [C. 32 q. 7, c. 13; Friedberg, i. 1143], *et in glosa xiiii d.* [xiiii d.: perhaps transposed from 'xiiii d.' in the next line] *et c.* Adulterii *et c. sequent.* [C. 32 q. 7 c. 15–6; Friedberg, i. 1144], *Extra de* excessibus prelatorum, Clerici [X 5.21.4: Friedberg, ii. 836], *et in glosa, xiiii. d.* Quod ait [D. 14 c. 1; Friedberg, i. 33], Gen. *xix* [Gen. 19]. *De hoc nota in* Speculo prelatorum [William of Pagula's treatise of canon law] *in prima parte, titulo de sacramento matrimonii,* § Quatuor de causis. *Set presbiter non dicet alicui modum per quem peccare potest contra naturam nisi peccator in confessione sua hoc sibi expresserit.*

Et istud est necessarium in ecclesia publicare,ut bene sciunt penitenciarii episcoporum quia multi sunt hiis diebus qui credunt in multis casibus peccatum contra naturam non esse peccatum, quod dolendum est.

Et ideo presbiter potest secure sci dicere inter parochianos suos, 'Scire debetis quod si quis semen coitus emiserit scienter et voluntarie aliter quam naturaliter cum uxore sua quocunque modo fecerit, quod graviter peccat, et qualiter sive quocumque mode fecerit [BL MS omits: *quod graviter . . . fecerit*] *debet dicere confessori sou.'*

Part 2

THE MAP OF THE WORLD

9

INHABITATION OF THE WORLD

There is the direct evidence: texts read and written by the literate minority. There is also a no-longer recoverable mental world of 'population geography': ordinary men and women's picture of the peopling of their own families, villages, towns, cities, kingdom, far-off countries, and the world. The texts look remote, for in style and content they went back to classical Greece and Rome and changes in them came about in part through intellectual developments in the schools. But there will have been connections as well as distances and differences between the mental world of a monk teaching geography at St Victor in Paris and the mental world of a trader or farmer in the Île-de-France, living in the same region and at the same time. 'Vanguard' and 'rearguard' are obvious themes here. Conservative preservation of classical knowledge and geographical literary conventions may have made some texts lag behind men of business and sailors, resisting the intrusion of new material based on these men's experience. On the other hand, the grappling with population that is found in the texts on the recovery of the Holy Land, which were drawn up and discussed by learned men in royal and papal courts and at general Church councils in 1274 and 1311, may have been in advance of common knowledge and outlook.

9.1 *Elementary education and natural philosophy*

In a tradition traceable back to early Carolingian times pupils in monasteries were taught the regions and places of the worlds, as they were known in epitomes of classical descriptions of the world. One textbook designed to help this was the *Descriptio mappe mundi*,[1] produced at the beginning of the 1130s by the principal figure at the abbey of St Victor in Paris, Hugh. While they were being taught, pupils will have had in front of them a coloured map of the world,[2] and verses were used to help them memorize facts, for example:

India habet in ipsa
Gentes plurimas . . .

India has in itself
Many peoples . . .[3]

[1] P. G. Dalché, *La 'Descriptio Mappe Mundi' de Hugues de Saint-Victor* (Paris, 1988).
[2] Ibid., pp. 100–1. [3] Ibid., p. 99.

This material came from the section *De terra et partibus* in the *Etymologies*, a compendium of classical knowledge written by Isidore of Seville (d. 636).

The general view of the world derived from classical thought.[4] The world was a sphere, upon which geographers' 'descriptions of the world' imposed parallel horizontal strips called 'climates'. These were divided into zones described as habitable or uninhabitable, *habitabilis, inhabitabilis*. One quarter of the surface of the known world was habitable, containing Asia, Africa, and Europe, and descriptions schematically listed their regions, mountains, rivers, and peoples. The broader part of this view, without the description of places, was transmitted in a work probably written between 1230 and 1245, John of Sacrobosco's *De spera*. Here the reader would find in chapter 1 an account of the sphericity of the world and the approximately accurate estimation of its circumference by Eratosthenes, and in chapter two the world's five zones. The two zones described by the Arctic and Antarctic circles were 'uninhabitable' because of coldness, and the zone between the tropics was 'uninhabitable' because of heat, while the two zones between the tropics and the Arctic and Antarctic circles were temperate and therefore 'habitable'. The location on the sphere of 'our habitable quarter' was given in chapter 3. At about 9,000 words John's work was usefully brief, and it became one of the commonest textbooks in mathematical education. Its 'manuscripts are legion',[5] and its account and its keywords, 'habitable' and 'uninhabitable', were commonplace.

'Knowledge of habitable places' was given philosophical attention by Albert the Great, in his *De natura loci*.[6] Divided into three treatises, its scope and character is readily shown by recapitulating its chapters' themes. Chapter 1 in the first treatise is devoted to the proposition that 'In natural science one ought to know the nature of place'. 'Place' is among the principles of nature. 'We ought to know the diversities of places in particular, and the cause of their diversity and accidents [i.e. characteristics]: then we may know those things which are generated

[4] I draw upon C. R. Beazley, *The Dawn of Modern Geography*, 3 vols. (London, 1897–1906); J. K. Wright, *The Geographical Lore of the Time of the Crusades: A Study in the History of Medieval Science and Tradition in Western Europe* (New York, 1925; repr. with corrections and same pagination, New York, 1965); G. H. T. Kimble, *Geography in the Middle Ages* (London, 1938); *Cartography in Prehistoric, Ancient and Medieval Europe*, ed. J. B. Harley and D. Woodward, in *The History of Cartography* (Chicago and London, 1987–), i; P. G. Dalché, *Géographie et culture: representation de l'éspace du VI au XIIe siècle* (Aldershot, etc., 1997).

[5] L. Thorndike, *The Sphere of Sacrobosco and its Commentators* (Chicago, 1949), p. 74; G. Beaujouan, 'L'enseignement de l'arithmétique élémentaire à l'université de Paris au XIIIe et XIVe siècles. De l'abaque à l'algorisme', *Hommenaje a Millás-Vallicrosa*, 2 vols. (Barcelona, 1954–6), i. 93–124. See Thorndike, *Sphere*, p. 50, listing commentators who raised questions about habitability.

[6] Albert announced his intention of writing the treatise thus: *pertinet hoc ad scientiam* de locis habitabilibus, *de qua nos, Deo volente, alibi faciemus tractatum, Meteora libri IV, Opera*, Borgnet, iv, II. iii. 2 (565). The *De natura loci* (*Opera*, Geyer, v, Part 2, 1–46) was written in Cologne 1251–4; *De natura loci*, p. vi; *Albertus and the Sciences*, pp. 566–7—where Weisheipl has *De natura loci* coming before *Meteora*, despite the latter containing this reference to Albert's intention of writing on habitable places in the future. See J. P. Tilman, *An Appraisal of the Geographical Works of Albertus Magnus and His Contributions to Geographical Thought*, Michigan Geographical Publications 4 (Ann Arbor, 1971), where the *De natura loci* is translated, pp. 25–145.

and corrupted in places.'[7] Chapters 6–9 address habitable and uninhabitable regions. Chapter 6, 'On the division of the world into habitable and uninhabitable places', describes the two principal ancient opinions (divisions by zones or climates), citing Aristotle and Avicenna and including their arguments by observation for the inhabitation of areas thought in principle to be uninhabitable. 'We have seen with our own eyes many who lived there.'[8] Chapter 7 asks whether the region between the equator and the south pole is habitable. Chapter 8 looks at regions regarded as uninhabitable because of cold. It carefully distinguishes between continuous and short-term habitation, and also points out that, because there are limits to sailing in the north and sailors turn back, the habitability of the furthest north 'is therefore not fully known to us'.[9] Chapter 9 is on the length and breadth of habitable places, and chapter 13 'On the diversity of the nature of places [arising] from the contingency of mountains, seas and woods'.

Albert's third treatise hints at history, both the history of habitation and also history of geographic knowledge. On the one hand, Albert uses one of the best pieces of information about Christ's birth to remind a reader that the discipline itself has its history: Caesar Augustus sent people in three directions to assemble a 'description of the world', an enterprise which took thirty-two years. On the other hand, 'habitation' of the world is itself historical. It grew, and 'there are [now] many large cities which did not exist then'.[10] Albert himself produced a schematic list of the world's places, and he appended to the whole work a map, which is no longer extant.

The work was apparently written in Cologne, between 1250 and 1254, very close in time to an important development in historical thought about place and inhabitation. 1260 is the probable date of William of Moerbeke's translation direct from Greek of Aristotle's *Meteorology*, and the certain date of his translation of Alexander of Aphrodisias's commentary on the *Meteorology*, again from Greek.[11] At one point in the *Meteorology* Aristotle deals with the fundamental characteristics of parts of the earth, dry or moist, cold or hot, as they affect human habitation. There have been changes in these qualities in regions of the earth, making them less or more able to feed peoples, and these happen so slowly and over such an immense time-span, in relation to human life, that they escape notice. In between, populations may be destroyed by disasters, wars, diseases, and sterilities. The transmigrations which happen—with some people leaving but others remaining until a region cannot feed a multitude—take place over such a long period that by the time of the last deserting of a region no one can remember

[7] *De natura loci*, I. i; p. 2. [8] Ibid., I. vi; p. 11.

[9] Ibid., I. viii; p. 15. [10] Ibid., III. i; p. 29.

[11] L. Minio-Paluello, 'Henri Aristippe, Guillaume de Moerbeke et les traductions latines médiévales des "Météorologiques" et du "De generatione et Corruption" d'Aristote', *Opuscula*, 57–86; W. Vanhamel, 'Biobibliographie de Guillaume de Moerbeke', *Guillaume de Moerbeke*, pp. 301–83 (pp. 309, 327, and 350). Moerbeke's translation is extant in 175 manuscripts, Alexander's commentary in nine; Alexander of Aphrodisias, *Commentaire sur les Météores d'Aristote: Traduction de Guillaume de Moerbeke*, ed. A. J. Smet, Centre de Wulf-Mansion, Corpus Latinum Commentariorum in Aristotelem Graecorum 4 (Louvain and Paris, 1968), p. xv.

the first. The same point applies to regions which become more able to feed people. Watery and marshy regions become drier, but this process and consequent inhabitation are so slow that no one remembers the beginnings, who the first people were, when they came, and what the lands were like.[12] Aristotle was expanded and given extraordinary clarity in the translation of the commentary by Alexander of Aphrodisias. For example, a brief phrase about 'sterilities', 'great' or 'moderate' (*sterilitates . . . magnae . . . secundum modicum*), becomes 'sterility of the earth', sterility of the earth itself happens either quickly or slowly, and correlatively 'transmigrations of peoples' happen quickly or slowly. In modern words, fertility decline and emigration, and varying rates in both.[13] Coming just a few years after Albert's treatise, this re-presentation of Aristotle's views would soon be providing clear encouragement to historical thought about rise and decline in fertility of place and the relationship between place, inhabitation, emigration, and immigration over a very long time-span.[14]

Albert's treatise was also very close to two notable events which advanced empirical knowledge of places. One was the completion in Germany, probably in Magdeburg and by the mid- to late 1240s, of Bartholomew the Englishman's

[12] Aristotle, *Meteorology*, I. xiv, from 351ª19. Moerbeke's text in Thomas Aquinas, *In libros Aristotelis Meteologicorum expositio*, I. xvii; *Opera omnia*, Leonine edn. iii. 380; in French paraphrase: Mahieu le Vilain, *Les Metheores d'Aristote: Traduction du XIIIe siècle publié pour la première fois*, ed. R. Edgren (Uppsala, 1945), pp. 68–9. The translation (and part paraphrase-commentary) into French was of Moerbeke's Latin; dedicated to a Count d'Eu, it dates perhaps from around 1270 or 1290, according to Vanhamel, 'Biobibliographie', p. 327.

[13] Alexander of Aphrodisias, *Commentaire*, ed. Smet, pp. 95–7: *Quare autem non fiant notae tales permutationes, causam inquit esse* omnem naturalem *permutationem* quae circa terram ex successione *et secundum modicum fieri,* et in temporibus *longis ut* ad nostram vitam. *Propter quod latet nos unumquodque ipsorum factum. Accidit enim gentium interitus fieri et corruptiones, ut non possint per memoriam retineri priora existentia neque ex successione. . . . Deinde autem, quae corruptiones et quomodo fiunt, propter quas non sunt in memoria talia eorum quae circa terram passiones, dicit. Et ait maximas quidem et celerrimas fieri corruptiones hominum* in bellis, *in quibus et civitates et gentes multas omnino interire accidit; alii* autem languoribus *pestilentibus corrumpuntur; hae autem propter sterilitatem terrae, propter quas transferuntur ab ipsa qui salvati fuerint; et ipsarum hae quidem subitae factae, hae autem paulatim steriliori facta terra. In quibus ait latere translationes gentium paulatim et non subitas factas: non enim omnes simul abierunt, sed hi quidem recedunt, hi autem manent, quousque regio alere potest, et hoc usque ad hoc facere, usquequo penitus destructa* regio non adhuc *aliquem* multitudinem possit alere; recessu *itaque primorum usque ad novissimos deserentes regionem,* verisimile fieri longa tempora, ita ut nullus *posterius recedentium memoretur quod primi aliqui recesserunt, quia multae generationes in medio extiterunt. Ut autem translationes gentium factae latent multotiens propter temporis processionem, sic inquit iterum* et inhabitantes latere, quando primo *inceperunt cohabitare gentes* in permutatas *terrae partes* et factas siccas ex aquosis et paludosis. *Paulatim enim et in his habitatio, et in multis fit temporibus additio, ita ut posteriores habitantes non cognoscant, quando incepit regionis illius eucrasia et cohabitatio.* Alexander's commentary is extant in nine manuscripts, ibid., p. xv.

[14] An earlier translation of the *Meteorology*, by Gerard of Cremona from Arabic before 1187, is still extant in 113 manuscripts; see the literature cited by R. Lemay, 'Gerard of Cremona', *DSB* xv. 173–92 (p. 180 no. 38). No attention is paid to habitability in the commentary on this passage produced by Alfred of Sareshel between 1190 and 1200: J. K. Otte, *Alfred of Sareshel's Commentary on the Metheora of Aristotle: Critical Edition, Introduction and Notes*, Studien und Texte zur Geistesgeschichte des Mittelalters 19 (Leiden, New York, Copenhagen, and Cologne, 1988), pp. 44–5. Much can be gained on commentaries on the *Meteorology*, ibid., pp. 28–30 and A. Dondaine and L. J. Bataillon, 'Le commentaire de Saint Thomas sur les Météores', *AFP* 36 (1966), 81–152 (pp. 117–40), but the general history of the many surviving commentaries has not been written.

De proprietatibus rerum, and the other was a lecture-tour, partly in Germany, by a traveller returning from the far east. Albert will not have been present when John of Pian di Carpine talked about his distant travels in Cologne in September 1245—he was in Paris—but presumably either the memory or the contacts[15] would have been there when Albert returned to Cologne in 1248. Albert was certainly to use material learnt from such returning travellers in later works.[16]

Most of Albert's treatise was abstract, and its list of regions and places is schematic, conservatively reproducing classical knowledge and excluding contemporary material. Albert's work can be viewed, however, as a high natural-philosophical counterpart of these empirical advances of the 1240s. In the *De natura loci* he established knowledge of place and what predominates in it, human habitation of place, as a branch of 'natural science' and a discipline with its own history. He systematized the raising and investigation of questions about habitation, parading both older classical writers and recently translated Greek and Arabic ones. While making more authorities known, he gave a place both for observation and the notion of current limits of knowledge, and he connected the knowledge of place, which was discussed in the text he produced, with its pictorial representation in a map.

We shall now turn to the first and least dramatic of the contemporary advances in specific knowledge about the habitable world.

9.2 *Bartholomew the Englishman*

The mid-thirteenth century was a classic period for the production of encyclopaedias, in particular the three compiled by Thomas of Chantimpré, Vincent of Beauvais, and Bartholomew. If Vincent's massive work (which is discussed below in Chapter 12) was the *Encyclopaedia Britannica* of its time, then Bartholomew's was the *Petit Larousse*, modest in scale, price, and ambition. It was probably intended as a resource-manual for preachers,[17] and it was very popular.[18]

After the first two books, on God and the angels, it provides a compendium of natural knowledge about man, the world, and the universe, with a considerable amount of precise data. As the rubrics of the late fourteenth-century English translation say, 'the fourteenth book deals with the world and its parts'—which meant features such as mountains, plains, and deserts. Its first chapter, on the earth, looks briefly at the natural causes of greater or lesser fertility, making it

[15] John had talked to an academic figure in Cologne, a *scholasticus*; R. A. Skelton, T. E. Marston, and G. D. Painter, *The Vinland Map and the Tartar Relation*, 2nd edn. (New Haven and London, 1995), pp. 39–40 n. 3.

[16] Albert, *De animalibus*, III. clcviii (i. 351), and John, *Ystoria Mongalorum*, IV and IX (Wyngaert, *Itinera*, pp. 49 and 117), on mare's milk drunk by Mongols.

[17] d'Avray, *Preaching*, p. 279; J. Ziegler, *Medicine and Religion c.1300: The Case of Arnau de Vilanova* (Oxford, 1998), pp. 194, 199, 201–2, and 208. On further use by Servasanto of Faenza, see Ch. 14 below, pp. 399–400 and nn. 56–7.

[18] See R. J. Long, *Bartholomaeus Anglicus On the Properties of Soul and Body* (Toronto, 1979), pp. 1–2.

'apter for human habitation' (*magis congrua hominum habitationi*). Although elsewhere in this chapter Bartholomew cites the *Meteorology*, which he will have known in the earlier translation from Arabic, there is no hint of history, long duration, or migration in his account.[19] 'The fifteenth book deals with regions and provinces', with 174 chapters listing the three continents, and many countries, regions, and provinces. In the descriptions Bartholomew recycles much classical and very early medieval material, notably the books on the 'parts of the world' in Pliny's *Natural History*[20] and the book 'On the earth and its parts' in Isidore's *Etymologies*.[21] But Bartholomew is richer than his classical sources, addressing more (and more varied) topics, and bringing in much new material. This is most marked in the descriptions of northern Europe, especially the north-western coast, Scandinavia, northern Germany, and the Baltic, where new information is inserted under old regions and new regions are added.[22] Appellation of origin connects Bartholomew to England and early teaching to Paris.[23] But in 1231 he went to Magdeburg,[24] and the geography of his later experience may be suggested by some of this new material in *De proprietatibus rerum*.

Describing a particular region or province Bartholomew deals with location ('bounded by such-and-such regions'), and then the physical features of mountains, plains, rivers, and forests, and fertility and types of produce. Alongside these he often put points about metals and minerals, trade (and sometimes industry), the people and their characteristics, populousness, towns and cities, and, more rarely, divisions of language[25] and cult and piety.[26] Physical features lead towards the fertility of the land and its produce: 'very fertile', 'abundant in crops'. The 'economic' map is sharp, with much on the metal and mineral resources of a region, and quite a lot on trade. There is an element of the conventions of praise—praise of a region for its riches in something or other—but the praise is

[19] *De proprietatibus rerum*, XIV. i; *Properties of Things*, XIV. i; ii. 694. I have used the Latin text in an edition of Nuremberg, 1519, which is cited by chapter number, apart from the German provinces, which are edited in Schönbach, 69–80, and the Italian provinces, edited in Lampen, 14–18. References are also given to Trevisa's middle-English translation, and where the chapter number is different in Latin editions I specify the latter in parentheses.

[20] Books 3–6. [21] Book 14.

[22] In alphabetical order, from the Estonian province of Reval onwards and when dealing with a north European area, Bartholomew sometimes cites as a source an 'Erodatus' and his work, which he refers to as *De regionibus et descripcione*. The name suggests a literary allusion, 'the Herodotus of our times'. It is possible that Bartholomew simply changed his style of citation when writing his Reval entry, in which case new material in regions listed *before* Reval could also come from Erodatus. Even though Barthlomew's written source and his own experience are no longer distinguishable, I attribute change to Bartholomew, since he chose, at least, the words pasted into his compendium.

[23] Lectured on the Bible. d'Avray, *Preaching*, p. 135 n. 2, warns against assuming that this was after he joined the Franciscans.

[24] At the newly established Franciscan *studium*, where he was *lector* in theology. He may have been the Bartholomew who was minister-provincial in Austria (elected in 1247 and still in office in 1249) and later minister-provincial in Saxony (elected in 1262, probably dying in office in 1272). See Long, *Bartholomaeus Anglicus*, pp. 2–5.

[25] Belgium, Schönbach, 70; *Properties of Things*, XV. xxvi; ii. 740.

[26] Schönbach, 73, 74, 75, 77, 78, and 80; *Properties of Things*, XV. lxxvii [lxviii], cix [cx], cxxv [cxxvi], cxxxix [cxl], cxlii [cxliii], and clxxi [clxxii]; ii. 777, 788, 800, 806, 808, and 822.

discriminating. At the most elementary level Bartholomew praises for one thing rather than another, for example abundance of pigs rather than sheep, and the reader can make an elementary map of sheep-rearing regions by making two lists, one of those regions where sheep are mentioned, another where they are not. There are nuances: for example, while wine is present in 'Francia', Anjou, and the Auvergne, it is given emphasis in Gascony through the mention of Gascony supplying other areas.[27] Further, although the land of most regions is 'fertile' in something or other, Bartholomew can duck conventional praise and bluntly state the opposite of fertility, as he does with Iceland, Asturias, and Finland.[28]

It is all very brief, and very realistic: physical features, then resources and trade, and then forms and intensity of habitation, towns, cities, and populousness. In modern terms, physical geography, economics, and demography are integrated.

Bartholomew's account of Africa is thin, as we would expect. Asia attracts comparison—Europe is 'smaller than Asia, but equal in number and nobility of peoples'[29]—and is given some summary verdicts. For example, 'Syria . . . is a most populous region'.[30] Bartholomew generalizes and summarizes a long tradition about the size of India, found ubiquitously in older descriptions of the world. India 'among all regions of the earth . . . is the most populous'.[31]

Europe has most of Bartholomew's attention, and, inside Europe, Germany and German fertility, populousness, wealth, and strength.[32] He mentions, or does not mention, towns, cities, and castles of particular regions, and he describes or does not describe these regions as 'populous', qualifying this attribute. His silences and qualifying comments repay attention.

We can put towns and cities on an ascending scale. Certain regions do not have towns and cities mentioned. In northern and central Europe these include Iceland, Finland, Reval, Denmark, Norway, Sweden, Hungary. Some countries or regions have no mentions of cities and towns, plural, but have one metropolitan city named, as in the case of Bohemia and Prague. Only castles and towns, but not cities, are listed for Apulia, Franconia, and Carinthia. A port appears along with the main town in the entry for Poitou—La Rochelle—and ports appear on their own in the description of Kent. Castles, towns *and* cities in the plural (and in various combinations) are listed for Aquitaine, Normandy, Belgium, Picardy, Meissen, Westphalia, and Saxony. Higher up the list, finally, are three regions of special emphasis. One is France, where this is underlined by separate entries for different

[27] *De proprietatibus rerum*, XV. xvi, xvii, lii, and clxvii; *Properties of Things*, XV. xvi, xvii, lvii, and clxvii; ii. 735, 759, 820.

[28] Schönbach, 80; *Properties of Things*, XV. clxxi; ii. 822.

[29] *De proprietatibus rerum*, XV. l: *minor quam Asia, et tamen par est in populorum numerosa generositate*; text in Milan, Ambrosian Library, MS A.147 Sup. fol. 181vb: *par est in numerosa popullorum generalitate vel generositate; Properties of Things*, XV. i; ii. 752: *is it per þerto in nombre and noblete of men.*

[30] Ibid., XV. clxvi: *Est autem regio populosissima; Properties of Things*, XV. cxlv; ii. 809.

[31] Ibid., XV. lxxiii: *Est autem India inter omnes regiones orbis . . . populosior; Properties of Things*, XV. lxxv; ii. 770.

[32] The fertility of *Germania* was an ancient theme, with a famous semantic explanation in Isidore, *Etymologiae*, XIV. iv: *propter fecunditatem gignendorum populorum Germania dicta est.*

regions, much as Germany's metal resources were underlined. One entry is for 'Francia' in general, in which there are 'many . . . cities', and in particular Paris. Here the flow of people and their support is commented upon. 'Paris receives people coming from all parts of the world, [and] supplies them with all necessities . . . it is particularly fitting in the suitability of its streets and houses for students.'[33] A second entry is for a particular 'province of Frenchmen . . . [which] has many towns and cities', 'Gallia Senonensis'. Defined negatively by the borders of Belgium, German Rhineland, 'Gallia Lugdunensis', Burgundy, and the Pyrenees, this province's entry and the description of Paris regionalize in a broad way Bartholomew's emphasis on northern French urban settlement. The second region is Flanders, 'famous for its most noble towns and sea-ports'.[34]

Bartholomew reserves his greatest emphasis, however, for Italy, which 'leads among all the western regions of Europe', among other things in its notable ports and walled cities. Whereas elsewhere Bartholomew usually mentions 'cities' or 'many cities', here he imports the attribute of populousness, deployed in a superlative adjective: Italy leads the way in western Europe in having, among other things, 'the most populous cities' (*civitates populosissime*).[35] Two other entries add to this, one for the province of Tuscany, with 'many glorious and noble cities'[36] which Bartholomew lists, Pisa, Siena, Lucca, Florence, and Arezzo, while also alluding to cities beyond Tuscany, including Milan, Padua, and Rome. The other is an independent entry for Venice, which also mentions Bergamo, Milan, and Mantua. A third entry, which was, however, rooted in classical sources, adds to the impression. Campania has 'many . . . populous . . . cities', *multae . . . civitates . . . populosae*, such as Naples and Pozzuoli.

Bartholomew notes a region's wealth in towns and cities partly because of the convention, in classical descriptions of regions, which dictated the naming or listing of famous cities, partly because they were there, and partly because they may be part, as well as a sign, of other things. Bartholomew can put towns and cities beside populousness, as in '*Gallia Senonensis* is a populous land, which has many cities and many towns',[37] but the connection here is that of *and*. For Bartholomew's proposition is '*Gallia Senonensis* is a populous land *and* has many cities and many towns', rather than 'The many cities and many towns of *Gallia Senonensis* express its extreme populousness'. Bartholomew only approaches this second proposition in his point about the extreme populousness of Italian cities.

We can put 'populous' on an ascending scale. Low down comes Savoy, with mention of its mountainous and deserted parts, and also low are those regions which may be praised but in whose descriptions the attribute 'populous' is

[33] *De proprietatibus rerum*, XV. lvii, and *Properties of Things*, XV. lvii; ii. 759.

[34] Schönbach, 71: *nobilissimis oppidis et portibus maris inclita*; towns are omitted from the translation in *Properties of Things*, XV. lviii; ii. 759.

[35] Lampen, 115; *Properties of Things*, XV. lxxix [lxxviii]; ii. 774.

[36] Lampen, 117: *plures habens inclytas et nobiles civitates; Properties of Things*, XV. clxiv [clxv]; ii. 818.

[37] *De proprietatibus rerum*, XV. cxlv: *Est autem terra populosa, habens civitates multas et oppida multa; Properties of Things*, XV. clxiv; ii. 808.

significant by its absence. Many of these regions are those which are not given the general description 'having cities and towns',[38] from countries in the eastern Baltic to Asturias in the south-west or Bohemia, Carinthia, and Hungary in the south-east. Higher come 'populous' regions, Brabant[39] and *Gallia Senonensis.* Higher also are regions where Bartholomew thinks of another and usually stronger phrase. Thuringia has 'numerous people': *populus numerosus,* while 'very populous', *multum populosa,* are Apulia, Belgium (*Belgia*), and Denmark—here unique among Scandinavian countries, and without an urban element in the description.[40] Picardy is 'abounding in peoples', *abundans populis,* and Zeeland is 'really very populous', *valde populosus.*[41] Higher is Flanders, for it occupies a 'small area of land', but the men there 'beget many children'. In modern terms, it is urbanized and densely populated, with a high birth-rate.[42] Remarkable is not only Bartholomew's concentration on populousness in the low countries, but also his reservation of special remarks for the populousness of regions of Germany. With its *populus numerosus,* as we have just seen, Thuringia has *number.* Franconia is 'extremely populous', *plurimum populosa.*[43] And, finally, there is the highest level, where Bartholomew states that a region is *over*-populated. Swabia is '*too* populous': *populosa nimis.*[44]

The map has regions missing. When dealing with his native Britain Bartholomew became distracted by a mixture of literary material, mythical origins, and the nature of its peoples, and, sadly, he let go hang the themes of towns, cities, and populousness. At the same time there is one additional 'demographic' feature which is of singular interest, in the entry for Frisia. Here Bartholomew addressed the theme of marriage-age from what we might call a moral-political-eugenic angle. 'This is a free people, not subject to the rule of another . . . they [the Frisians] keep their sons and daughters chaste up to the completion of adolescence. From this it happens that, with marriage then [viz. such late marriage], they generate full and strong offspring'.[45] Elsewhere in his encyclopaedia, in his

[38] I am putting to one side the mention of one important named city, for example Bohemia and Prague.

[39] Schönbach, 70: *terra . . . populosa; Properties of Things,* XV. xxv; ii. 739.

[40] Schönbach, 70; Lampen, 144; *De proprietatibus rerum,* XV. xlvii; *Properties of Things,* XV. xviii, xxvi, and xlvii; ii. 736, 740, and 751.

[41] *De proprietatibus rerum,* XV. cxxiii; Schönbach, 78; *Properties of Things,* XV. cxxii and cxlii; ii. 798 and 807.

[42] Schönbach, 71: *quamvis situ terre sit parvula . . . Gens . . . multiplex in sobole; Properties of Things,* XV. lviii; ii. 760: þei þis prouynce be litil in space . . . þe men þereof . . . geten many children.

[43] Schönbach, 71 and 79; *Properties of Things,* XV. lvi and clxv; ii. 758 and 819.

[44] Schönbach, 79; *Properties of Things,* XV. cliii; ii. 814. Worthy of remark is that Trevisa, writing in a period of population decline, drops the notion of 'too much', translating *gens populosa nimis* as 'þe men ben many'.

[45] Schönbach, p. 72: *Gens quidem est libera extra gentem suam, alterius dominio non subjecta . . . filios suos et filias usque ad completum fere adolescentie terminum castos servant, ex quo contingit, quod tunc temporis datos nuptui ipsorum soboles prolem completam generant et robustam; Properties of Things,* XV. lxi; ii. 762. This needs to be set beside Caesar's *De bello gallico,* VI. xxi (Loeb edn., pp. 344 and 346): *Germani . . . qui diutissime impuberes permanserunt, maximam inter suos ferunt laudem. . . . Intra annum verum vicesimum feminae notitiam habuisse in turpissimis habent rebus.* On the tradition of the text and medieval knowledge of it, see V. Brown, 'Caesar', *Catalogus Translationum et Commentariorum,* ed. F. E.

discussion of ages, Bartholomew had listed various views—adolescence ending at 21 in one source (the *Viaticum*), at 28 in another (Isidore), and at 30 or 35 according to the physicians. He takes his lead from Isidore in continuing on the theme of this as the time for bearing children.[46] If Tacitus's advocacy of high age of marriage and robust offspring was generally unknown until the rediscovery of his *Germania* in the Renaissance,[47] its role was to be filled during the later middle ages by Bartholomew's account of Frisia.

In effect Bartholomew took over the colourless lists of classical and earlier medieval tradition,[48] and gave a richer account of resources, economy, and urbanization. Integral to this was the category 'populous', and pasted onto many of the regions of Europe was a brief but realistically various picture of populousness. Outstanding in this was an emphasis on populousness of cities in parts of Italy, and density of population in general in parts of northern and north-western Europe.

The succinctness of Bartholomew's comments should not be mistaken for elementariness. Compare Bartholomew's account of one province with the writing of a slightly later mendicant, this time a Dominican of Alsace.[49] Bartholomew is brief when writing about the province of the Rhineland, just saying that it had 'many cities and strong towns'. The Alsace Dominican's picture of the upper reaches of the Rhineland is much more detailed. He contrasted its conditions in 1200 and around 1290. His main point is how simple, small, and *few* were things and *people* in 1200, as opposed to how more advanced, large, and *many* they were

Cranz and P. O. Kristeller (Washington, 1960–), iii. 87–139; see p. 90 on copying in the 11th century of the section on morals. In part comparable also is Ptolemy's *Quadripartitum*, II. iii, which associated love of liberty, bellicosity, and northern countries, including Britain, Gaul, and Germany; but, where Bartholomew writes of late marriage, Ptolemy had men's lack of passion for women and their preference for men. Ptolemy was translated into Latin by Plato of Tivoli in 1138; L. Minio-Paluello, 'Plato of Tivoli', *DSB* xi. 31–2; see also *DSB* ii. 435. Fertility, populousness, and bellicosity go hand in hand in Bartholomew's general account of Germany (*Alemannia*), without, however, any reference to marriage-age; Schönbach, p.69; *Properties of Things*, XV. xiii; ii. 732–3.

[46] *De proprietatibus rerum*, VI. i; *Properties of Things*, VI. i; i. 291–2.

[47] Tacitus, *Germania*, XX; *Texts and Transmission: A Survey of the Latin Classics*, ed. L. D. Reynolds (Oxford, 1983), pp. 410–11.

[48] An exception is Pliny's *Natural History*, whose four books describing the world's parts are densely packed and include, in a miscellaneous and unsystematic way, data reflecting Pliny's populationist outlook, e.g. numbers for a country's or a city's population, military manpower, or the results of a census (in a discussion of extremes of life-span). The extreme length of Pliny's work had militated against the multiplication of copies in the early middle ages, but abstracts were being made in the mid-twelfth century, and thereafter a few more copies of the whole work were appearing; *Texts and Transmission*, ed. Reynolds, pp. 307–16; C. G. Nauert, Jr., '*C. Plinius Secundus (Naturalis Historia)*', in *Catalogus Translationum et Commentariorum: Medieval and Renaissance Latin Translations and Commentaries, annotated lists and guides*, ed. F. E. Kranz and P. O. Kristeller (Washington, 1960–), iv. 297–422 (pp. 302–4 and 318); M. Chibnall, 'Pliny's *Natural History* and the Middle Ages', *Empire and Aftermath: Silver Latin II*, ed. T. A. Dorey (London, Boston, 1975), pp. 57–78. Increasing knowledge of Pliny may have encouraged Bartholomew's interest in population.

[49] *De rebus Alsaticis ineuntis saeculi XIII*, ed. P. Jaffé, *MGH SS* 17 (Hanover, 1861), pp. 232–7. In the extant manuscript, the anonymous text follows immediately annals from Basle and Colmar. On this Alsace school of Dominican historical writing, see the introduction to Rudolf von Schlettstadt, *Historiae Memorabiles: Zur Dominikanerliteratur und Kulturgeschichte des 13. Jahrhunderts*, ed. E. Kleinschmidt (Cologne and Vienna, 1974), pp. 27–32.

around 1290—though the later time is often implied rather than spelled out. There has been technological development, recently the appearance of iron on cartwheels, and the use of plaster in building houses, and expansion, whereas in 1200 there was not even a bridge over the Rhine. In 1200 the area covered by forests was larger and an estimated 1500 fisherman lived on the river Ill (Alsa), while the cities of Strasbourg and Basle were less grand, their houses having few and little windows and lacking light. The little cities of Colmar, Schlettstadt, Rouffach, and Mulhouse did not even exist in 1200, and there were at that time 'few men' in various groups—merchants, surgeons, doctors (*physici*), masters of mechanical arts, and Jews. Now, the contrast between Bartholomew's succinctness and lack of detail and the precision and variety of this Alsace text of around 1290 is only partly explained by the forty-year gap and things which had changed during these years. More is to be attributed to the differences of genre of the two texts. Behind Bartholomew and in his time, and among his later readers, there were people whose mental map of their regions will have had the precision and local examples of the anonymous Dominican. Bartholomew's epitome does not equal the population map in the mind of Bartholomew himself and others of his generation, rather it is that map reduced to the back of a postage stamp.

Bartholomew's populous picture of Europe was produced on the eve of a massive expansion in the west's picture of the far east.

9.3 *Asia and the far east: Mongolia and China*

India had long played the role of 'something very large and a long way to the east', containing many marvels and vast numbers of peoples and islands, and there is little to remark in Bartholomew's statement that 'India is amongst all regions of the earth . . . the most populous' beyond his characteristic choice of the superlative adjective *populosissima.* There were to be significant changes in the late thirteenth and early fourteenth centuries in physical knowledge of India, through the travels of merchants and and also friars engaged in missionary work and the setting up of dioceses. These brought about the first attested western visits to particular regions, which altered the mix of reality and fantasy in the western view of India, and therefore perhaps also the balance of these qualities in the picture of India's peopling. But the main lines of this picture were old.

What was new, however, was the development of a picture of the far reaches of northern and central Asia between the mid-thirteenth and mid-fourteenth centuries, Mongolia and China (Cathay).[50] This extension came in two stages, the first with the irruption and attacks on the west of the Tartars (Mongols), and consequent attention directed towards *them*, their geographical location, military

[50] Bartholomew had a bare two dozen words on 'Seres, a province in the east which has the name of a town', for he and his early medieval and classical predecessors had known virtually nothing of China; *De proprietatibus rerum*, XV. clxii; *Properties of Things*, XV. clxi (ii. 807); Yule and Cordier, *Cathay*, i.

strength, and numbers. The second came with the completion of the Tartar conquest of the southern mainland of Cathay, effected by 1276, and the subsequent opportunity for westerners to travel under the Mongol peace to the heart of China, to Canbalec (Peking/Beijing), and to the eastern coast and Kinsai (Hangchow) and beyond.

9.3.1 Mongolia[51]

The first serious reports of the Mongols came as the result of four journeys of Dominicans from Hungary between *c.*1230 and *c.*1237.[52] These were journeying to the area between the Volga and the Ural, in search of the 'Greater Hungary' which, it was said in Hungarian history, the Hungarians had left 'because the land could not support the multitude of inhabitants'.[53] Royal or national interest in this was sufficient for King Bela IV to pay the expenses of the second expedition. Journeying there, the friars came into contact with western outposts of Mongols, and learnt both from them and from those who knew something of them. Two reports survive. One of these, written by friar Julian and addressed to a papal legate at the Hungarian court, Benedictus Salvius de Salvis, bishop of Perugia, reported Tartar devastation of various kingdoms, including the destruction of the Volga Bulgars in autumn 1237. Julian's letter included material which had been supplied to him in writing by 'a certain Ruthenian [Russian] cleric'. It also included a translation into Latin of a letter from a Tartar Khan to the king of Hungary. This is the first such text to survive, but its reference to many previous emissaries,[54] sent to Bela IV, suggests that the Hungarian royal court was a repository of some experience by this time.

There were beginning to be persons and centres with special knowledge of the Mongols, and the lines of communication were rapidly multiplying. In St Albans Matthew Paris wrote under the year 1238 of Saracen emissaries coming to the kings of England and France, with reports about the Tartars, adding his famous observation on herring prices in Yarmouth, which were driven down because

[51] The most useful modern accounts of the themes treated in this section are Peter Jackson's introduction to his translation, *The Mission of Friar William of Rubruck*, ed. P. Jackson and D. Morgan, Hakluyt Society, 2nd ser. 173 (London, 1990), and F. Schmieder, *Europa und die Fremden: Die Mongolen im Urteil des Abendlandes vom 13. bis in das 15 Jahrhundert*, Beiträge zur Geschichte und Quellenkunde des Mittelalters 16 (Sigmaringen, 1994). My account begins in the 1230s, bypassing those western views of the later twelfth and early thirteenth centuries which were associated with the fabled Prester John; see ibid., pp. 5–6, and the comments of R. W. Southern, *Western Views of Islam in the Middle Ages* (Cambridge, Mass., 1962), pp. 45–7.

[52] See H. Dörrie, 'Drei Texte zur Geschichte der Ungarn und Mongolen. Die Missionsreisen des fr. Iulianus ins Ural-Gebiet (1234/5) und nach Rußland (1237) und der Bericht des Erzbischofs Peter über die Tartaren', *Nachrichten der Akademie der Wissenschaften in Göttingen*, Philologisch-historische Klasse (1956), 125–202 (pp. 125–31).

[53] Riccardus, *De facto Ungarie magne*, I, ed. Dörrie, 'Drei Texte', 151.

[54] Julian, [*Epistola de vita Tartarorum*], IV, ed. Dörrie, 'Drei Texte', 179. See Dörrie's comment on the high number of previous emissaries, 179 n. 4:9.

Frisian and Baltic merchants, terrified by the Tartar threat, had not turned up. Again in 1239 Matthew reported actions being taken by the kings of Hungary and Denmark in relation to the Tartars.[55] The events of December 1240 to late 1241 then preoccupied most of those in Latin Christendom who dealt with and thought about major world events.[56] News and reactions at the time are best conveyed in telegraphese. December 1240, the Tartars take Kiev, reducing it to 200 houses and piles of human bones which later travellers (such as John of Pian di Carpine) could still see. Conquest of southern Russia. 1241, through Poland and raiding down to Krakow, 18 March. 9 April, defeat of German and Polish army at Liegnitz in Silesia. Invasion of Hungary; defeat of Hungarian, Slavic, and German army near Mohi, late April or early May. July, raiding parties reach Neustadt by Vienna. Tartar withdrawal from these western parts on news of the death of Khan Ogotai.

The Tartars were what people *talked* about during this terrible period, as the flood of texts on the Tartars shows. See, for example, Matthew Paris. For 1241, he inserts a letter on the Tartars sent to the Duke of Brabant on the fourth Sunday in Lent. He reports the Duke writing to the bishop of Paris, William of Auvergne, and the archbishop of Cologne writing to Henry III of England. The emperor Frederick II's letter to Henry III is inserted, and also the addition at the end of the emperor's letter to the French king. People debated Frederick's letter, says Matthew, and they called into question some of what Frederick claimed about the Mongols, and Matthew reported a conversation between the French king and his mother about the Tartars.[57] A conversation between a renegade Englishman, who had served the Tartars, and had been one of their emissaries to the Hungarian royal court, was used in a letter written by Ivo, a renegade cleric from Narbonne, who saw the Tartars retreating from Vienna. Ivo sent the letter to Gerard Malmort, archbishop of Bordeaux, whom Ivo chose as his addressee not only because of Ivo's former service as a cleric to Gerard but also, as he said, because of Gerard's intermediate position between the kings of England, France, and Spain. The communication worked in at least one direction, since the letter found its way to St Albans and insertion into Matthew's chronicle under the year 1243.[58] Further urgent discussion is implied by the bundle of letters, mainly from eastern European religious, which Matthew copied into the appendix to his chronicle.[59]

The matter now moved to what was, when it met, the largest talking-shop of Latin Christendom: a general Church council. To the council which Innocent IV summoned at Lyons there came the emperor of Constantinople, the count of Toulouse and various other nobles, the patriarchs of Constantinople and

[55] Matthew Paris, *CM* iii. 488–9 and 639.

[56] See Matthew's summary of the past fifty years in his entry under 1250 for a self-conscious contemporary notion of 'major world events'.

[57] *CM* iv. 109–20.

[58] *CM* iv. 270–7. Its authenticity is exhaustively discussed in P. Segl, *Ketzer in Österreich: Untersuchungen über Häresie und Inquisition im Herzogtum Österreich im 13. und beginnenden 14. Jahrhundert* (Paderborn, Munich, Vienna, and Zurich, 1984), pp. 76–11.

[59] *CM* vi. 78–84.

Aquileia, and 140 archbishops and bishops from France, Italy, England, Ireland, Spain, Portugal, Bohemia, and eastern Europe. If the abbot of St Alban's did not go, as Matthew tells us, because of obesity and old age, the Tartars were the serious reason for the low turn-out, in particular the absence of all Hungarian bishops and most of the Germans. And when Innocent IV delivered his opening address to the Council on 28 June 1245, and used the five wounds of Christ to survey contemporary dangers, he identified the Tartars as the first wound. Some time before the council a Ruthenian Archbishop called Peter had come south, and had been questioned about the Tartars by a papal commission. What he had to say about the Tartars suggests that he may have been the 'certain Ruthenian cleric' who had supplied strikingly similar material to the Hungarian Dominican Julian, in or before 1237.[60] A further attraction of Peter may have been that he was a reputable source of information who was alternative to the famous information-letter which had been put round by the emperor Frederick II. At a council which was about to try to depose him, Frederick's name was mud. What is certain is that Peter now came to Lyons, appearing before the pope and assembled prelates of the council. He was taken through nine questions about the Tartars, to each of which he replied. The question on their population was the sixth in the list, which went as follows. 'First on their origin; secondly, on their belief; thirdly, on their cult; fourthly, on their way of life; fifthly, on their strength (viz. military); sixthly, on their multitude; seventhly, on their intentions; eighthly, on their observance of treaty [-obligations]; ninthly, on their reception of ambassadors'.[61] The buzz made by this session can still be picked up in the Burton Annals report of those prelates who, on their return home from the council, talked about it and about Peter's lack of languages and the need for an interpreter.[62]

There followed more missions by mendicant Friars, Dominicans and Franciscans. In 1245 Innocent IV commissioned the Franciscan John of Pian di Carpine and the Dominicans Andrew of Longjumeau, Ascelin of Cremona, and Simon of St Quentin to go on missions to the Great Khan, while Louis IX again commissioned Andrew in 1248. The Franciscans William of Rubruck and Bartholomew of Cremona, who left Acre in 1253, round off this early group. Among these, only two penetrated the eastern parts of the lands inhabited by the Mongols, John who came very close to Karakorum, and William who got there. Much of the returning material and the circumstances of its return and reception are now lost. For example, only some parts of a report written by Simon of St Quentin survive through their excerpting by a fellow Dominican—of which more in a moment. Where a report survives, such as William of Rubruck's, we can conjecture parts of its reception, at the French royal court and in the Franciscan Order, since it was addressed to the French king,[63] and we know of an intellectually eccentric English Franciscan who talked to William and incorporated parts of his book and conversation into a treatise he was writing in the 1260s, addressed to the Pope. But the

[60] On Peter see Dörrie, 'Drei Texte', 182–7. [61] Ibid., 188. [62] Ibid., 187.

[63] See Jackson, *Mission of Friar William*, p. 41, on William and the royal court.

rest is in the dark, and it has been suggested that the survival of this work only in English manuscripts indicates restricted readership.[64]

The case of John of Pian di Carpine is better known, and illustrates how returning reports spread. Commissioned by Innocent IV, John had left Lyons on 16 April 1245, arriving at an imperial camp near the Mongol capital, Karakorum, on 22 July 1246 and, after staying until November 1246, he journeyed back, regaining Lyons in November 1247. On his return, John wrote his *Historia Mongalorum* and gave lectures. In the concluding chapter of his work John wrote about its reception when it was still not complete. 'Those through whom [through whose regions] I journeyed, who live in Poland, Bohemia, and in Germany, and in Liège and Champagne, had eagerly [received] the history which is written above, [and] therefore rewrote it down before it had been completed and in fact [when it was still in a] very abbreviated [form], because we had not then had a period of calm to be able fully to complete it.'[65] One of the Franciscans who heard John lecturing in Krakow, Breslau, or Prague, a certain C. *de Bridia*, took down what he heard around the middle of July 1247, and produced a report which was in effect an adaptation of John's first short version. C. *de Bridia* finished this on 30 July 1247, and sent it to the minister of the Franciscans in Bohemia and Poland, Boguslas. A glimpse of John's later lectures comes from the Franciscan writer from Parma, Salimbene. He heard John at Sens during John's visit to Louis IX early in 1248, and he later described the way John 'had the book read aloud . . . whenever he found it too laborious to tell the story; and when readers were astonished or did not understand he himself expounded or discussed matters of detail'.[66] Salimbene was a witty observer of his fellow friars, and his light sketch is an early example of the portrait of a travel-bore.

Finally, a Dominican, Vincent of Beauvais, had been working with assistants and the French king's money at the Cistercian abbey of Royaumont on his massive three-part *Speculum Maius*, completing its first version between 1244 and 1246. At some date after 1248/9, he produced a revised second edition, and now the final book of one of the *Speculum*'s three parts, the *Speculum Historiale*, was largely given over to the Tartars. They were represented through extensive quotation and adaptation of John of Pian di Carpine's report, and excerpts from the lost report of Vincent's fellow Dominican, Simon of Saint Quentin.

The larger story of what was written and discussed in these years and in these milieux has often been told, and it is one which is appropriately dominated by military, political, and diplomatic themes, and the succession of western reactions, from early terror to the later opening out of the prospect of possible alliance with the Mongols against the Saracens, a prospect which was to play a role in western leaders' political and military calculations for a long time. Here we are going to pick out only one theme. This is the intrusion into western minds and the

64 Southern, *Western Views of Islam*, pp. 51–2; Jackson, *Mission of Friar William*, p. 51. See ibid., p. 282, for evidence of discussion of William in the Franciscan convent at Tripoli.

65 John of Pian di Carpine, *Ystoria Mongalorum*, IX. lii, Wyngaert, *Itinera*, p. 130.

66 Quoted in Skelton, Marston and Painter, *Vinland Map*, p. 39.

growth of a notion of the lands of the Mongols, their peopling of it, and their numbers, which had been the sixth item of enquiry at the council of Lyons.

There came, first of all, notions of the lands they inhabited, and the lands from which they had come. The theme is perhaps self-evident, but awareness of it would have been sharp in the minds of Hungarian friars who themselves had 'land of origin', 'inhabitation', and 'overpopulation' in mind, as they journeyed eastwards in search of Greater Hungary. The theme is already clear in the report written by Julian. 'It has been told to me by some that the Tartars used to inhabit land which the Cumans now inhabit . . . the land from which they earlier came is called Gotta (Cathay, China).'[67] Saracens appearing in the west in 1238 saw the Tartars as living to the north, in 'the Caspian mountains or places nearby', but also referred to 'extensive and rich lands to the east'. Location 'beyond the Chaldees', that is to say, far to the east, came in Ivo of Narbonne's letter, and then came the firm and clear information of the reports of the returning Franciscans. John of Pian di Carpine's first chapter was 'On their land'. C. *De Bridia*'s generalization of John shows, in its very crudity, the massiveness of the alteration of the view of the habitable world which was quickly occurring. 'According to the Tartars and some others the habitable fabric of the world is divided into two main parts, that is to say, the East and the West . . . For the western part begins [i.e. its eastern limits] in the country of Livonia and goes from Prussia to Greece and further and contains in itself the whole Church of the Catholic faith. . . . The remaining part, however, is called the eastern [part], and the land of the Tartars is placed in this, where the East joins the North [the Arctic], having next to it the ocean sea of the North [Arctic ocean], and it is called "Moal".'[68] The itineraries present in John's and William of Rubruck's reports provided a rough sketch—most of it still traceable by modern historical geographers—of the location and vastness of these tracts of the earth between Russia and modern Mongolia, and Mongolia itself, in this northern part of the 'eastern habitable world'.

As the location and extensiveness of Tartar lands took rough shape, ideas both of this land and what lay beyond it were forming. 'Desert' and 'devastation' were notions which quickly became commonplaces in relation to the Tartars: the results of what they *did*. Thus Matthew Paris's report about the kings of Denmark and Hungary in 1239 was of them sending Christians to 'reinhabit the provinces which had been reduced virtually to a desert by the Tartars'.[69] But 'desert', 'lack of settled habitation', and what we call nomadism came *also* to be commonplaces about the lands of the Tartars further to the east. The emphasis on westerners' settled habitation, which is found in the first extant Khan's letter in the 1237 report of the Dominican Julian, clearly implies the writer's contrasting lack of settled habitation. 'You', wrote the Khan [Ogotai], addressing the king of Hungary, '[who] inhabit houses and have towns and cities, how are you to escape my hands?'[70] The

[67] Julian, *Epistola*, I, Dörrie, 'Drei Texte', 167 and n. 1:2.

[68] C. *de Bridia, Hystoria Tartarorum*, II, ed. A. Önnerfors (Berlin, 1967), p. 4.

[69] *CM* iv. 669.

[70] Julian, [*Epistola de vita Tartarorum*], IV, ed. Dörrie, 'Drei Texte', 179.

Saracen reports, in 1238, of Tartar flocks and herds implied nomadism. Ivo of Narbonne described the Tartars as living 'in a great waste'.[71]

And then came the precision of John of Pian di Carpine and William of Rubruck. 'Their land is large', wrote of John, 'but viler than one can say.'[72] Only one hundredth part was fertile. 'There are not towns and nor any cities', apart from Karakorum.[73] John's ninth chapter, which is devoted to his itinerary, is flecked with words and phrases such as 'desert' and 'few men live [there]'.[74] William of Rubruck was more eloquent on the subject, repeatedly remarking the absence of towns and cities, quoting Hebrews 13: 14, 'they do not have anywhere "a lasting city" . . . Shepherds without a city . . . this vast solitude (*vasta solitudo*) . . . we journeyed for two months and never saw a town . . . for fifteen days we saw no people.'[75] He sometimes uses diminutives for fixed Tartar settlements, *casale* for a village, and the contemptuous *vilulla*, townlet, for Karakorum. Writing with his addressee in mind, the king of France, he used Parisian comparisons, saying that Karakorum was no better than the settlement round St Denis, and its palace ten times less than the monastery of St Denis.[76]

For what lay beyond Tartary (Mongolia) words had begun to emerge, *Gotta* (Cathay), in 1237 in Julian's report, and then 'the land of the Kitaians' (Cathayans) and Kitaia (Cathay). Slowly emerging also was the sense of a contrast between the poor and townless wastelands of the Tartars and what lay beyond. This is not yet clear in the 1238 reports of the Saracens, who stated that the Tartars 'had taken possession of extensive and rich lands to the east'. But it becomes clear in the late 1240s. For John, the land of Kitay is very wealthy.[77] There is more of this in William, as well as more precision about location. The Tartars' lands were thin, poor, and, as we have said, devoid of towns apart from Karakorum. To the north of Karakorum there were 'poor peoples' and there 'there is no city'. To the east of Karakorum 'there is no city'. But there was also *Cataia*, now in its medieval form as a name. While there is no direct description, William's reference to Nestorians existing 'in many of its cities', *civitates*, casually implies a land which is very different.[78]

'They are very numerous', the Saracens stated in 1238,[79] and one's first impression is that western writers simply repeated statements about infinite numbers of Tartars. Although such statements can be found, the impression is mistaken. From the very beginning there were attempts at precision, questions, and statements of quite large but not unthinkable numbers. All started, in the first instance, from preoccupation with the size as well as skill and techniques of the military threat posed by the Tartars. In 1237 the Dominican Julian was at pains to

[71] Matthew Paris, *CM* iv. 275. [72] John, *Ystoria*, I. vi; Wyngaert, *Itinera*, p. 32.

[73] Ibid., I. iv; p. 30. [74] Ibid., IX. xxii–xxiii; pp. 112–13.

[75] William of Rubruck, *Itinerarium*, II. i, IX. 4, XIV. i, XXI. i, XXII. ii, and XXXVII. xv; Wyngaert, *Itinera*, pp. 172, 189, 198, 219, 222, and 317.

[76] Ibid., XVII. iii, XIX. iii, XXIII. i, and XXXII. i; pp. 207, 212, 223, and 285.

[77] John, *Ystoria*, V. 10; p. 58.

[78] William, *Itinerarium*, XIV. i, XXVI. xi, and XXIX. xlv; pp. 198, 236, and 268–9.

[79] Matthew Paris, *CM* iii. 488: *numerosi nimis.*

observe militarily. The Khan sends out various armies, not one; one is described as 'copious'. The division into tens and hundreds, with one Tartar at the head of each, is rationalized as a way of ensuring loyalty in a system where Tartar numbers *are* reduced in war but can quickly be replenished by other peoples. In other words, the Tartars themselves do not supply limitless numbers. The enormously large (as opposed to a very large) estimate of Tartar numbers is given as a Tartar claim rather than fact. 'The Tartars claim that they have such a great multitude of warriors that it could be divided into forty parts, such that no power could be found on the earth that could resist one of these parts.' Julian does not comment on forty, but his use of the phrase 'they claim', *asserunt*, and his statement that the Tartars are coming to the west in four parts may suggest reserve. The forty units are probably fortieths of the numbers Julian provides. 'It is said that they have in their army 260,000 slaves not of their law [= religion], and 135,00 [who are] of their law.' In other words, the fortieth is (approximately) 10,000.[80] Julian is in no doubt of the military awesomeness of the Tartars, but he may have been thinking more of their techniques and record of invincibility than their claim of enormous multitudes.

Among the letters provoked by the disasters of 1241–2, it was the emperor's which laid unequivocal emphasis on vast numbers. Many Old Testament references can supply Frederick's 'multiplied like locusts', best of all Judges 7: 12: 'the eastern peoples . . . like a multitude of locusts'. Infinity and nothing are coupled in the letter. 'Trusting in their unlimited numbers . . . they have brought about universal depopulation.'[81] The letter's contents provoked a lot of discussion throughout Europe, Matthew Paris reported, and this included scepticism about the reports of their numbers. 'As there are only seven climates in the whole extent of the world . . . and these are not so remotely situated in the whole of the habitable world for travelling merchants not to explore them . . . where have so many and such people remained hidden up till now?'[82] Interest in and scepticism about the extravagances of Frederick's letter probably lie behind various of the questions which were put in open session at the council of Lyons to the Russian archbishop Peter, the sixth of which, as we have seen, was 'on their multitude'. Peter was cautious. '[Asked] about their multitude, he did not give a precise reply. However, he said that there have been gathered to them [into their population] peoples from virtually all nations and sects [religions].'[83] What largeness he would talk about, then, did not derive from Tartar multitude itself, but their conquests of others.

This was not the first attempt to find out. Ivo's letter to the archbishop of Narbonne contained the results, we may remember, of the interrogation of an

[80] Julian, *Epistola*, VI, Dörrie, 'Drei Texte', 182. Here I follow Dörrie, 182 n. 6:5, although he takes Julian's 395,000 as 400,00. 395,00 may have been the result of Julian carelessly trying to get three parts, in the ratio 2:1, out of 400,000.

[81] Matthew Paris, *CM* iv. 112–13. [82] Ibid., 120.

[83] Ibid., 192: *De multitudine non dedit certum responsum, tamen dixit quod quasi de omnibus nationibus et sectis universis sunt illis populi multi aggregati.*

1(a). This illustration to Nicole Oresme's translation of and commentary on Aristotle's *Politics* shows the good 'polity' in the top strip and the bad 'polity' in the lower, each strip containing, from left to right, poor, middling, and wealthy people. In a good polity middling people are proportionately numerous, while in a bad polity they are few and the poor look threatening. See pp. 314, 324, and 391.

1(b). The first indexes to books containing such headings as 'overpopulation' and 'birth-control' are found in manuscripts of Oresme's *Politiques d'Aristote*, which has such entries as 'Multiplication de peuple' (reproduced here) and 'Multitude d'enfans'. Readers are given book and chapter numbers of discussions of how to avoid over-population and the generation of too many children. See pp. 376–7.

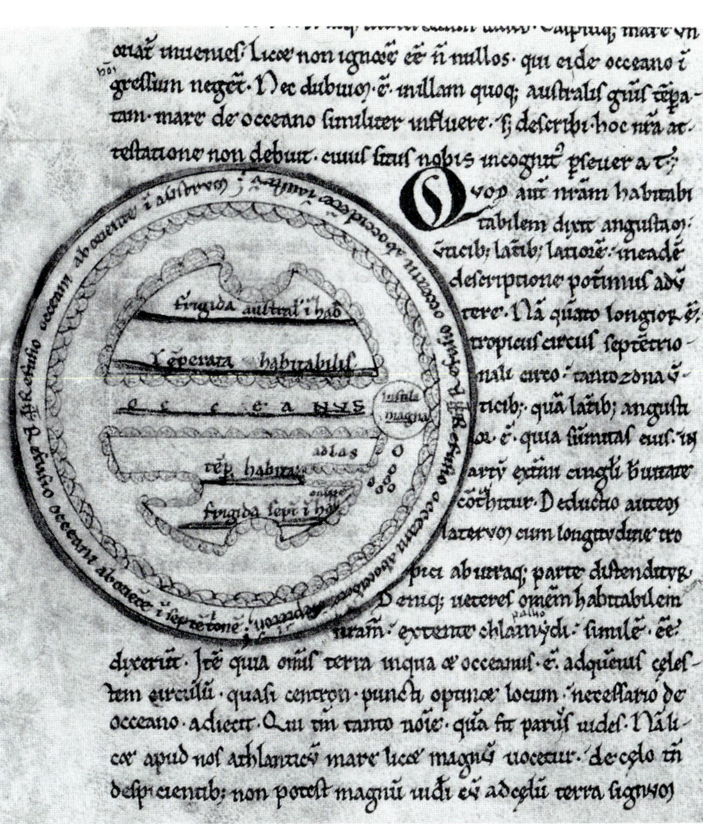

(a)

(b)

2(a) and (b). Many maps showed the world divided into five strips of zones or climates, with the north and south polar strips 'cold' and 'uninhabitable', the central equatorial strip 'torrid' and 'uninhabitable', and the other two strips 'temperate' and 'inhabitable'. Map (a) shows this in outline (and has north at the bottom), while map (b) shows how the known world could be accommodated into the schema. See pp. 218 and 248–9.

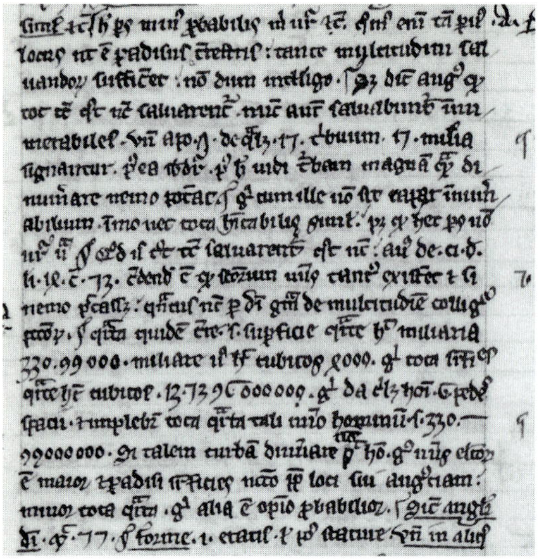

3. Large numbers are shown here in a manuscript of Richard Fishacre's *Sentences* commentary, which is an early attempt to bring them together with world-population. In this case Fishacre is calculating how many people would fit into a quarter of the world's surface if each person was given the same space, six feet by one mile. See pp. 244–6.

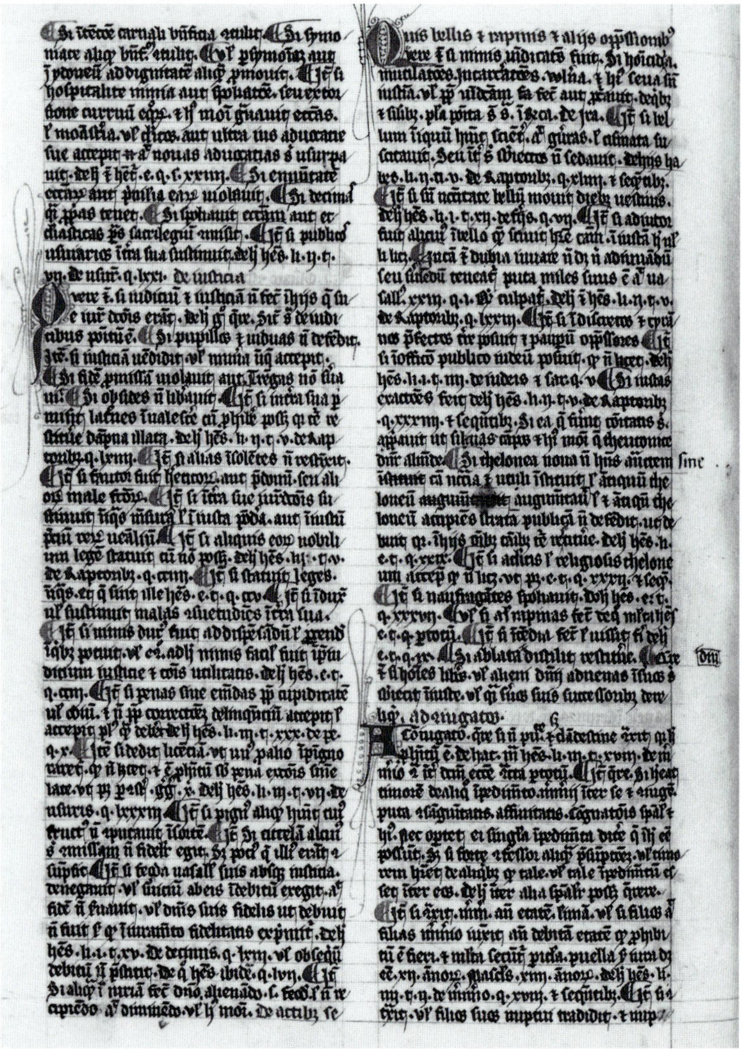

4. 'Did the wife effect some impediment to conceiving? And the same question to the husband. Or did she procure an abortion?' (*Item si aliquod impedimentum fecit ne conciperet; et idem de viro; vel si aborsum procuravit*). These conclude the questions to be put 'To Married people' (*ad coniugatos*) in confession, shown here in the second and third columns of a manuscript of the popular manual for confessors, John of Freiburg's *Confessionale* (1297–8). See pp. 197–9.

5. Tabular representation of defects in sexual intercourse, before, during, or after which lead to sterility, in a manuscript of the *Compilatio de conceptione*. This was one of several sex-tracts from Montpellier around 1300, which looked at failure to conceive. See. pp. 154.

In continuitate — Rhagadie / Vlcera — matris / aut virge — quod est in cancris / aut fistulis

Ex parte viri —
privatio vel defectus ipsius
sicut in etate decrepita
Nimia tenuitas et liquiditas eius
sicut in fleumaticis maxime
senibus et in pueris et
crapulosis et ebriis
Nimia caliditas ut in
febricitantibus et zenes
aut epar habentibus calidos
Nimia frigiditas ut in congelatis
aut in habentibus principalia
valde frigida
Nimia siccitas ut in
ethicis et consumptis
Nimia humiditas ut in ydropicis
Ab omni eius membro pro sperma
descendit et ideo principalium
cuiusque membri potest
ineptitudo reddi

Discrasia — calida / frigida / humida / sicca

Proprietas sterilitatis — In nullo / In nulla

Ineptitudo emissionis
Aversio mulieris in emittendo

post commixtionem —
Subita erectio mulieris
saltus maior ad posterius
Casus
Percussio
Furor
Clamor
Fletus
Sternutatio fortis
Olfactus horribilium
Adiutorium
Timor subitus
Terror vehemens
Subiacere medicinas
abortivas
Recipere eas per os
applicare eas exterius
quocumque modo
Explicit.

Certa signa impregnationis
sunt ista.
Retentio menstruorum assueta
Titillatio in orificio matricis
Gravitas ancharum
renum ac spine
Dolor in cruribus et
genubus
Calor colli
Siccitas spine
Delectantur in coitu
minus solito
Mamille duriores
Sentit matricem clausam
superius ac ad anterius
Sentit dolorem modicum
ab umbilico
deorsum ad receptionem
Finis est.

6(a) and (b). An estimate of Florence's population, 90,000 mouths (*bocche*) precedes the first existing sex-ratio figures, seen here (a) in a manuscript of the Giovanni Villani's *Chronicle*, where they are given under the year 1338. There were 5,000–6,000 babies per year, 'the male sex most times exceeding [the female] by 300 to 500 each year (*avanzando le piu volte il sesso masolino da CCC in D per anno*). The figures were based on counting girls and boys at baptism in Florence's Baptistry, the octagonal building seen here (b) in the centre in Florence in a fresco of 1342. See pp. 89 and 412.

Englishman, captured near Neustadt, who had served the Tartars. They aim at conquering the whole world. 'However, they cannot be computed at thousands of thousands', *nec possunt tamen millia millium computari*. This is shortly before the word *million* acquires common currency.[84] The words *computari possunt* suggest deliberate and self-conscious attempt to come to a numerical estimate. If we try to estimate their numbers, we should not think in millions. And these peoples live in a great waste, east of the Chaldees.

In John's and William's accounts, no number is mentioned, but the broad elements of their pictures match Ivo's report of what the captured Englishman had to say. Vast tracts of land, very thinly populated; and the 'ordas' or hordes of Tartars, gathered in a few encampments, each of which contains very many people, but not unthinkably large numbers. Modern demographic data for the Republic of Mongolia provide a picture of just under two million Mongols, hardly urbanized and living with a very low population density, just over three persons per square mile. The first traces of *that* part of western people's picture of the peopling of the habitable world are discernible around 1250.

9.3.2 *China*

After some respite in the previous twenty years, the Tartars renewed their pressure on the Sung state to the south in the 1250s. By 1279 they had overrun the whole of China. The Mongol capital had ceased to be Karakorum, and in 1267 was officially relocated to Canbalec: Khan-Baliq, 'the Khan's town', modern Peking or Beijing. In the same decade Tartar and Cathayan/Chinese administration had been merging, with Cathayan procedures and personnel predominating. Now, under the Tartar peace, the land route to Cathay was open to westerners, and was taken by those engaged in spreading the Catholic faith and trade. By the first half of the fourteenth century the far east was being carved up for missionary activities by the Franciscans and Dominicans. A Franciscan archbishop was entrusted with the province of Canbalec, a Dominican archbishop at Sultaniyeh in Iran was in charge of Iran and central Asia, and Dominicans were also allocated India. Alongside the friars were the western traders, who had previously got hold of far-eastern goods indirectly, after their transport to Alexandria and Damascus. Now, for nearly a century, they were doing it directly. Early traces of this story are the appearance of Chinese silk in Genoa in 1257 and the Chinese journey of the Marco Polos, father and uncle, Niccolo and Maffeo, in 1262–9. And a well-known emphatic testimony to the ordinariness of the treading of this long path and the dominance in it of the Genoese is the handbook written by a Florentine merchant, Pegolotti, in 1340, which detailed the stages, exchange-rates, and customs-duties of the route to Canbalec, while using Genoese measures.

[84] Ibid., 276. In his attentive and careful translation, J. A. Giles hesitantly suggested 'nor yet can they be reckoned at a thousand thousands'; *Matthew Paris's English History*, 3 vols. (London, 1852–4), i. 472.

From shortly before 1300 and for the next half-century there survives a welter of texts on all of this: letters from the missionaries in south and south-eastern Asia; treatises on the *Mirabilia* or wonders of the far east written by travellers, or by armchair travellers copying the real travellers; and specialized tracts. No detailed account can be given here, where we can only remark the profusion and ramification of this material, note some of the leading texts, and give some representative examples of the spread of information and the centres of its discussion. Some of the most important as well as representative are, among the letters describing missionary work, those written by the Franciscans John of Monte Corvino (*c.*1293–1306) and Andrew of Perugia (1326). Among the treatises, the *Divisament dou Monde* dictated by Marco Polo in 1298, the *Mirabilia Descripta* written in 1329 by the Dominican Jordan Catalani of Séverac, and the *Multe et diverse hystorie . . . de ritibus et condicionibus huius mundi et martirio IIII fratrum minorum* dictated by the Franciscan Odoric of Pordenone in 1330. Among specialist tracts, the *Livre de l'estat du Grant Caan*, written for Pope John XXII, probably by John de Cori.

Most of these authors were missionaries. John of Monte Corvino engaged in missionary work in the near east and Iran until 1289, and later in India (he visited the Madras region in 1291–2) and Cathay, where Clement V made him first archbishop of Canbalec in 1307. Jordan Catalani of Séverac worked as a missionary in India from 1321, and John XXII made him bishop of Quilon in south India in 1330. John de Cori was named the metropolitan of Sultaniyeh in Iran in 1330; Jordan Catalani was entrusted with taking the pallium to him. Odoric of Pordenone was a Franciscan whose activities—presumably missionary—are less clear than his travels, which took him from the Persian Gulf to India, Ceylon, possibly Madras, Sumatra, Java, possibly Borneo, Indo-China, and then up through various Cathayan cities to Canbalec. Marco Polo came from a family of long-distance Venetian traders who had already travelled to Cathay. He reached Chandu in 1275, entered Cathayan service, administering the city of Yang-Chau for three years, and after seventeen years in Cathay returned on a route which took him across India.

The missionary material partly circulated in various mission territories. One copy of John of Monte Corvino's second letter, which was written in Canbalec, was carried by Tartar postmen to friars in 'Khazar-land', while another copy was taken to Franciscans and Dominicans in Iran. Letters came back to mendicant convents in Italian cities. John's first letter, written in India around 1292–3, was sent to the Dominican Bartholomew of Santo Concordio, author of a famous confessor's manual, possibly in Tuscany,[85] and Andrew of Perugia's letter was sent to the Guardian of the convent in Perugia. Within the Orders back home there was concern to get the material produced and copied. Odoric was instructed to dictate his work to another friar in the convent in Padua.[86] Odoric's own fame was

[85] Bartholomew was called the 'Pisan' from his association with the convent of that city, and in 1297 he was in Florence.

[86] See *Les voyages en Asie au XIVe siècle du bienheureux Frère Odoric de Pordenone, religieux de*

strongest in north-eastern Italy, and his account of martyrdom in India appeared in frescoes in Padua and Verona, but his work spread very widely. Vernacular versions were made; there are still extant at last sixty-one copies of the Latin and thirty-four altogether of the Italian, French, and German translations.

Panoramic views and discussions of the eastern missions took place, of course, most intensely and at the highest level at the papal court. A copy of Odoric's work was being transcribed in Avignon the year after his death, Jean de Cori's general account of 'the state of the great Khan and Cathay' was produced for the pope, and Jordan of Séverac wrote his account of eastern marvels in Avignon. A variety of literate audiences received Marco Polo's work. Three copies carry a note that Marco Polo wanted it to be known throughout the world, and to be carried to noble parts of France. Even if this is a near-contemporary fabrication, retrospectively ascribing to Polo this express intention, it is useful in generalizing part of what happened. The work was written in French, and significantly prominent in the text's early history is a story of book-procurement in 1307. In that year a French nobleman, who was visiting Venice on a diplomatic mission, got hold of a copy from Polo itself, and the book went via his son to the brother of the king of France, Charles de Valois. Another audience was Latin-reading and clerical. A Dominican general chapter held in Bologna either in 1302 or 1314 gave instructions to a Bolognese Dominican to translate Polo's work into Latin, and the successful commission still survives in fifty-nine manuscripts. As we shall see in our final chapter, a Florentine businessmen, Giovanni Villani, who began writing his chronicle in the Tuscan vernacular in 1300, advertised the work, telling his readers that if they wanted to learn more about the Tartars they should go away and read Marco Polo and Hayton. The great Paduan philosopher and medical man, Peter d'Abano, had talked to Marco Polo and refers to him in two of his works. 'I heard from Marco', he writes, but it has been plausibly suggested that, when he writes that Marco 'has made known to us', the subject of these words *nobis . . . nuntiavit* is the book, and that what is being described is the book's impact: its impact on our knowledge of things.[87]

John of Monte Corvino concluded his 1305 letter from Cambalec by saying that no king or prince in the world could compare with the Cham in respect to the size of his country, and the multitude of its people, and the amount of his wealth.[88]

Saint-François, ed. H. Cordier, Recueil de voyages et de documents géographiques 10 (Paris, 1891), pp. lxv–cxvii and p. 2; Golubovich, iii. 374–94.

[87] This paragraph is based on L. F. Benedetto, *La tradizione manoscritta del 'Milione' di Marco Polo* (Turin, 1962 = reprint of the introduction to his edn. of 1928). On the production of a vernacular text followed rather than preceded by a Latin version, see A. Vernet, 'Les traductions latines d'oeuvres en langues vernaculaires au moyen âge', *Traductions et Traducteurs au Moyen Âge*, ed. G. Contamine, Documents, Études et Répertoires Publiées par l'Institut de Recherche et d'Histoire des Textes (Paris, 1989), pp. 221–41 (pp. 231 and n. 6 on Hayton, and 232 and n. 2 on Marco Polo). An illuminating account of Peter d'Abano's interest in inhabitation of the world and its regions is provided in N. G. Siraisi, *Arts and Sciences at Padua: The Studium of Padua before 1350*, Pontifical Institute of Medieval Studies, Studies and Texts 25 (Toronto, 1973), pp. 118–22.

[88] John of Monte Corvino, *Epistola II*, ix, Wyngaert, *Itinera*, pp. 350–1. Similar emphasis in Andrew of Perugia, *Epistola*, II; Wyngaert, *Itinera*, p. 374.

The accounts of Cathay all transmit a picture of an enormous land. The second point is the vast size of the population, but the enormous population is not set in a simple relation to geographical size. Odoric makes this point most explicitly when describing one of the provinces of Cathay. While he gives its large extent (via days of travelling) and its extreme populousness (according to him, the most populous province in the world), he uses the proximity of cities to underwrite his 'populousness' point. 'It has such a population that when you go out from one gate you see another.'[89]

In general the point is presented through the descriptions of the vast numbers of cities and the vast populations of some of them. Outstanding in the accounts are Cansay (Hangchow, Hangzhou) and Canbalec. Cansay is described as the greatest city in the world. Just as the village of St Denis had been used to make the point about how small Mongolian Karakorum was, the western travellers used sizeable cities from their own homelands to underline largeness. The Tartar emperor ruled over two hundred cities larger than Toulouse, wrote Jordan of Séverac, and with more men.[90] Neither Treviso nor Vicenza would count among the cities of the province of Manzi, wrote Odoric.[91] While his use implied that they were second-division western cities, just large enough to make his point, first-division cities were used in bigger comparisons. Zayton (Ch'uan Chow) was twice the size of Bologna, and Cansay three times the size of Venice.[92]

Other writers were to use statistics given for one or both of the two largest cities, including numbers of bridges, numbers of guilds, numbers of houses in each guild, numbers of markets, numbers of people frequenting these markets, and daily import of pepper and silk. Marco Polo gave a figure for prostitutes working in Cambalec—20,000—from which, he said, one could gain an idea of the city's population.[93] With the largest city, Cansay, a registration system was described by Marco Polo. Each townsman kept a list of the inmates of his house written over his door, striking out names on their deaths, and this was done so that the sovereign could know the population of the city. According to Marco Polo it contained 1,600,000 hearths.[94]

Transmitted by Marco Polo, this is part of a long and detailed text, coloured by exotic detail. Because of the high proportion of the fantastic in later travel-writing,

[89] Odoric of Pordenone, *Descriptio orientalium partium*, LXIV; Yule and Cordier, *Cathay*, ii. 327.

[90] *Description des merveilles d'une partie d'Asie par le P. Jordan ou Jourdain Catalani, natif de Séverac*, ed. C. De Montbret, Recueil de voyages et de mémoires publié par la Société de Géographie 4 (Paris, 1839), p. 59. See *SOPMA* iii. 51–2, and IV. 177.

[91] Odoric, *Descriptio*, XXVIII; ii. 309.

[92] Ibid., XXIX and XXX; ii. 309 and 310. The comparison could be feeble; e.g., Hayton wrote of Cambalec simply as 'plus grant que Rome', *La flor des estoires de la terre d'orient*, III. xii; *Recueil des historiens de la croisade, Documents Arméniens*, 2 vols. (Paris, 1906), ii. 160. Cities in the near east attracted similar comparisons; see e.g., the Franciscan Antonio dei Ribaldi of Cremona describing Damascus as two and a half Bolognas, in his *Itinerarium*, Golubovich, iii. 332.

[93] *The Book of Ser Marco Polo*, II. xxii, ed. H. Yule and H. Cordier, 3rd edn., 2 vols. (London, 1903), i. 414; Marco Polo, *The Description of the World*, ed. A. C. Moule and P. Pelliot, 2 vols. (London, 1938), i. 236.

[94] Marco Polo, II. lxxvi, ed. Yule and Cordier, i. 192; ed. Moule and Pelliot, ii. 339–40.

in particular Mandeville, it is tempting to depict later medieval reading of Marco Polo entirely in terms of projection of western fantasies or the 'otherness' of 'medieval' imagination. However appropriate for some readings, this suggestion does not apply to all. Peter d'Abano, for example, was serious. He wrote briefly about one of the earlier efforts by Genoese navigators, who in the late thirteenth and early fourteenth centuries sailed down the north-west coast of Africa, beyond previously known limits. In the same discussion he was reporting Marco Polo's statements as part of a general enquiry 'Whether there is habitation beyond the equator'. Half a century later than Albert the Great he was writing in a similar genre, on the frontier of academic knowledge of the extent of the habitable world.[95]

Sobriety characterized both Peter's academic concerns and the world-political and military interests of high ecclesiastical and royal courts. For essentially the same picture of Cathay's population as Marco Polo's is put over in reports compiled and submitted to the papal court, in particular the *Livre de l'estat du Grant Caan.* In this an account of royal government and religion is followed by a section on the condition of the realm of Cathay. This is partly about population and habitation. It is highly populated (*moult peuplez*), having many cities larger than Paris or Florence, and countless smaller inhabited cities. Because of the great population and the many waterways of Cathay, many people live on water. This section goes on to the production of food, and the next section briefly describes the two enormously populated cities of Cansay and Canbalec.[96]

Between the 1230s and the 1330s the west had received considerable extension to its picture of the habitable world and the character of its inhabitation. It acquired a view of the large but very thinly populated tracts of Mongolia, and of the land mass of China, with its enormous population. Of China's two most populous cities the west knew that one ran into millions, and that the number was known to the sovereign through its registration system and could be estimated by a westerner who multiplied the figure given for the number of hearths.

9.4 *Recovery of the Holy Land*

The reception of news and discussion in the mid-thirteenth century had a drama and intensity which were unique to this period, because of the devastation wrought by the Mongols, but the lines of circulation of information and arenas of debate in the west, at this time remained essentially similar for the next century. Mendicants went to the east, and returned, reporting, to kings and popes, and by

[95] See Pietro d'Abano, *Conciliator*, Differentia LXVII, 100vb–103va. On Peter's knowledge of Marco Polo, see Benedetto, *Tradizione manoscritta*, pp. ccxii–ccxiii; on his reading of John of Monte Corvino, see Wyngaert, *Itinera*, pp. 337–8 and n. 2. On Mandeville's fictions and the contrast with Marco Polo, see I. M. Higgins, *Writing East: The 'Travels' of Sir John Mandeville* (Philadelphia, 1997).

[96] *Le livre de l'estat du Grant Caan*, ed. M. Jacquet, *Nouveau Journal Asiatique* 6 (1830), 64–6. See C. R. Beazley, *The Dawn of Modern Geography*, 3 vols. (London, 1897–1906), iii. 207 and n. 3.

the early fourteenth century some were residing in far-eastern mission convents and writing back to western branches of their Orders.

Concurrently there was concern with the near east, preoccupation with the situation in the Holy Land and then, after the fall of Acre in 1291, with its recovery. Alongside intense debate at the second council of Lyons (1274) and the council of Vienne (1311–12) and at papal and royal courts, there came many writings on recovery. There were requests. Gregory X asked for written advice in his bull of summons to the council of Lyons (1272), and a master-general of the Dominican Order, Humbert of Romans, was one of several to respond, while in 1307 a former Armenian prince, Hayton, was dictating his advice at the behest of Clement V. Hearing of the project of crusade by the king of France, Philip VI, in 1331, a Dominican (possibly Raymond Stephani) sent in his own scheme, while one expert on the matter, the Venetian Marino Sanudo, bombarded the heads of Christendom with his writings.[97] In the later decades of the thirteenth and first half of the fourteenth centuries there was intense discussion at the principal centres of political, military, and ecclesiastical power in Latin Christendom, fed by and expressed in a large volume of writing.

In Chapter 3 above, William of Auvergne's view of Muslim population was depicted against a background of earlier and contemporary writings about Islam and the Holy Land, beginning in the first half of the twelfth century and concluding with reports reproduced by Matthew Paris in his chronicle in 1235. Even though the theme of 'recovery' after 1291 imposed a certain direction and sometimes supplied a title, these later Holy Land writings grew out of the earlier ones. There is much continuity of material and ideas. At the same time there is no strict demarcation from the far-eastern material we have just been examining. First seen as a threat and then as potential allies against Islam, the Tartars and their domains and military power came to be a part of 'recovery' literature, just as their faith came to be added to Mahomet's and others' as part of a map of the world's faiths. In another genre, the older and continuing one of the pilgrim's 'itinerary', there was neighbouring and also overlapping material in descriptions of the geography of the Holy Land and other countries passed through, with comments on peoples, faiths, and sometimes military capacity.

Maps were attached to copies of the text of a pilgrim-traveller, Burchard of Mount Sion, and also to the 'recovery' treatises written by the Genoese *medicus* Galvano da Levanto and Marino Sanudo. Comments here and there in such texts seem to be fragments of a larger mental cartography which rests on the knowledge of the near east which had been built up over the two hundred years since the First Crusade. The map is of physical geography, peoples and faiths, and agriculture and population.

[97] See C. J. Tyerman, 'Marino Sanudo Torsello and the Lost Crusade. Lobbying in the Fourteenth Century', *TRHS*, 5th ser. 32 (1982), 57–73. The discussions of this period are brilliantly evoked here and in the same author's 'Philip V of France, the Assemblies of 1319–20 and the Crusade', *Bulletin of the Institute for Historical Research* 57 (1984), 15–34, and 'Philip VI and the recovery of the Holy Land', *EHR* 100 (1985), 25–52.

One example is the 'itinerary' of the Franciscan friar Symon Semeonis, which describes his journey from Ireland to the Holy Land. As Symeon's text has him approaching Cairo he gives an account of Egypt's physical geography, its agriculture, the availability of food, and the cost of travel by water. Cairo's general situation is described, the character of its principal streets, running in a straight line and very crowded, and the numbers of asses kept at street-corners for hire as taxis or for other purposes. Amidst all this is population. Paris had impressed Symeon as 'the most populous of all cities which profess the Christian faith'. Carrying with himself its memory, Symeon used Paris to make a careful point about the relative size and population density of Cairo. 'In our judgement, and saving a better opinion, it is double Paris in size and quadruple in populousness, and if we were to say more we would not be overstepping the bounds of truth.'[98] Another example is the pilgrimage book of an Augustinian, James of Verona. This shows a mind interested in assessing wide areas, for example writing of the Bedouin moving around in groups of one or two hundred families, and describing the Arabian peninsula as a desert containing no cities, towns, or villages, and a nomadic population of something over 100,000.[99]

At the same time the military experts themselves had long been concerned with population in relation to the size of Muslim military resources. There was continuing expression of the old theme of their enormous numbers and the fewness of Christians. Among the 1274 texts there were repetitions of this. The Dominican William of Tripoli repeated the old picture of the Arabs as a great people of almost infinite population,[100] while Humbert of Romans attributed this view to those western Christians who opposed the crusade on the grounds of this particular Christian disadvantage. 'There we are very few in comparison to their multitude.'[101] Writing around 1291, but before the fall of Acre, the Franciscan Fidenzio of Padua insisted on the need for large numbers in a recovering and occupying force, entitling one chapter 'On the numerousness of Christians'.[102]

The detailed figures for Muslim forces by area and type of soldier which are given in one text commissioned by the Master of the knights hospitallers between 1289 and 1291, the *Devise des Chemins*,[103] suggest the precision that counted for the real soldiers, and one of the considerations which comes to dominate the

[98] Symon Semeonis, *Itinerarium al Hybernia ad terram sanctam*, LXVIII; ed. M. Esposito, Scriptores Latini Hiberniae 4 (Dublin, 1960), p. 72. For Symon Paris was the most populous of all Christian cities, ibid., VII; p. 28.

[99] James of Verona, *Liber peregrinationis*, IX; ed. R. Röhricht, 'Le pèlerinage du moine Augustin Jacques de Vérone (1335)', *Revue de l'Orient Latin* 3 (1895), 163–302 (pp. 213 and 248).

[100] William of Tripoli, *De statu Sarracenorum*, XXVII; ed. H. Prutz, *Kulturgeschichte der Kreuzzüge* (Berlin, 1883), p. 591.

[101] Humbert of Romans, *Opusculum tripartitum*, I. xiii; ed. O. Gratius, *Appendix ad fasciculum rerum expetendarum* (London, 1690), p. 193: *nos sumus ibi valde pauci in comparatione ad eorum multitudinem.*

[102] *De Christianorum numerositate*, Fidenzio of Padua, *Liber recuperationis terra sanctae*, XXIV; ed. Golubovich, iii. 28.

[103] *Itinéraires et descriptions de la terre sainte rédigées en français*, ed. H. Michelant and G. Raynaud, Société de l'Orient Latin, Série Géographique 3 (Geneva, 1882), pp. 239–52 ; see the figures by area and for type of soldier, pp. 240–1.

recovery literature indicates that 'vast populations and vast forces' had become an outdated cliché. Present in Fidenzio and Hayton, this theme was the dependence of Egypt on the import of slaves to keep up military numbers. It was given particularly forceful expression by Sanudo, who devoted a chapter to the diminution of inhabitants, and the Dominican William Adam, who wrote flatly that 'the Saracens of Egypt do not have sufficient men of themselves to inhabit it'.[104] The practical-minded Marino advocated Christian forces which were to be efficiently organized and directed, but relatively small.[105]

'Others say that . . .' One of these opinions reported by Humbert of Romans in 1274 concerned population and settlement. 'When we conquer their lands we do not have the people to populate and cultivate them'[106] was the view, echoing Roger Bacon's earlier comment that Christians conquer and then depart, leaving natives to multiply. Recovery literature's second concern was 'once recovered, how to preserve'. The old practical problem of sufficient immigration and settlement had not escaped earlier notice. Jacques de Vitry had commented on the lack of women in respect to men in the earlier Christian armies which supplied the Holy Land's settlers, and the consequent use of the nearest Latin Christian province, Apulia, as a source of supply of women for the settlers to marry.[107] But now it became the second leading theme in theoretical treatises, most of all in Pierre Dubois's famous *De recuperatione terre sancte* (1306–8), whose first part was dedicated to Edward I of England.[108]

Dubois begins with an echo of the older line of Jacques de Vitry. He writes that Muslims dedicate themselves to procreating and rearing as many children as possible, adding the further point that this is 'excepting no one'. In other words Muslim fertility was not held in check by a portion of the population being celibate. Resulting magnitude of population had led to the need to expand, and also the particular result that the Holy Land which the Saracens have now occupied was 'extraordinarily populated' by them, *mirabiliter populata.* Therefore, argued Dubois, this land cannot be occupied and *kept* occupied except by a very large number.[109] This introduces a treatise in which Dubois's 'populationist-colonial' outlook is often displayed, both in these ideas and in the prominence of such words (and their variants) as 'populate', 'inhabit', 'multitude' and 'settlers': *populare, inhabitare, multitudo, incolae.*[110] In the west the schools, which are to be insti-

[104] Marino Sanudo, *Liber secretorum fidelium crucis*, I. ii. 2; ed. J. Bongars, *Gesta Dei per Francos*, 2 vols. (Hanover, 1611), ii. 26; William Adam, *De modo Sarracenos extirpandi*, I; in *Recueil des historiens des croisades: Documents arméniens*, 2 vols. (Paris, 1869–1906), ii. 523: *Sarraceni Egipti non habent . . . sufficienter homines ad eam inhabitandum.* On William, see *SOPMA* ii. 81–2.

[105] Tyerman, 'Marino Sanudo', pp. 63–4.

[106] Humbert, *Opusculum*, I. xvi; p. 196: *quando obtinemus terras eorum, non habemus qui populant eas et excolant.*

[107] Jacques de Vitry, *Historia orientalis*, LXVIII; p. 125.

[108] P. Dubois, *De recuperatione terre sancte*, ed. C.-V. Langlois (Paris, 1891); many nuances of meaning are lost in W. I. Brandt's translation, P. Dubois, *The Recovery of the Holy Land* (New York, 1956).

[109] Dubois, *De recuperatione*, II; ed. Langlois, pp. 2–3.

[110] Note the language in the conclusion to Marino Sanudo's *Liber secretorum*, III. xv. 25 (ii. 208), which

tuted for the education of the boys and girls who are to emigrate to the Holy Land, are to be located according to the resources and population of particular regions.[111] Dubois envisages waves of immigrants coming into the Holy Land. As many 'colonists' as possible are to be sent out. Exile is to be used as a judicial punishment on western Christians 'in order to populate the Holy Land'. Intermarriage is to be an instrument of policy: girls well-instructed in the Christian faith 'are to be distributed in marriage to infidels'.[112]

The depth of Dubois's knowledge of Aristotle's *Politics* singles him out among the 'recovery' authors. He had heard Siger of Brabant lecturing on the *Politics* in Paris, and his own familarity is shown by his treatise's quotations from, or use of, passages from at least six of the eight books of the *Politics*. Now, book 2 of the *Politics* raised explicitly the theme of paucity of men, in relation to Sparta and a decline in its military numbers, and it discusses remedies, including the policy 'to induce (*provocare*) citizens to have more children'. Dubois does not directly depend on this passage, but his ready acquaintance with the *Politics* is very likely to have been an intellectual stimulus on this point.

One theme which *may* be present in Dubois' treatise is advocacy of the highest possible proportion of the occupying population being married and, consequently, opposition to their numbers including religious celibates. It was an obvious idea, alluded to in passing by Humbert thirty years earlier, when he wrote that the consequence of fearing fewness of numbers of Christians would be the rejection of virginity and the encouragement of everyone to marry, in order to multiply Christians.[113] Taken together, the initial point about Muslims 'excepting no one', Dubois's concern to reduce the numbers of inmates in western nunneries, and the enthusiasm with which Dubois envisaged western Christian girls marrying eastern clerics in the Holy Land[114] may well have hinted to a reader a thought which it would not have been politic to spell out. Among people who were thinking about how to ensure expansion of the new colonists' population there was certainly some toying with extreme ideas, one of which is glimpsed through Peter of la Palud's discussion of papal power of dispensation of the laws of marriage. The pope could not dispense the law against plurality of wives for any sort of necessity whatsoever, he wrote. Allowing plurality of wives would not be licit even 'for the necessity of Outremer, to bring about the multiplying of those inhabiting there'.[115]

Both in the earlier period which was discussed in Chapter 3 and in the later thirteenth and early fourteenth centuries, all these experiences—the conquering of the Holy Land, its occupation, preoccupation with the size of Saracen forces,

deals with 'how more easily and effectively to attract new colonists' to the Holy Land, *ad novos autem colonos gratius et utilius provocandos*.

[111] Dubois, *De recuperatione*, LX, ed. Langlois, p. 49: *secundum . . . populorum multitudines*.

[112] Ibid., IV and LXXXVI; pp. 7 and 71.

[113] Humbert, *Opusculum*, I. xii; p. 193.

[114] Dubois, *De recuperatione*, II, LXI, and CII; pp. 2, 51, and 82. See Brandt, p. 119 n. 18.

[115] Peter of la Palud, *In sententias*, IV. xxxiii. Q. 1 art. 1; 166ra: [*papa non*] *potest in pluralitatem uxorum, quod est contra legem naturalem, dispensare propter quamcunque necessitatem, puta ultramarinam, ut ibi multiplicentur habitatores*.

getting to know near-eastern geography, grappling with the effects on population of the permission of plurality of wives, and planning for a sufficiency of colonizing population—generated a rich complex of demographic thought. And it was the combination of thought about this area, thought about the Tartars, and more learned academic thought directed towards the limits of the habitable world, which brought about a very remarkable development in demographic thought, the creation of an elementary world 'population-geography' of faiths.

9.5 *The whole world*

So far we have seen populationist thought and awareness mapping *parts* of the world, Latin Christendom and the near east, the first driven by economic and demographic expansion, the second by the medieval equivalent of the problem faced today by Israel's colonists. We have seen the expansion of the area of the known habitable world, now to include the thinly inhabited Mongolian steppes and the enormous populations of mainland China. Based on the experience and preoccupations of rulers, soldiers, merchants, and missionaries, this is all at bottom empirical, but it coexisted with knowledge which was academic. This latter was the learning expressed in Sacrobosco's *De spera* and Albert's *De natura loci*, which mainly rested on a received earlier tradition of geographic knowledge, and envisaged a whole—the whole sphere of the earth and its habitable parts. Did the empirical and the abstract learned pictures connect? Clearly to some degree. Both Albert and Peter d'Abano used contemporary knowledge to press upon the limits of the world's habitability as laid down in classical geography.[116] But did they fuse in any deeper way? Was there any dim groping towards a sense of world population?

Yes—but not in a form which anticipates a United Nations Survey. Thought in this direction was encouraged by one rather arcane area of academic theology, and by concern about the faiths of the world. Theologians found singular freedom, as we saw in Chapter 4, when speculating about paradise and what would have happened if man had not sinned. Such themes as terrestrial paradise as a proportion of the world, the immortality of people in it, their numbers, and their eventual translation to celestial life encouraged thought about large spaces and large numbers, literally global thought. Let us look at a peculiar example found in an early Oxford commentary on the *Sentences*, produced by the Dominican Richard Fishacre.

Fishacre addresses the notion that there would have been generation in paradise until the completion of the number of the elect, at which point all would have transferred to a higher state. 'This part', wrote Fishacre, 'seems less probable

[116] There is a fine discussion of this theme, extension of the view of the habitable world, in P. G. Dalché, 'Les savoirs géographiques en méditerranée chrétienne (XIIIe s.)', in *Le scienze alla corte di Federico II*, *Micrologus* 2 (1994), 75–99 (pp. 76–83).

to me. I do not yet understand how such a little place as earthly paradise would be enough for such a great multitude [as is the multitude] of the saved.' He quotes, 'I saw a great multitude, which no man could number' (Apocalypse 7: 9). 'Since therefore this place, that is to say paradise, does not at all have the capacity for innumerable people . . . it is clear that this part [of Peter the Lombard's text] does not appear to be true.' After a brief reference to the numbers of the saved in the *City of God* he turns back to the size of a given area of the world, its capacity to hold people, and numbers.

One Arabic author whose astronomic-geographic work transmitted classical geographers' measurements of the globe was Al-Farghani, known as Alfraganus to our authors. His work had been translated into Latin twice in the twelfth century, and it was known to men who taught earlier in Oxford, to Alexander Nequam and to Robert Grosseteste. At roughly the same time as Fishacre was using Alfraganus in Oxford, he was also being imported into commentary on these distinctions in Paris. Alfraganus, then, provides Fishacre with his numbers. 'A fourth of the earth', he writes, 'that is to say the surface of a fourth, has 33,099,000 *miliaria* [square miles], according to Alfraganus, in *differentia* 8 [of his work].'[117] In fact, 33,104,100 would be better for the figures with which he was working. 'Now', Fishacre continues, 'a *miliare* contains 4,000 cubits. Therefore the whole surface of this fourth contains 132,396,000,000 cubits [= 33,099,000 × 4,000]. Therefore give each man six feet of space, and the whole fourth will be filled with this number of men, that is, 33,099,000,000.'[118] Fishacre goes on to the reduction to absurdity. A man *can* count this great multitude. Therefore the number of the elect (innumerable) is greater than this figure. Therefore there is a problem with the capacity of paradise.

Alfraganus had used 20,400 miles as the circumference of the earth; 6491 (rounded down by Fishacre to 6490) as its diameter (announced as dividing the first figure by π, which to him was three and one seventh); and a multiplication of circumference by diameter and division by four to arrive at 'the measure of the whole of a fourth part of the habitable world'. Just as in manuscripts of Fishacre, the figures vary in editions of the Latin translations of Alfraganus, and more research would be needed to establish the precise version of Alfraganus or perhaps an intermediary source which Fishacre used. But the figures are both very large

[117] The reference is to Ch. 8 of Alfraganus, *Liber de aggregationibus*, which provides measurements for the circumference and diameter of the earth. On Alfraganus see A. I. Sabra, 'Al-Farghānī', *DSB* iv. 541–5, and on the two twelfth-century translations R. Lemay, 'Gerard of Cremona', *DSB*, xv. 173–92 (p. 178). For the figures and their calculation, see Gerard's translation, Alfragano, *Il 'Libro dell'aggregazione delle stelle' (Dante, Conv., II, vi-134) secondo il codice Mediceo-Laurenziano PL. 29-Cod.* 9, VIII, ed. R. Campani (Città di Castello, 1910), pp. 89–90, and Campani's commentary, ibid., pp. 86–7 n. 1. I have not tried to identify which translation Fishacre (or his source) was using.

[118] I provide here the text from BL, MS Royal X.B.7, fol. 145ra, with variants from B [= Bologna, University Library, MS 1546, fol. 146vb], O [= Oxford, Oriel College, MS 43, fol. 186rb], P [= BN, MS Lat. 15754, fol. 107vb], V [= Vatican, MS Ottob. Lat. 294, fol. 339vb]:
Quomodo enim tam parvus locus ut est paradisus terrestris tante multitudini salvandorum sufficeret nondum intelligo . . . Ergo cum ille locus, scilicet paradisus, non sit capax innumerabilium . . . patet quod hec pars non videtur vera. . . . Quarta quidem terre, scilicet superficies quarte, habet miliaria 33,099,000 [a], *miliare*

and very close (33,105,000 in one edition, compared to Fishacre's 33,099,000) and the detailed citation of Alfraganus leaves no doubt about the ultimate source.

What can we say about what Fishacre's building on top of Alfraganus? Fishacre is taking an easy line with the maths of the large numbers, for his last figure is simply the first with three noughts added. Since the distinction between linear and square measurement was elementary and commonplace in contemporary textbooks, we should invoke something other than elementary error to explain Fishacre's quick and silent transition from area to linear measure. He envisages rectangles with two sides measuring one mile, and stretches a thousand men along each side at six-foot intervals. There is, then, for each man a strip measuring six feet by one mile.[119] All I can suggest is that where higher density and six-feet square might more readily spring to the mind of a man thinking of people in a town, lower density and thinking in terms of strips would be the image most likely to spring to the mind of a man thinking of people in the countryside: people visibly engaged in farming fields which were divided into strips. A man thinking of Oxfordshire rather than Oxford? That is conjectural. What we can do is juxtapose speculations separated by a century. When alluding to numbers generated since Adam and Eve, and writing in the first half of the twelfth century, Hugh of St Victor could do no more than allude weakly to thousands.[120] More than a century later Fishacre seizes the opportunity of a 'what if' theme to produce something which, however creaking and primitive, is nevertheless a significant early step. He takes the notional habitable quarter of the globe's surface, produces a large figure for its measurement, hypothesizes a given 'distribution' or 'density', and then extracts and states the resulting very high number of people. In one sense it is obviously an example of very abstract thought. It conjectures what *would be* the very large number of overall population, were the inhabitable quarter of the globe to be populated with an unvarying extreme density. That in itself suggests that the same mind could *think* the counterpart of this, namely the (extraordinarily) lower but still large figure, which would result from the varying and lower density inhabitation of the same habitable quarter of the globe.

vero habet cubitos 4,000, ergo tota superficies quarte habet cubitos 132,396,000,000 [b]. *Ergo da cuilibet homini sex pedes spacii, et inplebitur tota quarta tali numero hominum, scilicet 33,099,000,000. Sed talem numerum denumerare homo potest.*

[a] O: 33,190,000; P has 33,140,000 crossed out, and then the same figure.

[b] B: 137,396,000,000; V: 132, 356,000,000.

Fishacre's argument attracted critical attention from the Franciscan Richard Rufus, commenting on the *Sentences* in Oxford around 1250 (on the commentary, see Catto, 'Theology and Theologians', pp. 489–50). Rufus wrote: *Volunt autem quidam per comparacionem miliariorum quarte habitabilis terre ostendere quod tota superficies illius quarte non sufficeret omnibus salvandis. . . . non curo de hoc. Potuit enim Deus eis parare locum habitabilem maiorem vel minorem pro sua voluntate, et quartas plures si vellet*; Oxford, Balliol, MS 62, fol. 150va.

119 One problem among arithmetical examples in a fourteenth-century text—'how many hares there are in an acre if you give each one foot in length and a half in width?'—may come from a common tradition of such calculations; M. Curtze, 'Arithmetische Scherzaufgaben aus dem 14. Jahrhundert', *Bibliotheca Mathematica*, n.s. 9 (1895), 77–88 (p. 84),where Curze says that Gerbert (Sylvester II, d. 1003) posed a similar problem. Fishacre's long strip may be a deliberate diversion from this tradition.

120 Hugh of St Victor, *De sacramentis*, I. vi. 37; *PL* 176, 286.

Out in the real world, one hard reality with which men and especially clerics grappled was the number of Christians and the size of Christendom, and the dwarfing of Christian numbers and size by all the other faiths in the world. Thinking about this came nearer to, and then fused with, the learned geographical view of the globe. 'We Christians are few, the whole wide world is full of unbelievers': so Roger Bacon, in the 1260s, and this became a commonplace.[121] In Chapter 3 we saw the impact of the observation that the Saracens occupied much of the world, in the shrinking of men's sense of the size of the Christian part of it, and Peter the Venerable's articulation of this in his description of the size of the Christian proportion: a half or a third. The line on the graph representing western Christians' view of their own numbers and size in relation to the world continued downwards, albeit with one large blip. Briefly taken seriously at the highest level, by the pope and the crusaders encamped at Damietta in 1221, this was a piece of wishful thinking: credulity in a story that a Christian prince, King David (Prester John), was advancing from the far east with vast military numbers.[122] This had soon been replaced by a reality—Tartars advancing from the far east—which had varied effects. On the one hand it expanded the known world and its faiths and thereby broadly accelerated the shrinking of Latin Christians, while on the other hand it encouraged more moderation in looking at Saracen size and numbers. At the same time the unexpected numbers of oriental Christians in the far east helped to fill out and vary earlier observation of faiths in the near east, an example of which can be seen in Jacques de Vitry's *Historia orientalis.* Many of its chapters constitute, essentially, a geography of faiths. It begins with the Holy Land, but spreads out from it, looking first at Muslims and different Muslim groups, proceeding to pagans who rejected Mahomet's law (in Bulgaria and Cumania), and going on to include a variety of oriental Christians (Jacobites, Maronites, Georgians, Nestorians, Armenians, and Mozarabs) and various Jewish groups.

By 1300 the texts are increasingly displaying isolated patches of a 'population-geography' of these faiths. Through Ricoldo's writing, for example, there is a Baghdad of about 200,000 Saracens and several thousand Jews and oriental Christians, while James of Verona gives a figure of 30,000 for the numbers of oriental Christians in Egypt.[123] Texts come to have a section or a chapter devoted to the division of the world's parts according to faiths. In the mid-1260s Roger Bacon announces this as his intention in one part of his *Opus Maius*, though he only intermittently lives up to the plan, in 1274 Humbert had a brief stab at it,[124] and it continued in the fourteenth century. Marino Sanudo advised considering to what a small space of countries Catholics have been reduced, following this with a brief but efficient survey. 'Many scattered Christians inhabit other parts of Asia . . . a

[121] Southern, *Western Views of Islam*, p. 57; Ramon Lull, *Liber de fine*, in Lull, *Opera Latina*, IX, CCCM 35 (Turnhout, 1981), p. 250.

[122] Southern, *Western Views*, pp. 45–7.

[123] Ricoldo, *Itinerarium*, XXXIX; ed. J. C. M. Laurent, *Peregrinatores medii aevi quatuor* (Leipzig, 1873), p. 127; James, *Liber peregrinationis*, VIII; p. 244.

[124] Humbert, *Opusculum*, I. vi; p. 188.

few of the faithful inhabit Africa, albeit oppressed under the Saracen yoke.' Designed to make clear the residue which is inhabited by Latin Christians, Sanudo sketches their perimeter, in Spain, Romania, Hungary, Poland, and finally north to Lithuania.[125] There survives from 1332 a text which shows how remarkably this area of thought could develop. Already referred to, this was a 'recovery' treatise sent in by a Dominican to the king of France, Philip VI.[126] The author, who describes himself as having worked among infidels for twenty-four years, is said to have been Raymond Stephani, a friar from the Toulouse province who had preached in Persia and India and had been made Archbishop of Corinth in 1322. A separate section of his treatise is devoted to the second reason for crusade, expanding Christendom.[127] Latin Christians have been reduced. They are confined to a very tiny little bit of the inhabited world. Indeed, if the inhabited world were to be divided into ten parts, Latin Christians would not constitute one-tenth.[128] The author will demonstrate this.

The first argument has the author restating classical geography, which in the second argument he will attack. A quarter of the world is habitable; one half of that is taken by Asia, and the remaining half is sub-divided into two parts, one for Europe, one for Africa. In Africa there are no Christian people. Asia has many peoples and innumerable Christians, but these are not of the true Christian faith. That leaves only Europe. In Europe there are many pagan peoples bordering the Germans and Poles. There are Saracens in parts of Spain. Further to be excluded are the Ruthenians, Bulgarians, and inhabitants of Slavonia (roughly modern Yugoslavia). The author has no need to spell out the clear result of this first argument, namely 'much less than one quarter'.

The point can be demonstrated otherwise, writes the author, proceeding to his next proposition. This is that one section of the inhabited world devoid of Latin Christians is larger than is thought. He alludes to ancient geographers, without naming one in particular, writing that in the 'description of climates'—the ancient division of the globe into parallel horizontal strips—Asia is designated as having half the inhabited world. In fact, however, it has far more. He raises a historical question about past scholarship—why was Asia's capacity not adequately described?—and comes up with two conjectures. Either Asia was not so inhabited in *those* times, as, by implication, it is now. Or it *was* so inhabited, but this fact did not come to the attention of those writing descriptions of the world. An analogy is the way that we find places and provinces inhabited towards the Arctic pole, which are clearly beyond the last 'climate'. That is to say, these habitations exist,

[125] Marino Sanudo, *Liber secretorum*, I. v. 1; ii. 32.

[126] *Directorium ad passagium faciendum, Recueil des historiens des croisades: Documents arméniens*, ii. 367–517. *SOPMA* iii. 287–8, states that Raymond Stephani was the author; the work is given as anonymous in Tyerman, 'Philip VI', p. 35.

[127] *Directorium, De secundo motivo ad passagium faciendum*; pp. 381–5.

[128] Ibid.; p. 382: *Si enim, ut alias asserui et probavi, mundi pars habitata per homines in decem divideretur partes, nos qui veri Christiani sumus et dicimur orthodoxi, decima pars non sumus, qui tamen consuevimus esse totum.*

despite the fact that in the geography of 'climatic strips' there should be no human habitation north of the last strip.[129]

The author presents his third point as based on what he has seen and experienced himself, when travelling among peoples to preach the faith. In doing this he has crossed the equator, as have also trustworthy merchants. In other words, his own experience proves the truth of one disputed point in learned geography, the habitability of the world beyond the equator. In his recapitulation the author states that beyond the climates 'there is more inhabited to the east and the south', and adds that 'it is neither vain nor frivolous to designate the Antipodes [as habitable]'. The result is that Latin Christians are not just not a tenth, they are not even a twentieth part of the inhabited world.[130] The author had 'asserted and proved' all this elsewhere.[131] In other words, Raymond had written another work, earlier, in which he demonstrated more systematically that Latin Christians form less than a twentieth of the world. Unfortunately the work is lost.

Trustworthy merchants had also crossed the equator, and their experience, according to this Dominican, supported this expanded view of the inhabited world, in which Latin Christians were such a diminishing fraction, not even one twentieth of the whole world. Invoking their experience, the Dominican's text reminds us of *their* world-population view, clearly one that existed but has left no more than this indirect trace in a clerical text.

[129] Reading of Albert's *De natura loci* could be behind this point.

[130] *Directorium*, p. 384.

[131] See above, n. 128.

Part 3

ARISTOTLE AND MULTITUDE

10[1]

ANIMALS AND LIFE-SPAN

'Fat men are sometimes frigid . . . we have learnt the same about [fat] women', wrote William of Auvergne in his treatise *De matrimonio*. How had William *learnt* this? 'We have learnt this same thing from women, not from men's rumours or [general] opinion, [but] from experience itself and with certainty, in statements given in confession.'[2] William is footnoting himself, claiming evidence for his assertion, but other priests who heard confessions and wrote treatises did not make this point. The question remains, why was this particular confessor noticing the point, and then remembering it and writing about it?

It is easy to point to suggestive reading. William knew Aristotle's *On Animals* and he read widely in Avicenna. In the Latin translation of Aristotle used by William there occurred the proposition 'Very fat men rarely generate . . . and this happens similarly with [fat] women.' There was a wider but related statement in Avicenna's *On Animals*. 'Men whose complexion resembles womens' complexion will be fat, and their sperm will not be fertile.'[3] William did not copy these statements, which are not exactly the same as his, but reading Aristotle and Avicenna had programmed him. Alerted by the negative correlation between fatness and generative power, his mind was *now* ready to notice statements he heard from women in confession, about fat men and love-making, or from men about fat women, and his pen was now ready to report their observations.

William read these Greek and Arabic works in Latin translations which had only recently been made. Newly available texts were supplying William with information and sometimes spurring him to a particular thought. We have already met some other examples of this, in Chapter 7, where we saw newly

[1] In my references to Aristotle, the references containing digits sandwiching the letter 'a' or 'b' (e.g. 493a10) relate to the Bekker edition of the Greek text, and are given here because of their widespread use in such standard editions and translations as the Oxford Aristotle, Loeb, and Budé. Thus '493a10' will send the reader to D. W. Thompson's translation of the *Historia animalium*, in *The Works of Aristotle*, ed. J. A. Smith and W. D. Ross, 12 vols. (Oxford, 1910–52), iv, an otherwise unpaginated volume which contains these numbers in the margins—or to A. L. Peck and D. M. Balme's translation of the same work in the Loeb series, 3 vols. (Cambridge, Mass., 1965–91). Usually I only cite particular editions where they present the medieval Latin text.

[2] *De matrimonio*, IX; p. 525a.

[3] Aristotle, *De animalibus* (Scot), p. 39 [726a3–4]: *homines valde pingues raro generant . . . et similiter etiam accidit mulieribus*; Avicenna, *De animalibus*, XV. iii; 60vb: *mares quorum complexio assimilatur complexioni feminarum erunt pingues, et illorum sperma non erit generativum.*

translated medical works providing more knowledge about deliberate avoidance of offspring, and Chapter 3 where newly translated works on sex-determination were part of the intellectual climate in which Paris theologians began to think the thought of sex-ratio at birth and in the population. These were incidental to the main thrust of Part 1 of this book, but the broader phenomenon which they represent now becomes our main theme in Part 3. The most important development in the intellectual history of Latin Christendom in the central middle ages was translation. During this period the bulk of Greek and Arabian moral and natural philosophy and medicine was translated into Latin, circulated, absorbed, understood, and packaged to form the curriculum of institutions of higher learning, universities, and the higher *studia* of religious orders. This truth about western intellectual history in general is applied here to one sub-area of medieval thought. What was the impact of the translations from Greek and Arabic on 'demographic thought'? This is a question mainly about the Latin Aristotle.

There is an ascending significance in the order and size of treatment in Part 3. This chapter deals first with works which supplied a dense backcloth for 'demographic' thought, providing very detailed and plausible data about reproduction, and then, secondly, one 'demographic' theme, life-span. We shall concentrate on the treatises by Aristotle which were known in the middle ages as *On animals*, and in particular among these the *History of Animals* and the *Generation of animals*; Aristotle's tract *Length and Shortness of Life*; and a work attributed to Aristotle, the *Problems*. In addition there are Avicenna's *On Animals*, which contains much from Aristotle, and Averroes's epitome of *Length and Shortness of Life*. Set alongside these is just one representative and important example of medical texts, Avicenna's *Canon of Medicine*. The following three chapters address the most important moral-philosophical text, Aristotle's *Politics*. In the case of each text we shall be looking first at translation or translations, the diffusion of copies, the genesis of commentaries, and evidence for study in universities. In all of this we shall be using, principally, the data assembled by those scholars who have collaborated in the remarkable project to edit and study the transmission of the Latin translations of Aristotle, *Aristoteles Latinus*. Secondly we shall survey what was transmitted by the translated text, its themes and its distinctive and sometimes new vocabulary, before turning to look at how these texts were read. Earlier in this book we saw multiple, complex, and discernible connections between the realities of individuals living in a parish and discussion of marriage in the theology schools. Here by contrast we are dealing with a confined area of study, the Arts faculty and men reading newly arrived philosophical works, and the relationship of thought with the world outside is both narrower and more delicate and conjectural to establish. How do the preferences of the commentators show us glimpses of a thought-world formed, in part, by their reactions to the 'demographic' realities of the milieux in which they were living? How were the translated texts altering western capacity for 'demographic' thought?

10.1 The reproductive data and 'demographic' contents of the translations

'Forced by the lack of Latin [authors]', and 'among Latin books I could find no author that gave certain and reliable information.'[4] These phrases were written by two mid-eleventh-century monks at Monte Cassino called Alphanus and Constantine the African, as they explained why they had turned to texts on medicine and the physical nature of man written in Greek and Arabic, translating them into Latin. However qualified by a few earlier translations of medical works around the sixth century in Ravenna and evidence of continuity in southern Italy, the broad picture is there in the translators' commonplaces. There was a lack of learned medical texts in Latin in the west, and at the same time riches in Greek in Byzantium and in Arabic in Kairouan in north Africa and other advanced Muslim cities.[5] It was with the labours of Alphanus and Constantine that the serious business of putting this material into Latin got under way.

Some of the best modern study of the resulting translations has focused on the cultural construction of gender in past biology or medicine.[6] Here I shall not comment on gender. My theme is different and my starting-point more elementary. There were vast amounts of careful, detailed, and plausible data—biological and zoological in Aristotle's works on animals, descriptive of illnesses and wounds in the medical treatises. A fundamental fact of medieval history is the poverty of such material in the period up to about 1050, and the abundant and massive presence of such material which was brought about by the translating effort of the central middle ages. There was, further, remarkable communion between a natural philosophy in which biology played a large part, and a medicine which was very philosophical and drew much from Aristotle—matches which pitted Aristotle and medicine as opposing fighters took place precisely because of this.

Animals loomed large among the themes upon which Aristotle had accumulated encyclopaedic information, which was now transmitted to Christendom in Latin: the generation of animals, their mating patterns, their offsprings' inheritance of characteristics, the determination of their sex, their adaptation to their surroundings, their struggle for existence, their movement, growth, and nutrition. Large numbers of facts were collected and displayed in the very large *History of Animals*, organized according to various sorts of classification of animals and their qualities and parts and their degrees of similarity (e.g. *with* blood *or* bloodless), while the *Generation of Animals* addressed only the theme of its title. Sense and sensation, memory, length of life, and death were addressed individually in short tracts, which by the late thirteenth century were called *Parva Naturalia*, *The Little Natural Works*. Among the fundamental concepts informing this (in

[4] H. Bloch, *Monte Cassino in the Middle Ages*, 3 vols. (Cambridge, Mass.), i. 98 n. 5 and 103.

[5] See the map in Jacquart and Micheau, pp. 16–17.

[6] D. Jacquart and C. Thomasset, *Sexuality and Medicine in the Middle Ages*, trans. M. Adamson (Oxford, 1988); J. Cadden, *Meanings of Sex Difference in the Middle Ages: Medicine, Science and Culture* (Cambridge, 1993).

modern terms) zoological and biological material were the notions that all terrestrial bodies are composed of the four elements of fire, air, earth, and water; that natural things are mutable and in a process of 'coming-to-be and passing away', which was the title of one treatise, *Generation and Corruption*; and that life consists in the combination of warmth and moisture, and that its passing away and extinction come through the inevitable progression towards coldness and dryness. The thesaurus of words and phrases in which these themes, data, and theories were articulated was an inseparable element of what was transmitted.

Self-evidently narrower than this broad philosophical approach to all forms of terrestrial life was the concern in medical works with the human animal alone and with the preservation of health in the body and the cure of illness. Considerable amounts of data were assembled and systematized about the organization and functions of the body, its illnesses and malfunctions, and remedies. In the underpinning theory, prominent roles were played by the primary qualities of hot, cold, wet, and dry, whose balance made up a person's 'complexion', and the bodily fluids, blood, phlegm, red bile, and black bile, which constituted their 'humours' (sanguinary, phlegmatic, choleric, melancholic) and which were themselves 'complexionate'. These, together with age and sex, constituted the so-called 'naturals', while environment, air and region, exercise, food and drink, ingestion and evacuation made up the 'non-naturals. Complexional and humoral make-up varied both naturally and unnaturally. Thus a person's complexion was innate and natural according to sex—for example, the female was colder and damper; according to age—for example, old age was colder and drier; and region, and people's adaptation to a particular region's dampness or dryness, and heat or cold. At the same time complexion could go out of balance. This happened, for example, if someone whose natural complexion derived in part from a hot and dry region moved to live in a region which was cold and damp.

Aristotle's works *On Animals* and his *Little Natural Works* contained a large number of statements which both formed a backcloth to and also helped to contribute towards or to stimulate 'demographic' thought. Much was purely biological material, that is to say, data on human reproduction, where facts could slide into 'demographic thoughts' as they became the subject of generalizing, comparative, and quantitative statements. As I summarize this material in the following paragraph, I am following in the footsteps of the (usually anonymous) authors of anthologies entitled *Flowers* or *Authorities*, texts which were used by well-read Arts students of moderate ability, living around and after 1300. One such was the *Auctoritates Aristotelis*, compiled after 1280 and perhaps around 1300, and very popular, as its 153 still extant copies attest.[7] For many Aristotelian treatises it provides a brief anthology, simply listing a certain number of dicta taken from (or associated with) a treatise. Turning to its extracts from the *Length and Shortness of Life* the student found such sentences as 'Labour dries out and

[7] *Auctoritates Aristotelis*, pp. 24–35. This edition is based on early printed editions rather than the medieval manuscripts.

induces old age, and therefore those who labour much age more', followed by others taken from Averroes's epitome, for example, 'On account of paucity of coitus . . . females live more than males.'[8] Immediate context, connecting argument, and underlying principles, except where these are presented in a quotable extract, are omitted, and a complex philosophical original is reduced to a student's crib. In order to give an idea of what came across to readers in the Arts faculty, the following paragraphs imitate the *Authorities*, uprooting reproductive and demographic propositions from the texts in which they originated.[9]

Ages of generation and the generative span are addressed. The age at which intercourse begins varies,[10] but in any one kind of animal it is fairly standard.[11] The man as a rule begins to produce seed at 14,[12] and menses start in females at about the same time.[13] There is a difference between the age at which semen begins to be secreted and the age of generation. Men, though secreting from the age of 14, do not become able to generate until about 21; their seed is at first infertile and then becomes fertile.[14] Men can generate up to 60, or, if they exceed this, up to 70, while menses cease in most women about 40, but, when they exceed this age, some continue up to 50. None have continued longer. These later spans—men continuing to 70, women to 50—occur infrequently, and few people at these ages produce children. Generally the limit for men is 65, for women 45.[15] Age decreases both sexes' capacity for sex and conception,[16] and women who desire sex intemperately become settled and restrained after a number of births.[17] Within the generative span there are better and worse ages for conceiving. The offspring of the young—the too young—tend to be small, weak, and imperfect.[18] Young females conceive more readily, but having conceived they have more trouble in childbirth.[19] By 21 women have reached a good condition for child-bearing, and continue to improve thereafter.[20]

The breeding habits of humans are compared and contrasted to those of animals. For example, unlike other animals they are not seasonal, breeding in any season.[21] Home-building and monogamy have their parallels in bird-nesting and pigeons' keeping to single mates,[22] while comparison with human incest taboos is implicit in description of avoidance of sexual relations between female camels and horses and their male offspring.[23]

The physical conditions in women which are necessary for conception are regular but not excessive menstruation,[24] and appropriate condition of the womb. To

[8] Ibid., pp. 205 no. 117 and 206 no. 122.

[9] Modern editions of the medieval Latin *Historia animalium* have not yet been published, but the modern edition of the *Auctoritates Aristotelis*, pp. 209–17, provides the extracts quoted for that anthology.

[10] 544b12. [11] 544b20. [12] 544b25–6 and 581a12.

[13] 581a33–4. Also 727a4–6, Aristotle, *De gen. an.* (Scot), p. 42; (Moerbeke), p. 30.

[14] 582a17–32. [15] 545b27–31; 585b1–8. [16] 546a34.

[17] 582a25–6; 774a3–4; *De gen. an.* (Scot), p. 197; (Moerbeke), p. 143.

[18] 544b17–18. [19] 582a19–20. [20] 582a29. [21] 542a24–5.

[22] 612b18–20 and 612b32–613a8. [23] 630b32–631a8.

[24] 727b12–13; *De gen. an.* (Scot), p. 44; (Moerbeke), p. 32.

bring about conception, bring the womb to this opportune condition; to avoid conception, do the opposite. 'This is why some people oil that part of the womb with cedar oil . . .'[25] In a regularly menstruating woman conception occurs at the end of her period. While there is little further detail here, since the matter pertained more strictly to medicine, there is much on variations in fertility. There is individual variation. Some women do not menstruate, and some men remain virtually eunuchs.[26] Among women who do not conceive, some are enabled to do so by medical treatment. Fat men and women rarely generate, or are less prolific. There is variation with age. Some do not generate when younger, and only do so when older, or the other way round. Some generate females when young and males when older, or the other way round.[27] Some husbands and wives cannot produce with each other, but can with others. Some cannot generate when young, but can when older.[28] The same applies to the sex of offspring. Some husbands and wives produce males or females with each other, but the other sex when paired with others. Some women have difficulty conceiving, but after conceiving they bear to term; others conceive easily, but cannot bear to term.[29] Region and the qualities of a region—hot or cold, wet or dry—also produce variation, for example in some regions there is little generation, in others the generation of women.[30] On numbers of offspring produced on one occasion, humans are set within a wider range of animals, capable of production of one, several or many, but, usually and according to nature, only one.[31] In a particular region—Egypt is the example—more twins may be produced.[32]

One book of the *Generation of Animals* books is devoted to the determination of the sex of the baby. Ages and environment are invoked, with one or other sort of imperfection sometimes causing the generation of females. The young and the elderly are more likely to generate females, the mature to generate males. Those with more humid or female-like bodies are more likely to generate females.[33] The qualities of a region can affect the issue of fertility and sterility and the generation of one sex more than another,[34] and also the prevailing wind.[35]

Pregnancy is addressed in various ways. The theme of health and pregnancy is raised, and the period of gestation and incidence of miscarriages are discussed. Menstruation ceases upon conception; in a few women it continues, but this is rare. Most miscarriages occur early; their incidence in the fourth or eighth months brings much risk to the mother. Whereas the period of gestation is fixed among animals, it varies among humans,[36] from seven to ten months, with even a

[25] 583a17–27.

[26] 746b23–4; *De gen. an.* (Scot), p. 107; (Moerbeke), p. 78.

[27] Also 723a26–7; *De gen. an.* (Scot), p. 29; (Moerbeke), p. 22.

[28] 767a24–8; *De gen. an.* (Scot), p. 174–5; (Moerbeke), p. 127.

[29] 585b9–20.

[30] See also 909a32–5 (*Problems*, XIV. v; *Problemata Aristotelis*, 149rb), where warm and damp regions are conducive to female offspring.

[31] 772b2–3; *De gen. an.* (Scot), p. 192; (Moerbeke), pp. 139–40.

[32] 584b30–5.

[33] 766b29–32; *De gen. an.* (Scot), p. 173; (Moerbeke), p. 126.

[34] 767a28; *De gen. an.* (Scot), p. 175; (Moerbeke), p. 127.

[35] 766b34; *De gen. an.* (Scot), p. 173; (Moerbeke), p. 126.

[36] 772b8–10; *De gen. an.* (Scot), pp. 192–3; (Moerbeke), p. 140.

few women going to eleven. Babies born before seven months do not survive, while seven-month babies are the earliest that are capable of surviving. Fewer eight-month babies survive; more do not. [These passages present the following pattern: better survival for seven-month babies, worse for eight-month, and then better for nine- and ten-month babies]. Where survival is surprising or where there are reports of very long pregnancies, a mistake in calculation may explain things: a mother's mistake about the date of the conception.[37] There is regional variation in the survival of eight-month babies. Survival is good in Egypt and in places where women are good at giving birth and bearing lots of babies with ease, but in Greece few survive and the majority perish.

Whereas most animals give birth with little or no pain, humans do not. There are varying degrees of difficulty.[38] As already mentioned, age and region affect this. Young girls experience difficulty,[39] while women in some regions do it easily, and in others not. There are two more categories: women who work or are sedentary, and women who are weak-chested. Those who are sedentary and weak-chested experience difficulty, since the ability to control breathing determines the ease or difficulty of childbirth. One translation of *On Animals* makes it clear that among some peoples, where women work hard, the ability to control breathing will be higher and childbirth easier.[40]

The themes of defectiveness and mortality among babies appear briefly. At birth babies of either sex may be born defective. However, among humans more of these defective babies are male, whereas this difference is not found among other animals.[41] Most baby deaths occur before the seventh day.[42] Lactation is discussed—most lactating women do not menstruate[43]—and also the speed of resumption of conception after childbirth.[44] One translation of *On Animals* includes the statement that lactating women do not conceive.[45]

Much of the material articulated in Aristotle's *History* and *Generation of Animals* appears again in Avicenna's *On Animals*, in which only a few variations or differences of emphasis need noting. Where Aristotle appears to deny generative capacity in men between 14 and 21, Avicenna modifies. After 21 men produce good seed and seed which generates males, with the hint that before 21, while seed may be less good and productive of females, it is, nevertheless, generative.[46] Slightly different numbers are specified in statements about the end of the generative span. Avicenna has women generating up to 49 or 50.[47] In another passage they most frequently stop menstruating at 48, but sometimes continue until 50.[48] Men begin to be deficient in producing seed after 50, or later at 60.[49] Some men have procreated at 70, and their sperm is generative up to 78 and occasionally up to 90: but this is rare.[50] Region is briefly introduced. In warm regions men are capable

[37] For this paragraph see 584a35–585b26. [38] 586b27–587a5. [39] 582a20; 584b7–8.
[40] See discussion below and n. 100. [41] 775a4–5; *De gen. an.* (Scot), p. 201; (Moerbeke), p. 146.
[42] 588a8–10. [43] 587b30–1; 777a12–13; *De gen. an.* (Scot), pp. 207–8; (Moerbeke), p. 150.
[44] 587b1–5. [45] See discussion on p. 269 and n. 101 below.
[46] Avicenna, *De animalibus*, IX. i; 40va. [47] Ibid., V. ii; 34va. [48] Ibid., IX. v; 44ra.
[49] Ibid., V. ii; 34va. [50] Ibid., IX. v; 44ra.

only up to 60.[51] There are miscellaneous additions, such as the point about avoiding conception, in a story from Hippocrates about a woman giving a strong jump in order to eject seed.[52] Avicenna varies in his attitude to Aristotle. Often he accepts him, retailing him without saying so and without alteration, and occasionally he openly criticizes him. 'Aristotle says that', prefacing some statement, on occasion may suggest something in between: Avicenna disowning responsibility and raising a sceptical eyebrow. Avicenna also normalizes some of Aristotle, for example on human gestation, where he only includes eight and nine months, thereby avoiding the propositions of seven-month survival and eight-month non-survival.[53]

Aristotle's large themes are shot through with variations. Seasonal variation in mortality and illness is an especially strong theme in the (attributed) *Problems*. Diseases and mortality are seasonal; springtime sees many miscarriages. Regional variation and general differences in the progression through life of females and males are on the one hand prominent in the works *On Animals* and the *Problems*, and on the other hand serve to introduce the tract *Length and Shortness*. The principal propositions of the tract and supporting statements are already scattered through the *On Animals* and *Problems*, where the reader encounters the greater warmth of the male animal;[54] females' speedier progress through life-stages;[55] the speedier aging of men who are given over to too much sex and of women who bear many children;[56] the hierarchy of life-span among animals (with man's position in it);[57] the males' greater length of life than the female's;[58] and regional variation, slower aging in airy regions, quicker in low and marshy regions.[59] But Aristotle's ideas are gathered together and the theme given autonomous treatment in *Length and Shortness*, one of the *Little Natural Works*. One of the other *Little Natural Works* distinguishes between natural death and violent death, in a way which indicates an area of contingencies which are excluded.[60] Here, in *Length and Shortness*, the principal causes of long life and short life are put forward as matters for consideration and speculation. Are the causes the same throughout nature? Does illness necessarily go hand in hand with short life, and health with long life?[61] There are differences at different levels: between different kinds of animals

[51] Avicenna, *De animalibus*, V. ii; 34va. [52] Ibid., IX. ii; 41ra. [53] Ibid., IX. v; 44ra.

[54] 765b16–7; *De gen. an.* (Scot), pp. 169; (Moerbeke), p. 123; 891b21–4 (*Problems*, X. viii; *Problemata Aristotelis*, 99va).

[55] 583b27–8; 775a13–15, *De gen. an.* (Scot), p. 201; (Moerbeke), p. 146. [56] 582a22–4.

[57] 775b3–4; *De gen. an.* (Scot), pp. 209; (Moerbeke), p. 151; 891b29 (*Problems*, X. ix; *Problemata Aristotelis*, 99vb).

[58] 613a25; 896a35 (*Problems*, X. lxviii; *Problemata Aristotelis*, 116vb).

[59] 909b1–36 (*Problems*, XIV. vii–x; *Problemata Aristotelis*, 149rb–50rb).

[60] 478b22–5. I have excluded from discussion Aristotle's statement, in *On Generation and Corruption* (II. x; 336b10–12), that lives of all kinds of entities are measured by periods, shorter or longer, although a study of the reception of this proposition might well broaden our picture of scholastic thought on length of life. See, for example, Averroes, *Commentarium medium in Aristotelis De generatione et corruptione libros*, II. lviii, ed. P. H. Fobes, Corpus Commentariorum Averroes in Aristotelem, Versionum Latinarum 4/1 (Cambridge, Mass., 1956), pp. 150–1; Albert's commentary, *De generatione et corruptione*, II. iii. 5; *Opera*, Borgnet, iv. 450–1; *Opera*, Geyer, v, part 2, 206.

[61] 464b19–30; *De longitudine* (James), p. 405.

(for example, men are longer-lived than horses); within one kind of animal, differences between one animal and another, between one man and another; and differences between those living in distant regions.[62] There is a discussion of the principles, of what brings about destruction, how contraries are changed by contraries, and how all things are in the state of coming to be or passing away. Aristotle produces a hierarchy of the longest-lived in nature: the longest found among plants (the date-palm), then animals with blood, then those without, and so on. There is longer life in warm regions, shorter in cold.[63] According to nature an animal and its living consist in warmth and dampness, while old age and death consist in cold and dryness. What leads to dryness brings on quicker aging. Emission of seed can lead to such dessication. On account of this a mule (as a sterile animal) is longer-lived than a horse, and females are longer-lived than males if the males are very much given over to sex: male sparrows are an example of the latter. Labour also dries out and ages. Overall and by nature, males are longer-lived than females, because the male animal is warmer than the female, and warmth also explains longer life in warm regions.[64]

In his summary of the *Little Natural Works*, Averroes accorded separate treatment to the *Length and Shortness of Life*, providing a précis of Aristotle, followed by an appendix of the views of the 'ancients' on the subject.[65] The summary rearranges Aristotle's tract, putting the four qualities at the beginning; their importance is underlined by Averroes's repeated restatement and numbering of difference by genus, species, group, and individual. Concentration on groups as well as individuals highlights the categories—the groups of people who live in warm and moist or cold and dry regions, groups who live in maritime regions, and groups distinguished by age or sex. Passing away occurs to *groups* of people

[62] 465a3–12; *De longitudine* (James), pp. 405–6.

[63] 466b17–18; *De longitudine* (James), p. 409, quoted at the end of the next note.

[64] 466b8–16; *De longitudine* (James), p. 409: *supereffusa et multa semina senescunt cito; semen enim superfluitas est et amplius exsiccat abiectum. Et propter hoc est mulus longioris vite et equa et asino ex quibus fit, et femine maribus siquidem accedant masculi; ex quo passeres masculi breviores vite sunt feminis. Amplius autem, quecumque fatigantia sunt masculorum, et propter laborem senescunt magis; dessicat enim labor, senectus autem sicca. Natura enim sicut in homine est dicere, masculina feminis longius vivunt, quoniam maioris caloris est masculus femina. Sed que sunt in calidis, longioris vite sunt quam que in frigidis locis.* The same passage in Moerbeke's translation, Aristotle, *Opera* (Venice, 1496), 334v: *coitivi et multi sperma senescunt cito. Sperma enim superfluum et amplius dessicat emissum. Et propter hoc est mulus longioris vitae et asino, ex quibus genitus est. Et foemellae masculis si coitivi sint masculi: propter quod et pasceres masculi brevioris vitae foemellis. Adhuc autem quaecunque laboriosa masculorum propter laborem senescunt magis: dessicat enim labor; senectus tam[en] sicca est. Natura est ut ad omne dicere masculi foemellis longioris vitae. Causa autem quia calidius animal masculus est quam foemella. Eadem autem in calidis longioris vitae sunt quam in frigidis locis propter eandem causam.*

[65] Averroes, *Compendia librorum Aristotelis qui Parva Naturalia vocantur*, ed. E. L. Shields, Corpus Commentariorum Averrois in Aristotelem, Versionum Latinarum vol. 7 (Cambridge, Mass., 1949), pp. 129–49. The translation by H. Blumberg, Averroes, *Epitome of Parva Naturalia*, Corpus Commentariorum Averrois in Aristotelem, Versio Anglica 7 (Cambridge, Mass., 1961), pp. 54–61, is from the Arabic text, not the medieval Latin version. On Arab knowledge and possession of the *Little Natural Works*, see M. Steinschneider, 'Die *Parva Naturalia* des Aristoteles bei den Arabern', *Zeitschrift der deutschen morgenländischen Gesellschaft* 37 (1883), 477–92.

through the relations of their qualities and active and passive powers, but befalls *individuals* in two ways. One is 'naturally' (in the way that has just been said), while the other is 'contingently', through superfluities which nature cannot sort out and which, consequently, encourage illnesses.[66] Through Averroes's emphasis on this last theme, his text draws in more about human beings than there is in Aristotle's tract. There are references to Galen and doctors, and whereas the reader of Aristotle never loses sight of the theme of all living nature, in Averroes the predominant theme becomes the 'diversity of men in their course through life' (*diversitas hominum in vita*).[67] Noteworthy additions to and adaptations of Aristotle include the following. Aristotle's proposition that fat old people live longer is related to the quantity of warmth and dampness in large flesh.[68] Where Aristotle raised correlations of span and health or ill-health as a *question*, and raised it about all nature, Averroes rejects these correlations, concentrates on men, and introduces what 'we see' among men, the result of the lack of such correlations. 'We see many strong men who incur fatal illnesses and die before old age, and others of lesser strength, weak men, who arrive at old age.'[69] Medical art does not grapple with a person's complexion, which is the cause of length or shortness, for if the *medicus* were able to assess complexion, he would be able to assess length of life precisely.[70] In Averroes's text, much more than Aristotle's, there is a palpable sense of a world *out there*, outside the text: a world of human lives and human medicine.

In two further areas Averroes diverges significantly. There is little on sex difference, and no general statement about males living longer. The point comes up once, on aging and dessication through sex: 'on account of paucity of sex, the mule lives longer than the horse, and females longer than males' (*et propter paucitatem coitus vivit mulus plus quam equus et femine plus quam masculi*).[71] Where there was an 'if' in Aristotle, Averroes generalizes unconditionally. The Arts student reading them in 1300 would understand the two authorities to be in conflict. Secondly, whereas when summarizing Aristotle Averroes repeats longer life in warm and damp regions, only adding longer life for men living on islands in the sea rather than on farmland, in his appendix or postscript[72] he retails conflicting views on the subject, discusses them, and concludes that cold and dry places were conducive to long life.[73]

Avicenna's *Canon* represents learned medicine here.[74] The major part of this

[66] *Compendia*, p. 136; *Epitome*, p. 57.

[67] *Compendia*, p. 143; *Epitome*, p. 60.

[68] *Compendia*, pp. 138–9; *Epitome*, p. 58.

[69] *Compendia*, p. 142: *videmus quod multi graviter infirmi etiam vivunt multum, et multi bone consistentie moriuntur iuvenes*; *Epitome*, p. 60.

[70] *Compendia*, p. 142: *si esset nota, precise iudicaret medicus longitudinem et brevitatem vite*; *Epitome*, p. 59.

[71] *Compendia*, p. 139; *Epitome*, p. 58.

[72] When Averroes ends his summary of Aristotle, he appends a brief survey of the diverging views of the ancients, *Compendia*, pp. 147–9; *Epitome*, pp. 60–1.

[73] *Compendia*, p. 148: *loca frigida et sicca magis videntur esse cause longitudinis vite quam calida et sicca*; *Epitome*, p. 60.

[74] On the *Canon*, see Ch. 6 above, n. 61.

work addresses the body in great detail and enormous length: its parts and functions; illnesses and their cure; the various regimes for maintaining health that are appropriate from the first stages of infancy through to old age; and generation and its problems, overcoming sterility, the regime of the pregnant woman, avoiding conception, inducing abortion, and so on. The individual body is the subject, not a multitude of bodies, and the natural philosopher's interest in taxonomy and number is largely absent. However, in the first book's exposition of fundamental principles and the body's complexions and humours, both vocabulary and a philosophical and generalizing bent hold out a hand to natural philosophy. Further, the section devoted to common causes affecting the dispositions of the body ventilates a theme which was also in Aristotle.

This was diversity of incidence of illness and mortality according to seasons, years, and climates, which was a commonplace in much other medical literature, where it was the principal subject of the Hippocratic *Airs, Regions, and Places*. Avicenna devoted considerable attention to the last of these. Hot or cold and humid or dry places; high or low, stony, bare, mountainous and snowy, and marine places; northern, southern, eastern, and western regions: all are listed and discussed, and set in relation to health and, sometimes, length of life.[75] Humidity is linked to the incidence of fevers. Marshy land produces poor air, while stony and bare ground produces strong bodies. There are several strong correlations. Attributed to the north is longer life, rarity of miscarriages, and difficulty of childbirth.[76] In high places people are healthy, strong and 'live long'.[77] In hot and dry regions, 'the land of the blacks', there is the opposite: old age comes at thirty.[78] Finally, Aristotle had hinted at a correlation between health and occupation, in the less obvious pregnancy and easier childbirth of working women and the dessicating and aging effect of labour. Avicenna made the theme explicit and sharper, commenting on fullers and blacksmiths, whose work encourages an increase, respectively, in cold and humidity, or heat and dryness.[79]

[75] Avicenna, *Canon*, I. ii. 2. 11; 27rb–vb.

[76] Ibid., *De locis habitabilibus septentrionalibus: Et solet in eis esse . . . vite longitudo . . . dixerunt quidam . . . quod raro accidit eis ut abortum patiantur . . . Et partus advenit eis durus.* Compare Constantine the African, *Liber Pantegni, Theorica*, V. ix, in Isaac Israeli, *Opera omnia*, 2 vols. (Lyons, 1515), ii. 19vb, where in the north there is long life, women do not conceive much and do not abort, and many are sterile: *vita longa . . . Femine non multum concipiunt neque tamen abortiunt . . . Mulieres plurime sunt steriles.* Constantine says that the qualities of southerners are the opposite, spelling out short life (*vita eorum parva*) and women more frequently aborting.

[77] Avicenna, *Canon*, I. ii. 2. 11; 27rb–vb: *In locis habitabilibus altis morantes sunt sani, et fortes labores multum patientes, et vivunt diu.*

[78] Ibid., *De locis calidis*: *cito adveniet senium, sicut in terra nigrorum. Illis tamen qui ibi morantur adveniet senium in annis XXX.*

[79] *Canon*, I. ii. 2. 12, 28ra. There is similar comment in Constantine the African, *Liber Pantegni, Theorica*, I. xxiii and V. xii; 4rb and 20vb. The theme of professions and health was taken up by Arnau de Vilanova, *Speculum introductionum medicinalium*, lxxix, De artibus, in *Opera*, 26va, and by Bernard de Gordon in his *De decem ingeniis curandorum morborum*: L. E. Demaitre, *Doctor Bernard de Gordon: Professor and Practitioner*, Pontifical Institute of Medieval Studies, Studies and Texts 51 (Toronto, 1980), p. 156. It is discussed in my 'A "scientific" view of Jews from Paris around 1300', forthcoming in *Micrologus*.

Let us recapitulate the salient features of this sketch of what had become available by around 1300. First, someone making a statement about life-span around 1000 would probably be producing the spiritual commonplace of the brevity of man's life, drawing upon no more than the Psalms, Isaiah, Augustine's *City of God*, later Christian ascetic writing, and a tiny amount of science and medicine in Isidore's *Etymologies*. By 1300 statements about life-span would now have as their backcloth the massive, dense, and detailed biological and medical accounts of the animal world and of the human body which were available, lectured upon and studied in Arts and medical faculties.

Secondly, littering the biological works and also present in medical works are short phrases which now present in Latin such concepts as generative span, incidence of deformed babies, and length of life in a region: 'demographic' notions. In the *On Animals* they are miscellaneous. Some of these concepts receive no special emphasis. Others, such as the influence of region, are given more attention, and life-span is presented as a fully-fledged and autonomous subject for natural philosophical enquiry. Some concepts are only potentially there. That is to say, there are some propositions which are likely to encourage the emergence of a particular 'demographic' concept, as for example, large numbers of defective males at birth and the generation of females in particular regions and the genesis of the concept of sex-ratio. There is a stock of such concepts, then, and they were hedged about with qualifications and distinctions which encouraged ways of thinking about them. These included clear distinctions between individuals and groups, and between (*a*) the extreme possibilities in nature, and (*b*) 'what usually happens' or 'what applies to the majority of people'. Quantity plays *some* role, in elementary 'more' and 'less', or 'most frequently' and 'rarely'. Here and there precise numbers are in play, and in one case (gestation) numerical precision is edged into the picture by remarking its opposite, mistakes in calculation.

Arts students around 1300 were confronted with a massive example of empiricism *and* authority in Aristotle's *On Animals*, and the impact on them and their capacity or propensity to be empirical is a delicate problem. Further discussion of this theme is postponed until later in this chapter, when it crops up again in a discussion of commentaries on *Length and Shortness* and the possible influence upon them of the demographic realities of their own world.

10.2 *Translation*[80]

In western medicine the mid-eleventh century to the first half of the fourteenth century saw translations into Latin of Hippocratic works, Galen, and later Byzantine and Arabic authors. These were done from Greek or Arabic, and in some

[80] The following account of translations of Aristotle rests mainly upon AL *Codices 1–3* introductions, articles by Minio-Paluello (particularly those in his *Opuscula*), and *Guillaume de Moerbeke* for Aristotle, and the account of translations of Arabic medical works in Jacquart and Micheau. On Minio-Paluello,

cases from Arabic translations of Greek; later some of these Greek-to-Arabic-Latin translations were revised directly from the Greek original. Already mentioned above were the Abbey of Monte Cassino, and the monks Alphanus and Constantine the African. Important among later locations and figures were Toledo and Gerard of Cremona (d. 1187), who is accredited with at least eighty-two translations from Arabic, including Avicenna's *Canon* and twenty-three other medical works, and many others in the late thirteenth and early fourteenth centuries, culminating in the royal court at Naples and translation there of over fifty writings of Galen by Niccolò da Reggio (fl. 1315–48). Translations spread in manuscript copies. Largely from the labours at Monte Cassino a (fairly) standard anthology of texts emerged, known in the Renaissance as the *Articella.* It was being lectured upon in Salerno by 1170, and entered the curriculum in university medical faculties in the mid- to late thirteenth century. Parts of Avicenna's *Canon* were also entering the curriculum at the two centres which were the foundations of later medieval and renaissance university medicine, at Bologna under the influence of Taddeo Alderotti, and at Montpellier being formalized through the educational provisions of 1307, which were guided by Arnau of Vilanova. Modern studies of medieval medicine, especially in France, England, and the kingdom of Aragon, have patiently identified and compiled evidence about thousands of medical practitioners, nearly eight thousand, for example in France, and the élite among these studied medicine in universities. The Avicennan propositions discussed above, for example about place and health and longevity, were read in the first instance by these many men who had to learn these texts for university exams, and it was their minds which first received, adapted and were influenced by this material.

Let us turn to Aristotle's works and their translation, looking now in more detail at their further reception.

The principal translator of the first half of the twelfth century, James 'the Venetian and Greek', was in contact with philosophical schools in Constantinople, where he is himself briefly glimpsed in 1138, and he translated into Latin many of Aristotle's works, including *Length and Shortness*, directly from Greek manuscripts.[81] Over a century later, but at a date which is not precisely known, this translation of *Length and Shortness* was revised by the Flemish Dominican friar William of Moerbeke.[82] He was translating in Greece in 1260 and also probably

see J. Brams, 'Lorenzo Minio Paluello e l' "Aristoteles Latinus" ', L. Minio-Paluello, *Lughi cruciali in Dante: ultimi saggi, con un inedito su Boezio*, ed. F. Santi, Quaderni di Cultura Neolatina, Collana della Fondazione Ezio Franceschi 6 (Spoleto and Florence, 1993), pp. 13–25. As a broad-brush survey my account does not discuss the problem of versions of Aristotle known to early medics (upon which see D. Jacquart, 'Aristotelian Thought in Salerno', in *A History of Twelfth-Century Philosophy*, ed. P. Dronke (Cambridge, 1988), pp. 407–28), nor the miscellaneous 'outsiders' (d'Alverny's term), most notably David of Dinant, who used versions of the books *On Animals* and *Problems* which do not match the standard versions discussed here; see M.-T. d'Alverny, 'Translations and Translators', in *Renaissance and Renewal in the Twelfth Century*, ed. R. L. Benson and G. Constable (Oxford, 1982), pp. 421–62 (pp. 436–7).

[81] L. Minio-Paluello, 'James of Venice', *DSB* vii. 65–7; *Opuscula*, pp. 189–228 and 565–87.

[82] L. Minio-Paluello, 'Moerbeke, William of', *DSB* ix. 434–40 (p. 437). Until a modern edition appears

during his time at the papal court between 1267 and 1278, where he coincided with a bevy of scholars with scientific interests—we shall look at William more closely in the next chapter. Around 1260 Bartholomew of Messina, working for King Manfred whose court was at Palermo, was putting various pseudonymous Aristotelian works into Latin, including the *Problems*.[83]

All the translations so far mentioned were from Greek to Latin, as was the case with virtually all of the west's earliest translations of Aristotelian works, with only one significant exception,[84] where the earliest was a Latin translation of an Arabic text, which was itself a translation of Greek. The translator was Michael Scot, who worked first in Spain and later in Italy, in part at Frederick II's court in Palermo, which was, like the papal court, jostling with men of scientific interests.[85] He translated the three major parts of Aristotle's writings *On Animals* (*History, Parts, Generation*), before 1220 and in Toledo,[86] and also Avicenna's treatise *On Animals*. The latter is given a terminus by the date on one presentation copy to the emperor Frederick II, 1232.[87] The main Latin translation of Averroes's epitome of the *Little Natural Works*, including the *Length and Shortness*, has also been attributed to Michael Scot, but without any evidence.[88] Several decades later, possibly in 1260, Moerbeke redid part of Scot's work, retranslating Aristotle's *On Animals*, this time directly from Greek manuscripts.[89]

The west acquired, therefore, two translations of *Length and Shortness*, made a century or more apart but both directly from Greek. The west also acquired two translations of the majority of the works *On Animals*, separated by a shorter period (forty years or more), but much more divergent in character than the two translations of *Length and Shortness*. When turning to characterize Scot and Moerbeke as translators, the modern editors of the Latin Aristotle point out that Scot was dealing with a text which was already problematic, because it was itself a translation, and that tradition through Arabic script tends to produce more error than tradition through Greek or Latin. While insisting on the difficulty of Arabic, d'Alverny has suggested that translation often went through the vernacular, with

the translation has to be consulted in the Venice (1482) edition of Aristotle's Latin works or its reprints (*Guillaume de Moerbeke*, pp. 324 and 330). I have used it in the Venice (1496) reprint, 33v–5r.

[83] AL *Codices 1*, pp. 86–7; R. Seligsohn, *Die Übersetzung der ps-aristotelischen Problemata durch Bartholomaeus von Messina: Text und textkritische Untersuchungen zum ersten Buch. Inaugural Dissertation* (Berlin, 1934), pp. 16–18; Minio, *Opuscula*, pp. 112–13. Bartholomew's is the *antiqua* translation in *Problemata Aristotelis cum duplici translatione, antiqua et nova scilicet Theodori Gaze: cum expositione Petri Aponi* (Venice, 1501).

[84] Minio, *Opuscula*, p. 511.

[85] L. Minio-Paluello, 'Michael Scot', *DSB* ix. 361–5, and C. H. Haskins, 'Michael Scot in Spain', *Estudios eruditos in memoriam de Adolfo Bonilla y San Martin (1875–1926)*, 2 vols. (Madrid, 1927–30), ii. 129–34. See also C. Burnett, 'Michael Scot and the Transmission of Scientific Culture from Toledo to Bologna via the Court of Frederick II', in *Le Scienze alla corte di Federico II, Micrologus* 2 (Paris, Turnout, 1994), 101–26, although Burnett's main interest is in the astrological works.

[86] Haskins, 'Scot in Spain', 131 and n. 3. [87] AL *Codices 1*, p. 81.

[88] Averroes, *Compendia*, p. xiii; Minio-Paluello, 'Michael Scot', 363.

[89] Minio-Paluello, 'Moerbeke', 436; H. Drossaart Lulofs, preface to Aristotle, *De generatione animalium* (Moerbeke), pp. xix–xxv; *Guillaume de Moerbeke*, pp. 331–4.

an Arabic-reading assistant orally putting the Arabic into a romance vernacular, which the translator would render into Latin and write down; and she has pointed to Scot's use of two such assistants. The sequence therefore may have been long: Arabic to Greek, Greek to vernacular, and vernacular to Latin. Scot was intent on grasping the essential meaning of a passage rather than its precise literal translation, and he was prepared to suppress, expand, and not care too much about finer shades of meaning. Moerbeke, on the other hand, had the advantage of working directly from Greek, and his philosophy of translation was superior. He aimed at a precisely literal translation, without omission. He was willing, if need be, to create hybrid Greco-Latin words, and he wanted to preserve nuances.[90]

How do these contrasts show up in what western readers were getting, first, in the years after around 1220 from Scot, and secondly, in the years after 1260, from Moerbeke?[91] In the case of the Greco-Arabic-Latin and Greco-Latin translations of the *Generation of Animals* we are fortunate in having modern critical editions, and we can look at these side by side. In the first example the two translators are presenting a contrast between males and females after birth.

Scot	Moerbeke
. . . *citius crescunt feminae quam mares, et citius senescunt.*[92]	. . . *omnia prius perficiuntur, ut pubescentia, et status et senectus, femellis quam masculis.*[93]
. . . females grow more quickly than males, and they age more quickly.	. . . all things, such as puberty, maturity, and old age, are accomplished earlier in females than in males.

The two are only roughly the same. But while Scot makes two rather flat descriptive statements, Moerbeke's sharp phrasing produces a concept, 'the relative speed of progression through life's stages'.

Frequency and quantity are handled differently. This begins with slight differences. Where Michael Scot writes *raro*, 'rarely', William of Moerbeke writes *raro et in paucis*, 'rarely and among few people'. Our second example shows that the difference can be more significant:

[90] Minio-Paluello, 'Michael Scot', 362, 'Moerbeke', 435–6, and *Opuscula*, p. 272; H. Drossaart Lulofs, preface to Aristotle, *De generatione animalium* (Scot), pp. viii–ix; A. M. I. Van Oppenraay, 'Quelques particularités de la méthode de traduction de Michel Scot', in *Traductions et traducteurs de l'antiquité tardive au XIVe siècle*, Publications de l'Institut d'Études Médiévales, Textes, Études, Congrès 11, Rencontres de Cultures dans la philosophie médiévale 1 (Louvain, Cassino, 1990), pp. 121–9; M.-T. d'Alverny, 'Les traductions à deux interprètes, d'arabe en langue vernaculaire et de langue vernaculaire en Latin', *Traductions et Traducteurs au Moyen Âge*, ed. G. Contamine, Documents, Études et Répertoires Publiées par l'Institut de Recherche et d'Histoire des Textes (Paris, 1989), pp. 193–206 (see pp. 193 and 198). Note Minio-Paluello's suspicion that the use of vernacular as an intermediary in Arabic-Latin translation was the exception rather than the rule; *Opuscula*, p. 507.

[91] My concern here is not with fidelity to Aristotle and the earlier tradition, which would need the Greek and Arabic that I do not have: mine is only the elementary query about contrasts between Scot's and Moerbeke's Latin.

[92] 775a13; *De gen. an.* (Scot), p. 201.

[93] *De gen. an.* (Moerbeke), p. 146.

Scot	Moerbeke
. . . homines valde pingues raro generant . . . et similiter etiam accidit mulieribus.[94]	*. . . pingues autem minus prolifici videntur esse quam non pingues, et mulieres et viri.*[95]
. . . very fat men rarely generate . . . and this happens similarly with women.	. . . fat people, both men and women, seem to be less prolific than people who are not fat.

Moerbeke's neater Latin, his careful qualification ('it seems'), and his higher level of generalization (fat people overall) are the backdrop to a crucial divergence. Where Scot simply keeps the reader's eyes on events separated by long or short intervals, Moerbeke directs them towards the *quantitative result* of such events, fewer or more of something. Here is another example of the contrast between the numerical worlds they inhabit, in a passage on winds determining sex:

Scot	Moerbeke
. . . et cum ventus fuerit septentrionalis erit natus mas, et cum meridionalis femina.[96]	*. . . et borealibus masculotokein magis quam australibus.*[97]
. . . and when the wind is northerly a male will be born, and when southerly a female.	. . . and with northerly winds there is more bearing of male children than with southerly.

Scot presents the correlation as 1:1—north, females, south: males. A reader resisting the temptation to think at primary school level has first to think, 'Surely he cannot mean *only* females?' Moerbeke presents 'more', a tendency: north, *more* males. His reader is placed immediately above elementary thought. Moerbeke also produces a Greco-Latin hybrid word, to translate Aristotle's ἀρρενοτοκεῖν: his readers will have had a single word meaning 'to-male-child-bear', and here the phrase 'to-more-male-child-bear'. There are other such hybrids. One, for example, provides Moerbeke's readers with a new single Latin word (*monotokizo*) as the verb for an animal, such as man, which generally 'produces-one-offspring-at-one-birth'.[98]

Thirdly, Scot omits, Moerbeke does not. Here are two instances of what this meant:

Scot	Moerbeke
in pluribus autem mulieribus peioratur dispositio tempore impraegnationis, et hoc accidit propter quietem ex qua congregatur in eis multa superfluitas. In mulieribus autem operantibus et laborantibus non manifestatur impraegantio sicut in aliis, et forte pariet statim.[99]	*mulierum autem multe difficulter ferunt circa impraegnationem. Est quidem igitur causa aliqua horum et propter vitam: immote autem existentes ampliori replentur superfluitate, quoniam in quibus gentibus laboriosa mulierum vita neque impraegnatio similiter manifesta est, pariunt autem facile et ibi et ubicumque consuete laborare.*[100]

[94] 726a3–3; *De gen. an.* (Scot), p. 39.
[95] *De gen. an.* (Moerbeke), p. 28.
[96] 766b34; *De gen. an.* (Scot), p. 173.
[97] *De gen. an.* (Moerbeke), p. 126.
[98] 772b1 and 774b24; *De gen. an.* (Moerbeke), pp. 139 and 145.
[99] 774a30–4; *De gen. an.* (Scot), p. 202.
[100] *De gen. an.* (Moerbeke), p. 147.

However, among most women their condition gets worse during pregnancy, and this comes about on account of their rest, through which much superfluity gathers in them. But among women who work and labour, pregnancy is not so obvious and they may give birth instantly.	However, many women suffer [things] concerning pregnancy with difficulty. There is in fact some cause of these things, and it is because of their way of life. For, while living sedentarily, they [these women] are filled with more superfluity. Among those peoples where women's life [consists of] hard work, [however], pregnancy is not so obvious, and the women also give birth with ease. And [it happens this way] there, and wherever women are accustomed to working hard.

Both men have a comparison, but Scot simply leaves out 'peoples' and the subsequent 'there, and wherever', whereas Moerbeke's context for the point immediately carries the reader to comparisons of women's work among different peoples, and their differing experience of pregnancy and childbirth 'there, and wherever', throughout the world.

The second instance is the two men's treatment of lactation. Both translate Aristotle saying that lactating women in general do not menstruate, but then they diverge:

Scot	Moerbeke
[Scot's text does not continue: Scot simply omits the next statement]	... *neque concipiunt lactantes*.... nor do lactating women conceive.

For forty years, then, this thought about breast-feeding women not conceiving was not available to western readers. It became available with Moerbeke,[101] at around the same time that it was also becoming available through the translation of Averroes's *Colliget*, as we saw above in Chapter 6. The first translation of Aristotle's *On Animals* transmitted much of it, sometimes putting it into words which made it rather elementary and crude and sometimes omitting significant passages. Stimulating though this first exposure must have been to western scholars during the 1230s to 1250s, it must also have been on some points a brake on thought rather than an encouragement. The pithy and sharp Latin of the second translation transmitted to readers after 1260 a fuller and less elementary Aristotle. Now western readers were getting the stimulus to further thought provided by finer shades of meaning, previously omitted propositions, and higher conceptualization.

The case of the two Greco-Latin translations of *Length and Shortness* was different. Readers might choose Moerbeke's revision, to savour his sharper style. But there was scarcely any further variation between that version and James's.[102]

[101] 777a12–14; the omission is in *De gen. an.* (Scot), p. 207, and also in Avicenna, *De animalibus*, IX. v; 44rb, while the passage appears in *De gen. an.* (Moerbeke), p. 150.

[102] See the parallel passages quoted in n. 64 above.

10.3 *Diffusion and reception of the works* On Animals

Evidence of diffusion is provided by commentaries (and their extant copies), quotation, and university statutes and book regulations, and, before all this, the spread of copies of the texts themselves. Quite how many were there, how quickly were they made, and in what directions did they go? The raw materials for a study of this, namely the listing and description of manuscripts in the *Aristoteles Latinus*, have not been sufficiently exploited. The study would be in part a study of archaeological fragments. These are only the survivals, many are not precisely dated (and a few of the 'guestimates' in the pre-war *Aristoteles Latinus* catalogue might well prove to be unreliable), and location[103] and movement are only occasionally known.

Paris Arts faculty regulations in 1255 specified lectures on Aristotle's *On Animals*—self-evidently at this date Scot's version and presumably by some time in the 1260s either Scot or Moerbeke. Still extant are sixty-five manuscripts of Scot's translation, twenty-nine of Avicenna's *On Animals* (three of them copied with Scot), and forty of Moerbeke's translation, and the scripts of quite a few of these have been described as French, northern French, or Parisian.[104] One copy of Moerbeke has a note that the book had been in the hands of a 'corrector' of texts, Adam, who was living right in the heart of the city, Rue des Porees, in 1292. A list of prices of exemplars of texts held in 1304 by the Paris stationer André of Sens includes the *History of Animals* at thirty-two pence, and Albert the Great's reworking of Aristotle, his *Twenty-One Books on Animals*, at ten shillings: traces of a once lively system of supply in Paris.[105] Some college copies can be seen, in legacies which at the same time show earlier individual possession by masters. Thus the College of the Sorbonne's books included a Scot bequeathed by Master Gerard d'Abbeville on his death (around 1272);[106] two Moerbekes, one left by a

[103] In the following pages locations provided in AL *Codices* are used, with two caveats, one that any one known medieval location may only have been for a short time, the other that pointing to *current* location in an ancient library is only intended to raise the *possibility* that the manuscript in question was in that region in the middle ages. The materials for the study of reception through the further diffusion of commentaries on Aristotle are contained (*a*) in the lists of manuscripts drawn up by C. Lohr, 'Medieval Latin Aristotle Commentaries', in *Traditio* 23–30 (1967–74), and (*b*) later catalogues of manuscripts in particular countries. There is a convenient list of the latter in C. Flüeler, 'Die verschiedenen literarischen Gattungen der Aristoteleskommentare: zur Terminologie der Überschriften und Kolophone', in J. Hamesse (ed.), *Manuels, programmes de cours et techniques d'enseignement dans les universités médiévales*, Université Catholique de Louvain, Publications de l'Institut des Études Médiévales, Textes, Études, Congrès 16 (Louvain-La-Neuve, 1994), pp. 75–116 (pp. 75–7 n. 2).

[104] AL *Codices* 1–3.

[105] AL *Codices* 2, p. 904, no. 1305; *CUP* ii. 107, 111; R. H. and M. A. Rouse, 'The Book Trade at the University of Paris, ca. 1250–ca. 1350', in *La production du livre universitaire au moyen âge: Exemplar et pecia*, ed. L. J. Bataillon, B. G. Guyot and R. H. Rouse (Paris, 1991), pp. 41–114 (p. 83); see discussion of the stationers' lists in L. J. Bataillon, 'Les textes théologiques et philosophiques diffusées à Paris par exemplar et pecia', ibid., pp. 155–64. 81 extant manuscripts of Albert's work are listed in W. Fauser, *Die Werke des Albertus Magnus in ihrer handsriftlichen Überlieferung*, i. *Die echten Werke*, in Albert, *Opera*, Geyer, Tomus Subsidiarius, i. 139–59.

[106] AL *Codices* 1, p. 570 no. 684; see Glorieux, *Théologie*, ii. 356–60 no. 174.

Brabant Master Henri de Léau (d. 1355)[107] and the other by the Master Henri de l'Église;[108] and two books left by James of Padua, Master in 1354, one with parts of Avicenna's *On Animals* and both with fragments of Averroes's little-known commentary on *Generation of Animals*.[109] The direct traces of lecturing on the text are few.[110] One of two surviving compositions by a canon of Clermont, Gerard of Breuil, is an extensive commentary on Aristotle's *On Animals*, whose fair popularity can be judged by the seven copies in which it survives. Since Gerard's legacy of books to the Sorbonne locates his academic careeer in Paris, some time between 1268 and 1306, this work suggests lectures at Paris.[111] More is known precisely about John Vath, who was in the Arts faculty and rector of the University in 1289 and 1290, and composed *Questions upon the book On Animals* some time before 1295, using the Moerbeke text.[112] One Paris manuscript points to slightly later activity through the large numbers of quodlibetic questions it contains, many on themes from *On Animals*, which were raised and debated in the Arts faculty in Paris around 1300.[113]

Early fourteenth-century statutes in Oxford, codifying earlier practice rather than initiating, specified *On Animals* as one choice among several texts that someone incepting as a Master should have heard.[114] The commentaries in Oxford around 1250 by Adam of Buckfield on Aristotle's 'natural books' included all except the *On Animals*, one sign, perhaps, of lack of *great* interest in reception in England.[115] But the work spread early, and it was owned and was part of the intellectual formation of scholars in English universities as well. Some of the copies of the two translations were written by English hands,[116] and occasionally a copy bears marks of early English use. In one copy of Scot, early presence in England is attested by notes referring to English people and money and the date 1248, and early presence is also suggested by English glosses and the date 1289 in one copy of Moerbeke.[117] Still surviving Oxford and Cambridge college copies may not in all cases indicate *early* ownership, although in a few instances legacies

[107] AL *Codices 1*, p. 570 no. 685; see E. Wickersheimer, *Dictionnaire biographique des médecins en France au moyen âge*, 2 vols. (Paris, 1936, repr. Geneva, Paris, 1979), i. 285.

[108] AL *Codices 1*, p. 570, nos. 686; see Glorieux, *Arts*, p. 443 no. 1849.

[109] Ibid., pp. 561–3 and 569–79, nos. 671 and 683; see Glorieux, *Arts*, p. 443 no. 1852.

[110] See L. Cova, 'Le Questioni di Giovanni Vath sul de generatione animalium', *AHDLMA* 59 (1992), 175–287 (pp. 181–5).

[111] Ibid., 183 and n. 36. [112] Ibid., 190–1.

[113] BN, MS Lat. 16089. The questions in this and in Vienna, Nationalbibliothek, MS 2303 will be the subject of a monograph by Maaike van der Lugt.

[114] J. M. Fletcher, 'The Faculty of Arts', *HUO* i. 369–99 (pp. 384–5). Interest in Britain is discussed by C. Burnett, 'The Introduction of Aristotle's Natural Philosophy into Great Britain: A Preliminary Survey of the Manuscript Evidence', in *Aristotle in Britain during the Middle Ages*, ed. J. Marenbon, Société Internationale pour l'Étude de la Philosophie Médiévale, Rencontres de Philosophie Médiévale 5 (Turnhout, 1996), pp. 21–50 (pp. 33–5).

[115] J. A. Weisheipl, 'Science in the thirteenth century', *HUO* i. 435–69 (p. 462).

[116] AL *Codices 1*, pp. 246 no. 22, 527 no. 600, and p. 529 no. 604; see also p. 487 no. 518, and AL *Codices 2*, pp. 103–4, nos. 1470–1.

[117] AL *Codices 1*, p. 356 no. 253; AL *Codices 2*, pp. 1086–7 no. 1584. See also AL *Codices 1*, pp. 517–19 no. 583, and M. T. d'Alverny, '*Avicenna Latinus* IX', *AHDLMA* 36 (1970), 243–80 (pp. 251–2).

indicate earlier ownership by individual Masters' and later by colleges. Thus Master Henry of Cherwelton, fellow of Merton in 1299 and 1305, 'wrote' his copy of Scot, which came to Merton on his death in 1326, while John of Osmyngton, fellow between 1312/13 and 1319/20, also gave his copy of Moerbeke to Merton.[118]

How far should one use the picture of Paris and Oxford to hypothesize about other universities? One modern writer on Arts faculties in this period has emphasized custom and uniformity, in a way which would suggest much more going on than can be gleaned from the evidence directly bearing on any one university.[119] There was custom, unwritten and only sometimes codified by statutes, and when statutes were promulgated they were not necessarily instituting something new nor even complete in their description of existing practice. And universities tended to copy, especially Paris. Phrases like 'as is customary' in a new university statute, or 'as is customary' and 'as in Paris' in stationers' provisions, may indicate the adoption of much that is not spelled out in detail, the Parisian model taken over *en bloc*. They may support the conjecture of an unseen but much wider existence of these texts in Arts faculties outside Paris. This would fit the large numbers of extant copies of *On Animals*, large numbers written in northern hands, Flemish, German, southern hands, Italian, and Spanish. More detailed research would establish fragments of a wider diffusion of copies among European universities and lecturing and 'hearing' in Arts faculties. By the later middle ages Franciscan houses as far apart as Florence and Gdansk also own or have owned the book; copies of Aristotle's or Avicenna's *On Animals* and Aristotle's *Problems* which were once in Augustinian, Franciscan, or Dominican[120] hands are traces of the Arts training which was given in some Orders. Locations in libraries from Toledo to Cambrai[121] suggest further areas for enquiry, about diffusion in older monastic houses and cathedral chapters. One could also look to the diffusion of the crib, *Auctoritates Aristotelis*, as indirect evidence. Among the 156 surviving manuscripts, about two-thirds are from the fourteenth century, and some of these bear marks of ownership and use—one, for example, with the name of a liberal arts tutor to a nobleman in Montpellier.[122]

Among famous scholars who must have possessed the *On Animals* we know of one, Peter d'Abano, through his writing a note on it (it was the Moerbeke version) that he had bought it in Padua in 1309. Peter had deep medical interests, and the earlier owner of this book had been one 'F' (Francesco?), a *medicus* of Mantua:[123] a reminder of another important milieu, learned medicine, where the overlap of interest between medicine of the human body and Aristotle's comparative and systematic biology of animals was obvious. The connection is evident at an early

[118] AL *Codices 1*, pp. 383–4 no. 309 and 412 no. 366; see Emden, *BRUO* i. 395 and ii. 1408.

[119] J. A. Weisheipl, 'Curriculum of the faculty of arts at Oxford in the early fourteenth century', *Medieval Studies* 26 (1964), 143–85 (p. 145).

[120] AL *Codices 1*, pp. 361 no. 263 and 619 no. 785; AL *Codices 2*, pp. 810–11 no. 1140, 942–3 nos. 1370–1, and 1047–8 no. 1524; AL *Codices 3*, p. 177 no. 1753; M. T. d'Alverny, '*Avicenna Latinus* III', *AHDLMA* 30 (1964), 221–72 (pp. 248–9). See also AL *Codices I*, p. 586 no. 718.

[121] AL *Codices 1*, pp. 459–60 no. 458 and AL *Codices 2*, p. 852 no. 1231.

[122] *Auctoritates Aristotelis*, p. 40 n. 11.

[123] AL *Codices 2*, p. 897 no. 1296.

date. In 1232, when the scribe Henry of Cologne made his presentation copy for the Emperor Frederick II of Avicenna's *On Animals*, he used an exemplar which was made available to him by the imperial *medicus*, Master Wolmar, and he worked in Wolmar's house. Here, then, the earliest identifiable individual western owner of a work, much of which was based on Aristotle's, was a German *medicus* in southern Italy.[124] Another early copy, written in 1248, was made after an exemplar which was in the hands of a Master Bernard Colomb in Montpellier; there was a doctor of this name in Montpellier in 1301,[125] where tradition of profession in families and the custom of naming sons after fathers suggests that our Bernard was a father or grandfather. Suggestive is the chronological coincidence with a medical Master, Cardinalis, who is linked to Montpellier in 1240, and whose commentaries show much knowledge of Aristotle's *On Animals*.[126] Montpellier and its academic *medici* seem to be one early scene of reception of both authors' *On Animals*. 'I began my course in medicine on Monday 7 May, 1352' is a note in one copy of the Moerbeke translation.[127] It is representative of a wider point, *medici* ownership of a distinct minority of the copies, which is otherwise attested by medical notes inside the books, occasional binding together with medical works, and names of owners.[128] Their special position is evident in a passing reference in the statutes of the medical faculty of Montpellier in 1340, to the effect that the book *On Animals* was exempt from a general ban on lecturing on non-medical texts.[129]

Within the milieux sketched here, then, how were the works *On Animals* received? Rendering 'intelligible to the Latins' is a famous phrase, used by Albert the Great to describe his aim in reworking Aristotle's works, and it acquires special significance in the case of his *Twenty-One Books on Animals*, which were based on the obscurer Scot translation. The *Twenty-One Books* has an internal reference from 1260/1, which may indicate later composition or simply the date of a late addition. Albert repeats and clarifies. Statements acquire more emphasis, and, where they are autonomously the subjects of chapters or books, specific titles imply their conceptualization into topics: *On the signs of puberty*, *On the beginning of generation in man*, *On the variety of power of generating according to age*,

[124] AL *Codices* 1, p. 81.

[125] AL *Codices* 1, p. 669 no. 904, also described by M. T. d'Alverny, '*Avicenna Latinus* VII', *AHDLMA*, 34 (1968), 315–43 (331–2); Wickersheimer, *Supplément*, p. 35.

[126] M. R. McVaugh, 'Introduction', in Arnau de Vilanova, *Opera medica omnia* (Barcelona, 1975–), iii. 24.

[127] AL *Codices* 1, p. 308 no. 155.

[128] d'Alverny, '*Avicenna Latinus* III', 222–4, 230–1 (= AL *Codices* 2, p. 901 no. 1302) and 244–6 (= AL *Codices* 2, pp. 1058–9 no. 1540). D'Alverny, '*Avicenna Latinus* IV', *AHDLMA* 31 (1965), 271–86 (pp. 276–9) (= AL *Codices* 2, pp. 1104–5 no. 1613). D'Alverny, '*Avicenna Latinus* V', *AHDLMA* 32 (1966), 257–302 (pp. 284–6) (= AL *Codices* 1, p. 411 no. 364—see also Emden, *BRUO* iii. 1556–60); 289–91 (= AL *Codices* 1, p. 414 no. 373). D'Alverny, '*Avicenna Latinus* VII', 342 (= AL *Codices* 1, p. 753 no. 1096). D'Alverny, '*Avicenna Latinus* VIII', *AHDLMA* 35 (1969), 301–35 (pp. 306–7) (= AL *Codices* 2, pp. 836–7 no. 1198). D'Alverny, '*Avicenna Latinus* IX', 250–3 (= AL *Codices* 2, p. 1155 no. 1699). AL *Codices* 1, p. 571 no. 687. AL *Codices* 2, pp. 996 no. 1459 and 1197 no. 1794. See also Arnau de Vilanova, *Opera medica omnia*, iv. 196, and Siraisi, *Taddeo*, pp. 43–4, 152 and 192.

[129] Demaitre, *Doctor Bernard de Gordon*, p. 24 n. 121.

and *On impediments to generation.*[130] Here is an example illustrating how Albert underlines and adds. Albert repeats Aristotle's point that among humans, but not other animals, more males are born defective than females, and then adds a point about comparative movements inside the womb. 'Because of males' many movements while their members are still tender, more damage through breakages and lesions of members . . . happens to males than to females.'[131]

Some of Albert's enormous additional material comes from his wide reading in other sources, more than the lightly footnoted modern edition suggests. Thus when he refers to the dangers in childbirth of a girl under 15 conceiving, the specific age is plucked out of the air, while the adduced reason, her smallness of size, probably comes from Albert's reading of Avicenna's *Canon* on the danger to women who are narrowly built. The *Canon* is also his probable source for a woman rising up suddenly, moving and jumping in order to dislodge seed and avoid conception.[132] Other additional material is claimed to come from another source. 'I, Albert, *saw*'; 'We *see* woman at first not conceiving and then conceiving.'[133] Albert's work is frequently punctuated by such claims to personal observation,[134] often located in Cologne, the Harz mountains, or regions near the Baltic, and sometimes involving conversation with people such as shepherds, fishermen, miners, or midwives. Here is Albert on generative span:

> A man can generate up to 70, and very occasionally this power is extended in stronger men up to 80. A woman conceives and gives birth [= *can* conceive and give birth] up to the age of 50. And this happens rarely, and in fact to few women. However, in our times a woman has been found whose first-born was 40 years older than her last-born.[135]

The framework is Albert's repetition of Aristotle (*a*), but there is also (*b*) some light tinkering with numbers, and (*c*) the intrusion of claimed contemporary evidence. The immediate impact on the reader? The *History of Animals* was already a collection of facts, and both this and other parts of the *On Animals* acquired an even more empirical air and some colouring from a contemporary and northern, usually German, world. At the same time its air of serene scientific balance was ruffled, sometimes, by Albert's misogyny, and also his taste for the biggest this and the largest number of that. This taste for records may have been derived in part from the similar penchant displayed by Avicenna in his *On Animals*, and the parade of extreme cases of longevity, multiple births, and suchlike in Pliny's *Natural History*.

Not only Albert's prestige and erudition but also the vastness of his *Twenty-One Books on Animals* will have given this work reference status. If much of the later learned world read Aristotle through the *Twenty-One Books*, it was also pre-

[130] Albert, *De animalibus*, IX. i. 1 (i. 674), *De signis pubertatis*; IX. i. 2 (i. 680), *De principio generationis in homine*; IX. i. 6 (i. 697), *De varietate potentiae generandi secundum aetates*; X (i. 730), *De impedimentis generationis*.

[131] Ibid., XVIII. ii. 5 (ii. 1231).

[132] Ibid., X. ii. 1 and 3 (i. 748 and 754).

[133] Ibid., XV. ii. 3 (ii. 1023).

[134] See the over one hundred entries under 'Albertus (Ego)' in the index, ibid., ii. 1599.

[135] Ibid., V. ii. 1 (i. 431).

sented with a model of handling it in another work by Albert, his *Quaestiones super libris de animalibus.* This was part of an older tradition[136] of short questions and answers on medical, biological, and other natural scientific themes, miscellaneous and curious and ranging from the causes of thunder to the causes of crinkly hair. A powerful fillip to the genre came in 1258 and 1260—in 1260 with the translation of the *Problems,* and two years earlier, in Cologne in 1258, with the lectures delivered by Albert which raised and debated 448 *Questions* about material in the *On Animals.* The reported versions of these are short, and most of them are scholastic in form, stating a question, pro and con theses, these theses' support in arguments or authorities, and Albert's response. They conclude with the conventional addendum in which the disputant clears up anything not yet addressed. A few answers are shorter and simpler, thirty-word questions and answers. Here are examples. 'Juxtaposed questions on coitus . . . Why can a woman generate in her twelfth year, whereas a man, for the most part, does not generate before his fourteenth, but with regard to the final limit a woman ceases to conceive before a man ceases to generate?' 'Whether life is conserved longer in cold and humid regions, or cold and dry, or cold and humid?' 'At what time ought human generation to take place?' 'Whether the period of generation lasts longer in men than the period of conception in women?' 'Whether man grows more slowly outside the womb than woman?' 'Whether the male is of longer life than the female?' (This is translated in full in the next section).[137]

The scholastic form now encourages the entry and parading of conflicting authorities. It allows some freedom in relation to Aristotle. Aristotle's beginning of both male and female generation at 14, contrary perhaps to observation and certainly to canon law on the minimum ages for marriage, was quietly bypassed, and canon law minima were substituted: 12 for girls and 14 for boys. The raising of some of Aristotle's dicta as questions, and their ventilation, served further to conceptualize them. At the same time it helped to establish a canon, and, apart from the specific content of Albert's answers, his bequest was this canon. *These* are the questions which are going to be repeated and ventilated in later Arts faculty commentaries and quodlibetic questions, and *this* is how they are going to be approached. There were later developments. Avicenna was already strong in Albert's *Questions,* but the numbers of authorities, in particular medical authors, increased, as did also overlap and connections with questions which were aired in the medical faculty. Thus on the one hand it was a philosopher from the Bologna circle of *medici* around Taddeo Alderotti who took down the Paris *Questions* of John Vath,[138] and on the other hand the questions raised and ventilated by Taddeo and his circle substantially overlap the questions we have been encountering. Questions were added, but they were essentially similar in character. Taking up

[136] Surveyed in B. Lawn, *The Salernitan Questions: An Introduction to the History of Medieval and Renaissance Problem Literature* (Oxford, 1963).

[137] Albert, *Quaestiones de animalibus,* V. xi–xiv; (p. 160); VII. xxvii (pp. 182–3); IX. i (pp. 202–3); IX. iii–v (pp. 203–4); XV. viii (pp. 263–4).

[138] Siraisi, *Taddeo,* pp. 43–4.

other themes in *On Animals* were John Vath's question, 'Whether in the human species there are more deformed males than females',[139] and the quodlibetic question of a Paris manuscript, 'Whether a woman of fifty can conceive'.[140]

A typical later product of this tradition is the collection of quodlibets in an Erfurt manuscript.[141] 'Questions were raised about anything (*de quolibet*), which I shall determine acording to the order of the books.' Some are from *On Animals*. 'The fourth question was why a prostitute cannot conceive . . . The sixth was why a woman comes to growth more quickly than a man . . .[142] It is asked whether a woman of fifty years can conceive . . .[143] It is asked whether youths ought to generate females . . .[144] Whether sperm in the fourteenth year is apt for generation or not.'[145] Albert is liberally quoted, the seventh book of the *Politics* is added to the authorities on generative span,[146] and Avicenna's *Canon* is quoted very precisely by its distinctive part-name, the number of the 'fen' in a particular book. But there is little sign of further development. My impression is that there had been excitement as western intellectuals came into contact with Aristotle's data, followed by absorption as this material was clarified and expanded by Albert and then re-introduced in more advanced form by Moerbeke's translation; and that the long final stage was intellectually static.[147] During this last period the principal historical theme is spread and influence. Works like this Erfurt manuscript and others, which addressed these questions in the fourteenth century and later, joined hands with the copies of the translations in a common task: imprinting in the minds of a large number of fairly educated men a slightly expanded version of the miscellaneous collection of reproductive and 'demographic' information, ideas, and phrases which originated in the *On Animals*.[148]

10.4 *Diffusion and reception of* Length and Shortness

While the *On Animals* was a very long text and *Length and Shortness* tiny, it is the latter's history which is the larger affair. Translated earlier, *Length and Shortness* achieved wider diffusion. The greater evidence about its role as a curriculum text suggests a higher profile in Arts faculties, and a more long-lasting one. And the contents of commentaries and questions on it suggest that it was a more intellectually stimulating text.

[139] Cova, 'Questioni di Giovanni Vath', 273–4.

[140] BN, MS Lat. 16089, fol. 54vb: *Alia questio fuit* [*utrum*] *mulier 50ta annorum possit concipere*.

[141] Erfurt, Stadtbibliothek, MS. Fol 236, fol. 36ra–48vb.

[142] Ibid., fol. 37ra. [143] Ibid., fol. 38ra–b. [144] Ibid., fol. 38vb. [145] Ibid., fol. 39va.

[146] Ibid., fol. 38rb: *sed viri possunt generare usque ad LXX, et hoc tangit 14* de hystoria [animalium] *et in* de animalibus *et VIIo* politicorum.

[147] This verdict may well be qualified by the work announced in n. 113 above.

[148] Much of the material which has been discussed had a long undergound afterlife as the pseudo-science of modern times through its entry into the anonymous questions *Omnes homines* of around 1300 (ed. E. R. Lind, *Problemata Varia Anatomica: MS 1165 The University of Bologna*, University of Kansas Publications, Humanistic Studies 38 (Lawrence, Kan., 1968)) and the immense diffusion of this work in translation—Lawn, *Salernitan Questions*, pp. 99–102.

Some of James of Venice's translations of other works of Aristotle are known to have spread very early in northern France, where there seems to have been knowledge of them by the late 1160s, at the abbey of Mont St Michel and among people with whom John of Salisbury was in contact. A manuscript from St Michel written about 1200 and containing *Length and Shortness* might be a later trace of this.[149] A learned Englishman who was working in the decades around 1200 seems to have written a commentary on it, which is no longer extant.[150] The works of David of Dinant condemned in Paris in 1210 contain a short treatment of length of life. Whether based on *Length and Shortness* or only on parts of *On Animals*,[151] David's discussion is fumbling and primitive. Things become clearer during the second quarter of the thirteenth century, when a standard collection of Aristotle's works on natural philosophy was being put together, known as the *Older Corpus*. The *Little Natural Works*, including *Length and Shortness* of Life—formed part of this collection.[152] Of the hundred and one still extant copies of James's translation, eighty-three survive as part of a book containing this *Older Corpus*, and seventy-three were copied in the thirteenth century. Take one example, a thirteenth-century manuscript. Its 397 folios contain many of the texts of the *Older Corpus*, the *Length and Shortness* on four of them. At the end of a table of contents there is this note. 'Henry of Renham wrote this book, and heard [it] in the schools of Oxford, and he emended [its text?] and glossed it while hearing.'[153] This is a microcosm of the early university history of the tract, part of a standard collection of writings which was itself a (fairly) standard Arts faculty book.

There are still 156 copies of Moerbeke's revision, and their story is a repeat, set at a later date. The newer Greco-Latin translations were gathered into another fairly standard collection, the *Newer Corpus*, and virtually all the still extant copies of the Moerbeke revision of the *Length and Shortness* are found within the manuscripts of this collection, mainly written in the fourteenth and fifteenth centuries. One early fourteenth-century example contains the *Newer Corpus* in its 361 folios, the *Length and Shortness* on three of them. On one leaf a later fourteenth-century hand wrote this: 'Contained in this book are all the books of *The Little Natural Works* needed for the Master's degree, and various other things as [will appear] to the person who looks.'[154]

Through the *Aristoteles Latinus* descriptions of copies of both translations, and of the fifty-seven still extant manuscripts of Averroes's compendium of the *Length and Shortness*, we can see ownership among colleges and individual masters and

[149] Minio, *Opuscula*, pp. 180, 191, and 216–18; AL *Codices 1*, pp. 437–8 no. 408.

[150] Weisheipl, 'Science in the thirteenth century', p. 436 n. 4.

[151] David of Dinant, *Quaternulorum fragmenta*, ed. M. Kurdzialek, Studia Mediewistyczne 5 (Warsaw, 1963), p. 19. There is no clear citation of *Length and Shortness*; see d'Alverny, 'Translations and Translators', 437, on David's remarkably early access to versions of *On Animals* and *Problems*.

[152] When the tract *De longitudine et brevitate vitae* (*Length and Shortness*) is contained in this Older Corpus, its title is always *De morte et vita*; G. Lacombe, 'Medieval Latin versions of the *Parva Naturalia*', *The New Scholasticism*, 5 (1931), 289–311 (p. 305).

[153] AL *Codices 1*, p. 387 no. 317; C. Burnett, 'The Introduction of Aristotle's Natural Philosophy', p. 40.

[154] Ibid., pp. 680–1 no. 930.

spread over a wide area of Latin Christendom, all traces of the text's long and wide academic use. Its role as a standard text to be lectured on appears in statute evidence from Paris in 1255 and 1366, and Oxford in the early fourteenth century,[155] while in Bologna a Professor was charged with lecturing on the *Little Natural Works* in 1324[156] and the text appears again in the 1405 statutes.[157] Its standard status continues with the mushrooming of new university foundations in northern and central Europe which started in the mid-fourteenth century: the 1389 statutes of the new university of Vienna specify it.[158] Many copies bear signs of ownership or connections with houses of the new religious Orders. While a letter in one copy of the *Older Corpus* from the Bishop of Cambrai to Cambrai Dominicans, dated 1249, is one example of indication of ownership which is uncertain, one example of indications in which we can repose confidence is another copy, once in the Franciscan convent of Santa Croce, which has this note on the first folio. 'Brother Peter of John had this philosophy text on loan from the librarian, of the Florence convent, that is to say, Brother S. de Bucellis.' The inscription leads us into the organized library of a Franciscan convent in Florence, texts which were part of the Arts training in the Franciscan educational system, and, if 'Brother Peter of John' is, as seems likely, 'Brother Peter of John Olivi', it tells us of one occasion of this famous theologian's borrowing the book, probably during his two years teaching at Santa Croce (1287–9).[159] Once again, as with *On Animals*, diffusion of some of the copies suggests further enquiry about Arts teaching in older monasteries[160] and cathedral chapters[161] as well as the newer Orders,[162] and once again a minority of copies with medical notes or works or notes of ownership by *medici* attest circulation in another milieu.[163]

[155] Weisheipl, 'Curriculum', 159 and 174–5; see also 148 (prescribed in Toulouse in 1309). The *Little Natural Works* appear in the Paris stationers' list of 1304 (*CUP* ii. 107) in two groups. The first specifies the titles of three of them, not including *Length and Shortness*, which is presumably in the second: *de motibus animalium, et aliorum Parvorum*. The commentary *De etate* by Albert in the same list (*CUP* ii. 111) was presumably his commentary on *Length and Shortness*.

[156] Siraisi, *Taddeo*, p. 21.

[157] *Statuti delle Università e dei Collegi dello Studio Bolognese* (Bologna, 1888), ed. C. Malagola, p. 774.

[158] A. Lhotsky, *Die Wiener Artistenfakultät 1365–1487* (Vienna, 1965), pp. 243 and 252–3.

[159] AL *Codices 1*, pp. 523–4 no. 591. AL *Codices 2*, pp. 938–9 no. 1366.

[160] AL *Codices 1*, pp. 251–2 nos. 28–9; 260 no. 49; 266–7 no. 60; 267–8 no. 62; 272–3 no. 73; 273–4 no. 75; 282–3 no. 95; 419 no. 380; 443 no. 420; 443–4 no. 422; 446–7 no. 427; 447 no. 429; 503 no. 552; 545–6 no. 642; 547–8 no. 644; 609–10 nos. 769–70; 634–5 no. 818; 673 no. 914; 677 no. 923; 730 no. 1037; 732–3 no 1043; 736–7 no. 1053; 742–3 nos. 1071–2; 744–5 no. 1075. AL *Codices 2*, pp. 806 no. 1130; 889–90 no. 1286; 1096–7 no. 1600; 1100–1 no. 1609. Averroes: AL *Codices 1*, pp. 253–4 no. 34; 263–5 no. 57; 541–2 no. 634.

[161] AL *Codices 1*, pp. 326–7 no. 185; 329–30 nos. 194–5; 330–1 no. 197. AL *Codices 2*, pp. 831 no. 1187; 845 no. 1214; 856–7 no. 1239; 1126–7 no. 1652. Averroes: AL *Codices 1*, pp. 366–7 no. 273. AL *Codices 2*, p. 848 no. 1241.

[162] AL *Codices 1*, pp. 276–7 nos. 81–2; 468–9 no. 476; 491 no. 524; 512 no. 570; 593 no. 733; 748 no. 1085. AL *Codices 2*, pp. 810–11 no. 1140; 922 no. 1336; 936–8 no. 1365; 941–2 no. 1369; 947–8 no. 1377; 949–50 no. 1380; 981 no. 1436; 984–5 no. 1442; 1066 no. 1553; 1099–1100 no. 1607; 1216 no. 1835. Averroes: AL *Codices 1*, pp. 457–8 no. 454; 495–6 no. 534.

[163] AL *Codices 1*, pp. 504–5 no. 554. AL *Codices 2*, pp. 895–6 no. 1294; 1058–9 no. 1540; 1115–16 no. 1634. Averroes: AL *Codices 2*, pp. 1018–19 no. 1487; 1227–8 no. 1863.

Arts students 'heard' the *Little Natural Works* in the schools.[164] Simon of Faversham's commentary begins with a question 'Can there be knowledge (*sciencia*) of the causes of length and shortness of life?'[165] A field of knowledge and an academic discipline is defined, and the authoritative text is there, in place. Other extant commentaries similarly show the exercises of the schools, elementary level of line-by-line exposition and then the higher level of raising questions upon the text.

There are traces of such activity in many different places. Adam of Buckfield's commentary comes from mid-thirteenth-century Oxford,[166] and there is a long line from Paris: James of Douai (1270s?),[167] Peter of Auvergne (probably between 1296 and 1302),[168] Simon of Faversham (died 1306),[169] Walter Burley (1306),[170] and John de Jandun (died 1328).[171] One commentary difficult to date was produced by Peter of Ireland, whose scarcely known life points only to two locations, the University of Naples, where he was teaching around 1239/44, and King Manfred's court, where he is glimpsed in debate some time between 1258 and 1266.[172] Several other works which are not commentaries contain, nevertheless, treatments of the theme which suggest their authors' past engagement with *Length and Shortness* in Arts courses. The Austrian monk Engelbert of Admont studied at Prague's Cathedral school (1271–4), but, as we shall see in Chapter 11 below, it seems most likely that the Arts-Medicine faculty of Padua was the most likely place for Engelbert's meeting both *Length and Shortness* and the *Politics*, in the period *c.*1278–84.[173] The early studies of another reader, Peter d'Abano (1257–*c.*1315), were in Padua, to which he returned around 1303, and in between (certainly in 1295 and 1298) he had been in Paris.[174]

[164] Useful on the fortunes of *Length and Shortness* in the schools are O. Lewry, 'Study of Aging in the Arts Faculty of the Universities of Paris and Oxford', in *Aging and the Ages in Medieval Europe*, ed. M. M. Sheehan, Pontifical Institute of Medieval Studies, Papers in Medieval Studies 11 (Toronto, 1990), pp. 23–38, and M. Dunne's introduction to his edition of Peter of Ireland, *Expositio et quaestiones in Aristotelis librum de longitudine et brevitate vitae*, Philosophes Médiévaux 30 (Louvain, Paris, 1993). A list of commentaries is provided by J. De Raedemaeker, 'Une ébauche de catalogue des commentaires sur les "Parva Naturalia" parus aux XIIIe, XIVe et XVe siècles', *Bulletin de philosophie médiévale* 7 (1965), 95–108.

[165] Dunne, *Peter of Ireland*, p. 39.

[166] Lewry, 'Aging', pp. 26–8; Dunne, *Peter of Ireland*, pp. 33–8.

[167] Dunne, *Peter of Ireland*, pp. 14–15. On James see M. Grabmann, 'Jakob von Douai, ein Aristoteleskommentator zur Zeit des Heiligen Thomas von Aquin und des Siger von Brabant', in his *Mittelalterliche Geistesleben: Abhandungen zur Geschichte der Scholastik und Mystik*, 3 vols. (Munich, 1926–56), iii. 158–79 (pp. 163 and 165), and Glorieux, *Arts*, pp. 192–3 no. 209.

[168] Lewry, 'Aging', pp. 33–6; Dunne, *Peter of Ireland*, pp. 38–43. See E. Hocedez, 'La vie et les oeuvres de Pierre d'Auvergne', *Gregorianum* 14 (1933), 3–36 (pp. 16–17 and 29).

[169] Lewry, 'Aging', pp. 35–6; Dunne, *Peter of Ireland*, p. 39. See Simon of Faversham, *Quaestiones super libro elenchorum*, ed. S. Ebbesen, Pontifical Institute of Medieval Studies, Studies and Texts 60 (Toronto, 1984), pp. 3–6.

[170] Lewry, 'Aging', pp. 36–8; Dunne, *Peter of Ireland*, p. 15.

[171] Dunne, *Peter of Ireland*, pp. 15 and 39. See L. Schmugge, *Johannes van Jandun (1285/89–1328): Untersuchungen zur Biographie und Sozialtheorie eines Lateinischen Averroisten*, Pariser Historische Studien 5 (Stuttgart, 1966), pp. 15 and 131 (see p. 6 on John probably having been a pupil of Peter d'Abano).

[172] Dunne, introduction.

[173] G. B. Fowler, *The Intellectual Interests of Engelbert of Admont* (New York, 1947), pp. 59 and 73–83, and 'A medieval thinker confronts modern perplexities: Engelbert, Abbot of Admont, O.S.B. (C.1250–1331)', *American Benedictine Review* 1973 (33), 226–48 (pp. 233–4).

[174] L. Premuda, 'Abano, Pietro d'', *DSB* i. 4–5; Vescovini, G. F., 'Introduzione', in *Il 'Lucidator*

It is not clear where Peter of Spain (d. 1277) studied; since his use of the older translation presses us to look for an earlier date, it is worth noting that between at least 1245 and 1250 he was in Siena, and between 1250 and 1264 in Portugal.[175] Peter was professor of medicine at the university of Siena, and is glimpsed in 1250 with three other physicians submitting a consultation on contagious diseases to the city's authorities.[176] Questions about life-span are found among the medical questions of an anonymous author in a Paris manuscript,[177] and among the questions addressed by medical authors in Taddeo Alderotti's circle in Bologna, around 1300.[178] Peter d'Abano's great *Conciliator*, which contains his examination of life-span,[179] was a work whose very purpose was to explore differences between philosophers and medical authors. Even though *Length and Shortness* did not have the formal place among medical texts that it had among Arts texts, it was nevertheless read by *medici*.

Where modern scholarship has been preoccupied with only one theme among those who wrote on length of life, differences between the sexes, the medieval commentators were interested in three themes, in particular Old Testament longevity, differences between regions, and differences between men and women. Let us look at these in turn.

Old Testament longevity was an old topic, which had received lucid statement and sophisticated debate by Augustine.[180] After the extraordinary figures for longevity early in Old Testament history, there had been a return to ordinary spans: 'men today live to 70 or 80 or not much more.'[181] So, there was a problem, especially in unbelievers' incredulous reaction to scripture. Augustine had raised various possibilities. One could refer unbelievers to examples of extreme long life—one of 200 years—mentioned by Pliny. There was inconsistency in the figures given in the Hebrew and Greek versions of the Old Testament, but the differences were insignificant. Some had suggested that a different system of

dubitabilium astronomiae' di Pietro d'Abano: Opere scientifiche inedite, ed. G. F. Vescovini, Il mito e la storia 3 (Padua, 1988), pp. 17–52 (pp. 25–6).

[175] Peter of Spain, *Tractatus bonus de longitudine et brevitate vite*, ed. M. Alonso, *Pedro Hispano: Obras filosóficas*, iii. 413–90. See L. M. de Rijk, 'On the life of Peter of Spain, The author of The *Tractatus*, called afterwards *Summule logicales*', *Vivarium* 8 (1970), 123–54; Lewry, 'Aging', pp. 28–31; Dunne, *Peter of Ireland*, p. 28.

[176] de Rijk, 'Peter of Spain', 151.

[177] BN, MS Lat. 12331, which is described in J. Koch, 'Jakob von Metz O.P., der Lehrer des Durandus de S. Porciano, O.P.', *AHDLMA* 4 (1930), 169–232 (pp. 173–4).

[178] Siraisi, *Taddeo*, pp. 256, 260, 312 (Taddeo Alderotti: *Utrum terra calida et humida sit causa longe vite*), 319 (Dino del Garbo: *Queritur que complexio sit longioris vite*), 321 (Turisanus: *Utrum complexio longioris vitae cognoscatur*), and 330–3 (questions on aging).

[179] Peter d'Abano, *Conciliator*, Differentia ix; 14ra–15vb: *Utrum natura humana non sit debilitata ab eo quod antiquitus necne*; Differentia xxi; 32va–34vb: *Utrum complexio calida et humida sit longioris vite, necne*; Differentia cxv; 169vb–170ra: *Utrum in vere magis abbrevietur vita, quam in caeteris anni temporibus.* Peter discusses regions and longevity in his *expositio* of the *Problems*, XIV. ix–x (*Problemata Aristotelis*, 150ra–vb), referring to *Length and Shortness*, Averroes's commentary on this, and the contradiction between Aristotle on long life in warm regions and Avicenna's example in the *Canon* of habitable warm regions, where there is a 'very brief period of natural life' (*tempus brevissimumn est vite naturalis*) and old age comes after thirty years.

[180] Augustine, *City of God*, XV. ix–xiv. [181] Ibid., XV. xiv; see Psalms 89(90): 10.

calculation was in use in early biblical history, and that the figures should be divided by ten: but this did not work.

When we turn from the *City of God* to the biblical commentaries of around 1300, we see that the new natural philosophy and medicine have invaded the topic. Addressing the question why men lived so long, Nicholas of Gorran (d. *c.*1295) cites *On Animals* and provides a eugenic reply, that they waited till the right time to generate.[182] Peter of la Palud's first explanation was the 'well-complexioned' constitution of the first parents.[183] But theology in its turn also invaded natural philosophy and medicine, as abbreviation of life from antiquity became a topic in Peter of Spain's treatise, the Paris anonymous medical questions, and Peter d'Abano's *Conciliator*.[184] With Engelbert of Admont it became the subject of a substantial monograph.[185]

Such a rapid and large abbreviation of life: could this have happened by nature? Or was it supernatural, brought about by divine ordination? Some things in the Old Testament are clearly according to nature. But others are not, and Engelbert reviews the problematic data of the Old Testament, long ages and their diminution over time, and generation by the elderly Abraham and Sarah. He advances arguments for natural reasons for ante-diluvian longevity being unlikely, in particular the similarity of diet, constellations, and elements before and after the flood. He also uses examples of God's punitive abbreviation of life as precedents to make a positive case for divine ordination. Engelbert then goes on to the other tack in the second half of the treatise, arguing that abbreviation *did* proceed from natural causes. He devotes several chapters to outlining the general natural causes of length and shortness of life,[186] in what is basically a vigorous reworking of Aristotle and Averroes. Intrinsic cause (warmth and dampness, and their preservation or consumption) and extrinsic and contingent cause (place, time, diet, and so on) are clearly demarcated, and differences by region and sex are tackled

[182] BN, MS Lat. 14416, fols. 35vb–6ra: *Item super illud, vixit quoque Seth CV annis, etc., queritur quomodo homines tunc tantum vivebant et ita robusti erant. Respondeo quod tunc in perfecta . . . etate et robore generabantur. Nunc autem aliter est, quia propter libidinem non expectant tempora debite etatis ad generandum, que sunt post tria septima, ut ait philosophus vel* [*sic; possibly:* VII *politicorum* vel] *de animalibus.* On Nicholas (d. *c.*1295), see *SOPMA* iii. 165–8. On his postills, see B. Smalley, 'Some Latin commentaries on the Sapiential books in the late thirteenth and early fourteenth centuries', *AHDLMA* 18 (1950–1), 103–28 (pp. 106–16).

[183] Naples, Biblioteca Nazionale, MS VI. D. 74, fol. 115va: Lamech genuit . . . *Si autem queritur quo homines illius temporis ita diu vivebant, ad hoc potest racio multiplex assignari, prima ex bonitate complexionis primorum parentum. Fuerunt enim duo primi a Deo inmediate formati, et per consequens optime complexionati, et sic ad longiorem vitam dispositi.*

[184] Peter of Spain, *Tractatus bonus*, v; iii. 483–4; BN, MS Lat. 12331, fol. 180rb: *Item, quero propter quod vita hominum nunc existentium brevior est.* See n. 177 above. See also Conrad of Halberstadt, *Responsorium curiosorum* (Lübeck, 1478), II. dcxxvii: *Quare vita antiquorum aliquando existentium sit diuturnior quam modernorum*—and see Lawn, *Salernitan Questions*, p. 103 n. 3, on the author, either a Conrad active *c.*1321 or another who died after 1362. *SOPMA* i. 283, holds attribution to either Conrad as in question.

[185] Engelbert, *Tractatus de causis longaevitatis hominum ante diluvium*, in B. Pez, *Thesaurus anecdotorum novissimus*, 6 vols. (Augsburg, 1721–3), i. 439–502.

[186] Ibid., VII–XI; 454–8.

before Engelbert engages in his final intellectual gymnastics to prove his natural-ground case.

Similarities between Engelbert's treatise and Peter d'Abano's shorter discussion of the same theme, together with the vast array of authorities in Engelbert's treatise, suggest that there was wider debate of this theme, which had been developing its commonplaces for some years. By the early fourteenth century, then, Aristotle, Averroes, and medicine were being applied systematically to Old Testament life-span. Weaker, but still perceptible, was a world of 'today' which their encounter with Old Testament data coaxed into the open. Abraham's holding that conception was impossible at his centenarian age and Sarah's 90 years brings in this addition from Engelbert: 'although today some octogenarian men and sexagenarian women who have generated children may be found'.[187] Reduction in human life-span has brought it down to its natural period, 'which, as it is now, is believed to be eighty years, and at its maximum, one hundred'. In another part of the treatise, it 'is restricted to a hundred years, and bit more in some men, though only in a few'.[188] 'It is clear that many today who are 14, or a little more, or about that age generate children.'[189] 'Today' does not mean that these should be read as a series of precise modern observations. There is no clear distinction between 'today' meaning 'all post-diluvian time' and 'Engelbert's lifetime'. *On Animals* and Albert's penchant for records are likely to lie behind the point about elderly generation, while a variety of authorities, including the Old Testament, are influencing the figures for maximum natural life-span. A figure plucked from *On Animals* unites with canon law to produce the exaggeration of a eugenic criticism of modern times: boys do not wait for the right time. However useless to a historian of past demographic reality, these 'todays' have more significance for the historian of thought. Just as contingency is expressly present and contrasted with the fundamental causes of length of life, so also is there some sense of a long-continuing 'now': both encourage a sense of what actually happens in the real world.

Region was writ large in the authorities. To recapitulate: Aristotle's natural works transmitted propositions about variation of many vital matters according to region and environment, including fertility and sterility, sex-determination, ease of childbirth, and the production of single babies or twins, while Avicenna's *On Animals* added a hint about regional variation in generative span. Most prominent, however, was the statement, found both in *Length and Shortness* and *Problems*, that those living in warmer regions were of longer life than those living in cold regions. Region was also very important to medical authors. When we turn to the commentators, we find intense interest. The theme attracts sharp

[187] Engelbert, II; 444: *licet hodie inveniantur aliqui viri octogenarii et mulieres sexagenariae generasse.*

[188] Ibid., XX; 467: *ultimum spatium vitae humanae secundum suam speciem et naturalem periodum, qui ut nunc est creditur esse LXXX et ad maximum centum annorum*; xxviii: *usque ad centum annos et modicum ultra in quibusdam, licet paucis, hominum.*

[189] Ibid., XXV; 475: *constat autem quod hodie multi generant filios circa annum XIV et modicum ultra vel circa existentes, antequam tempus perfectae mensurae et roboris ipsorum suorum corporum circa annum tricesimum assequantur.*

attention in Albert's commentary on *Length and Shortness.* Virtually all commentaries upon Aristotle's text which took the form of questions raised region as a question—James of Douai,[190] Peter of Auvergne,[191] Simon of Faversham,[192] John of Jandun,[193] Walter Burley,[194] John Buridan.[195] It is also raised in questions, about *On Animals* and *Problems*, quodlibetic Arts questions, and medical questions.[196] Where a later treatise does not take the form of questions, as in the case of Engelbert's, the topic is still given a lot of attention. A core of references to authorities and material was rapidly established, and much of this was recycled from one text to another, but the treatment of the theme remained lively and spirited.

In the tradition the commentators were handling, they found a deep divide between Aristotle and virtually everyone else. Albert pointed out Aristotle's minority position in his commentary, which later people read. The anonymous author of the Paris medical questions, which may be quite early, paraded impressive medical authorities holding opposing views.[197] Aristotle's being in a minority position became standard knowledge. He was either wrong, or he could be 'saved' by taking his 'warm' to mean 'temperate' and his 'cold' to mean 'extremely cold', as John of Jandun does. Commentators adopted for their climatic/regional map of length of life 'Ethiopians', who stood for hot and dry regions. Or sometimes people and geography were articulated in reverse order: there was the south, where black men did not live beyond thirty. Everywhere, the opposite in this

[190] Leipzig, Universitätbibliothek, MS 1405, fol. 94ra (Vat = Vatican, MS Ross 569, fol. 197ra): *Queritur in qua regione homines sint longioris vite, utrum* [Vat adds: *scilicet*] *in calidis aut in frigidis* [Vat adds: *regionibus*].

[191] Cambridge, Peterhouse, MS 192, fol. 31ra: *Queritur de causis extrinsecis et primo utrum habitantes in locis calidis sint longioris vite quam habitantes in locis frigidis.*

[192] Oxford, Merton College, MS 272, fol. 397va: *Consequenter queritur utrum habitantes in regionis calidis sint longioris vite quam habitantes in regionibus frigidis.*

[193] John of Jandun, *Questiones de causa longitudinis et brevitatis vitae*, Q. 15, in John of Jandun, *Questiones Super Parvis Naturalibus* (Venice, 1570), 93v: *Utrum homines habitantes in regionis calidis sint longioris vite habitantibus in regionibus frigidis.*

[194] Oxford, Oriel College, MS 12, fol. 110va: *Queritur utrum habitantes in regionibus calidis sunt longioris vite quam habitantes in regionibus frigidis.* In his exposition of *Problems* Burley also addressed the question, *Quare australes sunt naturaliter longevi*, Oxford, Bodley, MS Digby 77, fol. 67va and Digby 153, fol. 123r; Burley refers to Peter d'Abano in the prologue.

[195] John Buridan, *Quaestiones in librum Aristotelis de longitudine et brevitate vite* (Paris, 1516), Q. 6, f. 51 va: *Utrum habitantes in regionis calidis sint longioris vite quam habitantes in frigidis.* On Buridan (last certain text 1358), see E. Faral, 'Jean Buridan. Maître ès Arts de l'Université de Paris', *HLF* 38 (1949), pp. 462–605.

[196] Erfurt, Stadtbibliothek, MS Quart. 323, fol. 212va: *Item, quodlibetum utrum habitantes in regionibus frigidis et siccis sint longioris vite quam in regionibus frigidis et siccis... Item, utrum habitantes in regionibus frigidis et siccis sint longioris vite quam habitantes in regionibus calidis et siccis*; Conrad, *Responsorium curiosorum*, II. dcxxii: *Quare sunt magis longevi qui in calidis locis habitant*; see nn. 178–9 above.

[197] The author refers to *Length and Shortness* under its title in the *Older Corpus*, *De morte et vita.* Against the warm and humid region being conducive to long life, he urges the authority of *Galeni in* libro complexionum... *Constantini in* pantegni... *Avicenne et aliorum auctorum.* There is citation of *Ypocras*, and ranged on on the other side *Haly... philosophus in* libro de morte et vita [Aristotle, *Length and Shortness*] ... *Galenus in* commento super ampheros [on the Hippocratic *Aphorisms*]. For Avicenna, see nn. 77–8 above. See *Burgundio of Pisa's Translation of Galen's 'De complexionibus'*, ed. R. J. Durling, Galenus Latinus 1 (Berlin, New York, 1976), pp. 67, 69, 80, 86, 88, 97, and 110, where region is dealt with, although I have not identified the passages to which the anonymous was referring.

climatic regional map was constituted by cold and dry regions, sometimes northern, to which longer life pertained. Surrounding the narrower point about length of life was a broader point about the superiority of peoples of certain regions and climates, which is partly rooted in the earlier literature. While being itself the subject of independent questions—which region confers greatest spiritedness or the best complexion—its character and occasionally its substance pervaded the question on region and length of life. An example is John Buridan's answer to the question 'Whether those living in warm regions are of longer life than those living in cold'. 'Some men are of rare complexion and weak constitution', wrote John, 'others of stronger complexion and more strongly put together. The former die quickly in cold regions, and live longer in warm ones . . . there is a powerful natural heat inside the latter. In cold regions such men are large and spirited, and of very long life.'[198]

The superiority and awareness of differences in peoples is also clearly a matter of strong current thought, feeling, prejudice, or even jokiness among the commentators. Albert writes that it is commonly said that men from warm regions are naturally cowardly and no good at war, and he introduces the French word *hardi* in a jibe about the French being bold but having no follow-up. A point about regions and diet (more food in warm regions, conducive to better conservation of life) has him tartly commenting that, nevertheless, Germans and Poles consume much more than the French and Lombards do.[199] German women are very fertile but experience difficulty in childbirth.[200]

The milieu should not be forgotten, in this case Germanophone. The first two of these three points were expressed by Albert, a man of Swabian noble origin, while he was going over Aristotle's work for the benefit of Dominicans in the Rhineland city of Cologne, in words which were taken down by a friar who is known simply as Conrad of Austria. Current thought and prejudice combine with the themes of ancient texts, in a picture whose most important elements have already been stated. There is the relegation of hot regions, where there is quick childbirth but short life, as represented by the thirty years of Ethiopian crinkly-haired black men. And there is pride in the superior spiritedness and physical strength of men in cold and dry regions. These regions are sometimes northern, and in them there is longer life. James of Douai extracts a point from Constantine the African, Saxon cities as an example of the milieux in which there is long life.[201]

[198] Buridan, *Questiones*, VI; 51vb: *aliqui homines sunt rare complexionis et debilis compositionis, alii vero sunt fortiores complexionis et fortius coagulati . . . et tunc in illis est calor naturalis valde fortis . . . tales homines sunt in regionibus frigidis magni et animosi et valde longe vite.*

[199] Albert, *Quaestiones*, VII. xxvii–xxviii; 182–3. Sanudo, *Liber secretorum*, II. iv. 18 (ii. 73) describes the Germans as great eaters through coming from frigid regions.

[200] Albert, *De natura loci*, II. iii; p. 27: *sed huius nos videmus instantiam in mulieribus germanicis, quae multum concipiunt fere ultra omnes mulieres, et difficillime pariunt.* This combines two traditions, on the one hand the notion of *Germania* being so called because of the fecundity of its people (see above, Ch. 9 n. 32), and on the other hand the notion of difficulty of childbirth in northern regions (found in Avicenna's *Canon*). On Avicenna, see n. 76 above.

[201] Vatican, MS Ross. 569, fol. 197ra (variants from Leipzig, Universitätsbibliothek, MS 1405, fol. 94ra = L): *Circa lectionem istam queritur in qua regione homines sint longioris vite, utrum in calidis aut in*

Blunter and most clearly expressive of the trend I have been describing is the anonymous author of the medical questions in the Paris manuscript. His conclusion, he says, is that 'a warm and humid region is not the cause of longer life, but rather men who live in it [in a warm and humid region] live less than those who live in cold countries, for example in England, Germany, and suchlike' (*calida et humida regio non est causa longioris vite, sed in ea minus vivunt homines quam qui in frigidis terris habitant, ut in Anglia, Almannia, et huiusmodi*).[202] Commentators are intermingling their own world and the worlds of their favoured authorities—everyone other than Aristotle—and doing it with considerable vigour.

The theme of differences according to sex cropped up in all of the Aristotelian works we have been discussing. Against the backdrop of faster female progress through life stages (*Generation*, *Problems*), there were the general statements. *According to nature* and *as a general* rule males [in the animal world] are longer-lived than females, with the possible exception of some birds (*History*). The male is longer-lived than the female (*Problems*, where context indicates that humans are at issue). *Contingently*, however, there could be faster aging and shorter life for men (*History*) or males in general (*Length and Shortness*), because of the drying out which resulted from too much sexual activity; faster aging for women through giving birth too many times (*History*); and greater aging for men through labour and its dessicating effect (*Length and Shortness*). In Aristotle's tract the most important statement comes after the two contingencies of emission of seed and labour. It is a sentence which concludes and generalizes, putting these two contingencies in their lesser place: 'By nature, however, and as a general rule, the male lives longer than the female, because the male is of greater heat than the female.'[203] While Averroes's compendium summarizes, it also reverses Aristotle's drift: 'because of paucity of intercourse . . . females live longer than males.' Aristotle's contingent variation—*if* males engage in excessive sex—has turned into an explanation which implies a general truth: there *is* such a lesser consumption of females through sex, which is the reason they live longer. The reader of Aristotle and Averroes encountered flat contradiction.

Those who commented on the meaning of *Length and Shortness*, such as Adam de Buckfield and Peter of Ireland,[204] devoted some time to clarifying and explaining. When we turn to those who raised questions on the text, we find the

frigidis. Et videtur quod in frigidis, primo auctoritate Avicene in maiori canone. Dicit enim quod habitantibus in calidis regionibus sit magnus [L: *magis*] *resolutio humidi et cito minuitur humidum et cito veniunt ad senium, quia sensus* [L: *senectus*] *causatur ex imutacione* [L: *minucione*] *humidi. Unde veniunt ad senectutem in XXX annis, sicut homines nigri. Idem eciam vld* [L: *vult*] *Constantinus in 5* penthegni, *vult enim quod habitantes sub polo et in civitatibus Saxonie sint longe vite.* Constantine the African, *Liber Pantegni, Theorica*, V. ix; 19vb: *Septentrionalis aer frigidus est et sic civitates ergo septentrionali polo supposite sicut sausonie leucicie frigidiores et sicciores esse comprobantur. His aqua clara est, aer clarissimus, corpora sanissima, color pulcher et rubicundus, corpora mobilia et fortiora, vita longa, mores asperi.*

202 BN, MS Lat. 12331, fol. 178vb. 203 See n. 64 above.

204 Adam de Buckfield, *Expositio*, Oxford, Merton College, MS 272, fol. 24ra; Peter of Ireland, *Expositio*, lectio VII, ed. Dunne, p. 145; see lectio VIII Q. 2, p. 148, where comparative life-span of the two sexes comes up, where the question asked is not life-span but why the female is colder.

theme coming up briefly under another general heading. With Buridan it is alluded to briefly under the question of which complexion pertains to longer life,[205] and with John of Jandun under a discussion of warm and humid qualities;[206] and Engelbert simply repeats Aristotle's drift, referring to the periods of males' lives being longer.[207] However, none of these writers raised the theme as an independent question: no one out of James of Douai, Buridan, Peter of Auvergne, Simon of Faversham, Burley, and John of Jandun. And where it came up under other headings it was not ornamented, as *region* was, with a glittering array of further authorities. With one exception, to be examined in a moment, the same point applies to questions upon *On Animals*, and more general Arts quodlibets. Commentators absorbed and understood the theme, but it aroused much less interest than region.

The one exception is Albert the Great. Not only did he deal with the theme in his commentary on *Length and Shortness*, but he also raised it as a question during his 1258 Cologne lectures. However digressive and intermittently original, Albert's commentary had the elementary aim of expounding Aristotle's meaning, and this is why Albert simply repeated him. 'Speaking according to nature, however, among men males are of longer life than females, unless contingently some exertion or sexual activity shortens their [males'] life.' When unfettered, however, as Albert was in his Cologne lectures, he did the opposite, and stated that contingently females lived longer. We shall return to this later in the chapter.

The introduction and reception of the *Length and Shortness of Life* constitutes, first of all, a chapter in the history of thought. It acquired a formal position in centres of higher learning, its subject acquired definition and status as a specific area of learned knowledge and discussion, and it was read, commented upon, questioned, and learnt in the schools. It had a higher profile than the miscellaneous information and concepts of the *On Animals*, and its instilling of certain vocabulary and themes in the minds of the learned minority in Latin Christendom, Arts students and also *medici*, will have been sharper and deeper. They also amounted to a clear overall picture, life-span as something dealt with comparatively by biology and medicine, a distinction of nature and contingency, differences between the sexes, and, above all, a distinct mental map of regions and peoples. The ideas were not only the property of the learned. Suggestive here is one mid-fourteenth-century text,[208] written by a Dominican called Conrad. The work has a preamble which owes something to literary conventions about introductions but which at the same time makes plausible statements about the real world. Conrad refers to his fellow Dominicans' task of 'being among men of various estates and

[205] Buridan, *Questiones*, VII; 51vb–2ra: *Que complexio sit longioris vite . . . Item, femelle in comparatione ad masculos sunt communiter flegmatice; sunt enim communiter magis frigide et magis humide. Et tamen communiter femelle sunt brevioris vite masculis, ergo flegmatica complexio est brevis vite.*

[206] John of Jandun, *Questiones*, XIII; 92r: *utrum calidum et humidum sint causa longe vite.* There is brief repetition of the point about emission of seed: *masculus etiam si sit multum coitivus est brevioris vitae quam femella, si sit casta.*

[207] Engelbert, *De causis longaevitatis*, XIII; 459–60.

[208] See n. 183 above.

conditions'. 'Many men want to ask about rare and curious things, and take pleasure in hearing and talking about them.'[209] So, in order to ease the friars' way among men, Conrad has compiled this material into a *Responsorium curiosorum*, a resource-manual to help in replies to such men's questions. The material in the compendium concerns the natural world, dealing with animals in general in its second book and man in its third.Two questions are 'Whether generative power lasts longer in men than power to conceive does in women?', and 'Whether the male is longer-lived than the female?'[210] The latter cites Albert and repeats him. Dominicans might preach faith and morals: but *these* were things people were really interested in, really delighted to chat about.

If the ideas became the ordinary mental furniture of later medieval men, they also had the capacity to stimulate the brightest of these to further thought. 'If, however, we compare its [summer's] illnesses to winter illnesses: for example, summer with thirty illnesses, winter on the other hand with seven. Certainly what happens is more people dying from the former's thirty than the latter's seven, since thirty is much more than seven. However, among the seven people [ill] in winter, proportionately more happen to die—let us say three [of the seven] as against six from the thirty [ill] in summer; unless the [summer] illness was a pestilence affecting many people.'[211] This is Peter d'Abano talking about seasonal incidence of illness and mortality, plucking numbers from the air, certainly, but *thinking* the application of number to the idea. A few decades later we can read the Dominican John Bromyard writing about death, ruminating about the evils of modern times, including overpopulation, and musing about the different illnesses which bring about death in infancy, youth, and old age. In the midst of this he thinks about the fraction of those who are born which does not reach eighty.[212] The span may come from the Psalms, and the fraction may be absurd (one tenth), but, like d'Abano a few years earlier, Bromyard is arithmetizing the idea.

10.5 *Observing contemporary demographic realities?*

What was the relation between people thinking *these* thoughts, and thinking about the demographic realities of the world in which they lived?

Let us think first of an ordinary student, and the impact upon him of the distinction between what happened according to nature and contingency. What would have been the relation in his mind between what the principles of nature

[209] Lawn, *Salernitan Questions*, p. 104 and n. 8.

[210] Conrad, *Responsorium*, III, ccclxxxiv: *utrum mas sit longioris vite quam femina*; ccclxxxvii: *utrum in viris plus durat virtus generacionis quam in feminis virtus conceptionis.* See also nn. 183 and 195 above.

[211] Peter d'Abano, *Conciliator*, Differentia, cxv; 170va: *Si enim comparemus aegritudines eius ad eas, quae hyemis, ut aestatis sunt 30 hyemis vero 7, ex 30 quidem illius plures contigit mori quam ex 7 huius, cum multum 30 7 excedant* [*r: excedat*]. *Ex 7 tamen hyemis plures proportionalitates* [*r: proportionaliter*] *accidit mori, puta tres, quam ex 30 estatis quia sex, nisi aegritudo fuerit pestilentia plurimos afficiens.*

[212] John Bromyard, *Summa praedicantium, Mors*, 2 vols. (Venice, 1586), ii. 71ra; also under *Vita*, ii. 436rb.

show and what actually happens? And what would have been the influence of the empiricism of the texts, which sometimes claimed this or that as a fact of observation, even though the texts' contents were mainly deductions from general principles? The formidable example of collecting and reporting data which was present in Aristotle's biological works, especially the *History of Animals*, was a mixed legacy. A principle was represented: but the Philosopher had spoken. The Philosopher was in fact contradicted by one authority on sex and life-span and by many on region, and Avicenna's criticism encouraged an attitude of less respect for Aristotle than is sometimes thought. However, the Arts student was primarily interested in passing exams. His first task was to master texts, and what he was trying to understand was other philosophical texts and some works, in particular the *Little Natural Works*, in which 'demographic' propositions were embedded in natural philosophical speculation. The contingencies of region, sex, and labour were investigated as general principles. The student's next aim was to widen his view to take in the sometimes discrepant views of other authorities—and to understand and sort these out. None of this means that such a student was never observant, only that his scholastic exercise was very abstract. This very abstraction, of course, may have encouraged awareness of the gulf between commentary in the academic hall and the facts of the world beyond its door. Commentary in the hall did not exclude contingency. The first statement in such a commentary, 'and thus (or therefore) we see that such men are long-lived, or whatever', is that it is clinching an argument, and is almost certainly derived from general principles (or another author). It is unlikely to be an observation which started the discussion. However, discussions which include contingency, what actually happens, and preface purported descriptions of the world with *vidimus*, 'we see' that people are like this, are likely to have some long-term influence on readers, however intangible: encouraging them to think about seeing, and to see.

Let us turn to the men who have left commentaries. They shared the outlook sketched in the previous paragraph, but they were men of exceptional learning and, occasionally, originality. Further, their works were not simply mirror-images of the emphases to be found in the authorities they were handling. Where their own commentaries display sharp features, it is legitimate to ask what is producing these, whether the particular outlook and experience of an individual author, or perhaps even some pressure being exerted on the minds of these men by the demographic realities of their world. The inordinate interest, consistent view, and occasional explicit importing of their own world which is found in commentators discussing region is the clearest example of the latter. The commentators were clerics from England, northern France, and Germany, and one widespread experience for such northerners was travel to southern Europe, especially to the papal court and Italy. Their texts contained some contemporary northerners' pride, proto-racial in character, and a comparative view of longevity, superior in the north, based not only on authorities but also almost certainly the crude contrasts lodged in their minds by travellers' experience in southern Europe. This last point cannot be proved absolutely, but the circumstantial case is strong.

The same cannot be said for Albert's statement about differences between the sexes. Or rather, it cannot be said as quickly. Let us begin with the question he raised in 1258,[213] which is here translated in full:

Further, there is the question whether the male or female is longer-lived.
(1) It seems that the female is. What is moist contributes to life in itself, what is hot however only contingently, for what is hot tends to consume what is moist. Since, therefore, the female is more moist and the male is hotter, the female will be longer-lived.
(2) Further, where illness is later, life will be longer; but the female becomes ill later; therefore etc.
The Philosopher says the opposite in *On the cause of shortness and length of life.*
It should be said that by nature the male is longer-lived, contingently however the female [is longer-lived].
Natural length of life subsists in radical moistness and temperate heat; shortness of life, however, arises from the consumption of radical moistness by heat. But temperate heat and radical moistness abound more in the male than in the female; therefore etc [therefore by nature the male is longer-lived].
However, contingently females are longer-lived, in this instance because they [females] work less, on account of which they are not consumed so much. They are more cleansed through the menstrual flow. And they are weakened less through coitus. Therefore they are more conserved. And these causes are contingent.
To the [two] arguments [advanced at the beginning].
[1] To the first it should be said that to consume is not [of the nature] of heat in itself—at least, not to consume is [of the nature] of the sort of temperate heat which is [found] in the male. And beyond this, moistness is twofold, namely aery and watery. Aery moistness contributes to life, as is said in the book *On the cause of length and shortness of life*, and watery moistness, which abounds in the female, does not [contribute to life]; the first, however [aery moistness], abounds in man; therefore etc.
[2] To the second argument it is to be said that illness is two-fold, namely [illness which occurs] by nature, and [illness which occurs] not by nature; illness not by nature occurs less in females than in males, and this is because their superfluities are purged more [than males' superfluities are, in the case of females] through menstruation. Illness according to nature occurs more in them than in men, because in males there is a stronger power to resist, in women a weaker power; therefore etc.

Albert says *femina* (female) rather than *mulier* (woman), *mas* (male) rather than *vir* or *homo* (man). Although a tiny doubt may linger about the exclusive application to humanity of Albert's debate of longevity, it seems likely that he was thinking mainly about humans. The veneer is broken three questions later, where

[213] Albert, *Quaestiones*, XV. viii; pp. 263–4.

the question says 'male' and 'female' but the subject—morals—very quickly has a heated misogynist replacing a cool natural philosopher and letting fly about 'men' and 'women'.[214] Albert's plumping for the female contingently living longer than the male was made famous by the demographic historian, David Herlihy, who had no hesitation on this point. Seeing this text as a reversal of general classical opinion, he published an article in which he used it alongside other evidence to argue that by Albert's time a deep sea-change in the life-expectancies of men and women had taken place: men were now living longer.[215]

What lay behind Albert's conclusion?

Contradiction of Aristotle on the other point, regions and length of life, was common, and this would have made the conclusion unshocking. An audience could have seen it simply as a lecturer preferring the alternative authority, Averroes. This was probably the case with Peter of Spain. After repeating Aristotle, Peter simply states, 'contingently, however the opposite happens', citing dessication through the emission of seed and 'the labour and *continuous motion*' of males (my italics indicate an addition in Peter).[216] There was more to Albert, however, than this. Just as he was unique in raising and debating the theme, so was he unique in the attention he displayed, in other texts, to health and aging in women. Albert returns again and again to the dangers of childbirth, adding to the authorities he is using. In *On Animals* he writes that if a young girl is impregnated, 'she suffers pain in childbirth *with a great pain*', and 'if they conceive before 21, *which happens most frequently*, they are *racked* with pain in childbirth'.[217] Distinguishing 'young' from 'under 15', he adds danger of death to this latter category, because of smallness of body,[218] and we saw him earlier dwelling on the prolificness of German women and their difficulty in labour. He connects bearing many children to good health, aging, and dying earlier. 'A woman who gives birth much is healthier, and she is made more quickly an old woman, and she dies sooner', and 'women who bear many children are made old and die quicker.'[219] 'Becoming old

[214] Albert, *Quaestiones*, XV. xi; pp. 265–6.

[215] D. Herlihy, 'Life Expectancies for Women in Medieval Society', in *The Role of Women in the Middle Ages*, ed. R. T. Morewedge (New York, 1975), pp. 1–22. Herlihy repeated the argument in an article published in 1978, which was reprinted in the posthumous collection of his essays edited by A. Molho, *Women, Family and Society in Medieval Europe: Historical Essays 1978–1991* (Providence and Oxford, 1995), pp. 57–68. The remarkable omission of these articles from the lists of his own works in Herlihy and Klapisch, *Tuscans and their Families*, and D. Herlihy, *Medieval Households* (Cambridge, Mass., and London, 1985) may indicate that he came to have reservations about the thesis.

[216] Peter of Spain, *Tractatus bonus*, III. ii; iii. 466–7: *Masculinus autem sexus naturaliter vitam prolongat magis quam femineus. Unde masculina animalia longius vivunt naturaliter eo quod calorem naturalem optinent fortiorem et virtutes fortiores, et machina corporis in ipsis est perfectioris et fortioris coagulationis, et idcirco tardioris resolutionis. Accidentaliter autem contingit contrarium.*

[217] Albert, *De animalibus*, IX. i. 2; iii. 680: *iuvenculae . . . cum impraegnantur, dolent in partu dolore magno . . . Si autem ante tempus vicesimi primi anni concipiunt, sicut frequentissime evenire solet . . . vehementer in partu cruciantur.*

[218] Ibid., X. ii. 3; i. 754. He probably derived the point from Avicenna.

[219] Ibid., X. ii. 1; i. 749: *mulier multum pariens est sanior et cito fit anus et citius moritur; sterilis autem ut in pluribus plurium est aegritudinum, sed diu perseverat iuvenilis et diutius vivit*; IX. i. 2; i. 680: *mulieres multos portantes infantos citius antiquantur et moriuntur.*

sooner' and 'dying sooner' are juxtaposed but not identical statements, for Albert is saying that women aquire the characteristics of old age quicker, and they may or do die sooner. The characteristics attract his attention. His word for women who bear many children being 'made old' is *antiquantur*: 'made ancient'. Elsewhere he details this: 'they go grey and get old women's wrinkles and features.'[220] Present in not precisely measurable portions are Albert the misogynist and Albert the scientist, obsessively curious about the particulars of physical phenomena. Albert goes on to apply sharply to women the distinction made by his authorities between ill health and short life. 'For the most part', he wrote (continuing from the sentence quoted about the health of the childbearing woman), 'the sterile woman has more illnesses. But she remains youthful for a long time, and she lives longer.' In Albert's debate in 1258 he made a not immediately clear distinction between natural and unnatural illness in males and females. It is reminiscent of the elementary learned medical distinction between 'naturals' (such a person's age, complexion, and sex), and 'non-naturals' (environment, exercise, diet, and outlook). 'Natural' may mean that which is constitutionally inherent in being a male or female, where the female's Aristotelian imperfection will clearly mean more illness, while 'infirmity not by nature' may mean all regular illnesses which affect *both* men and women. Within Albert's package of reasoning from first principles (such as female natural imperfection) and explaining *why* something is the case (such as more purging), there is one datum to which he is sticking. Albert's Aristotelian insistence on superior male natural power to resist distracts attention from the real point, which may be this: females suffer less from general illnesses.

Since Albert presented himself as a great observer of individual natural phenomena, it is likely that he conceived the material in the previous paragraph as lying both within his reading and his observation of women.[221] There is much evidence about Albert's omnivorous interest in *individual* phenomena; murkier, however, is his possible interest in quantity and number. Of course, in an unremarkable way he retailed small numbers relating to generative span, and he had a curiosity in record numbers. More significant, however, is that he does not display a particular taste for numerical comparisons, for proportions, and for giving estimates.

With these in mind, I suggest a reading of Albert thus.

[1] Albert may have been impressed by some pockets of long-lived women. Obvious candidates are two groups well-known to him, German aristocratic widows and communities of female religious, perhaps living longer than male religious.

[220] Ibid., IX. i. 3; i. 688: *et tunc canescunt et aniles accipiunt rugas et dispositiones.*

[221] The modern index to Albert's *De animalibus* (ii. 1599) contains an entry, 'Albertus, (ego)', referring to 119 passages, in most of which Albert says, 'I saw this', or makes an equivalent claim to direct experience. These are discussed in P. Hossfeld's *Albertus Magnus als Naturphilosoph und Naturwissenschaftler* (Bonn, 1983), pp. 76–96. Asking the question directly, 'Von welcher Qualität sind die eigenen Beobachtungen des Albertus Magnus?', Hossfeld has carefully scrutinized Albert's claims, in some cases remarking Albert's dependence on another written source, but also noting that there can be personal observation in cases where Albert formulates things impersonally. He notes the qualitative rather than quantitative character of Albert's observations (p. 94).

As we saw in Chapter 3, it was precisely the female religious of the milieu in which Albert spent his early mature years, Cologne, who made *one* sort of statistical impact. They impressed Matthew Paris by their very large numbers.[222]

[2] What lay between such observation of women, sharply-etched and miscellaneous, and the general proposition that contingently, that is to say in the real world and as it happens, women are longer-lived than men? I suggest that Albert had no great thought about overall numbers and proportions, or the difference between 'more', 'a little more', and 'much more', but simply made a long mental leap from black to white, from 'more one way' to 'more another way'.

[3] While Albert's statement *may* be better evidence than I am suggesting, it is clear that it is at best evidence about his view of the *existing* state of affairs: not evidence of a relatively *recent change*, as was inferred by David Herlihy.

10.6 Contemporary length of life

Real evaluation of the thought of the commentators needs to include in its considerations the relationship between this thought and contemporary levels of mortality, whether non-existent, out of kilter, or with some congruence. But the reality of contemporary mortality can never be more for us than the subject of controlled speculation. We lack mortality figures in themselves and also good evidence on diet, health, and disease.

The scarcity of evidence is an invitation to conjecture at will and fill the void with 'nasty, brutish, and short' lives. Girls married young and bred like rabbits, with death coming quickly to everyone. Using more respectable language, academic accounts describe a demographic regime in which high fertility is balanced by high mortality, in a population which remained fairly stable or only changed slowly. They add one nuance, the implications for fertility and mortality of the slow rise in population for three centuries up to around 1300, and decline thereafter. The particular sub-theme of differences between the sexes began to attract much attention in 1975, when David Herlihy published his article on women's life-expectancies. The context of Herlihy's argument was a general history of human life-span and mortality, which goes like this.[223] Whereas in pre-historic

[222] See Ch. 4 above, p. 106. For observation of great length of life among *male* religious celibates, see the comment on Carthusians living to 80 and even 100, helped by their vegetarian diet, in Arnau de Vilanova, *De esu carnium*, ed. D. M. Bazell, *Opera medica omnia*, xi (Barcelona, 1999), p. 131.

[223] G. Acsádi and J. Nemeskéri, *History of Human Life Span and Mortality* (Budapest, 1970), pp. 182–7, 221–5, and 259–63; D. Brothwell, 'Palaeodemography and earlier British Populations', *World Archaeology* 4 (1972), 75–87 (p. 83); G. J. Stolnitz, 'A Century of International Mortality Trends II', *Population Studies* 10 (1956–7), 17–42 (emphasizing complexity and variability of the problem of sex-differentials) and 'Recent Mortality Trends in Latin America, Asia and Africa. Review and Reinterpretation', *Population Studies* 19 (1965–6), 117–38 (pp. 136–7); W. Brass, 'Introduction: Bio-Social Factors in African Demography', in *The Population Factor in African Studies*, ed. R. P. Moss and R. J. A. R. Rathbone (London, 1975), 87–94 (p. 93); S. H. Preston, 'Causes and Consequences of Mortality Declines in Less Developed Countries during the Twentieth Century', in *Population and Economic Change in Developing Countries*, ed. R. A. Easterlin (Chicago, 1980), pp. 289–360.

civilizations and also in classical Rome some evidence points to men having better life chances than women, by the mid-twentieth century this pattern could only be found in underdeveloped countries, rural Guinea, Guatemala, parts of India, and so on. By contrast, in developed western countries women have had the advantage since census records began, and the advantage is increasing. When did the change-over start, when did women in Europe begin to claw back the difference, draw level with men, and then draw ahead? Herlihy argued that a changeover had occurred by the central middle ages. Higher compensations for injury to women than to men in barbarian law-codes indicated the scarcity of women, showing that women were still shorter-lived than men in dark-age Europe. However, by the central and later middle ages the flow of money and goods at marriage shows an excess of girls in the marriage market, and some later medieval German towns show a surplus of women. Women are living longer than men now, and this fundamental change finds its correlation in the move away from Aristotle's ancient statement that men lived longer—over to Albert's ringing declaration of the opposite in 1258.

Herlihy's specific arguments were weak. The first explanation of higher compensation in law-codes was the intention to give more protection to those who were more vulnerable, and the first question to be asked when one finds an excess of women in certain towns is, 'can higher immigration by women explain it?' Nevertheless, Herlihy's arguments convinced some scholars, leaving to them only further enquiry about how such a large change could have come about. In earlier times women's specific need for more iron, because of loss of blood between menarche and menopause, had been supplied inadequately, with fundamental debilitating effect. Women were thereby anaemic and more vulnerable to fatal illnesses. There were the beginnings of dietary change in the ninth century, with more meat, fish, cheese, and eggs, and then very significantly an increase in iron in their diet, in particular through the spread of the use of cooking-pots made of iron.[224] The leading expert on medieval diet, Christopher Dyer, points to the implausibility of sufficient spread of such pots, and, more damagingly, to the fact that most pots were copper.[225]

Herlihy in general thought of medieval Europe as a bloc, not distinguishing between the north-west and the south, and, although he thought about change between the early and central middle ages, he did not address the possibility of later long continuity, and of demographic history not finding a great divide, as has been found by political and religious history, between the '(late) medieval' and '(early) modern' periods. Divisions in Europe and long continuity have, however, been addressed by British historical demographers. Given the lack of evidence, their essays cannot provide sure answers, but they do mark off the ground upon which enquiry—or rather, informed and controlled speculation—should take place. Their mallets have driven in three pegs.

[224] V. Bullough and C. Campbell, 'Female Longevity and Diet in the Middle Ages', *Speculum* 55 (1980), 317–25.

[225] Conversation with the author.

[1] Looking back from what is known to speculate about the unknown seems the first principle, and the known here in England stretches back from modern census material to the patient reconstruction of the populations of some sixteenth-century communities. Wrigley took one of the latter, Hartland, as an example, in a powerful article which undermined assumptions about automatic very high levels of past mortality.[226] Hartland was not handicapped by the higher mortality expected in large and densely populated communities (and their propensity to infectious diseases) or in a low marshy location. It was a small and salubriously situated village, and from Elizabethan times until 1837 it showed expectation of life at birth of about fifty-five years, a level not achieved nationally until 1920. How should one look back from this four-century continuity towards the preceding the four centuries—through the higher mortality of the fourteenth century and back to the more favourable preceding period?

[2] In the sub-theme, the comparison of female and male life-expectancies, there is the possibility of some statistics even within the medieval period, albeit only for élite groups. Two studies in medieval northern Europe, Leyser's of aristocratic families in tenth-century Saxony and Hollingsworth's of English ducal families (1330–1479), showed greater female life-expectancies, and, where the figures allow some further break-down (Hollingsworth's), there is the particular datum that women were surviving better than men even through their childbearing years.[227]

[3] Wrigley's arguments about Hartland began with a reminder of the fundamental fact of his article's title, 'No death without Birth', that 'for most of human history fertility and mortality must have been at closely similar levels'. While low mortality in Elizabethan Hartland went hand in hand with such protections against infectious diseases as low density of habitation and extended maternal breast-feeding, at the level of demographic analysis it was the necessary counterpart of low fertility. Low fertility, itself, was mainly produced by a marriage-pattern in which the girls got married for the first time rather late, in their twenties, and in which a substantial proportion did not marry at all (see the fuller discussion of this in Chapter 12 below). Both factors put a limit on childbearing. There was a 'wide prevalence of [this] "European" marriage-pattern in Europe north of the Alps and the Pyrenees and west of the Oder'. In other words, in this region there was a general and reciprocal relation between the low fertility of the marriage-regime and low mortality, where the healthiest examples would be like Hartland. It has been shown that this marriage-pattern was already present in mid-thirteenth-century rural England. At the same time it has been suggested that

[226] E. A. Wrigley, 'No Death Without Birth: The Implications of English Mortality in the Early Modern Period', in *Problems and Methods in the History of Medicine*, ed. R. Porter and A. Wear (London, New York, Sydney, 1987), pp. 133–50.

[227] K. J. Leyser, *Rule and Conflict in an Early Medieval Society* (London, 1979), pp. 51–8; T. H. Hollingsworth, 'A Demographic Study of the British Ducal Families', repr. in *Population in History: Essays in Historical Demography*, ed. D. V. Glass and D. E. C. Eversley (London, 1965), 354–78 (pp. 358–9). See also comments in the introduction to *Life, Death and the Elderly: Historical Perspectives*, ed. M. Pelling and R. Smith (London and New York, 1991), pp. 10–11.

in at least one part of southern Europe, Italy, the marriage-pattern was to a large degree contrasting, with girls getting married very early, typically in their mid- to late teens, and only a tiny proportion of them never marrying.

Within the field thus demarcated, there is obvious invitation to speculate about [1] correlating levels of mortality, lower where the 'European' marriage-pattern prevailed (not to mention high ideals of maternal breast-feeding and baby-care), and [2] the possibility that women outside élite circles were also markedly outliving men. It is not my role to take these queries further, merely to point out that lower northern European mortality in reality would fit neatly with the preferences of the commentators, and (repeating Herlihy) that the pattern of women outliving men in northern Europe in the thirteenth century clearly fits the view of one commentator.

11

THE *POLITICS* (I): RECEPTION[1]

We turn to the last and most important of the texts examined in *The Measure of Multitude*, and it is now time to return to what was said in the introduction. For the case of the *Politics* is a microcosm of the case which is mounted in the book as a whole.

11.1 Historiography

Let us approach modern study of the *Politics* obliquely, looking at one very learned mid-thirteenth-century Dominican who wrote before it was translated, and one Paris master of about 1300 who had his own copy and used it heavily.

In mid-century some of the French king's money had been engaged in what a modern academic is tempted to represent as 'enlightened state funding of learning'. It went to help the Dominican Vincent of Beauvais and his assistants, working at the Cistercian abbey of Royaumont, in the production of a massive encyclopaedia. The venture and the resulting work remained the biggest until Diderot's and D'Alembert's *Encyclopédie*. The last finishing touches were being applied some time between 1256 and 1259, within ten years or less of the translation of the *Politics*.[2] One can turn to one of the three or four parts (the status of the fourth part has wavered), the *Speculum doctrinale*: approximately *Mirror of Learning*. One part of this *Speculum* is devoted to moral and practical science, and one sub-section of this part is on 'political science' (*scientia politica*). It deals with the science of civic as opposed to individual or domestic morals and rule. It is substantial, running to 109 columns in the 1624 folio edition.[3]

[1] Reference will be made (1) to Bekker numbers [see Ch. 10 above, n. 1], (2) to the best edition of Moerbeke's Latin translation of the *Politics*, Susemihl's (= Su), by page and line number, and also (3) to the widely available version printed in Spiazzi's edition of Aquinas's and Peter of Auvergne's commentary (= Sp), in this case by the numbers given by Spiazzi (1–1176) to the small units into which he divides Aristotle's text. These should not be confused with the numbers (1–1342) he allocates to the accompanying commentaries.

[2] The encyclopaedia was elaborated between 1244/6 and 1256/9, S. Lusignan, *Préface au Speculum Maius de Vincent de Beauvais: Réfraction et Diffusion*, Cahiers d'Études Médiévales 5 (Montreal and Paris, 1979), pp. 58–75. See M. Paulmier-Foucart, 'Vincent de Beauvais', *DSp* xvi. 806–13, and *Vincent de Beauvais: Intentions et réceptions d'une oeuvre encyclopédique au Moyen Âge*, ed. S. Lusignan, M. Paulmier-Foucart, and A. Nadeau (Paris and Montréal, 1990).

[3] Vincent, *Speculum doctrinale*, VII; 555–664.

When describing the first of the three parts of 'political science', Vincent says that it treats of cities and peoples. Pertaining to this, he writes, is 'variety of customs' ('customs' here probably covering laws and forms of government), a variety 'almost according to the number of cities and peoples'. At this point Vincent's notion of what political science might be is running ahead of what he can do. 'But', he continues, 'it is not within my capacity nor my intention to describe the customs and way of life of individual cities or regions.'[4] What can he, and what does he provide? He produces definitions from Isidore; the terrestrial city from Augustine; the moral instruction of the prince; soldiers; the just war; laws and law-giving. Vincent is anthologizing, sometimes via earlier thirteenth-century encyclopaedias, and where much material was available in twelfth- or earlier thirteenth-century translations of Greek and Arabic philosophy and science his anthology can look very up-to-date. The sections in the *Speculum doctrinale* on medicine and psychology have this aspect: but the section on political science does not. It makes no allusion to Aristotle's *Politics*. It was too early for this, by a whisker: the translation of the *Politics* from Greek into Latin came some time in the seventh decade of the thirteenth century.

Indulge speculation for a moment. How would Vincent's 'political science' have appeared had it been compiled late enough to use the *Politics*? It would no doubt have still been a rag-bag, as all his encyclopaedia is. But the extracts contained in the rag-bag would now have also included discussion of the human origins of civil associations; elements of Aristotle's systematic and detached observation of different forms of government and rule, as also of his comparative discussion of ideal forms of government; above all, the concepts and vocabulary used by Aristotle in these discussions.

Vincent's text is useful in several ways. It keeps our feet on the ground. Since it is an anthology, not a piece of original and innovative thought, it reminds us of the existence and importance of the slightly lower ground more commonly shared among literate men of no great intellectual distinction. It dispels the worries of anyone concerned with anachronism in the subjects pursued by modern historians and the language they use. Modern works with *History of Political Thought* in their titles which deal with some of Vincent's themes in their earlier chapters, before going on to deal with the impact of the *Politics*, under the banner of Augustinian pessimism about human society being replaced by Aristotelian naturalism, are reassuringly dealing with something which was *there*; something which had a reassuringly similar name, 'political science'; something which had a large place in a schema of knowledge such as that exemplified by the organisation and divisions of the *Speculum doctrinale*. In a modern *History of Medieval Thought*, the chapters devoted to the *Politics* and the revived study of Roman law and its notion of public authority may well subordinate this material to such a theme as 'Thought and the origins of the modern State'. Here a modern concern will be leading the way in the selection of the medieval material for discussion and

[4] Ibid., VII. v; 559. See also Flüeler, i. 6.

in its treatment. But the prominence and sharp definition of the modern concern means that everyone will be aware of what is going on. And it is possible for a historian to shuffle off that theme, and pay closer attention to what political themes actually interested *medieval* readers of the *Politics*: as is done in Jean Dunbabin's meticulous and penetrating analyses of the commentators.[5]

Let us leave this in suspense for a moment, and turn briefly to a second figure from about five decades later, for whom the *Politics* was easily available: a prominent master at the university of Paris at the turn of 1300, Godfrey of Fontaines. Godfrey possessed his own copy of the *Politics*, which he was to leave to the Sorbonne.[6] He had done some thumbing through this or another copy. In his own responses to 'what you will' questions in the Theology Faculty, his quodlibets, he made wide use of the *Politics*, quoting from or referring to passages in five of its eight books.[7] What interested Godfrey most? Not monarchy; not the origins of civil society; not the causes of revolution. What seems to have concerned Godfrey was what Aristotle said in the *Politics* on subjects like possessions and trade.

So, if one turns back and asks what people were interested in when reading the *Politics*, the answer is, 'not only political things, but much else, such as economic matters, or education'. These other things included thought about population. In the *Politics* population is seen historically. Political forms are related to different sizes of populations. There is speculation about optimum population. And interference with population is envisaged. Population looms largest as a theme in the commentaries on proposed ideal constitutions in book 2 and the discussion of marriage-ages and limitation of population in book 7. Medieval reading of these parts is the theme of this and the following two chapters.

It is important to be precise both about the force and the limits of the case which is being put forward. The relations, easy or tense, between Godfrey and Vincent and modern histories of medieval thought show several things. First, the conventional genre of history, the *history of political thought*, dominates, unifies, and simplifies. One drawback of this imperialism is that the variety of medieval interest in the *Politics* gets swept under the carpet. Godfrey of Fontaine's interests may be one example, while other men's interest in Aristotle on population is another. Secondly, the validity of the case does not depend on a vain attempt to overturn a large and evident truth, the much greater size and importance of conventional political thought, and the role of the introduction of the *Politics* in its history. That is not the proposal. What is being suggested is simple. The

[5] 'Aristotle in the Schools', in *Trends in Medieval Political Thought*, ed. B. Smalley (Oxford, 1965), pp. 65–85; Dunbabin, '*Politics*'; ead., 'Guido Vernani of Rimini's commentary on Aristotle's *Politics*', *Traditio* 44 (1988), 373–8. Some of the commentaries are used in her 'Government', in *The Cambridge History of Medieval Political Thought c.1350–c.1450*, ed. J. H. Burns (Cambridge, 1988), pp. 477–519.

[6] AL *Codices* 1, p. 575 no. 693.

[7] Godfrey of Fontaines, *Les quodlibets de Godefroid de Fontaines*, ed. J. Hoffmans, O. Lottin, A. Pelzer, and M. De Wulf, 5 vols., Les Philosophes Belges, Textes et Études 2–5 and 14 (Louvain, 1904–37), cited in the following by Textes et Études vol. numbers: Quodlibet VI, Q. 10 (iii. 212); Quodlibet VIII, Q. 11 (iv. 106, 108, 109, and 112); Quodlibet VIII, Q. 12 (iv. 128); Quodlibet XI, Q. 17 (v. 76); Quodlibet XII, Q. 7 (v. 109); Quodlibet XIII, Q. 9 (v. 252); Quodlibet XIV, Q. 1 (v. 304; *Quaestiones ordinariae*, III (xiv. 122).

camera-lens which normally points at a very large and clearly labelled mountain, political thought, is being turned in another direction, to point at a smaller hill (and perhaps a mistier one!), 'demographic' thought.

When emphasizing the impact of the introduction of the *Politics*, John Morrall talks of it enabling 'medieval political theory to come of age', and how one can 'imagine the excitement' of thirteenth-century thinkers encountering it.[8] This is equally true of its impact in areas other than political thought: men encountered in the *Politics* a much greater range of data and systematized thought about population than in any other previously available text. This is the first point to be made in recounting the place of the *Politics* in the history of demographic thought.

11.2 *Translation and study of the* Politics

The materials usable when writing the story of the introduction of the *Politics* are several. Part is the light so far shone on the history of the translation and the edition of the first, incomplete, effort; the modern edition of the later and full translation has not yet appeared. Another part is the data in the *Aristoteles Latinus* descriptions of manuscripts of the *Politics*, which we shall be examining, much as in Chapter 10, for what they show about the early location and movements of copies of the translations.

Some commentaries on the *Politics* have long been available in print—Thomas Aquinas's, with Peter of Auvergne's continuation, and Albert's—but few have had elaborate modern editions. The commentaries which have been given this treatment are those by Peter of Auvergne (the part on book 2 which overlaps with Thomas), Nicole Oresme, Aquinas, Engelbert of Admont (an epitome).[9] The current edition of Albert's works has not yet reached his commentary, which was last edited in the 1890s. This and the 1951 edition of the rest of Peter of Auvergne's commentary provide serviceable texts,[10] but the reader lacks those spasmodic illuminations of intellectual history which the minutiae of elaborate editions sometimes bring. This leaves a substantial part of the commentary material unpublished: principally Peter of Auvergne's questions on the *Politics*, other manuscripts containing questions closely related to Peter's, and the commentaries of Guido Vernani and Walter Burley. Within the *Mirror of Princes* genre (didactic

[8] J. B. Morrall, *Political Thought in Medieval Times*, 3rd edn. (London, 1971), p. 69.

[9] *The Commentary of Peter of Auvergne on Aristotle's Politics. The inedited part: Book III, less i–vi*, ed. G. M. Grech (Rome, 1967); see Flüeler, *Politica*, ii. 42–3. Oresme, *Politiques*; see Flüeler, *Politica*, ii. 38–9. Thomas Aquinas, *Sentencia libri Politicorum*, ed. H. F. Dondaine and L. J. Bataillon, *Opera omnia* (Rome, 1882–), xlviii—published 1971; see Flüeler, *Politica*, ii. 47. *Compendium Politicorum*, ed. G. B. Fowler in his 'Admont 608 and Engelbert of Admont', *AHDMLA* 44 (1978), 149–242 (pp. 191–205); see ibid., 51 (1983), 195–22 (pp. 219–22), 'Excerptum Aristotelis de Politica'; see Flüeler, *Politica*, ii. 10.

[10] Comparison of the Aquinas part of the 1951 edition by Spiazzi of the Aquinas–Peter commentary with the superior Leonine edition by Dondaine and Bataillon suggests that some of the textual problems of the Peter of Auvergne section may arise from defective editing.

literature for rulers), the principal treatises which make heavy use of the *Politics*, those by Giles of Rome, Engelbert of Admont, and Tolomeo of Lucca, lack modern critical editions.[11]

The state of secondary studies is better. A fundamental account of these medieval commentaries on the *Politics* was produced by Martin Grabmann,[12] and this theme was further developed in an unpublished Oxford D.Phil thesis by Fr Conor Martin,[13] supervised by the principal editor and guiding spirit of the Aristoteles Latinus project, Lorenzo Minio-Paluello, who also left a precious brief account of the impact of the *Politics*.[14] Since then a series of articles by Jean Dunbabin have provided acute and authoritative characterizations of the commentators and analyses of their responses to the *Politics*;[15] one would gain even more from a longer general account from her pen. Most recent is Christoph Flüeler's study of the later medieval reception of the *Politics*, based on searching examination of the manuscripts and authorship of later medieval commentaries, and taking as its example reactions to Aristotle's treatment of slavery.[16]

What are the outlines of the story which emerges? First, let us look at the translations themselves. The current conclusions of editors and scholars associated with the *Aristoteles Latinus* project about the translations are these.[17] Translating

[11] They have long been available in older editions, but the unique edition of Engelbert's *De regimine principum* is rare; I am grateful to Alexander Patschovsky for procuring a copy. A brief 'Excerptum ex Engelberti tractactu *De Regimine principum*' is edited in Fowler, 'Admont 608', AHDLMA 45 (1979), 225–306 (pp. 246–9); see ibid., 246 n. 1, announcing an edition of the *De Regimine principum* in the MGH series Staatsschriften des späteren Mittelalters. On projected editions of Giles of Rome, see C. F. Briggs, *Giles of Rome's De regimine principum: Reading and Writing Politics at Court and University, c.1275–c.1525* (Cambridge, 1999), p. 3 and n. 6.

[12] M. Grabmann, 'Die mittelalterlichen Kommentare zur *Politik* des Aristoteles', *Sitzungsberichte der Bayerischen Akademie der Wissenschaften*, Philosophisch-historische Abteilung (1941), 2, Heft 10.

[13] C. Martin, 'The commentaries on the Politics of Aristotle in the late thirteenth and fourteenth centuries, with reference to the thought and political life of the time' (unpublished D.Phil thesis, University of Oxford, 1949). This contains more than the principal article which emerged from it, 'Some medieval commentaries on Aristotle's *Politics*', *History* 36 (1951), 29–44. See also his 'The vulgate text of Aquinas's Commentary on Aristotle's Politics', *Dominican Studies* 5 (1952), 35–64, and 'Walter Burleigh' in *Oxford Studies Presented to Daniel Callus*, Oxford Historical Studies, n.s. 16 (Oxford, 1964), pp. 194–230.

[14] 'La tradition aristotélicienne dans l'histoire des idées', reprinted in his *Opuscula*, pp. 405–24 (pp. 415–9).

[15] See n. 5 above.

[16] Flüeler, *Politica*, in which the list of commentaries and secondary literature in vol. ii is valuable and up-to-date. See also his 'Die mittelalterliche Kommentare zur *Politik* des Aristoteles und zur Pseudo-Aristotelischen *Oekonomik*', *Bulletin de philosophie médiévale* 29 (1987), 193–229; 'Die Rezeption der "Politica" des Aristoteles an der Pariser Artistenfakultät im 13. und 14. Jahrhundert', in *Das Publikum politischer Theorie im 14. Jahrhundert*, ed. J. Miethke, Schriften des Historischen Kollegs, Kolloquien 21 (Munich, 1992), pp. 127–38 (several other studies in this volume bear upon the reception of the *Politics*); 'Die verschiedenen literarischen Gattungen der Aristoteleskommentare: zur Terminologie der Überschriften und Kolophone', in J. Hamesse (ed.), *Manuels, programmes de cours et techniques d'enseignement dans les universités médiévales*, Université Catholique de Louvain, Publications de l'Institut des Études Médiévales, Textes, Études, Congrès 16 (Louvain-La-Neuve, 1994), pp. 75–116. Reception in one region is considered by D. Luscombe, 'The Ethics and the Politics in Britain in the Middle Ages', in *Aristotle in Britain during the Middle Ages*, ed. J. Marenbon, Société Internationale pour l'Étude de la philosophie Médiévale, Rencontres de Philosophie Médiévale 5 (Turnhout, 1996), pp. 337–49 (pp. 345–9).

[17] W. Vanhamel, 'Biobibliographie de Guillaume de Moerbeke', *Guillaume de Moerbeke*, pp. 301–83 (p. 339); J. Brams, 'Guillaume de Moerbeke et Aristote', in *Traductions et traducteurs de l'antiquité*

the *Politics* from Greek into Latin took two attempts. The first was only of books 1 and 2 (up to chapter 11). It had many imperfections, and, although known by Albert, it had little success, surviving only in three manuscripts. The suggestion, made on the basis of internal evidence, is that this was a first stab by the Flemish Dominican William of Moerbeke; no external evidence of the identity of the translator survives. The date now put forward for this is 'before 1266'. Both internal and external evidence coincide to produce the proposition, which is never challenged, that William was the translator of the second version. A translation of all eight books of the *Politics*, this was done at a date which is now given as before 1270 or before 1268/9—the earlier suggestion was 'about 1260'. Though it would be rash to exclude the possibility of some use, after Albert, of the first translation, it seems that the second one, by William of Moerbeke, was *the* Latin text until Leonardo Bruni's translation in 1438.

Painstaking scholarship has assembled some fragments about earlier western awareness of the *Politics*. Knowledge that Aristotle had written on the state stretches back into the late twelfth century, and by the late 1240s it may have been quite widespread among those learned men reading references to the *Politics* in the *Ethics* and some translated commentaries. Further than this there is only conjecture: that some learned men were already wanting to have the characteristic Aristotle—systematic analysis and presentation of data—in 'political science'. The immediate context of Moerbeke's translation or translations is also subject to conjecture.[18] The meagre facts recovered about his life show him in three contexts. There are his appearances in Asia Minor (Nicaea) and Greece (Thebes, Corinth); his membership of the Dominican Order, some of whose members were so prominent in the early reception of Aristotle (Albert and Thomas); and his presence at various dates at the papal curia at Viterbo and Lyons, and in papal service as chaplain, papal penitentiary and, lastly, legate (1267, 1272, 1274, 1283/4). The contexts are suggestive. The papal curia was a centre of scholarship, and it was certainly the scene of Moerbeke's carrying out or finishing some of his translations. The curia may have been where he met such scientists and mathematicians as Campanus of Novara, Witelo and Henry Bate of Malines, and a papal physician, Rosellus of Arezzo. Thomas Aquinas's presence at the papal curia (not demonstrably overlapping with Moerbeke's) and an early hagiographic linking of the two produced the notion of a co-operative Aristotelian venture, which

tardive au XIVe siècle, Université Catholique de Louvain and Università degli Studi di Cassino, Publications de l'Institut des Études Médiévales, Textes, Études, Congrès 11, Rencontres de Cultures dans la Philosophie Médiévale 1 (Louvain and Cassino, 1990), pp. 317–36 (p. 320). The question is examined in Flüeler, *Politica*, ii. 15–29, where the conclusion is that the complete translation must predate 1268/9. P. Michaud-Quantin provided a critical edition of Moerbeke's first attempt, AL xxxix. 1; B. Schneider's edition of Moerbeke's second attempt will be AL xxix.2, and its introduction will supersede these discussions.

[18] For the following, see L. Minio-Palluelo, 'Moerbeke, William of', *DSB* ix. 434–40; Vanhamel, 'Bio-bibliographie de Guillaume de Moerbeke', pp. 301–18; A. Paravicini Bagliani, 'Guillaume de Moerbeke et la cour pontificale', *Guillaume de Moerbeke*, pp. 23–52, slightly revised when reprinted in his *Medicina e scienze della natura alla corte dei Papi nel duecento* (Spoleto, 1991), pp. 141–75.

modern scholars have been at pains to deny. What can be retained is this. The Dominican Order contained this prolific hunter after Greek manuscripts and translator; the Dominican Order also contained the two men who made very rapid use of Moerbeke's translation(s), Albert and Thomas; and scholarship and translation were notable at the curia in the 1260s–70s, especially, for officials, during the vacancies between papacies. At the same time, there is no specific evidence, such as a commission or request, directly bearing on the translation of the *Politics*.

The story of the *Politics* after its translation begins with its diffusion through copying of manuscripts of it, or through abbreviations of it, or through compendia of moral philosophy containing 'flowers' extracted from it. It continues with the composition of various levels of works based upon it: commentaries on it, abbreviated versions of it, formally posed and debated 'questions' raised upon it, and its use in independent treatises of the *Mirror of Princes* type. It goes on with the *Politics*' entry as a text to be read in institutions of higher learning, whether the Arts faculty of a university or the convents of the religious, mendicants and monks, and perhaps its entry into cathedral chapters.

The first salient impression one receives is speed of pick-up, especially French and in Paris. A great deal seems to have happened by the mid-1270s. Aquinas's commentary (only on books I–III. vi) has been dated to his second regency in the theology faculty at Paris, 1269–72,[19] while Albert's, on all eight books, is usually thought of as earlier than this,[20] and Siger of Brabant seems to have been determining a question on the *Politics* before 1277.[21] The settings here would probably be the *studium* of the Dominican convent in Cologne (Albert) and, as just indicated, the university of Paris (probably Thomas, Siger). About 1280[22] and in the milieu of the court of the French king, Philip III, we have the composition of a political treatise of *Mirror of Princess* type, Giles's *De regimine principum*, whose second and third books rely heavily on parts of the *Politics*. A work which made equally heavy use of the *Politics* and had the same title was written around 1291 by the Austrian Black Monk Engelbert of Admont, and this reminds us of the danger of exclusive concentration on Paris—for Engelbert had probably encountered the *Politics* in Padua.

Meanwhile, copying of texts was going on, and they were spreading. Quite how many, how quickly, and in what directions? If the listing and description of the manuscripts of the *Politics* in the *Aristoteles Latinus* have not yet been exploited, what would a study based upon them show? The data provided here also give an impression of earliness and speed of production. Since most of the dating is estimation, 'earliness' is also broadly defined. Twelve manuscripts are described as

[19] Dunbabin, 'Politics', 725; on Aquinas's early references, see Flüeler, 'Rezeption', 128–9, and *Politica*, i. 23–7.

[20] Dunbabin, 'Politics', 724; listed by Flüeler (*Politica*, ii. 2), but not discussed by him.

[21] Grabmann, *Mittelalterlichen Kommentare*, p. 24; Grech, *Commentary of Peter of Auvergne*, p. 9. On Pierre Dubois and Siger, see Ch. 9 above.

[22] Pre-1285, probably between 1277 and 1279.

from before 1300,[23] and the manuscripts from this period taken together with those from the turn of 1300 or described as early fourteenth century[24] amount to forty-nine, that is nearly half of the surviving manuscripts (108) were produced by the early fourteenth century. The hands listed are nearly all French (northern French, Flemish/French, or meridional) and Italian, occasionally also English and German. The data also provide fragments of a map of dispersion of copies, into the hands or libraries of university masters, religious houses, cathedral chapters, and even the occasional layman. These are used in the following sketch. When studying the 'impact of the *Politics*', if we are interested in 'impact on outlook' and not just the thoughts of a Thomas Aquinas, it becomes relevant not only to look at Thomas but also to trace copies into obscure libraries where an ordinary friar—say in Treviso or Lincoln—can read them.

Conventionally the next part of the story tells of the use of the *Politics* in the schools and in commentaries, principally by theologians who were members of religious orders. Here, for the sake of clarity, 'universities' and 'religious orders' are dealt with separately, at the risk of duplication. The evidence for the university story consists of university statutes, the names of masters known to have lectured on the text, and commentaries or questions raised on the text which are closely related to lectures. As in the cases of *On Animals* and *Length and Shortness*, Paris is easiest to document. The names associated with the *Politics* in Paris add up to something like a list. Thomas Aquinas has already been noted, perhaps producing his commentary during his second Paris regency (1269–72), and also Siger of Brabant, whose pupil Pierre Dubois later referred to Siger determining on a question in the *Politics*, presumably before Siger's appearance on heresy charges in 1276. Peter of Auvergne completed Thomas's commentary, also producing a commentary which goes over the part of book 3 upon which Thomas had left a commentary. In addition he left questions on the *Politics* which may be the *reportatio* of lectures.[25] John Vate, rector in 1290, determined five questions on the *Politics*.[26] Perhaps to be included at this point is Denis of Borgo San Sepolcro, producer of a no longer extant commentary on the *Politics*, and student of theology at Paris.[27] Nicholas of Autrecourt was lecturing on the *Politics* before the 1340s.[28] We could

[23] AL *Codices 1*, pp. 441 no. 415; 449 no. 433; 459 no. 457; 507–8 no. 562; 542 no. 637; 575 no. 693. AL *Codices 2*, pp. 839–40 no. 1206; 939–40 no. 1367; 1178 no. 1749; 1236 no. 1884. AL *Codices 3*, p. 132 no. 2140. The assessment of one manuscript as '13th–14th century' (AL *Codices 2*, pp. 852–3 no. 1230) is superseded by Minio-Paluello's estimate of *c.*1280, AL xxxiii (ed. alt.), p. 15.

[24] AL *Codices 1*, pp. 237 no. 1; 240 no. 9; 241 no. 11; 309 no. 157; 327–8 no. 188; 331–2 no. 200; 341 no. 219; 354 no. 249; 370 no. 282; 401 no. 345; 446 no. 426; 460 no. 460; 492 no. 526; 556–7 no. 662; 584 no. 713; 613 no. 777; 630 no. 808; 652 no. 860; 674–5 no. 918; 685 no. 941; 693 no. 953; 696–7 nos. 961–3; 722 no. 1016; 730 no. 1037. AL *Codices 2*, pp. 833 no. 1191; 1220 no. 847; 850 no. 1228; 851–2 no. 1230; 861 no. 1247; 935–6 no. 1363; 1053 no. 1532; 1192–3 nos. 1781–2; 1222 no. 1848; 1223 no. 1852.

[25] Martin, 'Commentaries', chs 4–5; Dunbabin, '*Politics*', 725–8; Flüeler, *Politica*, i, Ch. 2, and ii. 41–3.

[26] Martin, 'Commentaries', pp. 17–18; Flüeler, *Politica*, ii. 31.

[27] Flüeler, *Politica*, ii. 95.

[28] Martin, 'Commentaries', p. 19; Flüeler, *Politica*, ii. 98. It used to be thought that John Buridan (d. post-1358), Master of Arts about 1328 and a member of the faculty for over forty years, produced questions on the *Politics* at some point in this career, but Flüeler has shown that the real author of the questions attributed to John was Nicholas de Vaudémont, a late fourteenth-century Paris master.

go on from the lecturers and producers of commentaries or questions to look at other men making use of the text. A quick dip into the quodlibets of the theology faculty, for example, will immediately produce the Cistercian Jacques de Thérines (d. 1321),[29] or the secular master Godfrey of Fontaines (d. 1306 × 9), whom we have already seen possessing his own copy of the *Politics* and making heavy use of it. One point arises from the cautionary comment of Jean Dunbabin,[30] that the commentaries tended to come from mature theologians: a full account of the *Politics* in Paris would not be confined to one faculty.

Evidence about presence or dissemination of copies of the *Politics* or commentaries or derivative works tells another part of the story. From 1304 there survives a regulation for Paris stationers, specifying for the text of the *Politics* the number of pieces (*peciae*) to be parcelled out for copying (seventeen) and price (twelve pence).[31] The editor-designate of the complete Moerbeke translation has commented that the majority of its manuscripts descend from the exemplar of the university of Paris.[32] The stationers' regulations also include details for Thomas's commentary and Giles of Rome's *De regimine principum*, and a historian of *peciae* has analysed for what it can contribute to the history of this system a Paris copy of Albert's commentary, a manuscript of between 1270 and 1290, which was divided into forty-eight pieces.[33] The Sorbonne had copies: each of the secular masters Godfrey of Fontaines, Nicholas of Bar (d. 1310), Guillaume de Feuquières (mentioned around 1321) and James of Padua (mentioned 1356) left a copy to the Sorbonne;[34] in the case of Godfrey, presumably a well-read copy. And both the Sorbonne's little and large library inventories also list copies of Thomas's commentary, and its large library Albert's commentary, as well as Giles's *De regimine principum.*[35]

All of this looks like dense presence in Paris. It has been suggested that the most popular florilegium of Aristotle's (and others') works, the *Auctoritates Aristotelis*, was composed in Paris and for the use of Arts students.[36] It culled 150 dicta from the *Politics*, which was thereby reduced to about 1300 words.[37] The selection does not always seem very intelligent, and it is hard to envisage what was done with

[29] Jacques de Thérines, *Quodlibet*, I. ix, II. iii, II. viii, II. xv, and II. xix; ed. P. Glorieux, Textes Philosophiques du Moyen Âge 7 (Paris, 1958), pp. 140, 142, 214, 252, 300, and 314.

[30] In conversation. [31] *CUP* ii. 107.

[32] B. Schneider, 'Bemerkungen zum Aristoteles Latinus: Spuren einer Revision der Politikübersetzung des Wilhelm von Moerbeke', in *Aristoteles Werk und Wirkung*, ed. J. Wiesner, 2 vols. (Berlin and New York, 1987), ii. 487–97 (487).

[33] *CUP* ii. 110–11; L. Destrez, *La pecia dans les manuscrits universitaires du XIIIe et XIVe siècles* (Paris, 1935), p. 92; W. Fauser, *Die Werke des Albertus Magnus in ihrer handscriftlichen Überlieferung*, I, *Die echten Werke*, in Albert, *Opera*, Geyer, Tomus Subsidiarius, I, 186; see the listing of the 12 extant manuscripts ibid., pp. 184–6.

[34] AL *Codices 1*, pp. 556–7 no. 662; 561–3 no. 671 (only the beginning of the *Politics*); 575 no. 693; on this last see also L. Delisle, *Le Cabinet des manuscrits*, 4 vols. (Paris, 1868–81), iii. 60 no. 12. Guillaume: ibid., iii. 60 no. 15, and Glorieux, *Arts*, p. 441 no. 1779.

[35] Delisle, *Cabinet*, iii. 64 no. 41; iii. 72, C; iii., 78, AD; iii. 86, Ad. n and AB.c, AB.p, AD.r.

[36] *Auctoritates Aristotelis*, pp. 38–43 and 106.

[37] Ibid., pp. 252–63; extracts from the *Politics* are accompanied by extracts from the commentaries of Aquinas and Peter of Auvergne, ibid., p. 21.

these disjointed statements: 'It is useful for all animals to be ruled by man', 'It is not possible to live without food', 'The desire for riches tends to infinity', and so on. Learning by rote? If the *Auctoritates Aristotelis* is a guide to the likely amount and level of absorption of the *Politics* among ordinary students, our picture of dense presence in Paris needs to be qualified. The intellectual path from a Peter of Auvergne or Godfrey of Fontaines to the students whose grasp depended on cribs like this is long and downward.

Material is thinner outside Paris, but it exists. For example, there is a form from the Arts faculty in Oxford, from the early fourteenth century, which specifies the *Politics*.[38] We learn of an exposition of the *Politics*, Thomas's, among the philosophy books in Merton College library before 1325,[39] a text left to Oriel College library (perhaps in 1337),[40] and a text in the hands of a man who was lector of the Franciscans at Oxford *c.*1340.[41] There are Cambridge examples: around 1300 a text in the hands of a Peterhouse master and commentaries in the hands of a Cambridge Franciscan, and a copy left to Peterhouse by a man who was vicar of Wisbech in 1317.[42]

The question asked in Chapter 10 above—'How far should one use the picture of Paris to hypothesize about other universities?'—needs repeating here. The answer provided there recalled two commonplaces of modern scholarship on medieval universities and their statutes: that there was a great similarity between university curricula, and that statutes are very incomplete guides, often appearing only to alter existing customary practice. Not only does silence not mean absence, but one should assume roughly similar prescriptions of texts in other universities. These arguments need to be applied with caution here, for positive evidence about lecturing on the *Politics* in universities apart from Paris is thin. Further, we should pay heed to the fact that among Aristotle's moral works it is nearly always easier to find evidence about the *Ethics* than the *Politics*—more manuscripts, more commentaries, and more or quicker specification in regulations about texts to be read. This last point is seen in *later* medieval regulations, where one tends to find the *Ethics* specified without qualification as a text, while the *Politics* is not mentioned or is given as an alternative, for example 'either *On Animals* or the *Politics*'.

Only in one or perhaps two cases in Italian universities do the clouds part. 'Perhaps' qualifies the case of Padua, which begins with the Benedictine monastery of

[38] J. A. Weisheipl, 'Curriculum of the faculty of arts at Oxford in the early fourteenth century', *Medieval Studies* 26 (1964), 143–85 (161).

[39] F. M. Powicke, *The Medieval Books of Merton College* (Oxford, 1931), p. 102 no. 85.

[40] *BRUO* i. 450. W. J Courtenay, 'The fourteenth-century booklist of the Oriel College library', *Viator* 19 (1988), 283–90 (p. 285); see also M. B. Parkes, 'The Provision of Books', *HUO* ii. 407–83 (p. 409 n. 10).

[41] AL *Codices 1*, p. 237 no. 1—the text was given by Thomas of Ratford to the Franciscans in Lincoln. On Thomas, see *BRUO* iii. 1548.

[42] Martin, 'Vulgate text of Aquinas's Commentary, 62–4'; AL *Codices 1*, p. 354 no. 249; on Walter of Blascollisley, see A. B. Emden, *A Biographical Register of the University of Cambridge to 1500* (Cambridge, 1963), p. 64.

Admont in lower Austria. A copy of the *Politics* was once in its library,[43] presumably stemming from the earlier presence there of Engelbert, abbot of Admont. Apart from using the *Politics* in various treatises, Engelbert had composed a compendium of it; there is still in Admont a manuscript of this, which dates from *c.*1287 and has rubrics and emendations in Engelbert's hand.[44] Where did Engelbert encounter the text? In his own description of his education, he had studied grammar, logic and the *libri naturales* at Prague; at Padua, where the university (*studium generale*) was flourishing, logic and philosophy for five years under William of Brescia (who later taught in the Arts and Medicine faculty at Bologna); and theology for four years in the house of the Dominicans at Padua. His nine-year stay in Padua was from *c.*1278–87. 'Philosophy': the finger seems to point to the Arts-Medicine faculty of Padua as the most likely place for Engelbert's meeting the *Politics*, in the period *c.*1278–84.

The case of Bologna needs no such conjecture. Quentin Skinner has pointed to the use of the *Politics* by the Roman lawyers, in particular Bartolus of Sassoferrato,[45] while the presence of the *Politics* in the faculty of Arts and Medicine has been shown in Nancy Siraisi's study of a group of philosopher-doctors: Dino del Garbo, using the *Politics* (briefly) in a commentary, and Bartolomeo da Varignana using it very extensively in a commentary on the *Economics*.[46] It would be artificial to keep distinct from this law and Arts picture of Bologna the further part of a broader Bologna picture which has been sharply etched by Jean Dunbabin, in her account of an early fourteenth-century commentary on the *Politics*, that of Guido Vernani.[47] The commentary is set precisely in the context of the Dominicans and their house in Bologna, where Guido studied in 1297, was lector in 1312 and probably lived till 1324; and in the civic and lay world of Bologna the chancellor of the commune was the dedicatee of another of Guido's works, and Guido was writing his commentary on the *Politics* for a literate lay audience.

The presence of the *Politics* in the houses of the religious needs to come next, to be juxtaposed to our parade of universities. The elements of such an account partly comprise educational regulations specifying time and texts[48] for preparatory Arts or philosophy courses, the status of particular houses as provincial or general *studia*, and the presence of some in university centres. There are also the plains and the mountains: on the one hand the occasional demonstrably early presence of copies of the text or expositions in convent libraries, on the other hand the composition of commentaries by famous men. Clearly the Dominicans star, supplying, as we have seen, the greatest figures: the translator himself, and a line of commentators from the earliest (Albert and Thomas) to Guido Vernani.

[43] In an inventory of 1380; *Mittelalterliche Bibliothekskataloge Österreichs*, 5 vols. (Vienna, Graz, 1929–70), iii. 60.

[44] See n. 9 above.

[45] Q. Skinner, *The Foundations of Modern Political Thought*, 2 vols. (Cambridge, 1978), ii. 51–2.

[46] Siraisi, *Taddeo*, pp. 73, 83, and 88.

[47] See above, n. 5, and Siraisi, *Taddeo*, p. 77.

[48] See K. W. Humphreys, *The Book Provisions of the Medieval Friars, 1215–1400* (Amsterdam, 1964), pp. 67–8 and 77–8.

I would add Tolomeo of Lucca, whose continuation of Thomas's *De regno* has elements of a commentary. In 1315 the general chapter in Bologna laid down that the *Politics* (and *Ethics* and *Rhetoric*) should be 'read', and a Dominican chronicle provides under that year the name of the first friar to 'read' it (lecture upon it) in the convent at Milan. The *Aristoteles Latinus* catalogues and library inventories (many of which survive for Italy) enable us to map copies of the *Politics* together with commentaries and partly derivative works such as Giles's *De regimine principum*. An inventory of St Dominic's at Bologna from before 1386 shows a text of the *Politics*, and also a commentary, probably Albert's.[49] An inventory of Santa Maria Novella in Florence in 1489 shows two copies of the *Politics*, and also Albert's and Thomas's commentaries, and Giles's treatise.[50] In the mid-fourteenth century Saint-Eustorge in Milan had Burley's commentary (this seems suspiciously quick), as well as Tolomeo's continuation of Thomas's *De regno*, and Giles.[51] A copy of *c.*1300 was once in the convent of St Jacques in Paris.[52] An inventory of 1459 shows a text in the convent of St Augustine's at Padua,[53] while in St Dominic's at Perugia an inventory of 1430 shows a text, and an inventory of 1474–8 the commentaries of both Albert and Thomas.[54] St Dominic's at Ravenna once had Thomas's commentary with Peter of Auvergne's continuation,while a copy of Thomas's commentary was given to the convent of St Nicholas at Treviso in 1297.[55] These are positive indices: there are also many other medieval inventories of Dominican Italian libraries, which do not mention such texts. The lateness of some of the inventories clearly introduces a note of caution—has the copy only recently entered the library? Can one rely on the silence of other Italian Dominican inventories? How far is the prolificness of these lists and their efficient publication by Kaeppeli skewing this very Italian picture?

Other religious orders should not be underestimated. It is not much more difficult tracing these texts in the libraries of Franciscan houses. The shelves of Santa Croce in Florence, contained (or came to contain) two copies of the *Politics* written around 1300, and at some stage were to contain Burley's commentary and Giles.[56] The books examined at the convent of St Francis in Pisa in 1355 contained a chained text of the *Politics* and Thomas's commentary, for consultation only.[57] Assisi had the *Politics*,[58] while Siena's catalogue of 1482 includes two

[49] M.-H. Laurent, *Fabio Vigili et les bibliothèques de Bologne*, Studi e Testi 105 (Rome, 1943), p. 207 nos. 43 and 47.

[50] S. Orlandi, *La biblioteca di S. Maria Novella in Firenze dal sec. XIV al sec. XIX* (Florence, 1952), p. 42 nos. 314, 317, 322–3, and 326.

[51] T. Kaeppeli, 'La bibliothèque de Saint-Eustorge à Milan', *AFP* 25 (1955), 5–74 (pp. 15, 47, 48, and 57).

[52] AL *Codices* 1, p. 584 no. 713.

[53] L. Gargan, *Lo studio teologico e la biblioteca dei domenicani a Padova nel tre e quattrocento*, Contributi alla Storia dell'Università di Padova 6 (Padua, 1971), p. 243 no. 149.

[54] T. Kaeppeli, *Inventari di libri di San Domenico di Perugia, 1430–88*, Sussidi Eruditi 15 (Rome, 1962), pp. 64 no. 69, 217 no. 62, and 252 no. 189.

[55] Aquinas, *Sentencia libri Politicorum*, pp. A12 and A14.

[56] L. Minio-Paluello, 'Dante's Reading of Aristotle', in *The World of Dante: Essays on Dante and His Times*, ed. C. Grayson (Oxford, 1980), pp. 61–80 (p. 67), and AL *Codices* 2, pp. 935–6 no. 1363 and 939–40 no. 1367; Humphreys, *Book Provisions*, p. 114.

[57] Humphreys, p. 103.

[58] Humphreys, p. 107.

copies of Thomas's commentary.[59] An Oxford Franciscan's copy went to the Franciscans in Lincoln in the mid-fourteenth century.[60] The Franciscans may not have provided any of the great commentaries: one can only list from them a compendium of the *Politics* by a fourteenth-century Franciscan called Raymond Acger, apparently from Munich.[61] However quite a lot seems to have been going on at the humbler level of reading. 'For the use of the friars minor', the inscription on one (not otherwise more precisely located) Vatican text of the commentary of Thomas and Peter of Auvergne,[62] is the message of the list of texts in Franciscan libraries.

After the dazzling early example of Giles's use of the *Politics* in his *De regimine principum*, the Augustinians have little to show at the highest level. The commentaries of Denis of Borgo San Sepolcro, friend of Petrarch,[63] and Walter Kervyll (late fourteenth century), known through its presence in the library of Augustinians in York,[64] no longer survive. Though pride in their own Order will have encouraged copying and possession of Giles's treatise,[65] there are few traces of copies of the *Politics* itself: Santo Spirito in Florence was to acquire Boccaccio's copy.[66] It is not clear what texts in moral philosophy would have been covered by the decision of the 1338 chapter at Siena to specify three years study of philosophy.[67] The case of the Carmelites is similar. Giu Terré (d. 1342), prior general 1318–21, is alleged to have produced a no longer extant commentary.[68] Since the 1391 catalogue of the Florentine house is the principal source for medieval Carmelite holdings in general,[69] it may be significant that it includes a text of the *Politics*.[70]

At the same time, the older monastic orders should not be ignored, whether through the figure of an Engelbert, carrying the *Politics* into the world of Austrian Benedictine monasteries, or through the story of their opening up houses in university centres, as the Cistercians had done in Paris by shortly after 1250. There is a trail of copies of the *Politics* in Cistercian monasteries in German-speaking areas: a copy of *c.*1300 which was once in Keisheim (and is associated with a Keisheim monk at this date);[71] two fourteenth-century copies which were once (almost certainly in the fourteenth century) at St Mary's in Heilbronn;[72] one fourteenth-century copy of the *Politics*, and another of the same period with text

[59] K. W. Humphreys, *The Library of the Franciscans of Siena in the late Fifteenth Century* (Amsterdam, 1978), p. 23.

[60] See n. 41 above. [61] Flüeler, *Politica*, ii. 48 no. 54. [62] Aquinas, *Politics*, p. A13.

[63] A. Gwynn, *The English Austin Friars in the time of Wyclif* (Oxford, 1940), p. 102; see n. 27 above.

[64] *The Friars' Libraries*, ed. K. W. Humphreys, Corpus of British Medieval Library Catalogues (London, 1990), p. 64 no. 257.

[65] See Gwynn, *Austin Friars*, p. 17, for memory of the friars' love of Giles's work and their bringing it to England; Humphreys, *Book Provisions*, p. 117, on a copy in the Regensburg convent by 1347.

[66] Humphreys, *Book Provisions*, p. 121. [67] Gwynn, *Austin Friars*, p. 26.

[68] Flüeler, *Politica*, ii. 96 no. 194. [69] Humphreys, *Book Provisions*, p. 125.

[70] K. W. Humphreys, *The Library of the Carmelites at Florence at the end of the Fourteenth Century* (Amsterdam, 1964), p. 62 l. 14.

[71] AL *Codices* 1, p. 730 no. 1037. [72] Ibid., pp. 674–5 no. 918.

and the Thomas–Peter commentary at Lilienfeld.[73] Together they suggest another area of diffusion and study.[74]

Finally, there was a presence in courts—papal, royal, episcopal. The papal curia at Viterbo in the 1260s saw the translations, and it has been conjectured that the grand Toledo volumes of Aristotle's works of about 1280 (discussed below) were copied from a collection seen at the curia. We see a copy of the *Politics* and the Thomas–Peter commentary being made for John XXII about 1317,[75] and Burley presenting his commentary to Clement VI in 1343.[76] An inventory of the papal library in Avignon drawn up in 1369 confirms what one would expect, that it will have rivalled the Sorbonne, containing as it did two copies of the *Politics*, a third commented and glossed (viz. with the Thomas–Peter commentary?), Burley's commentary, the only so far-known copy outside Paris of the *Liber de ingenio bone nativitatis* (viz. the Aragon Anonymous commentary on Book 7),[77] and of course Giles.[78] A surprising number of copies of the *Politics* ended up (eventually?) in cathedral chapter libraries.[79] In one case, we have light cast on the distinguished scholarly setting of the production of a commentary. This was the circle of scholars around Richard of Bury, bishop of Durham, dedicatee of Burley's commentary on the *Politics*, which was also encouraged by another who had been in the circle, the bishop of London, Richard Bentworth.[80] Shortly afterwards Richard of Bury was to parade an elegant reference to the *Politics* in his *Philobiblon* (completed 1345), selected to illustrate the theme of the superiority of liberal over legal books.[81]

The earliest known episcopal interest was that displayed by Gonzales Pérez Gudiel, who is known to have examined the papal library in Viterbo when he was archbishop-elect of Toledo. From this source, it has been said, came the magnificent series of volumes, including a text of the *Politics*, which was put together around 1280 (one volume has 1279 date) and came into the possession of the cathedral chapter of Toledo.[82] The coincidence of Gudiel's proximity to the learned Castilian royal court and the fact of citation of the *Politics* in the royal Castilian law-code, *Las Siete Partidas*, points to a fascinating possibility of a track

[73] Ibid., pp. 256–7 nos. 39 and 41; Aquinas, *Politics*, p. A11.

[74] The Carthusians should be included. The Charterhouse of Salvatorberg (founded 1372), near Erfurt, had a copy of the *Politics*: *Mittelalterliche Bibliothekskataloge Deutschlands und der Schweiz*, ed. P. J. G. Lehmann *et al.* (Munich, 1918–), ii. 513.

[75] AL *Codices* 2, p. 1224 no. 1853, and Aquinas, *Politics*, p. A13.

[76] A. Maier, 'Zu Walter Burleys Politik-Kommentar', *Recherches de Théologie Ancienne et Médiévale* 14 (1947), 332–6 (pp. 334–5).

[77] See below, Ch. 12 n. 111.

[78] M. Faucon, *La librairie des papes d'Avignon: sa formation, sa composition, ses catalogues, 1316–1420*, 2 vols. (Paris, 1886–7), i. 122 no. 322; 127 no. 374; 129 no. 395; 140–1 no. 528; 146 no. 598; 164 no. 815; 169 no. 885; 175 no. 952.

[79] AL *Codices* 1, pp. 328–9 no. 191 (Prague); 459–60 nos. 457 and 460 (Cambrai); 613 nos. 777–8 (Tours). AL *Codices* 2, pp. 851–2 no. 1230 (Toledo); 1039–40 no. 1514 (Padua). See also *Mittelalterliche Bibliothekskataloge Österreichs*, iv., 41, on a fragment in the chapter at Salzburg.

[80] Martin, 'Burleigh', p. 222.

[81] Richard de Bury, *Philobiblon*, XI, ed. M. McLagan (Oxford and New York, 1970), pp. 118–19.

[82] L. Minio-Paluello, AL, xxxiii (ed. alt), pp. xv–xvi.

from papal court to archiepiscopal and then royal courts.[83] The period around 1280 also saw the composition of a treatise on the education of princes, which drew heavily upon the *Politics* and was closely connected with the education of the heir to the French throne: Giles of Rome's *De regimine principum*.[84] The royal house of Aragon provided the setting for the composition by the Aragon Anonymous of a commentary on book 7 of the *Politics*, apparently written for the heir to the throne, Jaime. The French court was again to provide a setting *c.*1371, this time for Nicole Oresme's translation into French and commentary for Charles V, luxury copies of which were to be disseminated in the royal and aristocratic libraries of France in the following century.[85]

Studies of the *Politics*' presence in Bologna and in particular Dunbabin's point about the audience of Guido Vernani's commentary, cultivated laymen, remind one both of the very strong presence of the *Politics* in Italian cities but also of the greater permeability of Latin and vernacular in them. Among the substantial minority of laymen in Italian cities who owned and read Latin texts—and even on occasion wrote theological treatises—we are not going to be surprised to find possible traces of lay ownership of copies of the *Politics*.[86] A very early translation into Italian (1288) of Giles's *De regimine principum* will have made for wide diffusion of some *Politics* at second-hand. There is some contrast with the picture among laymen in or from north-western Europe, more of whom were excluded by Latin. While northern vernaculars in general waited for a long time for their version of the *Politics*, there was an exception in the French language. The point has been made forcibly that Oresme's translation of *c.*1371 introduced into the vernacular many new words, bearing with them Aristotle's political concepts.[87] Close study would probably support some earlier intrusion, through the quick translations into French of Giles, the first of whose three versions, done in the 1280s, was into Picard French.[88] There was more direct intrusion a few years later, but its extent can no longer be seen. An obscure translator called Peter of Paris was producing translations into a French (which had traces of Venetian) in Cyprus around 1300. Dedications of other works are to Simon, marshal of Hospitallers at Cyprus between 1299 and 1310, and to Amauri of Lusignan, who was in Cyprus by

[83] Alfonso el Sabio, *Las siete partidas*, I. i. 6, 4 vols. (Madrid, 1844–5), i. 375.

[84] See Briggs, *Giles of Rome's De regimine principum: Reading and Writing Politics at Court and University, c.1275–c.1525* (Cambridge, 1999), pp. 9 and 13.

[85] Oresme, *Politiques*, pp. 34–9.

[86] AL *Codices* 2, pp. 939–40 no. 1367—a copy in the hands of the mother of John de Tasso in 1319 (on John see Glorieux, *Arts*, p. 208 no. 232); 1039–40 no. 1514—a copy in the hands of a nobleman (but perhaps also a prelate?) in 1356; 1193 no. 1782—a copy in the hands of a member of the Tornaquinci family of Florence.

[87] Oresme, *Politiques*, pp. 27–33. Oresme's statements about the right of the French language to receive learning are discussed in S. Lusignan, 'La topique de la *Translatio Studii* et les traductions françaises de textes savants au XIVe siècle', *Traductions et Traducteurs au Moyen Âge*, ed. G. Contamine, Documents, Études et Répertoires Publiées par l'Institut de Recherche et d'Histoire des Textes (Paris, 1989), 303–15 (pp. 311–12).

[88] See below, Ch. 14 n. 18, and, on the various vernacular translations, C. F. Briggs, *Giles of Rome's De regimine principum*, pp. 3–4 n. 7 and p. 14.

1306 and up to 1310. Through Peter's reference to and quotation from his own translation of the *Politics*, now lost, we know of this first effort, which is usually dated around 1305.[89] The French language, then, was already being coloured by this branch of Aristotelian terminology from the 1280s.

11.3 *Reception of the 'demographic' elements in the Politics*

When putting the demographic elements in the *Politics* and medieval western reactions to them side by side and noting what western thinkers received in the *Politics* and what they added, there are two questions which are our real concern. What is shown about these men's existing patterns of thought and thus what they were already, to some degree, in the habit of thinking? Beyond that is the more elusive matter: what went on in their minds as their reading of the *Politics* came up against those demographic realities of the world in which they lived which were most deeply impressed upon their minds?

The texts are at various levels. At one level there is the Latin translation (Moerbeke). At the next the extremely literal commentary, which is designed only to elicit Aristotle's meaning and does this through line-by-line paraphrasing (Albert). At the next level, the commentary which is still designed to elicit Aristotle's meaning but does this by analysis and restatement (Thomas–Peter). At the next, the raising of questions on the text, which may allow the intrusion of more independence on the part of the question-raiser (Peter of Auvergne in his questions, and some related anonymous questions, especially in a Milan manuscript). At the next, the writing of independent treatises, which use much of Aristotle's material but choose, organize, and range widely, displaying yet more independence (Giles of Rome, Engelbert of Admont, Tolomeo of Lucca). This ideal typification of the texts smooths out bumps: the possibility of quite independent material intruded into a usually close and dependent commentary; and the individual characters of various commentators—for which the reader should turn to Jean Dunbabin's accounts. The texts used here and in the next two chapters consist of Albert, usually taken first despite the lack of complete certainty about the date (and thus priority) of his commentary; the Thomas–Peter commentary, together with Peter's overlapping commentary on part of book 3 and his questions; Engelbert of Admont's epitome; the texts (whether commentaries or 'potted versions') of Guido Vernani[90] and Walter Burley; the commentary of Nicole Oresme; the treatise on book 7 of the *Politics* by the Aragon Anonymous;

[89] A. Thomas, 'Notice sur le MS latin 4788 du Vatican contenant une traduction française avec commentaire par maître Pierre de Paris de la *Consolatio Philosophiae* de Boèce', *Notices et extraits des manuscrits de la Bibliothèque Nationale et autres bibliothèques* 41 (1923), pp. 29–90 (p. 48): *Et qui vodra savour ceste estoyre, si lise en la* Politique *de Aristo*[*te*], *que nous avons translatee en Chypre*; p. 51: *Et nos mesmes determinamez ceste question soffizaument en le livre de la* Politique *de Aristo*[*te*], *que nos translatames dou Latin en franceis en Chipre.*

[90] I am grateful to Jean Dunbabin for lending me a microfilm of Venice, Marciana, MS 2492 containing this.

Giles of Rome's *De regimine principum*, Engelbert of Admont's *De regimine principum*, and Tolomeo of Lucca's continuation of Thomas's *On Rule*.

One exception to the chronology of this book, which elsewhere stops before the Black Death, is the inclusion of the text which Nicole Oresme produced in 1374. There is a case for doing this. Oresme's French is a substitute (however poor) for the historian of the Historians who address the lost French translation of *c.*1305 can find stimulus to their *conjectures* about its character and significance by looking at Oresme's later translation. Further, we have seen that study of the *Politics* was intense in the first half of the fourteenth century, but little has survived of the ideas of those who lectured on the text. Since Oresme seems to have entered the faculty of Arts around 1338/40 and to have been teaching in it from around 1345/6 until 1362,[91] he will have first encountered the *Politics* in the 1340s. When returning to the text thirty years later, his main task was producing a translation into French, for and at the request of Charles V, and it is unlikely that he would have radically rethought his interpretations of a text which he had learnt and (probably) lectured upon. In the glosses, therefore, Oresme *may* have transmitted *some* of the ideas about the *Politics* circulating in Parisian thought at this earlier period when he was in the faculty of Arts. However, the text which we have is late, and the reader is given an amber warning signal about its inclusion in a book otherwise devoted to thought *before* 1348.

What was conceptually 'demographic' in the *Politics* is presented here, and then some accentuations and additions, and a discussion of the introduction of an area of vocabulary and thought. Several areas of special emphasis are separately described in the following two chapters. There are two preliminary points, the first a reminder of this book's policy about words. The summary given in the next paragraph and later close discussions of texts or commentaries try to stick to very simple words in order to restrict the semantic colouring of *later* stages in the history of 'demographic' thought. Thus they use *multitude* where we usually use *population*, or *incite parents to generate more children* rather than *encourage the birth-rate*. Similar reasoning lies behind translating very literally, even to the extent of not smoothing out medieval Latin syntax. Modern readers should bear in mind that context usually suggests readers taking *city* as *city or wider political community*. Secondly, the summary of the demographic elements in the *Politics* does not use the cornucopia of scholarly literature which discusses Aristotle's Greek text and what Aristotle himself may have meant in his own time. It aims only to epitomize what may have come over to readers of Moerbeke's Latin version.

Here is population in the *Politics*. From one point of view, a city is a certain multitude.[92] A particular multitude inhabits an area—place and people go

[91] Oresme, *Politiques*, p. 14a. For a biographical sketch, see Nicole Oresme, *Expositio et quaestiones in Aristotelis De Anima: Édition, Étude Critique*, ed. B. Patar, Philosophes Médiévaux 32 (Louvain, Paris, 1995), 12*–14*.

[92] *Multitudo enim quaedam . . . est civitas*: 1261a18; Su p. 60 l. 8; Sp no. 122. Also 1274b41; Su p. 151 ll. 4–5; Sp no. 224.

together.[93] A multitude is virtually one half male and one half female,[94] and a multitude consists of or has marriages:[95] marriages are one of the forms of communication proper to cities.[96] The multitude is like a river which may have a name or identity although, since it always flows, it is never precisely the same: so a multitude, which always has some dying and some being born.[97] The multitude has history. There were the earliest humans, and perhaps the suggestion of a history of succeeding forms of habitation with the teleological progression from households onwards.[98] Reminiscent of the long historical duration of the *Meteorology* is a reference to early (known) earthdwellers possibly being the survivors of a disaster. In this there is a hint of a cyclical pattern of natural disasters bringing about drastic diminution of the multitude, followed by slow recovery, rehabitation of land, and re-increase of the multitude.[99] References to remote and different peoples with varying characteristics suggest the world-wide multitude (which is not, however, stated and discussed).[100]

The multitude can increase[101] or decrease. There can be paucity of men[102] or excess of multitude, and there can be great degrees of these. A city can be much greater than it was at the beginning,[103] and it can 'contain a very excessive number', or 'a very excessive multitude'.[104] Apart from the brief reference to a cyclical pattern in the multitude, the main pattern implied in past history is of growth from small multitude to large multitude.[105] In history, proceeding from the remote past to the recent past and current times [fourth century BC] the size of the multitude has had a close connection with other things. In remote times there were different forms of marriage: men buying brides.[106] When multitudes were smaller there was exchange in kind, while with the growth of multitudes (as well as quantity and diversity of possession) there came money.[107] When multitudes were small there were kingdoms, while with greater multitudes there have been democracies.[108]

[93] 1276a8–14; Su p. 159 ll. 1–7; Sp no. 230(4). See also 1260b19; Su p. 57 ll. 6–7; Sp no. 113.

[94] 1260b19; Su p. 57 ll. 6–7; Sp no. 113; Sp no. 180; 1269b15–17; Su p. 117 ll. 1–3.

[95] Implied throughout the discussion of different systems of marriage in book 2 and tinkering with marriage-age in book 7.

[96] 1280b16–7; Su p. 187 ll. 2–3; Sp. no. 270.

[97] 1276a34–40; Su p. 160 ll. 2–7; Sp no. 231.

[98] 1252b15–23; Su pp. 5 l. 5—6 l. 5; Sp nos. 13–15. See also 1297b16–28; Su pp. 431 l. 5—432 l. 3; Sp nos. 518–20.

[99] This hint is not spelled out: 1269a4–5; Su p. 113 ll. 2–3; Sp no. 174 (2). Aristotle's long-duration view of people and inhabitation is given in his *Meteorology*. See p. 322 below and n. 141.

[100] 1327b18–1328a21; Su pp. 268 l. 10—272 l. 5; Sp nos. 968–74.

[101] e.g. 1293a1–2; Su p. 401 ll. 9–10; Sp no. 452.

[102] 1270b15 and 1278a31–2; Su pp. 121 l. 7 and 172 l.5; Sp nos. 186 and 241(1): *paucitas hominum*.

[103] 1293a4, 1296b18–19, 1296b298, 1326a21–2, 1326b10, and 1326b12; Su pp. 259 l. 5, 261 ll. 9 and 11, 262 l. 6, 402 ll. 1–2, 425 ll. 6–7, and 426 l. 2; Sp nos. 452, 503, 504, 943, 949, and 951: *excessus multitudinis; excessus populi; excessus; excedere secundum multitudinem.*

[104] 1326a31, 1326b6; Su pp. 259 l. 14–260 l. 1, 261 ll. 4–5; Sp nos. 946–7: *valde autem excedens numerus; valde excedens multitudo.*

[105] 1286b8–22; Su pp. 223 l. 12—224 l. 14; Sp nos. 359–63.

[106] 1268b41; Su p. 112 l. 9; Sp no. 174(1).

[107] 1257a19–28; Su pp. 35 l. 12—36 l. 8; Sp no. 74.

[108] 1252a19, 1292b42–1293a2, 1297b22–8, and 1320a17–18; Su pp. 6 l. 1, 410 ll. 8–10, 431 l. 10—432 l. 3, and 476 ll. 9–10; Sp nos. 15, 452, 519–20, 854, and the passages in n. 100 above.

Within the multitude of a particular city there are groups who may be described as 'parts' of the unit but may also (with more 'populationist' emphasis) be described as 'multitudes'. These may be groups defined by job (soldiers, farmers) or wealth (the rich, the poor) or belonging and not belonging to a people (aliens). The multitude of a particular political community is a topic for discussion. A number for it or one of its parts can be suggested. The principal question is, what is the ideal multitude?[109] The multitude may have the sub-multitude of, say, 5000 soldiers.[110] The figure must be related to the greater numbers of families and members of other sub-multitudes (e.g. farmers)[111] when thinking of the overall multitude of a particular city and relating it to the surrounding region, which must be of an extent sufficient to feed this overall multitude.[112] The sub-multitudes are in a relation of size to each other, whose examples are given in numerically simple examples, usually obvious ratios: for instance, 1000 rich to 300 poor, or 10 to 20.[113] This relation can be out of kilter. Thus there may be a paucity of multitude or an excess of multitude of one group *vis-à-vis* another:[114] an excess of multitudes of rich and poor in relation to the middling, or of aliens in relation to those not alien. A form of inheritance (which in Sparta led to the devolution of two-fifths of property into the hands of women) may affect the multitude—in this case, reduce the number of soldiers.[115] Particular groups may be particularly reduced by deaths singularly or especially affecting them. For instance, deaths in battle may reduce the multitude of rich more than the multitude of the poor.[116] Or again, there will be more deaths among young girls in childbirth (than in maturer women in childbirth).[117] There is immigration and emigration,[118] and one emphasized theme is problems arising from the immigration and presence of aliens.[119] The overall multitude of the city may be various figures, 2000 or 10,000 or 'however many'.[120] The multitude can be maintained as the same (i.e. as a stable figure), given (among those born) the deaths of some of them and sterility (in some families),[121] and an overall balance between births and deaths.[122] It can also increase, and this increase can be described as without measure or determination. Considerable increase brings problems: poverty and sedition follow where numbers and possessions are out of balance.[123] It is envisaged that the legislator can intervene, to encourage

[109] Principally 1325b38–1326b24; Su pp. 257 l. 4—262 l. 8; Sp nos. 938–52; also 1276a32–4; Su pp. 159 l. 13—160 l. 1; Sp no. 230(6).

[110] 1265a10; Su p. 86 l. 9; Sp no. 138(2).

[111] 1319a15–19; Su p. 470 ll. 4–7; Sp no. 838.

[112] 1265a13–17; Su p. 87 ll. 1–3; Sp no. 140. See also 1327b30–2; Su p. 263 ll. 1–3; Sp no. 954.

[113] 1290a33–5 and 1318a34; Su pp. 389 ll. 8–9 and 465 l. 5; Sp nos. 412 and 825.

[114] 1302b33–1303a2; Su pp. 506 l. 9—507 l. 7; Sp no. 593.

[115] 1270a19–39; Su pp. 120 l. 5—122 l. 1; Sp nos. 185–6.

[116] 1303a4–5; Su p. 507 l. 9; Sp no. 594.

[117] 1335a17–18; Su p. 318 ll. 4–5; Sp no. 1073.

[118] Including deliberate settlement elsewhere of part of the population: 1273b19–20; Su p. 143 ll. 1–2; Sp no. 215.

[119] 1303a27–1303b2 and 1327a13–18; Su pp. 264 l. 10—265 l. 4 and 509 l. 9—510 l. 11; Sp nos. 599 and 958.

[120] 1262a3–9; Su p. 66 ll. 3–7; Sp no. 123(2).

[121] 1265a39–42 and 1265b7–10; Su pp. 89 ll. 5–6 and 90 ll. 3–6; Sp nos. 142(1) and 142(4).

[122] See n. 94 above.

[123] 1265a38–40 and 1265b10–12; Su pp. 89 ll. 4–6 and 90 ll. 6–8; Sp nos. 142 and 142(5).

people to have more children (as in Sparta).[124] Some measure and determination of the production of children is good, for it is insufficient to rely on the balance between fertility and generation and death.[125]

Much of what has been summarized so far comes from the earlier discussion in the *Politics* of various proposed ideal constitutions, and Aristotle's criticisms of them, and most of it crops up incidentally and miscellaneously. However, in the penultimate part of the *Politics*, book 7, 'population' themes occupy centre stage. The principal ones are the optimum size of a city; a legislator's 'good birth' (eugenic) intervention in marriage ages; and determining the multitude of children. A city's greatness should not be measured in terms of its multitude, and excess of multitude brings problems (already mentioned); such excess may also be excess of multitude of slaves or aliens. The best city will have a measured and determined multitude. A treatment of the stock of different peoples precedes a long section about the disposition of marriage-ages, 18 for women and 37 for men. This is to produce consonance of periods of generation and ages between spouses, to produce better births, to avoid less good births (when generation is by the too old or too young), and to avoid the larger number of deaths which occur when too young girls give birth, and to produce an appropriate relation of ages between parents and children. In relation to the notion that 'there ought to be a determined multitude of procreation of children' there is discussion of exposure of deformed children, and abortion before there is sense and life (in the foetus).

Let us begin our investigation of the impact of this material by looking closely at one short example in Moerbeke's Latin text, and what is done with it in paraphrases and commentaries.

Moerbeke:[126]

(*a*) *Inconveniens autem et possessiones adaequantem circa multitudinem civium non constituere,*
(*b*) *sed sinere puerorum procreationem infinitam,*
(*c*) *tamquam sufficienter utique respondentem ad eandem multitudinem propter sterilitates quantiscunque generatis,*
(*d*) *quia videtur hoc etiam nunc accidere circa civitates.*

In this (*b*) and (*d*) are straightforward for anyone with moderately good Latin. However, the display of Moerbeke's flair at turning an elegantly pithy phrase in parts of (*a*) and (*c*) makes them knottier. Many readers might need several readings and some thought to work out what these mean. A literal English rendering, which tries to leave in place some of the difficulty, could go thus:

(*a*) Moreover, [it is] strange for [someone who] is equalizing possessions not to lay down [something] about the multitude of citizens,
(*b*) but to allow the infinite procreation of children;

[124] 1270b1–3; Su p. 122 ll. 3–4; Sp no. 187: *provocat cives ut plures faciant pueros.*

[125] 1265a39–42 and 1265b6–10; Su pp. 89 ll. 5–6 and 90 ll. 1–6; Sp nos. 142(1) and 142(3): *oportere determinatam esse puerorum procreationem.*

[126] 1265a38–42; Su p. 89 ll. 4–8; Sp nos. 142–142(1). See Martin's characterization of Moerbeke's Latin and the commentator's task in his 'The vulgate test of Aquinas's Commentary', 37–40.

(*c*) [such procreation], so to speak, in any case corresponding sufficiently to the same multitude, on account of sterilities, however many have been generated:
(*d*) because this also now seems to happen in the case of cities.

Albert the Great goes through, expanding the text in his paraphrases in order to make Aristotle's meaning clearer. A literal English version of Albert could go like this:

Then, when he says, *Moreover,* [it is] *strange for possessions* etc, he criticizes Socrates—that when laying down a sufficiency of possession for the multitude he did not determine how great the multitude should be—saying: *Moreover,* [it is] *strange for* [someone who] *is equalizing possessions not to lay down,* add [here], how great the multitude ought to be, *but to allow the infinite procreation of children,* [such procreation], *so to speak, in any case corresponding to the same multitude,* that is, the possessions, so to speak, correspond to the infinite multitude to be procreated. And Socrates states that the cause of this is: *On account of the sterilities* of some matrons, through whose sterility the number of citizens is restricted, so that the possessions suffice for the others, *however many have been generated,* add [here], by [the matrons who are] not sterile.[127]

Real, translucent clarity only comes with Thomas. He goes further, distilling Aristotle's general intention into a brief introductory proposition, and then breaking down Aristotle's thought into several propositions, each of which is expanded for explanation. His initial summary and the first two points of his analysis go like this:

Then, when he says, *Moreover,* [it is], *strange.* He criticizes the position of Socrates for this, that when determining the quantity of possessions he did not determine the quantity of generation.
And on this he does six things. First, in fact, he points out that what Socrates was saying is strange. And he says that it is strange that someone should want to equalize the possessions of a city, that is reduce them to a certain quantity, and not institute together with this something to determine the multitude of citizens, but allow the generation of citizens to infinity, as Socrates did.
Secondly there, *so to speak sufficiently.* He points out the reason that was moving Socrates. It happens that many women in a city are sterile, and thus, although other women are generating many children, nevertheless the same multitude of the city will always be preserved, as we see occurs in cities now. And on account of this it did not seem necessary to Socrates for something to be determined about the generation of children.[128]

[127] Albert, *Politics,* p. 126(g): *Deinde cum dicit,* Inconveniens autem et possessiones etc., *reprehendit Socratem, quod constituens sufficientiam possessionis ad multitudinem, non determinavit quanta deberet esse multitudo, dicens:* Inconveniens autem et possessiones adaequantem circa multitudinem civium non constituere', *supple, quanta debet esse multitudo,* sed sinere puerorum procreationem infinitam, tamquam sufficienter utique respondentem ad eamdem multitudinem, *id est, tamquam possessiones respondeant multitudini infinitae procreandae. Et hujus causa dixit Socrates esse:* Propter sterilitates *aliquarum matronarum, quarum sterilitate restringitur numerus civium, ut posssessiones aliis sufficiant,* quantiscumque generatis, *supple, ex non sterilibus.*

[128] Aquinas, *Politics,* p. A142 (Spiazzi edn., pp. 77–8 nos. 232–3): *Deinde cum dicit* Inconueniens autem *etc., improbat positionem Socratis ex hoc quod determinans quantitatem possessionum non determinabat quantitatem generationis. Et circa hoc sex facit: primo quidem proponit esse inconueniens id quod Socrates dicebat. Et dicit quod inconueniens est quod aliquis uelit possessiones ciuitatis adequare, id est ad certam quantitatem reducere, et cum hoc non instituat aliquid ad determinandum multitudinem ciuium, set*

Thomas is analysing a wider section of the *Politics* than has so far been presented. Moerbeke's Aristotle had continued thus:[129]

(*e*) *Magis autem suspicabitur quis utique oportere determinatam esse puerorum procreationem quam substantiam,*	(*e*) In fact one will suppose that the procreation of children ought to be determined more than property [ought to be determined],
(*f*) *ut non numero quodam plures generentur, hanc autem multitudinem ponere adspicientem ad fortunas, si accidat mori quosdam generatorum, et ad aliorum sterilitatem.*	(*f*) so that no more than a certain number are generated, [and that one ought] to fix this multitude [= number] while taking account of chance, if some of those generated should happen to die, and [taking account of] the sterility of others.

This is how Thomas takes up the thread:

Fifthly there, [when he says], *so that not more than a certain number*, he shows what ought to be observed in such a determination. And he says that one ought to determine the multitude of children to be generated while taking account of fortuitous events, namely the deaths of those who are born and the sterility of women who do not conceive. That is to say, so that on one side the number of the generated should be permitted to grow in excess, to such a degree that it copes with the fortuitous deficiencies of this sort [on the other side].[130]

Guido writes after several decades of reading and attempting to understand the *Politics*, with the ready availability of such guides as Albert, Thomas, and Peter of Auvergne, and with a lay audience in mind. What he presents is brief, clear, and accessible:

Socrates erred because, while he determined in some way, as has been seen, about the quantity of possessions, he said nothing about the number of citizens, but allowed the city to grow without end. [Summarizes Aristotle's reason thus]: that since there are many sterile women in a city, however many children are generated from other [women], the same multitude will always remain in the city.[He continues, near the end of this section]: The multitude of a city ought to be determined—more than possession—such that the number of children being born does not exceed the quantity of possessions. Further, for the laying down of this multitude one ought to take account of fortuitous events, such as the death[s] of those who are born and the sterility of women.[131]

permittat generationem ciuium in infinitum fieri, sicut Socrates faciebat. Secundo, ibi Tanquam sufficienter *etc., ponit rationem que mouebat Socratem. Contingit enim in ciuitate multas mulieres esse steriles; et ita licet aliis mulieribus generantibus multos filios, tamen semper conseruabitur eadem multitudo ciuitatis, sicut nunc uidemus in ciuitatibus euenire. Et propter hoc Socrati non uidebatur necessarium quod circa generationem filiorum aliquid taxaretur.*

[129] 1265b6–10; Su p. 90 ll. 1–6; Sp nos. 142(3)–142(4).

[130] Aquinas, *Politics*, p. A142 (Spiazzi edn., p. 78 no. 235): *Quinto, ibi* Hanc autem multitudinem *etc., ostendit quod debeat obseruari in tali determinatione. Et dicit quod oportet determinare multitudinem filiorum generandorum respiciendo ad casus fortuitos, puta ad mortes eorum qui nascuntur et ad steriltatem mulierum que non concipiunt; ut scilicet tantum permittatur ex alia parte superexcrescere generatorum numerus, ut huiusmodi defectus suppleantur.*

[131] Venice, Marciana, MS 2492, fol. 73va–b: *Adhuc autem erravit Socrates, quia, cum aliqualiter ut visum est de quantitate possessionum determinaret, de numero civium nihil dixit sed permisit civitatem crescere*

Nicole Oresme translates Moerbeke into French—most of (*f*), for example, becomes:

Et pour determiner et limiter cest multitude il convient resgarder as fortunes qui pevent advenir par la mort de ceulz qui seroient engendrées et par la sterilité des femmes qui ne pourroit concevoir et des hommes qui ne pourroit engendrer.[132]

The humbleness of Oresme's genre—a translation with interspersed glosses—should not deceive us. A spirit of freedom and a richness of thought are everywhere apparent. The text is in a vernacular. The introductory gloss to the example is sharply direct: 'Then he states how such generation or procreation should be limited' (*Apres il met la maniere comment tele generation ou procreation doit estre limitee*). In expanding 'sterility' Oresme applies biological knowledge to a demographic pattern, breaking away from the tradition of Albert and Thomas ('the sterility of matrons') and substituting for it the broader 'the sterility of women who cannot conceive and of men who cannot engender'. His following gloss then pays attention to the relation between generation and sterility or deaths: *Et que l'en lesse faire generation selon l'estimation de la diminution qui pourroit avenir par lez dictes fortunes.* Here we have the mathematician Oresme introducing into this balance the phrase 'according to the estimate of diminution', a phrase whose arithmetic colouring now underlines the relation of generation, sterility, and death as a balance of numbers, a subject for 'estimation' or counting. More follows. After translating a few more lines, Oresme's gloss summarizes the drift:

And for this purpose, that the people should not multiply so greatly that it does not have enough upon which to live, it is appropriate to bring moderation and measure into this, according to philosophy and as best as one can through good laws and ordinances. And in many different ways according to the difference and diversity of regions and times and the conditions and customs of men.[133]

There then follows a long (about 750 words) gloss which is principally a historical survey of ways of controlling and limiting population. It is Oresme's historical knowledge and outlook, not Aristotle's which is displayed in this potted history: within its span, the first systematic history of population control. It is summarized and discussed in Chapter 13 below.

At the front of our minds we may have the blunt question, 'what was added to the *Politics*?', and excitement at seeing lift-off in Oresme. But we need to pause. We need to blank out of our minds whatever modern English translation of Aristotle we may have been reading, typically Ernest Barker's in the Oxford Aristotle. For such translations insidiously use phrases which come from later semantic-conceptual stages in the history of thought. And we should reflect on one avenue

sine fine. . . . Quia cum in civitate sint multe [? *id est*] *mulieres steriles, quotcunque filii ex aliis generentur semper remanebit in civitate eadem multitudo . . . Oportet ergo determinatam esse multitudinem civitatis magis eciam quam ipsa possessio, ita quod numerus nascentium filiorum non excedat quantitatem possessionum. Ad hanc autem multitudinem statuendam oportet habere respectum ad fortuitos casus ut ad mortem eorum qui nascuntur et ad sterilitatem mulierum.*

[132] Oresme, *Politiques*, p. 88b.

[133] Oresme's French is quoted below in Ch. 13 n. 58.

which was suggested in 1958 for tracing in general the influence of Aristotle. Thought in Latin and then in vernacular phrases and sentences is partly shaped by the possession and use of words such as form, matter, substance, accidents, quality, quantity, active, passive, energy, act, category. These words came into western languages in the first instance through Latin translations of Aristotle's logical and philosophical works.[134] In the case of the *Politics* we are not dealing with such formal logical and philosophical language, and the vocabulary in question may not have quite such a cut-and-dried history. However, the point still has much application to the vocabulary of the *Politics*, whether broadly of political topics or more narrowly of the 'demographic' topics which are discussed here. Translating from a Greek manuscript of the *Politics*, Moerbeke had been at great pains to produce precise equivalents in Latin—for which he has been duly praised in recent times. Something not immediately dazzling but very important has been taking place in Moerbeke's putting into the west's Latin these words and phrases, and then in the combined effort by readers of Moerbeke to understand Aristotle where Moerbeke's Latin was easy to follow, and to tease out its meaning where it was not. Powerful clarification and simplification is being brought about by Thomas's massive intellect: 'it happens that many women in a city are sterile: and thus while other women [are] generating many children, nevertheless the same multitude of the city will always be preserved.' An ever clearer way is being found to state the notion of a relationship between the sterility of some, the fertility of others, and the overall level of population. And there is a phrase: 'the same multitude remaining'. Conceptually and semantically this comes early in a line which leads to the more modern 'stable population and the conditions which maintain it', while Oresme's 'estimate of diminution' is in a line which leads to the thought of precise arithmetical measurement of those conditions. Not only are these phrases emerging and being sharpened or developed: they are being dinned in by repetition. Some other examples of this development of phrases and thoughts are given through close examination of other parts of the *Politics* in Chapters 12 and 13 below. These phrases can be brief: *excess of multitude* (leading to *over-population*), or *the multitude of men growing* (leading to *population growth*). They can be long: *the deaths of those who are born* (leading to *infant mortality*), or *if not more than a certain number are to be generated* (leading to *limitation of population*), or *incite parents to generate more children* (leading to *encourage the birth-rate*). And around 1305 such phrases were making their first (albeit abortive) entry into a western vernacular.

Here the point needs to be stated generally. Earlier chapters in this book have been examining 'demographic' elements in other sorts of texts, in part written before the introduction into the west of Aristotle's *Politics*. These show a particular range of thought and vocabulary existing in the west. There had been development of concepts—proportions of men and women ('sex-ratio', Ch. 4) or the

[134] L. Minio-Paluello, 'La tradition aristotélicienne dans l'histoire des idées', repr. in his *Opuscula*, pp. 405–24 (pp. 421–4); in its application to science the point is repeated in his 'Aristotle: tradition and influence', *DSB* i. 267–81 (pp. 277–9).

proportion of the married in a population (Ch. 5), for example—and of a generalizing mode of thought (about avoiding offspring, Ch. 8). Some of the earlier vocabulary may overlap with what now comes in the *Politics.* So, when describing Swabia in his *On the Properties of Things*, as we saw in Chapter 10 above, Bartholomew the Englishman had no problem writing that it was *over-populous* (*populosa nimis*). However, despite the overlap there is a significant gap between such descriptive phrases, adjectival, which ascribe one attribute to one region, and the noun or nouns which convey the concept, ripe for discussion as a generality, of *over-population* (*excessum multitudinis*). More important, however, is density. No text united so many of these phrases or so many 'demographic' concepts as the *Politics* and its commentaries, or had them so systematically analysed and related to other phenomena: and some of them were directly an accretion to the stock of concepts and phrases available in the west. This concentration and this accretion to the west's stock of phrases and therefore possible (or easier to think) thoughts was the first major importance for 'demographic' thought of the introduction of the *Politics.* And it is because this is a point *not* about one profound thought developed by Siger of Brabant or some other advanced thinker, but about the mentality, or mental world, of the literate in general, that so much attention was paid earlier in this chapter to a pointilliste picture of diffusion of copies of the *Politics* or derivative texts. For the case advanced here rests upon the many meetings of more ordinary literate men and the vocabulary in these texts, and thus the slow development among them of thinking 'demographically' in the ways spelled out in and stimulated by the *Politics.* Elusiveness of the theme may make it difficult precisely to trace and delineate this development. But this difficulty, and the necessary tedium of the demonstration of a few examples, should not obscure its fundamental importance.

To return to the contents of the *Politics.* Commentators struggle to understand it, and they restate it. They also bring their own emphases, by accentuating or, less obviously, underplaying parts of it, and they add, doing these things in a way which both shows them incorporating Aristotle into their own western European, Christian, and late thirteenth- or early fourteenth-century milieux and also sometimes casts fitful reflexive light on their outlook and these milieux.

There are two broad frameworks in the outlook of the commentators, frameworks into which the demographic contents of the *Politics* are being inserted. The first is the historical and geographical reaches of their view of the multitude in the world, and the second is their Christianity. Imagining and envisaging the multitude now and in the past comes easily to the commentators: a web of relations, a descending network of families, in Guido's pithy phrase, a 'succession of those dying and being born'.[135] The multitude has history. In Aquinas, Giles, Marsilio, and others Aristotle's teleological progression upwards from households becomes partly overlaid by a simpler historical account of fathers, children, and

[135] Venice, Marciana, MS 2492, fol. 85rb: *successionem decedentium et nascentium.*

grandchildren propagating in greater numbers.[136] Let us leave for a moment, until the next paragraph, the furthest projection of the multitude into the past, where commentators' view of the longer history of the multitude is inseparable from the Old Testament, and stay with geography. The *Politics* now merges, in commentators linking it with their reading of some of the geographic (and medical) texts surveyed in Chapters 10 and 11 above, and with the opening out which we discerned, towards a view of 'world population'. The world-wide extension of the multitude: this stimulates further comment principally where Aristotle comments on the characteristics of peoples. Albert imports climatic geography, Avicenna, and the astrologer Messehalla (whose writings had been translated from Arabic into Latin in the twelfth century) on the shortness of life of the Ethiopians. Again, in the central text on 'stock' Albert refers to his own work *De natura loci*,[137] while virtually all commentators, even Burley (who, apart from deliberately avoiding some of the history in the *Politics*, normally abbreviates), let rip with more material on the natural complexion and spirit of different peoples. The culmination comes with Oresme, whom we see elsewhere usually moving easily to a world-wide view. Thus, there is a universal multitude divided into kingdoms; the impossibility in such a universal multitude for men to live together civilly is the reason for the severalness of cities [= political communities]; the universal multitude is to be compared to a house with many children, from which it is expedient to make many houses. When Oresme turns to the stock of peoples he provides us with a massive excursus into earlier geographers and their divisions of the 'habitable world'. And the manuscripts of *his* translation of the *Politics* include at this point a diagrammatic map of the world.[138]

In the midst of a brief excursus on the remote past, with simple and barbaric laws, Aristotle alludes to early (or the earliest) humans, and whether they were generated out of earth or were the survivors of some cataclysm. Suddenly, brusquely, on the theme of the earliest projections into the past of the history of the multitude, commentators were confronted with the tensions between on the one hand their own knowledge of the multitude's descent from the first two created humans and its subsequent history as recounted in the Old Testament, and on the other hand the hints here of Aristotle's view. Thomas follows a brief reference to Aristotle's view with its contradiction: 'however, through ancient histories it is clear that regions began to be inhabited from a particular time, which seems contrary to the eternity of the world.'[139] He and the others hold the faith-versus-Aristotle topic at arms-length, and concentrate on two aspects of the point about survivors from a cataclysm: the particular theme of the Flood, and a cyclical up-and-down view of the long history of the multitude. Albert proceeds from the survivors to stating the theme as the new habitation of lands. Referring to 'astronomer philosophers' in general, and specifically Albumasar, he writes of

[136] Giles, *De regimine*, II. i. 2; p. 220. [137] Albert, *Politics*, pp. 330k and 663a.
[138] Oresme, *Politiques*, pp. 292b and 297a–299a.
[139] Aquinas, *Politics*, p. A160 (Spiazzi edn., p. 95 no. 292).

'the destruction of the habitations of ancient cities and the buildings and populating of new cities in provinces', and the causes of destruction, fire and water. Classical instances of both are given, Deucalion's flood, and destruction by fire in the fable of Phaethon in Ovid, in both of which a few were saved after universal destruction, from whom came the later inhabitants and cultivators of lands.[140] Thomas sees Aristotle as positing recurring phenomena: 'general desolations of lands happened many times through some floods or corruptions of some sort or other; and when these ceased regions began to be inhabited again.' After dismissing the one way in which this could happen (generation from earth) he proceeds to the other, reconciling it with the Old Testament: 'in a general destruction (*corruptione*), it could happen that a few men were saved in the mountains or in another way; just as we posit that Noah was saved in the ark at the time of the general Flood, and Deucalion was saved in the mountains in the flood which happened in the land of the Greeks . . .'[141]

Guido robustly and quickly rejects generation from earth. He then dwells on 'corruption', taking this further than earlier commentators. 'For destruction of land happens quickly and in a short time, and this in four ways, either from epidemic illness which occurs through corruption of the air; or from battles and wars; or from sterility of the region; or through the flooding of some sudden inundation. Sometimes a region which had been inhabited becomes uninhabitable, and the reverse, for long periods of time, which happens sometimes through the restriction of rivers and waters.'[142] Following Aristotle's *Meteorology*, he goes on to suggest long duration as the reason for our not being aware of such changes: 'because such a succession of regions happens over the longest times, such things are hidden [from us], because of our shortness of life.'[143] Guido also highlights more than previous commentators 'Christian truth', divine creation of the 'first inhabitors of the earth' and first parents, and the exemplification of Aristotle's 'survivors of destruction' through Old Testament history: 'Noah was saved after the Flood with his children . . . who were the first inhabitants of the earth after the Flood; and afterwards, having multiplied according to divine precept, they filled up the habitable earth.'[144] Oresme's excursus on various forms of 'depopulation'

[140] Albert, *Politics*, pp. 154–5f. The reference is to Albumasar, *De magnis coniunctionibus annorum revolutionibus ac eorum profectionibus* (Augsburg, 1489), a new edition of which is being prepared by C. Burnett. On Albumasar see D. Pingree, 'Ab Ma'Shar', *DSB* i. 32–9 (see p. 38 no. 8); on the manuscripts and editions of the Latin translation, see F. J. Carmody, *Arabic Astronomical and Astrological Sciences in Latin Translation: A Critical Bibliography* (Berkeley, 1956), pp. 91–2.

[141] Aquinas, *Politics*, p. A160 (Spiazzi edn., p. 95 no. 292). Here Albert, Thomas, and Guido are influenced by—and importing material from—Aristotle's *Meteorology*, I. xiv (from 351b9). Both Albert and Thomas had commented on the *Meteorology*; see Ch. 9 above, pp. 219–20.

[142] Venice, Marciana, MS 2492, fol. 77vb: *Terre autem corrupcio contingit attamen quidem cito et in pauco tempore, et hoc quadrupliciter, vel ex infirmitate epidemie que contingit ex corrupcione vel ex prealiis et guerris, vel ex sterilitate regionis, vel ex diluvio alicuius subite inundationis. Aliquando autem fit quidem regio inhabitabilis que prius fuerat habitata et econverso per multa et longa tempora, et fit quandoque per arctacionem fiuminum et stangnorum.*

[143] Ibid.: *quia talis successio regionum fit in longissimis temporibus, latent hic talia, propter brevitatem vite nostre.*

[144] Ibid., fol. 78ra: *salvatus* [sic] *Noe et filii sui cum uxoribus eorum . . . qui primi inhabitatores terre post*

through water, fire, corruptions, *mortalités*, and *pestilence* was to be even longer, and decked out with more scriptural, astrological, and classical erudition.[145]

Elsewhere the faith and the Christian practice and outlook of the commentators crops up only occasionally, miscellaneously, and for varying reasons. Something advocated by Aristotle may come up against the Old Testament or canon law. Three examples which crop up in Chapters 12 and 13 below are measure in the multitude, abortion to keep numbers down, and marriage-ages. Similarly, contemporary Christian practice may be evoked by passing allusions to contrasts in Greek practices. Examples of this in the next two chapters are the age of the priesthood, and invocation of a saint's help during childbirth.

These wider frameworks are not visible most of the time, where what we have is an effort to understand and expound a miscellany of 'demographic' themes and some tinkering to bring about a degree of rapprochement between what Aristotle says about these and the contemporary world. Effort to understand: focusing on the example of 5000 soldiers and the region of Babylon (used to illustrate the relation between size of a region and numbers it can support), Guido spells out the wife and servant of each soldier, each one generating either more children or at least one.[146] Or, looking at cities contemporary to himself, he lists words of relationship appropriate to one person: someone is a son to one person, a nephew to another, and so on.[147] The act of envisaging pulls Aristotle's world towards Guido's world. The tinkering in which the commentators engage may be only with the surface, or quite elementary. Thus where *city* is, or is being taken as, a *political community* it may be spelled out that what is meant is a kingdom.[148] Or the *city* may be an urban entity, and Oresme will refer to those which loom in his mind, Rouen and Paris.[149] Where Aristotle talks of a city as containing 2000 or 10,000 or 'whatever number', and most commentators decline to take up the challenge of the last phrase, Albert does take it up, and introduces 100,000:[150] a figure nearer to the size of the cities he lived in and knew so well, Cologne and Paris. The mention of a specific name—Guido, for example, bringing up Florentine greed in a discussion of the size of the region surrounding a city[151]—may provide the reader with a clear marker that some 'seeing how it fits' is going on. But it can also be going on where there are no such precise markers: and the reader needs to be more alert to spot these, as well as more tentative in asserting that they are happening.

diluvium, tandem multiplicati secundum divinum preceptum terra[m] habitabilem repleverunt. See also fol. 58va, where Guido smoothly blends Aristotle and the Old Testament, reciting Aristotle's progression from house to village and village to city and then simply adding that it was in this way that the human race was multiplied from Adam to the Flood and thence to the present day.

145 Oresme, *Politiques*, p. 98a.

146 Venice, Marciana, MS 2492, fol. 73rb: *Nam quilibet uxorem habet, famulum, et filios, forte plures vel saltem unum.*

147 Ibid., fol. 70ra.

148 Giles, *De regimine*, III. ii. 32 (pp. 541–4), is devoted to distinguishing *city* and *kingdom*; see also Engelbert, *De regimine*, I. xii (p. 31).

149 Oresme, *Politiques*, pp. 119b, 200b, 201b, 211b, 276a, and 286b.

150 Albert, *Politics*, p. 97 n.

151 Venice, Marciana, MS 2492, fol. 134rb.

Sometimes commentators fail to react to a theme. Only Guido and Oresme preserve Aristotle's hint that the division of the multitude into male and female is not exactly but only 'near' to half and half,[152] and neither they nor anyone else develop it or take up the opportunity to introduce the phrase which had been developed in *Sentences* commentaries for 'sex-ratio' in the multitude. As we have seen in Chapter 4 above, this phrase had developed by 1250, and in the early fourteenth century there comes the earliest record of attempts to count the sex-ratio, among babies when baptised. Why was there silence?

Other themes produce exposition, but no further reaction, while others do produce reactions. In these one can discern developments, sometimes only little, and occasional glancing contemporary allusions.[153] Subordinate parts or multitudes (Guido prefers the more 'populationist' word *multitude*) constitute a useful because middling example of a theme where we can see some but not very dramatic reactions and developments. Aristotle's discussion of disproportionate increase or decrease of particular parts or multititudes at one point attracts slightly more than usual attention from Albert, and then marked expansion and increased clarity from Peter of Auvergne. Through fortune, the deaths of soldiers and nobles in war may bring about the disproportionate decrease of their multitude, and thus the disproportionate increase of the poor, with the political consequences indicated by Aristotle.[154] Aristotle's discussion of middling people—proportionately larger in larger cities, and the likelihood that disturbance and sedition are absent where they outweigh the rich and the poor—attracts approving attention. There is clear restatement and expansion in Peter of Auvergne;[155] Giles devotes a whole chapter to it;[156] and Guido states that this peacefulness (where the middling are proportionately greater) is what 'we see by sense and observation' when looking at small and large cities.[157] Subordinate multitudes occasion brief contemporary references. Guido names mechanical crafts—leatherers, skinners, wool-workers, fullers, smiths[158]—and uses the military mariners of Venice and Genoa to exemplify Aristotle's reference to specialized concentrations of numbers in particular cities or areas.[159] On the other hand, when encouraged to think of a subordinate multitude in a city, the mind of the

[152] Venice, Marciana, fol. 68va: *Adhuc enim mulieres sunt ferre medietas liberorum qui sunt in civitate*; Oresme, *Politiques*, p. 99b. For Engelbert, *De regimine principum*, III. xxv (p. 85), women are straightforwardly *dimidia pars prolis.*

[153] In the *Politics*-inspired but independent treatises used here, in particular Engelbert's and Tolomeo's, there is much more explicit and detailed reference to the contemporary world than in the more constricted commentaries. Engelbert refers to contemporary cities, countries (Germany, Italy, France, Spain, and Greece) and Louis IX, *De regimine principum*, I. vii, I. viii, I. xvii, III. xxii, and VII. xxxiv; pp. 22, 23, 40, 75, and 251; on Tolomeo, see below Ch. 13 n. 10.

[154] Albert, *Politics*, pp. 442–3k–l; Peter of Auvergne, *Politics*, pp. 253–4 nos. 736–7.

[155] Ibid., pp. 222–3 no. 638.

[156] Giles, *De regimine*, III. ii. 33; pp. 545–7.

[157] Venice, Marciana, MS 2492, fol. 104rb: *videmus per sensum et experientiam.*

[158] Ibid., fol. 99vb: *Secunda pars [civitatis] est multitudo artificum mechanicorum, sicut sunt coriarii, pelliparii, lanarii, fullones, fabri et huiusmodi, sine quibus civitatem impossibile est habitari.*

[159] Ibid., fol. 100va: *bellatores autem marinarii in Athenis, nunc autem in nobilibus civitatibus Venetorum et Januensium.*

more north-western European Oresme seems automatically to envisage 'men of the cloth trade' (*gens de draperie*).[160] Such brief glimpses, here, of Guido's and Oresme's worlds have colour, but not the significance which is possessed by the relation of subordinate multitude and number. We see the allied themes of a relation between a region's size and fertility and the numbers it can support, and the ratios between different subordinate multitudes, inducing Engelbert of Admont to bring into his epitome the suggestion, which is not in the *Politics*, of a ratio between those engaged in agriculture and those fed by their labours of 4:1.[161] Engelbert is unique among the commentators in doing this. However, the paraphrased and commented restatements of Moerbeke's Aristotle were ramming home over and over again the notion of number and proportion on the subject of these subordinate multitudes of rich, middling, poor, soldiers, farmers, and other groups. The *idea* was there in the decades around 1300.[162]

Here and there, then, in the commentators' handling of the 'demographic' contents of the *Politics*, we can discern, sometimes clearly, sometimes tentatively, understanding, reactions, additions, and sometimes little chinks of light into their world. Sometimes the commentators' attention is noticeably sharper: they are concentrating hard. A mild example of this we have already seen in their interest in early men and the relation between long-term cycles of disasters and recovery of the multitude and Old Testament history of the multitude. The largest examples, however, were the themes of marriage-ages, and optimum size (and control) of the multitude, which are explored in the next two chapters.

160 Oresme, *Politiques*, p. 173b. 161 Engelbert, *Compendium Politicorum*, ed. Fowler, p. 201.
162 See the discussion of Giovanni Villani in Ch. 14 below.

12

THE *POLITICS* (II): AGE AT MARRIAGE

12.1 *The commentators and the marriage-ages of ordinary people*

One part of the *Politics* which attracted special attention was the discussion of marriage, in particular ideal ages of marriage, in book 7. Commentators added to it, and one writer even devoted a short treatise to it. What was in their minds as they wrote? Marriage-ages in Europe at this time have already cropped up incidentally in Chapters 6 and 10 above, and it is now time to give this theme more attention, as we try to see what may have shaped commentators' awareness of marriage-ages in their Europe, and, beyond this, *what* these realities were—or rather, what modern scholarship has conjecturally reconstructed.

There is an asymmetry in what is known with certainty about ages at first marriage in medieval Europe. While we have quite a lot of direct information about a minority, ruling and noble houses and their marriages, we have very little direct evidence about the majority, ordinary people and their marriages.

The position and power of the minority and the importance of its alliances mean that some information about these marriages has often survived. Even as early as the tenth century sporadic chronicle-entries can be put together to reconstruct some of the demography of such families, as Karl Leyser showed, and as time goes on increasingly complete genealogies of such families can be pieced together. Let us follow a few prominent examples which bear upon ages at first marriage for girls, taking them chronologically. We can look first at Leyser's analysis of the high aristocracy of tenth-century Saxony, where girls married early: examples of marriage at 13 are given.[1] Secondly, royal and aristocratic marriage in tenth- to twelfth-century Francia was under Georges Duby's microscope for several decades, and his generalization, for girls, was first marriage 'at a very young age'.[2] Third is T. Hollingsworth's statistical study of British ducal families, which showed for his earliest period, between 1330 and 1479, mean ages at marriage for girls of 17.1, and for men 22.4.[3] These examples may still leave much to be said. For example, various strata are being squashed in our discussion into 'minority'; and the effect of various forms of inheritance on men's age at marriage (low for the

[1] K. Leyser, *Rule and Conflict in an Early Medieval Society: Ottonian Saxony* (London, 1979), pp. 51–2.

[2] G. Duby, *Love and Marriage in the Middle Ages*, trans. J. Dunnett (Cambridge, 1994), p. 26—a rare comment from Duby, who was more interested in the age at first marriage of males.

[3] T. H. Hollingsworth, 'A Demographic Study of the British Ducal Families', in *Population in History*, ed. D. V. Glass and D. E. C. Eversley (London, 1965), pp. 354–78 (p. 365).

first-born but not for the rest in a system of primogeniture) is important. For our purposes, however, the broader sketch must suffice. And this sketch is the one which is familiar from the 'noble-woman' chapter in general accounts of medieval women: girls enter arranged marriages which sometimes have political and invariably have property dimensions, and they are very young.

'Material relating to a high social class is really only applicable to that class'.[4] Hollingsworth's dictum about historical demographic data in general applies particularly here, for there is no good ground for supposing that ordinary people's marriages resembled those of this minority. Since a famous article written by John Hajnal in 1965 the marriages of the many have been discussed within terms which he defined and described.[5] He distinguished two 'marriage patterns'. In one, the 'non-European' pattern, there were two features. Average age at first marriage for girls was very low, typically at or not long after the onset of puberty; and the nuptiality rate was extremely high, that is to say, virtually all adults will have been married at some time. The other, termed 'the European marriage pattern',[6] had the opposites of these. Average age at first marriage for girls was quite high, perhaps early twenties; and the nuptiality rate was quite low, that is, quite a large proportion of adults never married. Hajnal went further, suggesting that 'non-European' was what probably prevailed in medieval times, with a change towards European beginning in 'early modern' (sixteenth-century) Europe. From the late 1960s onwards, and culminating in a major monograph in 1978, there appeared a number of studies from David Herlihy and Christiane Klapisch.[7] These principally exploited and presented the rich data of a Tuscan census of 1427. This showed the mean age for girls' marriage of 17.6 (and the most common age 16), and a mean age for men approaching 38. Herlihy's comments on these figures—something 'European' in the men's pattern and 'non-European' in the women's—could encourage readers to think in an impressionist way of some sort of half-way house between the two, something perhaps to be expected in a very *late* 'medieval' society.

Several fundamental works by Richard Smith subsequently conquered and clarified the field. In 1979 he established that what is known for later medieval Tuscany is not good evidence for other parts of medieval Europe, in particular north-western Europe. Rather than looking at a chronological divide for Europe (one marriage pattern in 'medieval' Europe, another emerging in the 'early modern' period, as Hajnal had suggested), we should think of a geographical divide. On the one hand there is southern Europe, where in Italy there is evidence of the long duration of one marriage pattern. On the other hand there is north-western

[4] T. H. Hollingsworth, *Historical Demography*, The Sources of History: Studies in the Use of Historical Evidence (Cambridge, 1976 = re-issue of London, 1969), p. 211.

[5] J. Hajnal, 'European Marriage Patterns in Perspective', in *Population in History*, ed. Eversly and Glass, pp. 101–43; 'Two kinds of pre-industrial household formation system', in *Family Forms in Historic Europe* ed. R. Wall (Cambridge, etc., 1983), pp. 65–104.

[6] 'European' is best kept in quotation marks, since what is at issue is when and in what regions of Europe it prevailed.

[7] See Herlihy and Klapisch, *Tuscans and their Families*, and their further works, listed ibid., pp. 383–7.

Europe, where, especially in England, there is evidence of the long duration of a very different marriage pattern. What this latter was Smith argued in later articles.[8] These took the sort of marriage pattern to be found in rural England around 1800 and projected it back to the furthest point where there was (just about) statistically treatable evidence. For example, the geography of girls moving when getting married was about the same in the Lincolnshire villages of Weston and Moulton around 1800 as it was in these villages in the thirteenth century. Though difficult to treat, the statistical evidence, in particular serf-lists, seems to show that in parts of rural England in the mid-thirteenth century, girls' age at first marriage was already high.

Without exposition of what modern scholarship has further established about other related phenomena, such as size of families and co-residence of servants, let us turn to our commentators. If only we could interview them! The wish—and the frustration—reminds us that these men will have had in their minds and memories much that would be relevant to a Richard Smith. When turning to look at them we should remember two large elements shaping their experience of marriage-ages. The first is the families into which they were born. What were the backgrounds and milieux of our commentators, bright university men, who were mainly friars? We should not be misled by the ubiquity of one commonplace about thirteenth-century universities, upward social mobility. John Baldwin has repeated this theme. But he respects his data, and when summarizing his conclusions about those masters in Paris between 1179 and 1215 whose social origins are known, he wrote that 'at least half came from the landed "feudal" segment of society'.[9] More recently a searching study of the costs of education in medieval universities has cut down to size the notion of swarms of upwardly mobile talented lads, and has emphasized the high proportion of students who were of knightly or higher families.[10] Where we have information about them, our commentators are seen originating in the same milieux. Thus Albert the Great came from a family of lesser nobility, knights in the service of the counts of Bollstadt in Swabia. Thomas

[8] R. M. Smith, 'Some reflections on the evidence for the origins of the "European marriage pattern" in England', in *The Sociology the Family: New Directions for Britain*, ed. C. C. Harris, Sociological Review Monograph 28 (Keele, 1979), pp. 74–112; 'Hypothèses sur la nuptialité en Angleterre aux XIIIe–XIVe siècles', *Annales, Économies, Sociétés, Civilisations* 38 (1983), 107–36; 'Geographical Diversity in the Resort to Marriage in Late Medieval Europe: Work, Reputation, and Unmarried Females in the Household Formation Systems of Northern and Southern Europe', in *Woman is a Worthy Wight: Women in English Society c.1200–1500*, ed. P. J. P. Goldberg (Stroud, 1992), pp. 16–59; 'Marriage Processes in the English Past: Some Continuities', *The World We Have Gained: Histories of Population and Social Structure*, ed. L. Bonfield, R. M. Smith and K. Wrightson (Oxford, 1986), pp. 43–99; 'The People of Tuscany and their Families in the Fifteenth Century: Medieval or Mediterranean?', *Journal of Family History* 6 (1981), 107–28. See further P. J. P. Goldberg, *Women, Work and Life-Cycle in the Medieval Economy: Women in York and Yorkshire c.1300–1520* (Oxford, 1992), Ch. 5; 'Marriage, Migration and Servanthood: The York Cause Paper Evidence', in Goldberg, *Woman is a Worthy Wight*, pp. 1–15; P. Biller, 'Marriage Patterns and Women's Lives: A Sketch of a Pastoral Geography', ibid., pp. 60–107.

[9] J. W. Baldwin, 'Masters at Paris from 1179 to 1215: A Social Perspective', in *Renaissance and Renewal in the Twelfth Century*, ed. R. L. Benson and G. Constable (Oxford, 1982), pp. 138–72 (151).

[10] J. Dunbabin, 'Meeting the Costs of University Education in Northern France, *c*.1240–*c*.1340', *History of Universities* 10 (1991), 1–27.

Aquinas (used here as a representative example, though his commentary is not used in this chapter) was born into a family of lesser nobility in the far north-western reaches of the (then) Kingdom of Sicily. A late (and therefore not certain) tradition has Giles of Rome as a member of the powerful Roman Colonna family. Look at Aquinas. He continued to be concerned with his family, visiting relatives, and in one case acting as executor of a relative's will. That two of his sisters and a niece (or three sisters and not the niece) were married into comital families of the Terra di Lavoro is a reminder of ordinary experience in *his* family.[11] The norms, then, of marriage for their mothers, aunts, sisters, cousins, and nieces will have been in these men's minds: norms usually, we are suggesting, of marriage in the nobility. As we shall see, in addition to this there is the fact that two of our commentators were writing for royal heirs—Giles for the heir to the king of France, the Aragonese Anonymous for the heir to the king of Aragon—and both with acute awareness of age at marriage.

We need to recall a fundamental connection between the academic specialists and the pastors on the ground, which was described in Chapter 2 and exemplified in Chapter 8 above. For the second element shaping the awareness of marriage, among the commentators who were friars, was their membership of Orders most of whose members were pastoral specialists. Alongside the select few in universities were the 'common brothers' (*fratres communes*), who dealt day by day with the marriages of ordinary people in sermons and confession. There was no apartheid between the two groups of friars. It was for the common brothers that Aquinas wrote his beginners' manual, the *Summa theologiae*,[12] as Leonard Boyle has shown, and pastoral problems of everyday concern (including marriage) were quite prominent in the theology faculty at Paris. There was communication in both directions, and we should not expect of the famous theologians ignorance of what concerned parish priests and 'common' friars in general, and in particular one thing which was at the forefront of their minds: the marriages of ordinary people.

Let us now turn to the discussion in book 7 and reactions to it. These reactions fall clearly into two groups, the first of which is a line of close commentators from Albert to Oresme, the second two authors who directly adapt Aristotle to marriage in royal families (Giles of Rome and the Aragon Anonymous). As we shall see, these two groups provide a parallel to the asymmetry which is present in the more direct attempts of historical demographers to investigate medieval marriage-patterns. On the one hand in the reactions of the first group we can discern tension, and can conjecture that this tension was between what was encountered in the *Politics* and the commentators' world. The discerning is difficult, and the conclusions speculative. On the other hand the reactions in the second group are sharp and clear, and the relation with royal marriages sure, especially in the case of the Aragon Anonymous.

[11] See J. I. Catto, 'Ideas and Experience in the political thought of Aquinas', *Past and Present* 71 (1976), 3–21 (pp. 15–16).

[12] L. E. Boyle, *The Setting of the Summa Theologiae of Saint Thomas*, Pontifical Institute of Medieval Studies, The Étienne Gilson Series 5 (Toronto, 1982).

In the running commentaries, the tracing of the personal preferences of the authors and the tracking down of the quiet intrusions of the medieval world is not an easy task. It needs the application of a mental magnifying glass to a line-by-line examination of printed text and manuscript, coupled with a minute comparison of each line with what Aristotle himself says... One has to develop a nose for the slightest wind of any strange scent. One has to be on the look-out not merely for the plain introduction of new material, but also for the significant repetition, the significant misinterpretation or benign interpretation, the emphasis or enlargement of certain topics.[13]

Following Fr Martin's wise advice here and in the next chapter may sometimes mean going at the speed of a tortoise. In this chapter, here in section 1, we begin with a summary of Aristotle's discussion in book 7, so that we can then use the magnifying glass in what follows, scrutiny of the commentators in chronological order. Giles and the Aragon Anonymous are held over for section 2.

Book 7 contains a discussion of how to produce the best citizens, within which there is a treatment of the priority of the body over the soul and, consequent upon this, the importance of a 'good birth' policy to produce the best bodies. The following is what appears in Moerbeke's Latin text, mainly summarized rather than translated.

1067.[14] The legislator ought to see to the provision of the best bodies of those who are to be brought up, looking to marriage: when people should marry, and what sort of people.

1068. He ought to make laws about this, so that a man and a woman come together at the same stages of life, and to avoid dissonance of power to generate—one being able to generate when another cannot: this causes discords.

1069. He should also look to the succession of children, for children should neither be too far away from, nor too close in age to their parents. Elderly parents do not gain anything in return from children who are too young, and children who are too close in age may show less respect [or 'modesty'—translating *verecundia*] and may be quarrelsome about management [of the household].

1070. These ends can be secured in one way.

1071. Seeing that the end of generation is fixed—for the most part in men the last age is 70, but in women 50—one should fix also the ages at which marital intercourse begins for men and for women. The beginning of marriage ought to proceed down towards these times, observing the difference between the ages at which men and women stop generating and working down towards these ages [= working back from the later to the earlier ages].

1072. The sexual intercourse of the young is bad for procreation. In all animals the young produce imperfect offspring, more of which are female, and small in size. This must also be the case among men. The proof of this is that wherever there are cities where the young are free to marry, they have small and imperfect bodies.

[13] C. Martin, 'Some medieval commentaries on Aristotle's *Politics*', *History* 36 (1951), 29–44 (p. 38).

[14] Here I give the numbers into which Spiazzi divides Aristotle's text, Sp, pp. 396–7; 1334b29–1335b37, Su pp. 315 l. 6–324 l. 2.

1073. Another indication of this is that young girls suffer more in childbirths, and more die. *Propter quod et oraculum quidam aiunt factum fuisse propter talem causam Troezeniis, tamquam multis pereuntibus propter nubere magis iuvenculas, sed non ad fructuum productionem*: 'Some say that the oracle was done [the oracular pronouncement given] to the Troezens [people of Troezen] on account of this, with many dying through [men] marrying younger girls—[and the oracular pronouncement did not relate] to the production of fruit'. [This is deliberately left awkward in the translation given here. Modern translations make it clearer and also supply the oracular pronouncement which is missing in Moerbeke, 'plough not the young fallow.']

1074. Another point concerns temperateness of behaviour. It is more expedient for the older to engage in sexual intercourse, for young girls who have experienced it seem to be more intemperate.

1075. Further, 'the bodies of males seem to be harmed as far as growth is concerned, if they have had sexual intercourse while the body is still growing: and a certain time of this [growth] is determined, which does not go much beyond [this].'

1076 (a). 'So, on account of this it is fitting for [girls] to be married about the age of 18 years, for men however around 37 or a little [less]. For [in this way] there will be conjunction with perfect bodies for so much time, and they will come together suitably at times [encouraging] perfection in the procreation of children.'

1076 (b). 'If generation happens immediately [and] according to the reckoning, the succession of children will be, in fact, when the prime of life [*acme*] is beginning for them, [and] for those [the fathers when their] age has by now declined to the number of seventy years.'

There then follows brief discussion of periods of the year and other conditions which are best for procreation, and the care of pregnant women's bodies, before a return to marriage-ages:

1083 (a). Since the beginning of marriage has been determined, 'how much time they should devote to the procreation of children ought also to be determined'.

1083 (b). The offspring of the elderly like the offspring of the young are imperfect in mind and body; they are decrepit and weak.

1083 (c). A point [it is not immediately clear what point] is reached 'among most men—which some of the poets have stated, measuring ages by sevens—around the age of 50 years: so that someone who exceeds this age by four or five years ought to leave off from that which [leads] to manifest generation'.

We shall look at the commentators in sequence, beginning with Albert. Though the least interesting on the text, Albert was read by later commentators, and divergences from him as well as divergences from Aristotle set off clearly what is distinctive in them.

Marriage-age is the first of three parts in one chapter of Albert's commentary on book 7. Inside the chapter there is an analysis of Aristotle into these three parts, a restatement of Aristotle's opinion, and a literal paraphrase with some comment. Albert only provides a lengthy restatement of the first of the three parts, not the other two; in other words, he concentrates on marriage-age. The restatement is quite similar to what has been given above. But Albert massages the text. On the one hand he leaves out the question of age-gaps between parents and children [1072]—the reason is given below. On the other hand he highlights the evils which flow from procreation at too young an age:

In whatever cities youths and young girls are allowed to marry early, three unsuitable things happen. One is that men are born small and imperfect in body. The second is that young girls, accustomed to sex before the age of maturity, become lascivious, loving and yearning for incontinence. The third is that they are frequently endangered in childbirth, and die, and cannot help those who are born with the sustenance and care of milk and feeding. On account of all these things, says [Aristotle], the oracle determined that this [early marriage] was shameful for a male and female.[15]

Albert alters by grouping the three points under the cities where this happens, re-ordering them (the sequence is now 1072, 1074, 1073), and introducing the point about milk. This latter may in part draw on Aristotle's own recommendation of milk, which is given later, but it may also draw upon elements in Albert's own mind. One is Albert the biologist and the other may be Albert in touch with a strand which can be found in northern European pastoral writing, from the earlier Thomas of Chobham to the later William of Pagula, which instructed priests to urge upon their flocks the superiority of a mother's over a wet-nurse's milk.[16] Albert expands the difficult sentence about the oracle, making it a moral denunciation and one which applied to the early marriage of both sexes. In his literal paraphrase he further takes *pro eximiis* for *Troezenis*, therefore seeing the oracle as 'for nobles'.[17] Albert's line here was to receive varied reception among later writers, as we shall see.

Albert's restatement of Aristotle's 'opinion' has other traits, which also inform his literal paraphrase. As one would expect with such an encyclopaedic natural philosopher, Albert 'biologizes' what is in front of him, spelling out with more precision or more technical language such things or themes as 'members for generation', 'generative force', and menopause. In the paraphrase he expands the biological content with several quotations from Avicenna's and one from Aristotle's *On Animals*, on themes which include conception, defective foetuses, young women dying in childbirth, and growth. He also does this through referring to canon law on impotence.[18] Discernible also is a line about women. They become more prominent, mainly pejoratively, through Albert taking 1069 to refer to the age-gap between husband and wife rather than between parents and children. It

[15] Albert, *Politics*, pp. 733–4a: *in quibuscumque civitatibus laxantur juvenes et juvenculae cito conjugari, tria inconvenientia contingunt. Unum est quod homines parvi nascuntur corporibus et imperfecti. Secundum est, quod juvenculae assuefactae ad coitum ante tempus maturitatis, efficiuntur lascivae, incontinentiam diligentes et appetentes. Tertium est, quod frequenter periclitantur in partu, et moriuntur, et natis subvenire non possunt alimonia lactis et diligentia nutritionis. Propter omnia haec dicit, quod oraculum determinavit hoc turpe maris et foeminae.*

[16] Biller, 'Pastoral Geography', pp. 81–2.

[17] Albert, *Politics*, p. 736l. A future critical edition might show this as a corrupt reading.

[18] Albert, *Politics*, p. 735f, referring to X. 4. 15; Friedberg, ii. 704.

is bad for a man to marry an older woman, or for them to be the same age. 'Quarrelsome' and 'management' therefore, taken to apply to the husband-wife relation, suck in sharp comment on woman's nature and place. A wife should be respectful to her husband; since the husband ought to manage the house as its head, he ought like a wise man to surpass his wife in age; otherwise quarrels arise.[19]

The accentuation of points about women was distinctively Albertian. Albert's cast of mind, immensely and miscellaneously knowledgeable, was not likely to make Aristotle's text more generalized and more 'populationist'. However, although he does neither of these things, his account does contain some emphases: it gives sharp attention to marriage-age; it introduces learned reproductive biology; and it underlines youthful procreation as bad.

Immediately apparent in Peter of Auvergne is his greater clarity in interpreting and handling Moerbeke's Latin, but there is more, in what is eventually a quite remarkable commentary. The prejudicial points about women fall away, biology is there but it is different, and the overall colouring of the commentary is more 'populationist'. Most important, however, is the intrusion of a discussion of marriage-age into the commentary, a discussion which is notable both in itself and for the accent of opposition to youthful marriage.

Peter writes an introduction which briefly divides and subdivides the text into threes and twos, and then provides a quite long commentary on each proposition. He breaks this neat pattern with two long interjections (or one in two parts). The first is devoted to length of life, the second to the question of early marriages.

The staccato 'This . . . then that' of Peter's introduction highlights each point and makes it starker:

Because, as has been said, the good disposition of citizens depends firstly, on the good disposition of those generating, then on the disposition of the mother during pregnancy, thirdly however on suitable food and habit after birth . . . [The first is divided into two, the first of which is:] On the first he shows first when the nuptial joining should be. . . . [On this] he shows first that it ought to happen at a determined time and age. Secondly when he says *Since . . . is determined* [1071] he declares what are the determined time and age at which it ought to happen. He declares this first through an argument taken from caution about dissensions and diversity between those who are to be joined [1068]; secondly, when he says *Then to the succession of children etc.* [1069], through an argument taken from the succession of boys to their fathers; thirdly, when he says *To this also etc.* [1072], [through an argument] which is taken from the good future disposition of offspring or children.[20]

[19] Albert, *Politics*, pp. 735–6g.

[20] Peter of Auvergne, *Politics*, p. 399 no. 1225: *Et quoniam bona dispositio civium, sicut dictum est, primo pendet ex dispositione generantium; deinde ex dispositione matris, tempore gestationis; tertio autem ex convenienti alimento et consuetudine post nativitatem . . . Circa primum primo ostendit quando facienda est copula nuptialis . . . primo ostendit, quod oportet eam fieri tempore et aetate determinatis. Secundo, cum dicit* Quoniam enim determinatus est etc. *declarat quae sunt tempus et aetas determinata in quibus oportet fieri. Primum ipse primo declarat per rationem sumptam ex cautela dissensionum et diversitate copulandorum; secundo, cum dicit* Deinde ad puerorum successionem etc. *per rationem sumptam ex eis quae accidunt secundum successionem puerorum ad patres. Tertio, cum dicit* Adhuc autem etc. *ex ea quae sumitur ex bona dispositione prolis vel puerorum futura.*

As Peter continues from proposition to proposition he expands and clarifies. Thus Moerbeke's knotty forty-five words on age-gaps [1069], not clearly paraphrased by Albert, are unfolded into something four times as long, which smoothly expounds the effects of different age-gaps between parents and children on their mutual relations.[21] At the same time Peter, unlike Albert, adds no emphasis to Aristotle on the danger of women's intemperance; and Albert's extraneous material on women's nature and place is quietly dropped. On the oracle [1073] again Peter, unlike Albert, has *Troezinis*; 'nobles' do not appear. 'The oracle . . . was performed so that their pain should be alleviated with [this] help and the baby brought forth.'[22] The practice of women in childbirth invoking the help of a saint (usually St Margaret) or the Blessed Virgin Mary here informs Peter's understanding of the oracle. It is a rare reminder of how closely Peter *may* be shaping the commentary in relation to the refraction in his mind of the world in which he lived—even though he may provide no explicit reference to it.

Peter's presentation of four reasons for the unsuitability of the young for procreation is not Albert's, but it independently continues the tradition of adding emphasis. This begins with highlighting in the introduction to sections 1071–5:

Then, when he [Aristotle] says *Since* [1071]. He intends to declare, at what age it [marriage] ought to take place, from the term [beginning- and end-points] of generation in each, and from those unsuitable things which occur if it [marriage] happens too quickly.[23]

The four points [1072–5] are restated clearly and strongly. The first point [1072] has Peter spelling out twice that youthfulness (or otherwise) of *both* sexes is at issue: 'the coitus of the young, whether males or females', and 'where young men and young women are allowed to marry'. And there is a special twist to the point. Expanding 'cities' to 'cities and regions', Peter says that in whatever cities and regions young men and young women are allowed to marry, they generate children who are small and imperfect in body, adding to the original: 'and consequently less useful for military actions'.[24] Concern elsewhere in the *Politics* with soldiers and an allusion (soon to come) later in book 7 to the upbringing of children to this end[25] may be in the background here, but also a 'Frisian' tradition and the outlook of Peter's milieu, which are discussed later. Peter thinks through the implications of the point about ages of succession, adding the mother's age [1076b]: If when they marry, 'the women at 18 and the men at 36 or thereabouts, they immediately generate, the sons will succeed their parents at the beginning of the period when their bodies are perfect, that is to say, about the thirtieth

[21] Peter of Auvergne, *Politics*, p. 400 no. 1226.

[22] Ibid., p. 401 no. 1230: *factum esse oraculum . . . ut dolor eius adiutorio mitigaretur et foetus ad ortum produceretur.*

[23] Ibid., p. 400 no. 1228: *Deinde, cum dicit* quoniam enim, *intendit declarare qua aetate expedit eam fieri ex termino generationis in utroque, et ex inconvenientibus quae accidunt si fiat nimis cito.*

[24] Ibid., pp. 400–1 no. 1229: *coitus iuniorum, sive masculi sive femellae . . . in quibuscumque civitatibus et regionibus permittuntur iuvenes et iuvenculae coniugari, et permisceri ad generationem, generantur parvi et imperfecti secundum corpus, et per consequens minus utiles ad opera bellica.*

[25] Instilling a military habit in children through a diet of milk and exposure to cold, 1335b18–19, 1336a14–15; Su pp. 324 l. 12, 325 ll. 7–8; Sp nos. 1086, 1088.

year, with the mother in [her] fiftieth year, the father in [his] seventieth or thereabouts.'[26]

While this literal commentary is proceeding, there are two further, and connected, expansions. While Peter avoids Albert's broader biologizing style, he does introduce biological principles. Nutrition enters his account of the growth of young men's bodies [1075],[27] while there is much airing of the fundamental themes of medical and biological thought in Peter's time, 'radical humidity' and the balance of cold/hot and dry/wet in human beings at various stages in their lives. Secondly, implicit or explicit references to Aristotle's *Length and shortness* and 'life-span' appear frequently. In Peter's summary of 1067–8, the legislator aiming at the good future disposition of children should ordain laws and statutes about the nuptial communication of citizens, aiming at intrinsic perfection and disposition to good generation and also 'bearing in mind the time of life of each, of the male and the female—how much, that is to say, each can live according to nature'.[28] He adds to the theme of 'term[s] of generation' [1071], emphasizing variation—'in some people it is longer [and] in others shorter according to one or other material disposition'—and adding a statement of woman's briefer generative span, which is rooted in her lesser strength and warmth.[29] Then he concludes his discussion of the debilitation of male bodies through early sex [1075] with a reference to Aristotle's tract on life-span, giving its title and a summary of its account of span varying in relation to the emission of sperm, with the usual long life of sterile mules and short life of sparrows given over to sex.[30]

Although Albert had commented separately on Aristotle's tract on life-span, as well as raising questions on it in his 1258 Cologne lectures, he made no use of it here in his commentary on book 7. Peter had also commented on it, but unlike Albert he was convinced of its relevance to Aristotle's treatment of marriage-ages. He therefore pressed on with it in his commentary on book 7, and now made it the first of two themes in a long digression.[31] Differences in life-stages, as part of differences in life-span between the sexes, explained the proposed ideal marriage-ages. Although men and women are of the same species, strength of complexional make-up explains the duration of life of each of them, not common species, and the 'strength of complexion is much stronger in man than in woman on account of abundance of heat and its better proportion to other qualities; and therefore according to nature men are of longer life than women.' Peter does not qualify the statement of comparative life-span, but he will have been aware that in this summary he was only referring to 'according to nature', leaving out the loophole of

[26] *Politics*, p. 401 no. 1233: *si statim cum copulati sunt mulieres decemocto, viri triginta sex annorum existentibus, statim generent, succedent enim filii parentibus in principio status corpore perfecto, scilicet circa trigesimum annum matre agente quinquagesimum, patre septuagesimum vel circa.*

[27] Ibid., p. 401 no. 1232.

[28] Ibid., p. 399 no. 1225: *considerando ad tempus vitae utriusque, et maris et feminae; quantum scilicet uterque secundum naturam vivere potest.*

[29] Ibid., p. 400 no. 1228: *in aliquibus sit longior, in aliquibus brevior propter dispositionem materiae aliam et aliam.*

[30] Ibid., p. 401 no. 1232.

[31] Ibid., pp. 401–2 no. 1234.

'contingency', which Albert had used to state the opposite so devastatingly in one of his Cologne lectures, as we saw in Chapter 11 above. The principal point is age at maturity rather than age at death, and here, after stating the main comparison, Peter underlines variation. 'Therefore for the most part men need more time for perfecting than women: although on account of indisposition of matter it can happen the other way round.'[32] Aristotle's ideal ages are then repeated, as consequences of these differences in durations between men and women.

Peter then moves to an extension of this digression or, more accurately, a second digression. His commentary shifts in the following 350 words into a formal question, with Aristotle (late ages) and the objection (early ages) put forward as two opposed positions. There is an objection with two supporting arguments, a general response, and finally responses to the objection's two arguments:

If, however, it is objected that the nuptial tie ought to take place earlier than the Philosopher determines—
[1] Firstly, because generation occurs from superfluity of aliment, it seems therefore that this sort of joining ought to take place when superfluity of aliment first begins and males start to produce sperm. However this occurs a long time earlier than [the time] which the Philosopher determines, namely at the time of adolescence. Therefore it seems that it [marriage] ought to take place earlier.
[2] And furthermore laws, which seem to look to the common good, determine that marriages can take place when the woman is 12 [and] the man is 14 or thereabouts.

Peter's reply follows:

On this [matter], following the intention of the Philosopher, it is to be understood that if we consider the good disposition of those who generate and the good future condition of those who are to be generated, and consequently the common utility of the city or region, in themselves, it is better in most cases for this conjunction to take place when the bodies of each have been perfected [and] at the time determined by the Philosopher, or thereabouts. When their bodies have been perfected their strengths will be perfect, nor will they suffer any defect in growth nor [any defect] in their complexion as a consequence of [a defect] of this sort, except through superfluity, or something of this sort. And, as far as their bodies are concerned, children will be better disposed, because they will be generated by those who are more and better disposed, and consequently [they will be better disposed] as far as their souls are concerned, because good disposition of the body disposes to good disposition of the soul. And thus they will be more apt for virtues and civil acts.
Through some contingency, however, it can be expedient for it [marriage] to be later or earlier with some people, for example if their bodies are perfected earlier or later, or if fornication with aliens is feared, or something of this sort.

Peter then proceeds to reply particularly to the first argument:

Moreover, although superfluity of aliment and emission of seed may be found earlier in some, it does not follow that then [this earlier time] is better and more appropriate for

[32] *Virtus autem complexionis multo fortior est in viro quam in muliere propter abundantiam calidi et meliorem proportionem eius ad alias qualitates; et ideo viri longioris vitae sunt secundum naturam mulieribus. Et quia illud quod perfectius est pluri tempore indiget ad sui perfectionem . . . viri autem perfectiores sunt mulieribus; ideo pluri tempore indigent ad sui perfectionem quam mulieres, ut in pluribus: quamvis propter indispositionem materiae possit accidere e contrario.*

generation, as the argument [which takes the opposite] line was assuming. For it is not necessarily the case—among those things which are progressing from the imperfect to the perfect—that when it [something] can first [do something] it is not necessary that it can then [do it] perfectly; just as, when someone can first play the lute in some way or other, it does not follow that he can [then] play it perfectly—rather the other way round. In the course of generation the things which are earlier are certainly more imperfect; the things which are later, however, are more perfect, just as a man is more perfect than a child, as is said in the ninth [book] of the *Metaphysics*.
Further, [here Peter proceeds to the second argument] the laws do not determine that it is best for marriage to take place at the time of adolescence, that is when the woman is twelve, the man fourteen or thereabouts. But the laws allow it to take place for the first time then, because consent is valid, for the first time then, because of [the contracting parties'] use of reason, [which is] first present then or thereabouts, and because among most people some superfluity of aliment, however imperfect, first begins then.[33]

Peter briefly approached marriage-age in another of his writings. His *quaestiones* on the *Politics* included one, 'whether combination of male and female is from nature', which brought him again to marriage-ages through the theme of the long cohabitation (*commansio*) of male and female for the good education of children. Running against our expectation, the discussion does not have the sharpness and independence of Peter's nominally more passive and literal commentary. One could try to see significance in the way the numbers wander away from Aristotle's, the woman's up, the man's both down and up—'the woman around her twentieth and the man around his thirtieth, or even fortieth [year]'. Since these are multiples of ten, the significance *may* only be Peter's airiness when away from a close commentary and free.

[33] *Si autem obiicatur prius debere fieri coniugationem nuptialem quam determinat Philosophus; primo, quia generatio fit ex superfluo alimenti, quando igitur primo incipit esse superfluum alimenti, et masculi incipiunt spermatizare videtur quod deberet fieri talis copulatio, hoc autem contingit multo tempore prius quam determinet Philosophus, puta tempore pubescentiae; ergo prius videtur debere fieri. Et praeterea hoc iura determinant quae videntur considerare bonum commune, matrimonia scilicet posse fieri muliere existente duodecim annorum, viro existente quatuordecim vel circa.* [no. 1235] *Ad hoc est intelligendum, secundum intentionem Philosophi, quod si consideremus bonam dispositionem generantium et bonam habitudinem generandorum futuram, et per consequens utilitatem communem civitatis seu regionis per se, melius est coniunctionem istam fieri perfectis corporibus utriusque quod est tempore determinato a Philosopho vel circa, ut in pluribus: perfectis enim corporibus perfectae erunt virtutes, nec detrimentum aliquod patientur in augmento, aut complexione secundum quod huiusmodi, nisi propter superfluitatem, aut aliquid huiusmodi. Et pueri melius erunt dispositi quantum ad corpus, quia a magis et melius dispositis generabuntur, et per consequens secundum animam, quia bona dispositio corporis disponit ad bonam dispositionem animae; et sic magis apti erunt ad virtutes et actus civiles. Propter accidens tamen aliquod expedit tardius vel citius fieri in aliquibus, puta si tardius vel citius perficiantur corpora, aut si timeatur fornicatio cum alienis, aut aliquid huiusmodi. Quamvis autem prius in aliquibus inveniatur superfluum alimenti et emissio seminis, non tamen sequitur quod tunc melius et aptius sit ad generationem, sicut accipiebat ratio in oppositum. Non enim oportet in his quae procedunt de imperfecto ad perfectum quod quando aliquid potest aliquid primo quod tunc perfecte possit; sicut quando aliquis potest citharizare qualitercumque non sequitur quod optime possit, sed magis e contrario: quae enim sunt priora secundum viam generationis, imperfectiora sunt; quae autem posteriora perfectiora, sicut vir puero, ut dicitur nono* Metaphysicorum [see AL XXV.2, p. 178: *quia generatione posteriora specie et substantia sunt priora, ut vir puero*]. *Iura autem non determinant optimum esse fieri matrimonium tempore pubescentiae, scilicet muliere existente duodecim annorum vel circa, viro quatuordecim vel circa, sed tunc concedunt posse fieri, quia tunc primo potest valere consensus propter usum rationis, tunc primo vel circa inexistentis, et quia tunc primo incipit aliquod superfluum alimenti fieri, ut in pluribus, quamvis imperfectum.*

Peter's commentary was the most influential among the later writers of the north. It crisply clarified; it thought through implications and connections. It stands out first as an example of thought in this area. It is more 'populationist'. While some of Albert's straitjacket (of misogyny, for example) is shuffled off, the theme is 'biologized', in a different way. And, most significantly, there is systematic connection with another area of 'population' thought, the comparative durations of the sexes.

What also stands out in Peter's commentary is the larger number of traces of the thinking and expressing of these thoughts in terms of the real (and perhaps Peter's) world. Aristotle's 'city' is widened to 'cities and regions', inheritance ages are envisaged, and the understanding of the oracle seems to be rooted in the prayers and piety of contemporary young women. Much of the material Peter is pushing around may be tedious to our eyes; emission of seed and brevity of life have been pseudo-science in the sixteenth century and vulgar superstition and the material for jokes in the twentieth. However, in the thirteenth century they were 'natural philosophy' (science), and we must not miss, through amusement or contempt, the thrust of what Peter was doing with material which was, to him and his audience, serious stuff. Through his twists and turns this is what we see. There is a formally raised 'question' about marriage-age: should marriage take place earlier than Aristotle says? The answer attacks early marriage and promotes late marriage. Both are related to the 'common good', 'common utility': late marriages (through those generated in them) are better for civil actions, virtuous actions, and military activity. These are ideas about marriage-ages which were being aired in late thirteenth-century Paris.

In Guido's version this section's heading—'how those generating are to be disposed'[34]—does not draw special attention to marriage-ages. Guido's rendering carries hints of both Albert and Peter. Guido follows Albert's reading of the invocation of the oracle, now expanded to something done on behalf of 'great and noble women to reduce their pain', and by being geographically specific he reminds readers that a historical point is being made: 'in Greece many women died in childbirth because too young.'[35] Peter's envisaging of ages of succession is followed. Reasons for procreation by the young being bad are, as in Peter, 'fourfold'. However, although 'defect of heat' as the reason for more generation of females may come from Peter, Guido's wording is generally his own. Guido is short and simple, draining this proposition of the special emphasis it has in Albert and Peter. For example, 'cities and regions' are back to Aristotle's 'cities', and, far from spelling out twice, as does Peter, that what is at issue is the too young marriage of youths and young girls, Guido cuts back to *nimis iuvenes* marrying in such cities: a casual reader not referring back to Aristotle could take this to mean cities where *men* (*iuvenes*) marry too young, where *men* (*homines*) are (consequently)

[34] Venice, Marciana, MS 2492, fol. 139va: *Qualiter disponendi sunt generantes.*

[35] Ibid., fol. 139vb: *pro mangnis* [sic] *et nobilibus mulieribus, ut dolor mitigaretur et fectus produceretur ad ortum. In Grecia eciam multe multe mulieres moriebantur in partu quia nimis iuvencule.*

found to be physically small and imperfect. If Guido does underline he does this only on the point about girls' intemperance. He parades the ideal marriage-ages without fuss. There is no echo of Peter's two interjections, no reference to canon law, and in general no hint of sparks being created in Guido's mind by Aristotle's proposed marriage-ages.

Burley repeats virtually all of Peter of Auvergne, rewriting his section, including his two interjections, in shorter and yet starker form. There are two minor alterations to the four reasons for generation by the young being bad. Peter's third point, the intemperance of girls, a point he had rendered without changing Aristotle, is altered by Burley to refer to 'men': 'the sexual intercourse of the young makes *men* more intemperate.'[36] Whether or not 'men' is covering both sexes, we can see this as Burley taking one more step away from Albert's tedious misogynist reading. At the same time Burley follows exactly Peter's regionalism and continuation of Aristotle on too youthful girls as well as young men, and he accepts but also alters and adds to Peter's addition. 'A particular argument appears with men: for in whatever cities and regions youths and young women are permitted to marry and have intercourse for generation, *men* are generated who are small and imperfect in body and consequently useless (Peter has 'less useful') for military actions, as is patent in a region [which is] neighbour to us.'[37] Language is heightened, the reference to men is underlined for the first time, and the final contemporary reference is an addition—its significance is discussed later. The precise reference remains unclear. An Englishman, writing in 1338 or 1339 and thinking of English military success in very recent years, including the victory of Halidon Hill (1333),[38] could be envisaging the Scots. Very long-term political and military rivalry with the French suggests another candidate.

The last of the literal commentators examined here is Oresme. He emphasized variation in spans and ages, following Peter in spirit, though not to the letter. This is his gloss on the end of the generative span in males and females. 'One is to understand this as [applying] to the common course [of things], for some lose this power before these terms and others continue [to have it] beyond. . . . Item, one is to understand this [to apply] to regions where the people live to a sufficient age.'[39] Quotation below is going to show repetition of this point: unsurprising in a commentator who habitually discussed the globe and whose commentary contained a map of the earth,[40] is this more developed pre-occupation with variation around the world.

[36] Cambridge University Library, MS 1741, fol. 52ra: *coitus iuvenum facit homines magis intemperatos.*

[37] Ibid., fol. 51vb: *Et in hominibus apparet argumentum speciale: quoniam in quibuscumque civitatibus et regionibus permittuntur iuvenes et iuvencule coniugari et permisceri ad generacionem [et] generantur homines parvi et imperfecti secundum corpus et per consequens inutiles ad opera bellica, sicut patet in regione nobis vicina.*

[38] I owe the suggestion of Halidon Hill to Mark Ormrod.

[39] Oresme, *Politiques*, p. 331b: *Ce est a entendre de commun cours, car aucuns perdent ceste puissance avant ces termes et aucuns la continuent oultre. . . . Item, ce est a entendre es regions ou les gens vivent par eage souffisant.*

[40] Ibid., p. 297 and n. 2.

When Oresme turns to the oracle he follows the tradition of seeing in this an invocation for help. 'Young pregnant women or their friends went to a temple or an oratory ordained [for this], to make offerings or vows or prayers to a God or Goddess to help them give birth; Romans had a Goddess called Lucina, the Goddess of childbirth; just as in our faith women call upon St Margaret.'[41] In 1420 Thomasse, wife of Pierre de Brulli of Loches (in Poitou) was in labour for seven days. To her brother, who was among the husband and friends at her bedside, grieving at her agony, the women looking after Thomasse said, *Por Dieu, lisez la vie sainte Margarite sur votre seur, et au plaisir Dieu elle enfantera.*[42] Past tense and present tense: Oresme's use of his classical erudition marks the historical distance of Aristotle's world from his own. At the same time Oresme's contrasting present tense ('women call upon St Margaret'), at last brings a commentator's own world, here made of women like Thomasse, *unmistakably* right inside the commentary and quick with life.

Oresme's chapter's heading, unlike Guido's section heading, had indicated marriage-age as the topic,[43] and continuation of emphasis on opposition to early marriage is discernible in Oresme's digressive concluding gloss on the matter:

> And so, according to Aristotle, marriage which is very profitable for having children who have good complexional make-up and are naturally well disposed, is as far as woman is concerned, from 18 years to 50; and, as far as the man is concerned, from 37 or thereabouts right up to 70 years. And thus they will last together in good generative power for thirty-two or thirty-three years. And one should understand this as applying to temperate places and lands and times. And it is not to be understood that one cannot generate well before the times said above, or perchance after [them]; but this would not generally be [would not produce] such good fruit. And also the legislator can perfectly well put up with and tolerate marriages being earlier because of the malice of complexions [evil-doing brought about by complexional make-up]. But he ought to do what is in his power to hold, exhort, and induce citizens by laws and teaching, so that as far as is possible marriages are made at the times said above.[44]

Oresme is commenting at length, restating the point clearly, and putting it into a specific and partly regional setting. Along with a little futher development in the

[41] Oresme, *Politiques*, p. 332a: *Les jœnnes femmes grosses ou leur amis pour elles aloient a un temple ou oratoire ordené pour faire oblations et veux et prieres a un dieu ou a une deesse, afin qu'il leur aidast a enfanter. Et pour tele chose les Romains aoroient une deesse appellee Lucine: Lucina dea partus. Aussi comme en nostre foy les femmes reclaiment Saincte Marguerite.*

[42] *Livre des Miracles de Sainte-Catherine-de-Fierbois, 1375–1470*, ed. Y. Chauvin, Archives Historiques de Poitou 60 (Poitiers, 1976), pp. 42–3. See S. Laurent, *Naître au moyen âge: De la conception à la naissance: la grossesse et l'accouchement (XIIe–XVe siècle)* (Paris, 1989), pp. 194–5.

[43] Oresme, *Politiques*, p. 331a: *Ou .xxxive. chapitre il determine de l'eage de ceulz que l'en doit marier.*

[44] Ibid., p. 332b: *Et donques, selon Aristote, mariage tres profitable pour avoir enfans bien complexionnées et bien disposés par nature est quant a la femme de .xviii. ans a .l. Et quant a le homme de .xxxvii. ou environ jusques a .lxx. ans. Et ainsi il durent ensemble en bonne puissance generative par .xxxii. ou .xxxiii. ans. Et ce est a entendre en lieus ou païz et en temps bien attrempés. Et ne est pas a entendre que l'en ne puisse bien engendrer devant les temps desus diz et par aventure apres; mes ce ne seroit pas communement si bon fruit. Et aussi le legislateur peut bien souffrir et tollerer que mariages soient plus tost pour la malice des complexions ou des meurs des gens et pour eviter pluseurs inconveniens. Mes il doit a son povoir tendre, exhorter et enduire les citoiens par lays et par doctrine a ce que les mariages soient faiz es temps desus diz tant comme il est possible.*

'populationism' of thought, which is discernible in Oresme's discussion, and his characteristic display of classical historical knowledge, there is another sort of underlining in this concluding gloss on marriage-ages: realism and yet further thought displayed in the reflection on the gap between ideal and practice and how to bridge it.

When concluding we can look, first, at what has been shown about an area of thought. The Moerbeke translation introduced into the west both a locus for thought and discussion of marriage-ages and a number of propositions about them. These became very familiar, not just through the *Politics* itself and its commentaries but also through other texts which incorporated or quoted it or alluded to it, such as commentaries on the *Sentences* or the Pseudo-Aristotelian *Economics*. The area of thought itself experienced development. Biology entered, reproductive biology through Albert, and the physiology of stages of life in terms of 'radical humidity' through Peter of Auvergne. Material on the differing life-spans is added to material on generative spans. The Aragon Anonymous brings more, as we shall see, and by the time of Oresme the theme of variation by region and time comes in, and, as we have just seen, statement of ideal and practice and attempting to implement ideal, in a genre of thought which has slowly become more 'populationist'.

We can, secondly, juxtapose in our account what co-existed in the past: the commentaries, the men who wrote them, and the marriage patterns of the different regions and estates of their Europe. Grateful as we may be for the richer description which results, we are looking for more: connections. What have we found?

Marriage-age attracted special attention among some but not all: it loomed large in the minds of Albert, Peter, Burley, and Oresme, but little in Guido. It is crucially important not to force this contrast. The case against the contrast and seeing significance in it is that Guido is usually smooth; it is his style. The case for is that Guido made use of the earlier commentaries of Albert and Peter, but here preserves no trace of their emphases—utterly unlike the later Burley and Oresme. Rather than treading again over the same ground, we can look at another example, at north-western and southern European commentary on the Pseudo-Aristotelian *Economics*. Nancy Siraisi has brought into the light one commentator, again from Bologna, Bartolomeo da Varignana, a married layman who was teaching medicine in Bologna by 1292 and continued to do so until 1311, and was heavily involved in the affairs of the commune, producing medico-legal reports for the city authorities. His commentary on the *Economics* is full of practical discussions of economic (in the modern sense) themes such as finance, bullion, and trade. The section on marriage in book 1 produces much material on the subordinate position of women in the household. When the text turns to the theme of sex Bartolomeo provides a catalogue of categories: time, age, quantity, use, mode. 'All these things are talked about diffusely in book 7 of the *Politics*', he writes.[45] And

[45] *Hec omnia dicuntur diffuse 7° pollitice*; Venice, Padri Redentoristi, MS 3 (445), fol. 39r. I am grateful to Nancy Siraisi for lending me her microfilm of this manuscript. Bartolomeo and his commentary are discussed in her *Taddeo*, pp. 86–94.

Aristotle's ages and some of his justifying reasons are inserted. Apart from one emphasis (perfection of sperm at perfect age), which is clearly rooted in Bartolomeo's medical learning, all is smoothness. There is no accentuation; no tension. When we turn to Oresme, a few decades later, we see considerable intrusions into this section of the *Economics*.[46] However, Oresme, who knew book 7 of the *Politics* better than most, does not introduce Aristotle's marriage-ages.

There is one tempting avenue to explore. The social élite of Italian cities might well have found Aristotle's recommendations matching their marriage-patterns rather well. After all, his ideal ages fit like a glove the actual ages which were to be revealed in the Florentine catasto of 1427, and in fragmentary evidence earlier. Hence the smoothness, lack of ruffledness, of the inhabitants of a sophisticated Italian city like Bologna, when summarizing this material, as the friar Guido does, or when simply introducing it into the discussion of another text, as the engaged citizen and married medical man Bartolomeo does. On the other hand we have a south German mendicant who travelled widely, from the Baltic to southern Italy, but worked mainly in Cologne and Paris; a man from the Auvergne who worked in Paris; an Englishman, who travelled to Avignon, Toulouse, and Bologna; a Norman who worked in Paris. These men, in varying degrees northerners by birth and also men who had travelled in southern Europe, may have been aware of tensions. On the narrower front, they *may* have been aware of a tension between Aristotle's ideal age for men and the younger age of the marriages of first-born men in their own (high) milieux. More broadly, they *may* have been aware of the divergences of the marriage-ages of ordinary people in north-western and southern Europe, and the tension between what Aristotle proposed and the 'European' pattern of north-western Europe. Hence the sparks and crackle of their attention in commentaries on book 7; and—with caution because of the danger of arguing from silence—Oresme's *lack* of interest in introducing into the *Economics* ages which were less realistic?

It is important not only to state this tentatively, but also to spell out its limits. If there is a reaction, it is a muffled one. For its expression is ultimately an emphatic underlining of Aristotle, not, as perhaps it should be from northerners, a querying of what he says about the marriage-age of girls. If we follow conjecture to this point, we are presented with light reflexively cast on the first theme: the capacity of these men to observe and think 'demographically'. And this light makes this point. At this early stage in the history and development of this genre of thought, western commentators and writers observe and articulate thought about marriage-ages in their own world only at an individual level, as we shall see with the Aragon Anonymous. But it would be anachronistic to expect them to have both the capacity and the strength, when bound within the tentacles of Aristotle, to observe and articulate a generalizing Richard Smith point about marriage-patterns.

[46] Nicole Oresme, *Le livre de Yconomique d'Aristote*, ed. A. D. Menut, Transactions of the American Philosophical Society, n.s. 47, Part 5 (Philadelphia, 1957), pp. 811a–17a.

This is a tightrope of conjecture: perilous. But our observation of tension is not mistaken: something, however muffled, *is* going on. And one final sign of this is the curious presence of a 'Tacitean' or Frisian tradition in two northern commentators, Peter and Burley. The *Germania* contains a famous description which ascribes to Germans late marriage for both men and women and consequent vigour in the men, as well as a martial spirit and high moral standards—famous *now*, because of course the *Germania* was principally hidden from view during our period, hence the quotation marks around 'Tacitean tradition'. However, there was another text describing Frisia which was doing the work of the *Germania*, as we saw in Chapter 9. To recap: Bartholomew the Englishman's *De proprietatibus rerum* contained a description of a northern people whose elements are remarkably similar to those of Tacitus's *Germania*. The description is of a province within the confines of *Germania*. The people are strong: they use iron lances rather than arrows. Their's is a free race (*gens libera*), subject to no king, a race which will choose death rather than subjection to the yoke of servitude. The inhabitants 'preserve chastity wonderfully, and judge all immodesty severely, [and] they keep their sons and daughters chaste right up to the final completion of adolescence' (*usque ad conpletum terminum adolescencie*). (Elsewhere, in his account of 'age', Bartholomew begins with one view of 'adolescence' as ending at 21, but then proceeds to Isidore's view of it ending at 28, and physicians stretching it to 30 or 35.) 'And thus when they hand them over to marriage, they generate robust offspring.'

Here, then, was a widely available description—of an ideal? An ideal northern people, fierce and free, who preserved *girls* as well as boys to an appropriate (later) age of marriage, and consequently produced vigorous offspring. As we have seen, Peter of Auvergne's discussion contains elements of this. His strong defence of late marriage depends at one point on the weakness and lesser use for warlike actions of offspring generated in those cities and regions where youths and girls are allowed to marry young. And Burley not only made the military point more forcefully but added: 'as is patent in a region [which is] neighbour to us'. It is tempting to point to this northerner's experience of southern Europe, his visits to Avignon, Toulouse, and Bologna: but, as we have seen, the military reference may not be to a region which was south-east or south from England. We can conclude with this. Our tentative discerning of regional emphases among our commentators is getting some support not only from the echoes in Peter and Burley of the 'Tacitean' tradition, but also the willingness of the Englishman Burley to present this point explicitly as contemporary and regional, where 'regional' implies at least pride in England.

12.2 Book 7 and royal marriage-ages

Two other writers who dealt directly with Aristotle's marriage-ages, one briefly (Giles of Rome) and one extensively (the Anonymous of Aragon), shared a class of dedicatee and a preoccupation which both link them and set them apart from Albert, Peter, Guido, and Oresme: an heir to a throne and royal marriage. Royal marriage also concerned Engelbert.

The Augustinian Giles of Rome was in the Capetian capital from around 1260, and by 1281 his scholarly stature compelled a contemporary to say that among Paris theologians 'he is reputed to be the best in town on everything'.[47] This was near to the time when he acceded, as he wrote, to a 'friendly' royal 'request that I compose a certain book about the instruction of princes or the rule of kings'. He produced a work dedicated by his 'devoted' Giles to his 'special Lord',[48] the young prince Philip, heir to the French throne, who was then somewhere in his early teens. Philip in turn was later to use terms of personal warmth towards Giles when making a grant to the Paris Augustinians—'in consideration of [our] strongest inclination [towards] our close and beloved [friend] brother, Giles of Rome'. That such phrases may belong to literary conventions does not exclude them from simultaneously expressing some reality. Joseph Strayer, biographer of the later Philip the Fair, pours cold water on the notion of Giles's tutorship of the young Philip ('If Philip III really persuaded Egidius Romanus to act as his son's tutor . . .'), for which direct evidence is lacking. Strayer's scepticism and distaste extend to the treatise itself. 'One wonders whether an adolescent . . . ever read or had read to him the long and often ponderous treatise of Egidius.'[49] A matter of taste: this reader is struck by the seasoning of the treatise. It is salted with wit: 'just as Germans are barbarous to the Italians, and Italians barbarous to the English . . .'[50] With practicality: for example, recommending generals to have pictorial versions of itineraries, so that they can envisage military routes with their eyes, like seamen, who use maps in which ports, spaces, and other things are depicted in proportion, in order to see where to go, where they are and how to avoid danger.[51] With matter-of-fact directness: for example, when taking Aristotle's advice on prohibition of indecent art to mean that boys should not see pictures or statues of naked women.[52]

The second of the three books of the *De regimine principum* deals with rule of the household, with a large and central section on marriage. Like much of the rest of the treatise this makes very heavy use of the *Politics* and *Ethics*—and on marriage-ages, book 7 of the *Politics*. And there is unremitting concern to adapt this material to the exigences of ruling and royal houses. After the underlining or alteration of a point there is the incessant phrase, that it applies 'especially' or

[47] Godfrey of Fontaines, *Melior de tota villa in omnibus reputatur*; quoted in F. Lajard, 'Gilles de Rome, Religieux Augustin, Théologien', *Histoire Littéraire de France* 30 (1888), pp. 421–566 (p. 428).

[48] Giles, *De regimine*, preface, pp. 1–2: *Suo Domino speciali . . . suus devotus Fr. Aegidius . . . si vestra generositas gloriosa me amicabiliter requisivit, ut de eruditione principum sive de regimine regum quendam librum componerem.* In their account of Giles, F. Del Punta, S. Donati, and C. Luna ('Egidio Romano', *DBI* lxii. 319–41, at pp. 320–1) point out that at this time Giles had other young noblemen as dedicatees of his works and as pupils.

[49] J. Strayer, *The Reign of Philip the Fair* (Princeton, 1980), pp. 7–8.

[50] Giles, *De regimine*, II. i. 15; p. 263: *Sicut Theutonici sunt barbari Italicis, et Italici Anglicis.*

[51] See below, Epigraph, n. 3. [52] Giles, *De regimine*, II. ii. 10, p. 316.

'mostly' to kings and princes. Lack of children is a greater problem, more dangerous, in a ruling house.[53] Lack of care of royal offspring is more important, because of its consequences, than any other lack of care of offspring.[54] The traditional Christian view of marriage extending friendship (between kin) has the special application, at this level, of extending peace and dampening discords and wars.[55] One looks for nobility and multitude of friends in a wife, the last point applying more to kings and princes because of their status and the misfortunes which may result if they do not seek such things, for kings seek to abound more in civil power through the women they marry.[56] The common good and salvation of the kingdom depend on the offspring produced. Beauty in a wife will be especially important for kings and princes and, for good procreation, she should have a large body.[57]

When proceeding to his chapter on marriage-age,[58] Giles signals his intent to be specific. General maxims are not so useful in moral affairs, and he will descend to the particular. How should citizens, but especially kings and princes, use sex? In particular, at what age should one marry? 'In the seventh [book] of the *Politics* the Philospher touches upon four arguments which show that one should not engage upon marriage at too young an age.'[59] He then recites four reasons. The first consequence of too early marriage is the birth of children weak in body and imperfect, and therefore harmed in soul—deficient in reason and intellect. This is treated more lengthily than the following three reasons, the intemperance of women, danger to young women in childbirth, and harm to the growth of men.

The Giles whom we have seen carefully adapting material to the realities (or ideals) of monarchy now had a problem as he approached the specific age recommended by Aristotle. He was addressing a prince and heir, the first marriages of whose male forebears followed a pattern which he and Giles will have known and taken as a commonplace in the Capetian dynasty. In the middle of the previous century John of Salisbury had commented acidly on the love which this prince's great-great-great grandfather had felt for his wife, Eleanor of Aquitaine, writing that he loved the queen passionately, 'in an almost childish way', *fere puerili modo*.[60] In the first instance and principally, John's remark bears on Louis VII's personality—but it has a secondary bearing—on Louis's youthfulness at marriage. Consider the line going back from the young Philip. His father, Philip III, had married at 17; his grandfather, Louis (IX) at 20; his great-grandfather, Louis VIII, at 13; his great-great grandfather, Philip Augustus, at 14; his great-great-great grandfather, Louis VII, at 16. It was for a boy in this line, now perhaps about 12 years old, for whom Giles was writing: a boy who was to be knighted and married in 1284, at the age of 16 or perhaps 17—the year of his birth is uncertain.

[53] Ibid., II. i. 10; p. 249. [54] Ibid., II. i. 9; p. 243; II. i. 10; p. 249. [55] Ibid., II. i. 10; p. 247.

[56] Ibid., II. i. 12; p. 255. [57] Ibid., II. i. 13; pp. 256–7. [58] Ibid., II. i. 16; pp. 265–7.

[59] Ibid., II. i. 16; p. 265: *Tangit enim Philosophus* 7. Polit. *quatuor rationes probantes quod in aetate nimis iuvenili non est utendum coniugio.*

[60] John of Salisbury, *Historia pontificalis*, XXIX, ed. M. Chibnall (London, 1956), p. 61.

Giles at first seems to follow Aristotle. 'The Philosopher seems to want', writes Giles, 'that this time should be eighteen in the wife. In the man, however, more time is required.' Giles then abruptly cuts the Gordian knot, ignoring Aristotle. And he does not tell his readers what he is doing. 'For, if throughout the time of growing it is harmful for males to engage in marriage,' he continues, ' since the time of growth usually needed in men is three septennia, it seems that the due time for men to apply themselves to the task of conjugal intercourse is after the third septennium [after twenty-one].' He goes even further: 'However, because the generative power is too corrupt, if it seems expedient this time can be anticipated.'[61] Later, during the chapters devoted to the upbringing of children, Giles returns to marriage-age, and here he is open about his parting company with Aristotle: 'The philosopher shows at what age they ought to use marriage . . . saying (eighteen and thirty-six). . . . But because the generative force (as we said above) is too corrupt, it would be enough for youths to abstain from carnal intercourse for the whole time of growth, which usually lasts till the twenty-first year: because, if they engage in marriage within that time, they are encouraged to lasciviousness, and their growth is impeded . . .' A broad reference to tutors could have led readers who were aware that Giles had written for the young Philip to think of one element in the situation of young princes, advice from tutors, among others. 'If the tutors of children perceive that they cannot wait such a long time, this time can be anticipated as seems fit to them [the tutors].'[62] Giles has been doing a balancing act between Aristotle and youthful Capetian marriages, and when he talks about avoiding a too young age his readers know that he means something far less than 38. 'It is therefore proper for all citizens not to engage in marriage at a too young age. However, this is all the more proper for kings and princes, insofar as they should be even more concerned that their children should be physically handsome and elegant of body and mentally active.'[63]

'On the generation of royal offspring'[64] is one chapter in Engelbert's *De regimine principum*, specifying age as one of the three conditions upon which perfect generation rests, according to Aristotle in book 7 of *Politics*. Young parents generate imperfect children who do not live very long—they die quickly, especially the

[61] Giles, *De regimine*, II. i. 16; p. 267: *Videtur velle Philosophus, huiusmodi tempus in coniuge debere esse decem et octo annorum. In viro vero plus temporis requiritur. Nam si per totum tempus augmenti nocivum est masculis uti coniugio, cum ad tempus augmenti communiter in hominibus requirantur tria septennia, post tertium septennium in viris videtur esse debitum tempus dare operam copulae coniugali. Verum quia vis generativa est nimis corrupta, huiusmodi tempus anticipari poterit, si videbitur expedire.*

[62] Ibid., II. iii. 12; pp. 321–2: *In qua autem aetate debeant uti coniugio, ostendit Philosophus 7* Poli. *dicens . . . Sed quia vis generativa (ut superius diximus) est nimis corrupta, sufficeret toto tempore augmenti, quod durat communiter usque ad vigesimum primum annum, abstinere iuvenes a carnali copula: quod si infra tale tempus utantur coniugio, provocantur ad lasciviam, et impeditur eorum augmentum . . . si doctores puerorum percipiant iuvenes tantum tempus expectare non posse, poterit illud tempus anticipari prout eis videbitur expedire.*

[63] Ibid., II. i. 16; p. 266: *Decet ergo omnes cives non uti coniugio in aetate nimis iuvenili; hoc tamen tanto magis decet reges et principes, quanto ipsi plus debent esse solliciti, ut eorum filii sint formosi et elegantes corpore et industres mente.*

[64] Engelbert, *De regimine principum*, VII. xxii; pp. 225–8: *De generatione prolium regiarum.*

first ones; the Hippocratic *Aphorisms* are cited in support.[65] The children of the elderly will also be weaker, and there will be imperfect generation from a young man and old woman, or vice versa. Within their 'perfect' generative spans, 30 to 70 for men and 18 to 50 in women [*sic*], the 'most perfect' ages are respectively 50 and 33—although elsewhere, when discussing the Virgin Mary, Engelbert gives 31.[66] Engelbert's biographer reminds us of the members of noble families who were at the monastery of Admont, suggesting that Engelbert wrote for the 'express benefit' of the dukes and nobility of Austria.[67] His treatise, however, has no dedicatee, and his display of learning and recycling of Aristotle seems a more abstract exercise than Giles's.

In his sharp reduction of Aristotle's recommended age Giles had been doing something simple: brusquely adapting the *Politics* to the realities of the Capetian dynasty. The discussion of marriage-age in the tract by the Aragon Anonymous was similarly shaped by the marriage policy of a royal dynasty, but in a more dramatic way. This tract, entirely devoted to the marriage-age and 'good birth' section of book 7 of the *Politics*, is a remarkable work. Partly because it represents the most developed example of 'populationist' thought and is the most extended of all discussions of marriage-age in book 7, and partly because it is unprinted and has never had a place in accounts of commentaries on the *Politics*, it is given an extensive description here.[68]

Although the work is entitled *Libellus de ingenio bone nativitatis*, roughly translatable as *Tract about the art of good birth*,[69] 'good birth' is a peg for the real theme, marriage-age, not vice versa. The tract contains about 12,000 words, occupying ten folios in the one extant manuscript, which was once in the Sorbonne.[70] It begins thus: 'Since the question was put to me by the illustrious man the young Lord James, first-born [son] of the most serene prince Lord James, king of Aragon, "Whether by human art one can bring it about that parents generate good and perfect children?" . . .'[71] The reference to James as 'first-born' suggests that the work was written before James's renunciation of his rights of primogeniture at Tarragona on 22 December 1319,[72] while the anonymous author's adoption of a schema of ages in which the young fall between 21 and 31 suggests an

[65] Ibid., p. 226: *dicit Hippocrates in* Aphorismis, *quod nati parentis juvenibus membra principalia debiliora habent.*

[66] G. B. Fowler, *The Intellectual Interests of Engelbert of Admont* (New York, 1947), p. 80.

[67] Ibid., p. 114.

[68] A preliminary study appeared in P. Biller, 'Aristotle's *Politica* and "Demographic" Thought in the Kingdom of Aragon in the Early Fourteenth Century', *Annals of the Archive of 'Ferran Valls I Taberner's Library'*, 9/10 (1991), 249–64.

[69] This is contained in the explicit of the Paris manuscript, and in an inventory of the papal library drawn up in 1369. See n. 111 below.

[70] BN, MS Lat. 16133, fols. 74ra–83va. The manuscript has been described in AL *Codices 1*, no. 672, pp. 563–5, and M.-T. d'Alverny, 'Avicenna latinus II', *AHDLMA* 29 (1963), 217–33 (pp. 224–6).

[71] BN, MS Lat. 16133, fol. 74ra: *Postquam facta fuit michi questio per illustrem virum iuvenem Dominum Jacobum primogenitum serenissimi principis Domini Jacobi Aragonie Regis, 'Utrum possit humano ingenio procurari quod parentes bonos et perfectos filios generent?'*

[72] J. E. Martínez Ferrando, *Jaime II de Aragón: Su vida familiar*, 2 vols. (Barcelona, 1942), ii. 224–7, no. 305.

earlier terminus of 1317, when the 'young' James became 21. The author's identity is not known. When dealing with various learned opinions he writes of the *medicus*, the *phisicus*, the *naturalis philosophus*, and the *iurisconsultus*, without identifying himself as any of these, while his quotations are principally from works studied in the Arts and medical faculties. An apparent reference to courtiers and the text's opening question by James place him among the various learned men connected with the royal family of Aragon.

The tract is shaped by the statement of fourteen 'conclusions', which the author also calls 'laws'. Except for the first, each statement of a law is followed by a commentary. In the following translation, passages taken verbatim from the Latin text of the *Politics* are italicized.

1. The first law is, '*It is* certainly *necessary for the care of the body to be prior to that of the soul*' [1065–6]. However, the treatment here is different from that meted out to the other laws, in that it centres on the statement and discussion of a general introductory question, 'Whether the statesman who tries to make citizens best ought from the start to see *how the bodies* of the free men *who are to be brought up* in the city *can be best*?'[73]
2. '*First*, therefore, *one should take care about marriages, and what sort* [the spouses should] *be, and when one ought to make the nuptial* communication' [1067].[74] ['First' here should not lead to confusion: it is the second theme.]
3. 'Third law. The nuptial tie is completely forbidden between adolescents who are still growing, especially for the males' [1072–5].[75]
4. 'Fourth law. Nor are the young to be released to marriages. *The coitus of the young* is certainly *bad for the generation of children*' [1072].[76]
5. '*On account of time* those who are older *have withdrawn*, and having been *assigned to carry out holy rites* [988][77] they should be advised to desist from marriage' [1083].[78]
6. '*One ought* not only to *look to* the spouses but also *to the period of living* [life-stage] so *that they* communicate [Aristotle-Moerbeke: *come together*] *in ages at the same time, and are not dissonant in power, with* him *still being able to generate, she however not*' [1068].[79]

[73] BN, MS Lat. 16133, fol. 74ra: *Prima ipsarum hec est, 'Utrum politicus qui cives optimos facere studet a principio videre habet* qualiter optima fiant corpora *liberorum* qui *in civitate* educantur?' Priorem *enim* necessarium *est* esse curam corporis quam eam que anime (adapted from Moerbeke's Aristotle: *primo quidem corporis curam necessarium esse priorem quam eam quae animae*). In quotations from the Aragon Anonymous I use roman type to indicate verbatim copying of *Politics*.

[74] Ibid., fol. 75ra: Primo *ergo* curandum *est* circa coniugia *et* quales existentes *et* quando oportet facere nupcialem *communicacionem.*

[75] Ibid., fol. 75va: *Tercia lex. Copula itaque nupcialis inter puberes qui adhuc in augmento sunt prohibeantur omnino precipue masculis.*

[76] Ibid., fol. 76ra: *Quarta lex. Neque iuniores ad coniugia laxentur.* Iuniorum *enim* coitus pravus est ad puerorum generacionem.

[77] 1329a33–4; Sp p. 368; Su p. 279 ll. 5–7.

[78] Ibid., fol. 76va: *Seniores* propter tempus abdicati sunt *et* sanctificacionibus assigna*ti a coniugiis desistere moneantur.*

[79] Ibid., fol. 76vb: Oportet autem *non solum* aspicere ipsos *coniuges sed* ad tempus vivendi, ut

7. '[The statesman] should decide that *it is proper for* men *to be married about the age of thirty-seven years,* women *however about the age of eighteen years*' [1076, order of the sexes reversed].[80]
8. 'One ought however not only to look at age in the spouses but also at the time of year, so that as a rule they [marriages] are in winter while north winds are blowing' [1077].[81]
9. '*The habit* [of body] *of athletes* is not appropriate *for the procreation of children nor for good habit of political* [life], nor is the weak habit of body of someone *needing care and unhealthy* good for these things, *but* [a habit of body which is] *midway between these*' [1078].[82]
10. 'The married should engage in exercise [which is] *not violent nor* [devoted only] *to one* [purpose, as with athletes]' [1079].[83]
11. 'The married should neither be remiss nor [too] prompt [in applying themselves] to the act of generation.'[84]
12. '*Pregnant women* should be protected from every shock [*or* accident], and they should be fed with coarse *food*' [1080].[85]
13. '*On the keeping of those who are born, the* regulation (or *custom*) *of peoples prohibits the feeding of a defective* [baby] or any [baby] beyond *a determined number of children*' [1081, compressed].[86]
14. '*A diet abounding in milk is most appropriate for the bodies* of children, *moreover better without wine because of illnesses*' [1086].[87]

The fourteen 'laws' are mainly quotations, paraphrases, or compressed versions of dicta from a small part of book 7 of the *Politics*. The commentary which is given to each 'law' includes *citations* of other passages from the *Politics* and other moral and natural works by or attributed to Aristotle, and other authors named include Augustine, Averroes, Hippocrates, Galen, Avicenna, and Haly Abbas. Among commentators on the *Politics* use is made of Albert, who is named, and Peter of Auvergne, who is not. However, the Anonymous ranges away from the texts in book 7 of the *Politics* and these earlier commentators with notable freedom, as will be seen below. His own commentaries on particular 'laws' can be very long, sometimes for a time following the form of a proposition, the listing of a number

communicant etatibus ad idem tempus et non dissonent potencie, hoc quidem adhuc potente generare, hac autem non potente.

[80] Ibid., fol. 77rb: *Optet* quod *viros* congruit coniugari circa etatem XXXVII *annorum, mulieres* autem circa etatem XVIII annorum.

[81] Ibid., fol. 78vb: *Oportet autem non solum ad etatem respicere in coniugiis sed ad tempus anni ut regulariter in hyeme ventis borealibus flantibus fiant.*

[82] Ibid., fol. 79va: [A]thletarum habitus *non est oportunus* ad procreacionem puerorum neque *in* politicam bonam habitudinem, *nec extenuatus habitus* curis indigens et male habens *bonus est ad ista,* sed medius horum.

[83] Ibid., fol. 80ra: [*U*] *tantur coniuges exercicio* non violento neque ad unum.

[84] Ibid., fol. 80va: [*A*] *d actum generacionis coniuges neque remissi neque prompti fiant.*

[85] Ibid., fol. 81ra: [P]regnantes *ab omni occasione custodiri oportet, et grosso* cibo *alende sunt.*

[86] Ibid., fol. 81rb: De reservacione genitorum prohibet ordo gencium nullum orbatum nutrire *nec aliquem ultra* determinatam multitudinem puerorum.

[87] Ibid., fol. 82ra: [L]ac habundans alimentum maxime familiare *est* corporibus *puerorum,* magis autem sine vino propter egritudines.

of objections, 'Immediately someone might argue that . . .' and the reply to these by ordinal number, 'To the first [argument] . . .' The eighth 'law', for example, at one point gives rise to the statement of nine objections and nine answers.

Here the commentaries on 'laws' 2–7 are summarized, while description of the commentary on no. 13 is held over for the general discussion of commentaries on the theme of 'control' in the *Politics* which is given in Chapter 13 below.

Under (2) the author addresses the theme of the prince's duty to make his subjects good both for the sake of the common good and for his own good, and discusses the priority of concern for the body over concern for the soul. He looks at the border area between the 'statesman' (*politicus*) and the medical man (*medicus*). He says that on this theme the statesman puts on the 'shape of the natural philosopher'. Were a physician (*phisicus*) or a medical man to lay down the law in this area he would be going beyond his bounds, and his 'legislation' would have no effect.

Under (3) the author is concerned with the good or bad disposition of parents usually producing good or bad offspring, but not always. One particular proposition is extracted from Aristotle's text and given special emphasis:

> The third law. Sexual intercourse should be prohibited to adolescents who are still growing, particularly males. Here the legislator begins to descend to the times when marriages are suitable and those at which they are not. On this, it is to be understood that although boys produce sperm during adolescence, which lasts from the fourteenth year to twenty-one, marriages are not appropriate [for this period], nor also for [the period] from twenty-one up to thirty-seven, even though they can generate.[88]

The Aragon Anonymous's first point is one which is to remain his main one: the prohibition of early marriage to males. *Prohibited* is his word, *particularly males* his accentuation.

He then proceeds to an erudite disquisition on ages schemes. This is partly interesting for what it reveals about academic 'ages of man' thought in the early fourteenth century. Where the nearest dictionary to our author provides a definition only indirectly, 'ages in man vary according to the notable diverse variations in his condition',[89] the Anonymous provides a direct and philosophical definition. 'Age is nothing other than the condition of the natural disposition of a man as he is measured in time.' A clear and general survey of various schemes follows. 'For some have taken this natural diversification in relation to complexion, which varies in four ways throughout life.'[90] The combinations of the qualities of hot and

[88] BN, MS Lat. 16133, fol. 75rb: *Tercia lex. Copula itaque nupcialis inter puberes qui adhuc in augmento sunt prohibeantur omnino precipue masculis. Hic incipit legislator descendere ad etates in quibus non conveniunt et in quibus conveniunt coniugia, circa quod est intelligendum quod in pubescencia, que durat a XIIII° anno usque ad XXI, licet pueri spermatizent, non conpetunt coniugia, nec eciam a XXI usque ad XXXVII, licet generare possint.*

[89] J. Balbi, *Catholicon* (Mainz, 1470, repr. Farnborough, 1971), s.v. *Etas*: *variantur enim in homine etates secundum diversas notabiles varietates in statu ipsius.* On the author and work (1286), see *SOPMA* ii. 379–83.

[90] BN, MS Lat. 16133, fol. 75rb: *Etas nichil aliud est quam status naturalis disposicionis ipsius hominis ut tempore mensuratur. Hanc autem dispocionem naturalem quidam acceperunt racione complexionis, que*

cold and wet and dry in relation to the ages of childhood, youth, old age, and senility are then given. A second scheme follows. 'Some have taken this natural disposition in relation to growth and decline . . . And with these two modes some *medici* take four ages, while other *medici*, such as Hippocrates, distinguished seven ages according to the diversity of ailments which occur at various times. Therefore they call the first one which lasts from birth to 7 days "newly born". The second which lasts to 12 years they call the "teeth-growing [age]".'[91] The remaining five ages do not have their medical characteristics described.[92] The Anonymous then moves to note two points in Aristotle. One is that one approach adopted by Aristotle relates the succession of ages to different forms or stages of diet and education, which produces eight ages,[93] while the other is that Aristotle was opposed to dividing ages by sevens.[94]

Insofar as any scheme was standard, or a commonplace, it was that which could be found in Balbi's *Catholicon* and in many other books, all deriving ultimately from Isidore's *Etymologies.* In the simple definitions provided here, 7–14 was 'not yet apt for generating', 14–28 'adult for generating'. The contrast 'not yet apt' can be added to the fact that there is no reference to generation in relation to the third age (28–50). A straightforward reading, then, of the most widespread scheme of ages would indicate 14–28 as the (first?) period for generating, and the first 'appropriate' period. It is to circumvent this scheme and this statement that the the Aragon Anonymous is parading his elaborate erudition, displaying other schemes, displaying their variety, and underlining the fact that at their core was physical constitution and diet. It is also because Isidore's scheme mainly proceeded in (roughly) multiples of seven (to 7, to 14, to 28, to 50, to 70) that the Anonymous presses Aristotle's authority into service, for what he calls a 'prohibition' of dividing ages by sevens.[95]

He then goes on to quote virtually all of Peter of Auvergne's commentary on harmfulness of sexual intercourse for males who are still growing, adding to Peter material from Avicenna and Aristotle's *On the Generation of Animals,* using Moerbeke's translation. Possible objections are aired and answered. Someone could doubt, because of exceptions to the generalization about adolescent males having sex and not growing. Secondly, why does this point apply specifically to males and not to females? Referring briefly to the conflict between Aristotle (males only

diversificatur quadrupliciter in tota vita. I have not identified the source of the definition. For modern study of medieval ages schemes, see above, Ch. 1 n. 17.

[91] Ibid.: *Quidam acceperunt hanc naturalem disposicionem racione augmenti et decrementi . . . Et istis duobis modis accipiunt quidam medici quatuor etates. Alii medici sicut Ypocras distinxerunt VII etates secundum diversitatem morborum qui huiusmodi superveniunt in diversis temporibus. Unde primam etatem, que durat a principio nativitatis usque ad VII dies, vocant 'noviter genita'. Secundam, que durat usque ad XII annos, vocant 'dencium plantativam'.*

[92] Third age 'lasts to 14', 'boyhood'; fourth age 'lasts to 25 or 30', 'adolescence'; fifth age 'lasts to 35 or 40', 'youth'; sixth age 'lasts to 55 or 60', 'old age'; seventh age 'lasts for the rest of life', 'senility'.

[93] The eight ages are (1) the first three years, (2) the next two years to 5, (3) the next two to 7, (4) 7 to the 14th year, (5) 14th year to 37, (6) 37 to 55, (7) 55 to 70, and (8) 70 to the end of life.

[94] This is based on 1337a40–1; Su p. 331, ll. 6–7; Sp p. 398 no. 1099.

[95] BN, MS Lat. 16133, fol. 75va.

emitting seed) and medical authors (both sexes emitting), he uses his own Aristotelian position to state the physical answer—women not emitting seed and therefore not weakened—while retaining the point about the moral harm done to them through too early sex.

Under (4) the Anonymous's main concern is present and dealt with in the first sentence, in which he glosses the meaning of the 'younger' who are not to marry. 'By "younger" the legislator understands here between 21 and 37.'[96] He follows this with a justifying statement about the slowness of natural growth. Interwoven are three points about the drawbacks of too early generation, and here the commentary is for once less original than usual, more a conscientious plod. The first point is imperfect generation, of the female and small, where the Anonymous follows Peter of Auvergne but also quotes further from *On the Generation of Animals*. The second is dangers in childbirth, where he again follows Peter, adding a sentence to generalize, and perhaps switch back to both sexes: 'such early marriages are more for pleasure or some other usefulness than for production of fruit [good offspring]'.[97] The third is propinquity in ages, where he again follows Peter.

For (5) the Anonymous backtracks to an earlier part of book 7 which dealt with the elderly as a group deputed to priestly tasks, and the priesthood as a group desisting from marriage. Adding to the *Politics*, he moves it towards his own world when writing why priests do not marry. 'First, so that they can devote themselves more freely to divine worship when not preoccupied with household management; and therefore western Christians, who also take youths as priests, have forbidden marriage for priests, for this and other reasons.'[98] Other reasons come from our section of book 7, the imperfection of the offspring of elderly, and what follows if elderly men procreate, that is, the consequent difficulty of mutual help between elderly parents and small children, which the Anonymous adds is something which particularly applies to the poor. 'In this case both children and parents are miserable, and this is apparent particularly among humbler people, because of [their] indigence.'[99] Although the Anonymous is mainly interested in the prohibition of youthful marriage to young men, a symmetry is attracting him here—the prohibition of marriage to a group of males at the other end of life—and it is this which lies behind his introduction of this unusual theme.

In (6) the Anonymous expands the theme of dissonance of life-stages between spouses. The two evils—(1) the frustration of the principal effect of marriage, procreation, (2) the impeding of 'domestic communication'—are set within an argument about 'marriage from nature', which uses the terms of 'man as more a conjugal than political animal': a theme and terms which are commonplaces by

[96] BN, MS Lat. 16133, fol. 76ra: *Per 'iuniores' intelligit hic legislator illos qui sunt inter XXI anni et XXXVII.*

[97] Ibid., fol. 76rb: *Tale namque connubium magis est ad delectacionem vel ad aliquam aliam utilitatem quam ad fructuum produccionem.*

[98] Ibid., fol. 76va: *Primo ut non occupati administracione yconomica divinis obsequiis liberius vacare possint, et ideo christiani occidentales, qui eciam iuvenes in sacerdotes assumunt, propter hanc et alias causas prohibent coniugia sacerdotibus.*

[99] Ibid., fol. 76vb: *Nam in isto casu tam filii quam parentes miserabiles sunt, et hoc precipue apparet in humilioribus propter indigenciam.*

this period. More noteworthy is the sharpness of phrasing used by the Anonymous to distinguish between age and life-stages: 'it is to be understood that between man and wife there can be dissonance as far as the number of days is concerned [how old each one is], but not as far as their ages are concerned [the stage of life at which each one is].'[100]

'Law' (7) deals with the ideal ages. At last the Anonymous arrives at the central point, and now he produces his longest and most remarkable commentary. Aristotle was not stark enough on the one point which really mattered to the Anonymous. He laid down the ideal ages for generation for men of 37–55, and he laid down desisting *after* 55. But in the eyes of the Anonymous he was not blunt enough in specifying desisting *before* 37; and he did not use sufficiently extreme language. The commentary on this 'law' is primarily shaped by the concern of the Anonymous to supply these gaps.

All the goods of marriage will flow through observance of Aristotle's ideal ages: the generation of perfect offspring; no dissonance between husband and wife in generating; not a small succession of offspring; a relation of age between parents and children which means that children can help their parents.

The Anonymous then produces a detailed example. If one has a man of 18 who is betrothed (*sponsus*) and a girl (*sponsa*) of 7, he will be distant from marriage by 18 years, and she by 10. When the *sponsa* has come to the time of marriage she will have to wait 8 years before he comes to the age of marriage. [The author is aware of slight inprecisions in his calculations—later in the commentary he refers to ages being too little or too much by one or two years.]

> Therefore for the betrothed man and his friends [*amicis*—whose meaning in this context might include 'advisors and kin'] there is not a complaint about the minority of the betrothed, but rather, on the contrary, about the minority of the betrothed [boy]. For this reason the betrothed [boy] ought not to listen to the querulous moanings of [those] flatterers, who claim that his deploring of the minority of the betrothed girl is excessive. [Let] such people [beware] lest they incur [the punishment] which is threatened to those who call good 'evil', and evil 'good'. However, many of them speak more from ignorance than malice, and so they sin less.[101]

The ages are those we would expect in princely and ruling families, while a moral condemnation which is a commonplace from John of Salisbury's *Policraticus* onwards—courtiers as flatterers (*adulatores*)—suggests the setting of a court. The Anonymous proceeds immediately to state that 'from those things, which have been declared now and earlier, there follows one conclusion'. This conclusion is

[100] Ibid., fol. 77ra: *Intelligendum est quod inter virum et uxorem potest esse dissonancia quantum ad numerum dierum et non quantum ad etates.* This is supported by a reference to the *City of God* which I have not yet identified, and the commonplace, to the Anonymous, of ages starting quicker in woman because of her brevity of life relative to man's.

[101] Ibid., fol. 77va: *Et ideo non est querela sponso nec amicis eius de minoritate sponse, sed pocius econtra posset esse querela de minoritate sponsi, quare non debet sponsus attendere ad querulesas adulatorum lamentaciones, qui de minoritate sponse nimium dolere se asserunt. Tales enim ne illud incurrant quod comminatum est hiis qui bonum 'malum' et malum 'bonum' dicunt, verumptamen plurimi ex eis magis ex ignorancia quam ex malicia locuntur, et ideo minus peccant.*

that 'every joining of male and female in the human species which takes place outside certain ages of life (*aetates*) and without the nuptial tie is in a certain way unnatural'.[102]

After an expansion of this there follow the stating and answering of nine objections. They are long, and not listed here. Two of them recall the two stated by Peter of Auvergne in his excursus, the earliness of adolescence, and the lower minima stated by law. The Anonymous differs from Peter in that he almost dismisses law.

To the fourth [objection] one should say that according to the laws *consent makes marriage*. However, true consent is only in those who use marriage, and because boys in the fourteenth year and girls in the twelfth begin to reason then and begin then to be able to have sexual intercourse, which is a sign of generative power, the laws permit such marriages. But if the jurisconsult, putting on the garb of the natural philosopher, were to consider the unsuitable things stated above, which flow from such marriages, he would not consent to them.[103]

After his exhaustive answers to the objections, the Anonymous concludes with a lamentation about modern times. The law relating to ages 'is not commonly followed', he writes,

on account of two [things]. First, because of the incontinence to which the children of this age [or 'world'] are prone. For they cannot remain continent until the arrival of the age which is appropriate for generation, and therefore the paterfamilias prefers that his children marry during adolescence rather than unlawfully and unworthily engaging in lust, and thus, in order to avoid a greater evil, these not good marriages are produced. Secondly, on account of desire for succession of children. For the paterfamilias fears that the death of children will pre-empt the time [for generation] ordained by law, and that in this way he will be deprived of all succession [to him], and consequently his inheritance will devolve onto strangers; so he prefers to have imperfect descendants than, perhaps, none [at all]. But these two things come through failure to observe laws. On account of this in [this] modern time children desire to engage in lust more quickly, because they have been born of the imperfect [and are therefore themselves] imperfect. . . . [ending thus:] If anyone should begin to generate before the time laid down by law in order to have a greater multitude of children, this is entirely pointless, because it is better to have few children, who are perfect and long-lived, than many children who are imperfect and likely to die [young].[104]

[102] BN, MS Lat. 16133, *Sed ex hiis que nunc declarata sunt et prius sequitur una conclusio . . . Et est quod omnis commixtio maris et femelle que fit in specie humana extra certas etates et sine copula nupciali quoddammodo innaturalis est.*

[103] Ibid., fol. 78ra–b: *Ad quartum, dicendum quod secundum iura* consensus facit matrimonium (C. 27 q. 2. dict.; Friedberg, i. 1062). *Verus autem consensus non est nisi in hiis qui racione utuntur, et quia pueri in XIIII° anno puelle in XII° anno iam incipiunt racionari et incipiunt posse coire, quod est signum potencie generative, permittunt iura talia matrimonia. Sed si iurisconsultus induens formam philosophi naturalis consideraret supradicta inconveniencia que talia matrimonia consequuntur non consentiret ea.*

[104] Ibid., fol. 78vb: *Lex autem ista in qua etates eliguntur generacioni non preservatur communiter propter duo, primo quidem propter incontinenciam ad quam filii huius seculi proni sunt. Non enim possunt continere donec ad etatem generacioni debitam perveniant, et ideo pocius vult paterfamilias quod filii eius nubant in adolescencia quam quod inlegitime et inhoneste luxurientur, et sic ista non bona coniugia fiunt ad evitacionem maioris mali. Secundo propter desiderium successionis liberorum, nam paterfamilias, timens ne mors liberorum preocupet tempus statutum a lege et sic ab omni successione destituatur et per consequens hereditas eius devolvatur ad alienos, pocius vult inperfectos habere nepotes quam forte nullos. Sed ista duo ex inobservancia legum proveniunt. Propter hoc enim moderno tempore filii cicius luxuriari appetunt quia ex inperfectis inperfecti nati sunt. . . . Si aliquis ante tempus statutum a lege generare inceperit ut maiorem*

Although a little of the treatise still remains, this diatribe is the real conclusion to its main business.

This treatise's broader context is the Aragonese royal family, together with the learning and culture surrounding it, while its theme points to this family's marriages, and in particular the projected marriage of its dedicatee, the infante James. The very considerable intellectual interests of James's father, James II, are well known. Document after document in the standard collection of texts on medieval Catalan culture attests his driving interests, in translations and in the *dictamina* of Piero della Vigna, and they also draw the outlines of his scholastic provision for the infante James: his buying for him of a book of grammar in 1313, or payment to his *magister* Ramon of Benajac. His patronage of learned medical practitioners and his interest in medical texts has been described superbly and in a wealth of detail by Michael McVaugh.[105] An addition to our picture of the culture of James II's court and the infante James's household is provided by study of the *Libellus de ingenio bone nativitatis*: the raising of a question by the infante James, his intellectual connection with a learned natural philosopher, and the sharp and dramatic use of Aristotle's *Politics* to answer it. Beside the clear medical interests of the Aragonese royal family we must juxtapose Aristotelian moral philosophy.

Even better known than the intellectual interests of the Aragonese royal family is the peculiar nature of many of its marriages.[106] James II's grandfather, James I, had told in his autobiographical chronicle that he was hurried into marriage as young as possible, and that for a year he and his wife 'had not been able to do what man and woman should do, as we were still too young'.[107] James II was married four times, his first marriage (after a earlier dissolved contract) with a bride (Blanche of Anjou) of 12, when he himself was 28. This took place in 1295, and Blanche of Anjou produced ten children between 1296 and her death in childbirth in 1310. James II himself followed a matrimonial policy for his children which, it has been suggested, may have overstepped the bounds of the time—five daughters were espoused around the age of five.[108] The most notorious, however, is the case of the infante James.[109] He was born in 1296 of a mother who was probably

habeat multitudinem filiorum, hoc omnino vanum est quia melius est paucos perfectos et longevos habere filios quam multos inperfectos et moribundos.

[105] *Documents per l'História de la Cultura Catalana Mig-Eval*, ed. A. Rubio y Lluch, 2 vols. (Barcelona, 1908–21), ii. 3–4, 9, 12, 13, 17, and 21–2 (nos. 2, 11, 14, 15, 22, and 28). See also F. Elias De Tejada, *Las Doctrinas Políticas en la Cataluña Medieval* (Barcelona, 1950), Ch. 9 on the writings of James's brother Peter, and p. 125 on his allusions to Aristotle. I am grateful to Peter Rycraft for placing his knowledge of medieval Catalan culture at my disposal. See M. R. McVaugh's *Medicine before the Plague: Practitioners and their Patients in the Crown of Aragon, 1285–1345* (Cambridge, 1993), Ch. 1, 'The medical history of a royal family', and 'Royal surgeons and the value of medical learning: the Crown of Aragon, 1300–1500', in L. García-Ballester, R. French, J. Arrizabalaga, and J. Cunningham, ed., *Practical Medicine from Salerno to the Black Death* (Cambridge, 1994), pp. 211–36.

[106] An account is provided in R. Sablonier, 'The Aragonese royal family around 1300', in *Interest and Emotion: Essays on the Study of Family and Kinship*, ed. H. Medick and D. W. Sabean (Cambridge, 1984), pp. 210–39.

[107] Ibid., p. 213. [108] Ibid., p. 224.

[109] The following is based on H. T. Sturcken, 'The unconsummated marriage of Jaime of Aragon and Leonor of Castile (October 1319)', *Journal of Medieval History* 5 (1979), 185–201.

then aged thirteen. In 1312 Leonora of Castile was brought to the Aragonese court to be brought up there as James's future bride; she was then five, or older.[110] The infante James showed extreme reluctance to marry, and was eventually to enter religion. Between 1316 or 1317 and James's renunciation of his rights of primogeniture in December 1319 there unfolded the dramatic story of increasing tension and disputes between father and son, as the father, James II, brought increasing pressure on his son to marry.

It is in this context that some aspects of the *Libellus de ingenio bone nativitatis* acquire meaning: concern with ages of marriage in general; the provision of an arsenal of arguments *against* a man marrying while a *iunior*, viz. while under the age of 37, a marriage described with some hyperbole as *in a certain way unnatural*; the citing of one example of two young betrothed children whose age gap, eleven years, was probably that of the infante James and Leonora; and allusive angry reference to the pressure of courtiers. It is clear that in this case part of the reworking of the *Politics* in the *Libellus de ingenio bone nativitatis* had a precise purpose in the dispute over the infante James's projected marriage. Although the precise date of its commissioning and its precise role are not clear, there is one tantalizing clue. In the pursuit of his policy of putting pressure on his son, James II had obtained a letter from John XXII to the infante James, urging him to marry (Avignon, 19 September 1319). An inventory of 1369 shows that a copy of the *Tract about the art of good birth* had entered the papal library at Avignon:[111] perhaps originally as a result of the infante putting it forward to represent his side in debate?

We may well be impatient with the ponderousness of parts of these commentaries and the sheer slowness of their development, and contemptuous of some Aristotelian themes (such as debilitation through emission of seed), which for centuries have been consigned to the rubbish-heap of European thought. If so, we may be brought up short by the sense of humour displayed in a marginal note in the Sorbonne manuscript of the Aragon commentary. 'Few follow prudence in this act [sex].'[112] The tartness displayed here is on the margin of a text which one particular fourteenth-century reader was also finding heavy going—and perhaps distant from his experience of things? The *Politics* was, however, *the* text which he could read on the topic, the text which provided the themes and vocabulary for discussion of marriage-ages. The Aragon Anonymous and other commentaries represent the very beginnings of the history of systematic thought and discussion about marriage-ages, and we should not have anachronistic expectations of them.

[110] Sturcken, *Journal of Medieval History*, p. 199 n. 5.

[111] M. Faucon, *La librairie des papes d'Avignon: sa formation, sa composition, ses catalogues, 1316–1420*, 2 vols. (Paris, 1886–7), i. 127, no. 374: *Item, liber* de ingenio bone nativitatis, *coopertus coreo rubeo, qui incipit in secundo corundello primi folii* has autem *et finit in ultimo corundello penultimi folii* estis. After the sixty words of the opening statement the Paris manuscript continues with the words *Has autem conclusiones leges appello.*

[112] BN, MS 16133, fol. 77va.

13

THE *POLITICS* (III): MULTITUDE

13.1 *Optimum size*

The *Politics* contained a very flexible view of the actual multitude, a 'population' which had varied in the past and might be increasing, decreasing, or staying the same. It could be behaving in one of these ways under certain 'demographic' conditions of births, deaths, emigrations, and so on, and each of these ways had certain implications. While considering ideal and actual 'cities' and constructing the ideal 'city', Aristotle frequently had these implications at the centre of the picture: the implications of a certain size of overall multitude, or the proportional sizes of the multitudes of various parts of the 'city'. There are two important discussions of this in book 2, where the theme arises through the exposition and criticism of two proposed ideal constitutions (by Plato, in his *Laws*, and by Phaleas of Chalcedon), in which property is distributed equally. And there is a central discussion, where the theme is considered in its own right—'how many citizens?'—as part of the construction of the ideal 'city' in book 7. More of Aristotle's general drift was towards lower numbers and keeping them down, with however, as we shall see, one sharp exception.

What baggage of ideas and experience was being carried by the commentators who were confronting this? The first thing to reckon with in the experience of our commentators is their families. As we saw in Chapter 12 above, where we add the particulars of families of which we know something—those of an Albert or a Thomas Aquinas—to our more general picture of university masters and students, we find ourselves dealing with the military nobility, often of a lesser sort. Born in these families, the commentators will have been brought up in a particular mental world one constituent of which was norms about children, such as the importance of heirs, and numbers of children (perhaps varying according to estate and systems of inheritance). Disdain for lower estates, so easy to find among writers of noble origin, may have led here to condescension about 'popular multitudes'. The commentators were not only men from noble families lecturing in universities, they were also men born in the country who then lived in cities, cities among the largest in Europe: Cologne, Paris, Florence, and Prague. Country, town, and widespread travel formed them. Let us recall briefly the material (surveyed in Chapters 2 and 5 above) which those commentators who came to the *Politics* as mature theologians will have had introduced into their minds, dinned in and repeated until they were the commonplaces of thought. Principal among these were the emphasis on multiplication and the curse on sterility in the Old Testament; one of the Augustinian three goods of marriage, the good of offspring; and, from Augustine, Peter the Lombard, and *Sentences* commentaries, a more qualified biblical history of population. As we saw in Chapter 5 above, such themes as the good of population and the variation in the history of marriage as a binding precept could be used to express or approach the theme of too few or too many people.

Shaped by family, country, town, education, and travel, the earlier commentators, an Albert or an Aquinas, were passing their adult lives in the middle decades of the thirteenth century; a Peter of Auvergne or an Engelbert in its later decades; a Tolomeo then and into the third decade of the fourteenth century; a Burley into the mid-1340s. They lived through the demographic swings outlined in Chapter 5 above—in particular the growth towards the over-population of the years before and around 1300, and the famines and (possibly) the demographic downturn of the early fourteenth century (or earlier). Once again, the hypotheses their experience suggests are similar to those of Chapter 5. The simplest is that most of these men are likely to have been aware of or interested in these themes themselves: more interested in over-population than under-population. We can also ask whether living in an over-populated Europe may in itself have made them more in general—rather than in such a particular way—'populationist' in thought and outlook.

In a laboratory model for investigating the history of thought and outlook, we would look for a control. This could be the *Politics* being introduced to an under-populated western Europe. That did not happen. Nor is there a useful control in the later Oresme, writing well after the beginning of population downturn and also after the dramatic ravages of the Black Death. For by then so much in the western reception of the *Politics* had been done, so many of the lines of thought firmly set. There is little to be gained by hypothesizing and then asking 'is he less enthusiastic about the proposition "small is beautiful" than commentators who lived in an overpopulated Europe?' With the range of questions suggested by our earlier commentators' experience of population in the decades before and after 1300, let us now turn to look at their reception of Aristotle's ideas.

In book 2 Aristotle had criticized two schemes for constitutions. In one scheme, a number of 5000 soldiers had been suggested. This is criticized, for its lack of regard to the larger 'multitude' implied by this, and the very large territory—like the region of Babylon—which would be needed to support it. In the other, a scheme for equal distribution of property was criticized for failing to fix the corresponding numbers of citizens. Limiting the multitude is more necessary than limiting property. If one does not do so, poverty follows. The drift is in the other direction in book 4's discussion of actual constitutions. The most peaceful cities are those where middling men (*medii*) between the poor and the rich are more numerous, and they are relatively more numerous in larger cities; larger cities, therefore, are more peaceful. The theme is developed in the discussion of causes of revolution in book 5, which include the disproportionate increase of one group, especially rich or poor. There then follows in book 7 a long and important discussion of the optimum size of the multitude. Some may judge a city as great because it has more people. But this is to confuse size and greatness—one should look to power, not size. Very populous 'cities' have a problem with law, and they are difficult to rule. There is a necessary measure of size, and the best cities are those where this measure exists: not excessively small or large. The city needs to have enough multitude for the necessities of life, but it should not be too big.

'How large should be the multitude for an appropriate size of "city"?'[1] So runs the heading to the discussion of optimum multitude in Albert's commentary. The theme itself is now directly formulated in western thought. The restatements and explorations which remain close to Aristotle will then have as their most prominent feature the measured general discussion of book 7, which has just been summarized. Book 2 also has its legacy. In his *De regimine principum*, for example, Engelbert of Admont envisages the theme as a 'question of counsel'. 'One should . . . consider quality and quantity, that is to say, the multitude of inhabitants in a region, so as to know what sort and how big the region is, [and, given that] what sort of inhabitants and how many it can support at what quantity and quality of cost [= at what standard of living].'[2]

Despite book 7's prominence, we need to pause before sweeping book 4 under the carpet. Commentaries or questions do not directly tackle the opposition between those 'cities' of book 4, whose large size leads to lack of sedition, and the drift against very large size which is found elsewhere. But comparison of the commentators' approaches yields suggestive contrasts. Peaceful large 'cities' in book 4 attracted no very marked attention or extension. This needs to be juxtaposed to the passages in book 2 containing Aristotle's criticisms of ideal constitutions, where property but not multitude was determined, which did attract attention and extension. Moerbeke's text said that it was 'inappropriate not to lay down something about the multitude of citizens, but to allow the infinite procreation of children', and a little later it lays out the effect, 'the necessary cause of poverty for citizens; penury however brings about sedition and malignity'. Thomas smoothly expands this to 'if it is allowed that men generate to infinity without some determined number, *as generally happens in cities*, it necessarily follows that a cause of poverty among citizens will arise: *for there will be many poor children having only what their rich father had*; from the poverty of the citizens it will follow that they will be seditious and malign; *for while they do not have the necessities of life, they apply themselves to acquire them by frauds and extortions*.'[3] Guido repeats this with a little rephrasing, recasting the family example: 'as manifestly [happens] in a divided house [where] each child has less.'[4] Following Aristotle's almost identical

[1] Albert, *Politics*, p. 643: *Quanta debet esse multitudo ad convenientem civitatis magnitudinem?*

[2] Engelbert, *De regimine principum*, III. v; p. 59: *oportet . . . considerare qualitatem et quantitatem, id est, multitudinem habitantium in regione, ut sciatur, qualis et quanta regio, quales et quot habitatores, qualibus et quantis expensis valeat sustentare.*

[3] Aquinas, *Politics*, p. A142 (Spiazzi edn., p. 78 no. 237).

[4] Venice, Marciana, MS 2492, fol. 73vb: *Si autem permittatur augeri numerus civium sine fine sicud*

point in criticism of Phaleas of Chalcedon's equalization of property without limit of children—'many of the rich become poor; it is difficult for such men not to be insolent'—Thomas writes lengthily. He gives examples of what measures could be taken about the multitude of children (described in section 2 below). He points out how equalization of property is destroyed by births varying in families. 'For example, if one of two citizens, who have equal possessions, generates four children, the other however only one, it follows necessarily that their children will not have equal possessions, and through this, that the law [of equalization] will be dissolved.' 'There follows also another evil,' he continues, 'that is, that, while the substance of one rich man is divided among many children, men who are born from the rich become poor; and this is evil, because it is necessary for the peace of the city that the children of the rich, who can be insolent, are not poor, for [otherwise] they would become thieves.'[5]

These passages in book 2 are getting more attention and thought-out restatement, as well as some extension, while the development and repetition of the sequence 'uncontrolled generation leads to poverty leads to evil actions' is becoming, in effect, a counterweight to 'large cities are without sedition'. The point about size of cities and sedition entered the florilegium of Aristotle's statements, the *Auctoritates Aristotelis*. In the modern edition[6] Aristotle has been turned completely round: 'Large cities are more seditious than small.' When did this slip occur? The general climate of the commentaries has just been analysed—playing down the rare praise of large size in book 4, playing up criticisms of great size elsewhere—and it is possible that this encouraged the mistake which at some stage made the *Auctoritates* so directly misrepresent book 4. A 'Freudian-intellectual' slip?

Elsewhere, both in Moerbeke's Latin and the commentaries, the key-word is *excess*. In Moerbeke's Latin text two pairs of words did the donkey-work, 'excess of multitude' (*excessum multitudinis*) and 'the multitude exceeds' (*multitudo excedit*). Seemingly endless repetitions of these hit the eye of the reader of the commentaries, as well as the semantic variations or additions. The verb with 'multitude' may be *excrescere*, *superescrescere*, *supergredere*. There may be *viri superexcrescentes*; *excessum populi* and *multitudo superabundans*; *supremus excessus*. Oresme's French provides the degrees of excess thus: *excés de la multitude*; *grant excés de la multitude*; *multitude grandement excessive*; *tres grande multitude superhabondanment*.[7] Excess or growth 'towards infinity' is also frequent. One significance here is the sheer saturation of the texts with these phrases. Beyond the particular proposition about 'multitude' or size which a reader of, or listener to, a commentary might carry away with him, there will have been the less precisely

communiter fit in civitatibus, necesse est quod eveniat penuria inter eos, sicut manifeste in domo quasi divisa quilibet filius minus habet.

[5] Aquinas, *Politics*, p. A148 (Spiazzi edn., p. 84 no. 258).

[6] *Auctoritates Aristotelis*, p. 258 no. 79. Note that this provides an early printed text rather than one of the early manuscripts which were available in medieval universities.

[7] Oresme, *Politiques*, pp. 177a, 190a, 288b, and 334a.

definable but more fundamental effect of so much airing of these words. Further significant—and itself indicative of this climate of words—was the slight semantic shift achieved between Moerbeke's presentation of 'excess of multitude' and 'multitude excedes' and Walter Burley, who, about seventy years later, uses the phrase 'lest there should be excess multitude'.[8] Burley's readers could extract the subject of his subordinate clause, *multitudo excessiva*, 'excessive multitude'. Unlike the phrase developed some time before 1250 for 'sex-ratio' (discussed in Chapter 10), this is sharp and short, as is the modern 'over-population'. There is not yet a *Tractatus de multitudine excessiva, Treatise about excessive population*, nor does the phrase immediately suggest the abstraction and generalization towards an '-ism' (together with initial capital letters) which so many modern keywords or phrases, including 'over-population' seem to be acquiring in the early modern period. But the short phrase is there.

'Thou hast ordered all things in measure and number and weight' (Wisd. 11: 21). While Guido is fairly free in relating his presentation of the *Politics* to scripture and Christian doctrine, the others are austerely sparing. All the more significant, then, are their rare explicit references to scripture, theology, or canon law. Aristotle's discussion of optimum size, and the conclusion—that there should be a certain determined measure—acquires this weighty sanction from the Old Testament in Albert's commentary and, following him, Oresme's.[9] However, despite the acute awareness all the commentators will have had of the tension between the *Politics* and the Old Testament, only one writer decided to square up to the theme directly: Tolomeo of Lucca.

Though Tolomeo was not consistently a commentator nor, when he was, always precisely a literal one, parts of his continuation of Thomas Aquinas's *De regno* engaged very closely with particular parts of the *Politics*, including the ideal constitutions of book 2. Multitude seems to have particularly interested Tolomeo, and he shows this even where one cannot point unhesitatingly to originality. So, for example, he synthesizes two attitudes to 'birth-rate' outlined in book 2 into a crisp contrast: 'The Spartans were zealous for the multiplication of offspring, the Cretans not so much.'[10] Or he interjects, recasts, and appropriates. So, on the proposed constitution of Hippodamus, after writing that 'we can easily . . . see the error . . . for we cannot give a determined number in a polity', he adds his explanation of how the multitude increases in a polity. 'The people is multiplied in it either on account of the amenity of the place, or the fame of the region, or the fertility of the people.' He then immediately follows with this: 'again we see that the more cities abound in people the more powerful and famous they are adjudged to be.'[11] Tolomeo has appropriated and made into his own the point about what

[8] See n. 42 below. [9] Albert, *Politics*, p. 650i; Oresme, *Politiques*, p. 288a.

[10] Tolomeo, *De regimine*, IV. xviii; p. 347: *Lacedaemonii zelabant multiplicationem prolis, Cretenses non tantum.* On Tolomeo [Bartolomeo Fiadoni], see L. Schmugge, 'Fiadoni', *DBI* lxvii. 317–20.

[11] Ibid., IV. xi; p. 339: *faciliter errorem . . . percipere possumus . . . quia in politia determinatum numerum dare non possumus, sed multiplicatur in ea populus vel propter amoenitatem loci, vel propter famam*

many people *think*—the large and happy city—which is stated in order to be criticized at the beginning of book 7's discussion of optimum size, and his 'adjudged' probably implies similar detachment from this view, although he does go on to say that problems of rule are not necessarily incurred by such populousness.

Such examples of Tolomeo's particular interest in the multitude prepare the reader for one key passage where the *Politics* elicited from him a sharp and original reaction. What provoked him was the notion of government intervention not to keep down the 'birth-rate' but to encourage it: Spartan zeal 'to encourage the birth-rate' by rewards to the generators of certain numbers of children, freedom from public duties to the person who generated three children, freedom from tax for the person who generated four. Aristotle's criticism, that with many children many people would necessarily become poor, later expounded clearly by Thomas with the addition that this (many poor) is harmful to the city, was repeated by Tolomeo. 'This [many children] brought about the impoverishment of citizens, making them powerless to attack [their] enemies, and it was the cause of dissension among them, and thus the region diminished in strength.' Tolomeo turns from this mild extension of Aristotle–Thomas to a completely original attack on the notion that there is virtue in the mere ability to generate many. He begins by marking out those virtues which are both moral and, because of their good for others, worthy of reward. 'Reason shows that this [rewarding the generation of many] is reprehensible. For the fact that someone generates many does not arise from the virtue for which one merits reward, as for example fighting for the state, which comes from the virtue of courage; or giving counsel to the city, which pertains to prudence; or ruling citizens, which pertains to justice; or in conversing properly] with them, which pertains to prudence.' He goes on to point out that the virtue of generating, by contrast, does not rest on virtue in this sense, and therefore does not merit reward. 'But as for [the notion] that in generating someone should merit reward in the republic—this is not a matter of virtue, for even a vile man can possess a greater generative force: hence he should not be honoured for this, for honour is only owed to virtue.' Although the point is clearly based on a distinction between virtues which are moral and those which are not, the phrase 'vile man' may be ambiguous—a man both morally 'vile' and a member of a 'vile' estate. And we should not exclude the possibility that what is being expressed here is condescension towards generating (that is, very prolific generating) in the 'popular multitude'.

After briefly making a point about equating duty and reward, Tolomeo then turns to fertility and sterility in the Old Testament. 'And although the Mosaic Law brought a curse upon the sterile, as is manifest in Exodus [23: 26: 'There shall not be one fruitless nor barren in thy land'] and Deuteronomy [7: 14: 'No one shall be barren among you of either sex'], and the concession to have many wives was granted in order to multiply generation, this was only granted for virtue, in

regionis, vel propter foecunditatem gentis. Rursus videmus civitates, quod quanto magis abundant in gente, tanto maioris potentiae et famosiores iudicantur.

relation to [rapidly increasing the numbers of those dedicated to] the cult of God, as Augustine says in the *City of God*.'[12] The matter (with different Augustinian references) is from the standard treatment of diverse laws of marriage, through history, which is presented in the *Sentences*: curse on sterility and the concession of a plurality of wives then, when rapid increase of God's people was essential. Virtue *then* lay in increasing God's people. In bringing the *Politics* into contact with fertility in the theology of marriage and Augustine, Tolomeo could have chosen several things. What he passes over in silence is one of the Augustinian goods of marriage, offspring. What he selects is the theme of the historical emphasis on fertility in the Old Testament; useful, because it had passed. In so doing Tolomeo swiftly and easily achieves a concord between Christian theology of marriage, Aristotle's criticism of Spartan encouragement of birth, and Tolomeo's own additional fierce and possibly disdainful opposition to the notion that generating many is meritorious.

13.2 *Control of multitude*

While Moerbeke's text provided readers and commentators with notions both of too much and too little, 'excess of multitude' and 'paucity of men', it also gave them notions of doing something about these: 'determine what the multitude should be'; 'the procuring of children ought to be determined'; 'so that not more than a [certain] number are generated'; 'ordain the multitude of children'. The notion is highlighted by its opposite: 'not lay down [something] about the multitude of citizens, but allow the infinite procreation of children'. Occurring both where Aristotle describes ideas about ideal constitutions and where he refers to practical measures, words like 'determine' have meanings ranging from 'stipulate what population ought to be in an ideal world' to 'take measures to control population'. Commentators may slip from the first of these to the second. Variations on these phrases saturate the commentaries. Thomas on book 2 can be taken as an example. 'Apply measure to generation'; *mensurare generationem.* 'Concerning the generation of children, one should determine the multitude'; *oportet determinare multitudinem circa generationem filiorum.* 'No more citizens than some determined number should be generated'; *non generentur plures ciues aliquo numero determinato.* 'Determine the number of those to be generated'; *determinare*

[12] Ibid., IV. xv; pp. 343–4: *Hoc autem erat causa depauperandi cives: unde fiebant impotentes ad invadendum hostes, et hoc fuit in eis causa dissensionis, unde regio diminuta est in virtute. Istud autem reprehensibile est, in ratione fundatur, quia quod quis generet plures, non est virtutis, ex qua quis meretur praeeminentiam* [? *praemium*], *puta ut in bellando pro republica, quod est virtutis fortitudinis, vel in consulendo civitati, quod pertinet ad prudentiam, vel in regendo cives, quod pertinet ad iustitiam, vel in conversando oneste cum eis, quod pertinet ad temperantiam. Sed quod in generando quis mereatur praemium in republica, hoc non est virtutis, quia etiam vilis homo potest habere virtutem generativam meliorem: unde quod in hoc honoretur, non est dignum, quia honor non debetur nisi propter virtutem. . . . Et quamvis lex Mosaica sterili maledictione imprecetur, ut in Exod. et Deut. est manifestum, et ad multiplicandam generationem plurium uxorum sit facta concessio, hoc non fuit ibi concessum nisi ad virtutem, referendo ad cultum divinum, sicut Augustinus dicit* De Civ. Dei [XVI. xxxviii].

multitudinem filiorum generandorum. 'Ordain something about the multitude of children'; *aliquid ordinare circa multitudinem filiorum.* And the opposite: 'not institute something to determine the multitude of citizens, but permit the generation of citizens to infinity'; *non instituat aliquid ad determinandum multitudinem ciuium, sed permittat generationem ciuium in infinitum fieri.* 'If men are permitted to generate to infinity without some determined number'; *si permittatur quod in infinitum homines generentur absque aliquo determinato numero.*[13]

Engelbert's epitome of the *Politics* introduces 'regulate', in the phrase 'for the multitude of the generated to be regulated', *regulari*,[14] while 'check' or 'brake' enters with a phrase he presents in his *De regimine principum*: 'an unchecked multitude of citizens': *effrenata multitudo civium.*[15] With Oresme equivalent French phrases are appearing, for example, *nul terme quant a la multitude des citoiens* ('no limit with regard to the multitude of citizens'), and *mesure . . . en la generation ou multiplication des enfans* ('measure . . . in the generation or multiplication of children').[16] 'Appearing' with Oresme—yes, as far as extant evidence is concerned. Presumably the lost earlier French version had already pioneered such phrases.

We need to be detained only briefly by the theme of 'too few'. Book 2 briefly turns to paucity of men, following discussion of lack of men in Sparta, and hence the decline in numbers of the military. The defect was once supplied by giving citizenship to strangers, but 'it is better to refill the city with men through regulated possession [regulating the inheritance of property]'.[17] There is also the policy to 'encourage citizens to have more children' (*provocat cives quod plures faciant pueros*).[18] Commentators follow. Thomas expresses the point about inheritance with increased clarity—'if possessions devolved to the few, others would desert the city through poverty'[19]—and Tolomeo displays his weather eye for a correspondence between ancient Greece and the contemporary world, comparing the two-fifths inherited by Spartan widows to the half of goods inherited by widows in *Francia* (northern France).[20] Mentioned earlier, in Chapter 9 above, was the possibility of the *Politics* stimulating one author who was preoccupied with repopulation of a reconquered Holy Land, Pierre Dubois. I would expect these passages also to be of particular interest to readers aware of underpopulated areas of Spain, but I have not yet found evidence of this.

Among the northern European and Italian commentators surveyed here, greater attention is paid to excess of multitude, and looking at ways of avoiding it. In the exposition of the Cretan constitution one compact reference to the 'segregation of women, so that they do not have more children' and 'converse with

[13] Aquinas, *Politics*, pp. A141–2 and 148 (Spiazzi edn., pp. 77–8, 84 nos. 230, 232, 235–7, and 258).

[14] Engelbert, *Compendium Politicorum*, ed. Fowler, p. 195. The paraphrase 'to be subjected to rule' should be used if the reader is tempted to read *regulari* anachronistically as 'to be varied by push-button control'.

[15] Engelbert, *De regimine principum*, III. xxiii; p. 76.

[16] Oresme, *Politiques*, p. 88a.

[17] 1270b38–9; Su pp. 121 l. 11–122 l. 1: *melius per possessionem regulatam replere viris civitatem*; Sp no. 186.

[18] 1270b2–3; Su p. 122 ll. 3–4; Sp no. 187.

[19] Aquinas, *Politics*, p. A166 (Spiazzi edn., p. 101 no. 307).

[20] Tolomeo, *De regimine*, IV. xiv (p. 343).

men'[21] is smoothly expanded by Thomas. 'Desiring, however, that they should not procreate many children, in order to avoid the multitude of men exceeding the quantity of property, he wanted men not to mix much with women, and to this end he permitted shameful sex with males.'[22] While Albert and much later Oresme confine themselves to condemnations,[23] Guido is in Thomas's tradition in clearly expounding the policy of permitting homosexual acts as a way of controlling the multitude. 'He did not want men to be joined very frequently with women, so that women did not generate children and in order to avoid cities growing beyond the norm (*ultra modum*), and to this end he permitted them sex with males.'[24]

Here the Moerbeke text already has the point. Elsewhere the phrase 'ordain the multitude of children'[25] is not followed by specification in the Moerbeke text of what this might involve. 'For example', Thomas continues: and it is therefore examples in Thomas's own mind which follow. First is individual abstinence after a certain amount of generation in particular families: 'that a person should not apply himself further to generation after a certain number [of children]'. To abstinence he returned later in his commentary on book 2, in similar words: 'that they should not press on with generation after having a certain number of children'.[26] There followed, secondly, emigration to colonize, and thirdly a (deliberate?) vagueness about other methods: 'or that after children have been born in a certain number, that the superfluous men should be sent to set up other cities; *or by some other way* [my emphasis]'.[27]

Engelbert similarly extracted the theme of expulsion from book 2, but unlike Thomas he established a specific and contemporary setting. 'One should consider three things, the number or estimate of farmers and workers and the number of the idle and the size of [their] costs. Whence there is a law and custom in many cities—during a time of scarcity and hunger, estimating the number of those who have not lived long in those cities, and expelling them from the region.'[28]

This sharp attention which is paid in book 2 to methods of control, where control meant keeping numbers down in conditions of 'excess of multitude', is a

[21] 1272a23–6; Su p. 133 ll. 5–7; Sp no. 200.

[22] Aquinas, *Politics*, p. A174: *Volens etiam quod non procrearent multos pueros, ne multitudo hominum excederet quantitatem possessionis, uoluit quod homines non multum commiscerentur mulieribus, et ad hoc concessit turpem masculorum coitum*; Sp p. 108 no. 235.

[23] Albert, *Politics*, p. 102e; Oresme, *Politiques*, p. 106b.

[24] Venice, Marciana, MS 2492, fol. 81ra–b: *ut autem mulieres multos filios non gravarent* [r: *generarent*], *ne civitates crescerent supra modum, noluit quod mulieres frequenter mulieribus iungerentur, et ad hoc concessit eis coytum masculorum.*

[25] 1266b10; Su p. 97 ll. 8–9: *filiorum multitudinem ordinare*; Sp no. 155.

[26] Aquinas, *Politics*, p. A183: *ut scilicet non insisterent operi generationis postquam certum numerum filiorum generent* (Spiazzi edn., p. 116 no. 347).

[27] Aquinas, *Politics*, p. A148: *puta quod aliquis post certum numerum generationi operam non daret, uel quod postquam pueri <essent> nati in aliquo numero, quod super excrescentes uiri mitterentur ad alias ciuitates construendas, uel quocumque alio modo* (Spiazzi edn., p. 84 no. 258).

[28] Engelbert, *De regimine principum*, III. v; p. 60: *Unde etiam lex et consuetudo in multis civitatibus, quod tempore penuriae et famis solent aestimare numerum eorum, qui non multo tempore in civitatibus ipsis habitaverunt, et illos expellere de regione.*

leitmotif for the direct treatment of the theme in book 7. Aristotle's brief discussion in book 7 of exposure and abortion to keep numbers down attracted massive attention. Here precise delineation of what commentators did needs more patient exposition. Once again we begin with a deliberately literal and at times unclear translation of Moerbeke's difficult Latin,[29] followed by a parade of the commentaries.

[1081] *De reservatione autem et alimento genitorum sit lex nullum orbatum nutrire,*	On the preserving and feeding of those who are born, let there be a law [that one should] rear no defective [child].
propter multitudinem autem puerorum, ordo gentium [Albert's quotation of the *gentilium*] *prohibet nihil reservari genitorum:*	On account of the multitude of children, however, the regulation [*or*] custom of peoples forbids anything of those born [defective] being kept [I am taking the double negative in *prohibet nihil* as a single negative].
[1082] *oportet enim determinatam esse multitudinem puerorum procreationis, autem aliquibus fiant praeter haec combinatis, antequam sensus insit et vita, fieri oportet aborsum: quod enim sanctum, et quod non determinatum sensu et ipso vivere erit.*	The multitude of procreation of children ought, to be determined. If, however, [children] beyond [this determined multitude] are born to some who are coupled, there ought to be abortion before sense and life are present. What in fact is sanctioned [in this matter] will be marked off from what is not by [the presence of] sense and life itself.
[1083] *Quoniam autem . . .*	[Summary: the beginning of marriage has been determined, and the length of the period for the generation of children, and now one turns to the end of the generative period. There is no reference to controlling numbers.]

The general analysis and summary at the beginning of Albert's commentary is 'eugenic' rather than 'populationist'. 'He [Aristotle] says that if those who are born are conceived otherwise than has been said, completely incapable of a happy life, and prone to vices, it is better to procure abortion: for it is better for such [offspring] not to be than to be.'[30] As Albert goes through the text word by word,

[29] 1335b10–19, Susemihl, pp. 322–3. See W. L. Newman, *The Politics of Aristotle*, 4 vols. (Oxford, 1887–1902), iii. 473–4 for a part paraphrase and part translation of the Greek version of this difficult passage.

[30] Albert, *Politics*, p. 733: *dicit, quod si aliter concipiantur nati quam dictum est, omnino inhabiles sunt ad felicem vitam, et proclives sunt ad vitia, quod melius est procurare abortum: quia melius est tales non esse quam esse.*

however, he returns to the motive of keeping numbers down. Rather clumsily he gives a summary of Artistotle's intention in 1082–3 in the course of commenting on 1081, while returning under 1082, each time adding contemporary parallels. Under 1081: 'At the end he [Aristotle] adds what the law of the ancient gentiles was—and it still is of some, such as the Slavs, who are called Cumans: and they provide that no defective [baby who is] born deficient in members should be kept alive.' Well-known to any member of the Order were both the large role played in the life of the founder, Dominic, by the idea of a possible mission to the Cumans and the subsequent history of the Hungarian Dominican mission, from about 1220, under Paul of Hungary, and the first large conversions, of a Cuman prince and other leaders, in 1227.[31] It is probable that Albert's source was the general pool of observations by Dominicans of the mores of the Cumans, gathered during missionary work from this period. Albert immediately returns from his own contemporary example to Aristotle's past one.

They [the gentiles] ordained that there should be a determined number of children from parents, beyond which no [child] should be kept, [and they did this] in order to avoid a too great multitude growing further. But, because it is impious and against natural piety to kill one's own babies, he [Aristotle] rejects this law, and says that it will be less evil to ordain that mothers who become aware that they have conceived should procure an abortion of the conceived seed before the seed receives life and sense.[32]

He returns to this when expounding 1082. 'The *defective* are those who are born with defect of members, who are immediately killed by the aforesaid Slavs, as are also the old [who are *or* and those who are] useless for work. And the reason is, that they think it good to kill the man who lives in misery, so that he may be freed from misery.' Albert imports a text wrenched out of context from Aristotle's *Topics*: 'and this is what is said in the book of the *Elenchi* [sic], "It is good to slaughter fathers".' Once again, Albert returns to his own world, and this time to his own observations. These had been gathered during 1263–4, when he had been empowered by Urban IV to preach the crusade throughout German-speaking areas, and probably in autumn 1263, when he had been in the north-east.[33] 'And today', he goes on, 'the inhabitants of Saxony and Poland observe this rite, as I—who was nuncio of the Roman curia to those parts—saw with my own eyes, with the children showing me the tombs of the fathers they had killed in this way.' In his

[31] M.-H. Vicaire, *Saint Dominic and His times*, trans. K. Pond (London, 1964), pp. 55 and 299; J. Richard, *La papauté et les missions d'orient au moyen age (XIIIe–XVe siècles)*, Collection de l'École Française de Rome 33 (Rome, 1977), pp. 20–33. See the literature cited in *The Mission of Friar William of Rubruck*, ed. P. Jackson and D. Morgan, Hakluyt Society, 2nd ser. 173 (London, 1990), pp. 9 n. 1 and 70 n. 2.

[32] Albert, *Politics*, p. 739g: *In fine addit, quod lex Antiquorum gentilium fuit, et adhuc quorumdam est, sicut Sclavorum, qui Cumani dicuntur, et provident quod nullus orbatus natus deficiens in membris reservetur ad vitam. Statuerunt etiam ne nimia multitudo excrescat, ut determinatus sit numerus puerorum a parentibus, ultra quem nullus reservetur. Sed quia impium est et contra pietatem naturalem interficere proprios natos, reprehendit hanc legem, et dicit quod minus malum erit statuere, quod matres sentientes se concepisse, antequam semen accipiat vitam et sensum, si seminis concepti procurarent abortum.*

[33] H. C. Scheeben, *Albert der Große: Zur Chronologie seines Lebens*, Quellen und Forschungen zur Geschichte des Dominikanerordens in Deutschland 27 (Leipzig, 1931), p. 75.

commentary on the *Topics* Albert described their practices more fully. 'They kill crippled, lame, blind, and otherwise useless children, and fathers brought down by old age and the elderly to stop them living in misery. They are noble men, strong and fine.'[34]

His commentary on 1083 continues:

> Then he shows the reason for this law, *The multitude of procreation of children ought, nevertheless, to be determined*, lest, that is, [children] grow [in numbers] beyond [the multitude] which parents can feed. And because this law is against natural piety, he [Aristotle] adds: *If however children*, multitudes, that is, of children, *beyond this* [determined] procreation of children, *are born to some who are coupled*, [that] is, to those joined in marriage, *there ought to be abortion before sense and life are present*, that is to say [present] in the conceived members. For this is less evil than killing what is already born. And on account of this, according to the law of the Lord [Exod. 21: 22], he who strikes a pregnant woman [in a way] which brings about abortion of a not yet formed foetus, that is, [not yet] born [*sic*], should not be judged guilty of homicide; if the foetus is formed, he should be adjudged guilty of homicide.[35]

Such large and vivid importation of the contemporary world is very rare in any early commentary on any part of the *Politics*. Aristotle's dispassionate survey of exposure or infanticide of the deformed or abortion as methods of keeping numbers down is evoking a sharp response from Albert the Christian friar, and from Albert the response, characteristically, is the retailing of acute but miscellaneous observation. It is not the multitude, however, which is fascinating Albert, but killing. It is killing which encourages the addition of another sort of killing—of the elderly. And both these sorts of killing—killing of deformed children and the elderly—are located and vividly illustrated on or beyond the frontiers of Latin Christendom: norms *there*, among the pagans or barbarians, by implication the opposite, therefore, of the norms *here* in the west. Anecdotes are so rare that we

[34] Albert, *Politics*, p. 740t: Orbati *sunt qui cum defectu membrorum nascuntur, qui a praedi[c]tis Sclavis statim interficiuntur, sicut etiam decrepiti senes inutiles ad labores. Et causa est, quia bonum reputant interficere eum qui in miseria vivit, ut absolvatur a miseria. Et hoc est quod dicitur in libro* Elenchorum: Bonum est mactare patres. Bonum *enim dicunt, quod pium reputant. Et hunc ritum hodie servant habitantes in confinibus Saxoniae et Poloniae, sicut ego oculis meis vidi, qui fuit nuntius Romanae curiae ad partes illas, filiis demonstrantibus mihi sepulcra patrum quos ita occiderant.* The reference is to the *Topics*, not the *Elenchi* (AL 5. 1–3, p. 48 l. 21: *bonum patrem mactare*); this may be the fault of the manuscript transcribed in the edition used here. Albert on the *Topics*, *Opera*, Borgnet, ii. 329: *Est autem usque hodie servans illud pro religione, quod miserrimos in vita reputant pium esse occidere. Propter quod gibbosos, claudos et caecos vel aliter inutiles filios occidunt, et patres senio confectos, et senes ne in miseria vivant, occidunt et sepeliunt: et hoc reputant pia in terra ista. Igitur ego pro meipso et hoc ab incolis perquirens didici, et oculata fide aspexi, et tumulos sic occisorum (qui patres et matres occiderant) indicantibus aspexi. Sunt autem proceri homines, fortes et pulchri, usque hodie religionem patrum suorum in occisione parentum suorum observantes.*

[35] Albert, *Politics*, p. 740u: *Et ostendit rationem istius legis, ibi,* Oportet enim determinatam esse multitudinem puerorum procreationis, *ne scilicet excrescant ultra quam parentes possunt nutrire. Et quia haec lex est contra naturae pietatem, subdit:* Si autem aliquibus fiant, *multitudines scilicet puerorum*, praeter hoc, *id est, procreationem puerorum*, combinatis, [*id*] *est conjugio conjunctis*, antequam sensus insit, *membris scilicet conceptis*, et vita, fieri oportet abortum: *hoc enim minus malum est quam quod jam natus occidatur. Et propter hoc secundum legem Domini* (Exod. 21: 22): *Qui percutit mulierem praegnantem quod facit abortum de puerperio nondum formato, id est, nato, non inducatur homicidii reus: si autem puerperium formatum est, reus inducatur homicidii* (see Peter the Lombard, *Sentences*, IV. xxxi. 4; ii, pp. 445–6). Glossing *formato* as *nato* seems odd; the text may be corrupt.

cannot infer anything firmly from the absence of an anecdote about abortion. We can only (*a*) note that no anecdote is provided which similarly serves to distance it from western practice, and (*b*) draw attention to one feature which is clearly remarkable: Albert providing Old Testament accommodation for early abortion.

Albert does understand the motive of controlling numbers, and when re-presenting it he links the element of nutrition from 1082 to the motive in 1083 to produce 'children not being more numerous than parents can feed'. However, the motive was missing from his summary, he does not otherwise accentuate Aristotle, and he does not add to Aristotle's two methods. In all these he stood in contrast with later commentators.

Peter of Auvergne begins his account of 1081 by summarizing. Aristotle 'declares how children are to be dealt with after they are born, and [states] that it is not expedient to take care of all of them, or to take equal care', sharply dividing Aristotle's reasons, 'either on account of imperfection, or on account of multitude. And first he touches upon [the question of] how to deal with the defective, and where [children] exceed according to multitude.'[36] Peter's exposition provides a more extensive definition of the defective: 'defective in some sense or senses, member or members, through which they are [rendered] less useful for operations of understanding or to the community'. Side by side with this implicit justification for Aristotle's treatment is a softening of that treatment, in 'the law for none such to be fed: which is to be understood [to mean, not to be fed] with such care and diligence as [accompanies the feeding of] those born perfect'.[37]

Peter then moves on to 1082, and the theme of control and methods, and here he does two notable things. First, after restating the theme—'Then he says what is to be done if they exceed according to multitude'—he introduces an extraordinary long introduction on the need to keep the numbers of children down. It is much inspired by earlier parts of the *Politics*, but is original to Peter as a synthesis, in its wording, and as an importation into this part of book 7. It follows immediately after the statement of the theme quoted above, and is given here at length. 'It is to be understood', writes Peter,

> that since the city is a community sufficient in itself for life, citizens ought to be sufficient in themselves, and not poor. And therefore one should avoid in the city those things which bring poverty, that is, a multitude of children who ought to succeed to an inheritance. For a great and large inheritance from parents, when it is divided among a multitude of children, becomes a very slight [inheritance] for each one, especially in the third and fourth generation, as we see according to sense [= observe]. The Philosopher did not wholly like the law or custom of succession of the first-born, both because, although the first-born are single, those after them, however, are often many, [and] it follows that more of the free become poor

[36] Peter of Auvergne, *Politics*, p. 403 no. 1240: *Declarat qualiter pueri postquam sunt nati sint disponendi, et quia non expedit de omnibus curare, aut non aequaliter, aut propter imperfectionem, aut propter multitudinem. Et primo tangit qualiter se habendum est ad orbatos, et ubi excedunt secundum multitudinem.*

[37] Ibid.: *orbatos sensu aliquo vel sensibus, vel membro aut membris, quibus minus sunt utiles ad operationes intellectus et rempublicam . . . lex . . . nullum talem nutriri: quod intelligendum cum tanta cura et diligentia, cum quanta nutrienda sunt perfecti nati.*

rather than rich; and also because those who have possessions are parts of the city, [while] those who do not, [are] not. For citizens ought to have possessions, as has been said above. For which reason, if those born later do not succeed their parents in something, many of the free will not be citizens but will be expelled from the city. For those born later, like the first, can be born well [and therefore apt] for great things. However, [through] not having the wherewithal to do those things for which they are born, they will be forced to take from wherever [they can], setting upon [their fellow] citizens and others through theft, extortion and murder; and they will ally themselves to enemies. All these things are inopportune.

After this eloquent account of the civil dangers which flow immediately from poverty and ultimately from too many children, Peter proceeds to methods, and does a second remarkable thing. While not ignoring exposure or suppression of the defective as a means of keeping numbers down, he adds a method. He manoeuvres to link the method expounded in 1083 by Aristotle, abortion, with the theme of 1084 (termination of period of generation), to attribute two methods to an Aristotle who in fact had only advanced one. 'Supposing, therefore, that all ought to succeed to inheritance somehow', continues Peter,

he first puts forward the law or custom of some peoples for avoiding a superfluous multitude of children. In the first part he says, that in order to avoid a superfluous multitude of children, the order, that is law or custom of some peoples, prohibits any of the generated being kept beyond a determined multitude: because, for the city to be rich, there ought to be a determined multitude of them [children]. Otherwise, if anyone is allowed to generate any number whatsoever, the city will become poor. But since not keeping children alive is allowed, if this needs to happen he explains how it can be done with less guilt, saying that if some couples have more than is determined by law and they [those conceived] have to be exterminated, it is better to procure abortion before sense and life are present than [to do this] when they are. Procuring abortion after they [sense and life] are present is held by law to be murder; and they sin more. For what is sanctioned[38] is marked off from what is not by [the presence of] sense and movement. Therefore Aristotle does not speak thus, according to his intention, that some of the born should be exterminated; but according to the law of peoples; nor absolutely that abortion should be procured; but if they are to be killed by some people, this is better done before sense and life, not as a good in itself but as a lesser evil.[39]

[38] The Spiazzi edition has *semen*, presumably a mistake for the word used in Moerbeke–Aristotle, *sanctum* (from *sancio*).

[39] Peter of Auvergne, *Politics*, p. 404 no. 1241: *Declarat quid faciat si excedat secundum multitudinem. Est enim intelligendum quod, cum civitas sit communitas per se sufficiens ad vitam, oportet cives per se sufficientes esse, et non pauperes; et ideo cavenda sunt ita* [? *ista*] *in civitate quae inopiam inducunt, hoc autem est multitudo filiorum debentium succedere in haereditate: magna enim et multa haereditas parentum cum dividetur in multitudinem filiorum, valde tenuis erit secundum unumquemque, maxime in tertiam vel quartam generationem, sicut ad sensum videmus. Non enim placuit Philosopho lex seu consuetudo de successione primogeniti secundum totum: tum quia cum primogeniti sint singuli, posteriores autem multi ut frequenter, sequeretur plures liberorum esse pauperes quam divites: tum quia habentes possessiones sunt partes civitatis, non habentes autem, non. Civium enim oportet esse possessiones, ut dictum est prius. Quare si posteriores geniti non succederent in aliquo parentibus, plures liberorum non contingeret esse cives, sed expelli a civitate: tum quia posterius nati, sicut et primi, possunt esse bene nati ad magna: non habentes autem unde operentur ad quae nati sunt, compelluntur accipere undecumque, insidiantes civibus et aliis per furtum, per rapinam et per homicidia, et coniungunt se adversariis, quae omnia sunt inconvenientia. Supposito ergo quod omnes succedere debeant in haereditate qualitercumque, primo proponit ad vitandam superfluam multitudinem filiorum legem seu consuetudinem quarumdam gentium. Secundo, cum dicit* Quoniam autem principium quoddam, *ponit documentum ad hoc secundum intentionem suam magis. In prima*

Moving then to 1083, Peter makes control the first of its three purposes. 'First he shows how the time deputed for generation is to be determined to avoid superfluity of children.' After stipulating beginning and end ages deputed to generation (37–70, 18–50), Peter grafts his second method onto Aristotle: 'the time in between in which they can generate ought to be determined and shortened to avoid a superfluous multitude.'[40] He envisages a male span from 37 to 55 at most, female from 18 to 37.

Both Guido and Burley use Peter and follow him in this manoeuvre, but in contrasting ways. Guido is brief and unemphatic: 'the time between, rather in between, should be restricted to avoid a superfluous multitude of children and their imperfection.'[41] Burley, however, does much more than follow. To begin with, his treatment of this section vividly exemplifies Dunbabin's acute comment that Burley's characteristic wording and format impart a novel character and greater clarity to Aristotle. 'On account of multitude' is Burley's heading, and he continues, 'This is the second particle of this part, in which he teaches how one is to take care of the multitude, so that the multitude should not be excessive.'[42] As noted earlier, this is the first appearance of *multitudo excessiva*, and 'how one should take care of the multitude' is also novel. Burley follows Peter of Auvergne, with minor alterations which may compress but also add to and accentuate him. Thus citizens born, in Peter's remarkable preamble, for great works are now born 'for great *and virtuous* works'. In addition to following Peter's extraordinary emphasis on periods of generation he gives it a further element. On 1083, '*Whereas however the beginning*: however the teachings of Aristotle on avoiding a superfluous multitude of children are two.' Here comes Burley's addition:

The first is that a man and a woman ought not to mingle together before the time deputed for generation. Thus a superfluous multitude can be better avoided. If however they mix with each other indiscriminately at any time there will be a superfluous multitude of the generated. There is a determined time for generation in a man, that is to say 37 years, in a woman

parte dicit, quod ad vitandam multitudinem puerorum superfluam, ordo id est lex vel consuetudo gentium quarumdam prohibet nullum genitorum ultra multitudinem determinatam debere reservari: oportet enim, si debeat civitas esse dives, determinatam esse multitudinem ipsorum: aliter enim depauperaretur si dimitteretur quilibet generare quantumcumque. Sed quia datum est pueros non reservari ad vitam, declarat, si necesse sit istud fieri, qualiter cum minori culpa fiet: dicens quod si aliquibus coniugatis fiant plures quam sit determinatum a lege, et necesse est eos exterminari, magis procurandum est fieri abortum antequam sensus et vita insint quam cum infuerint: procurans enim abortum postquam infuerint, homicida a lege reputatur; et magis peccant; semen [recte: *sanctum*] *et non semen* [recte: *sanctum*] *determinatur per sensum et motum. Sic igitur Aristoteles non dicit secundum intentionem suam, quod debeant exterminari aliqui nati; sed secundum legem gentium; nec quod procurandus sit abortus absolute, sed si interficiendi sunt ab aliquibus, magis faciendum est hoc ante sensum et vitam, non sicut bonum secundum se, sed sicut minus malum.*

40 Ibid., p. 404 no. 1242: *Primo declarat qualiter determinandum est tempus deputatum ad generationem, ad vitandum superfluitatem puerorum . . . oportet tempus intermedium quo possunt generare magis determinari et breviari ad superfluam multitudinem vitandam.*

41 Venice, Marciana, MS 2492, fol. 140rb: *oportet quod tempus intermedium, magis intermedium, restringatur ad vitandam superfluam multitudinem filiorum et inperfectionem ipsorum.*

42 Cambridge, University Library, MS 1741, fol. 52va: Propter multitudinem *etc* [= 1082, *Oportet enim determinatam esse multitudinem*]. *Hec est secunda particula huius partis, in qua docet quomodo est curandum de multitudine, ne sit multitudo excessiva.*

however 17 or thereabouts, for it is then that they can first generate perfectly. The end of generation in men, among the majority, is the 70th year, in women the 50th or thereabouts, and in the middle period most of them can generate perfectly. And to avoid superfluous generation of children one ought to be careful that a man and a woman do not mingle together before or after the time naturally deputed for generation.[43]

After thus placing emphasis on abstinence before marriage and, presumably, delayed marriage, Burley imitates Peter's method but goes beyond him by pulling into the bag marked 'control' yet another passage in the *Politics* which originally has no such label: Aristotle's condemnation of adultery (1085). Here, states Burley, is 'the second doctrine for avoiding superfluous multitude', condemnation of adultery.[44]

Peter's, Guido's, and Burley's treatments are in, and establish, a recognizable tradition. As one would expect, the Anonymous of Aragon's is outside this line. Its originality is all the more marked for being displayed on a theme which did not have the importance that marriage-age had for its dedicatee, the infante James, and it shows how far an active mind could be moving on this theme by *c.*1319. We have already seen the remarkable 'eugenic' attack on the desire to have many offspring with which the Anonymous rounded up his treatment of marriage-ages, concluding that 'it is better to have a few perfect and long-lived children than many imperfect and illness-prone ones'. Moving on to 1081–2, which he treats together as forming one law, he begins by re-breaking the law into two. 'In this law two things are forbidden. Firstly, the feeding of children who are deformed is forbidden. Secondly, the feeding of children who are procreated beyond a fixed number is forbidden.'[45] His treatment of the first sheds light on his reading and interests—he refers to Albert, summarizing his observations, and giving the correct reference to the *Topics*.[46] But his originality comes in two later passages, in a general preamble to the second 'law', and the setting of both themes inside a discussion of the common good.

The preamble briefly and sharply puts forward an 'economic-demographic' argument for control. 'On the second', the Anonymous writes, 'one should understand that in confined and infertile countries, where there is scarcity of food and [where] perhaps [food] cannot be brought in by importation, there ought to be the fixing of a determined number of children who are to be fed in a city, in

[43] Cambridge, University Library, MS 1741, fol. 52vb: Quoniam autem principium: *documenta autem Aristotelis ad vitandam superfluam multitudinem puerorum sunt duo. Primum est quod vir et mulier non debent comisceri adinvicem ante tempus deputatum ad generacionem. Sic enim poterit melius vitari superflua multitudo. Si enim in quocumque tempore indifferenter comisceantur adinvicem, erit superflua multitudo generatorum. Est enim viro tempus determinatum ad generacionem, scilicet 37 anni, mulieris autem 17 vel circa, tunc enim primo possunt perfecte generare. Finis autem generacionis in viris ut in pluribus est 70 annus* [sic] *vel circa, in mulieribus 50us vel circa, et tempore medio possunt perfecte generare ut in pluribus, et ad vitandam superfluam multitudinem puerorum oportet cavere ne vir et mulier ante vel post tempus deputatum secundum naturam ad generacionem comisceantur ad invicem.*

[44] Ibid., fol. 53ra.

[45] BN, MS Lat. 16133, fol. 81ra: *In ista lege duo prohibentur. Primo enim prohibetur nutricio filiorum qui orbati sunt. Secundo prohibetur nutricio filiorum qui supra stabilitum numerum procreantur.*

[46] Presumably on the basis of a correct(ed) manuscript of Albert's commentary.

order to avoid the whole multitude of inhabitants suffering lack of food on account of the multitude of those [children] who are in excess.'[47] After expounding early abortion in the usual way, the Anonymous adds selling into slavery as another method. 'The Slavs however have found another better and less cruel way, because for lack of food they sell their own born to strangers, and thus throughout Italy the word "serf" was changed to the word "schiavi" [Slavs/slaves], so that serfs are called "schiavi".'[48] Abortion leads into a general discussion of killing, and this itself to a second remarkable passage. The author begins with a cliché of thought about the relation between the common good and the individual good. 'If, however, we consider a man in relation to the common good, which is more divine and better than any individual good, certainly it is permissible to kill some individual man if his life is harmful to the common good. In fact, the life of someone can be said to be harmful to the common good in four ways.' The first is commonplace. 'One way is on account of his evil deeds which arise from his evil constitution. Such are thieves and murderers who kill in an evil way; and such men are to be killed with a death [which is] hard, as the sin demands. For in civil communication these are to be compared to the body's rotten limbs, which have to be cut off completely so that the whole body does not rot.' The conventional nature of this group makes the alignment with it of the second category all the more startling. It is an 'economic-demographic' group. 'In another way the life of someone can be harmful [to the common good], only through the consumption of necessary food, as for example [the lives of some are harmful] because they are superfluous and excessive growths. And these are in no way to be killed, but are to be cast out of the city with some portion of goods, or at least in the way of the Slavs.' The third category, the defective, is also introduced by 'on account of consumption of food', and the fourth, the decrepit and mad are also introduced by this, more strongly worded: 'on account of the very lengthy and tedious work which citizens have in feeding some whose lives are completely useless to the community'.[49] The defective were to be given cheaper food and not allowed to marry.

[47] BN, MS Lat. 16133, fol. 81ra: *Circa secundum est intelligendum quod in terris arctis et sterilibus, in quibus est penuria nutrimenti nec forte per vectionem afferri potest, determinatum numerum puerorum alendorum in civitate stabilire oportet, ne propter excrescencium multitudinem tota incolarum multitudo in cibo paciatur defectum.*

[48] Ibid.: *Sclavi autem invenerunt aliam viam meliorem et minus crudelem, quia proprios natos alienigenis vendunt propter nutrimenti defectum, et ideo in tota Ytalia nomen 'servi' translatum est ad nomen 'sclavi', it quod servi 'sclavi' dicuntur.* See C. Verlinden, 'L'origine de "sclavus" = esclave', *Bulletin Du Cange* (*Archivum Latinitatis Medii Aevi*) 17 (1943 for 1942), 97–128.

[49] BN, MS Lat. 16133, fol. 81vb: *Si autem consideramus hominem in comparacione ad bonum commune, quod est divinius et melius omni bono particulari, bene licet aliquem hominem particularem interficere, si vita eius dampnosa est bono communi. Vita vero alicuius potest esse dampnosa bono communi quadrupliciter. Uno modo propter malas eius operaciones, que procedunt ex malo habitu. Quales sunt latrones et homicide qui malo modo occidunt, et tales sunt dura morte occidendi secundum exigenciam peccati. Isti enim in communicacione civili comparantur membris putridis in corpore, que omnino sunt abscidenda ne totum corpus putrefiat. Alio modo potest esse vita alicuius nociva solum propter consumpcionem alimenti necessarii, ut quia superflui et superexcrescentes sunt, et isti nequaquam interficiendi sunt, sed cum aliqua porcione bonorum vel saltem more Sclavorum a civitate sunt abiciendi. Alio modo potest esse vita alicuius nociva propter consumpcionem alimenti, et quia propagacionem liberorum in civitate vilescant. Quales sunt*

Observing that in some places the law permits the killing of those in the last category, the Anonymous discusses the restriction of the execution of useless parents to children. He seems to be following Albert here, and he carefully notes that these things are cruel and detested in the Christian religion.

A survey of commentators from Albert to Burley shows three salient features. First is the sheer vitality simply of the notion of keeping numbers down. This found sharp semantic expression, in a progression which led to the phrases avoidance of 'multitude [becoming] excessive' and 'how one should take care about the multitude'. It also found expression in the ways discussion of control was put in an ever more general setting, something done in order to avoid poverty and consequent disorder in the city (Peter), or as a consequence of consumption of food by superfluous individuals being against the common good (Anonymous). The common good is a matter of population here, as we have seen it on the particular theme of late marriage in Chapter 12, and in Chapter 5 in discussion of the non-generating celibate. Secondly, the lenient treatment meted out to one particular method (early abortion), especially by Albert, seems remarkable. This may have signified mainly commentators' concern to present Aristotle in a benign way, rather than contemporary mores. Clearly more relevant to these is the third and most striking feature among the commentators: that all of them (apart from Albert) were at one in *adding* to Aristotle's methods of keeping numbers down. In Aristotle they had found an allusion to homosexual acts, and more direct treatment of exposure and abortion. To these they added: avoiding procreating early (Burley) or desisting from procreation after a certain number of children (Aquinas) or after a certain time (Peter), an example of expulsion (Engelbert), emigration to colonize (Aquinas) or selling excessive numbers into slavery (the Anonymous), or strict morality (avoiding procreation through adultery), 'or some other method' (Aquinas).

Rather than any special emphasis on a particular method there seems to be a dwelling on number and variety of methods, through the concern to add to those proposed by Aristotle. On one method we need to note that the commentators were, nominally, prescribing rather than describing and were hemmed in by their being (mainly) Christian theologians. This underlies their silence over sexual practices which avoid conception, to which there may be allusion and the discretion of not specifying in Thomas's 'some other method'. The largest point seems to be the blunt way in which restriction within and before marriage is added and spelled out: contracting the period of generation within marriage (Peter). And numbers being kept down by the lack of generation before marriage at the specified (later) ages: an addition by the English commentator. It is difficult not to see

orbati, sicut prius dictum est. Et tales quia propter impotenciam et organorum defectum abici possunt ut alibi vivant. Precipit lex gencium ut non reserventur in vita, sed [unreadable; should be *licitum* or equivalent] *est reservare eos et saltem vilioribus nutrire ipsos. Verumptamen ad coniugia propter dictam causam minime recipendi sunt. . . . Quarto propter valde longam et tediosam occupacionem quam habent cives in nutriendo aliquos quorum vita omnino est inutilis rei publice, et tales sunt decrepiti* [*et*] *desipientes qui iam nec opere nec consilio rei publice deservire possunt, quos in quibusdam locis permittit lex interfici.*

the general high awareness, the variety of methods, and the emphasis coming from Burley, as the type of awareness one would envisage among intellectuals living in populations, especially in north-western Europe, in which 'preventive checks' played an important role in population movements.

By *c.*1340 among the 'demographic' sections of the *Politics* some of the sharpest attention had been devoted to 'control'. Most of this development was followed three decades later by Oresme, while the historian in him produced the most extraordinary addition to the theme seen anywhere in medieval commentaries.

Oresme's text continues the semantic history of this theme, as Aristotle's idea of control and methods finds its first extant written French form. Thus Oresme introduces 1081 and the following section, as forming a separate chapter [no. 36], which has this one theme. In it Aristotle 'treats of remedies against excessive multitude of children': *traicte des remedes contre excessive multitude des enfans.*[50] *Remedes* recurs for 'methods'.

Oresme preserves and transmits much of earlier commentators' additions. In his gloss on the first part of 1081 he refers to Peter's statement (though not to Peter by name): not nourishing the deformed as diligently as others. He then cites Albert, and repeats him on Slavs, and Albert having seen that the killing of parents was practised in Poland. Then he glosses the second part of 1081, 'the multitude of procreation of children ought to be determined', not following Peter of Auvergne, but like him recalling the broader issue of poverty in the city.

For if, as is often said, *city* is a multitude of moderate quantity and the region is of certain quantity and would not suffice to feed a greatly excessive multitude, it will follow that all or a large part are poor. From this follow evils, as was said in book 2, Chapter 9. And for this reason some legislators tried in the past to provide a remedy against such multiplication, such as not nourishing the defective; and also this, as far as the others are concerned, a remedy he mentions afterwards.[51]

The last words refer to abortion in 1082, whose translation follows, and then the gloss, where Oresme seems to condemn with a sharpness which is unmatched in earlier commentators and unlike Albert's apparent indulgence.

And so some pagans once ordained that when parents had enough children, when the woman was pregnant, one would procure abortion before the fruit had life in order to avoid homicide. For in truth, the later the remedy is applied in such a matter the greater the evil—as [in the case of] those who would wait till children are born and let them die or kill them, [something which] would be very evil; as king Pharaoh did in Egypt to the children of the Jews. Item, to procure abortion when the fruit already has life is evil; but, perchance, not as evil as to kill it when it is born. And in all ways, all this is evil.[52]

[50] Oresme, *Politiques*, p. 333b.

[51] Ibid., 334a: *Car si comme dit est souvent, cité est multitude de quantité moderee et la region est de quantité certaine et ne souffiroit pas pour nourrir une multitude grandement excessive, mes convendroit que tous ou une grande partie fussent povres. Et de ce s'ensuiroient pluseurs malz, si comme il fut dit ou .ix.ᵉ chapitre du secunt. Et pour ce, aucuns legislateurs tempterent jadis a mettre remede contre tele multiplication, si comme de non nourrir les defectueus comme dit est, et oveques ce, quant as autres, un remede qu'il touche apres.*

[52] Ibid.: *Et donques aucuns paiens ordenerent jadis que quant les parens avoient assés de enfans, que apres*

The gloss continues with other 'remedies' to which we shall return. Proceeding to the translation and glossing of 1083, Oresme again follows previous commentators and Peter and (or) Burley in seeing period of generation in marriage as a 'remedy'. 'And for this purpose [keeping the multitude down], Aristotle then states another remedy';[53] the text on commencement of age and how long one should devote oneself to procreation follows immediately. Oresme quotes Albert on the period of possible generation, and then writes,

> But I am with another commentator, according to whom one ought to understand that the term [= end-point] for good generation is 55 years as far as the man is concerned, and it begins at 37, as was said before; and for the woman from 18 years. And then the time of the woman ends around 36 or 37 years. And thus there are about 18 years in which they are in good vigour to make very good generation. But in the preceding chapter 32 years or thereabouts were provided for generation. And therefore he is providing here this restriction and this remedy against too great multiplication. For if the married are together for generation only for the times stated above, their fruit will be very good and they will not be in too great multitude.[54]

Oresme follows Burley in inserting into the condemnation of adultery the good of control. 'And thus is avoided excessive multiplication of children'.[55]

Oresme goes further than any predecessor, however, in raising awareness of the theme of control and methods of control. One way in which this is done is through the format of his work, in particular its indexing and cross-referring. In the index there are two entries. One is 'Multiplication of people',[56] whose direction is spelled out in an apposed clause, 'For what reason and in what way one can bring it about that the people does not multiply excessively': *Pour quele cause et en quele maniere l'en peut faire que le peuple ne se multiplie pas excessivement.* This entry provides three references (book 2, chapters 9, 16, 22), and cross-refers to the second index-entry, 'Multitude of children', *Multitude d'enfans.* 'Multitude of children' has two sub-headings, 'How it is not good to have too great multitude of children', *Comment ce ne est pas bon d'avoir tres grande multitude d'enfans,* which refers to book 2, chapter 9, and 'Several remedies against too great multitude of children or people', *Pluseurs remedes contre trop grande multitude d'enfans ou de peuple*—note the raising to the generality of 'people'. The latter refers to the

se la femme fust grosse, l'en procurast avortement avant que le fruit eust vie pour eviter homicide. Car selon verité, tant plus tart est mis remede en tele chose tant est plus grant mal, si comme qui attendroit que les enfans fussent nays et apres les lesseroient mourir ou les occirroit, ce seroit tres grant mal; si comme fist le roy Pharaon en Egypte des filz des Hebreux. Item, procurer avortement quant le fruit a ja vie est mal; mes, par aventure, non pas tant comme le occire quant il est nay. Item, procurer tele chose avant que le fruit ait vie est moins mal. Et toutesvoies, tout ce est mal.

[53] Oresme, *Politiques, Et pour ce, Aristote met apres un autre remede.*

[54] Ibid., p. 334b: *Mes je m'acorde a un autre expositeur, selon lequel l'en doit entendre que le terme de faire tres bonne generation quant a le homme est .lv. ans, et commence a .xxxxvii. ans, comme dit est devant; et de la femme a .xviii. ans. Et donques le temps de la femme fine environ .xxxvi. ou .xxxvii. ans. Et ainsi sunt environ .xviii. ans ou il sunt en bonne vigeur pour faire tres bonne generation. Mes ou chapitre precedent estoient mis quant a generation .xxxii. ans ou environ. Et pour ce, il met ici ceste restrainte et ceste remede contre trop grande multiplication.*

[55] Ibid.: *Et donques est evitee multiplication excessive d'enfans.*

[56] Ibid., p. 364b.

section which is summarized above, book 7, chapter 36. The passages cited also cross-refer. Let us follow Oresme's index, putting the principal references together, book 2, chapter 9, and book 7, chapter 36.

Oresme's gloss on 1082 (in book 7, Ch. 36), after treating abortion and mentioning that 'Aristotle states afterwards other remedies against too great multiplication', drifts towards establishing a wider setting, either of other ways in which the multitude declines, or of the ways in which now or in past history it has contained numbers who do not reproduce.

And also [there is this]. Since the times of the pagans some women suitable for marriage have been consecrated to God's worship in perpetual virginity. And in our polity those who are in holy orders and the religious are bound to chastity. And still there are other remedies which were touched upon in chapter 22 of the second [book]. And sometimes God and nature lessen the multitude by mortalities or by wars, or they incline one part of it to go and inhabit another region.[57]

The cross-reference back to book 2 is wrong (there is nothing relevant in Ch. 20). Chapter 9, findable through the index, was probably intended. Here, Oresme begins by glossing the theme of excessive multiplication leading to poverty, and this constraining men to sedition, wickedness, conspiracy, and division with a text from Ecclesiasticus 27: 1: 'Through poverty many have sinned.' 'And to this end', he continues, 'so that the people are not so greatly multiplied that they do not have a sufficiency with which to live, it is appropriate to provide, according to philosophy, moderation and measure in this [matter] as best as one can through good laws and good ordinances.' This is immediately given a wide geographical and historical dimension: 'and in many different ways according to the difference and diversity of regions and times and conditions and the mores of peoples'.[58] There then follows a general survey of various ways of restricting the multitude—avoiding polygamy, having groups who are not married, the effects of primogeniture, emigration, introducing measure into procreation (alluded to in passing)—or encouraging the growth of the multitude. Throughout Oresme provides historical examples, drawing upon his own erudite grasp of Old Testament, classical, or early medieval history.

The gloss proceeds thus (the numbers are mine):

[A. Keeping the multitude down]. (1) And as far as this is concerned, there could be an ordinance that it would not be allowed for a man to have several women together . . . And from this—that in past time [among] some [men] each one had a very great multitude of children

[57] Ibid., p. 334a: *Et pour ce, Aristote met apres autres remedes contre trop grant multiplication. Et ovecques ce, des le temps des paiens aucunes femmes habiles a mariage estoient consacrees au divin cultivement en perpetuele virginité. Et en nostre policie ceulz qui sunt es sains ordres et les religieux sunt obligiés a tenir chasteté. Et encor sunt autres remedes qui furent touchés ou .xx.ᵉ chapitre du secunt. Et aucune foiz Dieu et nature apetissent la multitude par mortalités ou par guerres ou il enclinent une partie de elle a aler habiter en autre region.*

[58] Ibid., p. 88b: *Et pour ce, afin que le peuple ne soit pas tant multiplié que il ne ait souffisanment de quoy vivre, il convient selon philosophie mettre en ce moderation et measure au miex que l'en peut par bonnes lays et par bonnes ordenances. Et en pluseurs manieres differentes selon la difference et diversité des regions et des temps et des conditions et des meurs des gens.*

and from several women—[evils flowed, demonstrated by examples culled from the Old Testament and classical history]. (2) Item, in returning to the theme, one other way of moderating generation is for persons of some estates not being able to marry but having to be chaste, as is the case here now with those who are in holy orders and in religion [= religious orders]. Item, a very long time ago and at a period when all men could marry, among the pagans there were some women, even noble women, [who were] consecrated to the cult of the Gods, such as Apollo and Vesta, [and living] in virginity and chastity, so it appears in histories. On the other hand, (3) without placing a rule or measure in the procreation of children, one can provide otherwise against too great multiplication of people in a region, (4) as when someone ordains that the oldest should have all the inheritances and the others should go off to serve and learn trades outside the country, just as Cato says: 'Since [sons] are born to you [give them not wealth, but instruct them in skills . . .' (5) Item, or that one sends part [of the multitude] to a foreign land, armed in order to conquer the country, as the Normans were sent to France, and as, according to the *History of the Lombards*, on several occasions those from parts of the north have come into parts of the south and have conquered several countries. And for this reason the land where more people are born than the country can feed was once called *Germany*, from *germinating*. And some other remedies for this are given in the 7th book in the 36th chapter. (B) Item, sometimes, to the contrary of what has just been said, one studies and applies oneself to multiplying generation, either to populate a region, or to make a lineage grow so that it becomes stronger, or for some other, just as Our Lord said to Abraham, 'I will multiply thy seed as the stars of heaven, etc.' [Gen. 22: 17].[59]

Within its brief span this (long) gloss provides the earliest systematic account of 'population control'. Scattered fragments which existed before—whether in classical histories, the Old Testament, Paul the Deacon, histories of central medieval conquests, including the Normans, Bartholomew's *De proprietatibus rerum*—are collected and united in an account which is partly a *history*. And thus that generically higher identity which a sense of the past confers was acquired by this notion, 'control of the multitude'.

[59] Oresme, *Politiques*, pp. 88b–89a: *Et quant ad ce, une ordenance pourroit estre que il ne fust pas souffert que un homme eust ensemble pluseurs femmes . . . Et de ce que aucuns ont eu ou temps passé chescun tres grant multitude de filz et de pluseurs femmes . . . Item, en retournant a propos, une autre maniere de moderer generation est que les personnes d'aucuns estas ne puissent estre mariés, mes que ils soient chastes, si comme il est ici maintenant, de ceulz qui sunt en sains ordres et en religion. Item, tres anciennement et ou temps que tous hommes se povoient marier, estoient entre les paiens aucunes femmes et mesmement des nobles consacrees au cultivement dez diez, si comme de Appollo et de Veste, en virginité et en chasté, si comme il appert per les histoires. D'autre partie, sans mettre regle ou mesure en procreation d'enfans, l'en peut bien pourvoir autrement contre trop grande multiplication de peuple en une region, si comme qui ordeneroit que les ainsnés eussent tous les heritages et les autres iroient servir ou apprendre artifices hors du paÿs, jouste ce que dit Chatonet:* Cum tibi sint nati (Cato, *Disticha*, I. 28). *Item, ou que l'en en envoiast partie en estrange paÿs armés pour conquerir terre, si comme les Normans furent envoiés en France, et si comme selon la* Histoire des Lombards, *pluseurs foiz ceulz des parties de spetentrion* [sic] *sunt venus es parties de midi et ont conquis pluseurs paÿs* (based on Paul the Deacon, *Historia Langobardorum*, I. i, where Paul describes the greater health and suitability for propagation of the north than the south, the consequent multitudes of the north, especially Germany, and therefore their southward movements). *Et pour ce, le paÿs ou plus de gens naissent que la terre ne peut nourrir fu jadis appellé* Germanie—a germinando (see Ch. 9 above, n. 32). *Et aucuns autres remedes sunt mis a ce ou .vii.ᵉ livre ou .xxxvi.ᵉ chapitre. Item, aucuns foiz au contraire de ce que fut dit devant, l'en estudie et se efforce l'en de multiplier generacion ou pour peupler une region ou pour acroistre un lignage afin qu'il soient plus fors ou pour autre cause, jouste ce que Nostre Seigneur dist a Abraham*: Multiplicabo semen tuum sicut stellas celi, etc. (Gen. 22: 17 and 26: 4).

13.3 *Aliens*

At several points in the *Politics* size of the city and excess of multitude are brought into relation with the theme of natives or foreigners in a city, or singleness or plurality of peoples. The first of the three passages is in book 2: 'concerning the magnitude of the city, however, that is to say how much and whether it is expedient for it to have one people [*gens*] or several, [these are questions from which] the statesman ought not to shrink'.[60] The second and third are parts of the discussion of optimum size in book 7, and Aristotle's criticism of the notion that one should value a city in terms of its multitude. Even if one does do this, one should not do it 'according to the contingent multitude, for it is perhaps necessary for a number of many servants [or slaves] and aliens and foreigners to live in a city'.[61] After developing the theme of problems of size in various directions—including the difficulty of ruling large multitudes by law—Aristotle's concluding point on the problems of a city of many men brings him back to this point again. 'However it is easy for foreigners and aliens to transform the polity; for with an excess of multitude it is not difficult [for them] to hide.'[62]

Peter of Auvergne took up and expanded the question of one people or several peoples, preferring one people, whose singleness of custom and constitution leads to peace among citizens, whereas 'cities which have been constituted out of various peoples have been destroyed because of the dissensions they had, brought about by diversity of customs; for one part would ally itself with enemies through hatred of another part.'[63] He glossed the second passage in a way which makes immigration clear—'a multitude of servants and a certain [multitude] of foreigners and aliens flowing into it [the city]'. He continues: 'These are not *per se* part of the city.'[64] These provided a platform for the third passage, which had already been underlined in Albert's literal gloss, which makes it clear who is leading to excess: '*for foreigners and aliens*, who, that is to say, are bringing about excess of multitude in the city, *easy*, supply it is [easy] *to take over the polity*, which is extremely bad and especially to be avoided'.[65] Peter of Auvergne now provides a specific exemplification, and expands. 'He proves this . . . thus. There happen to be many strangers and aliens and others who do not love the state in a city [which is already] of superabundant multitude. It is easy for foreigners and aliens and those who do not love the state to transform it, because of their multitude. Because of the excess of multitude it is not difficult [for them] to hide their plotting.'

[60] 1276a33–4; Su p. 160 ll. 1–2; Sp no. 230(6).

[61] 1326a18–20; Su p. 259 ll. 2–3; Sp no. 943.

[62] 1326b20–22; Su p. 262 ll. 4–6; Sp no. 951.

[63] *The Commentary of Peter of Auvergne on Aristotle's Politics. The inedited part: Book III, less i–vi*, ed. G. M. Grech (Rome, 1967), p. 91: *civitates quae constitutae sunt ex diversis gentibus propter dissensiones quas habuerunt propter diversitatem morum plures destructae sunt, quia una pars adiungebant* [sic] *se inimicis propter odium alterius.* This also appears in Thomas's commentary, in the Spiazzi edition, but not in the Leonine edition.

[64] Peter of Auvergne, *Politics*, p. 353 no. 1092: *quaedam multitudo servorum et quaedam advenarum et extraneorum confluentium ad ipsam. Tales autem non sunt per se pars civitatis.*

[65] Albert, *Politics*, p. 651p: Adhuc autem extraneis et advenis, *qui scilicet excessum faciunt multitudinis in civitate*, facile, *supple, est*, transumere politiam, *quod maximum damnum est, et maxime cavendum.*

He proceeds then to generalize this in support of Aristotle's general proposition about size. 'Those doing evil are more hidden in a larger multitude than a smaller one. This is bad for the city and against its nature. Therefore it is bad and against the nature of a city for it to be of superabundant multitude.'[66]

A populous city growing yet more populous, many resident and inflowing 'aliens', their 'machination': this may have fitted several cities and people's views of various alien groups. The case of Florence is discussed in Chapter 14 below. Here only one case is considered: the appeal of the combination of these elements to a commentator writing in Paris in the closing years of the thirteenth century. The 'scholarly guesses' at Paris's population around 1180 may be 60,000 or more; around 1250 100,000 or considerably more. Jordan's is the most recent general discussion of the demographic picture of the major group of aliens in Paris, Jews. A large influx in the second half of the twelfth century lies behind his first picture, from Philip Augustus's reign, of a very high ratio in the Île-de-la-Cité of about 1:5 (probably about 1000 Jews to about 5000 Christians), descending to a percentage in Paris as a whole of between 3% and 5%. In his second picture, around 1300, when a guess of about 70,000 is given for Jews in royal France as a whole, there is an Île-de-France and a Paris where Jews' demographic profile is dominated by movement. Harsh treatment in England from the mid-thirteenth century and various expulsions—from Gascony in 1288, Anjou in 1289, England in 1290—produced immigrations. Jews went from Gascony in various directions, including Poitou to the north; from Anjou towards the Île-de-France; from England a thousand (or more) to France, mainly Paris, which may also have had immigrants from Nevers. Despite this, the net number of Jewish residences in Paris was declining in the 1290s.[67]

There had long been extant written comment on Jewish immigration to Paris and their large numbers: not surprisingly, exaggerated comment. Philip Augustus's biographer Rigord had written that an 'extremely large multitude of Jews lived in *Francia* (northern France or the Île-de-France), having come there a long time before from many parts of the world', and they had settled in Paris. In his hostile eyes through their numbers and wealth 'they had taken over almost half the city'.[68] Rigord's account remained well-known—this part was copied into the historical volume of Vincent of Beauvais' encyclopaedia, slightly adapted. The extremely large multitude of Jews were living in *Paris* (rather than more broadly

[66] Peter of Auvergne, *Politics*, p. 355 no. 1100: *Probat idem . . . sic. In civitate superabundantis multitudinis contingit esse multos extraneos et advenas et alios non diligentes rempublicam. Extraneis autem et advenis et non diligentibus rempublicam facile est rempublicam transmutare propter multitudinem ipsorum. Non enim difficile est latere eorum machinationem propter excessum multitudinis. Magis enim latent male operantes in maiori multitudine quam minori. Hoc autem est malum civitati et contra naturam eius: ergo malum et contra naturam civitatis est ipsam esse superabundantis multitudinis.*

[67] W. C. Jordan, *The French Monarchy and the Jews: from Philip Augustus to the last Capetians* (Philadelphia, 1989), pp. 8–10, 113–14, 153–4, and 182–4.

[68] *Oeuvres de Rigord et de Guillaume le Breton, historiens de Philippe-Auguste*, ed. H. F. Delaborde, Société de l'Histoire de France, 2 vols. (Paris, 1882–5), i. 24: *multitudo maxima Judeorum in Francia habitabat, que a longis retroactis temporibus de diversis mundi partibus . . . ibi convenerat. . . . in tantum ditati sunt, quod fere medietatem totius civitatis sibi vendicaverant.*

in *Francia*).[69] Peter of Auvergne does not mention Jews specifically. Juxtapose, however, the two. On the one hand there was the presence of large but fluctuating numbers of Jews in Paris, immigrations, a tradition of exaggerated comment on their numbers and 'taking-over', their alien nature and accounts of their plots, and a sense of Paris as a city of 'superabundant multitude' in the late thirteenth century; and on the other hand Peter of Auvergne's sharp exemplification of Aristotle, and his particular emphasis on the large numbers of both (city population overall and alien sub-population), immigration of aliens, and their plotting (*machinatio*). It seems very likely that Peter has Paris Jews in mind. What remains delicate and difficult to discern is what Aristotle's text is doing to shape Peter's ideas and, conversely, how his pre-existing ideas are shaping his commentary.

Also suggestive is a quodlibetic question raised in the theology faculty by the Cistercian Jacques de Thérines. 'Should Jews expelled from one region be expelled from another [presumably the one into which they migrated]?'[70] This was in Paris at Christmas 1306. Jews expelled from Gascony in 1288, England in 1290, and, as we have seen, from France in August 1306 will have become refugees elsewhere: a problem for local authorities.[71] In the quodlibet (providing con and pro in standard fashion), Jacques's arguments con were the standard theological ones for preserving Jews. Now, Jacques's quodlibets *elsewhere* parade a wide range of explicit references to the *Politics*, including book 7. Although there is no such explicitness here in his brief pro argument, its shadow seems present. The argument goes as follows. 'It is to be understood, however, that they can multiply so much in some kingdom, and league together, and so seriously harm Christians and molest them, that they can for a time be expelled from some kingdom . . .' The emphasis on increasing numbers, 'leaguing together' (*confoederari*, also translatable as *to plot together*) and harming, has clear parallels both with the *Politics* and Peter's commentary, but these are only parallels, and there is no direct evidence of quotation from the *Politics* at this point. The suggestion has to remain tentative. The suggestion is that two Parisian texts from just before and just after 1300, Peter's and Jacques's, may show the *Politics* acting to systematize a cluster of thoughts which relate continuing growth and superabundance of city multitude and (perceived) large multitude of one part of this, a multitude of aliens—in Paris, a multitude of Jews—as a problem. If so, this should be set beside another development in Paris university which was happening in these years. This was the remarkable attempt of one (or perhaps two) northern masters to provide 'natural' (that is, according to medicine and natural philosophy) definitions of a Jew which showed how their 'social', psychological, and moral defects—timidity,

[69] Vincent, *Speculum historiale*, XXIX. xxv; 1194. See above, Ch. 9, pp. 226–7, on a view of Jews in Alsace: few in 1200 and (by implication) many in 1290. See hostile comment earlier, in the mid-eleventh century, on 'a considerable multitude' of Jews (*non modica multitudo*) living in the royal city of Orleans, Rodulfus Glaber, *Historiarum libri quinque*, III. vii; ed. N. Bulst, Oxford Medieval Texts (Oxford, 1989), p. 134.

[70] Jacques de Thérines, Quodlibet, I. xiv, in Jacques de Thérines, *Quodlibets I et II* and Jean Lesage, *Quodlibet I*; ed. P. Glorieux, Textes Philosophiques du Moyen Âge 7 (Paris, 1958), pp. 157–9.

[71] J. R. Strayer, *The Reign of Philip the Fair* (Princeton, 1980), pp. 148 and 235.

fleeing from society—flowed from their physical make-up, and the predominance in this of 'melancholy'.[72] There is nothing conjectural in the fact of this Arts faculty quodlibet, and its mobilization of Greek and Arabic natural philosophy and medicine to co-ordinate this 'natural' view of Jews. A mobilization of classical moral philosophy to co-ordinate 'populationist' views of a minority, the Jews, *may* have paralleled this, making the two, a 'populationist' as well as a 'scientific' approach to Jews, the academic contribution of Paris university to the development of thought about Jews at this period.

The theme of a minority in the population is presented here as a coda to our account of the *Politics* and 'demographic' thought: a small and speculative example. What it exemplifies is the intertwining around 1300 of several things: the realities of population, a sense of an excess of numbers, the inheritance of much earlier thought about the multitude (in this instance the multitude of aliens in it), and the various new thoughts about the multitude which had been flowing for thirty years or so from the Latin text of the *Politics*.

[72] P. Biller, 'A "scientific" view of Jews from Paris around 1300', forthcoming in *Gli Ebrei e le scienze nel Medio Evo e nella prima età moderna* in *Micrologus*.

Part 4

THE LIGHT OF COMMON DAY

14

THE BULGING CIRCUIT[1] OF FLORENCE

In 1288 a beginning was made to the new and third circuit of walls of the city of Florence. Planned four years earlier and completed fifty years later, the new walls enclosed 1,556 acres, nearly eight times the 197 acres enclosed by the earlier set of walls, which had been started in 1172.[2] The new walls expressed in stone two things. One was the past history of Florence's inhabitants between these dates, bulging inside and then breaking through the perimeter. The other was the view taken by Florentine planners, when deciding on the new perimeter, about likely expansion in the coming decades. On 28 November, there was a great ceremonious and public occasion, the blessing and laying in place of the first stone. Officiating were the bishops of Florence, Fiesole, and Pistoia, and there were in attendance all the prelates and religious of Florence, and all the Lords and higher ranks. The Florentine layman whose chronicle records this, Giovanni Villani, also adds that the audience included *popolo innumerabile*, 'countless ordinary people'.[3]

An extraordinary proportion of what was being thought at that time is lost: both the impressions and chat of the ordinary people of either sex who thronged around the blessing of the stone in 1284, and the inner reflective lives of the women whose marriages and bodies had supplied the babies.[4] So far this book has largely ignored high-ranking laymen and completely ignored all ordinary people and women of any rank, addressing only the thought of a tiny minority, clerical and male, simply because that is what survives. There is a little more that we can do about the thoughts of lay*men* in one particular case: Florence. We can look at laymen in the street in one case, a literate and sharply practical layman in another (Villani), and finally a very exceptional layman, the poet Dante. In this final chapter we shall look at these three examples. We shall still hear a lot about the views of

[1] *Circuit* here translates *cerchio* or *cerchia*, in this context an encircling wall.

[2] D. Waley, *The Italian City-Republics*, 2nd edn. (London, 1978), p. 17: from 80 to 620 hectares; see the map of the walls on p. 16.

[3] Villani, *Cronica*, VIII. xcix; i. 562. I am using Giuseppe Porta's 1990–91 edition of Villani, in which books 1 (chs. 1–37) and 2 (chs. 1–24) constitute what used to be book 1 (chs. 1–61) in earlier editions, with the consequence that the later Books in Porta's edition have a number which is one higher, e.g. Porta edition book 8 ch. 99 = older edition book 7 ch. 99.

[4] See the language of P. Brown, *The Body and Society: Men, Women and Sexual Renunciation in Early Christianity* (London, 1989), p. 99.

the religious, but here they will be treated as sources of, and subordinate to, the ideas of laymen.

Beyond common human experience, what 'vital' facts impressed themselves distinctively upon Florentine minds? The most obvious is what lay behind the event with which we started: theirs was a city subject to expansion in numbers from immigration, a city which planned and built a wider circuit of walls to encompass anticipated expansion of population. Precisely how norms or changes in other demographic areas, such as life-expectancy, or marriage-patterns, came over to Florentine eyes is not usually clear, although we shall soon be looking at some probabilities which are hinted at in the sermons which the Dominican Giordano of Pisa delivered to Florentines. Parents both in Florence itself and in the surrounding *contado* brought in their babies to be christened in the Baptistry, and there, as we saw in Chapter 4, the rector put down a black bean whenever he baptised a boy and a white bean when he baptised a girl. It is not clear when this started, but, by the time of Villani's mention of this in his account of Florence in 1338, the rector counted annually and had been doing this for a sufficient number of years to suggest annual variations within a certain range of numbers. Even if the precise figures were not widely known, the dramatic act of placing black and white beans in different groups for the purposes of counting would have familiarized reasonably bright parents with the notion of sex-ratio.

If we assume that basic demographic patterns usually change only very slowly, and that much of the Tuscany that was revealed in the *catasto* of 1427 can be read backwards, girls will have been getting married for the first time in their early to mid-teens, allying themselves to much older men. In middling and higher ranks marriage-brokers, called *sensali*,[5] will have mediated the haggling between families about dowries, in a way which will have made many people think of marriage as a market in which calculations took into account supplies of either sex and their ages. The disparity of age between girls and the older men they married will have made a married couple think about the husband's likely earlier death and the girl's likely middling years as a widow, and a sizeable proportion of women among the city's inhabitants who were already widows will have been a standing reminder of this. The men who dreamed of spending decades making their fortunes in northern Europe and returning to Florence to retire and enjoy themselves may have preferred not to think about life-span, as we shall see. Then there were the sober calculations of the administrators: leaders and officials who were concerned with war thinking about numbers of men in Florence and its *contado* who were technically of arms-bearing age, between 15 and 70; the same men, when concerned with taxation, thinking about men and property; and the same men again, when planning the buying and importation of grain, especially during periods of scarcity, thinking about the numbers of mouths that had to be fed in Florence. Finally, 'vital' facts from further afield entered Florence, whose international networks of companies

[5] On the Florentine *sensale*, see C. Klapisch-Zuber, *Women, Family and Ritual in Renaissance Florence*, trans. L. Cochrane (Chicago and London, 1985), p. 183.

and mendicant convents made it an extraordinarily good centre for news, as we shall see when we look at the geographical span of Villani's demographic data.

If these kinds of fact were matters of observation, assimilation, and reflection in the minds of Florentines, we need to think about the education of these particular minds. The statistics provided by Villani about elementary education in Florence in 1338—8,000 to 10,000 boys and girls learning to read, 1,000 to 1,200 learning the abacus and algorism, 550 to 600 learning grammar and logic[6]—are famous, but there is a frustrating lack of evidence with which to verify them and to assess their character. Giordano of Pisa may help us here. In sermons delivered in Florence (which we shall be looking at in more detail below), he implied much about those were listening to him. Books feature often, and 'reading' (*leggere*) as well as going to sermons is an act of piety.[7] Giordano likes numbers, and, when he uses lines in geometry, or the formula of three and one seventh (π), he is selecting these as the similes which he thinks will most effectively illustrate in the minds of lay Florentines the theological truths or moral exhortation which he wants to convey.[8] Giordano's assumptions about his audience's education are all the more telling because of their casualness.

We are reminded here of the general background, the growth in lay literacy in the twelfth and thirteenth centuries, and the development among many people in the same period of a numerate outlook, phenomena which have been illuminated by Michael Clanchy and Alexander Murray.[9] We are also reminded that when we look for high or low levels of the application of numbers to people, it is in Italian milieux that it is easy to find good examples. For instance, we can turn to treatises written by French, German, or Italian inquisitors, and look at the treatment of the size of heretical groups, which was a matter of both practical and theologico-polemical concern. A treatise from south-eastern Germany *c.*1266 contains the categories 'few' or 'many', whereas a treatise of a former Cathar and later Dominican, who came from Piacenza, contains a formidable array of precise numbers of different Cathar groups, variation in numbers through time, and an overall estimate of the numbers of Cathars in 1250: a unique exercise in inquisitorial literature of this period.[10] Counter-examples could easily be given—I am not aware of

[6] Villani, *Cronica*, XII. xciv; iii. 198.

[7] Giordano da Pisa, *Quaresimale fiorentino 1305–1306*, ed. C. Delcorno (Florence, 1974), pp. 84 and 222; *Prediche del beato F. Giordano da Rivalto dell'Ordine dei Predicatori recitate in Firenze dal MCCCIII al MCCCVI*, ed. D. Moreni, 2 vols. (Florence, 1831), ii. 220. Other editions of Giordano used in this chapter: Giordano of Pisa, *Prediche del beato F. Giordano da Rivalto dell' Ordine de' Predicatori*, ed. D. M. Manni (Florence, 1739); *Prediche sulla Genesi recitate in Firenze nel M. CCC. IV. Del Beato F. Giordano da Rivalto dell' Ordine dei Predicatori*, ed. D. Moreni (Florence, 1830); *Prediche inedite del B. Giordano da Rivalto dell' Ordine de' Predicatori recitate in Firenze dal 1302 al 1305*, ed. E. Narducci (Bologna, 1860). On the printed editions, see C. Delcorno, *L'exemplum nella predicazione volgare di Giordano di Pisa*, Istituto Veneto di Scienze, Lettere ed Arti, Memorie, Classe di Scienze Morali, Lettere ed Arti 36, fasc. 1 (Venice, 1972), pp. 9–10 n. 16.

[8] Giordano, ed. Manni, p. 38; Giordano, *Quaresimale*, p. 328.

[9] M. T. Clanchy, *From Memory to Written Record: England 1066–1307*, 2nd edn. (Oxford and Cambridge, Mass., 1993); A. V. Murray, *Reason and Society in the Middle Ages* (Oxford, 1978), chs. 7–8.

[10] See below and nn. 50–1.

a distinctly Italian input into the decisions by the Strasbourg and Naples general-chapters of the Franciscans to compile statistics of the Order[11]—but my impression is of readier Italian numeracy at this level.

At a higher level of mathematics, only one example occurs, but it is a very striking one, a new development in mathematics itself concerning the application of number to population, in this case animal population. Again, it is Italian. Leonardo of Pisa's *Liber Abaci* (written in 1202 and revised in 1228) goes over many mathematical problems which are applied to practical questions in contemporary life. Many of these deal with merchants' lives, trade and the exchange of different currencies, but there is also one problem which shows the application of number to a 'vital' theme, length of life. How long has a man lived if, after doubling his age and adding one-twelfth of this and one year, he has lived to one hundred?[12] In the midst of such briefly stated arithmetical problems comes the innovation in mathematical thought, in the—subsequently—famous rabbits problem. How many rabbits will you have at the end of a year if you begin with one pair, who produce two each month, who in turn . . .?[13] It can be put in other words. What is the formula for unlimited regular population expansion, when one leaves out mortality? Thought up in a crowded Italian city, this is a development of which one could easily make too much—but also too little, for Leonardo's text indicates wider natural experimental rather than just mathematical interest in the problem. He writes that someone, *quidam*, had put a pair of rabbits into a place enclosed by walls to see how many pairs would be produced in one year.[14] Unfortunately no more details are given—and in the present undeveloped state of scholarship on Leonardo one cannot totally exclude the possibility of a literary rather than contemporary source for this experiment. My suggestion, then, is that quite a few bright laymen in Italian cities will have brought ready numeracy to bear upon whatever population facts came into their minds.

What *ideas* were circulating in Florence in the decades around 1300—ideas, that is, which would have encouraged generalizing thought about 'vital' data and population? My tactic in answering this is, first of all, to take the considerable modern scholarship on Florentine culture in the decades around 1300 and look at its general statements, and then, in relation to each general statement, to ask 'What does this mean for "demographic" thought?' Thus, for example, a painstakingly compiled list of books known to have been in the Franciscan convent around 1300 has been taken as a guide to texts which were available to preachers and teachers at Santa Croce, and which were thus, through such Franciscans' use of this material, second-hand sources of Florentine laymen's ideas. Where this

[11] For these figures, see G. Golubovich, 'Series provinciarum O.F.M. saec. XIII–XIV', *Archivum franciscanum historicum* 1 (1908), 1–22 (pp. 19–20).

[12] Leonardo of Pisa [Fibonacci], *Liber Abaci*, ed. B. Boncompagni, *Scritti di Leonardo Pisano*, 2 vols. (Rome, 1857), i. 177. On Leonardo (d. after 1240), see K. Vogel, 'Fibonacci, Leonardo', *DSB* iv. 604–13 (pp. 606–7 on the rabbit problem); M. Muccillo, 'Fibonacci', *DBI* xlvii. 359–63.

[13] Leonardo, *Liber Abaci*, i. 283–4.

[14] *Quidam posuit unum par cuniculorum in quodam loco, qui erat undique pariete circundatus, ut sciret, quot ex eo paria germinarentur in uno anno.*

point is made about ideas in general, my question will be what 'demographic' concepts were contained in such books.

George Holmes has argued that we need to delete from our minds the later Florentine glories of the Renaissance when we turn back to 1300, when Florence in his view was markedly provincial and removed from the centres of thought. Looking at 'lay culture', he passed in review the elementary education of merchants, and the education of notaries in composition and Latin rhetoric, and when discussing its further sources he emphasized popularizing, vernacular, encyclopaedic works, in particular Brunetto Latini's, and the theme of interchange between Bologna and Florence. Juxtaposed with 'lay culture' was 'scholastic culture', trickling into Florence through several figures who had studied in Paris and who taught and preached at the Dominican and Franciscan convents of Santa Maria Novella and Santa Croce.[15] I am accepting this view and putting the question to each statement. In the following pages I catalogue the results, first of all what we find in the vernacular didactic works, secondly in the 'Bologna connection', and thirdly in the books and writings of the friars at Santa Maria Novella and Santa Croce.

14.1 *Vernacular books*

Among works in the first category examined here there is no question about the relevance of one, *Li Livres dou Tresor*, written by the author who, in Villani's words, 'began the process of civilizing the Florentines', Brunetto Latini.[16] I am also including a natural-philosophical encyclopaedia, intended for a vernacular-reading audience, by Restoro of Arezzo (1282),[17] the representation and elaboration of Aristotelian moral philosophy in Giles of Rome's treatise *De regimine principum*, which was available in an Italian version by 1288, *Del reggimento de' principi*,[18]

[15] G. Holmes, 'The Emergence of an Urban Ideology in Florence *c*.1250–1450', *TRHS*, 5th ser., 23 (1973), 111–34; *Florence, Rome and the Origins of the Renaissance* (Oxford, 1986), ch. 4. The foundations of this view were laid down by Grabmann and Minio-Paluello, and have been built on by Davis, Holmes, and d'Avray. See id. 'Remigio Girolami's *De bono communi*: Florence at the time of Dante's Banishment and the Philosopher's Answer to the Crisis', *Italian Studies* 11 (1956), 56–71 (see the references to Grabmann's works on p. 70); id., 'Dante's Reading of Aristotle', in *The World of Dante: Essays on Dante and His Times*, ed. C. Grayson (Oxford, 1980), pp. 66–7 and 71–2; C. T. Davis, 'Education in Dante's Florence' and 'An Early Florentine Political Theorist: Fra Remigio de' Girolami', reprinted in his *Dante's Italy and Other Essays* (Philadelphia, 1984), pp. 137–65 and 198–223; d'Avray, *Preaching of the Friars*, pp. 156–60.

[16] Villani, *Cronica*, IX. x; ii. 28. The edition of *Li Livres dou Tresor de Brunetto Latini* by F. J. Carmody (Berkeley and Los Angeles, 1948) underestimates the amount of Aristotle transmitted by Latini. For example, I. ccxx. 3 (p. 108, l. 15) comes from the *Physics*, book 1, 192b20–3; see the passage also in the later *Auctoritates Aristotelis*, p. 144 no. 50.

[17] *La Composizione del Mondo di Ristoro d'Arezzo: Testo Italiano del 1282*, ed. E. Narducci (Rome, 1859). Restoro d'Arezzo, *La Composizione del Mondo colle sue cascioni*, ed. A. Morino (Florence, 1976); see pp. xx–xxi on the Narducci edition.

[18] *Del reggimento de' principi di Egidio Romano volgarizzamento trascritto nel MCCLXXXVIII*, ed. F. Corazzini (Florence, 1858); see C. F. Briggs, *Giles of Rome's De regimine principum: Reading and Writing Politics at Court and University, c.1275–c.1525* (Cambridge, 1999), p. 13 n. 15, on another early Italian translation; *Li Livres du Gouvernement des Rois: A XIIIth Century French Version of Egidio Colonna's*

Hayton's *La Flor des Estoires de la Terre d'Orient*, and Marco Polo's *Divisament dou Monde*. Although there is less certainty about their specifically Florentine (as opposed to Tuscan or Italian) relevance, Giles's and Restoro's works were known and used by one Florentine layman, Dante,[19] and Hayton's and Polo's by another, Villani. What were the principal observations or generalizing propositions about 'vital' facts or population themes which were put over in these simplifying and vernacular works?

Li Livres dou Tresor, which Latini brought to Florence in 1266, provides a geography which transmits a view of this world as divided into habited and uninhabited, and the further notion of degrees of populousness, in this case of cities: cities in India are described as *bien peuplees*.[20] There is no special emphasis on these commonplaces. Latini does not omit entirely, nor does he underline, the 'wonders' (*mirabilia*) so favoured by his geographical source, Solinus. He includes some marvels of early gestation and brevity of life. This sort of material, which was present in other encyclopaedic works, perhaps in part catered for some people's taste for a cross between *Tales of the Fantastic* and the *Guinness Book of Records*—if so, it may tell one little about what was in the minds of others who were of more sober outlook. More significant is this, that the most obvious addition by Latini to his source is a piece of well-conceived population history. Where Britain may once have been uninhabited, Latini introduces the suggestion that this changed after population increase led to immigration: *Et por ce jadis i fu la fins des terres habitees, jus c'a tant que les gens crurent et multipliierent et k'il passerent en un ille ki est en mer . . . la grant Bretaigne.*[21]

There is no special emphasis in Latini's Old Testament history, which includes the longevity of the patriarchs, and a comment on Sarah's great age when bearing a child.[22] On the theme of marriage, Latini conveys the theological history we examined in Chapters 2 and 5 above—marriage as a precept in the old law, virginity praised in the new law—but without the usual population context of this history, namely variation in accord with a scarcity or sufficiency of people. When he is transmitting material from Guillaume Peyraut's *De vitiis et virtutibus*, however, there is more of interest. After emphasizing the procreative purpose of marriage, Latini goes on to underline the ideal of parity between those marrying. They should be equal both in lineage and age: *k'il se marie a son pareil de linage de cors et d'aage.*[23]

Treatise De Regimine Principum, ed. S. P. Molenaer (New York and London, 1899)—see p. xxvi on the translator.

[19] E. Moore, 'Appendix on Dante and Ristoro d'Arezzo', in his *Studies in Dante: Second Series* (Oxford, 1899), pp. 358–72; Minio-Paluello, 'Dante's Reading of Aristotle', pp. 59–80 (p. 69): 'Some remarkable coincidences point to Giles of Rome's *De Regimine Principum* as Dante's source of knowledge for the *Politics*.'

[20] *Tresor*, I. cxx; p. 113. [21] Ibid., I. cxxiii; p. 118.

[22] Ibid., I. xx, xxi, xl, and xxv; pp. 32–3, 34, 47, and 36. Villani commented on Sarah's age and her therefore supernatural conception, *Cronica*, XII. ii (iii. 18), and on Queen Constance conceiving when over 52, when this is almost impossible, *Cronica*, VI. xvi (i. 246): *in età di lei di più di cinquantadue anni, ch'è quasi impossibile a natura di femmina a portare figliuolo.*

[23] *Tresor*, II. lxxvii; p. 256.

Restoro d'Arezzo's treatise again provides an account of the *disposizione della terra*, part inhabited, part uninhabited, but more systematically than in *Li Livres dou Tresor*.[24] It pays attention to natural death and life-span, a *tempo e vita diterminata* in every animal, *lxx anni per natura, è piu e meno* in man. Averroes is cited on the terminus of growth at the age of 35; greater life-span is explained by *buona complessione* as well as good care.[25] There is astrology. Higher bodies are connected with epidemics and plagues, and Restoro conveys very powerfully the sense of revolutionary changes in regions over long periods of time, from city to forest, forest to city.[26]

Giles of Rome's treatise transmits some of the 'demographic' material in Aristotle's *Politics* which we saw in Chapter 11 above. There is political 'demography'—comparing the utility of many or few among the rich, the *gente di mezzo*, and the poor.[27] There is the theme of marriage-systems—a comparison of monogamy with polygamy, where Giles adds a reference to Saracens and other religions. There is the proposition that polyandry led to sterility or lesser fertility, based on the observation that prostitutes are more sterile than other women.[28] Prominent, as we saw in the previous chapter, was Giles's attention to marriage-age. Giles had pointed out four dangers of low age at marriage in his Latin text—the generation of imperfect children, inclining women to intemperance, the physical danger to women when giving birth at too young an age, and enfeeblement through men engaging in sexual relations too early—and here the conclusion was coming over in the vernacular. A man should not take a wife *essendo nel tempo di troppa giovinezza, ned infino che l'uno e l'altro, cioè la moglie e 'l marito, non sono in tempo convenevole.* Giles held up specific ages. *E dovemo sapere che a la femmina conviene avere diciotto anni e all'uomo ventuno, innanzi ch'ellino sieno in congiungimento naturale.*[29] Here, by omissions, something very different from Aristotle's 18 and 37 was achieved, an ideal of *tempo convenevole* in which there was a very small gap between the sexes. In both Giles's and Latini's didactic vernacular texts, then, there was attention to marriage-age, with the ideal of parity in ages upheld in Latini, and in Giles the notion of a 'suitable age' in both sexes and opposition to a low age.

With Marco Polo's *Divisament dou Monde* and Hayton's *La Flor des Estoires de la Terre d'Orient*, which was written for Clement V in 1307, we can be briefer, noting their Florentine readership, and the fact that they conveyed the material described in parts 3–4 of Chapter 9 above. Hayton transmitted a military-population survey of the near east, with a view to recovery of the Holy Land, and both his and Marco Polo's texts described the peopling of Asia. While both dwelt

[24] *Composizione del Mondo*, I. xx, xxiii, II. i. 3, and II. viii. 12. 1; ed. Morino, pp. 29–35, 37–48, 52–4, and 212–14.

[25] Ibid., I. xxii; ed. Narducci, pp. 23–4 and 193. This section is less developed in the manuscript followed by Morino, which lacks the references to Averroes and good complexion—*quegli che vivono più, cio è per la buona complessione ch'elli hanno.*

[26] Ibid., II. vii. 4; ed. Morino, pp. 183–90.

[27] *Del Reggimento de' principi*, III. ii. 30; pp. 276–7.

[28] Ibid., II. i. 7; p. 137.

[29] Ibid., II. i. 13; pp. 146–7.

on the vast size of Cathay, Polo was more statistical while Hayton was more impressionist, giving Beijing, for example, no numbers, and simply saying that it was larger than Rome.

14.2 *Florence and other cities*

'We must allow for a considerable intellectual interchange between Florence and the university of Bologna',[30] whose law and medicine were famous. Law I am postponing until we look at Santa Croce's books. Only Montpellier in this period rivalled Bologna in medicine. Taddeo Alderotti led a glittering circle of academic doctors in Bologna in the late thirteenth and early fourteenth centuries, men whose interests mingled medicine and Aristotle's moral philosophy. Florentine contacts begin with Alderotti, who came from Florence and married a Florentine, and they continue with the links or Florentine origin of some of Alderotti's pupils, and the fame of Alderotti and Dino del Garbo, which impressed their names into the writings of both Dante and Villani.[31] The significance of the doctors? We have seen in Chapter 10 the 'demographic' commonplaces of the standard textbooks of a doctor's training, for example, in Avicenna's *Canon* the ages of men, regional variation of human life-span, and many aspects of human reproduction, fertility, sterility, and avoidance of conception. In addition to the *Canon*, which was much studied and taught in Bologna, there are the emphases of the works of the Bolognese doctors themselves. In the *expositiones* of Alderotti, for example, we find a 'question' which refers to *Length and Shortness of Life* and debates Aristotle's opinion about regional variation in life-span, and elsewhere a lengthy treatment of the ages of man.[32]

Bartholomew of Parma was Lecturer in astronomy in Bologna in 1297.[33] 'Vital' facts are considered in his works, as in those of other astrologers, not just in relation to particulars—an individual, at a certain time—but also in relation to longer periods of time, and groups or sub-groups of people. Thus Bartholomew envisages considerable illness and mortality among men in general, or within sub-groups: among *young* men and women; or among a particular social group, men of 'low and servile condition, such as workers and peasants' (*villis et servilis conditionis, ut artificum et rusticorum*), or in the 'common people' (*vulgo)*; or a high incidence of miscarriages.[34] This suggests that the conceptualizations of

[30] Holmes, *Florence, Rome*, p. 86.

[31] Siraisi, *Taddeo*, 28–9, 28 n. 13, 40 and n. 76, 41 and n. 80, 56, 57, 58, 60, 64, 78–9 and n. 23.

[32] Taddeo Alderotti, *Expositiones in arduum aphorismorum* (Venice, 1527), 368v–9r and 375r.

[33] E. Narducci, 'Intorno al "Tractatus Sphaerae" di Bartolomeo da Parma astronomo del secolo XIII e ad altri scritti del medesimo autore', in *Bullettino di bibliografia e di storia delle scienze matematiche e fisiche*, ed. B. Boncompagni, 17 (1884), 1. See B. Nardi, 'Bartolomeo da Parma', *DBI* vi. 747–50.

[34] Narducci, 200–2. More could be said on the contribution of astrology to Italian thought at this period. Dante and Villani both mentioned Guido Bonatti (*Inferno*, XX. 118, and *Cronica*, VIII. lxxxi; i. 536), while Villani described Cecco d'Ascoli being executed by an inquisitor for astrology and necromancy (Cronica, XI. xli and xlii; ii. 570 and 572). Bonatti's *Liber astronomicus* diffused the notion of generalizing about regional illness and mortality, e.g. IV. xi: *De Saturno in ascendente . . . hora revolutionis*

astrological works, already briefly encountered in Restoro, may have disseminated generalizing and analytic habits of thought about 'vital' data.

'Florence–Bologna' is undoubtedly too narrow—it omits, for example, enquiry into possible influences from north-eastern Italy. Chapter 10's discussion of Engelbert of Admont and Peter d'Abano can be taken to suggest Padua as a centre of thought about life-span, and Chapter 9's discussion of Marco Polo reminds us of Venice as a centre of knowledge of far eastern populations—and, as we shall be seeing, Villani knew Marco Polo's work and used it precisely to learn about the Tartars.

14.3 Heretics

The third preoccupation of modern historians of Florentine lay culture in this period is the channelling of ideas into Florence through the religious, in particular the Franciscans and Dominicans and their books at Santa Croce and Santa Maria Novella. Among these 'religious', one group tends to be forgotten: heretical preachers. In the repression of Cathar heretics, a far greater role was played in Italian cities than in Languedoc by debate and polemical discussions, which could and did include the literate layman—one of the earliest anti-Cathar treatises was written in Piacenza by one such layman. Such debate will have brought about wide diffusion of Cathar themes. Cathars had a long history in Florence, and varied evidence attests to their continuing presence there. In a deposition made to the inquisitor Bernard Gui there is casual reference to staying with a Cathar and meeting a number of Cathar believers in Florence in 1300,[35] and the two most prominent late thirteenth-century preachers in Florence were concerned with the Cathars. The danger posed by the Cathar Church could stimulate thought about relative numbers, while, more directly, Cathar teaching that marriage and procreation were wrong could stir people to thought about the continuation of the human race. In fact there is some evidence, though slight, suggesting that this theme was stimulated by Cathars in Florence, and also discussion of the relative numerical size of Church and sect; this evidence is summarized later in this chapter.

. . . *significat detrimentum illius regionis . . . et pestilentias, ut sunt infirmitates, mors, fames; De astronomia* (Basle, 1550), 512a. The little that is known of his life and the sources cited by Guido suggest a mid- to late thirteenth-century date. Cecco goes a step further in finding contemporary examples, illustrating regionalism with a point about Romagna experiencing [high] mortality while the Marches did not; *In spheram mundi enarratio*, ed. L. Thorndike, *The Sphere of Sacrobosco and its Commentators* (Chicago, 1949), pp. 344–411 (p. 375). An illuminating introduction to astrology in Italy *c.*1300 is given in M.-T. d'Alverny, 'Pietro d'Abano et les "naturalistes" à l'époque de Dante', *Dante e la cultura veneta*, ed. V. Branca and G. Padoan (Florence, 1966), pp. 207–19. On Bonatti, see C. Vasoli, 'Bonatti, Guido', *DBI* xi. 603–8.

[35] P. van Limborch *Liber Sententiarum Inquisitionis Tholosanae* (Amsterdam, 1692), p. 81. One recent account emphasizes the scarcity of evidence for later Cathars in Florence, another stresses their continuing strength there in the later thirteenth century: C. Lansing, *Power and Purity: Cathar Heresy in Medieval Italy* (New York, 1998), pp. 71–6 and 211 n. 79, and M. D. Lambert, *The Cathars* (Oxford, 1998), pp. 278–9. For Giordano of Pisa they were a spent force, *Prediche*, ed. Moreni, i. 28.

14.4 Mendicant convents and their libraries

Cathars were few, and undoubtedly usually under cover and only talking to a few. Far more numerous and visibly talking to any Florentine who cared to listen were the mendicant friars, in particular the Franciscans and Dominicans at Santa Croce and Santa Maria Novella. 'In the thirteenth and into the fourteenth centuries the Dominican and Franciscan convents must have been the major centres for the diffusion of ideas into the city.'[36] These convents belonged to two extraordinarily far-flung and busy international networks, and they were, therefore, first of all receivers and disseminators of news. Travel to and information about eastern lands is an immediate example. Glimpses of this are given in the cases of Gerard of Prato, sent off from Santa Croce to journey to the Mongols,[37] and Riccoldo of Monte Croce, who returned to Santa Maria Novella in 1301, bringing back travel information which included a high population estimate for a distant population—according to Riccoldo there were about 200,000 Saracens living in Baghdad.[38]

Northern scholastic culture existed in the convents in part through the presence of some friars who had studied in Paris, in part through books. 'If we look at about twenty manuscripts of the late thirteenth and early fourteenth centuries, which used to be contained in four or five shelves in the library of Santa Croce in Florence and are now in the Laurentian library',[39] we find Aristotle's works *On Animals*, the *Little Natural Works* and Averroes's epitomes of these, including *On the Length and Shortness of Life*, and the *Politics*. If we look at a list of Santa Croce books which were *certainly* at Santa Croce in this period we see certain standard works which are commentaries on, compendia of, or related to Peter the Lombard's *Four Books of the Sentences*, and these include copies of William of Auxerre's *Summa Aurea*, Bonaventure's commentary on the fourth book of the *Sentences*, and in addition a recent compendium of the *Sentences* composed by Gerard of Prato while lector in Florence, while the canon law of Bologna and elsewhere is represented by such standard works as Gratian's *Decretum* and Gregory IX's *Five Books of the Decretals*, with glosses, together with Huguccio on Gratian, and Bernard of Parma on the *Decretals*.[40] The fact that a manuscript was written in the late thirteenth century and was in the library at Santa Croce does

[36] d'Avray, *Preaching*, p. 157.

[37] Salimbene de Adam, *Cronica*, ed. G. Scalia, 2 vols. (Bari, 1966), i. 302 and 305–6.

[38] Riccoldo, *Itinerarius*, XIX, ed. J. C. M. Laurent, *Peregrinatores Medii Aevi Quatuor* (Leipzig, 1864), p. 127: *In hac itaque ciuitate creduntur esse plus quam ducenta milia Saracenorum.* Riccoldo's description of Baghdad is discussed by U. M. de Villard, *Il libro della Peregrinazione nelle Parti d'Oriente di Frate Riccoldo da Montecroce* (Rome, 1948), pp. 76–89.

[39] Minio-Paluello, 'Dante's Reading of Aristotle', p. 66.

[40] C. T. Davis, 'The Early Collection of Books of S. Croce in Florence', *Proceedings of the American Philosophical Society* 107 (1963), 399–414. A useful comparison is the reconstruction of books—from a slightly earlier date (mainly 1278) and in a Dominican convent—by F. Pelster, 'Die Bibliothek von Santa Caterina zu Pisa, eine Büchersammlung aus den Zeiten des Hl. Thomas von Aquin', in *Xenia Thomistica*, ed. S. Szabó, 3 vols. (Rome, 1925), iii. 249–80. Since this convent was where Giordano of Pisa studied, its books also bear on the flow of ideas into Florence.

not necessarily mean that Santa Croce had this manuscript in the late thirteenth century. A minority of Santa Croce manuscripts bear inscriptions—such as the date of the bequest of the book to Santa Croce—which enable the painstaking compiling of the 'certain' list which was used above. Scholarly caution, then, is needed, and at the same time historian's realism. For the 'certain' list must only represent a fraction of what was once there at Santa Croce, and Santa Croce was only one convent among others. Santa Croce's library will have been shaped in part by its status as a 'centre of higher study' (*studium generale*) in the Franciscan Order, as also will have been the library of the Augustinian convent of Santo Spirito, made a 'centre of higher study' in 1287. Although the Dominican Santa Maria Novella did not yet have this status, it was already in the late thirteenth century one of the most important centres of Dominican education at the middling 'provincial' rank, between an ordinary convent school and a centre for higher study, and in turn its library will have reflected this. Between them these convent libraries will have had many of the other much-copied standard works we have been using, such as Bartholomew the Englishman or Aquinas on the *Sentences* or the Pseudo-Aristotelian *Problems.*

The first salient point about the Santa Croce library is that it contains the majority of the fundamental texts upon which the earlier chapters of this book have been based. Further, close to each other on these library shelves will have been different texts which approached the same theme. Thus the *Decretum* and the *Decretals* dealt with age at marriage from the point of view of the minimum age according to canon law, while Huguccio's commentary, referring to the *physici*, introduced the theme of medical or natural philosophical opinion on the age of sexual maturing, and Aristotle's *Politics* showed how ages at which men and women married could be dated. The theological and canon-legal works approach avoidance of conception in various ways, and the *Politics* raised control as a theme. Gregory IX's *Decretals*[41] and the theological works brought up and discussed variations of marriage in relation to paucity or expansion of human population, while a compendium of the *Sentences* written by a Santa Croce friar, Gerard of Prato, contained an abbreviated version of this,[42] William of Auxerre's *Summa aurea* contained a trenchant statement of current sufficiency, and the *Politics* discussed optimum size and encouraged the thought of 'excess of multitude'.

In Florentine convents, and in the minds of the friars who had access to these libraries, such juxtaposition will have had the potential of producing the 'Eisenstein effect'. When discussing the impact of printing, Elizabeth Eisenstein[43] suggested that what was stimulating further thought was the fact that it was now easier to have the older standard texts side by side on the same shelves. Creative,

[41] See *Gaudemus in Domino*, X. 4. 19. 8; Friedberg, ii. 723–4.

[42] *Il Breviloquium super libros Sententiarum di Frate Gherardo da Prato*, ed. M. da Civezza (Prato, 1882), p. 147.

[43] E. L. Eisenstein, *The Printing Press as an Agent of Change*, 2 vols.(Cambridge, 1980), i. 76–7. I am grateful to Peggy Smith for drawing my attention to the earlier importance of George Sarton in propounding this line of thought.

new, thought was produced by readers noticing much more frequently the links and areas of friction between old texts. The Eisenstein effect is something which could apply in any large earlier accumulation of books, and we must add to it another creative link. Take a friar in Santa Croce picking up and opening one of its copies of William of Auxerre's *Summa aurea.* When reading its early account of the sex-ratio—God ordaining the production of more males than females—he could have connected this with the black and white beans being piled up at christenings in the Baptistery. When reading William of Auxerre's statement that 'now the people of God has expanded throughout the world, and countless marriages nowadays generate a sufficiency of children of God', he could have connected this with the sprawling of numbers beyond Florence's earlier walls.

14.5 *Three mendicant preachers: Remigio dei Girolami, Servasanto of Faenza, Giordano of Pisa*

Ideas moved outside the walls of Santa Croce and Santa Maria Novella as the friars taught—Dante wrote that he attended lectures and disputations at the schools of the religious, probably the schools of these convents. In the barn-like church buildings of the mendicants and the squares in front of them ideas were broadcast to larger audiences, in sermons. Florence was a centre of preaching,[44] and we can glimpse some of the material that was being put across in this medium by three notable preachers of the period. One was the Dominican Remigio, lector of Santa Maria Novella after his studies in Paris and a prominent preacher in Florence, where he lived most of the time from 1260 to his death in 1319.[45] Another prominent preacher, the Franciscan Servasanto of Faenza—'the greatest moralist of the thirteenth century'—received orders between 1244 and 1260, and preached in Italian cities, principally in Tuscany, and especially in Florence, where he spent most of his life and died, probably around 1300.[46] The third has already been mentioned, the Dominican Giordano of Pisa. Giordano was born in Rivalto around 1260, studied in Pisa, Bologna, and Paris, and preached in Florence between January 1303 and spring 1307; he died in Piacenza in 1311.[47] The surviving traces of

[44] d'Avray, *Preaching of the Friars*, pp. 156–60. D. R. Lesnick, *Preaching in Medieval Florence: The Social World of Franciscan and Dominican Spirituality* (Athens, Ga., and London, 1989), should be used with caution, because the contrast between 'scholastic' Dominicans and affective 'experiential' Franciscans is based on a comparison of different genres. Dominican sermons (pp. 96–133) are set against Franciscan devotional writings (pp. 142–71); the very 'scholastic' Franciscan Servasanto of Faenza is ignored.

[45] On Remigio, see the works cited in n. 15 above, the bibliography in Remigio, *Contra falsos ecclesie professores*, ed. F. Tamburini, preface by C. T. Davis, 'Utrumque Ius', Collectio Pontificiae Universitatis Lateranensis 6 (Rome, 1981), and Lesnick, *Preaching*, pp. 108–11. I am grateful to David d'Avray for lending me his microfilm of the Florence manuscript of Remigio's sermons (see below, n. 49).

[46] d'Avray, *Preaching of the Friars*, p. 76, quoting from Oliger. See further ibid., pp. 76 n. 5, 155 n. 2, 158 n. 60, and 160, and L. Oliger, 'Servasanta da Faenza O. F. M. e il suo "Liber de virtutibus et vitiis"', in *Miscellanea Francesco Ehrle*, i. Studi e testi 37 (Rome, 1924), pp. 148–89.

[47] C. Delcorno, *Giordano da Pisa e l'antica predicazione volgare*, Biblioteca di 'Lettere Italiane' 14 (Florence, 1975), pp. 3–28.

their preaching vary in richness and immediacy. Latin sermons of Remigio survive, and a treatise, *Contra falsos professores ecclesie*, which, it has been suggested, was intended to supply material for sermons; Latin sermons of Servasanto also survive, again together with works designed to furnish materials for preachers, his *Summa de paenitentia* and his *Liber de exemplis naturalibus*. More vivid and often precisely dated and located—usually a particular day in the piazza in front of Santa Maria Novella—are the sermons of Giordano. A story survives about a cloth-worker who followed Giordano through churches and streets, but even more eloquent testimony to Giordano's success comes from the anonymous literate lay Florentines, probably members of confraternities of Santa Maria Novella, who took down many hundreds of pages of the sermons, preserving them in the vernacular.[48]

Let us begin with Remigio, who had a concern with number and magnitude which he showed, first of all, in relation to heresy. His marriage sermon on the text *Nupcie facte sunt* refers to Cathar condemnation of marriage, as does also a sermon of Servasanto, who defends marriage as natural and necesary for conserving the species.[49] In Remigio's case the interest in heresy and number went further. Polemic against sects sometimes concentrated on their size—going in one of two, contrary, directions. If you wanted to warn about the danger posed by heretics, you wrote about how many they were and how widespread, while if you wanted to prove that they were not the true Church, you wrote about how they were not very widespread or many, and thus not conformable to Psalm 18 and Romans 10: 18: 'their sound hath gone forth into all the earth, and their words unto the ends of the whole world.' Before looking at Remigio's concern with the second theme, the Church's big size, let us see a German Dominican putting the point in the 1260s. The Church is the true Church, not heresy, partly because of its geographical spread—the 'spread of its faith' and because heretics are 'in few countries'—and partly because of its hold among many people, especially those in higher milieux. 'The multitude of believers [shows we are the true Church], because every sort of men holds our faith, that is, philosophers, the learned, and princes, but only a few hold the faith of heretics, and these only the poor and workmen and women and the illiterate.'[50] Remigio takes up the point of the true Church's large size in his

[48] Ibid., pp. 18 and 70.

[49] Remigio refers to 'hereticos qui dampnant nuptie carnales' near the beginning of his *Nupcie facte sunt* sermon, Florence, Biblioteca Nazionale, MS Conv. soppr. G.4.396, fol. 22vb. Servasanto's *Nupcie facte sunt*, BL, MS Harley 3221, fols. 72r–74r, defends marriage against those who condemn it, referring to heretics in language which might indicate contemporaneity, fols. 72v–3r: *in novissimis temporibus discedunt quidam a fide, attendentibus spiritibus erroris etc, et prohibentes nubere et abstinere a cibis quos Deus creavit. Manifestum ergo est quod omnes illi errant qui nupcias damnant, et cibos alis comedere vetunt. Sed ista faciunt patarini.* See also the references in fol. 217r, *sunt enim heretici qui olim dicti sunt manichei, nunc autem communi usu appellantur patareni, qui . . . duo ponunt esse principia*, and to heretics who heed Mani not Christ and hide their doctrine, [talking] with lowered voices, in Bonaventure, *Opera omnia*, ed. A. C. Peltier, 15 vols. (Paris, 1864–71), xiv. 8; see n. 54 below on this edition of Servasanto. Servasanto, marriage, and heresy are discussed by D. d'Avray, 'Some Franciscan Ideas about the Body', *Archivum Franciscanum Historicum* 84 (1991), 343–63.

[50] The Passau Anonymous, cited here from a later recension edited by J. Gretser, *Maxima Bibliotheca*

Contra falsos professores ecclesie, where he inserts it into an odd and interesting schema of the Church having and knowing the seven liberal arts. The Church has arithmetic. Absolutely speaking, arithmetic is concerned with multitude, but according to common use it concerns measure. There is prophecy about both the numerous (that is to say, countable) multitude and the innumerable multitude of the people of God, and the Church has this multitude in persons and other things. The Church of the faithless, however, cannot be said to be this Church. To support this Remigio then provides a notably precise citation of a text of Rainier Sacconi on the Cathars—its date of composition (1250) and Sacconi's career first as a Cathar and then as a Dominican are specified. Remigio's statistic is then quoted. In the whole world, counting Cathars of both sexes, there are not four thousand in number. Sacconi's basis for this statement is also given: the said computation was formerly made several times among them (the Cathars).[51]

Distinctive in Remigio's deployment of this stock polemical theme is his statistical precision—which was unique among medieval polemicists—in digging out a precise figure for the numbers of heretics and saying how this figure was obtained. And unique is the abstractness of his setting of the theme, which in Remigio's words becomes, in effect, 'the Church has large population'. There are parallels with Remigio's concern with counting heretics in Villani and to a lesser extent Dante,[52] and the question whether a large population in Florence is or is not a good is much in the minds of all three lay Florentines we shall be looking at.

Just as large population was a good for ecclesial communities, in Remigio's eyes, it was also a good in political communities. Turning his eyes to the city in one of his sermons, Remigio stated that God had granted Florence seven good things—if a man used these things properly illumination (illustriousness or glory) ensued, but if improperly blindness. Coming third among the seven good things, after abundance of money and nobility of coinage, was 'multitude of people', *multitudo populi.* Trusting in God as the author of multitude of people, who was thereby giving one an instrument of strength, was the proper use, which brings illustriousness.[53]

Servasanto had a wide knowledge of Aristotle's works, medicine, and the material on the natural world found in Bartholomew's *De proprietatibus rerum*, and therefore his sermons and compendia of material for sermons contain the sort of

Veterum Patrum, ed. M. de La Bigne, 28 vols. (Lyons, Geneva, 1677, 1707), xxv. 263–4; see A. Patschovsky, *Der Passauer Anonymus: Ein Sammelwerk über Ketzer, Juden, Antichrist aus der Mitte des XIII. Jahrhunderts*, Schriften der Monumenta Germaniae historica, 22 (Stuttgart, 1968), p. 109. The theme is analysed in D. Kurze, 'Häresie und Minderheit im Mittelalter', *Historische Zeitschrift* 229 (1979), 529–73.

[51] Remigio, *Contra falsos professores ecclesie*, XXXVIII (ed. Tamburini, pp. 80–3); Rainier Sacconi, *Summa de Catharis et Leonistis seu Pauperibus de Lugduno*, ed. F. Sanjek, *AFP* 44 (1974), p. 50.

[52] Villani gave Dolcino's followers a number, 3000 men and women, *Cronica*, IX. lxxxiv (ii. 170), and Dante was concerned with heretics' numbers, that there have been many more than one thinks, *Inferno*, IX. 127–9. Giordano of Pisa provided a figure, more than 8000, for Jews being converted in Apulia around 1290, *Prediche*, ed. Moreni, ii. 231.

[53] See Davis, 'An Early Florentine Political Theorist: Fra Remigio de' Girolami', in his *Dante's Italy*, p. 206 and n. 30. I am grateful to David d'Avray for providing me with a photostat of the manuscript Davis quotes here; Remigio does not develop further the point about Florence's population.

things we looked at in Chapter 10 above.[54] The commonplace of brevity of life takes him to Aristotelian and medical material on death and life-span, as he discusses the consumption of 'radical humidity', uses the image of a burning candle for life and death, and cites Aristotle's *Length and Shortess of Life*. Tuscan audiences will have received through Servasanto, then, a scientization of these themes.[55] In the midst of all of this there is one point of unusual interest, Servasanto's attention to age at marriage. Servasanto selected for entry into his *Liber de exemplis naturalibus*[56] a text from Bartholomew's *De proprietatibus rerum*, which we discussed in Chapter 9 above, dealing with a far-off people, situated within the confines of *Germania*, the Frisians. This particular people is ideal in several ways, including its military prowess. 'This is a free people, not subject to the rule of another . . . they [the Frisians] keep their sons and daughters chaste up to the completion of adolescence. From this it happens that, with marriage then, they generate full and strong offspring.' Servasanto's text is almost identical to that in early printed editions of Bartholomew, and it is possible, therefore, that what Servasanto put into his *Liber de exemplis naturalibus* was an exact copy of the reading in the (unknown) manuscript which he used.

At this stage, the significance is that a friar working in Florence and producing a compilation of preachable materials should have chosen this particular text for inclusion. The next stage was Servasanto's reworking of and selection from this passage, in one of his *Sermons about Saints*. This was in a sermon on St Agnes, at a point where Servasanto holds up her virginity against the morals and practices of his own times. 'The virgins of our times are never like that [St Agnes]', he writes; 'they are corrupted before they are ready:'

It is necessary to hand them over to marriage before they reach the time of puberty, to avoid their being debauched, perhaps, before they are handed over to their husbands. The Christian girls among the Frisians are not like that. For this Frisian people is extremely zealous for chastity, and punishes very severely any of either sex who transgress. The Frisians keep their daughters in their houses, therefore, for a long time, nor do they allow them to marry before, almost, thirty. And for this reason they [these Frisian daughters] do not, like our girls, generate weak and little children, but strong and big ones, as is proved by experience.[57]

[54] I have used the *Antidotarium Animae* [= *Summa de paenitentia*] in the Louvain, 1484/7 edn. (see Oliger, 'Servasanto', pp. 148 and 153–6); BL, MS Arundel 198 for the *Liber de exemplis naturalibus* (it contains extracts—see Oliger, 'Servasanto', pp. 156–62). For sermons I have used BL, MS Harley 3221, and those incorrectly attributed to Bonaventure and printed in Bonaventure, *Opera omnia*, ed. Peltier, xiii. 493–636 and xiv. 1–138 (on Servasanto's authorship, see Oliger, 'Servasanto', p. 167). I am grateful to David d'Avray for referring me to the British Museum MSS.

[55] In Bonaventure, *Opera*, xiii. 556, 559, and 623, and xiv. 60; *Antidotarium animae*, V. 22, 23.

[56] MS. Arundel 198, fol. 79vb.

[57] In Bonaventure, *Opera omnia*, ed. Peltier, xiii. 519: *Sic* [like St Agnes] *nunquam virgines nostris temporibus sunt tales, quae ante sunt corruptae quam aptae . . . et oportet quod nuptui prius tradantur, quam ad tempus pubertatis attingant, ne prius forte stuprentur, quam maritis tradantur. Unde dicitur . . . Non sunt tales apud Frisones christianae puellae. Nam gens illa Frisonum miro modo castitatem zelat, et gravissime punit, si quos, vel si quas transgressores inveniant* [sic]. *Filias ergo suas in domibus propriis diu servant, nec ante triginta quasi annos permittunt quod nubant: et ideo non, sicut nostrae, filios debiles et parvos generant, sed robustos et magnos, sicut experientia probat.*

Servasanto has selected and omitted. Political liberty no longer appears. It is the chastity and marriage-age only of *girls* which is at issue, not of both sexes. The pressures behind this selection could be simultaneously the exigencies of a sermon about a female virgin and contemporary practice. A detail is inserted that is not found in Bartholomew, one which would have been a commonplace in Servasanto's milieu: families keeping daughters 'in their own houses'. Servasanto's other sermons make it clear that 'here and now' is in Italy, and one part of Italy, north of Rome. 'Our Italians flee the ultramontanes'; merchants travel across the Alps; 'who except a fool would go to France via Rome?' Most of his references are to Florence.[58] It is this part of Italy which is invoked, then, when he refers to 'our' girls as being handed over to marriage very early, and generating weak offspring. The first is linked to lack of chastity, and not, as we shall see in Villani and Dante, to dowry. Both Servasanto and Dante choose as the opposite of contemporary practice the exemplification of the ideal of high marriage in a remote people. It is a geographical remoteness with Servasanto, far away in north-western Europe, and, as we shall see in Dante, chronological remoteness, far away in much earlier, smaller and chaster, Florence. Unlike Dante, but like Villani, Servasanto inserts a precise figure for marriage-age in his remote ideal. Servasanto's number is not present in Bartholomew's description of the Frisians, though it is one of four numbers given in his earlier discussion 'on ages', when looking at what is meant by 'completion of adolescence': in the twenty-first year, or up to twenty-eighth, or up to thirtieth, or up to thirty-fifth. What was the significance of thirty? Servasanto had considerable knowledge of written sources on periods of life and life-span, although I have not found in his works knowledge of the discussion of marriage-age in the *Politics*. On this point he was not copying. One hundred and thirty years later the Florentine catasto shows girls in fact marrying around fifteen. Was Servasanto simply choosing a very high number to underline the contrast—possibly, in a mental world of white and black, ideal and its opposite? A rounded figure which was double the norm of practice in the milieu in which he and his audience lived?

It is difficult also to be sure about the meaning of his reference to 'experience' showing the robustness of Frisian offspring. Physical robustness of the *Germani* in general was a literary commonplace—well-known enough to his audience to supply the mental framework of their observation of actual men from northern Europe? What is clear, however, is the special significance of a great Franciscan preacher, working in Tuscany, asserting the low age at marriage of 'our' girls in 'our times', basing a eugenic point on this, and upholding an ideal of the opposite, an ideal which he located in a people in north-western Europe.

One of Servasanto's favourite commonplaces is the superior morality of animal as opposed to human behaviour, and on at least two occasions he uses this to make a point about sex in marriage. In one sermon, there is the ideal of conjugal

[58] In Bonaventure, *Opera omnia*, ed. Peltier, xiii. 568 and 598, and xiv. 24; Oliger, 'Servasanto', pp. 182–6.

continence, and no adultery, whereas the opposite is the case among human beings: 'in fact there is more adulterous or incestuous coitus than lawful; more against nature, than through the natural act.'[59] The point about sex against nature in marriage is spelled out more in another sermon. 'Beasts come together for generation, to conserve the species, man generally for the pleasure of the flesh . . . A beast in the carnal act does not alter the mode of nature but, apart from a few, observes it; but men more often change the mode of nature, and do not observe it with their wives.'[60] The theme was also tackled by Giordano, in a sermon in which he said that *è dato il matrimonio a potere usare, e sodisfare alla natura secondo Iddio, e non se ne trova quasi nel centinaio uno che ben l'osservi.*[61] There is an analogous statement made in a much later vernacular sermon by Bernardino of Siena who said, when preaching about marriage, 'Of 1000 marriages, I believe 999 are the devil's.' This has been interpreted as a reference to the practice of one form of the sin against nature, withdrawal, and is one of the texts used to suggest that this 'was the kind of contraceptive behaviour most frequently encountered' in the thirteenth to fifteenth centuries.[62] The interpretation is just as plausibly applied to Giordano's and Servasanto's sermons, and to their context, where in Giordano's case one can be precise: thought and practice among members of his audience, the Florentines to whom he was talking, in the vernacular, at Santa Maria Novella on 5 August 1304.

Whereas Dante could have heard Servasanto, and may even have had Remigio as a teacher, he could not have heard Giordano in Florence, because in 1302 he became an exile. Like Remigio, our third preacher, Giordano, grappled with the facts of Florentine life, but whereas Remigio's was an intellectually exalted concern with the application of political theory to major political crises, Giordano's was more grainy and miscellaneous. His sermons bristle with workshops, prices, exchange, and Florentine merchants and bankers coming back from France.[63]

Where Remigio was interested in the Church's possession of arithmetic, and defining it as a liberal art, Giordano overlapped in his general interest. His sermons are shot through with mathematics: Pythagoras on the virtue of numbers,[64]

[59] In Bonaventure, *Opera omnia*, ed. Peltier, xiv. 2: *Nam inter pisces continentia conjugalis servatur, et nullum inter pisces adulterium committitur, cum hoc inter homines non servetur; imo plures sunt coitus adulterini, et incestuosi, quam legitimi; plures contra naturam, quam opere naturali.*

[60] In Bonaventure, *Opera omnia*, ed. Peltier, xiv. 92–3: *Bruta coeunt ad generationem, unde suam valeant conservare speciem; homo communiter ad solam delectationem carnis: unde nec cessat a muliere praegnante, cum multa sin[t] animalia, quae post conceptum foetum abstinen[t] a foemina. Bruta etiam in actu carnali modum naturae non mutant, sed servant, praeter pauca; sed homines naturae modum saepius mutant, et cum uxoribus non servant.*

[61] Giordano of Pisa, *Prediche*, ed. Moreni, i. 240. See also his *Prediche*, ed. Narducci, p. 436: *quando nel matrimonio usassi quelle cose che non dovessi.* Worth comparing are the clear references to avoidance of offspring and abortion in the vernacular and Latin sermons delivered by Federigo Visconti in Pisa between the early 1240s and 1277, A. Murray, 'Archbishop and Mendicants in thirteenth-century Pisa', in *Stellung und Wirksamkeit der Bettelorden in der städtischen Gesellschaft*, ed. K. Elm, Berliner Historische Studien 3, Ordensstudien 2 (Berlin, 1981), pp. 19–75 (p. 49 and nn. 116–17).

[62] Noonan, *Contraception*, pp. 226–7.

[63] Delcorno, *Giordano da Pisa*, pp. 44–66.

[64] Giordano, *Quaresimale*, pp. 47–8, *Prediche*, ed. Narducci, pp. 261–2. On the science of numbers see also *Prediche*, ed. Manni, p. 208.

talking about squared and cubed numbers,[65] different lines in geometry,[66] and examples of a tiny quantity (the thousandth of a thousandth of a point) or a very large one.[67] So often a point is being made about *number*: for example, the distinction in countability of a thousand thousands on the one hand and thousands of thousands on the other, or a comment on a number such as a thousand being stated as a *large* number rather than, by implication, precisely a thousand.[68] One spiritual commonplace often hammered home is, unsurprisingly, the brevity of human life compared to eternity, and here audiences will have been familiar with Giordano fleshing out his examples with numbers rather than just saying 'short' or 'long'. How long do you expect to live? To 50? To 60? A favourite with Giordano is the example of the Florentine banker accumulating wealth in France in order to enjoy retirement back in Florence. Giordano spells out the long years of toil in France and the short number of years—given brevity of life—of the banker's not-so-enjoyable retirement.[69] Attacks on astrological determination of natural life-span again bring in suggested numbers of years of life-span on the one hand and of actual length of life (through violent accidental death) on the other. You may have natural length of life, or you may be killed and only live to 20.[70] Giordano is being impressionist, not providing Florentine actuarial tables. He plucks figures from the air, and no doubt he knew one or two Florentine businessmen who spent their middle lives in France and then died in Florence at the age of 60. What is significant is that some sort of number is penetrating everywhere.

Giordano shares with Servasanto medicine and natural philosophy. His sermons frequently invoke primary qualities or humours of the body, and medicine and the working of medicine—a passing comment, for example, will have incorrect diet (overeating) leading to more illness and shorter life.[71] In general, as with Servasanto, there is a presentation and 'scientization' of various themes. When we call to mind the material which we surveyed in Chapter 10 above—Aristotelian natural-philosophical and medical data about reproduction and life-span—and turn to Florence, we see that some of the content and much of the language and colouring of this material was in the air and in the sound-waves between these preachers and lay Florentines.

[65] Giordano, *Quaresimale, Prediche sulla Genesi*, p. 84. [66] Ibid., *Prediche*, ed. Manni, pp. 37–8.

[67] Ibid., *Prediche*, ed. Manni, p. 39; *Quaresimale*, pp. 190 and 204 (on a number so large that it was beyond any abacus in the world).

[68] Ibid., *Prediche*, ed. Manni, pp. 149 and 218.

[69] Ibid., *Prediche*, ed. Manni, p. 78; *Prediche sulla Genesi*, p. 83; *Prediche*, ed. Moreni, i. 207 and 283, and ii. 153 and 300; *Prediche*, ed. Narducci, p. 211; *Prediche*, ed. Narducci, p. 296. Note that the library of the Dominican convent in which Giordano studied at Pisa contained Albert the Great's commentary on Aristotle's *Length and Shortness of Life*; Pelster, 'Die Bibliothek von Santa Caterina zu Pisa', 265. It must not be forgotten that behind Giordano's words also lies a long tradition of ascetic writing, culminating in Innocent III's treatise on the misery of the human condition, which retailed abbreviation of life since the Psalmist's seventy or eighty. 'Few now last to forty, extremely few to sixty' (*Pauci nunc ad quadraginta, paucissimi ad sexaginta annos perveniunt*); Lotario dei Segni [Innocent III], *De miseria condicionis humane*, I. ix, ed. R. E. Lewis (Athens, Ga., 1978), p. 107. See ibid., pp. 3–4 on this work's popularity and the 672 extant manuscripts.

[70] Ibid., *Prediche*, ed. Manni, p. 105; *Prediche sulla Genesi*, pp. 75–6.

[71] Ibid., *Quaresimale*, p. 46; *Prediche*, ed. Narducci, p. 260.

In the air between them—going only in one direction? The arrangement of this chapter suggests friars and books as sources and our laymen as receivers of ideas, but as we draw near to the end of our look at preaching friars, it is worth pausing and musing about this. Giordano's sermons had a lot of impact in Florence, says the modern master of this subject and Giordano's editor, Carlo Delcorno, who goes on to write that public conditions structured Giordano's discourse and provided its content.[72] Broadly, this means that Giordano thought about *cui* or *quibus*, 'to whom' he was talking, Florentines, and that he shaped his material accordingly, tailoring theological truths and moral exhortations to their everyday lives and material concerns. Thus 'the brevity of life in this world' becomes the brevity of retirement of the successful Florentine businessman, while guardian angels are like *sensali*, marriage-brokers.[73] Reduced to essentials then, (*a*) this or that piece of learned natural philosophy is being transmitted *to* lay Florentines, and (*b*) this or that theological or moral point is being transmitted to lay Florentines, dressed up in an image taken from observation of their lives. This last points to something going in the reverse direction, *from* lay Florentines *to* the friars. The sense of two-way traffic is strengthened if we add 'thought' to other concerns: 'tailored to their everyday lives and material concerns and patterns of *thought*'. Let us reflect on this further, looking at three areas which stand out in Giordano's sermons.

First, in one instance of sermonizing about length of life, Giordano chooses to relate it to how much you eat: one *moggio* (eight bushels) of grain in a year. Now, we are going to see Giovanni Villani taking a figure for quantity of grain eaten by one person, and providing multiples of this figure for particular dates in Florence—multiples from which Florence's population figures at those dates can be derived mathematically. Here Giordano does something similar, but goes towards one person's long life rather than population at a given date. His figure means, he says, that a man who lives to 80 eats eighty *moggia* of grain during his life.[74] If Villani's is the thought of an informed and important layman in a particular milieu, in a city whose commune looked carefully to population and consumption and buying grain to anticipate scarcity, the Dominican Giordano's is quite simply borrowed from this milieu, to be adapted to moral didactic purposes.

Second, when we piece together from different parts of Giordano's sermons the broad lines of his general historical and geographical view of the habitation of the world, we *mainly* find echoes of the learned texts we have been examining in previous chapters. The sphere of the world, with lands and waters; some 'well-inhabited countries'.[75] Fishacre's concern with the density of population in the earthly paradise has something of a counterpart in Giordano's rhetorical question how all Jews past, present, and to come could fit into such a small area as the Holy Land.[76]

[72] Delcorno, *Giordano da Pisa*, pp. 29 and 44–66.

[73] Giordano, *Prediche*, ed. Manni, p. 237. For the Florentine *sensale*, see Klapisch-Zuber, *Women, Family and Ritual*, p. 183.

[74] Ibid., *Quaresimale*, p. 190.

[75] Ibid., *Prediche*, ed. Manni, p. 22; *Prediche*, ed. Moreni, i. 28.

[76] Ibid., *Quaresimale*, p. 362.

The power and spread of the Saracens over the world and the minimization of Christianity is reminiscent of the world geography of faiths described in Chapters 3 and 9, though Giordano does not apply number directly to it.[77] However, when dealing with Old Testament numbers, Giordano hints at a parallel between on the one hand the small numbers then who did not bend the knee to Baal, 7,000, and the more than a million in King Solomon's Israel, and on the other hand the world now: presumably the small numbers of Christians set against the rest of the world.[78] So far, mainly echoes. Let us look more closely at Giordano's handling of Old Testament numbers. First, where 1 Chronicles 1: 25 says, 'and the number of Israel was found, a thousand thousands and a hundred thousands of men that drew the sword', Giordano rounds the figure down to a thousand thousands and alters the qualification of the number from 'men that drew the sword' to 'without the women': 'more than a thousand thousands without the women'.

Presentation of the Old Testament is being coloured with concern for a total population figure, even if under-fifteens are not being counted. Whose concern, though? Let us look at another example, noting on the one hand that Exodus and Numbers give Israel in the Mosaic period as having 600,000 (rounded) or the more precise 603,550 arms-bearing men, and on the other hand that Giovanni Villani used the figure 5:18 as the ratio between arms-bearing men and overall population. Thus 30,000 arms-bearing men would be multiplied by three and three-fifths to arrive at a total population of 108,000, counting everyone. Now, Giordano refers to the 600,000 that Moses wanted to rule, casually slipping in that this was *più due volte che tutta Toscana*, 'more than double the whole of Tuscany'.[79] With Villani's multiplier, this is 2,160,000, a figure which makes abundantly clear the figure of which it is 'more than double': one million. Or, rather, in Giordano's and his audience's minds, one thousand thousands. Is it a Dominican friar who is *telling* a Florentine audience that the total population of Tuscany is a thousand thousands? Or is it the general view in this audience that one thousand thousands is the total population of Tuscany? The second seems to me more likely. It is the thoughts and ideas of lay Florentines that are impressing themselves on Giordano.

Thirdly, there is marriage, where Giordano's ideas are again *mainly* echoes of the theology of the schools. Reminiscent of the theological history of marriage and population discussed in Chapters 2 and 5 above are several sermons, one in which Giordano describes plurality of wives as conceded, in olden times, on grounds of necessity (to expand population fast),[80] others in which the theme of virginity and celibacy comes up—the world would perish if all were celibate—and another on the alternating utility of virginity and marriage, according to population. In one case the transcript of the sermon spells out interchange: someone

[77] Giordano, *Prediche*, ed. Manni, p. 81. [78] Ibid., *Quaresimale*, p. 332.

[79] Ibid., *Prediche*, ed. Moreni, ii. 274. Data about population in parts of Tuscany are discussed in Herlihy and Klapisch, *Tuscans and their Families*, ch. 3. Richard Smith informs me that Giordano's estimate accords with what one would project from this chapter.

[80] Ibid., *Prediche*, ed. Moreni, ii. 119–20.

in the audience asks Brother Giordano if the world would perish were everyone *religioso*, a member of a religious order.[81]

In another, Giordano presents himself as conveying to the audience what the fathers and scholastic authorities say: *Dicono i Santi.* And Giordano's drift is generally reminiscent of William of Auxerre in his *Summa aurea*—copies of which were in Florence—in a passage which was discussed in Chapter 5. 'Now, however, marriage is by way of remedy, not precept, rather by permission. For now the people of God is increased throughout the whole world, and everywhere innumerable marriages sufficiently generate children of God.' However, Giordano's slant is individual. The authorities say that *al mondo hae gente troppa; e però chi può tenere verginità è ottimo. Anticamente era più necessario il matrimonio; ma oggi ci n'hae troppi: e però Iddio ne scema spesse volte.*[82] 'The world has too much people; and therefore best is the person who can hold to virginity. In olden times marriage was more necessary; but today there are too many of them [too many marriages]; and therefore God often diminishes them [cuts down the number of marriages].' Clearly Giordano is reproducing a commonplace, but heightening it. God positively acts to prune the number of marriages in given population conditions: as it were a Divine setter of the marriage-rate. And the stark vernacular *troppa gente*, 'too much people', *may* be rooted more in the language and minds of the Florentines Giordano was addressing than in the *Sentences* commentaries which Giordano had read as a student.

14.6 Lay Florentines (a): Anonymous

In 1233 a great devotional movement sweeping through northern Italian cities was helped on its way by the fiery sermons of various preachers, among them the Dominican John of Vicenza. Noise of John's doings and miracles spread—was it really true that he had raised eighteen men from the dead? News about John produced reaction in Florence, and at some stage a witticism. In turn this witticism was remembered and passed on, perhaps embellished, and finally it was preserved in writing by the Franciscan Salimbene, in the 1280s. In his chronicle Salimbene devoted a special section to such things—witticisms, buffooneries, or jokes—headed *De truffis.* The Florentines are presented as great *truffatores*, mockers or jokers, exchanging broad comments in the street. Watching a friar walking through Florence in the winter, for example, Florentines laugh when he falls headlong on the ice, one of them asking the friar whether he wanted anything else under him, and getting back in reply,'Yes! Your wife'. 'He's one of us!' was their laddish reaction to being thus outstripped in coarseness.[83]

Salimbene's next example of Florentine humour was their formulation of a witticism in response to John of Vicenza. 'One time, when these [Florentines]

[81] Ibid., *Prediche*, ed. Narducci, pp. 117–18. See also *Prediche*, ed. Manni, p. 92.

[82] Ibid., *Prediche*, ed. Manni, p. 240.

[83] *De nostris est.*

heard that the Dominican John of Vicenza wanted to come to their city, they said, "For God's sake, he mustn't come here! For we have heard that he raises the dead, and we are so many that our city can't hold [all of] us!" And the Florentines' words sound really good in their language.'[84]

In 1233 these Florentines were still 'held' within the circuit of 1172, and the tightness of the compression which they felt is manifest in the logic of the witticism: the intolerableness of adding to the living just eighteen or so of the dead. However good was Salimbene's own remarkably pliant and verbally inventive Latin, here he was remembering and replaying the joke in his mind in the vernacular. For it sounded even better in Tuscan, in vivid words which are now lost.

14.7 *Lay Florentines (b): Giovanni Villani*

A more serious character was writing about a century later, an important man. Born on or before 1276,[85] Giovanni Villani was a businessman in the first half of his life, joining a leading trading and banking firm, the Peruzzi, bankers to the king of France, and by 1322 investing in the rival Buonaccorsi firm. In the later part of his life, between 1316 and 1341, he held various Florentine official positions, and he died in 1348. It is not known when he began his *Nuova Cronica*—not earlier than the 1320s or 1330s, it is thought. It is to this Tuscan vernacular text that we are now turning, the work of a literate Florentine, reader of Latin, French, and Italian, an experienced traveller, and a Florentine administrator. Villani was familiar with biblical history; he read chronicles and used the Latin *Chronica de origine civitatis*;[86] he read the French vernacular works of Hayton and Marco Polo. He will have been exposed to the *sort* of sermons we have been examining.[87] I say 'sort of' in order to except Giordano, whom Villani probably missed, for between 1302 and 1307 he was mainly in Flanders, representing the Peruzzi. Experienced travel and continuing interest in northern Europe underpin Villani's account of hunger in

[84] Salimbene, *Cronica*, I, 117: *Hi [Florentini], quadam vice audientes, quod frater Iohannes de Vicentia ex ordine Predicatorum... Florentiam ire volebat, dixerunt, 'Pro Deo non veniat huc. Audivimus enim quod mortuos suscitat, et tot sumus, quod civitas nostra capere nos non potest'. Et valde bene sonant verba Florentinorum in ydiomate suo.*

[85] My account of Villani is based on L. Green, *Chronicle into History: An Essay on the Interpretation of History in Florentine Fourteenth-Century Chronicles* (Cambridge, 1972), ch. 1. Giovanni Villani's chronicle was extremely popular. Still extant are 111 manuscripts: G. Porta, 'Censimento dei manoscritti delle cronache di Giovanni, Matteo e Filippo Villani', *Studi di Filologia Italiana* 34 (1976), 61–129 (pp. 64–114), 37 (1979), 93–117 (pp. 95–116), and 44 (1986), 65–7.

[86] Ed. O. Hartwig, *Quellen und Forschungen zur ältesten Geschichte der Stadt Florenz*, 2 vols. (Marburg, Halle, 1875–80), i. 35–65. Some aspects of Villani's free use and 'completion' of it are studied by N. Rubinstein, 'The Beginnings of Political Thought in Florence', *Journal of the Warburg and Courtauld Institute* 5 (1942), 198–227 (pp. 214–24). Comparison of the *Chronica de origine civitatis* and Villani's *Nuova cronica* shows the latter overlaying population themes on the former. See also C. T. Davis, 'Topographical and historical propaganda in early Florentine Chronicles and in Villani', *Medioevo e Rinascimento* 2 (1988), 33–51.

[87] Villani was a connoisseur of the genre—see his critical comments on one Dominican's sermons, *Cronica*, XII. xxiii; iii. 67.

1316, where he lists Germany, Holland, Frisia, Zeeland, Brabant, Flanders, Hainault, and Burgundy, and estimates mortality in the population at over one third.[88] Through his official positions in Florence his eyes were trained on many of our concerns in this chapter. So, in 1321 he was superintending the continuing construction of the new circle of walls.[89] During the years of scarcity, 1328–30, he was one of the officials trying to cope with the need to import food, whose job involved calculation about Florence's inhabitants and their consumption.[90] In 1331 as a representative of the Calimala guild, guardian of the structure of the baptistry of St John, he was superintending the work on the door whose master was Andrea Pisano:[91] in intimate contact with the building in which the rector counted male and female babies.

Florence and its population are at the centre of the *Nuova Cronica*, where they are given a chronologically long and geographically wide setting. Old Testament population history is reduced to a brief rationalization of great expansion. 'With long life and having more wives, the patriarchs had many children and descendants, and multiplied into a large people.'[92] Of the world's three parts, the first and largest is Asia, containing more than half of the inhabited world; Africa has savage provinces and deserts but is populated; and the third part, Europe, is confined but 'is by far the most populated part of the world' (*è dal tanto la più popolata parte del mondo*).[93] Bartholomew the Englishman's words, which we looked at in Chapter 10, were quite likely to have been aired by a mendicant preacher in Florence—Europe as 'smaller than Asia, but equal in number and nobility of peoples'—but behind Villani's words there may be more, both his own observation and changes in the population during the seventy or eighty years since Bartholomew wrote. In modern terms Villani's words about Europe are 'it is by far the most *densely* populated part of the world'.

Villani's account of marriage in Islam is the populationist one which we examined in Chapters 3 and 9. Mahomet made a law that 'anyone could have and use as many wives and concubines as he could support, to generate children and increase his people'.[94] Featuring also in the *Nuova Cronica* are the enormous size of Baghdad, the wide geographical spread through the world of the Saracens,

[88] Ibid., X. lxxx; ii. 285: *più che 'l terzo de la gente morirono.* Northern chroniclers' accounts of mortality during the famines of 1315–17 are edited in F. Curschmann, *Hungersnöte im Mittelalter: Ein Beitrag zur deutschen Wirtschaftsgeschichte des* 8. bis 13. Jahrhunderts, Leipziger Studien aus dem Gebiet der Geschichte 6/1 (Leipzig, 1900), pp. 208–17. This collection of texts is convenient for the study of the degrees of quantitative precision displayed by chroniclers over six centuries, beginning with (*a*) 'men died' or 'there was mortality', and going through (*b*) 'many many died' (or 'there was great mortality', (*c*) fractions such as a half or a third, (*d*) qualifications of fractions (such as Villani's more than a third), and (*e*) ending with precise figures, usually quite small figures for local mortality. See p. 95 (under the year 838) for a remarkable presentation of precise computation of mortality in Frisia—2437—from the Carolingian period.

[89] Ibid., X. cxxxvii; ii. 338. [90] Ibid., XI. cxix; ii. 672. [91] Ibid., XI. clxxv; ii. 742.

[92] Ibid., I. ii; i. 6: *in lunga vita, avendo più mogli, aveano molti figliuoli e discendenti, e multiplicaro in molto popolo.*

[93] Ibid., I. iii–v; ii. 6–10.

[94] Ibid., III. viii; i. 116: *a ciascuno fosse lecito d'avere e usare tante mogli e concubine quante ne potesse fornire, per generare figliuoli e crescere il suo popolo.*

their multitudes, and the great numbers of Arabs from all parts—'the Saracens of the infinite universe in Arabia'—continuing to supply men and money to maintain the outpost kingdom in southern Spain, Granada. Villani compares this to the way western Christians had supported the Holy Land.[95] The large numbers of the Tartars and the large space of the world occupied by them also figure, though Villani advises readers who want further information to go off and read Marco Polo and Hayton.[96]

The coming-to-be of inhabitation and population, and their increasing and (perhaps) passing away are commonplace themes in Villani; witness, for example, this early passage. 'Note that in ancient times the coasts were much inhabited, and [although] just inland there were few cities and few inhabitants, yet in Maremma and the Marittima towards Rome and the coast of Campagna there were many cities and many peoples, which today are consumed and brought to nothing by corruption of the air.'[97] Tuscany and Florence itself are to have this theme, as we shall see, from the original Tuscany which was found by Atlas, a good and healthy place but 'utterly uninhabited by human kind' (*tutto disabitata di gente umana*), through to the bulging population figures of his own life-time which Villani provides for his readers. Villani's historical sense is more than just cycles and long chronology. When talking about the large size of Florence's population in a particular remote past, he sets it against the different values of that particular past. It was a good-size city *for that period*. When more recent events are at issue, there is careful measuring comparison between, as we shall see, 1280 and 1338.

While Villani's passion for measure and number were most famously shown in the long entry for 1338, a set of statistics of many sorts of people and things in Florence, the character of this passion is also on display elsewhere, albeit more quietly. From the 1260s onwards entries often detail exact military numbers. Villani provides a qualifying adverbial phrase to indicate that a figure is an approximation,[98] and indicates a gap between belief and fact. At first it was thought that 3000 were dead, but in fact it was 300.[99] This concern for precision may partly explain his leaning towards proportions and fractions. While he may provide an overall figure for mortality or population, at the same time he may say that population is a quarter of what it later was,[100] or that mortality was at least one per family.[101] Again, Villani shows a penchant for breaking figures down. Quite apart from the statistics of 1336–8, there are frequently passages where he says that mortality affected to a greater or lesser degree certain categories, male or female, young or old, the poor, or town and country; and he also looks at mortality in battle in relation to sizes of city populations.[102]

[95] *Cronica*, III. viii (i. 118–19); III. xvii (i. 136); VIII. xxxvii (i. 470–1); XII. xcix (iii. 210); XII. cxx. 120 (iii. 239).

[96] Ibid., VI. xxxix (i. 255–6); IX. xxxv (ii. 53–7); X. xxxli (ii. 419–20).

[97] Ibid., II. xiii; i. 78–9. [98] Ibid., XIII. lxxxiv; iii. 485: *albitrando al grosso.* [99] Ibid., XII. i; iii. 9.

[100] Ibid., V. vii; i. 174: *non v'avea abitanti il quarto forse ch'è oggi*; XII. cxiv; iii. 226: *morinne più che 'l sesto de' cittadini.*

[101] Ibid., XII. cxiv; iii. 226: *non rimase famiglia ch' alcuno non ne morisse, o dove due o tre o più.*

[102] Ibid., VIII. xxxi; i. 464: *Siena, a comparazione del suo popolo, ricevette maggiore danno de' suoi cittadini in questa sconfitta, che non fece Firenze a quella di Montaperti.*

If passion for the idea of numbers is found variously among the preaching mendicants, sophistication in its practice is found in Villani. Villani shows occasional glimmers of their interests. His numbering of the followers of the heresiarch Dolcino, 3,000, is reminiscent of Remigio's interest in heretics and number. The city increased in size and vices, he wrote at one point—a cliché with many possible sources, including the mendicant commonplace (echoed by Giordano of Pisa)[103] that cities contain more sinners than elsewhere. And we shall see that Villani and Servasanto approach each other on marriage-age. Villani also shares 'medicalization' with the preachers of around 1300: such themes as seasonal or environmental incidence of illness and mortality appear readily in them and in Villani.[104] Thus the summer of 1335 brings smallpox. Affecting children in Florence and the contado, it brings more than 2000 deaths of both sexes.[105] Where we find Villani very ready to bring astrology to bear on events, including population,[106] we are not only reminded of the possible influence of Restoro of Arezzo and Bartholomew of Parma, but also of Giordano of Pisa's denunciation of this sort of thing.

At the centre was Florence. Both the earlier legendary part of Villani's history and the later part, replete with the facts of Florentine and imperial political history, are draped round a sturdy framework: Florence's foundations, the construction of successive circuits of walls, and the varying periods of inhabitation, immigration, and expansion of population. The sequence is this:

1. Atlas found Tuscany an excellent and healthy place, but utterly devoid of human habitation.[107]
2. The first circuit: in 70 BC Caesar built and walled Florence. 'We do not find a chronicle which specifies the area and circuit of the city', but, when Totila destroyed it, it was very large.[108]
3. It was 'populated', *popolata*, grew and muliplied, and became 'quickly a good city for that time': *buona città secondo il tempo d'allora.*[109]
4. In AD 450 Totila destroyed Florence.[110]
5. Between 450 and 801 it was a ruined city, with just a few inhabitants around the cathedral.[111]
6. In 801 Charlemagne rebuilt the city and rewalled it. Villani keeps harping on the relative smallness (*piccolo, minore*) of the area (*sito*) and the 'circuit' (*giro*) of the walls, and traces the line of the walls in great detail in relation to current buildings.[112]
7. Many immigrants came in, and Florence rapidly became 'well populated', *bene popolata*, and 'very well inhabited . . . and [with a] large people, according to [the standards of] that time': *molto bene abitata . . . e grande popolo, secondo il tempo d'allora.*[113]

[103] Giordano, *Quaresimale*, p. 41.
[104] Villani, *Cronica*, II. xiii (i. 78–9); X. ccxxii (ii. 406–7); XI. lxxii (ii. 596).
[105] Ibid., XII. xxxiii; iii. 81.
[106] Ibid., II. xiii (i. 79); X. lxxx (ii. 285); XII. c (iii. 211); XIII. xli (iii. 393).
[107] *Cronica*, I. vii; i. 12.
[108] Ibid., II. i; i. 61.
[109] Ibid., II. ii (i. 63) and II. v (i. 67).
[110] Ibid., III. i; i. 98.
[111] Ibid., III. xxi; i. 141.
[112] Ibid., IV. i (i. 145) and IV. ii (i. 146 and 148).
[113] Ibid., IV. iii; i. 150–2.

The account of increase is spread over many years. In the early eleventh century Florence has 'much increased in people and power, in relation to its little site', and much immigration into Florence follows its destruction of Fiesole in 1010. Eventually, with their coming, it was necessary 'to increase the wall and circuit of the city'.[114]

8. The circuit of 1078: the city 'filled' more, and there came more suburbs outside the little old city, and so 'of necessity it became expedient to increase the circuit'. Villani sets the beginning of the new wall in 1078 (a century too early, in fact), and continues with minute and precise description of where this *secondo cerchio* went. Villani's description of relentless expansion continues. In the entry under 1107, Florence's population growth lies behind extension of the *contado* and Florentine lordship over it.[115]

9. The circuit of 1283: the circuit with which this chapter opened was ordained because of further population growth, Florence yet further 'increased in people', *cresciuta di popolo.* In the next forty years of his chronicle Villani continues to attend to the last circuit, detailing its moats and the dismantling of old walls in 1310, additional walling in 1316, his own role in supervising its construction in 1321, and concluding with two detailed chapters in 1323, 'On the large size and building of the city of Florence and the new circle and wall', which contain his measuring of the barbicans and the circuit, given as five miles.[116]

10. Finally, Villani noted emptiness within the 1283 circuit. While he provided a picture of population pressure pressing on previous walls, he carefully noted in his final account of the last circuit, in 1323, that it enclosed much space which was empty of houses but filled with orchards and gardens.[117]

Interwoven with the succession of circuits are two strands of comment about population. One is numerically impressionist, with statements about 'large' growth and considerable immigration, the other consists of precise figures, as follows.[118]

1 [= no 3 above]. Before Totila's destruction of the city in 450, Florence had grown to 22,000 men-at-arms, without the [male] elderly and [male] children.[119] With the ratio of arms-bearing men and overall population which Villani found in 1338, 5:18, this means he was probably suggesting a total population before 450 of 79,200—or a round 80,000.

[114] *Cronica*, IV. v (i. 156), V. vi (i. 171), and V. vii (i. 173).

[115] Ibid., V. viii (i. 175–8) and V. xxv (i. 208).

[116] Ibid., VIII. xcix (i. 562), IX. xxxi (ii. 49), X. x (ii. 218–19), X. lxxvii (ii. 280), X. cxxxvii (ii. 338), and X. cclvi–vii (ii. 428–34).

[117] Ibid., X. cclvii; ii. 433.

[118] On the utility of Villani's figures for the study of demographic and economic *realities*, see E. Fiumi, 'La demografia fiorentina nelle pagine di Giovanni Villani', *Archivio Storico Italiano* 108 (1958), 78–158; A. Sapori, 'L'attendibilità di alcune testimonianze cronistiche dell'economia medievale', *Archivio Storico Italiano* 12 (1929), 19–30; A. Frugoni, 'G. Villani, Cronica, xi. 94', *Bullettino dell'Istituto storico italiano per il medio evo* 77 (1965), 229–55.

[119] Villani, *Cronica*, III. i; i. 97.

2 [= nos. 7–8 above]. While ascribing the wall of 1078 (correctly speaking, 1172) to great population growth, Villani was at pains to stress that this was great *for that time*. In modern terms it was still small. 'It was not a great people in comparison with the one of our times; for the city of Florence was a small site [area], as has been mentioned and as one can still see [by looking] at the first circuit [of walls], and of inhabitants it did not have a quarter of today's.'[120] If he was bearing in mind 1338's 90,000 mouths, then he was thinking of less than 22,500 at this time.

3. In 1280 the city needed 800 *moggia* of grain a week.[121] This appears in the entries for 1338, which, containing as they do both (*a*) the number of mouths in Florence, and (*b*) the consumption by that number of *moggia* per day, encourages the reader to work out what this means—about 73,500 mouths.

4. In 1300 the city had more than 30,000 citizens, and more than 70,000 men capable of bearing arms in the part of Tuscany under Florence's control.[122] Multiplied, this seems to mean Florence itself containing more than 105,000 inhabitants, and its *contado* about 245,000 inhabitants.

5. In 1338 there were about 25,000 arms-bearing men in Florence, that is, men aged between 15 and 70, and there were about 90,000 mouths overall.[123] Further, 'We find from the parish priest who baptised the babies—inasmuch as he put down a black bean for each male he baptised in San Giovanni and for each female a white [bean], in order to have the number—he found that in these times there were each year from 5,500 to 6000 [with] the male sex most times surpassing [the female] by 300 to 500 each year.'[124]

[120] Ibid., V. vii; i. 174: *nonnera di grande popolo a comparazione ch'ella è a' nostri tempi; che.lla città di Firenze era di piccolo sito, come fatto è memzione, e ancora si vede al primo giro, e non v'avea il quarto ch'è oggi.*

[121] Ibid., XII. xciv; iii. 200. [122] Ibid., IX. xxxix; ii. 62.

[123] Ibid., XII. xciv; iii. 197–8: *Trovamo diligentemente che in questi tempi avea in Firenze circa XXV^M d'uomini da portare arme da XV in LXX anni, cittadini . . . Istimavasi avere in Firenze da LXXXX^M di bocche tra uomini e femmine e fanciulli.*

[124] Ibid., XII. xciv. 28–34; iii. 198: *Trovamo dal piovano che battezzava i fanciulli (imperò che per ogni maschio che battezava in San Giovanni, per avere il novero, mettea una fava nera, e per ogni femmina una bianca) trovò ch'erano l'anno in questi tempi dalle V^MD in VI^M, avanzando le più volte il sesso masculino da CCC in D per anno.* Economists and historical demographers have long worked to make sense of and use these figures. See N. Rodolico, 'Note statistiche su la popolazione fiorentina nel xiv secolo', *Archivio storico italiano,* 5th ser. 30 (1902), 241–74 (250–2)—Rodolico addresses only the birth-rate, not the ratio; Fiumi, 'Demografia fiorentina', 85–7; R. Mols, *Introduction à la Démographie Historique des Villes d'Europe du XIVe au XVIIIe siècle*, 3 vols. (Louvain, 1954–6), i. 85 and n. 4, and ii. 288; J. C. Russell, *Late Ancient and Medieval Population,* Transactions of the American Philosophical Society, n.s. 48, part 3 (Philadelphia, 1958), p. 16; Frugoni, 'Villani', 249–51; Herlihy and Klapisch, *Tuscans and Their Families,* pp. 131–4. They have juxtaposed them with figures for overall Florentine population and pointed out that these figures relate not to 1338 but to a series of years 'in these times'. They have addressed the problem of the high ratio. For 5500 a male excess between 300 and 500 provides ratios in the range of 111.5:100 to 120:100, while for 6000 they are in the range of 110.5:100 to 118.2:100. These are remarkably higher than the figure one would normally expect, about 105:100. This is at birth, while Villani's figures are at baptism. They are the figures compiled by the priest at San Giovanni, who may have been less numerate than the statistically-minded chronicler who took them over from him. Frugoni has pointed out that numbers will have been cut down by deaths before baptism (Frugoni, 'Villani', 249). Fiumi had already pointed to babies being brought in from the countryside for baptism in Florence, with a view to Florentine citizenship, and the possibility of disproportionately high numbers of males among this group of babies contributing to the high male excess (Fiumi, 'Demografia fiorentina', 86 and n. 90). More recently, when addressing the sex-ratio in their study of the Florentine catasto of 1427, Herlihy and

Villani's words show him arriving at these figures. First of all, there is direct examination of data. *Trovamo diligentamente*: 'we *find* after diligent enquiry' that there are 25,000 arms-bearing men. *Istimavasi*: 'it was estimated' that there were some 90,000 mouths. As a Florentine official Villani will have had access to records which enabled a calculation, which he has then rounded. Note the contrast with the 1300 figures, which are presented plainly, without any of these hints of consultation of records and calculation. *Trovamo dal piovano*: 'we *find* from the parish priest' who baptised babies in the Baptistery the numbers of baby girls and boys, as we discussed in Chapter 4 above. As someone supervising work at the Baptistery in 1331, Villani was in contact, and here he is taking directly from a priest at the Baptistery records kept year by year over a number of years of female and male baptisms. Either the priest or Villani—but Villani is the more likely—has performed operations on these figures. Clearly they are annual computations, and quite a few years have been preserved. Presumably they were precise figures. Villani or the priest has looked at them, massaged them into round figures, and then noted minima and maxima in order to provide two ranges, one of overall numbers of baptisms and the other of the sex-ratio. From *aviso*, 'information' about the bread needed continuously in the city, it was 'estimated' that there were 90,000 mouths. Even a Dominican friar like Giordano had a formula for a weight of grain and one person's consumption. As an official concerned with food imports during the scarcity of 1328–30, Villani will have had access to the very best 'information', and he clearly had a formula in his mind, n weight of grain = food for one person for a day. On the basis of this formula, then, he estimated the overall number of mouths in Florence that had to be fed; or, someone else estimated and Villani reported. When Villani provides a figure of grain imports per week in 1280, rather than the number of mouths, this is because of immediate context, which is figures for other imports. The formula and a calculation of mouths in 1280 are implied.

Secondly, Villani is also doing some more speculative estimation. How does he arrive at earlier figures, those of pre-450 and pre-1078 (correctly 1172)? For the pre-450 figure he is likely to have worked backwards from the circuits of walls, equipped with some formula he devised, x space = y mouths. He then divided this figure by three and three-fifths to arrive at the number of arms-bearing men. With the pre-1078 figure he could have done this more simply, taking the circle of 1078 (= 1172) and seeing this as enclosing less than a quarter of the circle which *would have* just contained the population of his own time. In other words, something like the area of the 1283 circle, minus the empty spaces. But this is at best good guesswork, for in these things Villani does not spell out what he is doing.

Klapisch produced a ratio which is interestingly near to the lower ratios produced from Villani's figures: 110:100 (*Tuscans and Their Families*, p. 132), but what predominates in their account is looking for reasons which may have skewed the figures, such as undervaluing and under-recording of female babies, who were possibly out in larger numbers with wet-nurses, rather than investigation of the possible reality of such a large excess (ibid., pp. 131–2, 135–6).

Villani's experience and knowledge of the new circuit and current Florentine population had its counterpart, then, in his construction of Florentine history in which the fundamental element in the remote past as well as the present was also the circuit and population. Villani's pride in size, including large population, is reminiscent of the Dominican Remigio's commendation of large population as one of seven gifts bestowed by God on Florence, and more broadly its literary expression in his *Nuova Cronica*, and especially in the many (and large) figures, which he lists in 1338, make modern scholars see it as belonging to the fertile genre of 'praise of city'.[125] It is quite likely that Villani's reading of the statistics of far-eastern cities in Marco Polo led him to compare. However smaller and less fabulous, Florence, like Beijing, was to have its parts enumerated. It is also worth recalling here the possibility of a more indirect influence which was raised in Chapter 11 above. Disseminated in the decades around 1300, the ideas contained in the *Politics* included the notion, repeatedly dwelt upon, of number and proportion in relation to the subordinate multitudes of rich, middling, poor, soldiers, farmers, and other groups. This is a plausible element in the ancestry of Villani's producing 'statistics' for each of various subordinate 'multitudes' in Florence in 1338, magnates, knights, aliens and transients, judges, notaries, and other groups. At the same time Villani also goes *against* praise of large size, which he links with vice. The duality of approach echoes duality among the friars, Remigio's praise of size on the one hand and on the other hand mendicant sermons about cities containing many sins.[126] But Villani's 'demographic' outlook is not reducible to the learned 'analogues' and possible 'sources' we can suggest. Though a more sophisticated man than the coarse jokers of 1233, Villani had a concern with the theme of size and population which was clearly, at bottom, shared also by street-corner Florentines. His view of the new circuit of 1283 will have overlapped heavily with the innumerable ordinary people who saw its first stone being blessed and placed in position.

Most difficult to locate is one 'demographic' theme which has not so far been mentioned: marriage-age. 'And the majority of the maidens were 20 or more years old before they went to husband' (*e le più delle pulcelle aveano XX o più anni anzi ch'andassano a marito*).[127] This is part of a picture of an ideal Florence in a specific period in the past, which has a close counterpart in Dante—and much scholarship has been devoted to the possibility that Villani read Dante, or that both had a common source,[128] reasonable suggestions which, however true, are unlikely to be more than a small part of the picture. I repeat: an author is not reducible to a source. Even if there is only one source, and it is copied, the choice of the source reflects the author.

In the background were the realities of Florence in Villani's time, or, rather, Villani's view of those realities. Since what these realities were is clearly and

[125] See J. K. Hyde, 'Medieval Descriptions of Cities', repr. in his *Literacy and its Uses: Studies on Late Medieval Italy*, ed. D. Waley (Manchester and New York, 1993), pp. 1–32 (pp. 25–8).

[126] Villani, *Cronica*, VI. xxxii; i. 259.

[127] Villani, *Cronica*, VII. lxix; i. 364.

[128] See C. T. Davis, 'Il buon tempo antico', repr. in his *Dante's Italy*, pp. 71–93.

precisely implied by the contrasting style and manners which are attributed to the Florentines of the past golden period, let us spell out what is implied for *now*, meaning in the early fourteenth century: Florentines live ostentatiously and with great expenditure, consuming fine food and buying (especially the women) costly and elaborate clothing. Dowries are extraordinarily high, and the majority of girls get married very young.

Part of attention to marriage-age also comes through concentration on this in vernacular works used or available in Florence, and sermons: Brunetto's upholding of parity of age; Giles's upholding of particular (quite close) ages for men and women and eugenic aims; and, most of all, Servasanto. As we saw, Servasanto criticizes the current low age at which 'our' girls get married, and upholds a high age, which is associated with a remote ideal—geographically remote—a people of military prowess, liberty, and virtue. Villani chooses to set his ideal in a chronologically remote period, 1250, which perhaps has *liberty*, for it was the year of the death of the oppressor of the liberty of many cities, Frederick II, and also of the formation of Florence's first 'popular' government. It certainly has *military prowess*, for it appears in a book dozens of whose chapters are devoted to Florentine military victories. And it had *virtue* and success, as Villani spells out. 'With their simple way of life they did greater and more virtuous things' than we do in our days. If we seek parallels, Servasanto is closest, but I am not suggesting him as a single source. The concatenation of texts we have been examining and the very close parallels, which we shall be seeing between Villani and Dante, indicate that both over-population and the low marriage-age of girls were matters of general concern.

14.8 *Lay Florentines (c): Dante*

We turn finally, then, to another Florentine, overlapping in his life and experience with Villani, though in many ways so different and one of the greatest of all poets. Our interest lies in cantos 15–16 in the *Paradiso*, written by Dante probably some time between 1315 and 1318.[129] Born in 1260 and christened in that baptistery where at some—later?—stage the priest would be casting a black bean for such a male baby, Dante lived, learnt, and breathed in the air of Florence, until exile in 1302, which lasted until his death in 1321. In his obituary notice Villani commented on Dante being very learned in virtually every discipline, *grande letterato quasi in ogni scienza*, and it has been plausibly suggested that we should credit Dante's statement that he attended the schools of the religious, being taught possibly by mendicants at Santa Maria Novella, such as Remigio, or at Santa Croce. Certainly Dante was more likely than Villani to have extensive knowledge of the

[129] I use Natalino Sapegno's text of the *Divina Commedia*, 3 vols., 2nd edn. (Florence, 1968), and, unless otherwise noted, the translation of the old parallel text Temple Classics edition, whose literalness often has the merit of *not* deciding between conflicting interpretations.

predominantly scholastic texts which this book has been discussing. We are not surprised to find Dante, for example, citing one of Aristotle's *Little Natural Works* in relation to variation in the 'ages of man', which he discussed in his philosophical treatise *Convivio.*[130] At the same time we would be surprised to find in him quite the passion for population figures evinced by the hard-headed man of affairs who was Villani.

Everyone was conscious of exile and its effects. The Dominican Giordano of Pisa commented on exiles' natural desire to return,[131] and after saying that Dante 'denounced and cried out' too much, Villani suggested that 'perhaps his exile made him do this'. Again, where Villani is more prosaic, there is the passion of both exile and poet whenever Dante engages with Florence in the *Comedy.* Set in 1300, this long poem recounts a vision granted to Dante, the Dante-personage whom the real Dante made into one of the characters of the *Comedy.* In this vision the Dante-personage is led through Hell, Purgatory, and Heaven. Coming from a crowded earthly city, Dante depicted its counterpart in the afterlife, in a Hell, and, to a certain extent a Purgatory, which are teeming with crowds and multitudes, often 'more than a thousand'. They are skilfully choreographed, and a thesaurus of 'crowd' words and similes is ransacked to describe them. One parallel was Rome during the jubilee year in 1300, when a system of two-way traffic was adopted to handle and keep moving the visiting pilgrims, who, according to Villani, increased the city population throughout that year by 200,000.[132] Coming from a population circled by a wall, whose circumference was an initial guide to its numbers, Dante depicts sinners contained in Hell's circuits and describes Virgil addressing the Dante-personage and telling him how to arrive at the number of sowers of discord:

> *Pensa, se tu annoverar le credi,*
> *che miglia ventidue la valle volge*
>
> Consider, if thou thinkest to number them,
> that the valley goes round two-and-twenty miles.[133]

Amidst Dante's immense 'cast-list'[134] there are many Florentines, and meeting them or talking about Florence are the occasions of everything from pathos to extremes of bitterness. Through encountering these the reader is slowly led forward and prepared for the climax of Dante's treatment of his loved and hated native city, cantos 15–16 in the *Paradiso.* Here there is an occasion of deep emotion,

[130] *Convivio,* IV. 23. Dante's discussion of ages is analysed in J. A. Burrow, *The Ages of Man: A Study in Medieval Writing and Thought* (Oxford, 1986), pp. 6–8, 32–6, and by E. Sears, *The Ages of Man: Medieval Interpretations of the Life-Cycle* (Princeton, 1996), pp. 103–4. I do not discuss the encyclopaedic scholastic culture shown by Dante in his *Convivio,* whose index of authors and texts coincides frequently with the index to *The Measure of Multitude.*

[131] Giordano, *Prediche,* ed. Narducci, p. 403.

[132] *Inferno,* XVIII. 26–32; Villani, *Cronica,* IX. xxxvi; ii. 57.

[133] *Inferno,* XXIX. 8–9.

[134] The phrase is used in an article to which I am much indebted, J. Usher, '"Più di mille": Crowd Control in the Commedia', in *Word and Drama in Dante: Essays on the "Divina Commedia"*, ed. J. C. Barnes and J. Petrie (Dublin, 1993), pp. 55–71.

the extraordinary meeting of Dante and his forebear Cacciaguida. Introducing himself as Dante's great-great-grandfather, Cacciaguida immediately launches into a long and eloquent account of the wonderful state of Florence in his time, the mid-twelfth century. Like Villani's account of the good former time, this was a mirror to 'now', which in the case of the *Comedy* was 1300. At its core was the notion of Florence's purity when it was within the older circuit,

Fiorenza dentro dalla cerchia antica
Florence, within the ancient circling.[135]

Peace and simplicity of dress are immediately followed by the theme of 'measure' in dowry and girls' marriage-age.

Non faceva, nascendo, ancor paura
la figlia al padre; ché 'l tempo e la dote
Non fuggíen quinci e quindi la misura.

As yet the daughter's birth struck not the father
with dismay; for wedding day and dowry
evaded not the measure due on this side and on that.[136]

Villani echoed that theme, but not the next one.

Non avea case di famiglia vote;
non v'era giunto ancor Sardanapolo
a mostrar ciò che 'n camera si pote.[137]

There were no houses empty of family;
Sardanapalus[138] had not yet arrived
to show what may be done within the chamber.[139]

When Cacciaguida had finished and Dante came to question him, he asked about his ancestry and then the former size of Florence's population.

[135] *Paradiso*, XV. 97.

[136] *Paradiso*, XV. 103–5. See Sapegno's note, quoting the *Ottimo Comento*, to the effect that they used to wait to 'sufficient age' (*etade sufficiente*) to marry them, but now marry them in the cradle. Mark Musa's translation in the Penguin Classics edition runs thus: In those days fathers had no cause to fear | a daughter's birth: the marriageable age | was not too low, the dowry not too high.

[137] *Paradiso*, XV. 106–8. [138] A classical figure of lust.

[139] This could mean *either* ostentatious and too big to live in, which is the interpretation in Musa's translation (houses too large to live in were not built), *or* empty because of exiles, *or* devoid of offspring because of vice. See Sapegno's note. He prefers the third, *vuote di prole, a cagione di costumi corrotti*, 'empty of offspring by reason of immoral practices'. Parallels between Giles of Rome's *Del Reggimento de' principi* and the *Commedia* include the notion of a house without offspring not being perfect (II. i. 3; pp. 131–2) and the presence of Sardanapalus as a figure of lust (I. ii. 16; p. 52): *Sardanapolo . . . tutte le sue parole, et tutto il suo intendimento era ne la camera in seguire le sue malvagie volontà di lussuria.* When one compares Latin and French versions—*omnes collocutiones eius erant in cameris ad mulieres*, and *toutes ses paroles estoient en chambres as dames*—there appears special emphasis in the added *tutto il suo intendimento . . . malvagie volontà di lussuria.* The most likely interpretation—offspring lacking in Florentine houses in 1300, in contrast to the purer days of 1150, through sexual practices—accords with what Servasanto and Giordano were saying.

ditemi dell'ovil di San Giovanni,
quanto era allora . . .?

Tell me of the sheepfold of St John [= the Baptistery],
how great it then was . . .?[140]

The answer from Cacciaguida, a knight, was that

Tutti color ch'a quel tempo eran ivi
da poter arme tra Marte e l'Batista,
eran il quinto di quei ch'or son vivi

At that time all who were there, between Mars
and the Baptist, [boundaries of the city] capable of arms, were but the
fifth of the now living ones.[141]

The older circuit casts a long shadow, as Cacciaguida compares past and present numbers, laments youthful marriage, and alludes darkly to lack of children. If the bringing together of these themes and the changes wrought by the passing of 150 years may be worthy of remark, in the climate of Florentine thought around 1300 it is not extraordinary.

But Dante distilled this matter into poetry. And there they stand, these three moral and historical 'demographic' observations: at the climax of the *Comedy*'s depiction of the ideal and corrupt versions of the city of Dante's birth, and at the high point of medieval poetic art. Even into the vision of paradise, where there would be no marrying or giving in marriage, Dante carried his thoughts, and those of his ancestors and contemporaries, about the generation and multitude of men and women on earth.

[140] *Paradiso*, XVI. 25–6. [141] *Paradiso*, XVI. 46–8.

EPIGRAPH

THE CLIMATE OF THOUGHT

The title of this book can plead 'Not guilty' to the charge of anachronism of word or phrase, for *The Measure of Multitude* could have been understood in the thirteenth century. But what of the enterprise overall? That is to say, what of the anachronism of the individual discipline: demographic thought—in the middle ages?

I see no danger of crude anachronism of parts of the discipline. Only comic ignorance would make one look for a Law of Population or Princeton Life-Tables in thirteenth-century Paris. Nor is there a problem in the lack of systematic statics, unless one thinks that an area of thought is defined by all the characteristics of its most advanced version, such that all earlier versions must fall away. There is clear grappling with many aspects of population long before the union of this intellectual discipline with mathematics and the invention of the word *démographie* in 1855.[1] And, as we have seen, quantity enters to some degree even in the more primitive demographic thought of our period.

There is more of a problem when the whole is considered. The difficulty is not a lack of demographic concepts and vocabulary, for when we turn the lens in their direction we find a great deal to look at. We can also find a lot brought together. William of Auvergne addressed fertility in western Christian marriages, avoidance of offspring, sterility among prostitutes, the relation of a polygamous system to the sex-ratio in a population, and the comparative population densities of a polygamous Islamic and monogamous Christian country: all in one treatise. And within just a few lines of one canto in Dante's *Comedy* there is an equally remarkable concatenation of 'demographic' themes. How far is genre a problem? A modern textbook will be entitled *Demography*, but where can I point to a medieval equivalent? William's was a treatise on the sacrament of marriage, and Dante's a visionary poem. This point has some force. I can urge that the lack of a medieval treatise *De multitudine, On population*, is parallelled by the lack of medieval treatise *On Economics*, in the modern sense of the word 'economics'. However, this may not be much of a defence, rather an indication that there is something inherently shaky not only in my project but also in others, such as modern histories of *Medieval Economic Thought. History of Medieval Political Thought* before the translation of the *Politics* is similarly vulnerable.

[1] Dupâquier, *Histoire de la démographie*, p. 403. Forms of the English *demography* (*-er, -ic* and *-y*) are first attested by the *Oxford English Dictionary* in 1880–2, and forms of *demographical* (*-al*, -ally) in 1902.

The climate of thought has seldom been described . . .[2]

The opening line of this poem by Robert Graves is unexpectedly useful. What of the 'climate of thought' in one particular area, modern demography? In its impersonal reduction of humans to quantity and its odd mix of bits of biology, geography, and sociology, it does have a distinctive climate: rather odd and cold. When reading many of the texts used in this book—let us say, a commentary in which marriage-ages are combined with Aristotle on length of life and some reproductive biology—I have often sensed a similar climate. I advance this impression not to persuade anyone, but only to inform the reader who is curious about what I really think.

I am uncertain. While writing this book I have gone from conviction to doubt and back again. The subject seems to me much like different ways of looking at one fourteen-century survival, the Gough map of England. From one aspect this green map looks comic. England is all green, it lies on its side and much of it is out of kilter.[3] But when I think about earlier medieval maps, another aspect appears. Most earlier maps represented geographical areas schematically and symbolically, rather than realistically. Seen in the light of these, the Gough map looks different. Distorted it may be, but it is England: depicted roughly to scale and perfectly recognizable.[4] It can even be seen as a breakthrough of realism.

By the first half of the fourteenth century, is medieval demographic thought a Gough map: rough and primitive 'demographic thought' that is recognizably *there*?

[2] 'The Climate of Thought' is both the title and first line of a poem in which Robert Graves addressed the weather, seasons, and landscape of thought: *Collected Poems 1975* (London, 1975), p. 113.

[3] Other maps which have not survived may well have been better-proportioned. Giles of Rome described proportion in contemporary seamen's maps, *De regimine*, III. iii. 11; p. 584: *Sic etiam marinarii faciunt, qui videntes maris pericula, ne eorum naves patiantur naufragium, descripserunt maris mappam, ubi portus marini, discrimina maris, et cetera talia proportionaliter sunt descripta, qui marinarii intuentes, statim percipiunt qualiter debeant pergere, et in quo loco existant, et in quibus debeant se cavere.*

[4] *Cartography in Prehistoric, Ancient and Medieval Europe and the Mediterranean*, ed. J. B. Harley and D. Woodward, *The History of Cartography* (Chicago and London, 1987–), i. plate 80 and p. 496. Harley's historiographical essay in this volume, 'The Map and the Development of the History of Cartography' (pp. 1–42), is useful on the study of maps as expressions of ideas and outlook.

BIBLIOGRAPHY

This bibliography lists works cited in the book. Part 1 contains primary sources, part 2 reference works and catalogues of manuscripts and libraries, part 3 secondary material. Only those manuscripts whose contents have been used are listed in part 1. Not listed there are those manuscripts mentioned in the book solely in order to map the diffusion and reception of a work.

1. PRIMARY SOURCES

Adam de Buckfield, commentary on Aristotle, *De longitudine et brevitate vitae*, Oxford, Merton College, MS 272.

Alain de Lille, *De fide, Liber quartus contra paganos*, ed. M.-T. d'Alverny, *Cahiers de Fanjeaux* 18 (Toulouse, 1983), pp. 323–50.

—— *Liber poenitentialis*, ed. J. Longère, 2 vols., AMN 17–18 (1965).

—— '*Liber poenitentialis*: les traditions moyenne et courte', ed. J. Longère, *AHDLMA* 32 (1966), 169–242.

Albert the Great, *Commentarii in octo libros Politicorum Aristotelis*, in *Opera*, Borgnet, viii.

—— *De animalibus libri XXVI*, ed. H. Stadler, 2 vols., BGPTM 15–16 (1916–20).

—— *De generatione et corruptione*, *Opera*, Borgnet, iv. 345–457; ed. P. Hossfeld, *Opera*, Geyer, v, part 2.

—— *Meteora libri IV*, *Opera*, Borgnet, iv. 477–808.

—— *De natura loci*, *Opera*, Geyer, v, part 2, 1–46; trans. J. P. Tilman, *An Appraisal of the Geographical Works of Albertus Magnus and His Contributions to Geographical Thought*, Michigan Geographical Publications 4 (Ann Arbor, 1971), pp. 25–145.

—— *Opera omnia*, ed. A. Borgnet, 38 vols. (Paris, 1890–99).

—— *Opera omnia*, ed. B. Geyer *et al.*, 50 vols. (Aschendorff, 1951–).

—— *Quaestiones super De animalibus*, ed. E. Filthaut, in *Opera*, Geyer, xii.

—— *Scripta in IV. libros sententiarum*, 5 vols. (1893–4), in *Opera*, Borgnet, xxvi–xxx.

Albumasar, *De magnis coniunctionibus annorum revolutionibus ac eorum profectionibus* (Augsburg, 1489).

Alexander of Aphrodisias, *Commentaire sur les Météores d'Aristote: Traduction de Guillaume de Moerbeke*, ed. A. J. Smet, Centre de Wulf-Mansion, Corpus Latinum Commentariorum in Aristotelem Graecorum 4 (Louvain and Paris, 1968).

Alexander of Hales, *Glossa in quatuor libros sententiarum Petri Lombardi*, 4 vols., Bibliotheca Scholastica Medii Aevi 12–15 (Grottaferrata, 1951–57).

—— *Quaestiones disputatae antequam esset frater*, 3 vols., Bibliotheca Scholastica Medii Aevi 19–21 (Grottaferrata, 1960).

—— *Summa theologica*, 4 vols. in 6 parts (Quaracchi, 1924–79).

Alexander III, *Sententiae*, ed. A. M. Gietl, *Die Sentenzen Rolands nachmals Papstes Alexander III* (Freiburg-im-Breisgau, 1891).

Alfonso el Sabio, *Las siete partidas*, 4 vols. (Madrid, 1844–5).

Alfraganus, *Liber de aggregationibus*, in Gerard of Cremona's Latin translation: ed. R.

Campani, Alfragano, *Il 'Libro dell'aggregazione delle stelle' (Dante, Conv., II, vi–134) secondo il codice Mediceo-Laurenziano PL. 29-Cod. 9*, VIII (Città di Castello, 1910).

Alfred of Sareshel, *Commentary on the Metheora of Aristotle: Critical Edition, Introduction and Notes*, ed. J. K. Otte, Studien und Texte zur Geistesgeschichte des Mittelalters 19 (Leiden, New York, Copenhagen, and Cologne, 1988).

Al-Kindi, *Apologia* or *Risālat* [*Risālat 'Abdillāh ibn-Ismā'īl al-Hāshimi ila 'Abd-al-Masīh ibn Ishāq al-Kindi wa-Risālat al-Kindi ila al-Hāshimi*], ed. J. Muñoz Sendino, 'Al-Kindi, Apología del Cristianism', *Miscelánea Comillas*, 11–12 (Comillas, Santander, 1949), pp. 337–460.

Alsace Anonymous: see *De rebus Alsaticis*.

Alvarus Pelagius, *De planctu ecclesie* (Venice, 1560).

Andrew of Perugia, *Epistola*, ed. Wyngaert, *Itinera*, p. 373–7.

The Anglo-Saxon Missionaries in Germany, ed. and trans. C. H. Talbot (London, 1954).

Anonymous commentaries on *Sentences*:

—— BN, MS Lat. 3681.

—— BN, MS Lat. 14307.

—— BN, MS Lat. 14308.

—— Erfurt, Stadtbibliothek, MS Fol. 108.

—— Leipzig, Universitätsbibliothek, MS 418.

—— Leipzig, Universitätsbibliothek, MS 558.

—— Vatican, MS Vat. Lat. 782.

Anselms von Laon systematische Sentenzen, ed. F. Bliemetzrieder, BGPTM 18, parts 2–3 (1919).

Anselm of Laon, school of: *Das Schrifttum der Schule Anselms von Laon und Wilhelms von Champeaux in deutschen Bibliotheken*, ed. H. Weisweiler, BGPTM 33, 2 vols. (1936).

Antoninus of Florence, *Confessionale* (Cologne, *c.*1470).

—— *Theologia moralis*, ed. P. Ballerini, 4 vols. (Verona, 1740).

Antonio Andrès, *In quatuor sententiarum libros opus longe absolutissimum* (Venice, 1578).

Antonio dei Ribaldi of Cremona, *Itinerarium*, ed. Golubovich, iii. 331–42.

Aragon Anonymous, commentary on Aristotle, *Politics*, BN, MS Lat. 16133.

Aristotle, (*a*) medieval Latin translations:

(*a*) i *De animalibus* (*On Animals*) = *History of Animals, Parts of Animals*, and *Generation of Animals*:

—— *Michael Scot's Arabic-Latin Translation. Part Two. Books XI–XIV: Parts of Animals*, ed. A. M. I. Van Oppenraaji, Aristoteles Semitico-Latinus 5 (Leiden, Boston, and Cologne, 1998).

—— *Michael Scot's Arabic-Latin Translation. Part Three. Books XV–XIX: Generation of Animals*, ed. A. M. I. Van Oppenraaji, Aristoteles Semitico-Latinus 5 (Leiden, New York, and Cologne, 1992).

—— William of Moerbeke's Greek-Latin trans.: *Generation of Animals: De generatione animalium: Translatio Guillelmi de Moerbeka*, ed. H. J. Drossaert Lulofs, AL xvii. 2.v.

(*a*) ii *De longitudine et brevitate vite* (*On Length and Shortness of Life*):

—— James of Venice's Greek-Latin trans.: Peter of Spain, *Obras Filosóficas*, ed. M. Alonso, Consejo Superior de Investigaciones Cientificas, Instituto de Filosofia 'Luis Vives', Series A 4, 3 vols. (Madrid, 1941–52), iii. 405–11.

—— William of Moerbeke's Greek-Latin trans.: Aristotle, *Opera de naturali philosophia* (Venice, 1496), 33v–35r.

(*a*) iii *Meteorologica* (*Meteorology*):

—— William of Moerbeke's Greek-Latin trans. in Thomas Aquinas, *In libros Aristotelis Meteologicorum expositio*, I. xvii; *Opera omnia*, Leonine edn., iii. 323–421.

—— French translation/paraphrase: *see* Mahieu le Vilain.

(*a*) iv *Politica* (*Politics*):

—— Moerbeke's Latin translation, first incomplete attempt: *Politica (Libri I–II. 11)*, ed. P. Michaud-Quantin, AL xxix. 1 (Bruges and Paris, 1961).

—— Moerbeke's second and complete Latin trans.: *Aristotelis Politicorum Libri Octo, cum vetusta translatione Guilelmi de Moerbeka*, ed. F. Susemihl (Leipzig, 1882). Also available in Thomas Aquinas, *In libros politicorum Aristotelis expositio*, ed. R. M. Spiazzi (Turin and Rome, 1951).

—— French trans.: *see* Nicole Oresme.

(*a*) v (Pseudo-Aristotle), *Problemata* (*Problems*) [attributed], Bartholomew of Messina's Greek-Latin trans.:

—— book I: R. Seligsohn, *Die Übersetzung der ps-aristotelischen Problemata durch Bartholomaeus von Messina: Text und textkritische Untersuchungen zum ersten Buch*, Inaugural Dissertation (Berlin, 1934).

—— *Problemata Aristotelis cum duplici translatione, antiqua* [= Bartholomew of Messina] *et nova scilicet Theodori Gaze: cum expositione Petri Aponi* (Venice, 1501).

See also *Auctoritates Aristotelis.*

Aristotle (*b*): modern English translations:

—— *The Complete Works of Aristotle: The Revised Oxford Translation*, ed. J. Barnes, Bollingen Series 71/2, 2 vols. (Princeton, 1984).

—— *The Works of Aristotle*, ed. J. A. Smith and W. D. Ross, 12 vols. (Oxford, 1910–52).

Arnau de Vilanova, *Breviarium practice* [dubiously attributed to Arnau], in *Opera nuperrime revisa*, 150ra–205rb.

—— *Compilatio de conceptione* [attributed to Arnau], in *Opera nuperrime revisa*, 213va–4ra.

—— *De esu carnium*, ed. D. M. Bazell, *Opera medica omnia*, xi (Barcelona, 1999).

—— *Opera medica omnia*, ed. M. R. McVaugh *et al.* (Barcelona, 1975–).

—— *Opera nuperrime revisa* (Lyons, 1532).

—— *Speculum introductionum medicinalium*, in *Opera nuperrime revisa*, 1ra–36ra.

Astesanus of Asti, *Summa de casibus conscientiae* (pre-1479, place unknown).

Auctoritates Aristotelis: un florilège médiéval. Étude historique et édition critique, ed. J. Hamesse, Philosophes Médiévaux 17 (Louvain, Paris, 1974).

Augustine, *De civitate Dei*, ed. B. Dombart, Teubner edn., 2 vols. (Leipzig, 1877).

—— *City of God*, trans. H. Bettenson (Harmondsworth, 1972).

Averroes, *Colliget* (Venice, 1497).

—— *Commentarium medium in Aristotelis De generatione et corruptione libros*, ed. P. H. Fobes, Corpus Commentariorum Averroes in Aristotelem, Versionum Latinarum 4/1 (Cambridge, Mass., 1956).

—— *Compendium* of Aristotle's *De longitudine et brevitate vitae: Compendia librorum Aristotelis qui Parva Naturalia vocantur*, ed. E. L. Shields, Corpus Commentariorum Averrois in Aristotelem, Versionum Latinarum 7 (Cambridge, Mass., 1949), pp. 129–49.

—— modern trans. of Arabic (not the medieval Latin version): H. Blumberg, *Averroes, Epitome of Parva Naturalia*, Corpus Commentariorum Averrois in Aristotelem, Versio Anglica 7 (Cambridge, Mass., 1961), pp. 54–61.

Avicenna, *Abbreviatio de animalibus*, in Avicenna, *Opera* (Venice, 1508, repr. Frankfurt-am-Main, 1961), 29r–64r.

—— *Liber canonis medicine* (Venice, 1527, repr. Brussels, 1971); BL, MS Royal 12.G.6.

—— *Liber de philosophia prima sive scientia divina*, ed. S. Van Riet, Avicenna Latinus, 3 vols. (Louvain and Leiden, 1977–83).

Baldwin, archbishop of Canterbury, letter, *PL* 207, 306–8.

Bartholomew the Englishman [Bartholomaeus Anglicus], *De proprietatibus rerum* (Nuremberg, 1519); Milan, Ambrosian Library, MS A.147 Sup.

—— Book 15, German, Low Countries, Scandinavian, and Baltic provinces: ed. A. E. Schönbach, 'Des Bartholomaeus Anglicus Beschreibung Deutschlands gegen 1240', *Mitteilungen des Instituts für österreichische Geschichtsforschung* 27 (1906), 54–90.

—— Book 15, Italian provinces: ed. W. Lampen, 'L'Italia nel pensiero di Fra Bartolomeo Anglico O.F.M.', *Studi Francescani* 14 (1928), 111–18.

—— *On the Properties of Things: John Tevisa's translation of Bartholomaeus Anglicus De Proprietatibus Rerum*, ed. M. C. Seymour *et al.*, 3 vols. (Oxford, 1975–88); i–ii contain the text, iii variant readings.

Bartholomew of Bruges, questions on Ps-Aristotle, *Economics*, BN, MS Lat. 16089; Vatican, MS Vat. Lat. 2167.

Bartholomew of Exeter, 'Penitential', ed. A. Morey, *Bartholomew of Exeter, Bishop and Canonist: A Study in the Twelfth Century* (Cambridge, 1937), pp. 175–300.

Bartholomew of Parma, *Tractatus Sphaerae*, ed. E. Narducci, *Bullettino di bibliografia e di storia delle scienze matematiche e fisiche*, ed. B. Boncompagni, 17 (1884), pp. 43–120 and 165–215.

Bartolomeo da Varignana, commentary on Ps-Aristotle, *Economics*, Venice, Padri Redentoristi, MS 3 (445).

Bérenger Frédol the Older [attributed], *Summula in foro poenitentiali, In primis debet sacerdos*, BN, MS Lat. 3265.

Bernard de Gordon, *Lilium medicinae* (Lyons, 1574).

Bernard Gui, *Liber sententiarum*: P. van Limborch, ed., *Liber Sententiarum Inquisitionis Tholosanae* (Amsterdam, 1692).

Bernard of Pavia, *Summa decretalium*, ed. E. T. A. Laspeyres (Regensburg, 1860, repr. Graz, 1956).

Bonaventure, *Commentaria in quatuor libros sententiarum*, 4 vols. (Quaracchi, 1882–9) = *Opera omnia*, 11 vols. (Quaracchi, 1882–1902), i–iv.

—— *Opera omnia*, ed. A. C. Peltier, 15 vols. (Paris, 1864–71: see below, Servasanto of Faenza, sermons.

Breviarium practice: see Arnau de Vilanova.

Brunetto Latini: *Li Livres dou Tresor de Brunetto Latini*, ed. F. J. Carmody (Berkeley and Los Angeles, 1948).

C. de Bridia, *Hystoria Tartarorum*, ed. A. Önnerfors (Berlin, 1967).

Capitula Episcoporum, ed. P. Brommer, MGH, 1- (Hanover, 1984–).

Cecco d'Ascoli, *In spheram mundi enarratio*, ed. L. Thorndike, *The Sphere of Sacrobosco and its Commentators* (Chicago, 1949), pp. 344–411.

Chartularium universitatis parisiensis, ed. H. Denifle and E. Chatelain, 4 vols. (Paris, 1889–97).

Chronica de origine civitatis, ed. O. Hartwig, *Quellen und Forschungen zur ältesten Geschichte der Stadt Florenz*, 2 vols. (Marburg, Halle, 1875–80), i. 35–65.

Cicero, *De inventione*, trans. W. M. Hubbell, Loeb edn. (London, Cambridge, Mass., 1949).

Claudius Ptolemaeus: *see* Ptolemy.

Conrad of Halberstadt, *Responsorium curiosorum* (Lübeck, 1478).

Constantine the African, *Liber Pantegni*, in Isaac Israeli, *Opera omnia*, 2 vols. (Lyons, 1515).

Corpus iuris canonici, ed. E. Friedberg, 2 vols. (Leipzig, 1879).

Councils & Synods with other Documents Relating to the English Church I, AD 871–1204, ed. D. Whitelock, M. Brett and C. N. L. Brooke, 2 vols. (Oxford, 1981).

Councils & Synods with other Documents Relating to the English Church II, AD 1205–1313, ed. F. M. Powicke and C. R. Cheney, 2 vols. (Oxford, 1964).

Curtze, M., ed., 'Arithmetische Scherzaufaben aus dem 14. Jahrhundert', *Bibliotheca Mathematica*, n.s. 9 (1895), 77–88.

Dante, *Commedia*, ed. N. Sapegno, 3 vols., 2nd edn. (Florence, 1968).

—— *The Divine Comedy*, trans. M. Musa, 3 vols. (Harmondsworth, 1984–6).

David of Dinant, *Quaternulorum fragmenta*, ed. M. Kurdzialek, Studia Mediewistyczne 5 (Warsaw, 1963).

De Coniugio, ed. F. Bliemetzrieder, 'Théologie et théologiens de l'école épiscopale de Paris avant Pierre Lombard', *RTAM* 5 (1931), 272–91 (pp. 274–87).

Decretum Dei fuit, ed. H. Weisweiler, *Das Schrifttum der Schule Anselms von Laon und Wilhelms von Champeaux in deutschen Bibliotheken*, BGPTM 33, 2 vols. (1936), i. 361–79.

De rebus Alsaticis ineuntis saeculi XIII, ed. P. Jaffé, *MGH SS* 17 (Hanover, 1861).

Deus de cuius principio, ed. H. Weisweiler, 'Le recueil des sentences "Deus de cuius principio et fine tacetur" et son remaniement', *RTAM* 5 (1933), 245–74.

Devise des Chemins, ed. H. Michelant and G. Raynaud, *Itinéraires et descriptions de la terre sainte rédigées en français*, Société de l'Orient Latin, Série Géographique 3 (Geneva, 1882), pp. 239–52.

Dominic Grima, commentary on Genesis, BN, MS Lat. 362.

Dörrie, H., 'Drei Texte zur Geschichte der Ungarn und Mongolen: Die Missionsreisen des fr. Iulianus ins Ural-Gebiet (1234/5) und nach Rußland (1237) und der Bericht des Erzbischofs Peter über die Tartaren', *Nachrichten der Akademie der Wissenschaften in Göttingen*, Philologisch-historische Klasse (1956), 125–202.

Duns Scotus, *Quaestiones in libros sententiarum*, 6 vols.; *Opera omnia*, 12 vols. (Lyons, 1539), v–x.

Durand of St. Pourçain, *In Petri Lombardi sententias theologicas commentariiorum libri IV* (Venice, 1571, repr. in 2 vols. Ridgewood, NJ, 1964).

Engelbert of Admont, *Compendium Politicorum*, ed. G. B. Fowler, 'Admont 608 and Engelbert of Admont', *AHDMLA* 44 (1978), 149–242 (pp. 191–205).

—— *De regimine principum libri seu tractatus VII*, ed. J. G. T. Huffnagl (Regensburg, 1725).

—— 'Excerptum Aristotelis de Politica', ed. G. B. Fowler, 'Admont 608 and Engelbert of Admont', *AHDMLA* 51 (1983), 195–22 (pp. 219–22).

—— 'Excerptum ex Engelberti tractactu *De Regimine principum*', ed. G. B. Fowler, 'Admont 608', *AHDLMA* 45 (1979), 225–306 (pp. 246–9).

—— *Tractatus de causis longaevitatis hominum ante diluvium*, in B. Pez, *Thesaurus anecdotorum novissimus*, 6 vols. (Augsburg, 1721–3), i. 439–502.

Fidenzio of Padua, *Liber recuperationis terra sanctae*, ed. Golubovich, iii. 9–60.

Fredericq, P., ed., *Corpus Documentorum Inquisitionis Haereticae Pravitatis Neerlandicae*, 5 vols. (Ghent and 'S Gravenhage, 1889–1906).

Fulcher of Chartres, *Historia Hierosolymitana*, trans. F. R. Ryan and ed. H. S. Fink, *A History of the Expedition to Jerusalem, 1095–1127* (Knoxville, 1969).

Galen, *Burgundio of Pisa's Translation of Galen's ΠΕΡΙ ΚΡΑΣΕΩΝ 'De complexionibus'*, ed. R. J. Durling, Galenus Latinus 1 (Berlin, New York, 1976).

Gandulph of Bologna, *Sententiarum libri quatuor*, ed. J. De Walter (Vienna and Wrocław, 1924).

Gentile da Foligno, question *An sit licitum provocare aborsum*: ed. R. J. Schaefer, 'Gentile da Foligno über die Zulässigkeit des artifiziellen Abortes (ca. 1340)', *Archiv für die Geschichte der Naturwissenschaften und der Technik* 6 (1913), 321–8 (pp. 325–6).

Geoffrey of Poitiers, *Summa*, BN, MS Lat. 15757.

Gerald of Wales, *De principis instructione*, ed. G. F. Warner, in *Opera omnia*, 8 vols., RS 21 (1861–91), viii.

Gerard of Prato: *Il Breviloquium super libros Sententiarum di Frate Gherardo da Prato*, ed. M. da Civezza (Prato, 1882).
Giles of Rome [Aegidius Colonna], *Del reggimento de' principi di Egidio Romano volgarizzamento trascritto nel MCCLXXXVIII*, ed. F. Corazzini (Florence, 1858).
—— *De regimine principum libri III* (Rome, 1607, repr. Darmstadt, 1967).
—— *Li Livres du Gouvernement des Rois: A XIIIth Century French Version of Egidio Colonna's Treatise De Regimine Principum*, ed. S. P. Molenaer (New York and London, 1899).
—— *In secundum librum sententiarum* (Venice, 1581).
Giordano da Pisa, *Prediche del beato F. Giordano da Rivalto dell' Ordine de' Predicatori*, ed. D. M. Manni (Florence, 1739).
—— *Prediche del beato F. Giordano da Rivalto dell'Ordine dei Predicatori recitate in Firenze dal MCCCIII al MCCCVI*, edited by D. Moreni, 2 vols. (Florence, 1831).
—— *Prediche inedite del B. Giordano da Rivalto dell' Ordine de' Predicatori recitate in Firenze dal 1302 al 1305*, ed. E. Narducci (Bologna, 1860).
—— *Prediche sulla Genesi recitate in Firenze nel M. CCC. IV. Del Beato F. Giordano da Rivalto dell' Ordine dei Predicatori*, ed. D. Moreni (Florence, 1830).
—— *Quaresimale fiorentino 1305–1306*, ed. C. Delcorno (Florence, 1974).
Glossa ordinaria [on the Bible]: *Biblia sacra cum glossis*, 6 vols. (Lyons, 1545).
Glossa ordinaria on Gratian's *Decretum: Decretum divi Gratiani . . . unacum variis scribentium glossis et expositionibus* (Lyons, 1560).
Godfrey of Fontaines, *Les quodlibets de Godefroid de Fontaines*, ed. J. Hoffmans, O. Lottin, A. Pelzer, and M. De Wulf, 5 vols., Les Philosophes Belges, Textes et Études 2–5 and 14 (Louvain, 1904–37).
Goldberg, P. J. P., *Women in Medieval England c.1275–1525*, Manchester Medieval Sources (Manchester, 1995).
Golubovich, G., *Biblioteca bio-bibliografica della Terra Santa e dell'Oriente francescano*, 4 vols. (Quarrachi, 1906–23).
Gui of Orchelles, *Tractatus de sacramentis ex eius summa de De sacramentis et officiis ecclesiae*, ed. D. and O. Van den Eynde, Franciscan Institute Publications, Text Series 4 (New York, Louvain and Paderborn, 1953).
Guibert de Nogent, *Autobiographie*, ed. E.-R. Labande (Paris, 1981).
Guido Bonatti, *De astronomia* (Basle, 1550).
Guido of Monte Roterio, *Manipulus curatorum* (Albi, c.1475).
Guido Vernani, commentary on Aristotle's *Politics*, Venice, Marciana, MS 2492.
Guillaume Peyraut, *Summa de virtutibus et vitiis*, 2 vols. (Antwerp, 1571).
Guillaume de Peyre Godin, [*In sententias*], Naples, Biblioteca Nazionale, MS VII.C.30.
Guillem Rubió [Guillielmus de Rubione], *Disputatorum in quatuor libros Magistri Sententiarum libri quatuor* (Paris, 1518).
Guiraud d'Ot, [*In sententias*], BN, MS Lat. 3068.
Hayton, *La flor des estoires de la terre d'orient, Recueil des historiens de la croisade, Documents Arméniens*, 2 vols. (Paris, 1906), ii. 113–253.
—— Latin trans., *Flos historiarum terre orientis*, ibid., 255–363.
Henry of Brussels and Henry the German, *Questiones quodlibetales*, BN, MS Lat. 16089.
Henry of Ghent, commentary on Genesis, BN, MS Lat. 15355.
—— *Quodlibet VI*, ed. G. A. Wilson, *Opera omnia* (Louvain, 1979–), x.
Henry of Susa (Hostiensis), *Summa aurea* (Venice, 1574, repr. Turin, 1963).
Hermann of Tournai, *De restauratione abbatiae Sancti Martini Tornacensis*, XVIII, *PL* 180, 39–130.
Horrox, R., ed., *The Black Death*, Manchester Medieval Sources (Manchester, 1994).
Hostiensis: *see* Henry of Susa.

Hugh of St Cher, [*In sententias*], BN, MS Lat. 3073; MS Vat. Lat. 1098.
Hugh of St Victor, *Descriptio Mappe Mundi*, ed. P. G. Dalché, *La 'Descriptio Mappe Mundi' de Hugues de Saint-Victor* (Paris, 1988).
—— *De sacramentis, PL* 176, 174–613.
—— trans. R. J. Deferrari, Hugh of Saint Victor, *On the Sacraments of the Christian Faith (De sacramentis)* (Cambridge, Mass., 1951).
Hugo of Novo Castro, [*In sententias II*], BN, MS Lat. 15865.
—— [*In sententias*, IV], Vatican, MS Chigi. B. VI. 96.
Humbert of Garda, [*In sententias*], Vatican, MS Vat. Lat. 1098.
Humbert of Romans, *Opusculum tripartitum*, ed. O. Gratius, *Appendix ad fasciculum rerum expetendarum* (London, 1690), pp. 185–229.
Isidore of Seville, *Etymologiarum sive originum libri XX*, ed. W. M. Lindsay, 2 vols. (Oxford, 1911).
Ivo of Chartres, *Decretum, PL* 161.
—— *Epistolae, PL* 162, 11–299.
Jacques Fournier [Benedict XII]: *Le registre d'inquisition de Jacques Fournier, évêque de Pamiers (1318–1325): Manuscrit no. Vat. Latin 4030 de la Bibliothèque Vaticane*, ed. J. Duvernoy, 3 vols., Bibliothèque Méridionale 2nd series, 41 (Toulouse, 1965).
—— J. Duvernoy, *Le registre d'inquisition de Jacques Fournier, évêque de Pamiers (1318–1325): Corrections* (Toulouse, 1972).
—— *Le registre d'inquisition de Jacques Fournier, évêque de Pamiers (1318–1325)*, ed. and trans. J. Duvernoy, intr. E. Le Roy Ladurie, 3 vols., École des Hautes Études en Sciences Sociales, Centre de Recherches Historiques, Civilisations et Sociétés 43 (Paris, Hague, and New York, 1978).
Jacques de Thérines, *Quodlibets I et II*, ed. P. Glorieux, Textes Philosophiques du Moyen Âge 7 (Paris, 1958).
Jacques de Vitry, *Historia Occidentalis*, ed. J. F. Hinnebusch, *The Historia Occidentalis of Jacques de Vitry: A Critical Edition*, Spicilegium Friburgense 17 (Fribourg, 1972).
—— *Libri duo, quorum prior Orientalis, sive Hierosolymitanae, alter Occidentalis Historiae nomine inscribitur*, ed. F. Moschus (Douai, 1597, repr. Farnborough, 1971).
James of Douai, commentary and questions on Aristotle, *De longitudine et brevitate vitae*, Leipzig, Universitätsbibliothek, MS 1405; Vatican, MS Ross. 569.
James of Verona, *Liber peregrinationis*, ed. R. Röhricht, 'Le pèlerinage du moine Augustin Jacques de Vérone (1335)', *Revue de l'Orient Latin* 3 (1895), 163–302.
John Bromyard, *Summa Praedicantium*, 2 vols. (Venice, 1586); BL, MS Royal VII.E. 4.
John de Balbi, *Catholicon* (Mainz, 1470, repr. Farnborough, 1971).
John de Bassoles, *Opera in quatuor libros sententiarum*, 2 vols. (Paris, 1516–17).
John de Burgo, *Pupilla oculi* (Strasbourg, 1518).
John Buridan, *Quaestiones in librum Aristotelis de longitudine et brevitate vite* (Paris, 1516).
John Duns Scotus: *see* Duns Scotus.
John of Erfurt, [*In sententias*], Leipzig, Universitätsbibliothek, MS 556; MS 558.
John of Freiburg, *Confessionale*, BN, MS Lat. 3532; Oxford, Bodleian Library, MS Laud Misc. 278.
—— *Summa confessorum* (Augsburg, 1470).
John of Gaddesden, *Rosa Anglica* (Venice, 1516).
John of Jandun, *Quaestiones de causa longitudinis et brevitatis vitae*, in John of Jandun, *Quaestiones Super Parvis Naturalibus* (Venice, 1570), cols. 85b–95a.
—— questions on Ps-Aristotle, *Economics*, Erfurt, Stadtbibliothek, MS Quart. 188.
John of Monte Corvino, *Epistolae*, ed. Wyngaert, *Itinera*, pp. 340–55.

John Peckham, *Quodlibeta quatuor*, ed. J. Etzkorn, Bibliotheca Franciscana Scholastica Medii Aevi 25 (Grottaferrata, 1989).

John of Pian di Carpine, *Ystoria Mongalorum*, ed. Wyngaert, *Itinera*, pp. 27–130.

John Quidort of Paris, *Commentarium in libros sententiarum*, ed. J.-P. Muller, 2 vols., Studia Anselmiana 47 and 52 (Rome, 1961–4).

John of Sacrobosco, *De spera*, ed. and trans. L. Thorndike, *The Sphere of Sacrobosco and its Commentators* (Chicago, 1949), pp. 76–142.

John of Salisbury, *Historia pontificalis*, ed. M. Chibnall (London, 1956).

John of Sterngassen, [*In sententias*], MS Vat. Lat. 1092.

John Vath, *Questiones*, ed. L. Cova, 'Le Questioni di Giovanni Vath sul de generatione animalium', *AHDLMA* 59 (1992), 175–287.

Jordan Catalani of Séverac, *Mirabilia descripta*, ed. C. De Montbret, *Description des merveilles d'une partie d'Asie par le P. Jordan ou Jourdain Catalani, natif de Séverac*, Recueil de voyages et de mémoires publié par la Société de Géographie 4 (Paris, 1839), pp. 37–64.

Julian, [*Epistula de vita Tartarorum*], ed. Dörrie, 'Drei Texte', pp. 165–82.

Leonardo of Pisa, *Liber Abaci*, ed. B. Boncompagni, *Scritti di Leonardo Pisano*, 2 vols. (Rome, 1857).

Le livre de l'estat du Grant Caan, ed. M. Jacquet, *Nouveau Journal Asiatique* 6 (1830), pp. 57–71.

Livre des Miracles de Sainte-Catherine-de-Fierbois, 1375–1470, ed. Y. Chauvin, Archives Historiques de Poitou 60 (Poitiers, 1976).

Lotario dei Segni [Innocent III], *De miseria condicionis humane*, ed. R. E. Lewis (Athens, Ga., 1978).

Macer Floridus: *see* Odo of Meung.

Mahieu le Vilain, *Les Metheores d'Aristote: Traduction du XIIIe siècle publié pour la première fois*, ed. R. Edgren (Uppsala, 1945).

Mansi, J. ed., *Sacrorum Conciliorum Nova et Amplissima Collectio*, 31 vols. (Florence and Venice, 1759–98).

Marchesino of Reggio Emilia, *Confessionale*, in Bonaventure, *Opera omnia*, ed. A. C. Peltier, 15 vols. (Paris, 1864–71), viii. 359–92.

Marco Polo, *The Book of Ser Marco Polo*, ed. H. Yule and H. Cordier, 3rd edn., 2 vols. (London, 1903).

—— *The Description of the World*, ed. A. C. Moule and P. Pelliot, 2 vols. (London, 1938).

Marino Sanudo, *Liber secretorum fidelium crucis*, ed. J. Bongars, *Gesta Dei per Francos*, 2 vols. (Hanover, 1611), ii.

Master Martin, *Summa*, BN, MS Lat. 14526.

Matthew Paris, *Abbreviatio Chronicorum*, in *Historia Anglorum*, ed. F. C. Madden, 3 vols., RS 44 (London, 1866), iii.

—— *Chronica majora*, ed. H. R. Luard, RS 57, 7 vols. (1872–83).

—— trans. J. A. Giles, *Matthew Paris's English History*, 3 vols. (London, 1852–4).

—— *Historia Anglorum*, ed. F. C. Madden, 3 vols., RS 44 (London, 1866).

Mondino de' Liuzzi, *consilium* attributed to: ed. N. G. Siraisi, *Taddeo Alderotti and His Pupils: Two Generations of Italian Medical Learning* (Princeton, 1981), p. 283 n. 61.

Montpellier Anonymous, *Tractatus de sterilitate*, ed. E. M. Cartelle, *Tractatus de sterilitate: Anónimo de Montpellier (s. XIV) (Atribuido a A. De Vilanova, R. De Moleriis y J. De Turre)*, Lingüística y Filología 16 (Valladolid, 1993).

Nicholas of Gorran, *Postillae*, BN, MS Lat. 14416.

Nicholas of Ockham, [*In sententias*], Oxford, Merton College, MS 134.

Nicole Oresme, *Le livre de Politiques d'Aristote*, ed. A. D. Menut, Transactions of the American Philosophical Society, n.s. 60, part 6 (Philadelphia, 1970).

—— *Le livre de Yconomique d'Aristote*, ed. A. D. Menut, Transactions of the American Philosophical Society, n.s. 47, Part 5 (Philadelphia, 1957).

Odo of Meung (attributed): *A Middle English Translation of Macer Floridus de Viribus Herbarum*, ed. G. Frisk (Upsala, Copenhagen, and Cambridge, Mass., 1949).

Odoric of Pordenone, *Descriptio orientalium partium*, ed. Yule and Cordier, *Cathay*, ii. 278–336.

—— trans. ibid., 97–277.

—— French trans. by John of Ypres, *c*.1350, ed. H. Cordier, *Les voyages en Asie au XIVe siècle du bienheureux Frère Odoric de Pordenone, religieux de Saint-François*, Recueil de voyages et de documents géographiques 10 (Paris, 1891).

Omnes homines, anonymous medical and scientific problems and questions: ed. E. R. Lind, *Problemata Varia Anatomica: MS 1165 The University of Bologna*, University of Kansas Publications, Humanistic Studies 38 (Lawrence, Kan., 1968).

Passau Anonymous, treatise against heretics, Jews, and Antichrist, later recension: ed. J. Gretser, *Maxima Bibliotheca Veterum Patrum*, ed. M. de La Bigne, 28 vols. (Lyons and Geneva, 1677 and 1707), xxv. 262–77.

Peter d'Abano, *Conciliator controversiarum quae inter philosophos et medicos versantur* (Venice, 1565, repr. Padua, 1985).

—— *Expositio Problematum Aristotelis*, in *Problemata Aristotelis cum duplici translatione, antiqua et nova scilicet Theodori Gaze: cum expositione Petri Aponi* (Venice, 1501).

Peter Aureoli: Peter of Aquila [= incorrect attribution], *Quaestiones in quatuor libros sententiarum* (Speyer, before 1487).

—— *Scriptum super Primum Sententiarum*, Franciscan Institute Publications (New York, Paderborn, and Louvain, 1953).

Peter of Auvergne, commentary and questions on Aristotle, *On Length and Shortness of Life*, Cambridge, Peterhouse, MS 192.

—— commentary on Aristotle, *Politics*: Thomas Aquinas, *In libros Politicorum Aristotelis expositio*, ed. R. M. Spiazzi (Rome, Turin, 1951); the commentary is Peter's from III. vi (p. 142).

—— *The Commentary of Peter of Auvergne on Aristotle's Politics. The inedited part: Book III, less i–vi*, ed. G. M. Grech (Rome, 1967).

—— questions on Aristotle, *Politics*, BN, MS Lat. 16089.

Peter the Chanter, *Summa de sacramentis et animae consiliis*, I, II, III(1), III(2a), III(2b), ed. J.-A. Dugauquier, AMN 4, 7, 11, 16, 21 (1954–67); refs. to III are to text edited in III(2a–b), in which pagination is continuous; III (1) contains editorial matter.

Peter of Ireland, *Expositio et quaestiones in Aristotelis librum de longitudine et brevitate vitae*, ed. M. Dunne, Philosophes Médiévaux 30 (Louvain, Paris, 1993).

Peter of John Olivi, *De perfectione evangelica*, Qu. 6, *An virginitas sit simpliciter melior matrimonio*, ed. in A. Emmen, 'Verginità e matrimonio nella valutazione dell' Olivi', *Studi francescani* 64 (1967), 11–57 (pp. 21–57).

—— [Quaestiones de matrimonio], Vatican, MS Vat. Lat. 4986.

Peter of la Palud [Petrus de Palude], *In quartum sententiarum* (Venice, 1493).

—— [*In secundum sententiarum*], Vatican, MS Lat. 1073.

—— [*Postillae in Bibliam*], Naples, Biblioteca Nazionale, MS VI. D. 74.

Peter the Lombard, *Sententiae in IV libris distinctae*, ed. I. Brady, 2 vols., Spicilegium Bonaventurianum 4–5 (Grottaferrata, 1971–81). I part 2 contains books 1–2 of the *Sententiae*, and II contains books 3–4 of the *Sententiae*. I part 1 contains the editor's introduction; see below Brady, *Prolegomena*.

Peter of Poitiers [chancellor of Paris], *Sententiae*, ed. P. S. Moore, J. N. Garvin, and M. Dulong, 2 vols., Publications in Medieval Studies, The University of Notre Dame 7 and 11 (Notre Dame, 1943–50).

Peter of Poitiers [of St Victor], [*Summa de confessione*] *Compilatio praesens*, ed. J. Longère, CCCM 51 (1980).

Peter of Spain [John XXI], *Tractatus bonus de longitudine et brevitate vite*, ed. M. Alonso, *Pedro Hispano: Obras Filosóficas*, ed. M. Alonso, Consejo Superior de Investigaciones Cientificas, Instituto de Filosofia 'Luis Vives', Series A 4, 3 vols. (Madrid, 1941–52), iii. 413–90.

Peter of Tarentaise [Innocent V], *In IV. Libros sententiarum commentaria*, 4 vols. (Toulouse, 1652, repr. Ridgewood, NJ, 1964).

Peter the Venerable, *Contra Petrobrusianos liber*, ed. J. Fearns, CCCM 10 (1968).

—— *Summa totius haeresis Saracenorum*, ed. J. Kritzeck, *Peter the Venerable and Islam* (Princeton, 1964), pp. 204–11.

Petrus Alfonsi, *Dialogi contra Iudaeos, PL* 157, 535–672.

Petrus de Trabibus, [*In sententias*], Florence, Biblioteca Nazionale, MS D. 6. 359; Leipzig, Universitätsbibliothek, MS 524.

Pierre Dubois, *De recuperatione terre sancte*, ed. C.-V. Langlois (Paris, 1891).

—— trans. W. I. Brandt and P. Dubois, *The Recovery of the Holy Land* (New York, 1956).

Pliny the Elder, *Naturalis Historiae libri XXXVII*, ed. L. Janus, Teubner edn., 6 vols. (Leipzig, 1865–80).

—— ed. and trans. H. Rackham *et al.*, *Natural History*, Loeb edn., 10 vols. (Cambridge, Mass., and London, 1942–63).

Poenitentiale Hubertense 56, ed. F. W. H Wasserschleben, *Die Bußordnungen der abendländischen Kirche* (Halle, 1851), pp. 377–86.

Poenitentiale Pseudo-Romanum, ed. F. W. H Wasserschleben, *Die Bußordnungen der abendländischen Kirche* (Halle, 1851), pp. 360–77.

Prepositinus of Cremona, *Summa*, BN, MS Lat. 14526.

Ptolemy, *Quadripartitum* [also known as *Tetrabiblos*], ed. and trans. F. E. Robbins, Loeb edn. (Cambridge, Mass., and London, 1948).

Questiones medicales, anonymous, BN. MS Lat 12331.

Questiones quodlibetales, medical and scientific, anonymous, Erfurt, Amplon., MS. F. 236.

Questiones quodlibetales, medical and scientific, anonymous, Erfurt, Amplon., MS Q. 323.

Rainier Sacconi, *Summa de Catharis et Leonistis seu Pauperibus de Lugduno*, ed. F. Sanjek, *AFP* 44 (1974), 31–60.

Ramon Lull, *Liber de fine*, in Lull, *Opera Latina*, ix, CCCM 35 (Turnhout, 1981).

Ralph Glaber, *Historiarum libri quinque*, III. vii; ed. N. Bulst, Oxford Medieval Texts (Oxford, 1989).

Ranulph Higden, attributed, *Speculum curatorum*, Cambridge University Library, MS MM.i.20.

Rasis, *Continens* (Venice, 1542).

—— *Liber ad Almansorem* (Venice, 1497).

Raymond of Peñafort, *Summa de poenitentia et matrimonio, cum glossis Ioannis de Friburgo* (Rome, 1603, repr. Farnborough, 1967); the glosses attributed to John of Freiburg are in fact by William of Rennes (below).

Raymond Stephani [attributed], *Directorium ad passagium faciendum*, *Recueil des historiens des croisades: Documents arméniens*, 2 vols. (Paris, 1869–1906), ii. 367–517.

Regimen animarum, anonymous, Oxford, Bodley, MS Hatton 11.

Regino of Prüm, *Libri duo de synodalibus causis et disciplinis ecclesiasticis*, ed. F. G. A./F. W. A. Wasserschleben (Leipzig, 1840, repr. Graz, 1964).

Le registre de l'officialité de Cerisy, ed. M. G. Dupont, Mémoires de la Société des Antiquaires de Normandie, 3rd ser. 10 (Caen, 1880).

Remigio, *Contra falsos ecclesie professores*, ed. F. Tamburini, preface by C. T. Davis, 'Utrumque Ius', Collectio Pontificiae Universitatis Lateranensis 6 (Rome, 1981).

—— sermons, Florence, Biblioteca Nazionale, MS Conv. Soppr. G. 4. 396.

Restoro d'Arezzo, *La Composizione del Mondo colle sue cascioni*, ed. A. Morino (Florence, 1976).

—— *La Composizione del Mondo di Ristoro d'Arezzo: Testo Italiano del 1282*, ed. E. Narducci (Rome, 1859).

Riccardus, *De facto Ungarie magne*, ed. Dörrie, 'Drei Texte', pp. 151–61.

Richard de Bury, *Philobiblon*, ed. M. McLagan (Oxford and New York, 1970).

Richard Fishacre, [*In sententias*], BL, MS Royal X.B. 7; BN, MS Lat 15754; Bologna, University Library, MS 1546; Oxford, Oriel College, MS 43; Vatican, MS Ottob. Lat. 294.

—— *Super s. Augustini Librum de Haeresibus*, ed. R. J. Long, 'Richard Fishacre's *Super s. Augustini Librum de Haeresibus Adnotationes*: An Edition and Commentary', *AHDLMA* 60 (1993), 207–79.

Richard of Middleton, *Super quatuor libros sententiarum Petri Lombardi*, 4 vols. (Brescia, 1591, repr. Frankfurt-am-Main, 1963).

Richard Rufus, [*In sententias*], Oxford, Balliol, MS 62.

Ricoldo of Monte Croce, *Itinerarium*, ed. J. C. M. Laurent, *Peregrinatores medii aevi quatuor* (Leipzig, 1873), pp. 105–41.

Rigord, *Oeuvres de Rigord et de Guillaume le Breton, historiens de Philippe-Auguste*, ed. H. F. Delaborde, Société de l'Histoire de France, 2 vols. (Paris, 1882–5).

Robert of Courson, *Summa*, BN, MS Lat. 14524.

Robert of Flamborough, *Liber poenitentialis*, ed. J. J. F. Firth, Studies and Texts 18 (Toronto, 1971).

Robert Grosseteste, sermon *Ego sum pastor bonus*, ed. O. Gratius, *Appendix ad fasciculum rerum expetendarum* (London, 1690), pp. 260–3.

Robert de Melun, *Questiones [theologice] de Epistolis Pauli*, ed. R. M. Martin, Spicilegium Sacrum Lovaniense 18 (Louvain, 1938).

Robert de Sorbon, *De confessione*, in *Maxima Bibliotheca Veterum Patrum*, ed. M. de La Bigne, 28 vols. (Lyons and Geneva, 1677, 1707), xxv. 352–8.

Roger Bacon, *Opus minus*, in *Opera quaedam hactenus inedita*, ed. J. S. Brewer, RS 15 (London, 1859), pp. 311–89.

Roland of Cremona, [*In sententias*], Paris, Bibliothèque Mazarine, MS Lat. 795.

Rufinus: *The Herbal of Rufinus*, ed. L. Thorndike (Chicago, 1945).

Rymer, T., *Foedera, Conventiones, Literae . . .*, 3rd edn., 10 vols. (Hague, 1745, repr. Farborough, 1967).

Sacerdos igitur, anonymous, Vatican MS Pal. Lat. 719.

Salimbene de Adam, *Cronica*, ed. G. Scalia, 2 vols. (Bari, 1966).

Select Cases from the Ecclesiastical Courts of the Province of Canterbury c.1200–1301, ed. N. Adams and C. Donahue, Selden Society 95 for 1978–9 (London, 1981).

Selge, K.-V, ed., *Texte zur Inquisition*, Texte zur Kirchen- und Theologiegeschichte 4 (Gütersloh, 1967).

Sententiae Berolinenses, ed. F. Stegmüller, 'Sententiae Berolinenses. Eine neugefundene Sentenzensammlung aus der Schule des Anselm von Laon', *RTAM* 11 (1939), 33–61.

Sententie Magistri A, ed. Reinhardt, *Anselm von Laon*, pp. 167–244.

Servasanto da Faenza, *Antidotarium Animae* [= *Summa de paenitentia*] (Louvain, 1484/7).

—— *Liber de exemplis naturalibus*, BL, MS Arundel 198.

—— sermons, BL, MS Harley 3221.

—— sermons [incorrectly attributed to Bonaventure], in Bonaventure, *Opera omnia*, ed. A. C. Peltier, 15 vols. (Paris, 1864–71), xiii. 493–636 and xiv. 1–138.

Simon of Faversham, commentary and questions on Aristotle, *De longitudine et brevitate vitae*, Oxford, Merton College, MS 272.

Statuti delle Università e dei Collegi dello Studio Bolognese, ed. C. Malagola (Bologna, 1888).

Les statuts synodaux français du XIIIe siècle (Paris, 1971–).

—— I. *Les statuts de Paris et le synodal de l'ouest (XIIIe siècle)*, ed. O. Pontal.

—— II. *Les Statuts de 1230 à 1260*, ed. O. Pontal.

Stephen of Bourbon, *Tractatus de diversis materiis praedicabilibus*, ed. A. Lecoy de la Marche, *Anecdotes historiques, légendes et apologues tirés du receuil inédit d'Étienne de Bourbon, Dominicain du XIIIe siècle* (Paris, 1877).

Summa Parisiensis on the Decretum Gratiani, ed. T. P. McLaughlin (Toronto, 1952).

Summa penitentie fratrum predicatorum, anonymous, ed. J. Goering and P. J. Payer, 'The "Summa penitentie fratrum predicatorum": A Thirteenth-Century Confessional Formulary', *MS* 55 (1993), 1–50.

Symon Semeonis, *Itinerarium ab Hybernia ad terram sanctam*, LXVIII; ed. M. Esposito, Scriptores Latini Hiberniae 4 (Dublin, 1960).

Taddeo Alderotti, *I 'Consilia'*, ed. G. M. Nardi (Turin, 1937).

—— *Expositiones in arduum aphorismorum* (Venice, 1527).

Thomas Aquinas, *Opera omnia*, 25 vols. (Parma, 1852–73).

—— *Scriptum super libros sententiarum*, 3 vols; *Opera omnia*, vi–viii.

—— *Sentencia libri Politicorum*, ed. H. F. Dondaine and L. J. Bataillon, *Opera omnia* (Rome, 1882–), xlviii (1971).

—— *Summa theologiae*, Blackfriars edn., 60 vols. (London, 1964–76).

Thomas of Chantimpré, *Bonum Universale de Apibus* (Douai, 1627).

Thomas of Chobham, *Summa confessorum*, ed. F. Broomfield, AMN 25 (Louvain and Paris, 1968).

Thomas of Strasbourg, *Commentaria in IIII. Libros sententiarum*, 2 vols. (Venice, 1564, repr. Ridegewood, NJ, 1965, 2 vols. in 1).

Tolomeo of Lucca [Bartolomeo Fiadoni], *De regimine principum* (= Tolomeo, *Continuatio* to Thomas Aquinas, *De regno*), in Thomas Aquinas, *Opuscula pholosophica*, ed. R. M. Spiazzi (Turin, 1954), pp. 280–358.

Trois sommes de pénitence de la première moitié du XIIIe siècle, ed. J. P. Renard, 2 vols., Lex Spiritus Vitae 6 (Louvain, 1989).

'Trotula' text, *Cum auctor*, ed. I. Spach, *Gynaeciorum sive de mulierum tam communibus tam gravidorum, parientium et puerporum affectibus et morbis* (Strasbourg, 1597), pp. 42–60.

Vidal de Four, *In sententias*, Vatican, MS Vat. Lat. 1095.

Giovanni Villani, *Nuova cronica*, ed. G. Porta, 3 vols. (Parma, 1990–91).

Vincent of Beauvais, *Speculum quadruplex, sive Speculum maius*, 4 vols. (Douai, 1624, repr. Graz, 1965).

Walter Burley, commentary and questions on Aristotle, *On Length and Shortness of Life*, Oxford, Oriel College, MS 12.

—— commentary and questions on Aristotle, *Politics*, Cambridge, University Library, MS 1741.

—— commentary and questions on Aristotle, *Problems*, Oxford, Bodley, MS Digby 77.

Walter of Bruges, [*In sententias*], MS Vat. Chigi B.VI.94.

Walter of Mortagne, *De sacramento coniugii* [printed as book 7 of the *Summa sententiarum*], *PL* 176, 153–74.

—— *Epistolae*, ed. E. Martène and U. Durand, *Veterum scriptorum et monumentorum historicorum, dogmaticorum, moralium amplissima collectio*, 9 vols. (Paris, 1724–33), i. 834–48.

Wasserschleben, F. W. H, ed., *Die Bussordnungen der abendländischen Kirche* (Halle, 1851).

William Adam, *De modo Sarracenos extirpandi*, in *Recueil des historiens des croisades: Documents arméniens*, 2 vols. (Paris, 1869–1906), ii. 521–55.

William of Auvergne, *De legibus*, *Opera omnia*, i. 18a–102b.

—— *De matrimonio, Opera omnia*, i. 512b–28b; BN, MS Lat. 14842; Vatican, MS Vat. Lat. 849.

—— *Opera Omnia*, ed. F. Hotot and B. Le Feron, 2 vols. (Orléans and Paris, 1674, repr. Frankfurt-am-Main, 1963).

William of Auxerre, *Summa aurea*, ed. J. Ribailler, 4 vols. in 7 parts, Spicilegium Bonaventurianum 16–20 (Paris and Grottaferrata, 1980–87). The *Summa*'s book numbers and the series numbers co-ordinate thus: Lib. 1 = 16; Lib. 2 parts 1–2 = 17 (in two parts not differentiated by number); Lib. 3 part 1 = 18a; Lib. 3 part 2 = 18b; Lib. 4 = 19. The editor's *Introduction* = 20.

William of Conches, *Dialogus de substantiis physicis* (Strasbourg, 1567).

William de la Mare, [*In sententias*], Florence, Biblioteca Nazionale, MS Conv. Sopp. A. 2. 727.

William Doune, *Memoriale presbiterorum*, Cambridge, Corpus Christi College, MS. 148;

—— in part ed. and trans., M. Haren, 'The Interrogatories for Officials, Lawyers and Secular Estates of the *Memoriale Presbiterorum*', *Handling Sin*, pp. 123–63.

William of Malmesbury, *De gestis regum Anglorum*, ed. W. Stubbs, 2 vols., RS 90.

William of Pagula [Paull], *Letter to Edward III*, ed. J. Moisant, *De speculo regis Edwardi III* (Paris, 1891).

—— *Oculus Sacerdotis*, BL, MS Royal VI.E. 1; Oxford, Bodley, MS Rawlinson A. 361; MS Rawlinson A. 370.

—— *Speculum Prelatorum ac religiosorum et parochialium sacerdotum*, Oxford, Merton College, MS 217.

William of Rennes, glosses on Raymond of Peñafort: the glosses attributed to John of Freiburg in Raymond of Peñafort, *Summa de poenitentia et matrimonio, cum glossis Ioannis de Friburgo* (Rome, 1603, repr. Farnborough, 1967).

William of Rubruck, Itinerarium, ed. Wyngaert, *Itinera*, pp. 164–332.

—— trans., *The Mission of Friar William of Rubruck*, ed. P. Jackson and D. Morgan, Hakluyt Society, 2nd ser. 173 (London, 1990).

William of Tripoli, *De statu Sarracenorum*, ed. H. Prutz, *Kulturgeschichte der Kreuzzüge* (Berlin, 1883), pp. 575–98.

Wyngaert, A. Van den, ed., *Itinera et relationes fratrum minorum saeculi XIII et XIV*, Sinica Franciscana 1 (only vol. published) (Quarracchi, 1929).

York, Borthwick Institute of Historical Research, Cause Paper F. 261.

Yule, H., *Cathay and the Way Thither, Being a Collection of Medieval Notices of China*, revised by H. Cordier, 4 vols., Hakluyt Society, 2nd ser. 33, 37, 38, and 41 (London, 1915–16).

2. WORKS OF REFERENCE AND LIBRARY AND MANUSCRIPT CATALOGUES

Alszeghy, Z., 'Abbreviationes Bonaventurae. Handschriftliche Auszüge aus dem Sentenzkommentar des hl. Bonaventura im Mittelalter', *Gregorianum* 28 (1947), 474–510.

Aristoteles Latinus, Codices:

—— Lacombe, G., assisted by Birkenmajer, A. Dulong, M., and Franceschini, E., *Codices, Pars Prior*, Corpus Philosophorum Medii Aevi (Rome, 1939).

—— Lacombe, G., assisted by A. Birkenmajer, M. Dulong, and E. Franceschini, rev. L. Minio-Paluello, *Codices, Pars Posterior*, Corpus Philosophorum Medii Aevi (Cambridge, 1955).

—— Minio-Paluello, L., *Codices, Supplementa altera*, Corpus Philosophorum Medii Aevi (Bruges and Paris, 1961).

Avicenna Latinus:

—— d'Alverny, M.-T., 'Avicenna Latinus', I, *AHDLMA* 28 (1962 for 1961), 281–316; II, 29 (1963 for 1962), 235–338); III, 30 (1964 for 1963), 221–72; IV, 31 (1965 for 1964), 271–86; V, 32

(1966 for 1965), 257–302; VI, 33 (1967 for 1966), 305–27; VII, 34 (1968 for 1967), 315–43; VIII, 35 (1969 for 1968), 301–35; IX, 36 (1970 for 1969), 243–80; X, 37 (1971 for 1970), 327–61; XI, 39 (1973 for 1972), 321–41.

—— *Avicenna Latinus: Codices* [= reprint of 'Avicenna Latinus', I–XI, *AHDLMA* 2839 (1962–73 for 1961–72), with addenda by S. van Riet and P. Jodogne (Louvain and Leiden, 1994).

Bloomfield, M. W., *et al.*, *Incipits of Latin Works on the Virtues and Vices, 1100–1500 A.D.* (Cambridge, Mass., 1979).

Carmody, F. J., *Arabic Astronomical and Astrological Sciences in Latin Translation: A Critical Bibliography* (Berkeley, 1956).

Courtenay, W. J., 'The fourteenth-century booklist of the Oriel College library', *Viator* 19 (1988), 283–90.

Davis, C. T. 'The Early Collection of Books of S. Croce in Florence', *Proceedings of the American Philosophical Society* 107 (1963), 399–414.

De Raedemaeker, J., 'Une ébauche de catalogue des commentaires sur les "Parva Naturalia" parus aux XIIIe, XIVe et XVe siècles', *Bulletin de philosophie médiévale* 7 (1965), 95–108.

Delisle, L., *Le Cabinet des manuscrits*, 4 vols. (Paris, 1868–81).

Die deutsche Literatur des Mittelalters: Verfasserlexikon, 2nd edn., ed. K. Ruh and others (Berlin and New York, 1979–).

Dictionary of Scientific Biography, ed. C. C. Gillispie, 16 vols. (New York, 1970–80).

Dictionnaire d'Histoire et de Géographie Ecclésiastiques (Paris, 1912–).

Dictionnaire de Spiritualité, 17 vols. (Paris, 1937–95).

Dictionnaire de théologie catholique, 15 vols. (Paris, 1903–50).

Doucet, V., *Commentaires sur les Sentences: Supplément au répertoire de M. Frédéric Stegmüller* (Quaracchi, 1954). [See Stegmüller below.]

Emden, A. B., *A Biographical Register of the University of Cambridge to 1500* (Cambridge, 1963).

—— *A Biographical Register of the University of Oxford to A.D. 1500*, 3 vols. (Oxford, 1957).

Faucon, M., *La librairie des papes d'Avignon: sa formation, sa composition, ses catalogues, 1316–1420*, 2 vols. (Paris, 1886–7).

Fauser, W., *Die Werke des Albertus Magnus in ihrer handscriftlichen Überlieferung*, i. *Die echten Werke*, in Albert, *Opera*, Geyer, Tomus Subsidiarius, i.

Flüeler, C., 'Die mittelalterliche Kommentare zur *Politik* des Aristoteles und zur Pseudo-Aristotelischen *Oekonomik*', *Bulletin de philosophie médiévale* 29 (1987), 193–229.

Frantzen, A. J., *Mise à jour du fascicule no. 27* (Turnholt, 1985): revision of C. Vogel, *Les 'Libri paenitentiales'*, Typologie des sources du moyen âge occidental 27 (Turnholt, 1978). [See Vogel below.]

Gargan, L., *Lo studio teologico e la biblioteca dei domenicani a Padova nel tre e quattrocento*, Contributi alla Storia dell'Università di Padova 6 (Padua, 1971).

Giles of Rome [Aegidius Romanus/Colonna], *Catalogo dei manoscritti*, in *Opera omnia*, Corpus Philosophorum Medii Aevi, Testi e Studi 12, (Florence, 1987–).

Glorieux, P., *La faculté des arts et ses maîtres au XIIIe siècle*, Études de Philosophie Médiévale 59 (Paris, 1971).

—— *La littérature quodlibétique*, 2 vols., Bibliothèque Thomiste 5 and 21 (Paris, 1925–35).

—— *Répertoire des maitres en théologie de Paris au XIIIe siècle*, 2 vols., Études de Philosophie Médiévale 17–18 (Paris, 1933–4).

Histoire littéraire de la France (Paris, 1733–).

Humphreys, K. W., *The Book Provisions of the Medieval Friars, 1215–1400* (Amsterdam, 1964).

—— ed., *The Friars' Libraries*, Corpus of British Medieval Library Catalogues (London, 1990).

—— *The Library of the Carmelites at Florence at the end of the Fourteenth Century* (Amsterdam, 1964).

—— *The Library of the Franciscans of Siena in the late Fifteenth Century* (Amsterdam, 1978).

Jacquart, D., *Dictionnaire biographique des médecins en France au moyen âge: Supplément* (Geneva and Paris, 1979). [See Wickersheimer below.]

Kaeppeli, T., *Inventari di libri di San Domenico di Perugia, 1430–88*, Sussidi Eruditi 15 (Rome, 1962).

—— 'La bibliothèque de Saint-Eustorge à Milan', *AFP* 25 (1955), 5–74.

—— and Panella, E., *Scriptores Ordinis Praedicatorum medii aevi*, 4 vols. (Rome, 1970–93).

Kibre, P., *Hippocrates Latinus: Repertorium of Hippocratic Writings in the Latin Middle Ages*, rev. edn. (New York, 1985) [= revision of articles of same title which appeared in *Traditio* 31–38 (1975–82).

Laurent, M.-H., *Fabio Vigili et les bibliothèques de Bologne*, Studi e Testi 105 (Rome, 1943).

Lehmann, P. J. G., *et al.*, *Mittelalterliche Bibliothekskataloge Deutschlands und der Schweiz* (Munich, 1918–).

Lohr, C. H, 'Medieval Latin Aristotle Commentaries', *Traditio* 23 (1967), 313–414; 24 (1968), 149–246; 26 (1970), 135–216; 27 (1971), 251–352; 28 (1972), 281–396; 29 (1973), 93–198; 30 (1974), 119–44.

—— 'Aristotelica Matritensia', *Traditio* 53 (1998), 251–308.

Manitius, M., *Geschichte der lateinischen Literatur des Mittelalters*, 2 vols. (Munich, 1911–23).

Mittelalterliche Bibliothekskataloge Österreichs, 5 vols. (Vienna, Graz, 1929–70).

Orlandi, S., *La biblioteca di S. Maria Novella in Firenze dal sec. XIV al sec. XIX* (Florence, 1952).

Pelster, F., 'Die Bibliothek von Santa Caterina zu Pisa, eine Büchersammlung aus den Zeiten des Hl. Thomas von Aquin', in *Xenia Thomistica*, ed. S. Szabó, 3 vols. (Rome, 1925), iii. 249–80.

Porta, G., 'Censimento dei manoscritti delle cronache di Giovanni, Matteo e Filippo Villani', *Studi di Filologia Italiana* 34 (1976), 61–129 (pp. 64–114); 37 (1979), 93–117 (pp. 95–116); and 44 (1986), 65–7.

Powicke, F. M., *The Medieval Books of Merton College* (Oxford, 1931).

Stegmüller, F., *Repertorium commentariorum in Sententias Petri Lombardi*, 2 vols. (Würzburg, 1947). [See Doucet above.]

Theologische Realenzyklopädie, i– (Berlin, 1976–).

Thorndike L., and Kibre, P., *A Catalogue of Incipits of Medieval Scientific Writings in Latin*, 2nd edn. (London, 1963).

Vanhamel, W., 'Biobibliographie de Guillaume de Moerbeke', *Guillaume de Moerbeke*, pp. 301–83.

Vogel, C., *Les 'Libri paenitentiales'*, Typologie des sources du moyen âge occidental 27 (Turnhout, 1978). [See Frantzen above.]

Wickersheimer, E., *Dictionnaire biographique des médecins en France au moyen âge*, 2 vols. (Paris, 1936, repr. Geneva and Paris, 1979). [See Jacquart above.]

Wippel, J. F., 'Quodlibetal Questions, Chiefly in Theological Faculties', in *Les questions disputées et les questions quodlibétiques dans les facultés de théologie, de droit et de médecine*, ed. B. C. Bazan, G. Fransen, D. Jacquart, and J. W. Wippel, Typologie des sources du moyen âge occidental 44–5 (Turnhout, 1985), pp. 153–222.

3. SECONDARY SOURCES

Acsádi, G., and Nemeskéri, J., *History of Human Life Span and Mortality* (Budapest, 1970).

Baldwin, J. W., *The Language of Sex: Five Voices from Northern France around 1200* (Chicago, 1994).

Baldwin, J. W., 'Masters at Paris from 1179 to 1215: A Social Perspective', in *Renaissance and Renewal in the Twelfth Century*, ed. R. L. Benson and G. Constable (Oxford, 1982), pp. 138–72.

—— *Masters, Princes and Merchants: The Social Views of Peter the Chanter & His Circle*, 2 vols. (Princeton, 1970).

—— *The Medieval Theories of the Just Price: Romanists, Canonists and Theologians in the Twelfth and Thirteenth Centuries*, Transactions of the American Philosophical Society, n.s. 49, part 4 (Philadelphia, 1959).

Balič, C., *Les commentaires de Jean Duns Scot sur les quatre livres des sentences: Étude historique et critique* (Louvain, 1927).

Bartlett, R., *Gerald of Wales 1146–1223* (Oxford, 1982).

Bataillon, L. J., 'Les textes théologiques et philosophiques diffusés à Paris par exempla et pecia', in *La production du livre universitaire au Moyen Âge: exemplar et pecia*, ed. L. J. Bataillon, B. G. Guyot, and R. H. Rouse (Paris, 1991), pp. 155–63.

Beaujouan, G., 'L'enseignement de l'Arithmétique élémentaire à l'université de Paris au XIIIe et XIVe siècles. De l'abaque à l'algorisme', *Hommenaje a Millás-Vallicrosa*, 2 vols. (Barcelona, 1954–6), i. 93–124.

Beazley, C. R., *The Dawn of Modern Geography*, 3 vols. (London, 1897–1906).

Benedetto, L. F., *La tradizione manoscritta del 'Milione' di Marco Polo* (Turin, 1962 = repr. of the introduction to his edn. of 1928).

Berlioz, J., 'Les ordalies dans les *exempla* de la confession (XIIIe–XIVe siècles)', *L'Aveu: Antiquité et moyen-âge*, Collection de l'École Française de Rome 88 (Rome, 1986), pp. 315–40.

—— and Ribaucourt, C., 'Images de la confession dans la prédication au début du XIVe siècle. L'exemple de *l'Alphabetum narrationum* d'Arnold de Liège', in Groupe de la Bussière [= M. Sot and others], *Pratiques de la confession, des Pères du désert à Vatican II: Quinze études d'histoire* (Paris, 1983), pp. 95–115.

Biller, P., 'Applying Number to Men and Women in the Thirteenth and Early Fourteenth Centuries: An Enquiry into the Origins of the Idea of "Sex-ratio"', in *The Work of Jacques Le Goff and the Challenges of Medieval History*, ed. M. Rubin (Woodbridge, 1997), pp. 27–52.

—— 'Aristotle's *Politica* and "Demographic" Thought in the Kingdom of Aragon in the Early Fourteenth Century', *Annals of the Archive of 'Ferran Valls I Taberner's Library'*, 9/10 (1991), 249–64.

—— 'Birth-control in the West in the Thirteenth and Early Fourteenth Centuries', *Past and Present* 94 (1982), 3–26.

—— 'Cathars and Material Women', in *Medieval Theology and the Natural Body*, ed. P. Biller and A. J. Minnis, York Studies in Medieval Theology 1 (York, 1997), pp. 61–107.

—— 'The Common Woman in the Western Church in the Thirteenth and Early Fourteenth Centuries', in *Women in the Church*, ed. D. Wood, SCH 27 (Oxford, 1990, pp. 127–57.

—— 'Confessors' Mannuals and the Avoiding of Offspring', *Handling Sin*, pp. 165–87.

—— '"Demographic Thought" around 1300 and Dante's Florence', in *Dante and the Middle Ages: Literary and Historical Essays*, ed. J. C. Barnes and C. Ó Cuilleanáin (Irish Academic Press: Dublin), pp. 57–92.

—— 'John of Naples, Quodlibets and Medieval Theological Conncern with the Body', in *Medieval Theology and the Natural Body*, ed. P. Biller and A. J. Minnis, York Studies in Medieval Theology 1 (York, 1997), pp. 3–12.

—— 'Marriage Patterns and Women's Lives: A Sketch of a Pastoral Geography', in *Woman is a Worthy Wight: Women in English Society c.1200–1500*, ed. P. J. P. Goldberg (Stroud, 1992), pp. 60–107.

—— *Handling Sin: Confession in the Middle Ages*, York Studies in Medieval Theology 2 (York, 1998).

—— 'Northern Cathars and Higher Learning', in *The Medieval Church: Universities, Heresy and the Religious Life. Essays in Honour of Gordon Leff*, ed. P. Biller and [R.] B. Dobson, SCH, Subsidia 11 (Woodbridge, 1999), pp. 25–53.

—— 'A "scientific" view of Jews from Paris around 1300', forthcoming in *Gli Ebrei e le scienze nel Medio Evo e nella prima età moderna*, in *Micrologus*.

—— 'Women and Texts in Languedocian Catharism', in *Women, the Book and the Godly*, ed. L. Smith and J. H. M. Taylor (Cambridge, 1995), pp. 171–82.

—— 'Words and the medieval notion of "religion"', *Journal of Ecclesiastical History* 36 (1985), 351–69.

—— and Minnis, A. J., ed., *Medieval Theology and the Natural Body*, York Studies in Medieval Theology 1 (York, 1997).

Binkley, P., 'John Bromyard and the Hereford Dominicans', in *Centres of Learning: Learning and Location in Pre-Modern Europe and the Near East*, ed. J. W. Drijvers and A. A. MacDonald (Leyden, New York, and Cologne, 1995), pp. 255–64.

Bloch, H., *Monte Cassino in the Middle Ages*, 3 vols. (Cambridge, Mass.).

'Bonaventura', *DBI* xi. 612–30 (author not given).

Børresen, K.-E., *Subordination et Equivalence: Nature et Rôle de la Femme d'après Augustin et Thomas d'Aquin* (Oslo and Paris, 1968).

Bologne, J.-C., *La naissance interdite: Stérilité, avortement, contraception au Moyen Âge* (Paris, 1988).

Boyle, L. E., 'The date of the *Summa praedicantium* of John Bromyard', *Speculum* 48 (1973), 533–7.

—— *Pastoral Care, Clerical Education and Canon Law, 1200–1400* (London, 1981) [reprinted articles].

—— 'The Quodlibets of St. Thomas and Pastoral Care', no. II in *Pastoral Care*.

—— *The Setting of the Summa Theologiae of Saint Thomas*, Pontifical Institute of Medieval Studies, The Étienne Gilson Series 5 (Toronto, 1982).

—— '*Summae confessorum*', in *Les genres littéraires dans les sources théologiques et philosophiques médiévales: Définition, critique et exploitation*, Université Catholique de Louvain, Publications de l'Institut d'Études Médiévales ser. 2/5 (Louvain, 1982), pp. 227–37.

Brady, I., *Prolegomena*, vol. i, part 1 of Peter the Lombard, *Sententiae*.

Brams, J., 'Guillaume de Moerbeke et Aristote', in *Traductions et traductueurs de l'antiquité tardive au XIVe siècle*, Université Catholique de Louvain and Università degli Studi di Cassino, Publications de l'Institut des Études Médiévales, Textes, Études, Congrès 11, Rencontres de Cultures dans la Philosophie Médiévale 1 (Louvain and Cassino, 1990), pp. 317–36.

—— 'Lorenzo Minio Paluello e l'"Aristoteles Latinus" ', L. Minio-Paluello, *Lughi cruciali in Dante: ultimi saggi, con un inedito su Boezio*, ed. F. Santi, Quaderni di Cultura Neolatina, Collana della Fondazione Ezio Franceschi 6 (Spoleto and Florence, 1993), pp. 13–25.

Brass, W., 'Introduction: Bio-Social factors in African Demography', in *The Population Factor in African Studies*, ed. R. P. Moss and R. J. A. R. Rathbone (London, 1975), 87–94.

Brentano, R., *Two Churches: England and Italy in the Thirteenth Century* (Princeton, 1968).

Briggs, C. F., *Giles of Rome's De regimine principum: Reading and Writing Politics at Court and University, c.1275–c.1525* (Cambridge, 1999).

Brooke, C. N. L., 'Gregorian Reform in Action: Clerical Marriage in England, 1050–1200', in *Medieval Church and Society: Collected Essays* (London, 1971), pp. 69–99.

Brothwell, D., 'Palaeodemography and earlier British Populations', *World Archaeology* 4 (1972), 75–87.

Brown, P., *The Body and Society: Men, Women and Sexual Renunciation in Early Christianity* (London, 1989).

Brown, P., 'St Augustine', in *Trends in Medieval Political Thought*, ed. B. Smalley (Oxford, 1965), pp. 1–21.

Brown, V., 'Caesar', *Catalogus Translationum et Commentariorum*, ed. F. E. Cranz and P. O. Kristeller (Washington, 1960–), iii. 87–139.

Brundage, J. A., *Law, Sex and Christian Society in Medieval Europe* (Chicago, 1987).

—— *Medieval Canon Law* (London and New York, 1995).

Bullough, V. L., 'The prostitute in the early middle ages', in *Sexual Practices and the Medieval Church*, ed. V. L. Bullough and J. Brundage (Buffalo, NY, 1982), pp. 34–42.

—— and Campbell, C., 'Female Longevity and Diet in the Middle Ages', *Speculum* 55 (1980), 317–25.

Burnett, C., 'Michael Scot and the Transmission of Scientific Culture from Toledo to Bologna via the Court of Frederick II', in *Le Scienze alla corte di Federico II, Micrologus* 2 (Paris and Turnhout, 1994), 101–26.

——'The Introduction of Aristotle's Natural Philosophy into Great Britain: A Preliminary Survey of the Manuscript Evidence', in *Aristotle in Britain during the Middle Ages*, ed. J. Marenbon, Société Internationale pour l'Étude de la Philosophie Médiévale, Rencontres de Philosophie Médiévale 5 (Turnhout, 1996), pp. 21–50.

Burrow, J. A., *The Ages of Man: A Study in Medieval Writing and Thought* (Oxford, 1986).

Cadden, J., *Meanings of Sex Difference in the Middle Ages: Medicine, Science, and Culture* (Cambridge, 1993).

Callewaert, P. S., 'Les pénitentiels du moyen âge et les pratiques anticonceptionelles', *La Vie Spirituelle* 74, Supplement (1965), 339–66.

Campbell, M. C., *The Witness and the Other World: Exotic European Travel Writing 400–1600* (Ithaca, NY, 1988).

Cannuyer, C., 'La date de rédaction de l'"Historia Orientalis" de Jacques de Vitry (1160/70–1240), évêque d'Acre', *Revue d'Histoire Ecclésiastique* 78 (1983), 65–72.

Cartography in Prehistoric, Ancient and Medieval Europe, ed. J. B. Harley and D. Woodward, in *The History of Cartography* (Chicago and London, 1987–), i.

Catto, J. I., 'Ideas and Experience in the political thought of Aquinas', *Past and Present* 71 (1976), 3–21.

—— 'Theology and Theologians 1220–11320', *HUO* i. 471–517.

Chibnall, M., 'Pliny's *Natural History* and the Middle Ages', *Empire and Aftermath: Silver Latin II*, ed. T. A. Dorey (London, Boston, 1975), pp. 57–78.

Clanchy, M. T., *From Memory to Written Record: England 1066–1307*, 2nd edn. (Oxford and Cambridge, Mass., 1993).

Cohen, J., *"Be Fertile and Increase, Fill the Earth and Master it": The Ancient and Medieval Career of a Biblical Text* (Ithaca, NY, and London, 1989).

Colish, M. L., *Peter Lombard*, Brill's Studies in Intellectual History 41, 2 vols. (Leiden, New York and Cologne, 1994).

Cox, P. R., *Demography*, 4th edn. (Oxford, 1970).

Curschmann, F., *Hungersnöte im Mittelalter: Ein Beitrag zur deutschen Wirtschaftsgeschichte des 8. bis 13. Jahrhunderts*, Leipziger Studien aus dem Gebiet der Geschichte 6/1 (Leipzig, 1900).

Dalché, P. G., *Géographie et culture: representation de l'éspace du VI au XIIe siècle* (Aldershot, etc., 1997).

—— 'Les savoirs géographiques en méditerranée chrétienne (XIIIe s.)', in *Le scienze alla corte di Federico II, Micrologus* 2 (1994), 75–99.

—— *See* Hugh of St Victor above.

d'Alverny, M.-T., 'Alain de Lille et l'Islam. Le "Contra Paganos"', *Cahiers de Fanjeaux* 18 (Toulouse, 1983), pp. 323–50.

—— 'La connaissance de l'Islam au temps de saint Louis', in *Septième centenaire de la mort de saint Louis* (Paris, 1976), pp. 235–46.

—— 'Deux traductions latines du Coran au moyen âge', *AHDLMA* 16 (1948), 68–131.

—— 'Pietro d'Abano et les "naturalistes" à l'époque de Dante', *Dante e la cultura veneta*, ed. V. Branca and G. Padoan (Florence, 1966), pp. 207–19.

—— 'Les traductions à deux interprètes, d'arabe en langue vernaculaire et de langue vernaculaire en Latin', *Traductions et Traducteurs au Moyen Âge*, ed. G. Contamine, Documents, Études et Répertoires Publiées par l'Institut de Recherche et d'Histoire des Textes (Paris, 1989), pp. 193–206.

—— 'Translations and Translators', in *Renaissance and Renewal in the Twelfth Century*, ed. R. L. Benson and G. Constable (Oxford, 1982), pp. 421–62.

Daniel, N., 'Crusade Propaganda', in *A History of the Crusades*, ed. K. M. Setton, 6 vols. (Madison, 1969–89), vi. 39–97.

—— *Islam and the West: The Making of an Image*, 2nd edn. (Oxford, 1993).

Davis, C. T., 'Il buon tempo antico', in *Dante's Italy*, pp. 71–93.

—— *Dante's Italy and Other Essays* (Philadelphia, 1984).

—— 'An Early Florentine Political Theorist: Fra Remigio de' Girolami', in *Dante's Italy*, pp. 198–223.

—— 'Education in Dante's Florence', in *Dante's Italy*, 137–65.

—— 'Topographical and historical propaganda in early Florentine Chronicles and in Villani', *Medioevo e Rinascimento* 2 (1988), 33–51.

d'Avray, D. L., *The Preaching of the Friars: Sermons diffused from Paris before 1300* (Oxford, 1985).

—— 'Some Franciscan Ideas about the Body', *Archivum Franciscanum Historicum* 84 (1991), 343–63.

Delcorno, C., *L'exemplum nella predicazione volgare di Giordano di Pisa*, Istituto Veneto di Scienze, Lettere ed Arti, Memorie, Classe di Scienze Morali, Lettere ed Arti 36, fasc. 1 (Venice, 1972).

—— *Giordano da Pisa e l'antica predicazione volgare*, Biblioteca di 'Lettere Italiane' 14 (Florence, 1975).

Del Punta, F., 'The Genre of Commentaries in the Middle Ages and its Relation to the Nature and Originality of Medieval Thought', in *Was ist Philosophie im Mittelalter?*, Veröffentlichungen des Thomas-Instituts der Universität zu Köln 26 (Berlin and New York, 1998), pp. 138–51.

—— Donati, S., and Luna, C., 'Egidio Romano', *DBI* lxii. 319–41.

Demaitre, L. E., *Doctor Bernard de Gordon: Professor and Practitioner*, Pontifical Institute of Medieval Studies, Studies and Texts 51 (Toronto, 1980).

—— and Travill, A. A., 'Human Embryology and Development in the Works of Albertus Magnus', in *Albert and the Sciences*, pp. 405–40.

Destrez, L., *La pecia dans les manuscrits universitaires du XIIIe et XIVe siècles* (Paris, 1935).

Detloff, W., 'Alexander Halesius', *TRE* ii. 245–8.

—— 'Bonaventura', *TRE*, vii. 48–55.

Devereux, G., *A Study of Abortion in Primitive Societies* (London, 1960).

Diepgen, P., *Frau und Frauenheilkunde in der Kultur des Mittelalters* (Stuttgart, 1963).

Dondaine, A., and Bataillon, L. J., 'Le commentaire de Saint Thomas sur les Météores', *AFP* 36 (1966), 81–152.

Dossat, Y., *Les Crises de l'Inquisition Toulousaine au XIIIe siècle* (Bordeaux, 1959).

Doucet, V., *Prolegomena*, in Alexander of Hales, *Summa Theologica*, 4 vols. (Quaracchi, 1921–48), iv, part 1.

Dove, M., *The Perfect Age of Man's Life* (Cambridge, 1986).

Drossaart Lulofs, H. J., 'Preface', Aristotle, *De generatione animalium* (Scot), pp. vii–xv.

Dubois, H., and Zink, M., *Les âges de la vie au moyen âge*, Cultures et Civilisations Médiévales 7 (Paris, 1992).

Duby, G., *Love and Marriage in the Middle Ages*, trans. J. Dunnett (Cambridge, 1994).

—— *Rural Economy and Country Life in the Medieval West*, trans. C. Postan (London, 1968).

Dunbabin, J., 'Aristotle in the Schools', in *Trends in Medieval Political Thought*, ed. B. Smalley (Oxford, 1965), pp. 65–85.

—— 'Government', in *The Cambridge History of Medieval Political Thought c.1350–c.1450*, ed. J. H. Burns (Cambridge, 1988), pp. 477–519.

—— 'Guido Vernani of Rimini's commentary on Aristotle's *Politics*', *Traditio* 44 (1988), 373–8.

—— *A Hound of God: Pierre de la Palud and the Fourteenth-Century Church* (Oxford, 1991).

—— 'Meeting the Costs of University Education in Northern France, *c.*1240–*c.*1340', *History of Universities* 10 (1991), 1–27.

—— 'The reception and interpretation of Aristotle's *Politics*', in *The Cambridge History of Later Medieval Philosophy*, ed. N. Kretzmann, A. Kenny, and J. Pinborg (Cambridge, 1982), pp. 723–37.

Dupâquier, J. and M., *Histoire de la démographie: La statistique de la population des origines à 1914* (Paris, 1985).

Ebbesen, S., 'Introduction', in Simon of Faversham, *Quaestiones super libro elenchorum*, ed. S. Ebbesen *et al.*, Pontifical Institute of Medieval Studies, Studies and Texts 60 (Toronto, 1984), pp. 1–22.

Ellenblum, R., *Frankish Rural Settlement in the Latin Kingdom of Jerusalem* (Cambridge, 1998).

Ehrle, F., 'S. Domenico, le origini del primo studio generale del suo ordine a Parigi e la somma teologica del primo maestro, Rolando da Cremona', in *Miscellanea dominicana, in memoriam VII anni secularis ab obitu patris Dominici (1221–1921)* (Rome, 1923), pp. 85–134.

Eisenstein, E. L., *The Printing Press as an Agent of Change*, 2 vols. (Cambridge, 1980).

Elias De Tejada, F., *Las Doctrinas Políticas en la Cataluña Medieval* (Barcelona, 1950).

Esmein, A., *Le mariage en droit canonique*, 2nd edn. rev. R. Génestal and J. Dauvillier, 2 vols. (Paris, 1929–35).

Eynde, D. Van den, *Essai sur la succession des écrits de Hugues de Saint-Victor*, Spicilegium Pontificii Athenaei Antoniani 13 (Rome, 1960).

Faral, E., 'Jean Buridan. Maître ès Arts de l'Université de Paris', *HLF* 38 (1949), pp. 462–605.

Fildes, V., *Wet Nursing: A History from Antiquity to the Present* (Oxford, 1988).

Filthaut, E., *Roland von Cremona O.P. und die Anfänge der Scholastik im Predigerorden* (Vechta, 1936).

Finch, A., '*Repulsa uxore sua*: marital difficulties and separation in the later middle ages', *Continuity and Change* 8 (1993), 11–38.

Fiumi, E., 'La demografia fiorentina nelle pagine di Giovanni Villani', *Archivio Storico Italiano* 108 (1958), 78–158.

Flandrin, J.-L., untitled review [of the French translation of J. T. Noonan, *Contraception* (Cambridge, Mass., 1966)], *Annales de Démographie Historique 1969* (1970), 337–59.

Fletcher, J. M., 'The Faculty of Arts', *HUO* i. 369–99.

Fletcher, R. A., *The Conversion of Europe: From Paganism to Christianity 371–1386 AD* (London, 1997).

Flüeler, C., 'Die Rezeptionder "Politica" des Aristoteles an der Pariser Artistenfakultät im 13. und 14. Jahrhundert', in *Das Publikum politischer Theorie im 14.* Jahrhundert, ed. J. Miethke, Schriften des Historischen Kollegs, Kolloquien 21 (Munich, 1992), pp. 127–38.

—— *Rezeption und Interpretation der Aristotelischen Politica im späten Mittelalter*, Bochümer Studien zur Philosophie 19, 2 vols. (Amsterdam, Philadelphia, 1992).

—— 'Die verschiedenen literarischen Gattungen der Aristoteleskommentare: zur Terminologie der Überschriften und Kolophone', in J. Hamesse, ed., *Manuels, programmes de cours et techniques d'enseignement dans les universités médiévales*, Université Catholique de Louvain, Publications de l'Institut des Études Médiévales, Textes, Études, Congrès 16 (Louvain–La-Neuve, 1994), pp. 75–116.

Fournier, P., and Le Bras, G., *Histoires des collections canoniques en Occident depuis les Fausses Décrétales jusqu'au Décret de Gratien*, 2 vols. (Paris, 1931–2).

Fowler, G. B., *The Intellectual Interests of Engelbert of Admont* (New York, 1947).

—— 'A medieval thinker confronts modern perplexities: Engelbert, Abbot of Admont, O.S.B. (*c*.1250–1331)', *American Benedictine Review* 1973 (33), 226–48.

Frantzen, A. J., *The Literature of Penance in Anglo-Saxon England* (New Brunswick, NJ, 1983).

Friedmann, A., *Paris, ses rues, ses paroisses du moyen âge à la révolution* (Paris, 1959).

Frugoni, A., 'G. Villani, Cronica, xi.94', *Bullettino dell'Istituto storico italiano per il medio evo* 77 (1965), 229–55.

García-Ballester, L., McVaugh, M. R., and Rubio-Vela, A., *Medical Licensing and Learning in Fourteenth-Century Valencia*, Transactions of the American Philosophical Society 79, part 6 (Philadelphia, 1989).

Gaudemet, J., 'La définition romano-canonique du mariage', in his *Église et société au moyen âge* (London, 1984), no. XIV.

—— *Le mariage en occident: Les mœurs et le droit* (Paris, 1987).

Génicot, L., 'On the Evidence of Growth of Population in the West from the Eleventh to the Thirteenth Century', in *Change in Medieval Society: Europe North of the Alps, 1050–1500*, ed. S. Thrupp (London, 1965), pp. 14–29.

—— *Le XIIIe siècle Européen*, Nouvelle Clio 18 (Paris, 1968).

Geremek, B., *The Margins of Society in Late Medieval Paris*, trans. J. Birrell (Cambridge and Paris, 1987).

Gilson, E., 'Avicenne en Occident au moyen âge', *AHDLMA* 36 (1970), 89–121.

—— *History of Christian Philosophy in the Middle Ages* (London, 1955).

Glorieux, P., 'Sentences (commentaires sur les)', *DTC* xiv (1941), cols. 1860–84.

Goldberg, P. J. P., 'Marriage, Migration and Servanthood: The York Cause Paper Evidence', in Goldberg, *Woman is a Worthy Wight*, pp. 1–15.

—— *Women, Work and Life-Cycle in the Medieval Economy: Women in York and Yorkshire c.1300–1520* (Oxford, 1992).

—— ed., *Woman is a Worthy Wight: Women in English Society c.1200–1500* (Stroud, 1992).

Golubovich, G., 'Series provinciarum O.F.M. saec. XIII–XIV', *Archivum franciscanum historicum* 1 (1908), 1–22.

Grabmann, M., 'Jakob von Douai, ein Aristoteleskommentator zur Zeit des Heiligen Thomas von Aquin und des Siger von Brabant', in his *Mittelalterliche Geistesleben: Abhandlungen zur Geschichte der Scholastik und Mystik*, 3 vols. (Munich, 1926–56), iii. 158–79.

—— 'Die mittelalterlichen Kommentare zur *Politik* des Aristoteles', *Sitzungsberichte der Bayerischen Akademie der Wissenschaften*, Philosophisch-historische Abteilung (1941), 2, Heft 10.

Gras, P., 'Le registre paroissial de Givry (1334–1357) et la Peste Noire en Bourgogne', *Bibliothèque de l'Ecole des Chartes* 100 (1939), 295–308.

Green, L., *Chronicle into History: An Essay on the Interpretation of History in Florentine Fourteenth-Century Chronicles* (Cambridge, 1972).

Green, M. H., 'The Development of the *Trotula*', *Revue d'Histoire des Textes* 26 (1996), 119–203.

—— 'Documenting medieval women's medical practice', in *Practical Medicine from Salerno to the Black Death*, ed. L. García-Ballester *et al.* (Cambridge, 1994), pp. 322–52.

Green, M. H., review, untitled [of J. M. Riddle, *Eve's Herbs* (Cambridge, Mass., London, 1997)], *Bulletin of the History of Medicine* 73 (1999), 308–11.

—— 'Women's Medical Practice and Health Care in Medieval Europe', in *Sisters and Workers in the Middle Ages*, ed. J. Bennett *et al.* (Chicago, 1989), pp. 39–78.

—— and Schleissner, M., 'Trotula (Trota), "Trotula"', *Vf* ix (1996), 1083–8.

Grundmann, H., *Religiöse Bewegungen im Mittelalter*, 2nd edn. (Hildesheim, 1961).

Guillaume de Moerbeke: Recueil d'études à l'occasion du 700e anniversaire de sa mort (1286), ed. J. Brams and W. Vanhamel, Ancient and Medieval Philosophy, De Wulf-Mansion Centre, Series 1, 7 (Louvain, 1989).

Guillemain, B., *La cour pontificale d'Avignon, 1309–1376: Étude d'une société* (Paris, 1966).

Gwynn, A., *The English Austin Friars in the Time of Wyclif* (Oxford, 1940).

Haggenmüller, R., 'Zur Rezeption der Beda und Egbert zugeschriebenen Bußbücher', in *Aus Archiven und Bibliotheken: Festschrift für Raymond Kottje zum 65.* Geburtstag, ed. H. Mordek, Freiburger Beiträge zur mittelalterlichen Geschichte 3 (Frankfurt, Berne, New York, and Paris, 1992), pp. 149–59.

Hajnal, J., 'European Marriage Patterns in Perspective', in *Population in History: Essays in Historical Demography*, ed. D. V. Glass, and D. E. C. Eversley (London, 1965), pp. 101–43.

—— 'Two kinds of pre-industrial household formation system', in R. Wall, ed., *Family Forms in Historic Europe* (Cambridge, etc., 1983), pp. 65–104.

Hamm, M., 'Johannes von Freiburg', *Vf* iv. 605–11.

Haren, M., 'Confession, Social Ethics and Social Discipline in the Memoriale Presbiterorum', in *Handling Sin*, pp. 109–22.

—— 'Social Ideas in the Pastoral Literature of Fourteenth-Century England', in *Religious Belief and Ecclesiastical Careers in Late-Medieval England: Proceedings of the Conference held at Strawberry Hill, Easter 1989*, ed. C. Harper-Bill, Studies in the History of Medieval Religion 3 (Woodbridge, 1991), pp. 43–57.

Harley, J. B., 'The Map and the Development of the History of Cartography', *Cartography in Prehistoric, Ancient and Medieval Europe and the Mediterranean*, ed. J. B. Harley and D. Woodward, *The History of Cartography* (Chicago and London, 1987–), i. 1–42.

Harvey, B. F., 'Introduction: the "crisis" of the early fourteenth century', in *Before the Black Death: Studies in the 'crisis' of the early fourteenth century*, ed. B. M. S. Campbell (Manchester and New York, 1991), pp. 1–24.

—— 'The population trend in England between 1300 and 1348', *TRHS*, 5th ser. 16 (1966), 23–42.

Haskins, C. H., 'Michael Scot in Spain', *Estudios eruditos in memoriam de Adolfo Bonilla y San Martin (1875–1926)*, 2 vols. (Madrid, 1927–30), ii. 129–34.

Heers, J., *Le moyen âge, une imposture* (Paris, 1992).

Heinzmann, R., *Die 'Institutiones in sacram paginam' des Simon von Tournai: Einleitung und Quästionsverzeichnis*, Münchener Universitätsschriften, Theologische Fakultät, Veröffentlichungen des Grabmann-Instituts, n.s. 1 (Munich, Paderborn, and Vienna, 1967).

Helmholz, R. H., *Canon Law and the Law of England* (London and Ronceverte, 1987).

—— *Marriage Litigation in Medieval England* (Cambridge, 1974).

Hemptinne, T. de, 'Les épouses des croisés et pèlerins flamands au XIe et XIIe siècles: L'exemple des comtesses de Flandre Clémence et Sibylle', in *Autour de la première croisade*, ed. M. Balard, Série Byzantina Sorbonensia 14 (Paris, 1996), pp. 83–95.

Herlihy, D., 'Life Expectancies for Women in Medieval Society', in *The Role of Women in the Middle Ages*, ed. R. T. Morewedge (New York, 1975), pp. 1–22.

—— *Women, Family and Society in Medieval Europe: Historical Essays 1978–1991*, ed. A. Molho (Providence and Oxford, 1995).

—— and Klapisch-Zuber, C., *Tuscans and their Families: A Study of the Florentine Catasto of 1427* (French edn., Paris, 1978; Eng. trans. New Haven and London, 1985).

Hewson, M. A., *Giles of Rome and the Medieval Theory of Conception: A Study of the 'De formatione corporis humani in utero'* (London, 1975).

Heynck, V., 'Der Skotist Hugo von Novo Castro OFM. Ein Bericht über den Stand der Forschung zu seinem Leben und seinem Schrifttum', *Franziskanischen Studien* 44 (1962), 244–70.

—— 'Zur Datierung des Sentenzkommentars des Petrus de Palude', *Franziskanische Studien* 53 (1971), 317–27.

Higgins, I. M., *Writing East: The 'Travels' of Sir John Mandeville* (Philadelphia, 1997).

Himes, N. E., *A Medical History of Contraception* (Baltimore, 1936).

Hissette, R., *Enquête sur les 219 articles condamnés à Paris le 7 Mars 1277*, Philosophes Médiévaux 22 (Louvain and Paris, 1977).

Hocedez, E., 'La vie et les oeuvres de Pierre d'Auvergne, *Gregorianum*, 14 (1933), 3–36.

Hollingsworth, T. H., 'A Demographic Study of the British Ducal Families', repr. in *Population in History: Essays in Historical Demography*, ed. D. V. Glass and D. E. C. Eversley (London, 1965), 354–78.

—— *Historical Demography*, The Sources of History: Studies in the Use of Historical Evidence (Cambridge, 1976 = re-issue of London, 1969).

Holmes, G., 'The Emergence of an Urban Ideology in Florence *c.*1250–1450', *TRHS*, 5th ser. 23 (1973), 111–34.

—— *Florence, Rome and the Origins of the Renaissance* (Oxford, 1986).

Hossfeld, P., *Albertus Magnus als Naturphilosoph und Naturwissenschaftler* (Bonn, 1983).

Hunt, R. W., *The Schools and the Cloister: The Life and Writings of Alexander Nequam (1157–1217)*, rev. M. Gibson (Oxford, 1984).

Hyde, J. K., 'Medieval Descriptions of Cities', repr. in his *Literacy and its Uses: Studies on Late Medieval Italy*, ed. D. Waley (Manchester and New York, 1993), 1–32.

Humphreys, K. W., *The Book Provisions of the Medieval Friars, 1215–1400* (Amsterdam, 1964).

Iung, N., *Un franciscain, théologien du pouvoir pontifical au XIVe siècle: Alvaro Pelayo, évêque et pénitencier de Jean XXII* (Paris, 1931).

Jacquart, D., 'Aristotelian Thought in Salerno', in *A History of Twelfth-Century Philosophy*, ed. P. Dronke (Cambridge, 1988), pp. 407–28.

—— 'Principales étapes dans la transmission des textes de médecine (XIe–XIVe siècle)', in *Rencontres de cultures dans la philosophie médiévale: traductions et traducteurs de l'antiquité tardive au XIVe siècle*, ed. J. Hamesse and M. Fattori (Louvain and Cassino, 1990), pp. 251–71.

—— 'La réception du *Canon* d'Avicenne: comparaison entre Montpellier et Paris au XIIIe et XIVe siècles', in *Histoire de l'école médicale de Montpellier: colloque* (Paris, 1985), pp. 69–77.

—— and Micheau, F., *La médecine arabe et l'occident Médiéval* (Paris, 1990).

—— and Thomasset, C., *Sexuality and Medicine in the Middle Ages*, trans. M. Adamson (Oxford, 1988).

Jordan, W. C., *The French Monarchy and the Jews: from Philip Augustus to the las Capetians* (Philadelphia, 1989).

—— *The Great Famine: Northern Europe in the Early Fourteenth Century* (Princeton, 1996).

Karras, R. M., *Common Women: Prostitution and Sexuality in Medieval England*, Studies in the History of Sexuality (Oxford, 1996).

Kedar, B. Z., *Crusade and Mission: European Approaches toward the Muslims* (Princeton, 1984).

Kimble, G. H. T., *Geography in the Middle Ages* (London, 1938).

Kealey, E. J., *Medieval Medicus: A Social History of Anglo-Norman Medicine* (Baltimore and London, 1981).

Kempshall, M. S., *The Common Good in Late Medieval Political Thought* (Oxford, 1999).

Kienzle, B. M., 'The Prostitute-Preacher: Patterns of Polemic against Medieval Waldensian Women Preachers', in *Women Preachers and Prophets through Two Millennia of Christianity*, ed. B. M. Kienzle and P. J. Walker (Berkeley, Los Angeles, and London, 1998), pp. 99–113.

Klapisch-Zuber, C., *Women, Family and Ritual in Renaissance Florence*, trans. L. Cochrane (Chicago and London, 1985).

Kleinschmidt, E., introduction to Rudolf von Schlettstadt, *Historiae Memorabiles: Zur Dominikanerliteratur und Kulturgeschichte des 13.* Jahrhunderts, ed. E. Kleinschmidt (Cologne and Vienna, 1974).

Koch, J., 'Jakob von Metz O.P., der Lehrer des Durandus de S. Porciano, O.P.', *AHDLMA* 4 (1930), 169–232.

Kolmer, L., *Ad Capendas Vulpes: Die Ketzerbekämpfung in Südfrankreich in der ersten Hälfte des 13. Jahrhunderts und die Ausbildung des Inquisitionsverfahren*, Pariser Historische Studien 19 (Bonn, 1982).

Kottje, R., 'Ehe und Eheverständnis in den vorgratianischen Bußbüchern', in *Love and Marriage in the Twelfth Century*, ed. W. Van Hoecke and A. Welkenhuysen, Mediaevalia Lovaniensia, Series 1, Studia 8 (Louvain, 1981), pp. 41–58.

Kritzeck, J., *Peter the Venerable and Islam* (Princeton, 1964).

Kurze, D., 'Häresie und Minderheit im Mittelalter', *Historische Zeitschrift* 229 (1979), 529–73.

Lacombe, G., 'Medieval Latin versions of the *Parva Naturalia*', *The New Scholasticism* 5 (1931), 289–311.

Lajard, F., 'Gilles de Rome, Religieux Augustin, Théologien', *Histoire Littéraire de France* 30 (1888), pp. 421–566.

Lambert, M. D., *The Cathars* (Oxford, 1998).

Landgraf, A. M., *Introduction à l'histoire de la littérature théologique de la scolastique naissante* (Montreal and Paris, 1973).

Langholm, O., *Economics in the Medieval Schools: Wealth, Exchange, Money and Usury according to the Paris Theological Tradition, 1200–1350*, Studien zur Geistesgeschichte des Mittelalters 29 (Leiden, New York, and Cologne, 1992).

Langosch, L., 'Caesarius von Heisterbach', *Vf* i. 1152–68.

Lansing, C., *Power and Purity: Cathar Heresy in Medieval Italy* (New York, 1998).

Laqueur, L., *Making Sex: Body and Gender from the Greeks to Freud* (Cambridge, Mass., and London, 1990).

Laurent, S., *Naître au Moyen Âge. De la conception à la naissance: la grossesse et l'accouchement (XIIe–XVe siècle)* (Paris, 1989).

Lawn, B., *The Salernitan Questions: An Introduction to the History of Medieval and Renaissance Problem Literature* (Oxford, 1963).

Lemay, R., 'Gerard of Cremona', *DSB* xv. 173–92.

Lecoy de la Marche, A., *La chaire française au moyen âge*, 2nd edn. (Paris, 1886).

Le Goff, L., *La naissance de purgatoire* (Paris, 1981).

Le Roy Ladurie, E., *Montaillou, village occitan de 1294 à 1324* (Paris, 1975).

—— English trans. and abridgement: *Montaillou: Cathars and Catholics in a French Village 1294–1324* (London, 1978).

Lesnick, D. R., *Preaching in Medieval Florence: The Social World of Franciscan and Dominican Spirituality* (Athens, Ga., and London, 1989).

Lévy, J.-P., 'L'officialité de Paris et les questions familiales à la fin du XIVe siècle', in *Études d'histoire du droit canonique dédiées à Gabriel Le Bras*, 2 vols. (Paris, 1965), ii. 1265–94.

Lex, L., 'L'enregistrement des décès et des mariages au XIVe siècle', *Bibliothèque de l'École des Chartes* 51 (1890), 376–78.

Leyser, H., *Hermits and the New Monasticism: A Study of Religious Communities in Western Europe, 1100–1150* (London, 1984).

Leyser, K. J., *Rule and Conflict in an Early Medieval Society: Ottonian Saxony* (London, 1979).

Lhotsky, A., *Die Wiener Artistenfakultät 1365–1487* (Vienna, 1965).

Lewry, O., 'Study of Aging in the Arts Faculty of the Universities of Paris and Oxford', in *Aging and the Ages in Medieval Europe*, ed. M. M. Sheehan, Pontifical Institute of Medieval Studies, Papers in Medieval Studies 11 (Toronto, 1990), pp. 23–38.

Lindner, P. B., *Die Erkenntnislehre des Thomas von Strassburg*, BGPTM 27 (Münster, 1930).

Long, R. J., introduction to *Bartholomaeus Anglicus On the Properties of Soul and Body*, ed. R. J. Long (Toronto, 1979).

Longère, J., *Oeuvres oratoires des maîtres parisiens au XIIe siècle: Étude historique et doctrinale*, 2 vols. (Paris, 1983).

Lottin, O., *Le droit naturel chez Saint Thomas d'Aquin et ses prédécesseurs*, 2nd edn. (Bruges, 1931).

—— 'Roland de Crémone et Hugues de Saint-Cher', *RTAM* 12 (1940), 136–43.

Luscombe, D., 'The *Ethics* and the *Politics* in Britain in the Middle Ages', in *Aristotle in Britain in the Middle Ages* (see above under Burnett), pp. 337–49.

Lusignan, S., *Préface au Speculum Maius de Vincent de Beauvais: Réfraction et Diffusion*, Cahiers d'Études Médiévales 5 (Montreal and Paris, 1979).

—— 'La topique de la *Translatio Studii* et les traductions françaises de textes savants au XIVe siècle', *Traductions et Traducteurs au Moyen Âge*, ed. G. Contamine, Documents, Études et Répertoires Publiées par l'Institut de Recherche et d'Histoire des Textes (Paris, 1989), 303–15.

———ed., with M. Paulmier-Foucart and A. Nadeau, *Vincent de Beauvais: Intentions et Réceptions d'une oeuvre encyclopédique au Moyen-Âge* (Paris and Saint-Laurent, 1990).

McVaugh, M. R., 'Introduction', in Arnau de Vilanova, *Opera medica omnia* (Barcelona, 1975–), iii, 11–39.

—— *Medicine before the Plague: Practitioners and their Patients in the Crown of Aragon, 1285–1345* (Cambridge, 1993).

—— 'Royal surgeons and the value of medical learning: the Crown of Aragon, 1300–1500', in L. García-Ballester, R. French, J. Arrizabalaga, and J. Cunningham, ed., *Practical Medicine from Salerno to the Black Death* (Cambridge, 1994), pp. 211–36.

Maier, A., 'Zu Walter Burleys Politik-Kommentar', *Recherches de Théologie Ancienne et Médiévale* 14 (1947), 332–6.

Martin, C., 'The commentaries on the Politics of Aristotle in the late thirteenth and fourteenth centuries, with reference to the thought and political life of the time' (Unpublished D.Phil thesis, University of Oxford, 1949).

—— 'Some medieval commentaries on Aristotle's *Politics*', *History* 36 (1951), 29–44.

—— 'The vulgate text of Aquinas's Commentary on Aristotle's Politics', *Dominican Studies* 5 (1952), 35–64.

—— 'Walter Burleigh' in *Oxford Studies Presented to Daniel Callus*, Oxford Historical Studies, n.s. 16 (Oxford, 1964), pp. 194–230.

Marshall, C., *Warfare in the Latin East, 1192–1291* (Cambridge, 1992).

Martínez Ferrando, J. E., *Jaime II de Aragón: Su vida familiar*, 2 vols. (Barcelona, 1942).

Mayer, H. E., 'Der Brief Kaiser Friedrichs I. an Saladin vom Jahre 1188', *Deutsches Archiv* 14 (1958), 488–94.

McDonnel, E. W., *The Beghards and Beguines in Medieval Culture, With special emphasis on the Belgian Scene* (New Brunswick, NJ, 1954).

Meens, R., 'The Frequency and Nature of Early Medieval Penance', in *Handling Sin*, pp. 35–61.

—— *Het tripartite boeteboek: Overlevering en betekenis van vroegmiddeleeuwse biechtvoorschriften (met editie en vertaling van vier tripartita)* (Hilversum, 1994).

Merlo, G. G., 'Sulle "misere donnicciuole" che predicavano', *Valdesi e valdismi medievali II, Identità valdesi nella soria e nella storiografia* (Turin, 1991), pp. 93–112.

Mols, R., *Introduction à la démographie historique des villes d'Europe du XIVe au XVIIIe siècle*, 3 vols. (Louvain, 1954–6).

Michaud-Quantin, P., *Sommes de casuistique et manuels de confession au moyen âge (XII–XVI siècles)*, AMN 13 (1962).

—— 'La "Summula in foro poenitentiali"', *Studia Gratiana* 11 (1967), 145–67.

Minio-Paluello, L., 'Aristotele dal mondo Arabo a quello Latino', Minio-Paluello, *Opuscula*, pp. 501–35.

—— 'Aristotle: tradition and influence', *DSB* i. 267–81.

—— 'Dante's Reading of Aristotle', in *The World of Dante: Essays on Dante and His Times*, ed. C. Grayson (Oxford, 1980), pp. 61–80; Italian trans. in Minio-Paluello, *Lughi cruciali in Dante*, pp. 29–49.

—— 'Henri Aristippe, Guillaume de Moerbeke et les traductions latines médiévales des "Météorologiques" et du "De generatione et Corruption" d'Aristote', Minio-Paluello, *Opuscula*, pp. 57–86.

—— 'James of Venice', *DSB* vii. 65–7.

—— *Luoghi cruciali in Dante: ultimi saggi, con un inedito su Boezio*, ed. F. Santi, Quaderni di Cultura Neolatina, Collana della Fondazione Ezio Franceschi 6 (Spoleto and Florence, 1993).

—— 'Michael Scot', *DSB* ix. 361–5.

—— 'Moerbeke, William of', *DSB* ix. 434–40.

—— *Opuscula: The Latin Aristotle* (Amsterdam, 1972).

—— 'Plato of Tivoli', *DSB* xi. 31–2.

—— 'Remigio Girolami's *De bono communi*: Florence at the time of Dante's Banishment and the Philosopher's Answer to the Crisis', *Italian Studies* 11 (1956), 56–71; Italian trans. in Minio-Paluello, *Luoghi cruciali in Dante*, pp. 111–29.

—— 'La tradition aristotélicienne dans l'histoire des idées', Minio-Paluello, *Opuscula*, pp. 405–24.

Molin, J.-B., and Mutembe, P., *Le rituel de mariage en France du XIIe siècle au XVIe siècle*, Théologie Historique 26 (Paris, 1974).

Monnot, G., 'Les citations coraniques dans le "Dialogus" de Pierre Alfonse', *Cahiers de Fanjeaux* 18 (Toulouse, 1983), pp. 261–77.

Moore, E., 'Appendix on Dante and Ristoro d'Arezzo', in his *Studies in Dante: Second Series* (Oxford, 1899), pp. 358–72.

Morpurgo, P., 'L'ingresso dell'Aristotele latino a Salerno', in *Rencontres de cultures dans la philosophie médiévale: traductions et traducteurs de l'antiquité tardive au XIVe siècle*, ed. J. Hamesse and M. Fattori (Louvain and Cassino, 1990), pp. 273–300.

Morrall, J. B., *Political Thought in Medieval Times*, 3rd edn. (London, 1971).

M. Muccillo, 'Fibonacci', *DBI* xlvii. 359–63.

Müller, M., *Die Lehre des Hl. Augustinus von der Paradiesehe und ihre Auswirkung in der Sexualethik des 12. und 13. Jahrhunderts bis Thomas von Aquin* (Regensburg, 1954).

Murray, A., 'Archbishop and Mendicants in thirteenth-century Pisa', in *Stellung und Wirksamkeit der Bettelorden in der städtischen Gesellschaft*, ed. K. Elm, Berliner Historische Studien 3, Ordensstudien 2 (Berlin, 1981), pp. 19–75.

—— 'Confession before 1215', *TRHS* 6th ser. 3 (1993), 51–81.

—— *Reason and Society in the Middle Ages* (Oxford, 1978).

Musallam, B. F., *Sex and Society in Islam: Birth Control before the Nineteenth Century* (Cambridge, 1983).

Nardi, B., 'Bartolomeo da Parma', *DBI* vi. 747–50.

Nardi, E., *Procurato aborto nel mondo greco romano* (Milan, 1971), pp. 669–79.

Nauert, C. G. Jr., '*C. Plinius Secundus (Naturalis Historia)*', in *Catalogus Translationum et Commentariorum: Medieval and Renaissance Latin Translations and Commentaries, annotated lists and guides*, ed. F. E. Kranz and P. O. Kristeller (Washington, 1960–), iv. 297–422.

Needham, J., *A History of Embryology*, 2nd edn. (Cambridge, 1959).

Newman, W. L., *The Politics of Aristotle*, 4 vols. (Oxford, 1887–1902).

Noonan, J. T. Jr., 'An Absolute Value in History', in *The Morality of Abortion* (Cambridge, Mass., 1970), ed. J. T. Noonan Jr., pp. 1–59.

—— *Contraception: A History of its Treatment by the Catholic Theologians and Canonists* (Cambridge, Mass., 1966).

—— 'Intellectual and Demographic History', *Daedalus* 97 (1968), 463–85.

North, J. D., 'Astrology and the Fortunes of Churches', *Centaurus* 24 (1980), 181–211.

O'Boyle, C., *The Art of Medicine: Medical Teaching at the University of Paris, 1250–1400*, Education and Society in the Middle Ages and Renaissance 9 (Leiden, Boston, and Cologne, 1998).

Oliger, L., 'Servasanto da Faenza O.F.M. e il suo "Liber de virtutibus et vitiis"', in *Miscellanea Francesco Ehrle*, I, Studi e testi 37 (Rome, 1924).

Oppenraay, A. M. I. Van [Oppenraaij, A. M. I. van], 'Quelques particularités de la méthode de traduction de Michel Scot', in *Traductions et traducteurs de l'antiquité tardive au XIVe siècle*, Publications de l'Institut d'Études Médiévales, Textes, Études, Congrès 11, Rencontres de Cultures dans la philosophie médiévale 1 (Louvain, Cassino, 1990), pp. 121–9.

Otis, L. L., *Prostitution in Medieval Society: The History of an Urban Institution in Languedoc* (Chicago and London, 1985).

Paolini, L., 'Italian Catharism and Written Culture', in *Heresy and Literacy, 1000–1530*, ed. P. Biller and A. Hudson (Cambridge, 1994), pp. 83–103.

Paravicini Bagliani, A., 'Guillaume de Moerbeke et la cour pontificale', *Guillaume de Moerbeke*, pp. 23–52.

—— rev. repr., *Medicina e scienze della natura alla corte dei Papi nel duecento* (Spoleto, 1991), pp. 141–75.

Park, K., *Doctors and Medicine in Early Renaissance Florence* (Princeton, NJ, 1985).

Parkes, M. B., 'The Provision of Books', *HUO* ii. 407–83.

Patar, B., 'Introduction', Nicole Oresme, *Expositio et quaestiones in Aristotelis De Anima: Édition, Étude Critique*, ed. B. Patar, Philosophes Médiévaux 32 (Louvain, Paris, 1995).

Patschovsky, A., *Der Passauer Anonymus: Ein Sammelwerk über Ketzer, Juden, Antichrist aus der Mitte des XIII. Jahrhunderts*, Schriften der Monumenta Germaniae Historica, 22 (Stuttgart, 1968).

Paulmier-Foucart, M., 'Vincent de Beauvais', *DSP* xvi. 806–13.

Payer, P. J., 'Early Medieval Regulations concerning marital sexual relations', *Journal of Medieval History* 6 (1980), 353–76.

—— *Sex and the Penitentials: The Development of a Sexual Code, 550–1150* (Toronto, 1984).

Pelling, M., and Smith, R., ed., *Life, Death and the Elderly: Historical Perspectives* (London and New York, 1991).

Perrin, C.-E., 'Le manse dans le Polyptyque de l'abbaye de Prüm à la fin du IXe siècle', *Études historiques à la mémoire de Noël Didier* (Paris, 1960), pp. 245–58.

Perrin, C.-E., *Recherches sur la seigneurie rurale en Lorraine d'après les plus anciens censiers (IXe–XIe siècle)*, Publications de la Faculté des Lettres de l'Université de Strasbourg 71 (Paris, 1935).

Peters, F. E., *Aristotle and the Arabs: The Aristotelian Tradition in Islam* (New York and London, 1968).

Phillips, J. R. S., *The Medieval Expansion of Europe* (Oxford, 1988).

D. Pingree, 'Abū Ma'Shar', *DSB* i. 32–9.

Prawer, J., *Crusader Institutions* (Oxford, 1980).

—— *The Latin Kingdom of Jerusalem: European Colonialism in the Middle Ages* (London, 1972).

Premuda, L., 'Abano, Pietro d'', *DSB* i. 4–5.

Preston, S. H., 'Causes and Consequences of Mortality Declines in Less Developed Countries during the Twentieth Century', in *Population and Economic Change in Developing Countries*, ed. R. A. Easterlin (Chicago, 1980).

Pycke, J., 'Heriman de Tournai', *Dictionnaire d'Histoire et de Géographie Ecclésiastiques*, xxiii. 1453–8.

Raunié, E., 'Couvent des Filles-Dieu. Notice historique', in E. Raunié and M. Prinet, *Epitaphier du vieux Paris*, 4 vols. (Paris, 1890–1914), iv. 317–52.

Reinhardt, H. J. F., *Die Ehelehre der Schule des Anselm von Laon: Eine Theologie- und kirchenrechtsgeschichtliche Untersuchung zu den Ehetexten der frühen Pariser Schule des 12.* Jahrhunderts, BGPTM, n.s. 14 (Aschenbach, 1974).

Reynolds, P. N., *Marriage in the Western Church: The Christianization of Marriage during the Patristic and Early Medieval Periods* (Leiden, New York, and Cologne, 1994).

Richard, J., *La papauté et les missions d'orient au moyen âge (XIIIe–XVe siècles)*, Collection de l'École Française de Rome 33 (Rome, 1977).

Riddle, J. M., 'Ancient and Medieval Chemotherapy for Cancer', *Isis* 76 (1985), 319–30.

—— *Contraception and Abortion from the Ancient World to the Renaissance* (Cambridge, Mass., London, 1992).

—— *Eve's Herbs: A History of Contraception and Abortion in the West* (Cambridge, Mass., London, 1997).

Rijk, L. M. de, 'On the life of Peter of Spain, The author of The *Tractatus*, called afterwards *Summule logicales*', *Vivarium* 8 (1970), 123–54.

Rodolico, N., 'Note statistiche su la popolazione fiorentina nel xiv secolo', *Archivio storico italiano*, 5th ser. 30 (1902), 241–74.

Roisin, S., 'L'efflorescence cistercienne et le courant féminin de piété au XIIIe siècle', *Revue d'Histoire écclésiastique* 39 (1943), 342–78.

Rossiaud, J., *Medieval Prostitution* (Oxford, 1988).

Rouse, R. H. and M. A., 'The Book Trade at the University of Paris, ca. 1250–ca. 1350', in *La production du livre universitaire au moyen âge: exemplar et pecia*, ed. L. J. Bataillon, B. G. Guyot, and R. H. Rouse (Paris, 1991), pp. 41–114.

—— 'Le développement des instruments de travail au XIIIe siècle', in *Culture et travail intellectuel dans l'occident médiéval*, ed. G. Hasenohr and J. Longère (Paris, 1981), pp. 115–44.

—— '*Statim invenire*: Schools, Preachers and New Attitudes to the Page', in *Renaissance and Renewal in the Twelfth Century*, ed. R. L. Benson and G. Constable (Oxford, 1982), pp. 201–25.

Rubinstein, N., 'The Beginnings of Political Thought in Florence', *Journal of the Warburg and Courtauld Institute* 5 (1942), 198–227 (pp. 214–24).

Rubio y Lluch, A., ed., *Documents per l'História de la Cultura Catalana Mig-Eval*, 2 vols. (Barcelona, 1908–21).

Russell, J. C., *Late Ancient and Medieval Population*, Transactions of the American Philosophical Society, n.s. 48, part 3 (Philadelphia, 1958).

Sablonier, R., 'The Aragonese royal family around 1300', in *Interest and Emotion: Essays on the Study of Family and Kinship*, ed. H. Medick and D. W. Sabean (Cambridge, 1984), pp. 210–39.

Sabra, A. I., 'Al-Farghānī', *DSB* iv. 541–5.

Sapori, A., 'L'attendibilità di alcune testimonianze cronistiche dell'economia medievale', *Archivio Storico Italiano* 12 (1929), 19–30.

Scheeben, H. C., *Albert der Große: Zur Chronologie seines Lebens*, Quellen und Forschungen zur Geschichte des Dominkanerordens in Deutschland 27 (Leipzig, 1931).

Schmaus, M., 'Neue Mitteilungen zum Sentenzkommentar Wilhelms von Nottingham', *Franziskanische Studien* 19 (1932), 195–223.

Schmieder, F., *Europa und die Fremden: Die Mongolen im Urteil des Abendlandes vom 13. bis in das 15 Jahrhundert*, Beiträge zur Geschichte und Quellenkunde des Mittelalters 16 (Sigmaringen, 1994).

Schmugge, L., 'Fiadoni', *DBI* lxvii. 317–20.

—— *Johannes van Jandun (1285/89–1328): Untersuchungen zur Biographie und Sozialtheorie eines Lateinischen Averroisten*, Pariser Historische Studien 5 (Stuttgart, 1966).

Schneider, B., 'Bemerkungen zum Aristoteles Latinus: Spuren einer Revision der Politikübersetzung des Wilhelm von Moerbeke', in *Aristoteles Werk und Wirkung*, ed. J. Wiesner, 2 vols. (Berlin and New York, 1987), ii. 487–97.

Sears, E., *The Ages of Man: Medieval Interpretations of the Life-Cycle* (Princeton, 1996).

Segl, P., *Ketzer in Österreich: Untersuchungen über Häresie und Inquisition im Herzogtum Österreich im 13. und beginnenden 14. Jahrhundert* (Paderborn, Munich, Vienna, and Zurich, 1984).

Shahar, S., *Growing Old in the Middle Ages: 'Winter clothes us in Shadow and Pain'* (London and New York, 1997).

Sheehan, M., 'Marriage Theory and Practice. The Diocesan Legislation of Medieval England', *MS* 40 (1978), 408–60.

Simon, A., *L'ordre des pénitentes de S. Marie-Madeleine en Allemagne au XIIIe siècle* (Fribourg, 1918).

Siraisi, N. G., *Arts and Sciences at Padua: The Studium of Padua before 1350*, Pontifical Institute of Medieval Studies, Studies and Texts 25 (Toronto, 1973).

—— *Avicenna in Renaissance Italy: The Canon and Medical Teaching in English Universities after 1500* (Princeton, 1987).

—— *Taddeo Alderotti and His Pupils: Two Generations of Italian Medical Learning* (Princeton, 1981).

Skelton, R. A., Marston, T. E., and Painter, G. D., *The Vinland Map and the Tartar Relation*, 2nd edn. (New Haven and London, 1995).

Skinner, Q., *The Foundations of Modern Political Thought*, 2 vols. (Cambridge, 1978).

Smail, R. C., *Crusading Warfare (1097–1193)* (Cambridge, 1956).

Smalley, B., 'Some Latin commentaries on the Sapiential books in the late thirteenth and early fourteenth centuries', *AHDLMA* 18 (1950–1), 103–28.

—— 'William of Auvergne, John of La Rochelle and St. Thomas Aquinas on the Old Law', in *Studies in Medieval Thought and Learning from Abelard to Wyclif* (London, 1981), pp. 121–81.

Smith, L., 'William of Auvergne and confession', *Handling Sin*, pp. 95–107.

—— 'William of Auvergne and the Jews', *Christianity and Judaism*, ed. D. Wood, SCH 29 (1992), pp. 107–17.

Smith, R. M., 'Demographic developments in rural England, 1300–48: a survey', in *Before the*

Black Death: Studies in the 'Crisis' of the Early Fourteenth Century, ed. B. M. S. Campbell (Manchester and New York, 1991), pp. 25–77.

Smith, R. M., 'Geographical Diversity in the Resort to Marriage in Late Medieval Europe: Work, Reputation, and Unmarried Females in the Household Formation Systems of Northern and Southern Europe', in Goldberg, ed., *Woman is a Worthy Wight*, pp. 16–59.

—— 'Human Resources', in *The Countryside of Medieval England*, ed. G. Astill and A. Grant (Oxford, 1988), pp. 188–212.

—— 'Hypothèses sur la nuptialité en Angleterre aux XIIIe–XIVe siècles', *Annales. Économies. Sociétés. Civilisations* 38 (1983), 107–36.

—— 'Marriage Processes in the English Past: Some Continuities', *The World We Have Gained: Histories of Population and Social Structure*, ed. L. Bonfield, R. M. Smith, and K. Wrightson (Oxford, 1986), pp. 43–99.

—— 'The People of Tuscany and their Families in the Fifteenth Century: Medieval or Mediterranean?', *Journal of Family History* 6 (1981), 107–28.

—— 'Some reflections on the evidence for the origins of the "European marriage pattern" in England', in *The Sociology of the Family: New Directions for Britain*, ed. C. C. Harris, Sociological Review Monograph 28 (Keele, 1979), pp. 74–112.

Southern, R. W., 'Aspects of the European Tradition of Historical Writing: 2. Hugh of St. Victor and the Idea of Historical Development', *TRHS*, 5th ser. 21 (1971), 159–79.

—— *Robert Grosseteste: The Growth of an English Mind in Medieval Europe*, 2nd edn. (Oxford, 1992).

—— *Western Society and the Church in the Middle Ages* (Harmondsworth, 1970).

—— *Western Views of Islam in the Middle Ages* (Cambridge, Mass., 1962).

Sprandel, R., *Altersschicksal und Altersmoral: Die Geschichte der Einstellungen zum Altern nach der Pariser Bibelexegese des 12.–16. Jahrhunderts*, Monographien zur Geschichte des Mittelalters 22 (Stuttgart, 1981).

Stangeland, C. E., *Pre-Malthusian Doctrines of Population: A Study in the History of Economic Theory* (New York, 1904).

Steinschneider, M., 'Die *Parva Naturalia* des Aristoteles bei den Arabern', *Zeitschrift der deutschen morgenländischen Gesellschaft* 37 (1883), 477–92.

Stevenson, K., *Nuptial Blessing: A Study of Christian Marriage Rites* (Oxford, 1983).

Stolnitz, G. J., 'A Century of International Mortality Trends, II', *Population Studies* 10 (1956–7), 17–42.

—— 'Recent Mortality Trends in Latin America, Asia and Africa. Review and Reinterpretation', *Population Studies* 19 (1965–6), 117–38.

Strayer, J., *The Reign of Philip the Fair* (Princeton, 1980).

Sturcken, H. T., 'The unconsummated marriage of Jaime of Aragon and Leonor of Castile (October 1319)', *Journal of Medieval History* 5 (1979), 185–201.

Tentler, T. N., *Sin and Confession on the Eve of the Reformation* (Princeton, 1977).

Texts and Transmission: A Survey of the Latin Classics, ed. L. D. Reynolds (Oxford, 1983).

Theissing, H., *Glaube und Theologie bei Robert Cowton OFM*, BGPTM 42(3) (Münster, 1970).

Thomas, A., 'Notice sur le MS latin 4788 du Vatican contenant une traduction française avec commentaire par maître Pierre de Paris de la *Consolatio Philosophiae* de Boèce', *Notices et extraits des manuscrits de la Bibliothèque Nationale et autres bibliothèques* 41 (1923), pp. 29–90.

Thomson, R. M., 'William of Malmesbury and Some Other Western Writers on Islam', *Medievalia et Humanistica*, n.s. 6 (1975), pp. 179–87.

Tierney, B., *Medieval Poor Law: A Sketch of Canonical Theory and Its Application in England* (Berkeley and Los Angeles, 1959).

Titow, J. Z., 'Some differences between manors and their effects on the conditions of the peasantry in the thirteenth century', *Agricultural History Review* 10 (1962), 113–28.

Tolan, J., *Petrus Alfonsi and His Medieval Readers* (Gainesville, etc., Fla., 1993).

Traductions et traducteurs au moyen âge, ed. G. Contamine, Documents, Études et Répertoires Publiées par l'Institut de Recherche et d'Histoire des Textes (Paris, 1989).

Traductions et traducteurs de l'antiquité tardive au XIVe siècle, Université Catholique de Louvain and Università degli Studi di Cassino, Publications de l'Institut des Études Médiévales, Textes, Études, Congrès 11, Rencontres de Cultures dans la Philosophie Médiévale 1 (Louvain and Cassino, 1990).

Tyerman, C. J., *England and the Crusades 1095–1588* (Chicago and London, 1988).

—— 'Marino Sanudo Torsello and the Lost Crusade. Lobbying in the Fourteenth Century', *TRHS*, 5th ser. 32 (1982), 57–73.

—— 'Philip V of France, the Assemblies of 1319–20 and the Crusade', *Bulletin of the Institute for Historical Research*, 57 (1984), 15–34.

—— 'Philip VI and the recovery of the Holy Land', *English Historical Review*, 100 (1985), 25–52.

Usher, J., '"Più di mille": Crowd Control in the Commedia', in *Word and Drama in Dante: Essays on the "Divina Commedia"*, ed. J. C. Barnes and J. Petrie (Dublin, 1993), pp. 55–71.

Valois, N., *Guillaume d'Auvergne évêque de Paris (1228–1249): Sa ie et ses ouvrages* (Paris, 1880).

Vasoli, C., 'Bonatti, Guido', *DBI* xi. 603–8.

Vaultier, R., *Le folklore pendant la guerre de Cent ans d'après les lettres de rémission du Trésor des Chartes* (Paris, 1965).

Vaux, R. de, *Notes et textes sur l'Avicennisme latin aux confins des XIIe et XIIIe siècles*, Bibliothèque Thomiste 20 (Paris, 1934).

Verdon, J., 'La gynécologie et l'obstétrique aux IXe et Xe siècles', *Revue française de Gynécologie*, 71 (1976), 39–47.

Verlinden, C., 'L'origine de "sclavus" = esclave', *Bulletin Du Cange* (*Archivum Latinitatis Medii Aevi*) 17 (1943 for 1942), 97–128.

Vernet, A., 'Les traductions latines d'oeuvres en langues vernaculaires au moyen âge', *Traductions et traducteurs au moyen âge*, ed. G. Contamine, Documents, Études et Répertoires Publiées par l'Institut de Recherche et d'Histoire des Textes (Paris, 1989), pp. 221–41.

Vescovini, G. F., 'Introduzione', in *Il 'Lucidator dubitabilium astronomiae' di Pietro d'Abano: Opere scientifiche inedite*, ed. G. F. Vescovini, Il mito e la storia 3 (Padua, 1988), pp. 17–52.

Viard, P. 'Guillaume d'Auvergne', *Dsp* vi (1967), cols. 1182–92.

—— 'Guillaume d'Auvergne', *DHGE* xxii (1988), col. 848.

Vicaire, M.-H., *Saint Dominic and His Times*, trans. K. Pond (London, 1964).

Villard, U. M. de, *Il libro della Peregrinazione nelle Parti d'Oriente di Frate Riccoldo da Montecroce* (Rome, 1948).

Vincent de Beauvais: Intentions et réceptions d'une oeuvre encyclopédique au Moyen Âge, ed. S. Lusignan, M. Paulmier-Foucart, and A. Nadeau (Paris and Montreal, 1990).

Viollet, P., 'Bérenger Frédol, canoniste', *Histoire littéraire de la France* 34 (1914), 62–178.

Vogel, K., 'Fibonacci, Leonardo', *DSB* iv. 604–13.

Wakefield, W. L., 'Some unorthodox popular ideas of the thirteenth century', *Medievalia et Humanistica*, n.s. 4 (1973), 23–35.

Waley, D., *The Italian City-Republics*, 2nd edn. (London, 1978).

Weigand, R., *Die bedingte Eheschliessung im kanonischen Recht: Ein Beitrag zur Geschichte der Kanonistik von Gratian bis Gregor IX* (Munich, 1963).

—— 'Die Rechtsprechung des Regensburger Gerichts in Ehesachen unter besonderer Berücksichtigung der bedingten Eheschließung nach Gerichtsbüchern aus dem Ende des 15. Jahrhunderts', repr. in his *Liebe und Ehe im Mittelalter*, Bibliotheca Eruditorum 7 (Goldback, 1993).

Weisheipl, J. A., ed. *Albertus Magnus and the Sciences: Commemorative Essays 1980* (Toronto, 1980).

—— 'Curriculum of the faculty of arts at Oxford in the early fourteenth century', *Medieval Studies* 26 (1964), 143–85.

—— *Friar Thomas d'Aquino, his Life, Thought and Works* (Oxford, 1975).

—— 'The Life and Works of St Albert the Great', in *Albertus and the Sciences*, 13–48.

—— 'Science in the thirteenth century', *HUO* i. 435–69.

Wright, J. K., *The Geographical Lore of the Time of the Crusades: A Study in the History of Medieval Science and Tradition in Western Europe* (New York, 1925; repr. with corrections and same pagination, New York, 1965).

Wrigley, E. A., 'No Death Without Birth: The Implications of English Mortality in the Early Modern Period', in *Problems and Methods in the History of Medicine*, ed. R. Porter and A. Wear (London, New York, Sydney, 1987), pp. 133–50.

Xiberta, B., *De scriptoribus scholasticis saeculi XIV ex ordine Carmelitarum* (Louvain, 1931).

Zeimentz, H., *Ehe nach der Lehre der Frühscholastik*, Moraltheologische Studien, Historische Abteilung 1 (Düsseldorf, 1973).

Ziegler, J., 'Medicine and Immortality in the Terrestrial Paradise', in *Religion and Medicine in the Middle Ages*, ed. P. Biller and J. Ziegler, York Studies in Medieval Theology 3 (forthcoming).

—— *Medicine and Religion c.1300: The Case of Arnau de Vilanova* (Oxford, 1998).

Zumkeller, A., 'Thomas de Strasbourg', *Dsp* xv. 872–3.

INDEX OF MANUSCRIPTS

GENERAL INDEX